NATIVE AMERICAN RHETORIC

Native American Rhetoric

Edited by Lawrence W. Gross

University of New Mexico Press | Albuquerque

© 2021 by the University of New Mexico Press
All rights reserved. Published 2021
Printed in the United States of America

First paperback printing 2023

ISBN 978-0-8263-6321-3 (cloth)
ISBN 978-0-8263-6562-0 (paper)
ISBN 978-0-8263-6322-0 (electronic)

Library of Congress Control Number: 2021944783

Founded in 1889, the University of New Mexico sits on the traditional homelands of the Pueblo of Sandia. The original peoples of New Mexico —Pueblo, Navajo, and Apache—since time immemorial have deep connections to the land and have made significant contributions to the broader community statewide. We honor the land itself and those who remain stewards of this land throughout the generations and also acknowledge our committed relationship to Indigenous peoples. We gratefully recognize our history.

Cover illustration: "Coyote, Looking Deeply." Acrylic on canvas. 18 × 13.75 in. Copyright Inés Hernández-Ávila. Used by permission.
Designed by Felicia Cedillos

Composed in Huronia Navajo 10.25/14.25

DEDICATION FOR INÉS TALAMANTEZ

For Inés Talamantez
Indigenous Academic Auntie
Dancing into spirit
This world and beyond

For Inés Talamantez
Inspirational strength and wisdom
Thank you for your guidance

For Inés Talamantez
Your generosity knew no bounds

For Inés Talamantez
May we speak and work as you did.
Boldly. And with great love.

For Inés Talamantez
Forever remembered as a bold, nurturing
feminist warrior

For Inés Talamantez
For inspiring las generaciones de Apache, Xican@, e Indígena scholars,
nimitztlazohtla

For Inés Talamantez
Great Mother whose embrace of wisdom
Heals

For Inés Talamantez
A Mother, a Spiritual Guide, a beautiful soul
You are loved

For Inés Talamantez
Lolito's first Elder, Bellita's ceremonial mother,
Mi hermana, mi amiga, mi compañera en esta vida

For Inés Talamantez
Mom
You taught us all to love and respect the mother earth
We will miss you terribly

For Inés Talamantez
I hear your voice now
and then
my heart sings

For Inés Talamantez
Thank you for seeing me
Stoking my power
Thank you for helping me see myself

For tita, Inés Maria Talamantez
My grandmother, mentor, and exemplary woman
Thank you for sharing your wisdom and love

To Inés Talamantez, my beloved grandmother, Tita, Strawberry
Grandma, my teacher, matriarch, fellow poet, sibling Scorpio

To Inés Talamantez, my dear hermana, tocaya,
We walked a long way together, older sister.
Grácias to your beautiful spirit, in memory of your honor, courage, and fierce
dignity, always.

Inés Talamantez
October 31, 1930 to September 27, 2019, 3:33 a.m.

Photograph of Inés Talamantez. Digital photograph. Created by Josef Sanchez, grandson of Inés Talamantez. Used by permission.

Her Spirit Rides on the Wings of the Eagle

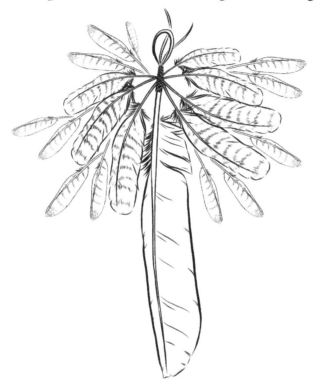

In Loving Memory
of Our Mother, Grandmother, Great Grandmother,
Sister, Professor, Healer,
Medicine Woman, Mentor, and Friend

INEZ TALAMANTEZ
10/31/1930 - 9/27/2019
3:33

"Her Spirit Rides on the Wings of the Eagle." Graphic illustration. Created by Annalise
Brolaski, granddaughter of Inés Talamantez. Used by permission.

CONTENTS

ILLUSTRATIONS

PREFACE

I would like to exercise my privilege as the editor for this volume to say a few more words about Inés Talamantez. In many ways, and as I used to like to tell her, I viewed her as my academic mother. In some ways I meant that in a literal fashion. Dr. Talamantez was born on October 31, 1930. My own mother, Cecelia Gross (née Beaulieu), was born on November 8, 1930, a mere eight days after Dr. Talamantez. Dr. Talamantez had seven children. My mother had nine. In my conversations with her, Dr. Talamantez told me how she did not use corporal punishment with her children, but instead used her Apache ways to raise her children. My mother did not hit or spank us either, but instead used her Anishinaabe ways to raise us. Dr. Talamantez had both a high emotional intelligence and intelligence quotient, as did my mother. Dr. Talamantez liked to dance. My mother was noted for her dancing skills. Finally, Dr. Talamantez was beautiful, and that is not just me saying that. My own mother was, and is still, beautiful. I love Dr. Talamantez with all my heart and soul. I love my own mother with all my heart and soul. But, at this point we part ways a bit because I have to confess, I love my own mother with all my heart and soul a bit more than Dr. Talamantez, but only a wee bit more. I am sure the reader will forgive me and understand why I love my own mother more than I do Dr. Talamantez.

When she was still with us, I tried to show my respect to Dr. Talamantez as best I could. So, at our annual meetings of the American Academy of Religion (AAR), I spent as much time as I could with her and tried to pay attention to her needs as best I could. The AAR is the professional organization for academics and others in the field of religious studies. So, for example, we were in a session once and Dr. Talamantez said she could not hear the speaker. I was sitting on her right-hand side, and the speaker was to our right. I said, try one of my hearing aids. So, I took the hearing aid out of my right ear and put it in her ear. She exclaimed how much better that was! I gave her the contact information for my audiologist. Eventually, she went to go see him to get her own hearing aids.

But here is another confession. I have to confess that it was not just because I wanted to make sure that her needs were attended to that I spent as much time as I could with Dr. Talamantez at our annual meetings of the AAR. I wanted to spend as much time with her as I could because, for me, it was so rare to get to spend time with her and I knew she would not be with us forever. I wanted to glean as much wisdom as I could from her while she was still here. However, I will note I was not the only one to follow Dr. Talamantez around the AAR. There used to be some number of us who would do so. I liked to joke that Dr. Talamantez was the mother duck with all her little ducklings in a row following after her.

And now, she is gone. I find myself thinking about her often and telling stories about her. Certainly, stories about Dr. Talamantez are part of my teaching. So, I am trying to keep her memory alive in whatever small way I can, including making sure we dedicated this book to her. I am also thinking about how to carry on her legacy. Of course, Dr. Talamantez was a giant in the field. She more or less single-handedly created the field of Native American religious studies as it exists today in the United States. It is pretty much the case that Dr. Talamantez worked with just about everybody who is anybody in the field. She most definitely paved the way for us to have the space to do Native American religious studies in the academy and at the AAR as Native people, thinking and theorizing about Native traditions from within the traditions themselves instead of imposing Western theories on Native cultures. She was a singular person, and there will never be another person like her.

So, how can I honor her memory and carry on her legacy? I am doing that in part with my scholarship. As I hope these pages make clear, we are thinking and theorizing about Native cultures from within the cultures themselves. But, what about her legacy of mentorship? I am finding more and more that it is now time for me to step forward and mentor young scholars, just as Dr. Talamantez did. I am grateful she has a number of other students who are now senior scholars in the field and who are helping to mentor young scholars, too. With the number of students she had, Dr. Talamantez left a broad base of support so the field can continue to grow and prosper. But one of the best lessons she taught us was to be good relatives and to take care of one another. I look forward to working with my colleagues to carry on the work of Dr. Talamantez and will do my best to be a good relative and take care of others.

I would be remiss if I also did not say a few words about Phyllis A. Fast (1946–2019), who also passed away while this book was still in production. Dr. Fast was another remarkable Native American woman. She was a Koyukon Athabascan who was raised on a farmstead in rural Alaska. She is much to be admired for earning her PhD in anthropology from Harvard University. From there, she spent many years teaching in the University of Alaska system, first in Fairbanks and later in Anchorage, where she retired as a professor emerita in 2014. Dr. Fast was a gifted artist who had her works displayed at multiple museums. I never had the fortune of meeting Dr. Fast myself. But I share in the loss with her family, friends, and colleagues. She was another pioneer in the field of Native American studies, and especially Alaska Native studies. I am sure she was an inspiration for many. She, too, will be missed.

Lawrence W. Gross
San Manuel Band of Mission Indians
Endowed Chair of Native American Studies
University of Redlands,
Redlands, CA
December 11, 2020

ACKNOWLEDGMENTS

I will keep my acknowledgments short and simple. I will start off by thanking Elise McHugh at the University of New Mexico Press. She advocated for this project to be published by her press and led the hard work to shepherd it through the production process. I of course have to thank my colleagues who contributed essays to this volume. I appreciate that they recognized the value of the topic and used their valuable time to write essays for the book.

I am also thinking quite a bit lately about my relatives. I recently started weekly Zoom meetings so my relatives and I can study the Ojibwe language together. It turns out, our meetings are part Ojibwe language class, part family reunion, and part gossip session, with a heavy emphasis on the latter! We have a good time in our sessions. But, at this point I am also reminded of a story about my Anishinaabe grandmother, Christine Beaulieu (1899–1982). My sister Ann told me a story about how they were in Lengby, Minnesota. Lengby is a town near the northern border of the White Earth Reservation. They decided to stop in the bar to see who was around. As the story goes, three people came up to Grandma and talked with her for a while. After they got done talking, my sister Ann asked, "Who were those people?" Grandma then went into these long genealogical connections that no doubt wound all around the reservation. But, after she was done, she said, "But just because they're related to us, it doesn't mean we have to claim them." So, I am sure I have my fair share of relatives who do not care to claim me. But no matter our status and how we stand at any one time, I want my relatives to know I love them one and all. They help ground me. That is, they give me a place to stand as a human being on this earth. I know where I stand in my culture because through our ancestors I am connected to our cultural history, and through our children and their children, I am connected to our cultural future. So, my relatives ground me in both space and time. That helps me live as a fulfilled human being. It is a blessing to have relatives, and for that, I will be eternally grateful.

Publication Credits

"Haudenosaunee Thanksgiving Address: Greetings to the Natural World" originally published as: *Thanksgiving Address: Greetings to the Natural World*, Copyright © 1993 Six Nations Indian Museum and The Tracking Project. ISBN 0–9643214–0-8. Reprinted by permission.

Chapter 3 Epigraph: *Native Voices: American Indian Identity and Resistance* edited by Richard A. Grounds, George E. Tinker, and David E. Wilkins published by the University Press of Kansas, © 2003. www.kansaspress. ku.edu. Page 209. Used by permission.

William Blackwater, 1927, from *O'odham Creation & Related Events as Told to Ruth Benedict in 1927 in Prose, Oratory, and Song* by Donald Bahr. © 2001 The Arizona Board of Regents. Reprinted by permission of the University of Arizona Press. Pages 22–23.

Unnamed Composite Storytellers, 19XX from: Dean Saxton and Lucille Saxton, *Legends and Lore of the Papago and Pima Indians* (Tucson: University of Arizona Press, 1973), 6–8. Used by permission.

"The Rattlesnake Receives His Fangs" from *Pima Indian Legends* by Anna Moore Shaw. ©1968 The Arizona Board of Regents. Reprinted by permission of the University of Arizona Press. Pages 17–19.

Manuel Havier, 1976–1978 from: Donald M. Bahr, "Four Rattlesnake Songs," in *Speaking, Singing, and Teaching: A Multidisciplinary Approach to Language Variation: Proceedings of the Eighth Annual Southwest Areal Language and Linguistics Workshop*, ed. Florence Barkin and Elizabeth A. Brandt, Anthropological Research Papers, no. 20 (Tempe: Arizona State University, 1980), 118. Used by permission.

Jane H. Hill, "What Is Lost When Names are Forgotten," in *Nature Knowledge: Ethnoscience, Cognition, and Utility*, ed. Glauco Sanga and Gherardo Ortalli (New York: Berghahn Books, 2003), 176. Used by permission.

David Kozak and David Lopez, "Echoes of Mythical Creation: Snakes, Sex, Voice," *Wicazo Sa Review* 10, no. 1 (1994): 54–55. Published by the University of Minnesota Press. Copyright 1994 by the Association for American Indian Research. Used by permission.

Peter Blue Cloud, "The Cry," in *Elderberry Flute Songs: Contemporary Coyote Tales*, 4th ed. (New York: White Pine Press, 2002), 8–9. Used by permission.

Introduction

LAWRENCE W. GROSS

THIS BOOK EXAMINES RHETORICAL practices in Native American traditions. There has been extensive scholarship on how Native Americans use rhetoric to resist colonization, as will be discussed below. However, there is comparatively little scholarship on the nature of rhetoric within individual Native communities.[1] In other words, the conventions and practices of how Native Americans address each other, especially in the public realm, is an area in need of further exploration. Our book seeks to fill that gap. As an overarching thesis, we argue that Native American rhetorical practices have their own interior logic grounded in the moral thinking and religious practices of the given tradition. Once the ways in which the rhetorical practices are grounded in the culture of a tradition is understood, the phenomenological expression of the speech patterns makes sense.

The larger goal of this project is to continue to articulate and validate Native American cultural practices. Too often, Native American cultural forms are devalued, denigrated, and dismissed within the mainstream culture. The assaults on Native cultures can have the deleterious effect of causing Native people to adopt the stance of the mainstream culture and so turn away from their own practices. Native American rhetoric is one example of this phenomenon. For example, I have heard Native Americans joke about punishing misbehaving children by making them go listen to an elder if they do not start behaving themselves! Even though it is said in jest, still, it is not unusual for young Native Americans to avoid elders because the young do not know how to listen to their senior citizens. However, as stated above, we will demonstrate Native American rhetoric has its own methods of operation based firmly in their religions, cultures, and morality that lend it a power equal to anything found in the West. So, while we seek to validate Native American rhetoric, we intend to further demonstrate the value of the Native American traditions from which they arise.

As such, the questions informing our book will include such concerns as: What are the conventions of tradition of interest, and why are they used? What strategies are used for listening to the rhetorical conventions in a given tradition? How do the conventions in question relate to other aspects of the culture?

One especially weak point in the scholarly literature is the lack of analysis regarding the conventions used in different Native American cultural practices. I made an attempt to begin this process, looking at the conventions of Anishinaabe rhetoric, such as how the speaker is guided by spiritual values and personal experience.[2] But beyond that, we have very little discussion of the strategies underlying Native American rhetoric in different traditions.

By the same token, listening to Native American rhetoric is an art in itself. No doubt, many Native Americans fall into the practice of listening to speakers within their own traditions without much formal training. However, it cannot be taken for granted that people within a tradition will actually learn how to listen to speakers from their communities. As pointed out above, this is especially a problem with young Native Americans who too often view listening to their elders as a chore and a bore. Not knowing how to listen results in young Natives missing out on the wisdom their elders have to convey, which leads to the further erosion of Native American cultures. So, it can be seen how critical it is to articulate the methods for listening to elders so as to better encourage young people to seek out their wisdom.

However, it is clear that Native American rhetoric does not exist in a cultural vacuum. Instead, it is connected to and is informed by other aspects of the culture, especially those found within the sphere of religion and morality. The essays in this book explore the various ways in which this reality plays out in various traditions. For example, my paper will discuss how the use of digressions in Anishinaabe rhetoric is connected to the religious idea that all things are connected. The use of digressions in Anishinaabe rhetoric thus is based on and gives witness to that religious idea. The essay by Philip P. Arnold examines the Thanksgiving Address found in Haudenosaunee society. In the Thanksgiving Address, the people repeatedly state how they are now of one mind as they seek consensus in their decision-making processes. The concepts of the one mind and the importance of consensus come from the traditions brought to the Haudenosaunee by the Peacekeeper, and so are firmly grounded in the religious ideals of the people. So, it can be seen when we examine Native American rhetoric, we are not simply looking at speech patterns. Instead, with Native American rhetoric grounded firmly in the cultural and religious ideals of a given tradition, that rhetoric is imbued fully with the sacred power of the traditions.

Unfortunately, as stated above, all too often non-Indian people are not familiar with the conventions of Native American rhetoric. As such, there is a tendency to slight Native American rhetorical practices. In fact, it is not uncommon for non-Indians to completely tune out Native American speakers. Again, as stated above, all too often young Native Americans pick up these very attitudes from the mainstream society. But dismissing Native American rhetoric based on Western standards is yet one more way in which Native cultures are under assault. It is a way to silence Native American voices from speaking in a manner that best fits their traditions and expresses their religious values. As such, clearly articulating the conventions of Native American rhetoric and the ways in which they are grounded in the morality of the people is an essential task in continuing the efforts to validate Native American cultures and so keep them alive and vibrant. We hope our book will make a contribution to that effort.

The paucity of writing about the traditions and values informing Native American rhetoric add to the necessity of our work. In that regard, much of the scholarly literature to date on rhetoric coming out of the field of Native American studies has emphasized the role rhetoric is playing in resistance and survivance. However, as we turn to an examination of the scholarly literature on the topic, we will start with one of the most important works in the field and one that is referenced a number of times throughout this collection, "Rhetorical Sovereignty: What Do American Indians Want from Writing?" by Scott Richard Lyons, who is Minnesota Ojibwe.[3]

Much as we are attempting here, Lyons is concerned with Native Americans laying claim to their own forms of writing and communication. He does frame the issue as part of the effort by Native Americans to resist colonization.[4] But the goal of this decolonization effort is for Native Americans to take control of writing, both the practice and the teaching, in order to strengthen the sovereignty of Native nations. He writes, "Attacks on sovereignty are attacks on what it enables us to pursue; the pursuit of sovereignty is an attempt to revive not our past, but our possibilities. Rhetorical sovereignty is the inherent right and ability of peoples to determine their own communicative needs and desires in this pursuit, to decide for themselves the goals, modes, styles, and languages of public discourse."[5] This clear commitment to rhetoric serving the interests of sovereignty has made Lyons's article a touchstone in the field.

Another important term originates from the writings of Gerald Vizenor, another Minnesota Ojibwe. In his book *Manifest Manners: Narratives on Postindian Survivance,* Vizenor introduces the term "survivance" in support of his argument that Native people need to build new societies based on our traditional cultures but responsive to the modern day. He defines "survivance" as follows: "Survivance is an active sense of presence, the continuance of native stories, not a mere reaction, or a survivable name. Native survivance stories are renunciations of dominance, tragedy and victimry."[6] When Vizenor talks about renunciations of tragedy and victimry, he means Native people need to move beyond being victims of colonization in order to create new forms of being Native in the world. The term "survivance" has become common in the field of Native American studies and is used by a number of contributors to this volume, much like the phrase "rhetorical sovereignty."

Those notions of sovereignty and survivance helped set the stage for commentators on Native American rhetoric to emphasize how Native people use rhetoric to resist colonization. One example of this approach can be found in the collection of essays, *Rhetoric of the Americas: 3114 BCE to 2012 CE,* edited by Damián Baca and Victor Villanueva. Writing in the introduction to the book, Baca focuses on the manner in which Native American rhetoric presents a "discourse of critique of Anglo- and Eurocentric ideologies.[7]" He goes on to list a number of questions informing the book, with the majority of them discussing resistance to the hegemonic power of the West. Thus, while we will admit the authors represented in this collection strive to illuminate indigenous forms of discourse, the examination invariably involves how

Native American rhetoric resists colonization.[8] Baca concludes his introduction by discussing the need to decolonize the field of rhetoric more generally speaking. He advocates examining rhetoric from the point of view of the colonized. Such a project, he asserts, will not only necessitate rethinking the assumptions underlying Western rhetoric, but also entail affirming our own ideologies, cultural meanings, and historical narratives."[9] However, by remaining entranced by the West, and speaking almost entirely in the language of resistance to colonization, little in the way of actually elucidating Native American rhetoric can be gleaned from this collection. Additionally, the essays focus on Mexico, Central and South America, and the Caribbean, and there is nothing in the way of studies of traditions north of the border. So, while we admire this effort, and we certainly share a common concern in wanting to affirm Native rhetorical practices, more could be said about indigenous discourse, especially by leaving the West behind and examining and theorizing Native American rhetoric from within the traditions themselves, as we attempt here. Hopefully, our project will further the efforts of affirming the rhetoric indigenous to the Americas.

Without going into detail, other works follow in the same vein. Looking at a few select examples in chronological order of publication, Richard Morris and Philip Wander examine how Native people use rhetoric to create social cohesion, or "social hegemony," in the face of colonization.[10] In this case, they are particularly interested in how the Lakota people used rhetoric to maintain their identity through the difficult times in the late nineteenth century. In her essay, "Rhetorics of Survivance: How American Indians Use Writing," Malea Powell turns her attention to the early twentieth century. She is interested in how the Native intellectuals Sarah Winnemucca Hopkins and Charles Alexander Eastman worked to create a new understanding of what it meant to be Indian.[11] As can be seen, her work features an emphasis on both rhetoric and survivance. So again, her project is to demonstrate how Native people use rhetoric to resist colonization. For their part, John Sanchez and Mary Stuckey focus on the 1960s and 1970s and how Native people used rhetoric during the Red Power movement.[12] That is, they explore how rhetoric was put into the service of activism. In the 2006 book edited by Ernest Stromberg, *American Indian Rhetorics of Survivance: Word Medicine, Word Magic,* we again see an interest in rhetorics of survivance.[13] The essays cover both historical examples of Native rhetoric and current-day issues related to the topic. But again, as the title indicates, the book overall stresses the manner in which Natives use rhetoric vis-à-vis colonizing forces. Returning to the nineteenth century for one last example, Jason Black is interested in how Native people of the Southeast used rhetoric as a strategy of decolonization in his essay, "Native Resistive Rhetoric and the Decolonization of American Indian Removal Discourse."[14] Although this review of the literature is limited in scope, the general idea can be gleaned that the typical approach to date has been to examine Native rhetoric as a response to colonization. We hope to move the dialogue in a different direction with this collection of essays. Of course, we cannot escape the gravity well of mainstream society, and the topic of using rhetoric to resist colonization will appear from time to time. However, for the most part our work sheds a light on the cultural factors that give Native American rhetoric its power.

In thinking about Native American rhetoric as a way of resisting colonization, I believe one critical problem arises. In resisting colonization, the purpose of this type of rhetoric seems to be confrontational, that is, standing up to the oppressive forces of the settler state. The problem is, within Native American cultures, rhetoric seems to play an entirely different role, one that seeks harmony, consensus, and unity. In that regard, the ultimate purpose of Native American rhetoric is completely different from the goal of rhetoric in the Western tradition, and here we cannot escape looking at Aristotle. In his book on the subject, Aristotle defines rhetoric as follows: "Rhetoric may be defined as the faculty of observing in any given case the available means of persuasion."[15] More to the point, rhetoric in this conception of the term is the art of argumentation. It is mainly intended for the political realm. Note, though, that as a form of argumentation, the underlying assumption is that argumentation involves confrontation. That is, each respective orator argues for his or her point of view vis-à-vis other positions. In this regard, it is not surprising that one realm of rhetoric as conceived by Aristotle was the law. Argumentation is used to determine the guilt or innocence of the alleged criminal. However, the legal system in the West is one of confrontation. The representatives of the plaintiff and defense confront each other in the court of law.

I would argue the underlying purpose of Native American rhetoric is not one of confrontation, trying to best one's rhetorical opponent. Instead, the goal of Native American rhetoric is, as I said above, the creation of harmony, consensus, and unity. The idea is to create social cohesion, especially by respecting the autonomy of individuals to decide for themselves. If we keep this idea in mind, many of the chapters start to make better sense. For example, as will be explained below, the Thanksgiving Address of the Haudenosaunee has one purpose of creating a unified mind, "now our minds are one." This approach is important in Haudenosaunee political deliberations because the idea is not to best one's opponents, but to reach consensus. As another example, the Tohono O'odham have their way of talking to rattlesnakes. The move is not to immediately kill the rattlesnake, but to talk to it and inform it of the consequences of being around humans. Killing the snake is more of a last resort. In effect, the Tohono O'odham tell the rattlesnake the way it should act in order to maintain harmony between snakes and people.

So, I will ask the reader to keep the underlying purposes and goals of Native American rhetoric in mind. If the text is approached with Western assumptions about the function of rhetoric, it becomes easy to devalue, denigrate, and dismiss the discussions of Native American rhetoric presented in these pages. Conversely, viewing the chapters through the lens of the goals of Native American rhetoric will make it easier to understand the power of those goals. To the degree that harmony, consensus, and unity are part of their religion, culture, and worldview, we can say we have reached the bedrock of Native American rhetoric. Native American rhetoric rests on the foundation of the importance of social cohesion and good relations in Native traditions. It is that driving force to maintain social cohesion and good relations that ultimately gives Native American rhetoric its power.

As we turn to a summary of the chapters, then, I would like to start out by discussing three of the essays that are of particular importance because they exemplify Native American rhetoric. That is, they transfer as much as is possible the forms and conventions of Native American rhetoric into written form. As such, I want to give them special consideration. The three works, in order they appear in this collection, are by Philip P. Arnold, Seth Schermerhorn, and Inés Talamantez. They present examples, respectively, of Haudenosaunee, Tohono O'odham, and Apache rhetoric.

Philip P. Arnold in his essay in chapter 1, "'And Now Our Minds Are One': The

Thanksgiving Address and Attaining Consensus among the Haudenosaunee,"
provides a deep understanding of Haudenosaunee rhetorical practices. The
example of Native American rhetoric in the chapter is the Thanksgiving Address
he presents at the beginning of his essay. As Arnold explains, the Haudenosaunee
customarily open formal gatherings by reciting a greeting of thanks and
gratitude to the people in attendance and to the other-than-human "people"
who comprise the natural world. As he clearly states, this is not a prayer intended
as a form of worship. Instead, the greeting expresses thanks for all the gifts
humans receive from the natural world. This act of thanksgiving reaffirms the
Haudenosaunee connection to the different elements of the natural world.
However, just as importantly, the greeting brings the people together as one. At
the end of each section, a refrain is repeated: "And now our minds are one." That
statement reminds the people of the important Haudenosaunee value of
consensus in decision-making. This rhetorical practice reflects the religion,
worldview and morality of the Haudenosaunee people. Reminding the people
that "our minds are one" reinforces the Haudenosaunee principles of unity,
consensus, and peaceful coexistence. So, while the greeting may appear simple
on the surface, it both celebrates and creates unity between humans and the
natural world and within the human community.

I would like to take a slight digression at this point and talk a bit more
about the Thanksgiving Address presented in the opening of the chapter. The
Thanksgiving Address constitutes about half the chapter. It might seem like
a waste, a chore, and a bore to have to read the whole thing. I would caution
the reader against adopting that attitude. Instead, I am reminded of a story. A
spiritual leader for one of our local Native nations came to campus to give a
blessing before an event. Before the event started, he asked how much time
he had. Oh! He made me so mad! So, I looked at him and said, "These things
are sacred matters. You don't put sacred matters on the clock!" He said, "Thank
you." Now, that spiritual leader knows that whenever he comes to our campus
to give a blessing, he can take as much time as he needs to do it in a good way.
So, by presenting the Thanksgiving Address here, we are trying to do so in a
good way.

I would therefore advise the reader to instead take the Thanksgiving
Address in its intended spirit, that is, to put oneself in a good spiritual place so
that our minds may be one. So, relax into the Thanksgiving Address, take the

time to read it through without skimming over it, and feel the calming power of the prayer and understand how the Thanksgiving Address really can help create the conditions such that now our minds are one. Then, the reader really will be able to understand the power of the rhetoric that is the Thanksgiving Address of the Haudenosaunee people.

Returning to the chapter discussions, Seth Schermerhorn takes another unique angle on Native American rhetoric in his essay in chapter 5, "'O'odham, Too': Or, How to Speak to Rattlesnakes." I appreciate the way Schermerhorn challenges one of the underlying assumptions of this book—that we discuss how Native Americans talk to each other—and expands the definition of what it means to be a human. In this case, the Tohono O'odham view animals, including rattlesnakes, as human, too. So, the question becomes, how does one talk to humans in the form of rattlesnakes? What is unique about this essay is the primary material Schermerhorn includes in his discussion. He has both interviews that he conducted with a Tohono O'odham with whom he works and Tohono O'odham stories about rattlesnakes. The interviews are published verbatim, so they provide an unpolished look at how teachings about rattlesnakes are presented in the culture. For their part, the stories provide the cultural understanding of rattlesnakes in the culture. In this case, the stories do not present a unified picture; they have their differences in details and other considerations. Together, the teachings and stories present how a Tohono O'odham would come to understand rattlesnakes in the culture and how to speak to them. However, the teaching and stories are not straightforward. They are, in a way, loose around the edges. But this is, in fact, closer to the way Native American rhetoric functions as a living practice. That is, the rhetoric is as much affective as anything else. It takes time and patience to bring the various teachings together to create a feel for how to talk to rattlesnakes. Schermerhorn thus presents how Native American rhetoric actually functions as a living reality, and so is worth special attention.

Inés Talamantez has perhaps the purest form of Native American rhetoric presented in this volume in chapter 7. She is principally interested in how Apache rhetoric reflects and is informed by the Apache notion of *diiyii*, or "sacred power," although the English translation does not do full justice to the complex manner in which the term functions in Apache culture. Be that as it may, Talamantez opens with an introduction to diiyii and its relationship to

Apache rhetoric. However, from there she spins out the implications of the connection in many different forms, following a thread of thought that takes her through many of her personal experiences and concerns, including the importance of learning one's indigenous language, the various reactions by non-Native and Native students learning about Native American ways, and, since it was her primary area of personal and research interest, the Apache girl's coming-of-age ceremony. The material covers a lot of ground, not all of it seemingly directly connected to the main topic of Apache rhetoric. However, as I tell my students, in listening to Native American elders, and for many of us in the field, Inés Talamantez was our elder, it is important to remember that even though what they are saying may not seem relevant to the issue under discussion, they are giving the listener, or, in this case, the reader, things they can be and should be thinking about for the rest of their lives. I know for myself this is how I always approached listening to Dr. Talamantez. I approach her essay with this same spirit.

We should also address the power Native American rhetoric can have on the listeners, which is a topic that is not covered to any large degree in the scholarly literature. Chapter 10 by Gabriel Estrada provides an example of this phenomenon. As will be explained below, Estrada examines the film, *My Own Private Lower Post*, directed by Duane Gastant' Aucoin. At the end of the chapter, Estrada discusses how the film had a healing effect on zir and other two-spirit Native people. Ze provides personal testimony about zirs life story and how the film had an impact on his healing journey. So, I am pleased we have an essay that speaks to the power Native American rhetoric can have on the listeners from the listeners' point of view. It is a topic of inquiry we hope other scholars will pursue.

As for the rest of the book, the layout for the chapters will take something of a circle around the North American continent. I will provide more detail about the respective chapters below. However, by way of a short summary, we will begin our inquiry in the northland with Philip P. Arnold's essay on the Thanksgiving Address in the Haudenosaunee tradition. My essay on another northern people, the Anishinaabeg (plural of Anishinaabe), will follow. From there we will by necessity make a rather abrupt jump to the borderland of the south. Delores Mondragón explains her experience having mixed identities as related to her upbringing in El Paso, Texas We next venture into Mexico with an examination of Nahua rhetoric. We return to the borderland experience as Seth Schermerhorn looks at a borderland people, the Tohono O'odham. We will spend time with other Southwest traditions with essays on the Navajo and Apache. From there we move to the West Coast with a study of the Hupa people of northern California. Moving further up the coast, our next stop takes us to the Lower Coast Salish. Moving further north, we arrive at the land of the Teslin Tlingit in the southern Yukon area of Canada. We finish the tour in Alaska with an essay on riddles in Athabascan culture. We conclude the work with a thorough presentation of "Coyotean rhetoric."

Another metaphor that serves as an organizing principle for the book is the path of the sun during the day. So, we start off with the east, the dawn. It seems like good practice to start the day with a prayer. And we do so with the Thanksgiving Address in Arnold's work. As the sun climbs the sky, we move to the southeast and south. We place the essay by Inés Talamantez near the middle of the book, the zenith. Dr. Talamantez belonged to the Sun Clan. And there is a way her students, including myself, revolved around her. So, Dr. Talamantez stands in the middle at the height of the book, and the rest of us revolve around her. As the day progresses, we move to the west and finally come to the end of the day. Inés Hernández-Ávila finishes her piece with the cry of the coyote. So, as the day comes to an end and night starts to fall, the coyote sings, and we are reminded it is time to retire and how the day was blessed. Our journey through Native American rhetoric thus has both a geographic and temporal component to it.

Turning now to the individual chapters, we discussed Arnold's piece on the Haudenosaunee above. So, looking at my essay in chapter 2, my main goal is to demonstrate how the use of digressions in Anishinaabe rhetoric is informed by and reflects our religion and worldview that all things are related. First, I explain how digressions are used. In effect, speakers invariably circle back to their main point. So, this is not stream-of-consciousness speaking. Instead, it would be better to say Anishinaabe speakers are exploring the connections between different topics. Exploring connections between topics relates to the worldview of the Anishinaabeg. In Anishinaabe thinking, all things are related. This is also part of their moral thinking. So, Anishinaabe rhetoric both reflects and demonstrates the worldview and morality of the Anishinaabeg. This piece is placed second in the book in order to provide an understanding of some of the foundations of Native American rhetoric. The intent is to make it easier to understand some of the observations that will reoccur throughout the book, such as the role of storytelling in relation to rhetoric in various traditions.

Next, in chapter 3, Delores Mondragón looks at how indigenous and Chicana, Chicano, and Chicanx scholars insert indigenous worldviews in their work and so develop forms of survival scholarship and build commitments to solidarity with their respective communities. One of the first challenges is to assert the indigenous and Chicana, Chicano, and Chicanx presence in academia by naming their experience. Drawing on the writings of Gloria Anzaldúa, the concept of mestiza consciousness is used to understand and name the real-world experiences of the indigenous and Chicana, Chicano, and Chicanx scholars. By naming their experience, these scholars can then better assert their presence and help them find ways to navigate the often treacherous waters of academia. In asserting their presence, space is opened within academia for the indigenous and Chicana, Chicano, and Chicanx voice, and the Native worldview can join the conversation in advancing scholarship.

In chapter 4, Felica Lopez provides a close reading of the Nahua codices to bring to light the rhetorical traditions from Mexico and Central America. The codices were written using a system of glyphic and pictorial writing. Only a limited number of the codices remain because the invading Spanish destroyed the large corpus of written works extant at the time. However, enough remains that we can develop an understanding of Nahua rhetoric by combining the written history as found in the codices with the religious traditions and the language of the people. Lopez demonstrates how the rhetoric related in the codices relates to women's concerns, such as childbirth. However, without knowing the cultural context and worldview of the Nahua, it is easy for the codices to escape easy understanding. A thorough knowledge of the Nahua worldview, then, is necessary to appreciate the full rhetorical power of the codices.

As discussed above, Seth Schermerhorn explains how to talk to rattlesnakes in Tohono O'odham culture in chapter 5.

Meredith Moss examines current-day rhetorical practices among the Diné, or Navajo, people in chapter 6. As she demonstrates, maintaining the distinct identity of the Navajo is an integral part of their public discourse. Thus, even though public discussions are often conducted in English, especially with regard to politics, the Navajo have specific strategies to incorporate the use of the Navajo language, such as using Navajo discourse markers and pronunciation. Most importantly, though, the Diné will bookend their talks with statements in the Diné language. So, while on the one hand the use of the Diné language and other conventions of Diné rhetorical patterns will mark the speaker as being Diné, those same considerations help maintain the solidarity of the people. By establishing their identity as Diné in this manner, the individual will have a stronger rhetorical foundation from which to speak.

The essay on Apache rhetoric by Inés Talamantez discussed above appears in chapter 7.

While Inés Hernández-Ávila will discuss Coyotean rhetoric in chapter 12, Cutcha Risling Baldy discusses salmon rhetoric among the Hupa Indians of northern California in Chapter 8. For Risling Baldy, salmon rhetoric arises from the close connection the Hupa people have to the salmon. It is based on the knowledge that is generated from the importance of salmon to the Hupa in many different ways. So, salmon rhetoric involves living close to the land and the water of the rivers that are central to their culture. It involves the sacred stories that talk of the relationship between the salmon and the Hupa. It also concerns the ceremonial relationship the Hupa have with the salmon. In effect, the Hupa have generated knowledge about the salmon that is equal to and in many ways superior to Western "scientific rhetorics" about salmon. Risling Baldy thus argues that the Hupa people and other Native people in northern California concerned about the survival of the salmon should center salmon rhetorics in their efforts to influence state and federal policies and regulations that govern the fate of the salmon.

Danica Miller focuses more on interpersonal relationships in her discussion of the Lower Coast Salish in Chapter 9. There are two aspects of Lower Coast Salish rhetoric she reviews: introductions and teasing. The Lower Coast Salish introduce themselves by stating their relatives and clans. This expresses the Lower Coast Salish cultural value of relationships. For its part, teasing plays a role in Lower Coast Salish culture by "nudging" people in a good direction. That is, it is not the art of argumentation as in Western rhetoric, but a means to gently guide people. Both of these aspects of Lower Coast Salish rhetoric are further based on a central cultural value: familial love and respect. So, the

Lower Coast Salish use the conventions of their introductions and teasing to promote healthy relationships between people.

In chapter 10, Gabriel Estrada discusses healing from historical trauma in a film by the Tlingit film producer, Duane Gastant' Aucoin. Estrada examines Aucoin's movie *My Own Private Lower Post*. The film mainly centers on the healing process Aucoin's family went through to recover from the trauma inflicted on her mother in boarding school. However, Aucoin is also interested in asserting the presence of two-spirit people in traditional Tlingit culture to heal the trauma endured by two-spirit individuals in Native communities. To that end, the film ends with a depiction of a traditional Tlingit story that involves an affirmation of two-spirit identity. As such, Estrada argues, the film is a powerful rhetorical device for healing from both the more general trauma brought about by colonization and the more specific trauma of two-spirit people.

One aspect of the rhetorical practices of specific tribes that is rarely studied involves riddles. In chapter 11, Phyllis A. Fast addresses that shortcoming by examining the traditional use of riddles in the social practices of the Koyukon Athabascan people of Alaska. In the past, the riddles often involved different aspects of nature. The interlocuter posed a riddle about some specific aspect of nature. The answer was hidden both within the complex language of the Koyukon people and the workings of nature. That is, in order to answer the riddle, one needed to know both the intricacies of the language and the environment. Unfortunately, because of language loss and colonization, the power of the riddles has been lost in Koyukon society. However, aspects of riddling continue in the form of teasing to help the Koyukon maintain their distinct cultural identity. So, while the forms of the rhetoric may have changed, the cultural values of the importance of knowing the land and maintaining good relations are still expressed in Koyukon rhetoric.

The above exploration of Native American rhetorical practices only begins to skim the surface of the conventions whereby Native people speak to each other. But, as can be gleaned, standing behind these rhetorical practices are the religions, cultures, and worldviews of the various traditions. Having captured a glimpse of the depth of Native American rhetoric, religions, cultures, and worldviews, the manner in which Native American rhetoric finds its way into academia and public discourse in general takes on a whole new level of meaning. The last essay in the book provides an example of how that process works.

In chapter 12, Inés Hernández-Ávila discusses what she introduces as the "Coyotean rhetoric" of the Mohawk writer Peter Blue Cloud. Hernández-Ávila argues that when looking at how Coyotean rhetoric functions in Native societies, the emphasis should not be on the more predictable notions of this Trickster figure, but instead, on the deeper and more complex facets of this well-known sacred being. By considering Blue Cloud's full and complicated rendition of Coyote, a Coyotean rhetoric emerges that encompasses teachings about humans' (flawed) relationships with the land, the gentle love elders (even Coyotes) have for the young, and Coyote in the role of peacemaker (and not always troublemaker). As she argues, Coyote is all those things and more. It is that multivalent nature of Coyote that makes Coyotean rhetoric so powerful and, as she concludes, provides the thread that ties all the essays in this collection together. By tying all those threads together, and with the ending cry of the coyote, the chapter makes for a fitting essay to conclude our collection.

Our work therefore covers a wide range of topics and traditions. Thus, even though the topic of our book is Native American rhetoric, it is of course true that there is no one, single rhetoric that covers all the diverse cultures indigenous to the Americas. Indeed, in truth our collection is a mere passing glance at the richness of rhetorical practices that exist among Native people. Still, we hope our efforts will shed some light on the topic. More to the point, we hope our study constitutes a starting point for further work on the cultural factors that give Native American rhetoric its power. We also hope it will inspire Native people to continue to claim their cultural practices and assert their legitimacy. So, in some ways, by focusing on how Native Americans talk to each other and ignoring the colonizers to as great a degree as possible, we are actually engaging in an act of resistance ourselves. We are saying we do not have to define ourselves by the colonizers or limit our understanding of our cultures only as they exist to resist colonization. We assert our cultural practices are good enough in and of themselves. By taking that stand, we perform the ultimate act of resistance. We hope that message shines clear in the pages that follow.

Notes

1.   Lawrence W. Gross, *Anishinaabe Ways of Knowing and Being* (Farnham Surrey, UK: Ashgate, 2014), 199–200.

2.   Lawrence W. Gross, "Anishinaabe Rhetoric," chap. 8 in *Anishinaabe Ways of Knowing and Being* (Farnham Surrey, UK: Ashgate, 2014), 199–200.

3.   Scott Richard Lyons, "Rhetorical Sovereignty: What Do American Indians Want from Writing?," *College Composition and Communication* 51, no. 3 (February 2000): 447–68.

4.   Lyons, "Rhetorical Sovereignty," 449.

5.   Lyons, "Rhetorical Sovereignty," 449–50.

6.   Gerald Vizenor, *Manifest Manners: Narratives on Postindian Survivance* (1994; repr., Lincoln: University of Nebraska Press, 1999), vii.

7.   Damián Baca and Victor Villanueva, eds., *Rhetorics of the Americas: 3114 BCE to 2012 CE* (New York: Palgrave Macmillan, 2010), 2.

8.   Baca and Villanueva, *Rhetorics of the Americas*, 2.

9.   Baca and Villanueva, *Rhetorics of the Americas*, 12.

10.   Richard Morris and Philip Wander, "Native American Rhetoric: Dancing in the Shadows of the Ghost Dance," *Quarterly Journal of Speech* 76, no. 2 (May 1990): 164–91.

11.   Malea Powell, "Rhetorics of Survivance: How American Indians Use Writing," *College Composition and Communication* 53, no. 3 (2002): 396–434, https://doi.org/10.2307/1512132.

12.   John Sanchez and Mary E. Stuckey, "The Rhetoric of American Indian Activism in the 1960s and 1970s," *Communication Quarterly* 48, no. 2 (2000): 120–36.

13.   Ernest Stromberg, ed., *American Indian Rhetorics of Survivance: Word Medicine, Word Magic* (Pittsburgh: University of Pittsburgh Press, 2006).

14.   Jason E. Black, "Native Resistive Rhetoric and the Decolonization of American Indian Removal Discourse," *Quarterly Journal of Speech* 95, no. 1 (2009): 66–88.

15.   Aristotle, "Rhetoric," August 21, 2008, https://web.archive.org/web/20080821121058/http://www.public.iastate.edu/~honeyl/Rhetoric/rhet1-2.html.

CHAPTER ONE

"And Now Our Minds Are One"

The Thanksgiving Address and Attaining Consensus among the Haudenosaunee

PHILIP P. ARNOLD

Introduction

The Ganoñhéñ·nyoñ', which is called the "Thanksgiving Address" in English, translates to "The Words before All Else." It is a protocol, referred to as the "opening," used by the Haudenosaunee (Iroquois) before and after every gathering and also as a greeting of a new day and at other public ceremonial events. At ceremonial events, it is recited in a Haudenosaunee language (Mohawk, Oneida, Onondaga, Cayuga, Tuscarora, or Seneca), but it has also been translated into English and a variety of other languages.[1] Often, it will be asked that the recitation of the Thanksgiving Address not be recorded at public events, but there are several recitations that have been recorded in a variety of contexts, from the opening of the United Nations Forum in Indigenous Issues each year, to a small gathering at Onondaga Lake, near Syracuse, New York.

For the Haudenosaunee, the Thanksgiving Address is something that was given to them at Creation. It is an ancient process, used for millennia, that brings minds together "as one," all beings involved in the basic material necessities of life. What follows is the "Thanksgiving Address" in English and Mohawk.

Haudenosaunee Thanksgiving Address: Greetings to the Natural World[2]

THE PEOPLE

Today we have gathered and we see that the cycles
of life continue. We have been given the duty to
live in balance and harmony with each other and
all living things. So now, we bring our minds
together as one as we give greetings and thanks to
each other as people.
Now our minds are one.

ONKWEHSHÓN:'A

Onwa wenhniserá:te ionkwakia'taró:ron ne
iorihwá:ke ne aitewaka'eniónnion tsi niiohtonhá:kie
tsi na'titewátere ne onkwehshón:'a tánon' tsi ní:ioht
tsi rokwatákwen ne ohontsià:ke. Ne ne á:ienre'k
akwékon skén:nen tsi tewanonhtón:nion ne tsi
niionkwè:take kenhnón:we iahitewaia'taié:ri oni tsí
inonkwata'karí:te iah thahò:ten tekionkwakia'tónkion
ne kanonhwa'kténhtshera'. Ne kati ehnón:we
iorihwá:ke tsi entewátka'we ne kanonhweratónhtshera.
Éhtho niiohtónha'k ne onkwa'nikón:ra.

THE EARTH MOTHER

We are all thankful to our Mother, the Earth, for
she gives us all that we need for life. She supports
our feet as we walk about upon her. It gives us joy
that she continues to care for us as she has from the
beginning of time. To our Mother, we send
greetings and thanks.
Now our minds are one.

IETHI'NISTÉNHA OHÓNTSIA

Onen nón:wa ehnón:we nentsitewate'nikonhraié:ra'te
Iethi'nisténha Ohóntsia tsi ne'e taiakohtka'wenhá:kie
tsi naho'tèn:shon ionkionhéhkwen. Iotshennón:nia't
tsi shé:kon teionkhihsniékie tsi ní:ioht tsi
shakohrienaién:ni ne shahakwatá:ko ne tsi
ionhontsiá:te. Ne ionkhihawíhshon ne onkwehshón:'a
tánon' kario'ta'shon:'a tsi nikarí:wes ohontsià:ke
entewátka'we ne kanonhweratónhtshera.
Éhtho niiohtónha'k ne onkwa'nikón:ra.

THE WATERS

We give thanks to all the waters of the world for
quenching our thirst and providing us with
strength. Water is life. We know its power in many
forms—waterfalls and rain, mists and streams,
rivers and oceans. With one mind, we send
greetings and thanks to the spirit of Water.
Now our minds are one.

OHNEKA'SHÓN:'A

Onen ehnón:we ientsitewakié:ra'te ne
ohneka'shón:'a tsi rawé:ren tsi enkahnekónionke ne
tsi ionhontsiá:te. Ne ehonón:we nitewéhtha ne
aionkwaha'taná:wen nó:nen enionkwania'táthen.
Nia'teka'shatstenhserá:ke tewaienté:re—tsi
ieiohnekénshon, tsi iokennó:re's, tsi iaonhawí:ne's
tánon' tsi kaniatarahrón:nion. Khénska tsi
entewahwe'nón:ni ne onswa'nikón:ra ne
iorihwá:ke tsi entewátka'we ne
kanonhweratónhtshera.
Éhtho niiohtónha'k ne onkwa'nikón:ra.

THE FISH

We turn our minds to the all the Fish life in the water.
They were instructed to cleanse and purify the
water. They also give themselves to us as food. We
are grateful that we can still find pure water. So,
we turn now to the Fish and send our greetings
and thanks.
Now our minds are one.

KENTSIONSHÓN:'A

Tánon' kati ehnón:we nikontí:teron ne
khia'tekéntsiake tánon' otsi'nonwa'shón:'a. Ne'e
teshakó:wi ne takontohtáhrho tsi kahnekarón:nion.
Ne oni taionatka'wenhákie ne onkwatennà:tshera
ne ionkwaia'tahnirá:tha. Ne ne iotshennón:nia't tsi
shé:kon iorihwató:ken ionkwatshenrionhákie ne ne
kahnekí:io. Ehnonkwá:ti entewakié:ra'te ne
entewátka'we ne kanonhweratónhtshera.
Éhtho niiohtónha'k ne onkwa'nikón:ra.

THE PLANTS

Now we turn toward the vast fields of Plant life.
As far as the eye can see, the Plants grow, working
many wonders. They sustain many life-forms. With
our minds gathered together, we give thanks and
look forward to seeing Plant life for many
generations to come.
Now our minds are one.

TSI SHONKWAIENTHÓ:WI

Ne onen ehnón:we nentsitewakié:ra'te netsi ní:ioht
tsi tekahentaién:ton. Ia'teiotkahróktha ohontsiakwé:kon

taiohnio'onhákie ne shonkwaienthó:wi ne
nia'tekonti'satstenhserá:ke ne ohonte'shón:'a.
Aiá:wens kiótkon aitewatkahthóhseke ne tsi ní:ioht
tsi rowinentá:'on. Enska tsi entewahwe'nón:ni ne
onkwa'nikón:ra tánon' tsi ia'teiotihtehrón:ton
entitewahawihtánion ne kanonhweratónhtshera.
Éhtho niiohtónha'k ne onkwa'nikón:ra.

THE FOOD PLANTS

With one mind, we turn to honor and thank all the
Food Plants we harvest from the garden. Since the
beginning of time, the grains, vegetables, beans,
and berries have helped the people survive. Many
other living things draw strength from them too.
We gather all the Plant Foods together as one and
send them a greeting and thanks.
Now our minds are one.

KAIEN'THÓHSHERA

Enska tsi entewahwe'nón:ni ne onkwa'nikón:ra
tánon' ehnón:we nentsitewakié:ra'te ne ne
onkwatenná:tshera tsi ní:ioht tsi shonkwaienthó:wi.
Ne teionkwahsniékie ne kaienthóhsera tsi nikarí:wes
ohontsià:ke teionkwatawénrie. Nia'teiotikióhkwake
ne ká:nen, osahè:ta tánon' kahi'shón:'a
tewaienthókwas ne ionkwaiatahnirá:tha. Ne oni
iononhéhkwen ne kwah tsi naho'tèn:shon róhshon
ne ohontsià:ke. Ne tsi nentewá:iere ne kati
enkiethihwe'nón:ni ne kaienthohtshera'shón:'a tsi
wa'tiiethinonhwerá:ton.
Éhtho niiohtónha'k ne onkwa'nikón:ra.

THE MEDICINE HERBS

Now we turn to all the Medicine Herbs of the
world. From the beginning they were instructed to
take away sickness. They are always waiting and
ready to heal us. We are happy there are still
among us those special few who remember how to
use these plants for healing. With one mind, we
send greetings and thanks to the Medicines and to
the keepers of the Medicines.
Now our minds are one.

ONONHKWA'SHÓN:'A

Ne onen ehnón:we nentsitewakié:ra'te ne
ononhkwa'shón:'a iorihwá:ke. Ne tsi nihoié:ren
ohontsiakwé:kon tethohráhthon ne
ononhkwa'shón:'a. Ne ionateríhonte a'é:ren
kontihawíhtha ne kanonhwa'kténhtshera. Kiótkon
iotiharékies tánon' ionatatewinentá:on
aiakótsien'te'. Iotshennónnia't tsi shé:kon
teiontonkwe'taiestáhshion ne ronné:iahre tsi
niiotiianerenhshero'tén:shon ne ononhkwa'shón:'a.
Onen kati nen'ne tentsiethinonhwerá:ton ne
ononhkwa'shón:'a tánon' tsi niionkwè:take ne'e
tehotíhkwen tsi rontenonhkwá:tsheranonhne.
Éhtho niiohtónha'k ne onkwa'nikón:ra.

THE ANIMALS

We gather our minds together to send greetings
and thanks to all the Animal life in the world. They
have many things to teach us as people. We see
them near our homes and in the deep forests. We
are glad they are still here, and we hope that it will

always be so.
Now our minds are one.

KONTÍRIO

Enska tsi entewahwe'nón:ni ne onkwa'nikón:ra
tánon' teniethinonhwerá:ton ne kontí:rio ne ne
ohontsiakwé:kon shakotká:wen. Ókia'ke
iethí:kenhs teionatawenriehákies aktónkie tsi
ionkwataskwahrónnion oni tsi kaskawaién:ton.
Iotshennónnia't ehnón:we iorihwá:ke tsi shé:kon
iethí:kenhs ne kontí:rio oni aiá:wens kiótkon
ehnaiohtónhake.
Éhtho niiohtónha'k ne onkwa'nikón:ra.

THE TREES

We now turn our thoughts to the Trees. The Earth
has many families of Trees who have their own
instructions and uses. Some provide us with
shelter and shade, others with fruit, beauty, and
other useful things. Many people of the world use
a Tree as a symbol of peace and strength. With one
mind, we greet and thank the Tree life.
Now our minds are one.

OKWIRE'SHÓN:'A

Onen nón:wa ehnón:we nentsitewate'nikonhraié:ra'te
ne iorihwá:ke ne okwire'shón:'a. Ohontsiakwé:kon
kahwatsiraké:ron iotihnió:ton ne ne khia'tekakwí:rake.
Ne ne tsi naho'tèn:shon ionaterihón:te ne khia'tekaién:take
ókia'ke' thonón:we nitewaterahkwawehosthákhwa
tánon' ókia'ke' iohien'tón:nion oni tsi ne

iontenonhshatariha'táhkhwa tánon' oni ne ionniá:ton ne
tsi ionkwataskwahrónnion. Iotka'tákie ronatkwirarákwen
ne onkwehshón:'a ne ne ohontsiakwé:kon
kahwatsiraké:ron tsi ne'e shonehiahráhkhwen ne
skenen'kó:wa tánon' ka'shasténhsera. Ensaka tsi
entewahwe'nón:ni ne onkwa'nikón:ra tsi
wa'kiethinonhwerá:ton ne okwire'shón:'a.
Éhtho niiohtónha'k ne onkwa'nikón:ra.

THE BIRDS

We put our minds together as one and thank all the
Birds who move and fly about over our heads. The
Creator gave them beautiful songs. Each day they
remind us to enjoy and appreciate life. The Eagle
was chosen to be their leader. To all the Birds—
from the smallest to the largest—we send our
joyful greetings and thanks.
Now our minds are one.

OTSI'TEN'OKÓN:'A

Enska tsi entewahwe'nón:ni ne onkwa'nikón:ra
tánon' teniethinonhwerá:ton ne otsi'ten'okón:'a tsi
ionkwatenontsistaténion kontikienónkie's. Ne kati
ne'e shakorenná:wi ne akonterennó:ten ne ne
skén:nen akaién:take tsi ionhontsiá:te. Ókia'ke oni
ne entewatekhwaiéhstahkwe. Oni ne rorákwen ne
tsi niká:ien entkonwatikowanenháke ne ne á:kweks
nihohshennó:ten. Iotshennónnia't tsi shé:kon
Iethí:kenhs akwé:kon ne otsi'ten'okón:'a ne
nihonná:sa oni ne raktikowá:nen's. Onen kati
tentsiethinonhwerá:ton ne otsi'ten'okón:'a.
Éhtho niiohtónha'k ne onkwa'nikón:ra.

THE FOUR WINDS

We are all thankful to the powers we know as the
Four Winds. We hear their voices in the moving air
as they refresh us and purify the air we breathe.
They help us to bring the change of seasons. From the
four directions they come, bringing us messages
and giving us strength. With one mind, we send
our greetings and thanks to the Four Winds.
Now our minds are one.

OWERA'SHÓN:'A

Onen nón:wa ehnón:we nentsitewate'nikonraié:ra'te
ne tsi ní:ioht tsi rokwatá:kwen rawé:ren enkaién:take
ne ka'shatstenhsera'shón:'a ne ne kaié:ri nikawerá:ke.
Ne iethiwennahrónkha ratiwerarástha ne tsi
ionhontsiá:te á:se shonnón:ni ne tsi ní:ioht tsi
tewatón:rie oni tsi ne tehotitenionhákie ne tsi
niionkwakenhnhó:tens. Kaié:ri niiokwén:rare tsi nón:we
thatiienhthákhwa tsi ionkhi'shatstenhsherá:wihs.
Ne tsi nentsitewá:iere enska tsi entewahwe'nón:ni
ne onkwa'nikón:ra tánon' teniethinonhwerá:ton ne
ne kaié:ri nikawerá:ke.
Éhtho niiohtónha'k ne onkwa'nikón:ra.

THE THUNDERERS

Now we turn to the west where our Grandfathers,
the Thunder Beings, live. With lightning and
thundering voices, they bring with them the water
that renews life. We bring our minds together as
one to send greetings and thanks to our Grandfathers,
the Thunderers.
Now our minds are one.

RATIWÉ:RAS

Onen ehnón:we ientsitewakié:ra'te ne tsi
ia'tewa'tshénthos nón:we thatiienhthákhwa ne
ionkhisho'thokón:'a ratiwé:ras.
Tewahni'nakara'wánionhs nó:nen á:re
tontaiaonharé:re tahatihnekenhá:wi ne á:se
enshonnón:ni ne tsi ionhontsiá:te. Ne tsi
nentewá:iere enska tsi entewahwe'nón:ni ne
onkwa'nikón:ra tánon' teniethinonhwerá:ton ne
ionkhisho'thokón:'a ratiwé:ras.
Éhtho niiohtónha'k ne onkwa'nikón:ra.

THE SUN

We now send greetings and thanks to our eldest
Brother, the Sun. Each day without fail he travels
the sky from east to west, bringing the light of a
new day. He is the source of all the fires of life.
With one mind, we send greetings and thanks to
our Brother, the Sun.
Now our minds are one.

KIONHKEHNÉHKHA KARÁHKWA

Onen nón:wa ehnón:we nentsitewate'nikonraié:ra'te
ne tsi karonhiá:te rorihwató:ken éhtho tehaiahiá:khons
ne tshionkwahtsí:'a kionhkehnéhkha karáhkwa.
Ne tehoswa'thé:ton tsi niaonkwenonhákie tánon'
ne ro'tariha'tonhákie ne tsi ionhontsiá:te ne ne
skén:nen tsi akontonhahtén:ti ne tsi nahò:ten
shonkwaienthó:wi. Ne tsi nentsitewá:iere enska tsi
entewahwe'nón:ni ne onkwa'nikón:ra tánon'
tentshitewanonhwerá:ton ne tshionkwahtsí:'a
kionhkehnéhkha karáhkwa.
Éhtho niiohtónha'k ne onkwa'nikón:ra.

GRANDMOTHER MOON

We put our minds together to give thanks to our
oldest Grandmother, the Moon, who lights the
nighttime sky. She is the leader of woman all over the
world, and she governs the movement of the ocean
tides. By her changing face we measure time, and it
is the Moon who watches over the arrival of children
here on Earth. With one mind, we send greetings
and thanks to our Grandmother, the Moon.
Now our minds are one.

AHSONTHENHNÉHKHA KARÁHKWA

Ne tsi nentsitewá:iere enska tsi entewahwe'nón:ni
ne onkwa'nikón:ra tánon' teniethinonhwerá:ton ne
ne ahsonthenhnéhshon ehnón:we kiekonhsarákies
ne ne ionkhihsótha karáhkwa. Ohontsiakwé:kon ne
tekontatenen'tshí:ne ne tsiona'thonwí:sen. Oni tsi
ní:ioht tsi wat'nekoriá:nerenhs ohontsiakwé:kon
akaónha ne ehnón:we iakorihwaientáhkwen.
Akaónha iakote'nientenhsthonhákie ka'nikahá:wi
tsi tehotita'onhákie ne ratiksha'okón:'a. Oni ne
tewate'nientenhstáhkhwa tsi ní:ioht tsi teiakotenionhákie tsi
nikiakotkonhsaierá:ton ne'e onkwatenhni'tashetáhtshera.
Onen kati enska tsi entewahwe'nón:ni ne onkwa'nikón:ra
tánon' teniethinonhwerá:ton ne ionkhihsótha karáhkwa.
Éhtho niiohtónha'k ne onkwa'nikón:ra.

THE STARS

We give thanks to the Stars who are spread across
the sky like jewelry. We see them in the night,
helping the Moon to light the darkness and
bringing dew to the gardens and growing things.
When we travel at night, they guide us home. With

our minds gathered together as one, we send
greetings and thanks to the Stars.
Now our minds are one.

OTSISTANOHKWA'SHÓN:'A

É:neken nentsitewakié:ra'te ne ne
otsistanohkwa'shón:'a tentsiethinonhwerá:ton.
Ahsonthenhnéhshon iethí:kenhs shakotiienawá:se
ne ionkhihsótha karáhkwa tehotihswathé:ton. Oni
tsi ne'e ron'aweiástha ne ne skén:nen tsi
akontonha'tén:ti ne tsi nahò:ten shonkwaienthó:wi
tánon' tsi ionkwathehtaké:ron. Ne oni
tewate'nientenhsthákhwa tsi iah thaitewakia'táhton
tsi niahonkwennonhákie. Enska tsi
entewahwe'nón:ni ne onkwa'nikón:ra tánon'
teniethinonhwerá:ton ne otsistanohkwa'shón:'a.
Éhtho niiohtónha'k ne onkwa'nikón:ra.

THE ENLIGHTENED TEACHERS

We gather our minds to greet and thank the
Enlightened Teachers who have come to help
throughout the ages. When we forget how to live
in harmony, they remind us of the way we were
instructed to live as people. With one mind, we
send greetings and thanks to these caring Teachers.
Now our minds are one.

SHONKWAIA'TÍSON RAONKWE'TA'SHÓN:'A

Enska tsi entewahwe'nón:ni ne onkwa'nikón:ra
tánon' teniethinonhwerá:ton ne tsi niká:ien ne
ronateríhonte ne ahonten'nikón:raren ne tsi

kahwatsiraké:ron ne tóhsa' thé:nen ne
akieróntshera ahonataweiá:ten. Ne
tsionkhiiehiahráhkhwa tsi ní:ioht tsi rawé:ren ne
taiontawén:rie ne onkwehshón:'a.
Entewahwe'nón:ni ne onkwa'nikón:ra tánon
teniethinonhwerá:ton ne Shonkwaia'tison
Raonkwe'ta'shón:'a.
Éhtho niiohtónha'k ne onkwa'nikón:ra.

THE CREATOR

Now we turn our thoughts to the Creator, or Great
Spirit, and send greetings and thanks for all the
gifts of Creation. Everything we need to live a
good life is here on this Mother Earth. For all the
love that is still around us, we gather our minds
together as one and send our choicest words of
greetings and thanks to the Creator.
Now our minds are one.

SHONKWAIA'TÍSON

Onen ehnón:we iatitewawennanihá:ra ne ne tsi
nón:we thotatenaktarakwén:ni ne Shonkwaia'tíson.
Akwé:kon ehnón:we nikiawé:non ne ka'shatsténhsera.
Akwé:kon ne tahotka'wenhákie ne tsi nahò:ten ne
ne skén:nen tsi aitewanonhtonnionhá:ke tsi nikari:wes
ohontsià:ke teionkwatawénrie. Iotshennónnia't ne
taiontkahthónnion ne orihwakwé:kon á:ienre'k
shonkwanorónhkwa tsi shé:kon iotiio'tákie ne tsi
ní:ioht tsi shakorihwaientá:te. Entitewateweién:ton
ehnón:we entewatewennaié:ra'te ne ne ísi na'karón:iati
ne kati wahi entewátka'we kanonhweratónhtshera.
Éhtho niiohtónha'k ne onkwa'nikón:ra.

CLOSING WORDS

We have now arrived at the place where we end
our words. Of all the things we have named, it was
not our intention to leave anything out. If
something was forgotten, we leave it to each
individual to send such greetings and thanks in
their own way.
Now our minds are one.

SAKARIHWAHÓ:TON

Onen ehnón:we iahétewawe ne ieióhe
onsaitewarihwahó:ton. Ne tsi naho'tèn:shon
wetewana'tónnion, iah ki teionkwa'nikonhrón:ni
toka nahò:ten'k saionkwa nikónhrhen. Tsi
sewaia'tátshon ki ne onen wakwarihwaientáhkwen
ne entisewatka'we kanonhweratónhtshera.
Éhtho niiohtónha'k ne onkwa'nikón:ra.

The "Thanksgiving Address"

According to Oren Lyons, and other Haudenosaunee leaders, this address is
the true origin of the Thanksgiving holiday that is celebrated throughout
North America. Immigrant people who colonized these lands missed the
depth of this message of Thanksgiving, however, by neglecting the human
responsibilities to Creation upon which the Thanksgiving Address focuses.

From the version presented above, the Thanksgiving Address can be seen
to focus on the activity of bringing minds together as one around the
importance of maintaining a material balance with the world around the
human world. The Great Law of Peace works on consensus. Decisions must be
achieved by complete agreement and, as such, achieving the unity of minds is
critical for the success of any gathering.

The gathering of minds to one is seen here as including the nonhuman
world. It is a world of persons too, but nonhuman persons. It is often said that
each and every part of the Creation—to which the Thanksgiving Address is

given—has their duties and responsibilities to the rest of Creation. The activity of Creation, as expressed in the Thanksgiving Address, is a continuous activity that human beings need to focus on before their minds can be focused on the task at hand. The rhetorical strategy of the Thanksgiving Address is to Skä·noñh—Peace and Wellness that comes when human beings are in proper balance with the natural world. It also encompasses agriculture—referred to as the Three Sisters (corn, beans, and squash). It also encompasses the organization of leadership and governance set down by the Peacemaker at Onondaga Lake as well as the diplomacy achieved with wampum and condolence between Indigenous nations and settler-colonial people. Staying with the protocols of the Thanksgiving Address for thousands of years has been the reason that the Haudenosaunee have survived at a number of different levels.

The Thanksgiving Address acknowledges the process in which gifts are exchanged as a regular feature of life. This is a profound insight into the workings of the sacred world upon which human beings depend. As is often repeated, it is not a prayer but an address. I have taken this to mean that it is not a petition to the Creator for some perceived lack or need, but rather a simple expression of gratitude for the gifts of life that have already been given. As an address, it is seen as a communication between human and nonhuman people and not as a wish for something—as it would be with a prayer.

As for the structure of the Thanksgiving Address, it can be seen as both pliable, or changed depending on the circumstances, and as having formal segments or parts. The Thanksgiving Address is an oral ceremonial event and therefore is amenable to any circumstance. Writing it down constrains its living presence. This is one reason why the Onondaga Nation does not want the Thanksgiving Address textualized or recorded. There is a rhythm to the Thanksgiving Address in all of its versions. Even nonspeakers who have heard the address numerous times can hear the rhythm in the cadence. Moreover, it works. I have witnessed it working to bring different contentious voices into accord even when there is no one other than the speaker who understands what is being said.

For a full appreciation of the "Thanksgiving Address," however, one needs a better understanding of the Haudenosaunee. The discussion below includes our continuing work at the Skä·noñh—Great Law of Peace Center, which—as is described—is an educational center that was created by a collaborative and led by the Onondaga Nation leadership. Important in this discussion is how to culturally contextualize the "Thanksgiving Address" within Haudenosaunee values.

The Haudenosaunee

The Haudenosaunee are a confederacy of originally five separate nations: the Mohawk, Oneida, Onondaga, Cayuga, and Seneca. In the early 1700s, the Tuscarora joined as that sixth nation. French Jesuits first referred to them as the Iroquois, and the English referred to them as the Six Nations. Figure 1.1 depicts an image of the "Confederacy Belt," or "Hiawatha (Hayenhwátha') Belt,"[3] which is an ancient belt whose image is at least one thousand years old and made of wampum (a worked bead of purple and white carved from the quahog shell, which is found along the Atlantic seaboard from Cape Cod to Long Island). From left to right, the symbols represent the Seneca, Cayuga, Onondaga (symbolized by Great Tree of Peace in the center), Oneida, and Mohawk Nations.[4] Underneath the Hiawatha Belt is a depiction of a Longhouse that extends across upstate New York with five fires, representative of the five original nations in the Confederacy.

The Hiawatha Belt was repatriated to the Haudenosaunee in the late 1980s from a museum of anthropology at the State University of New York at Albany (SUNY Albany). The return of this belt was the result of a protracted struggle between the Onondaga Nation, who are the wampum keepers, and the "Iroquoianists," who are a group of non-Haudenosaunee academics who purportedly made careers writing about them. This struggle had been ongoing for generations and illustrates the distinctive ways in which Indigenous and academic communities have had different interpretive locations and also a lack of collaborative tools—on the part of the academics.[5] Since the wampum belt's return to the Onondaga Nation, its image has come to represent the Haudenosaunee as a flag and can be seen displayed prominently by Haudenosaunee people throughout the Central New York region, and now, around the world. This single repatriation of the Hiawatha Belt has resulted in a cultural renaissance of the Haudenosaunee and represents a victory of Indigenous peoples over the colonizing orientations of the academy. This

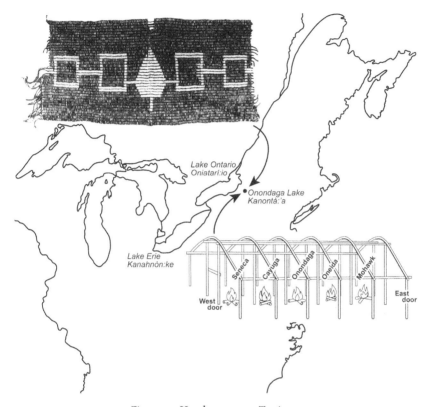

Figure 1.1. Haudenosaunee Territory.

illustrates why a collaborative methodology must emerge from the category
of Indigenous religions. Describing this category requires a shift in the ways
the work by scholars must move from the objectification of the indigenous
"other" to a collaborative venture with a vision of a shared viable future.

Hiawatha (Hayenhwátha') Wampum Belt and Haudenosaunee Longhouse
tradition referred to as "The Great Law of Peace" was founded at Onondaga
Lake, near the current city of Syracuse, New York, in upstate New York, in
their heartland. Mohawk names of waterways are indicated. Haudenosaunee
influence extended from Nova Scotia to the Mississippi and from the upper
Great Lakes to Georgia.[6]

The Hiawatha Belt also depicts the founding of the Haudenosaunee
Confederacy through their acceptance of the Great Law of Peace. This is a

complex protocol that was delivered by the Peacemaker to Jikonsaseh, Hiawatha, and the Tadodaho, and that spread to all Five Nations. The Central Tree in the Belt represents the Onondaga Nation, and also the geographical location of Onondaga Lake, where this Great Law of Peace was founded. Once the five warring nations accepted the Peacemaker's message, a White Pine was uprooted to reveal a swift running stream below. Into its roots were cast the weapons of war, and it was replanted so its White Roots of Peace would spread in the four directions. The White Pine, with its needles growing in clusters of five, represents the united Haudenosaunee Confederacy of five nations. Onondaga would be the Keepers of the Fire, or the capital. Today, of the 566 "tribes" federally recognized by the United States, only three are still governed by their ancient, pre-Colonial traditional clan systems. All three are Haudenosaunee, and the Onondaga are still Keepers of the Center Fire. Although all Six Nations are still represented in Grand Council meetings at Onondaga, the US government only recognizes three of these traditional governments. The others have been replaced with elected Bureau of Indian Affairs (BIA) chiefs, who do not follow the Haudenosaunee Longhouse protocol of the Great Law of Peace, which is over one thousand years old.[7]

Longhouse people are matrilineal in that they are identified by their mother's clan. Male "chiefs," or *hoyane*, in the Onondaga language (which actually translates as "good mind") are raised into their clan offices by the Clan Mothers, who are female clan representatives and sit beside their respective male representative. These offices are chosen by consensus and remain for life. The Haudenosaunee system of governance greatly impressed and influenced the Founding Fathers of the United States in the eighteenth century and also the women who launched the women's rights movement in 1848 with their first convention held in Seneca Falls, New York—right in Seneca Nation territory.

The Message of the Skä·noñh—Great Law of Peace Center

The Skä·noñh—Great Law of Peace Center opened in November 2015 to tell the story of the Haudenosaunee and their founding over one thousand years ago at Onondaga Lake. Now surrounded by a county park of the same name, the lake is also the most chemically polluted body of water in the United

States. Visitors learn about the Haudenosaunee at the Center, as well as their first contact with Jesuit missionaries in 1656. The Thanksgiving Address, however, is woven throughout the Center as a fundamental principle of the Haudenosaunee. The Thanksgiving Address is now associated with the Great Law of Peace and diplomatic relationships all through the period of contact from 1613 until the present time. Below is an outline of the message of the Skä·noñh—Great Law of Peace Center.

Onondaga Lake is culturally distinctive in two ways. First, it is the founding place of the "Great Law of Peace" (discussed below) on or before 909 CE. Second, it is the site where the first Europeans resided in the middle of Onondaga Nation territory from 1656 to 1658.

The Skä·noñh—Great Law of Peace Center collaborative was responsible for its content. The collaborative is composed of academics, researchers, and teachers from local educational institutions; community leaders; and other persons who are committed to the task of presenting to the general, non-Haudenosaunee public their values from a genuinely Haudenosaunee perspective. The collaborative, which crafted the Center's narrative, clearly wanted to amplify the voice of the Onondaga Nation. We did not want to achieve a balanced view of history but rather wanted to present Haudenosaunee culture and history only from a Haudenosaunee perspective. One can read the Jesuit and other historical accounts of the "Iroquois" in any library. To hear this history from the perspective of the Haudenosaunee leadership themselves has been our focus. Ironically, it is the high-tech environment of video screens and touch pads that allows for the Indigenous message of the Haudenosaunee to filter through. Over thirty hours of interviews, mostly with the leadership of the Onondaga Nation, has been edited down to six videos, each four minutes long. This was an appropriate number to provide the basic information about the core issues important for the Center.

There are six separate messages that are communicated at the Skä·noñh—Great Law of Peace Center. These are all accompanied by signage and a video. These are:

1. Skä·noñh—Onondaga welcome greeting Peace and Wellness only obtained through proper relationship with the Natural World

2. Thanksgiving Address, "Words before All Else"
3. Creation—natural world prepares the earth for human beings
4. Great Law of Peace
   a. Peacemaker, Jikonsaseh, Hiawatha, Tadodaho
   b. Established at Onondaga Lake over one thousand years ago
5. European Contact and Genocide
   a. Doctrine of Christian Discovery, Jesuit Missionary Fort
   b. Two Row Wampum, Colonialism, Sullivan-Clinton Campaign, George
   Washington's Canandaigua Treaty Belt, Boarding Schools
6. Haudenosaunee Influences
   a. Western Democracy, Women's Movement, Lacrosse, Environment,
   Food, United Nations

Skä·noñh: The visitor is welcomed to the Skä·noñh Center with the phrase "Nya weñha Skä·noñh" on the wall. It is a welcoming greeting that means "Thank you for being well" in the Onondaga language. People who watch and listen to this welcome video learn that Skä·noñh is also the Onondaga word for "peace." As Clan Mother Freida Jacques says, "Peace, but in a deep way." In the Haudenosaunee worldview, peace is only attained when human beings are in a balanced relationship with the natural world. This is the theme that unifies the values of the Haudenosaunee and is woven throughout Skä·noñh Center. In this welcome exhibit, we introduce visitors to the Haudenosaunee, who were wrongly labeled as "Iroquois" by the French Jesuits who first coined the phrase. One also learns about the importance of maintaining language and ceremonies as fundamental to the survival of the Haudenosaunee. The video is designed for the non-Haudenosaunee visitor, but we have already found that people from all kinds of different communities can benefit from these lessons.

Thanksgiving Address: The second stop on the tour is dedicated to the "Thanksgiving Address" (as it is usually translated into English) or the Ganoñhéñ·nyoñ'("Words That Come before All Else") and is the subject of this paper. This is an ancient protocol that has eighteen separate parts and which is recited before and after (often called an "opening" and "closing") before every meeting in conversation in the Longhouse. It is also recited regularly at many other ceremonial events. It is not a prayer, but an address where different living beings who have duties for keeping the world going are thanked. These beings are People, Mother Earth, Water, Fish, Plants, Food Plants, Medicine Herbs, Animals, Trees, Birds, Four Winds, Thunderers, Sun, Grandmother Moon, Stars, Enlightened Teachers, Creator, and Closing Words. The recitation of the Thanksgiving Address can last for hours or for a few minutes, depending on the context and the wishes of the orator. After each nation of beings is thanked there is the refrain "Now our minds are one." This is said to unify the assembled human group around the human need to continue to support life—all life—not just human life. As Freida Jacques says in the video, "Human beings are just a part of Life."

Creation: The ancient Haudenosaunee story of creation is long and involved. It can take a week or more to recite the entire story in the Longhouse. We have had to reduce this story to just four minutes to keep the attention of the visitor. We have thus settled on focusing on the values of the Haudenosaunee that the Creation story seems to emphasize. It recounts how the natural world prepared the Earth for human beings. The focus of the story is Sky Woman, because the central feature of the story is that a pregnant woman from the Sky-world falls to earth, which is covered with water at the time. Aquatic birds rise up to break her fall and gently put her on the Great Turtle's back. As Robin Kimmerer says in the video, this demonstrates that the first interaction between humans and animals is one of care. Deciding to make her a new home, the animals try to dive into the waters to get some earth. After three animals cannot dive deep enough, it is the muskrat that finally comes to the surface with a bit of earth under his claw. With that bit of earth, Sky Woman dances on Turtle's back and spreads out the land. From that action, the North American continent is formed and called Turtle Island. It also indicates that the earth is alive and is feminine.

As time goes on Sky Woman gives birth to a girl—First Woman, who thrives on the new earth. One night she is impregnated and gives birth to twins—The Creator Twins. The first is born the normal way, and the second breaks through her armpit and kills her. From her body sprout the Three Sisters of Corn, Beans, and Squash. The twins are raised by Sky Woman, but they are continually in conflict with one another. When the benign twin creates a rose, the mischievous one puts thorns on it. The fights and conflicts get so bad that the Creator separates the Creator Twins as Day and Night, Sky and Earth, Life and Death. The twins express how the world works between two opposing forces in it. As John Mohawk says, these forces are ascending and descending forces of Creation that are associated with the different twins.[8] Values of balance between human beings and the natural world are evidenced in this epic story of Creation. Skä·noñh is the primary element of this story as well.

Great Law of Peace: The focal point of the Skä·noñh Center is what is referred to in English as the "Great Law of Peace," which was founded at Onondaga Lake over one thousand years ago (see above). Like the Creation Story, the account of the founding of the Great Law of Peace takes ten days to recite. Today, Haudenosaunee gather in greater and greater numbers to attend the "reading" from respected elders who recite it in their respective languages (Mohawk, Oneida, Onondaga, Cayuga, Seneca, and Tuscarora). At these readings the ancient wampum belts are displayed, and everyone is encouraged to touch them so as to make contact with those original instructions. Essentially, the Great Law of Peace defines the Haudenosaunee as the people they are today. It is the basis of their survival and their influence throughout the world. It is also a continuation, or a revitalization, of the values expressed within the Thanksgiving Address since time immemorial.

This is the story as told at the Skä·noñh Center:

The Haudenosaunee forgot the Original Instructions of the Creator and fell into a state of violence. There was constant killing as warriors roamed across this land, causing great suffering among the Haudenosaunee. At this time came the Peacemaker, who was a man of special powers, talents, and abilities. He was born to a virgin girl of the Huron Nation near the Bay of Quinte on the northern shore of Lake Ontario. His grandmother had a dream where a Spirit Being told her that "he will be a messenger of the Creator and will bring peace and harmony to the people on earth."

The Peacemaker carved a White Stone Canoe, a remarkable vessel, and paddled it into Haudenosaunee territory. He embarked to change the hearts and minds of the most dangerous people he could find, in order to restore Skä·noñh, the Good Mind, and bring unity to all people. One way he demonstrated the power of unity was by explaining that one nation alone is like one arrow—it could be easily broken. However, five nations when united are like five arrows bundled together, which are not so easily broken.

Jikonsaseh (Tsikúsáhsę̃ "Wide Face") was a woman of the Erie Nation who helped the warriors and enjoyed their stories of murder and mayhem. She would provide aid and comfort by feeding them, mending their clothes, and encouraging them to continue on their path of violence. But those warriors caused much harm among the Haudenosaunee. To prevent her from further enabling the warriors, the Peacemaker used his Good Mind and reason to change Jikonsaseh's mind, and to work for peace. Because she was the first to accept his message of Skä·noñh, the Peacemaker declared that women would have positions of prominence in their clan and have the responsibility to nominate male clan chiefs (Hoyane "Good Mind"). To this day, Haudenosaunee women continue this tradition. For every male chief there is a Clan Mother who heads each of the various families. Skä·noñh also means that there will be equity and no prejudice in the Good Mind.

After meeting Jikonsaseh, the Peacemaker then traveled to spread the message of Peace to all Five Nations.

As the Peacemaker traveled from village to village, he encountered the most difficulty in convincing the Onondaga to accept his message. Here lived the Tadodaho (Thadodá•ho'), a man so feared it is said his body was twisted and snakes grew from his head. He was a powerful sorcerer and a cannibal who ate human flesh. Also in Onondaga territory was Hiawatha (Hayenhwátha'), who likewise was dedicated to establishing peace. However, at this time, he was in deep grief due to the murders of his beloved daughters. He was unable to function and wandered aimlessly throughout the territory for many days. He arrived south of Onondaga at Tully Lake and spoke a command to the birds, and then he witnessed the waterfowl rise up from the water with such force that they carried the water with them. As he walked along the lake bottom, he picked up small shells of freshwater clams and placed them in his deerskin pouch. After he had passed across the lake, the waterfowl returned the water. On the shore he began making strings of shells, which is the first use of wampum. He said, "If I found or met anyone burdened with grief as I am, I would use these shell strings to console them. I would lift the words of condolence with these strands of beads, and these beads would become words with which I would address them."

Hiawatha then met the Peacemaker, who made fourteen more wampum strings that related to his body. With the wampum strings, the Peacemaker's words lifted the grief of Hiawatha and removed the lump from his throat so he could speak, wiped the tears from his eyes so he could see, and brushed away the dust of death from his ears so he could hear. This ceremony uplifted the mind, spirit, and body of the grieving Hiawatha, restoring him to a fully functioning human being once again. This wampum ceremony became the way in which all visitors are to be greeted by the Haudenosaunee. The recognition of loss was seen as fundamental in helping to clear hearts and minds, and restoring Skä·noñh, before each gathering.

It was determined by the Peacemaker over one thousand years ago that the Condolence Ceremony would be used to install all chiefs, and to also console families through the loss of any loved ones. The Haudenosaunee continue to raise their chiefs through the Condolence Ceremony today.

Over one thousand years ago, the Five Nations were brought together in peace at Onondaga Lake by the Peacemaker and Hiawatha (Hayenhwátha'). Together they planted the Great Tree of Peace (Skaẹhetsi'kona) and created the Haudenosaunee Confederacy. This is where Skä·noñh began anew.

The Tree of Peace is a metaphor for how peace can grow if it is nurtured. Like a tall tree, peace can provide protection and comfort. Like a pine tree, peace spreads its protective branches to create a place of peace where we can gather and renew ourselves. Like the White Pine, peace also creates large white roots (tsyoktehækẹæta'kona) that rise out of the ground so people can trace their journey to the source. If anyone truly desired peace, they could follow the sacred white roots of peace to the capital of the Confederacy, here at Onondaga, where they would learn of the words of the Peacemaker. His message is that we all can nurture the "Tree of Peace."

The Peacemaker had the warriors uproot a great white pine, which left a gaping hole underneath it. The fifty chiefs and warriors threw their weapons of war under the Great Tree, where an underground stream carried the weapons away, and then the tree was lifted back upright. This is the origin of the phrase "bury the hatchet." The Peacemaker said that the chiefs will be standing on the earth like trees, deeply rooted in the land, with strong trunks, all the same height (having equal authority) in front of their people, to protect them, with the power of the Good Mind—not by use of physical force. On top of the tree sits an eagle who serves as an ever vigilant protector of the Peace. The Five Nations also came together to play Deyhontsigwa'eh (They Bump Hips) to solidify the Great Peace—today the game is known as lacrosse.

The Peacemaker united with forty-nine chiefs to use the power of their good to transform Tadodaho's thinking from that of a seeker of death to that of a maker of peace. The Peacemaker negotiated an important role for Tadodaho in the newly established Confederacy as the fiftieth chief: He would have the authority to call the Grand Council together, which would meet in his territory at Onondaga and also be responsible to ensure that all of the chiefs would keep the Good Mind and maintain Skä·noñh. The Peacemaker and his helpers then combed the snakes from Tadodaho's hair. They also straightened his body that was twisted in seven places. Using their combined strength, the Peacemaker and Hiawatha restored the Tadodaho's humanity. Once a grotesque mass of evil, the new Tadodaho now stood erect like a tall tree. Deer antlers were placed upon his headdress to represent his new status as the defender of the Great Law of Peace.

This decisive moment when the circle of unity was completed through the transformation of the most evil of minds in the land was many years coming. The lesson for all of us is that no matter how demented one may have been in the past, the mind has the capacity of being restored. Once we apply our minds in the way it was intended, we will naturally find ourselves in Skä·noñh—the state of peacefulness and wellness.

There are several important values expressed in this story that have had a profound effect on the world. The transformation through words and songs of the first Tadodaho, who was an evil sorcerer who devoured his enemies, into the leader of the Confederacy demonstrates that even the most twisted person can be changed to be an agent of peace.

European Contact and Genocide

The initial friendly exchange between Europeans and the Haudenosaunee in the early part of the seventeenth century led to an eventual clash of values. The natural world that had been honored and nurtured by the Haudenosaunee was exchanged for the manufactured goods of the Europeans. The

Haudenosaunee world was turned upside down by the invasion of European colonists. Radical ideas invaded and upset the state of Skä·noñh (Peace, balance with the natural world).

The people of Turtle Island were shocked by ideas like "private landownership" because it was inconceivable that human beings could own Mother Earth. As with other Indigenous peoples, the Haudenosaunee understand that human beings belong to the land, but Europeans believed the land belonged to them. Related to the idea of property, and that human beings were in control of the natural world, was a patriarchal worldview that men were superior to women.

Europeans used religion to justify their right of conquest and the subjugation of Indigenous peoples of the "New World" to take possession of their land. This created catastrophic cultural, spiritual, environmental, and political consequences that resulted in profound turmoil, including the loss of untold human lives through warfare and disease, as well as the loss of most of their homelands.

What happened in 1656 between the Onondaga and the French Jesuits at the site of the mission of Sainte Marie is a microcosm of the larger story. As discussed above, the Skä·noñh—Great Law of Peace Center was repurposed from what was once called "Sainte Marie among the Iroquois" that continued the narrative of the French Jesuits occupation of the site from 1656 to 1658. The Jesuits arrived with the deed to more than six hundred square miles of land in Onondaga Nation Territory. While the Jesuits professed to only be there to learn and teach the Onondaga about their religion, they were actually there to dispossess them of their lands and traditions. After only twenty months, the Jesuits were forced to leave, and the accounts by the Jesuits and by the Onondaga are very different from one another.[9] To this day a Roman Catholic church has not been allowed to be built on the Onondaga Nation Territory as a consequence of this event from the seventeenth century.

This episode is reflective of the Doctrine of Christian Discovery, which originated in a fifteenth-century papal bull to the monarchs of Portugal and Spain that fueled the Age of Discovery. Essentially, the implication was that when a Christian explorer sets foot in lands of non-Christians, their bodies, wealth, and lands reverted to the sponsoring monarch and the church (that is, the Vatican). In 1823 this idea was codified as a principle of US property law in the US Supreme Court decision *Johnson v. McIntosh* (21 U.S. 543) and has been used since then up to the present day to maintain federal control over Native lands. When the Jesuits arrived in the seventeenth century, the relationship of Christianity and appropriation of land was a well-organized doctrine.[10]

Continuance and Contributions

From its founding over one thousand years ago at Onondaga Lake until today, the Onondaga Nation, Central Fire of the Haudenosaunee Confederacy, has continued to use the Great Law of Peace to guide its people. Thanksgiving ceremonies are performed each season in Longhouses throughout Haudenosaunee traditional territories. Clan leaders are elected and raised into office by means of the Condolence Ceremony process. In spite of attempts to assimilate and destroy the Haudenosaunee, the Longhouse tradition has survived due to strong and forward-thinking leadership. Its lowest ebb was during the early 1900s, but now there are signs of language revitalization, a greater interest in the ceremonies and governmental process by the youth, and a greater level of support by allies around the world.

Remarkably, the Onondaga Nation survived the tidal waves of colonization and continues to live within their original homelands. Their council fire still burns. The Great Law of Peace still continues to inspire the decisions of the chiefs, Clan Mothers, and Faithkeepers.

Most United States citizens are unaware of how profoundly their culture has been shaped by the Haudenosaunee as a result of what took place here at Onondaga Lake. Many of the best and most admired attributes of American society have their roots here.

In the Haudenosaunee people, the colonists saw freedom and liberty at work. It was a practical model of how a society could respect the rights of all living beings, yet have everyone work toward the common good.

Ideas such as popular initiatives, town meetings, caucuses, women's rights, and representative government were being practiced here long before the American Revolution. The colonial leaders took great inspiration in the Haudenosaunee Confederacy practice of the Great Law of Peace. They studied Haudenosaunee political protocols and employed them for many generations in making peace treaties with many other Native nations.

The Haudenosaunee inspired the Founding Fathers of Western democracy and the Founding Mothers of the women's rights movement. Settlers and contemporary agriculturalists have long recognized the importance of our food ways and medicines, just as scientists continue to be inspired by our traditional ecological knowledge and practices.

Conclusion

The Skä·nonĥ—Great Law of Peace Center has given a wider voice to the values expressed in the Thanksgiving Address. At a time of great climate change, this message continues to carry an important message for all human beings. It can be seen as a rhetorical device whereby people of divergent opinions and commitments can eventually bring their "minds together as one" and discuss in peace and respect the most pressing issues facing us all. It can also be seen as holding on to a set of ageless Indigenous values that appreciate the relationship of peace between human beings as also requiring a balanced relationship with the natural world.

We want to make sure people know how to understand the Thanksgiving Address. It is not Indians worshiping nature. There is a cultural context that needs to be understood in order to understand how the Thanksgiving Address fits into and expresses the culture of the Haudenosaunee and, in turn, expresses the religion, values, and worldview of the people. The Thanksgiving Address implies that human beings exist only because of the generosity of other-than-human beings. Our existence is contingent on the existence of others. This contradicts the colonial and modern ideas of the primacy of human lives as expressed in the Doctrine of Discovery, for example. These ancient processes serve to remind us of how humility and respect are not just a matter of being polite, but are also the way human beings can survive.

Notes

1.   The Tracking Project publishes a version of the Thanksgiving Address in Mohawk and ten other languages: English, German, Swedish, Japanese, Portuguese, Spanish, Bisayan, French, Hawaiian, and Italian. Thanks to the vision of Chief Jake Swamp and his Tree of Peace Project, these versions are still sold around the world.

2.   Originally published as: *Thanksgiving Address: Greetings to the Natural World*,

This translation of the Mohawk version of the Haudenosaunee Thanksgiving Address was developed and published in 1993. English version: John Stokes and Kanawahienton (David Benedict, Turtle Clan/Mohawk); Mohawk version: Rokwaho (Dan Thompson, Wolf Clan/Mohawk); original inspiration: Tekaronianekon (Jake Swamp, Wolf Clan/Mohawk). See John Stokes, David Benedict, and Dan Thompson, *Thanksgiving Address: Greetings to the Natural World* (Corrales, NM: The Tracking Project; Onchiota, NY: Six Nations Indian Museum, 1993). The English version may be found here: https://americanindian.si.edu/environment/pdf/01_02_Thanksgiving_ Address.pdf.

3.   The name of Hiawatha is the anglicized rendering of the Haudenosaunee name of Hayenhwátha', who is an important person in the founding of the Great Law of Peace at Onondaga Lake over one thousand years ago. Due to the Henry Wadsworth Longfellow poem "Hiawatha," the name Hiawatha is more recognizable, even though in the Longfellow poem, he lives on Lake Superior rather than Onondaga Lake and the poem relates the story of the Anishinaabe cultural hero Wenabozho. The common spelling of "Hiawatha" will be used here.

4.   The Tuscarora Nation became the sixth to join the Haudenosaunee in the 1720s when they came north from South Carolina to escape the slave traders and aggressive appropriations of their lands by European settlers.

5.   A particularly important book that details this ongoing interpretive controversy is Oren Lyons, ed., *Exiled in the Land of the Free: Democracy, Indian Nations, and the U.S. Constitution* (Santa Fe, NM: Clear Light Publishers, 1992).

6.   Special thanks to Joseph Stoll, who created this map depicting the heartland and influence area of the Haudenosaunee.

7.   Dating the origins of the Haudenosaunee Confederacy is a matter of scholarly debate. The best estimate, however, is 1142 CE. See Barbara A. Mann and Jerry L. Fields, "A Sign in the Sky: Dating the League of the Haudenosaunee," *American Indian Culture and Research Journal* 21, no. 2 (January 1997): 105–63, https://doi.org/10.17953/ aicr.21.2.k36m1485r3062510. Using the same methodology, more recent excavations are pushing this date back further to August 18, 909 CE. See Jack Rossen, "Epilogue: Challenging Dominant Archaeological Narratives of the Haudenosaunee," in *Corey Village and the Cayuga World: Implications from Archaeology and Beyond*, ed. Jack Rossen (Syracuse, NY: Syracuse University Press, 2015), 197. Many Haudenosaunee people insist, however, that the real date of the founding is thousands of years earlier, and that the Confederacy could be ten thousand years old.

8.   John Mohawk, *Iroquois Creation Story: John Arthur Gibson and J. N. B. Hewitt's Myth of the Earth Grasper* (Buffalo, NY: Mohawk Publications, 2005).

9.   We are left with only two sources of information by which we try to understand this past: The accounts of the seventeenth-century Jesuits who traveled to Onondaga Lake in 1656 and were forced to leave in 1658, and the oral history with wampum belts of the Onondaga. The accounts are very different from one another and will be emphasized

in the current fort in coming years. By looking back to the first encounters, we can examine the lingering impacts of these events.

10.   For more information, see these websites: Indigenous Values Initiative and American Indian Law Alliance, "Doctrine of Discovery," https://doctrineofdiscovery.org/; and Indigenous Values Initiative, "Indigenous Values Initiative," https://indigenousvalues. org/.

CHAPTER TWO

The Use of Digressions in Anishinaabe Rhetoric as a Moral Act

*Connecting Speech to the Religious Idea
That All Things Are Related*

LAWRENCE W. GROSS

IN MY BOOK *Anishinaabe Ways of Knowing and Being*, I included a chapter on Anishinaabe rhetoric.[1] I began my discussion by relating how my students thought I engaged in digressions too often during my lectures. To deal with this situation, I began teaching my students about the conventions of Anishinaabe rhetoric so they would know how to listen to me. I went on to explain the conventions used by Anishinaabe speakers, such as being informed by spiritual values and personal experience. I also discussed how to listen to Anishinaabe rhetoric, such as the importance of not tuning out or interrupting the speaker. Further, I went into some detail about the use of storytelling and repetition by Anishinaabe speakers, which, along with digressions, are two features of Anishinaabe rhetoric. In the end, though, I did not go into great detail about digressions themselves in my book chapter. So, I did not discuss the nature of digressions in Anishinaabe rhetoric and the religious and moral ideals informing that practice. This essay will address that shortcoming and detail the nature of digressions in Anishinaabe rhetoric. I will argue that in using digressions, Anishinaabe speakers are exploring the connections between all things. The notion that all things are related, however, arises from Anishinaabe morality. So, in effect, the use of digressions by Anishinaabe speakers is at heart a moral act in that the use of digressions both expresses and affirms the moral universe of the Anishinaabeg. I will start off by briefly covering the other aspects of Anishinaabe rhetoric, that is, storytelling, the use of personal experience, and speaking from the heart. I will also summarize some points about how to listen to Anishinaabe rhetoric. Although I covered those topics in my book, I will quickly review them so that we have a common understanding of the phenomenon. From there I will address the use of digressions and their connection to Anishinaabe morality.

There are several aspects of Anishinaabe rhetoric that we can identify. In addition to the use of digressions, Anishinaabe rhetoric is marked by the use of storytelling, the use of personal experience, and repetition. There are good reasons the Anishinaabe take this approach to rhetoric. First and foremost is the importance of the spirits and spiritual values. We take it for granted that Anishinaabe orators speak in good faith for the most part, although we also recognize some of them do not. They want to convey the best information they have. The best information we have is that knowledge that is derived from the spiritual realm through prayer and meditation or is at least guided by time-tested spiritual values. The use of personal experience relates to the epistemology of the Anishinaabeg. From what I have been taught, the Anishinaabeg believe the things we experience are put here by the Creator or the spirits for us to experience. Thus, if we wish to speak in good faith, there is no higher knowledge we can convey than that provided to us by the spiritual realm for us to experience.

Speaking from the heart does not mean speaking emotionally, or wearing one's heart on one's sleeve, as it were. Instead, the intention is to convey a sense of who the speaker is as a human being. In other words, the attempt is made to show what values are important to the speaker as a human being. This aspect is related to the way leadership functioned in our traditional societies. Prior to permanent contact, we did not have the coercive instruments of state—such as police, courts, and prison—for leaders to impose their will on the people. Instead, the only tools leaders had at their disposal were setting a good example and persuasion. Leaders therefore spoke from the heart to show people who they were as human beings, to demonstrate that their values were good, and their intentions were to help people and not seek personal gain. It was then up to the people to decide the degree to which the individual was trustworthy and so worth listening to and following, or instead if the individual was speaking in bad faith. That tradition of speaking from the heart is still with us to this day.

When listening to Anishinaabe speakers there are four things to keep in mind: do not tune out the speaker; do not interrupt the speaker; do not worry if the original question was not answered; and do not worry if there is no moral to any story the speaker might tell. These four elements can be grouped into the first two and the last two. In regard to the first two, it is important not to tune out or interrupt the speaker because in doing so the listener might miss something important. For example, the speaker might drop in a gem of wisdom that could change one's life. However, if one tunes out the speaker, one might miss out on the precious pearl of wisdom that was being offered. If one interrupts the speaker, one might not hear important information the speaker was getting around to. For example, one might have heard the same story from a speaker before and the temptation might be to interrupt the speaker to let him or her know that one knows the story and so he or she does not have to tell it again. But one never knows. The speaker might go on to add information the listener had not heard before. In that case, interrupting the speaker would result in the listener forgoing a chance at learning new information. With regard to the last two items, there are three considerations at work. First, practically speaking, the speaker cannot know exactly what the listener needs. That would be a bit of hubris on the part of the speaker. Instead, the speaker simply offers the gift of his or her comments and allows the listener to decide for himself or herself if the information is useful. Also, the speaker respects the intelligence of the listener and trusts the listener will be able to figure out the meaning of the speaker's words for himself or herself. Finally, the speaker is giving the listener something the listener can, and probably should, be thinking about for the rest of his or her life. If the speaker gave the moral of the story, for instance, that would effectively kill the story. Instead, by not giving the moral of the story, the listener can keep going back to the story and perhaps find new ways the story applies to his or her life as the listener grows and changes.

With that brief summary of some of the conventions of Anishinaabe rhetoric, we are ready to delve more deeply into the topic of digressions. Let us begin by considering an important foundation for Anishinaabe morality, the concept of *bimaadiziwin,* or the Proper Conduct of Life.

When it comes to bimaadiziwin, I will mainly reference my chapter on the topic from my book, *Anishinaabe Ways of Knowing and Being.*[2] There are a couple of aspects of bimaadiziwin that should be kept in mind. The term itself has a rather simple linguistic structure. The root of the word is the animate, intransitive verb (VAI), *bimaadizi,* which simply means, "he/she/it lives." Since the pronoun is included in VAI verbs and VAI verbs are gender-neutral and can include beings Westerners categorize as inanimate, such as drums, pipes, and feathers, the word is translated with the "he/she/it" in the subject position. Adding the suffix *win* turns the verb into a noun. Thus, technically, bimaadiziwin could simply be translated as "life." Indeed, the Ojibwe People's dictionary website translates bimaadiziwin as meaning "life."[3] In reference to moral teachings, it is not uncommon for *mino,* "good," to be attached as a prefix, resulting in the term *mino-bimaadiziwin,* or the "Good Life."

For all its linguistic simplicity, however, the word is rich in extended meanings. As Roger Spielmann outlined, it is difficult, if not impossible, to translate the term as it is used in the moral teachings of the Anishinaabeg. When he asked bilingual speakers to translate the term, such themes emerged as "a worthwhile life," "a long, fulfilling life," "our walk in life," "walking the straight path in this life," and others.[4] One of my elders, Thomas Shingobe, translated the term as the "Proper Conduct of Life." When we look at how the teaching actually manifests itself in the lives of the Anishinaabe people, the rationale Shingobe had in mind in translating the word the way he did quickly becomes apparent.

First and foremost, we should note that the Anishinaabeg do not have a given set teaching for bimaadiziwin. As I explain in *Anishinaabe Ways of Knowing and Being,* the Anishinaabeg are loath to write the teaching down or otherwise limit the teaching in any way. Instead, one is expected to be mindful of the teaching and be on the constant lookout for new opportunities to learn. Assisting in that endeavor is the degree to which the teaching permeates Anishinaabe life. As Rupert Ross argued,

> I think I was bothered by the fact that such teachings were not written
> down. I therefore assumed that they couldn't have been clearly known to

everyone, and as such couldn't have the force of real "law." In that respect, I didn't understand that there was no need to write them down because they were stated everywhere, in every activity, at virtually every hour of the day.[5]

In some respects, it is understandable that the Anishinaabeg would not want to codify the teaching of bimaadiziwin. Life, after all, is infinite in its variety and ever changing in its form and necessities. So, to limit the teaching in any way would in some ways be an attempt to limit life, hardly a desirable pursuit. Instead, the Anishinaabeg know it is better to not try to capture or limit life in any way, but instead be on the constant alert for new knowledge to be gained in how to live the Proper Conduct of Life. For example, it is not the case that elders are viewed as the only individuals who hold wisdom and knowledge. As Roger Spielman has pointed out in regard to Anishinaabe pedagogy, all people are at the same time teachers and learners.[6] That means we can learn about the Proper Conduct of Life even from children. When the opportunities are thus so broadly conceived, it can be seen why the Anishinaabeg do not codify the Proper Conduct of Life explicitly and indeed leave it to life itself to teach us about life.

Still, it can be argued there are two important aspects of bimaadiziwin, protecting one's life and being a good relative. In regard to the former, Spielmann provides a good example in his book on Ojibwe discourse. He includes a verbatim teaching from the monolingual Ojibwe elder Okinawe. Without going into great detail, Okinawe stressed being very careful to not engage in activities that could endanger one's life and to not either indulge oneself in negative emotions or to let adverse circumstances cloud one's judgment. Thus, for example, he states it is best to not go around where people are drinking or to swim while drunk, but also to not drive one's car during bad weather and to be careful walking on ice. He also teaches the importance of forgiveness when treated badly by others so as to not get carried away and cause harm to any individual. Interestingly enough, he also says it is important to not panic if one gets lost in the bush. If one panics, one might literally start running around and so injure oneself.[7]

This last point reminds me of a funny story involving my grandmother, Christine Beaulieu, and her sister, Delphine Darco, or Diamond, as they called her. Diamond was visiting my grandmother at her place back "in the sticks," as we referred to the location of her house on the White Earth Reservation. They went out for a walk, but somehow got lost. Diamond asked my grandmother what they should do. My grandmother suggested they take a nap. Diamond said, "OK." So, they laid down and took a nap for a while. When they got up, Diamond looked around and said, "Oh, there's your old house right over there." My grandmother replied, "I guess so." So then, they just simply walked back to her house. Who takes a nap when they are lost in the woods? My grandmother and her sister, I guess. They did not panic. They kept their cool. And, even got in a nice little nap. That is Okinawe's teaching in action. One always remains calm and keeps control of oneself. Doing so, one can avoid doing potentially harmful things to oneself or others under trying circumstances, and live to tell the tale, as happened with my grandmother and her sister.

Being a good relative is another important component of bimaadiziwin, however. As the above teaching by Okinawe suggests, one is careful to protect one's life. But, when we consider aspects of his teaching on a deeper level, we can see that maintaining good relations, being a good relative, figures greatly in his approach. This is especially true when it comes to practicing forgiveness. Okinawe stressed that one practices forgiveness so as to not bring harm to oneself or others. The practical effect in practicing forgiveness, though, is that one can live as a good relative, keep the peace, and maintain social harmony. My own late spiritual mentor, Greg Kingbird Sr., taught the importance of forgiveness as well. We were discussing difficult relationships at one point, and he said to me, "The old people taught, forgive, forgive, forgive." So, in his teaching and that of his elders, forgiveness held a very important place. As stated above, that emphasis on forgiveness helps make one a good relative.

Beyond the human realm, being a good relative extends to other-than-human relatives as well. The term "other-than-human" relatives is the phrase used by A. Irving Hallowell to capture the manner in which the Anishinaabeg see animals and other elements of the natural world as having human status, but not human form.[8] They are thus "other-than-human" relatives. As I argue in my book, however, relationships with other-than-human relatives are fundamentally moral in nature.[9] Thus, one is to treat animals and other resources one harvests with the outmost respect and humility. For example, before harvesting plants, one is expected to offer tobacco and give thanks for the sacrifice the plants are about to make to sustain one's life. My late spiritual mentor even taught me a song I should sing whenever I harvest plants or any part of them, such as their fruit, and I still sing that song to this very day, and am sure I will as long as I am still able to harvest plants.

What we want to note here for our purposes, though, is that by seeing elements of the natural world as relatives, the Anishinaabeg thus recognize they are connected to all elements of the universe writ large. When I say, "universe writ large," I mean that in as expansive as manner as I can. Thus, the connections include the spiritual realm as well as the physical, although it might not be quite technically correct to separate the two as such. As Thomas Shingobe taught and as he said, "The whole world is spiritualized." So, there is a sense the physical world and the spiritual world are one and the same. Additionally, the connections of which I am speaking are not limited to our planet, Earth. Both Thomas Shingobe and my late spiritual mentor talked about life on celestial bodies outside of the Earth, most especially the moon. I have heard other Anishinaabe teachers talk about life on other planets as well. The spiritual journeys of the Anishinaabeg have taken them across the universe. And so, when they talk about life and our connection to the world, those connections are in some ways infinite in variety. So, the question thus arises, do the Anishinaabeg really think all things are connected? As we will explore in the next section, the answer is a resounding yes.

In 2010, Brent Debassige studied how the concept of mino-bimaadiziwin can be used to inform an Anishinaabe research methodology. He is primarily concerned with bringing a spirit-centered approach to research that is informed by Anishinaabe values and worldview. One aspect of the Anishinaabe worldview in which he is particularly interested is the "wholistic" nature of Anishinaabe thought. As he explains in a footnote on the subject,

> I include the "w" at the beginning of the term holistic because I concur with Antone, Gamlin, and Turchetti (2003) when they make the distinction as follows: "Wholistic describes the Aboriginal philosophy in which 'everything is related' by virtue of shared origins and in which, by extension, the human being is considered an entire whole; that is, mentally, physically, spiritually and emotionally as an individual, with one's family and

extended family, one's people, and with the cosmos in sacred relationships. This is distinct from a "holistic" philosophy in which the term 'related' is taken as meaning 'all things are interconnected' by virtue of sharing an environment in which action leads to a type of 'domino effect' in a secular world."[10]

The key to understanding the above quotation involves the difference between "related" and "interconnected." The latter, as Debassige indicates, concerns linear cause-and-effect relations. So, on the one hand, it could be argued that siblings are interconnected because they have the same parents. But that strictly cause-and-effect relationship does not even begin to capture the depth of the connections that exists between family members. When it comes to human relationships, what matters more than the simple blood relationships is the manner in which we are interconnected through heart-to-heart connections. Saying "heart-to-heart connections" is another way of saying we are connected by love and kind regard for each other. As such, heart-to-heart connections involve the spiritual and emotional life of humans, rather than simply being limited to linear cause-and effect relationships, although we do not want to dismiss those ties completely, either.

By the same token, even though we want to recognize the importance of cause-and-effect relationships that exist in the natural world and between humans and the natural world, the emphasis in Anishinaabe thinking is not constricted to that narrow conceptualization of all things being related. Instead, we exist in a web of relationships in which it is possible to draw connections between all things. An infinite world of possibility awaits any explorer, whether in the physical world or in the mental, emotional, and/or spiritual life of human beings.

Roxanne Struthers, Valerie Eschiti, and Beverly Patchell made much the same observations in their article, "The Experience of Being an Anishinabe Man Healer: Ancient Healing in a Modern World":

Traditional stories have long been the keepers of information, offering guidance and solutions for the hardships endured on the human journey. For too long, the old ways and teachings have been seen as unnecessary in the modern world. The philosophy advocated by traditional Native people, respect for all living things and honoring the connections that exist between them, is being embraced by more people who believe it is necessary for them and for all of humanity sharing this earthly path.[11]

This quote encapsulates both the points we made about the Proper Conduct of Life and the recognition that all things are connected. Thus, respect for all living beings is certainly an important component of the Proper Conduct of Life. However, it is not enough to simply hold that respect; one must also honor it so that one's attitudes are reflected in one's actions. So, the Proper Conduct of Life, having respect and honoring the connections that exist between all elements of life, whether animate or inanimate, near at hand or far removed, is a very important lesson conveyed through traditional stories.

As one final example, Deborah McGregor provided a similar take on traditional stories, this time regarding the so-called Earth Diver story of the Anishinaabeg in which their cultural hero remakes the world after it has been flooded. The Anishinaabeg are supposed to only use his name when there is snow on the ground. To circumvent circumstances in which individuals may wish to discuss him, they will use a euphemism with which to refer to him during other times of the year: Bebaamosed, or "The One Who Walks Around." I will refer to him by that euphemism here. In any case, there are different versions of the Earth Diver story, but in the one with which I am most familiar, the muskrat retrieves mud from the bottom of the flooded world after the beaver, otter, and mink have all failed. The story has an environmental aspect to it in that Bebaamosed and his nephew, the wolf, upset the harmony of the natural order by overhunting. To protect themselves, the animal spirits in council decide to kill the wolf. The leader of the underwater creatures, Mishibizhii, volunteers to do so, and he is successful in his task. To get revenge for killing his nephew, Bebaamosed kills Mishibiizhii in turn. Finally, to get their revenge, the followers of Mishibiizhii make it start raining until the whole world is flooded. That is how Bebaamosed found himself in the position to remake the world after it was flooded. But, as can be seen, the whole dilemma came about because Bebaamosed and the wolf did not follow the Proper Conduct of Life, were not good relatives, and so wound up throwing the world out of balance. Writing about this story, McGregor states,

An environmentally-minded ecologist would nod at this story and agree that, yes, we know we are all connected, and what happens in one part of the ecosystem will impact another. This was not a new principle to the Anishinaabe people.[12]

She goes on to quote Battiste Henderson: "All aspects of knowledge are interrelated and cannot be separated from the traditional territories of the people concerned."[13] So, while the quotation above focuses more on cause-and-effect relationships, the second quote adds depth to our understanding of what she means when she talks about how "we know we are all connected." As stated earlier, the obvious importance of cause-and-effect relationships is acknowledged. But, beyond that, knowledge itself is interrelated as well, and, just as importantly, cannot be separated from the land. Recognition that knowledge is interrelated arises from the experience gained from living close to the land and seeing that, indeed, all things are interrelated.

The above examples provide compelling evidence that the Anishinaabeg do indeed hold the belief that all things are connected. However, we still need to establish that the Anishinaabeg use digressions when they speak. From my experience, that certainly is the case. Rupert Ross has discussed this same phenomenon in talking about speech patterns among the Anishinaabeg in Ontario.[14] He included an account of a speech he gave using the conventions of Anishinaabe rhetoric to an audience of First Nations people in Yellowknife, Northwest Territories.

> It took a whole to get going—as if I was floundering around trying to catch a rhythm. Once I did, however, it felt like being swept up in an adventure of some sort, more like following something that was alive on its own rather than trying to breathe life into something flat and bloodless on the page. Stories led into other stories, following their own logic, not mine. I found myself going through connections I had not seen before, then arriving at destinations that touched me in ways that were new. There were moments when I could feel tears welling up, there were moments when I felt great love and joy, and there were moments when there was such pain that only silences could capture them—and they did.[15]

Two other researchers who have commented on the use of digressions, or circular speech patterns, are Roxanne Struthers and Cynthia Peden-McAlphine. They explored the considerations scholars need to keep in mind when conducting phenomenological research among indigenous people. They write,

> Thus, it is paramount and necessary to understand the culture, language, and how the people speak to each other (Banks-Wallace, 2002). This is particularly important in indigenous societies, as talk is usually circular, not linear. Indigenous people consider the world as one circle, moving endlessly and eternally, perpetually and for perpetuity (Einhorn, 2000). Examples of circular talk taken from research excerpts include initiating a dialogue when asked the question, Tell me what it is like to be a women [*sic*] healer in your community. After explaining her experience for a while, the participant told a story about a seemingly unrelated topic. Then, she talked about another distinct, third topic and told another story to exemplify that subject matter. Thereupon, she returned to finish talking about the first topic under discussion. This type of circularity continued throughout the whole interview (Struthers, 1999) and was repeated for each new question that arose during the discussion. This type of expression can be difficult for a linear thinker to follow and can present a challenge during data analysis, when a researcher is searching for the essence of the lived experience. However, if one knows how to talk circularly, it is not viewed as unusual. Thus, defining a story in a manner consistent with the population under investigation is a critical part of the research process. It is not just what is said but how it was said and who said it that determines the meaning of a particular story (Banks-Wallace, 2002).[16]

Yes, indeed, it is important to consider how things are said when dealing with indigenous populations, including the Anishinaabeg. For the purposes of our discussion, we want to examine more deeply the relationship between these speech patterns that are circular in nature, that is, that employ the use of digressions, and the worldview of the Anishinaabeg. As we have seen, an important component of the worldview of the Anishinaabe people is the concept of the Proper Conduct of Life. Further, the Proper Conduct of Life includes a recognition that all things are connected. With that understanding in place, we are ready to explore how the use of digressions in Anishinaabe rhetorical practices both manifest and validate the worldview of the Anishinaabeg.

It is not uncommon for individuals using the conventions of Anishinaabe rhetoric to make use of digressions. However, it needs to be understood that the use of digressions does not mean or involve stream-of-consciousness thinking. Instead, it would be better to refer to this phenomenon as directed digressions in that the speaker invariably circles back around to the original point. In effect, the speaker is exploring the connections between different subjects. Exploring how the connections between different subjects works has a number of specific nuances. First and foremost, the number of subjects explored can be many and varied. Thus, the speaker might explore the connections between two to three topics, or may choose to go on a longer digression involving many more topics. The number of topics touched upon in this manner is theoretically infinite, but for practical purposes is necessarily limited in scope. By the same token, the nature of the topics brought up for analysis are not set in any fashion. So, a digression might concern itself with topics A, B, and C or just as easily focus on topics D, E, F, and G. Further, the time and spatial dimensions of the digression are open as well. A digression could cover past events only; past and future events; present, future, and past events; or any other temporal combination. The same type of practice can be applied to matters pertaining to the spatial dimension as well. There may even be digressions within digressions. So, there really are an infinite number of ways in which a digression can unfold. In the end, though, the discussion will invariably come back around to the original topic, closing the circle and tying all the seemingly unrelated strands of thought together.

The impact of the use of digressions in Anishinaabe rhetoric on the listener needs to be considered as well. There are at least three aspects about the listener that can be considered. First, in listening to digressions, the listener gets a look at the way the mind of the speaker functions. The way the human mind functions is fascinating. It can be characterized as the world's most advanced supercomputer. By bringing up unexpected connections, the listener is able to see receive a glimpse into the workings of another mind. The fascinating way in which the mind works in making unexpected connections can serve to keep the listener engaged and attentive to what comes next. Second, in drawing unexpected connections, the listener will see the world in new ways. New vistas of the imagination will be opened, helping to deepen the listener's understanding and appreciation for the complex nature of reality. Third, having new vistas of the imagination opened for the listener invites the listener to exercise his or her own imagination. The field of possibilities has been opened up, and new thoughts and ideas can potentially spring to life. In effect, the use of digressions by the speakers invites the listener to explore unexpected connections for himself or herself. All these acts—glimpsing the workings of another mind, hearing unexpected connections, and making one's own novel connections—reinforce the power contained within the use of digressions for the listener.

The power contained within the use of digressions is directly related to Anishinaabe religion and morality. In Anishinaabe thinking, all things are connected. Thus, there is an infinite variety of ways in which connections can exist between things. However, if that proposition is true, then there should be ways in which that truth claim can be tested. That is, we should be able to illustrate that all things actually are connected in some way. In this regard, Anishinaabe rhetoric both takes seriously and demonstrates the Anishinaabe philosophical and religious notion that all things are connected. In some ways, it can be argued the use of digressions involves explorations of reality. As stated above, there is an infinite variety of ways in which things can be connected. Also, as stated above, there is no one set way in which those connections must manifest themselves. Thus, while a digression that runs from X to A, B, and C, and then back to X is valid, a digression that runs from X to D, E, F, and G, and then back to X is just as valid. And, more to the point, the two do not cancel each other out. The use of digressions as a common rhetorical practice by the Anishinaabeg continuously demonstrates that indeed all things are connected. Establishing the truth claim that all things are connected thus validates the morality of the Anishinaabeg. As a result, the use of digressions on the one hand and the religion and morality of the Anishinaabeg on the other mutually reinforce each other. The use of digressions validates Anishinaabe religion and morality. In turn, Anishinaabe religion and morality give Anishinaabe rhetoric its power. It should come as no surprise, then, that, true to the religion and morality of the Anishinaabeg, their rhetoric, religion, and morality are intimately connected together.

Given the above, we can see the depth of the cultural conflict that results when digressions are labeled as bad or wrong by Western rhetorical standards. The claim that digressions are bad insults not only Anishinaabe speech practices, it also belittles and undermines their religion and morality upon which those digressions are based. This is why it is so important for the Anishinaabeg to articulate and validate their own forms of rhetorical practice. In affirming the use of digressions, we further affirm the religion and morality of the Anishinaabeg.

In the end, we should not be surprised the use of digressions by the Anishinaabeg has its ultimate roots in the religion and morality of the culture. As I demonstrated in my book chapter, other aspects of Anishinaabe rhetoric share this feature as well, although they manifest different aspects of Anishinaabe religion. By more fully articulating the underlying logic of Anishinaabe rhetoric, we can gain an even deeper appreciation of this complex cultural phenomenon. As such, we can see Anishinaabe rhetoric has its own power and indeed stands equal to any other rhetorical forms that exist in the world.

Notes

1.   Lawrence W. Gross, "Anishinaabe Rhetoric," chap. 8 in *Anishinaabe Ways of Knowing and Being* (Farnham Surrey, UK: Ashgate, 2014).

2.   Lawrence W. Gross, "*Bimaadiziwin*, or the Good Life of the Anishinaabeg," chap. 9 in *Anishinaabe Ways of Knowing and Being* (Farnham Surrey, UK: Ashgate, 2014).

3.   "Bimaadiziwin," The Ojibwe People's Dictionary, accessed December 31, 2019, https://ojibwe.lib.umn.edu/main-entry/bimaadiziwin-ni.

4.   Roger Spielmann, *"You're So Fat": Exploring Ojibwe Discourse* (Toronto: University of Toronto Press, 1998), 159.

5.   Rupert Ross, *Returning to the Teachings: Exploring Aboriginal Justice* (Toronto: Penguin Books, 1996), 271.

6.   Spielmann, *You're So Fat*, 91–92.

7.   Spielmann, *You're So Fat*, 154–58.

8.   A. Irving Hallowell, "Ojibwa Ontology, Behavior, and World View," in *Culture in History: Essays in Honor of Paul Radin*, ed. Stanley Diamond (New York: Columbia University Press, 1960), 30–34.

9.   Gross, *Anishinaabe Ways of Knowing*, 209–10.

10.   Brent Debassige, "Re-Conceptualizing Anishinaabe Mino-Bimaadiziwin (the Good Life) as Research Methodology: A Spirit-Centered Way in Anishinaabe Research," *Canadian Journal of Native Education* 33, no. 1 (2010): 24n6. Footnote in original.

11.   Roxanne Struthers, Valerie S. Eschiti, and Beverly Patchell, "The Experience of Being an Anishinabe Man Healer: Ancient Healing in a Modern World," *Journal of Cultural Diversity* 15, no. 2 (Summer 2008): 75.

12.   Deborah McGregor, "Coming Full Circle: Indigenous Knowledge, Environment, and Our Future," *American Indian Quarterly* 28, no. 3/4 (Summer–Autumn 2004): 388.

13.   McGregor, "Coming Full Circle," 390.

14.   Ross, *Returning to the Teachings*, 170–74.

15.   Ross, *Returning to the Teachings*, 173.

16.   Roxanne Struthers and Cynthia Peden-McAlpine, "Phenomenological Research among Canadian and United States Indigenous Populations: Oral Tradition and Quintessence of Time," *Qualitative Health Research* 15, no. 9 (November 2005): 1271. Footnotes in original.

CHAPTER THREE

Chicana/o/x Rhetoric

Relevance and Survival through Naming, Space, and Inclusion

DELORES MONDRAGÓN

We knew that what we were reading in the scholarly texts minimized and in many ways vilified our people's cultures and histories. Many, like myself, wanted to change the way academia portrayed American Indians, and we wanted to learn about our traditions in ways that did not relegate us to specimens of evolutionary development. Michelene E. Pesantubbee

In writing this piece, I delve briefly into multiple forms of knowledge transfer. Some of the ways I write will be accessible and familiar to some readers and for others my writing will seem ambiguous and foreign. I know how you feel. I invite the reader to approach this work with patience and compassion. It is part of understanding these familiar ways of Chicana/o/x rhetoric. If, to be rigorous in the academy, we are expected to learn Hegelian, Kantian, Nietzschean, Durkheimian, Foucauldian thought, et alia, and also are required to learn German and/or French to understand the zeitgeist, I invite the reader to consider investigating the languages and forms used by Chicanas, Chicanos, and Chicanx who have their languages, too, and other ways of knowledge transference with, by, and for La Raza. I respectfully acknowledge and remember the many scholars before me and those who made and continue to make great strides so that I can continue to benefit from their wisdom—it is medicine to me. I continue to feel a sense of gratitude because I and many others are able to share knowledge formations through different modalities—as many as are needed to continue thriving and/or surviving. I also simultaneously acknowledge that there were and continue to be many of our peoples whose stories wait to be re-remembered.

I will delve into *testimonio,* as a necessary form, to share a glimpse into some of the ways *nosotrxs* and *lxs otrxs* communicate. Dolores Delgado Bernal, Rebecca Burciaga, and Judith Carmona write about testimonio in the ways that I will refer to it in this writing. They argue that testimonio is "an approach that incorporates political, social, historical, and cultural histories that accompany one's life experiences as a means to bring about change through consciousness-raising. In bridging individuals with collective histories of oppression, a story of marginalization is re-centered to elicit social change."[1] So, my goal is that in sharing different ways of knowing, including by *testimoniando* from witnessing, what helped me develop my own identity and rhetoric, I am able to "elicit social change" in spaces where our ways of communicating are still invisible, erased, or delegitimized. That is, this chapter addresses the rhetoric that causes de-indianization and the rhetoric that could reverse it. I will provide examples of the names and shifting identities that are used in daily life and the scholarship that both seeks to de-indigenize and indigenize Chicana/o/x communities and their members. As stated, I will especially use testimonio to make my case but will point to other ways of knowing. I know we have been testimoniando since time immemorial and that we need to continue honoring this way of knowing and learning. Indigenas including Chicanas/os/x have been orating and continue this practice because it has and continues to be accessible across generations. I humbly add *mi granito de arena aqui* to reassure myself and others that we are continuing to strive to center indigenous scholarship, even if other scholarship can seem, and in many cases can be, detrimental to our minds, bodies, and spirits.

In the spirit of thanksgiving, I want to acknowledge that my work builds on the work of past and current Elders who have strived for liberation inside and outside the academy. I am in gratitude for community teachers such as my mother Jennifer Mondragón, who continues to teach me compassion; Ana Becerra, who pours our women's sweat lodge; Deborah Guerrero, who carries Kaya, a grandmother drum and continues the ancestors' songs; Linda Woods, who carries Migizi, a veteran woman's Eagle Staff; and Moses Mora, who is steadfast in his commitment to our collective ceremonies. I thank them for not only talking the talk but also for walking the walk. And, I am grateful for my academic Elders Inés Talamantez, Cherrie Moraga, Grace Chang, Gloria Anzaldúa, and the *mujeres* quoted here who occupied those liminal spaces of feminism that I needed to witness as a woman of color and to so many others for creating the language and carving out the spaces in academia by finding the *palabras* to have the subaltern be heard.[2] They complicated indigenous identities, borders, and histories through different lenses while interweaving interstitial spaces to help illuminate the complexities of our shared colonization. They are inspiring subsequent generations as they create sacred, safe, and physical spaces in academia and outside of it for us to thrive in so many ways.

As I share this story of identity and the rhetoric around it, I also keep in mind the shared similarities in Chicana/o/x shifting and *movimiento* and Kaupapa Māori, that is, "localizing" and "strategic positioning" as discussed by Linda Tuhiwai Smith.[3] I will also employ Margaret Kobach's approach of introducing the self.[4] Both of their insights of indigenous methodologies is essential for this work.

As I have learned, testimonio, including that informed by embodied knowledge, is a site of authority. I have learned from my teachers and through ceremony that testimonio is a necessary tool for survival because, first and foremost, these ways in which we Chicanas, Chicanos, and Chicanx share knowledges as we move around these dangerous spaces require particular forms of rhetoric of and for survival and of and for thriving. I begin this testimonio, more specifically my testimonio, to illustrate how Chicana/o/x rhetoric often develops, functions, facilitates, and influences identity formation and how it educates and helps some of us Chicanas/os/x decolonize from our prior indoctrinations—indoctrinations that are in keeping with genocidal practices by institutions designed for the sole purpose of terminating "Indians" like me.

A testimonio: I became Chicana as an undergraduate student at the University of Texas at El Paso. I learned about the Brown Buffalo, Oscar Zeta Acosta. I learned about Cesar Chavez and his hunger strike, Reies Lopez Tijerina's incarceration, and Rodolfo "Corky" Gonzales and *Joaquin*. I did not learn about Martha Cotera, Dolores Huerta, Jovita Idar or of any Mexican-American women or Chicanas for a long time. But I finally had the agency to call myself something that was not imposed on me. I had spent a long time tied to military identities as a seaman, dual-military member, dependent, and veteran. I was not only a mother, auntie, and grandmother who happens to be a student veteran, I learned I was a borderlander and a two-spirit indigenous mujer who still lives with contradictions. I am more comfortable now that I know about strategic positioning and locating myself as I shift to face what confronts me.

I was dangerously on the way to spending my life in an ambiguous state of not knowing who or where I came from or who I was. Knowing and learning about myself and my identity was honestly, I thought, a luxury I could not afford spending my time thinking about. I had to hustle to survive. I, like many indigenous women, live not only with an ideological and genocidal war here at home but also with American wars overseas. It took a lot of privileges and advantages to find out what I did not know. I straddled borders, literally and figuratively! Gloria Anzaldúa taught me that. This queer Tejana pulled me in with a quote of *El Otro Mexico* by Los Tigres del Norte in her *Borderlands.*[5] She localized knowledge for me. I had been singing *El Otro México* and *La Puerta Negra* by Los Tigres del Norte, *con mi padre* since I was a kid. My dad, Rogelio Mondragón, who migrated from Mexico, used this song to educate me about the discrimination he experienced from my mother's Chickasaw family. He also used *La Puerta Negra* as a metaphor for the border. He explained that every border crossing was a *Puerta Negra*—a black door he had to push through, to get into the United States without losing his humanity. And he often reminds me that "esta cosa de la inmigración a sido una cosa de siempre," when talking about the everyday inhumanities experienced at the border.

When I heard Rodolfo "Corky" Gonzales's epic poem "I Am Joaquin" in a Chicano studies classroom where the professor's expressed intention was to make us proud and highlight our shared Chicano identities, I was inspired though recoiled at the wailing woman heard in the background of the recording. When Aztlán was described as both a mythical and real place, of and for Chicanos, I felt I had found my homeland. I was no longer *ni de aqui ni de alla*. I was part of a community because it was a space created for someone like me, that is, until a Chicano studies professor said Aztlán was located in Santa Barbara, California—home of the Chumash peoples. I was lost again. When Caló was described as the language of resistance among Mexican American youth, including Zootsuiters and Chicanos, I became proud to speak and understand most of it, because I had been shamed by many *adultos* and teachers for using it . . . and Spanish. I was finally proud to be from Chucotown, *donde te whachas de la chota* on your way to your *cantón y tu jefita*. I still recall the laughter that overtook my Spanish class at the Defense Language Institute Foreign Language Center located at the Presidio of Monterey, California, where I was shamed, questioned, and belittled for bringing in Caló. It was humiliating . . . at the time. I now know that it has value but still appreciate that it can still be humiliating for some of those kids I grew up with—for those *carnalitas/os/x* before and after me who speak cautiously. Caló is natural and it shows you belong *en el barrio*—it is part of *la cultura*. Eliminating it is genocide because it is language born of and for survival.

When I encountered Anzaldúan scholarship in a Chicano studies class, and then an aptly named Chicana studies class, I realized we would not be scolded or humiliated for speaking like *mi gente*. I learned about mestiza consciousness, La Raza, El Movimiento, Brown Berets, school walkouts, Teatro Campesino, grape strikes, pesticides, murals, and all I would eventually learn as a doctoral candidate in Chicana and Chicano studies at the University of California, Santa Barbara. I was encouraged to embrace my Chicana identity because it meant I was fighting for social justice—versus my father's antiquated definition of a *raza* betraying Border Patrol "Chicanilla" wearing a border patrol uniform. I felt relief. I felt relevant. But soon things became complicated when I started bringing in my Chickasaw identity. I felt confused. I felt disconnected, again.

I was a different sort of mestiza, not quite like my peers. My mother is Chickasaw and white. I, like Cherrie Moraga, was *La Güera* in El Paso because my mom (like Cherrie's dad) was neither Mexican nor Mexican American, so this complicated things.[6] I was also not sure if I was "Azteca" because my family hailed from the region of Mexico where the Mazahua (*Jñatjo*) people originated. Unfortunately, because of *mestizaje mi familia en* Mexico and my dad claimed to be *descendientes de los Españoles* and nothing else, their indigenous bodies, practices, and locations complicate this belief—for me.

As a Chicana/o studies graduate student, I helped students understand Chicana and Chicano knowledges. It did not take long for generalized identities and histories to become convoluted. My cohort alone was complicated. It was made up of one Chicano and three mujeres who identified themselves with multiple identities. One was Puerto Rican/Chicana, another Salvadorian and Mexican American, and then there was me, a Chickasaw Chicana. My students, too, started asking critical questions that I had not asked or was not brave enough to ask at the time. I was desperate for inclusion. I was probably as desperate as the Chicanos in El Movimiento. Did you notice that? I said Chicanos. I learned and taught about Chicanos. It was what was assigned. It took feminist classes and scholarship by Chicanas and Chicanx, Latinas and Latinx, Tejanas and Tejanx as well as Native women to shift my lens once more. I am still learning as I write this.

The development of my studies would come into a deeper and critical stage with the work of Dr. Horacio Roque Ramirez, a queer Salvadorian professor. In his life and after his transition into the spirit world, he helped me realize that critical questions were necessarily everywhere and that unfortunately not everyone had been included in my learning and teaching. He purposely did not identify as Chicano, and I often wonder if this act of pushing against impositions contributed to his early death. He challenged Chicana and Chicano scholars to think beyond ascribed definitions and boundaries. He embodied a different sort of borderlander, one defining himself and his spaces at the university, in the most compassionate ways. His propositions of critical thought through a queer lens stay with me today. It is what helps me appreciate the shift that occurred with the name el Movimiento Estudiantil of Progressives for Change (MEPA), although I will have more to say on this later.[7] What I am learning is that trying on names and looking for safe spaces has shifted my notions about identity and challenged my developing indoctrination into Chicana/o/x rhetoric. Names and spaces, to learn and try on names, was and is important to my continual striving toward liberation from colonization. I rarely see this admittedly unknown fluidity of identities practiced or acknowledged in the academy—being static is a luxury for those not concerned with genocide.

Flashback: A recent attendance in a required religious studies course challenged my mind, body, and spirit as I experienced the trauma of Western philosophical rhetoric. When Kant and Heidegger were introduced and assigned, I panicked as students in the class shared Heidegger's unrepentant membership in the Nazi party nonchalantly. Later, I would read about Kant's hierarchical order and his characterization of indigenous peoples as "uneducable; for they lack affect and passion," "are not amorous, and so are not fertile," and "care for nothing and are lazy," revealing his racism toward people like me.[8] I experienced cognitive and cultural dissonance and learned to develop a *conciencia con compromiso*, as expressed by Linda Prieto and Sofia A. Villenas.[9] It became hard to absorb what I was being taught and who I needed to learn from, including the "foundational" scholars like Heidegger, especially because those teachings had not contended with indigenous philosophies and because there was no pause or reflection on accepting the teachings from racists. I did not have the words for what I was experiencing but Dolores Delgado Bernal did. She pointed to epistemological racism. I yearned for and was grateful to read her writings on "Using a Chicana Epistemology in Educational Research," where she states that "in education, what is taught, how it is taught, who is taught, and whose fault it is when what is taught is not learned are often manifestations of what is considered the legitimate body of knowledge."[10] She "criticized conventional notions of objectivity and universal foundations of knowledge for erasing the specific intersectionality and location of Chicana experiences."[11] Mujeres like her laid the foundations of Chicana, Chicano, and Chicanx epistemological rhetoric fundamental to Chicana, Chicano, and Chicanx ontologies and indigenous Chicana, Chicano, and Chicanx scholarship.

Chicana, Chicano, and Chicanx ways of understanding are often personal and continuously merging into and bridging onto the realms of US and Mexican indigenous scholarship, creating exciting spaces for contradictions, uncomfortableness, solidarity, and compassion, which are all desirable for the true decolonization of work, research, and daily life. Creating bridges between the north and the south continues to be complicated, but we need to learn and understand how so we can move forward as whole peoples. The national project of *mestizaje*, for example, continues to "de-indianize" the indigenous people in Mexico and elsewhere, and this makes it hard to participate in collective actions for social change and environmental justice here in our communities and abroad. Many have quoted Guillermo Batalla, but his wisdom bears repeating because we are still struggling to acknowledge deep fractures that have occurred as a result of the ethnocide happening in Mexico. He writes,

> De-Indianization is a historical process through which populations that originally possessed a particular and distinct identity, based upon their own culture, are forced to renounce that identity, with all the consequent changes in their social organization and culture. De-Indianization is not the result of biological mixture, but of the pressure of an ethnocide that ultimately blocks the historical continuity of a people as a culturally differentiated group.[12]

Many incredible teachers are actively reclaiming their indigenous identity and are re-indigenizing themselves by claiming their roots, through naming with the development of words like Xicana and through the creation of spaces like the Xicana Sacred Space. They are challenging the status quo on university campuses and establishing bridges from the academy back to the communities many of us want to stay connected to and help improve through the tools we acquire on university campuses and from our Elders.

Andrés Reséndez pointed out that "a world of exceedingly fluid identities" subsisted in the Southwest. He used George J. Sanchez's analysis of "how Mexican immigrants became Mexican American in Los Angeles by focusing on things like their changing employment and consumer patterns and how these adaptations affected their perception of collective self," to see the myriad of identities forming in the early frontier.[13] The history of naming, whether to oppress or empower along with the why and how, are important in order to recontextualize and appreciate the continued practice of this form of decolonizing rhetoric and in order to understand the tensions and disconnects between indigenous peoples north and south of the US border.

Along with the continued de-indianization of our ancestors, early generations of activists reappropriated and redefined the word "Chicano" for themselves and rehabilitated its meaning in creating a positive identity. It worked for a while, but the word Chicano with its patriarchal residue was gendered and erased the contributions of women and others *en La Causa*. Those on the margins understood this problematic truth. Many Chicanas, like

Martha Cotera, resisted the justifications, by Chicanos, of their erasure by challenging Chicanos to make space for intersectional conversations on race, class, and gender, and by highlighting the contributions of *mujeres en el Movimiento*. Later, we would have self-identifying gender nonconforming peoples push against the gendered imposition placed on them with the use of Chicana, Chicano, and Chican@, and so we moved toward the more inclusive term Chicanx. Prior to this "strategic positioning," mestizaje became suspect and was rejected as an identity by indigenous people that embrace their indigenous identities and rejected or practiced decentering the Spanish roots of the word "mestizo."[14] Vigil reminds us that we should not forget the strategic moves in history nor the residue of the past where "many mestizos, especially those who looked Spanish, followed the racist colonial ideology [and] many Indians followed this strategy by 'passing' as mestizos. They attempted to change racial membership and thereby gain wider socioeconomic opportunities."[15] Though it is evident that "acculturation and identity change over generations did not move immigrants from their foreign category into a single, homogeneous American identity . . . migrants acculturated to and changed their identities into a series of races that formed over the course of American history," and this includes the identities that continue to change as needed so we can push against oppression and all other traumas that come with colonization.[16]

While some Chicanos/as/x rejected mestizaje because the Spaniards had never conquered their people or rejected Aztlán because they did have an immediate homeland, others rejected Chicana, Chicano, and Chicanx because they did not find a place to belong within that terminology and hence created names for themselves once again. They wanted their own names and spaces—names and spaces that were more inclusive—names and spaces that continued their decolonial projects—out of the danger of remaining static and susceptible to genocide. Younger generations and old progressives are learning to shift and change with and without fear because of this real threat. They are renaming themselves as they move forward as a people, despite the legacy of patriarchy, homophobia, colorism, and Catholic guilt. We see this movement clearly with the recent renaming of MEChA. This acronym, which originally stood for Movimiento Estudiantil Chicano de Aztlán, was later inclusive of Chicanas, followed by Chican@, then Chicanx. Later, the organization dropped Chicanx and Aztlán, while recalibrating, to become a more inclusive Movimiento Estudiantil of Progressives for Change, or MEPA. In their reassurance to the *veteranos/as/x* of the *lucha*, they shared the following:

> Ultimately, the heated, multi-generational debate is reflective of shifts happening elsewhere in the Latino community. In 2017, The National Council of La Raza, the largest Latino advocacy organization, changed its name to UnidosUS, in an attempt to be more inclusive and appeal to younger generations. Likewise, the growing adoption of the gender non-binary term "Latinx," is an effort to create a label that is inclusive of women and the LGBTQ community (recently, MEChA also adopted the X, changing Chicano to Chicanx.) These proposed shifts in language represent the changing lens through which younger generations view diversity and inclusion, and also remind us that there has never been consensus around the terms that should define our complex communities. After all, the young Chicanos of the '60s rebelled against Mexican-American terminology they felt didn't represent them or their values.[17]

Resistance to the name change was loud but ultimately reminiscent of other changes within this community and other communities that must maneuver constantly to maintain their agency and sovereignty.

Many subaltern communities are finding safe spaces or creating sacred spaces for their outrage, most of the time. Some Chicanas/os/x are naming their identities for the first time. They are queer, indigenous, farm workers, maids, children of undocumented parents and/or deported parents, who were publicly shamed and whose identities were depicted as undesirable and "alien." The beautiful thing I witnessed was that some students in required diversity studies courses discovered their Elders in ethnic, queer, or feminist studies classrooms. I have witnessed the awe when Gloria Anzaldúa, Cherrie Moraga, Dolores Huerta, the Combahee River Collective, Wounded Knee Occupation of 1973, or El Plan de Santa Barbara are discovered by students. These scholars and movements represent the legacies and the foundations for their bodies to exist inside and outside the academy where they can continue to create sacred spaces. Lourdes Diaz Soto et al. shared an example of the journey and importance of such a space when they wrote about the development of a Xicana Sacred Space. They wrote,

> Our original intent—to develop a methodology that focuses a Chicana lens on action research—resulted in the recognition of a Xicana Sacred Space (XSS). The space emerged and was created as a result of dialogic and collaborative tensions, intentions, and complexities. We named the experience to capture not only the physical space that it provided us but also a figurative space affording theoretical explorations. The XSS made room for freedom and for intense dialogue, creating an intimate circle for collective reflexivity; shared subjectivities; the transformation of identities; a source of strength, direction, and knowledge; and a springboard for powerful research and community projects.[18]

Suzy Zepeda, too, highlights the creation of space through naming by explaining that "the use of the 'X' in the term Xicana signals a conscious politicized identity that insists on intentionally remembering Indigenous cultures, languages, roots, and hidden histories of Mesoamerica."[19]

The creation of their own safe spaces and other related activities are empowering in further contextualizing the perceived contradictions in everyday life. These activities also renew our appreciation for our *veteranos/as/x en la lucha* like muralist Moses Mora. He continued *la lucha* through his work with the help of artist and activist MB Hanrahan, who collectively created a space to tell the story of the Tortilla Flats neighborhood, which was overtaken by the construction of US Highway 101 in Ventura, California, as he related the story to me at the Bell Arts in April 2015. The nonviolent occupation by Chicanas/os/x and other Latinas/os/x of Dodger Stadium, built over a destroyed and stolen Mexican immigrant and Mexican-American community known as Chavez Ravine, is another example of the creation of this type of space.

As I, and many others, continue entering spaces not made for Chicanas/os/x, where the Anzaldúan mestiza consciousness "embraces the contradictions and ambiguity of those who live in more than one culture" kicks in and where body language such as side-eyes and deep breaths confront indigenous bodies, we recognize the need for naming and for spaces of inclusion for the mere survival of queer people of color (QPOC) like us.[20] We also name the Missing and Murdered Indigenous Women and Girls and Two-Sprit Peoples (MMIWG2S) and yet hold on to the realization that we are actively hunted. When a predator enters a room, Chicanas/os/x and other indigenous peoples alike recall the disproportionate amount of sexual violence at the hands of perpetrators past and/or remember warnings from sisters about the *wasi'chu* (Lakota: white person, but literally "greedy person") because the numbers do not lie and neither does the evidence of the violence done to indigenous bodies. So, much like ceremony informs and adds to our spiritual and practical knowledge production for survival, silence, murals, and other shifting language is rhetoric that has the same usefulness.

Another flashback: As I wrote this chapter from Huatulco, Oaxaca, Mexico, I was reminded of the violence back home in the United States. On the day I was writing this, a white male in his twenties killed twenty-three people and wounded twenty-three more in El Paso because he hated immigrants and Hispanics. My parents, who walk the mall where this mass shooting happened, thankfully were in Huatulco with me. This shooting quickly reminded me of the mass shooting and perpetrator who killed six students near my school in Santa Barbara in May 2014. Both gunmen had manifestos. I mention this briefly here because our mental health needs protection, too. As recipients of historical, insidious, and intergenerational trauma who navigate academic and other institutional spaces, it is important to acknowledge that many of us suffer from complex traumas, traumas that will influence what we feel can be shared safely. Hence, we must always walk with gentle and compassionate hearts as we talk and learn from and with our communities. Audre Lorde always reminds us that "the master's tools will never dismantle the master's house," so we should not replicate the violence. As Dr. Inés Talamantez always told her students, we need to speak from the heart and find ways to be compassionate.[21] She would say this was the only way to walk in a good way, while being ever mindful of the historical truth of our collective oppression.

People are often surprised by the warnings that are not usually shared outside of safe spaces, but I will try to provide my own warning in part here so that I, too, remember. We warn about all those who might put us in danger, even indigenous Chicanx academics who have been colonized to talk, write, and sound like the oppressor, delivering colonizing blows to the mind, body, and spirit of the brown body, leading many of those same colonized indigenous academics to their early deaths once they have become tokenized and suffocated as they enforce what is "legitimate" scholarship, while ironically quoting racists like Heidegger and Kant in order to feel included and respected. But it is the maestrx, the Elders—the ones often entrusted to take care of their communities—who are the ones we need to pay attention to and learn from. They are the ones to be respected, not because they ask to be respected or because other people say they should be respected, but because those Elders are the ones most interested in the survival of our babies, our bodies, and our histories.

So, after growing up on the border of El Paso and Ciudad Juárez, where names like *chucos*, cholas, Tejanas, *Juareñx*, Tarahumaras, *mojados* are always developing and changing, I came to appreciate witnessing the uniquely courageous practice of naming the self. The recent public self-naming of a student as undocumented (and later others as UndocuQueer and UndocuTrans) was a display of courage and liberation that remains overwhelming and humbling, when one understands the risk. Yet, it is also evident that it is a necessary action that has always taken place. I continue to witness these forms of shifts and movimientos outside of the university, too, but not as frequently, especially under the leadership of the forty-fifth president of the United States where we witnessed that one can lose one's children or parents. The stakes are higher now that those choosing to name themselves can be deported or worse, risking one's self and one's children to detention in our country's concentration camps. We all witnessed the all-too-familiar state violence on indigenous bodies, including sterilizations. We all have witnessed the naming of Deferred Action for Childhood Arrivals, or DACA, people not too long ago when they were guaranteed a path to citizenship. Now they live with uncertainty because of ineffectual legislation. The dangerous, yet courageous, rhetorical actions taken by these undocumented people are worthy of acknowledgment and remembering so that we do not forget the strengths and risks our communities are willing to take for the betterment of the whole.

Juan Gonzalez, again, reminds us of the intergenerational trauma inflicted by the state, wherein unjust violence was imposed on Mexican and American indigenous people alike. As he writes,

In July 1954, the federal government unleashed one of the darkest periods in immigrant history—"Operation Wetback." Brutal dragnets were
conducted in hundreds of Mexican neighborhoods as migrants were summarily thrown into jails, herded into trucks or trains, then shipped back
to Mexico. Many of those abducted were American citizens of Mexican
descent. The government, ignoring all due process, deported between 1 and
2 million people in a few short months.[22]

This injustice is ever present today as the detention centers are filled with
indigenous peoples.

The experience of indigenous people, as witnessed by the deportations of
the 1950s and the concentration camps of today, remind us of the need for social
change and how the power of space, including testimonios, can help affect that
change. This is why understanding knowledge transfer based on indigenous
methods and methodologies is so crucial. In closing this piece, I am reminded of
a recent encounter with a Māori activist and storyteller who made me aware of
the shared commonalities indigenous peoples share in their respective ways
of shifting, movement, and knowing. The Māori Elder told me that after periods
of community orating, it was expected that an action would follow their
orating. Once the action was completed, time was allocated to reflect on the
given action. After reflecting on the consequences of the action and seeing how
it worked, it was important to congregate and orate once again, making the
appropriate adjustments after finding out what worked and what did not work
for the community. The Elder informed me that the most important aspect of
this process was the recalibration that occurred in this continuous circular
process. Striving for the betterment of the community was key. With this Māori
Elder's words in mind, I share this testimonio as an action toward bringing
examples of Chicana/o/x rhetoric into conversation within this collection,
praying that it leads to further reflections, recalibration, and new actions in our
shared efforts to hear ourselves, our subaltern, speak and be heard.

Notes

Note to Epigraph: *Native Voices: American Indian Identity and Resistance* edited by
Richard A. Grounds, George E. Tinker, and David E. Wilkins published by the University
Press of Kansas, © 2003. www.kansaspress.ku.edu. Page 209. Used by permission.

1. Dolores Delgado Bernal, Rebeca Burciaga, and Judith Flores Carmona, "Chicana/Latina Testimonios: Mapping the Methodological, Pedagogical, and Political," *Equity & Excellence in Education* 45, no. 3 (2012): 363.

2. Emma Pérez, *The Decolonial Imaginary: Writing Chicanas into History* (Bloomington: Indiana University Press, 1999), 31–51. For more on the subaltern being heard, see Jay Maggio, "'Can the Subaltern Be Heard?': Political Theory, Translation, Representation, and Gayatri Chakravorty Spivak," *Alternatives* 32, no. 4 (2007): 419–43.

3. Linda Tuhiwai Smith, *Decolonizing Methodologies: Research and Indigenous Peoples*, 2nd ed. (London: Zed Books, 2012), 188.

4. Margaret Kovach, *Indigenous Methodologies: Characteristics, Conversations and Contexts* (Toronto: University of Toronto Press, 2009), 91, 110.

5. Gloria Anzaldúa, *Borderlands/La Frontera: The New Mestiza*, 2nd ed. (San Francisco: Aunt Lute Books, 1999), 23.

6. Cherríe Moraga, "La Güera," in *This Bridge Called My Back: Writings by Radical Women of Color*, ed. Cherríe Moraga and Gloria Anzaldúa (Watertown, MA: Persephone Press, 1981), 27–34.

7. Aaron E. Sanchez, "Why Student Group MEChA's Proposed Name Change Has Set Off a Fierce, Multi-Generational Debate," Remezcla, April 4, 2019, https://remezcla.com/features/culture/mecha-name-change-debates.

8. Immanuel Kant, *Lectures on Anthropology*, ed. Allen W. Wood and Robert B. Louden, trans. Robert R. Clewis et al. (Cambridge: Cambridge University Press, 2012), 320. For more on Kant's racism, see Mark Larrimore, "Sublime Waste: Kant on the Destiny of the 'Races,'" in *Civilization and Oppression*, ed. Catherine Wilson, (Calgary, AB: University of Calgary Press), supplement, *Canadian Journal of Philosophy* 25 (1999): 99–125. For a list of some of the scholarly literature on Kant's racism, see Wulf D. Hund, "'It Must Come from Europe': The Racisms of Immanuel Kant," in *Racisms Made in Germany*, ed. Wulf D. Hund, Christian Koller, and Moshe Zimmermann (Zurich: LIT-Verlag, 2011), 78n28. For more on racism in Western philosophy in general, see Bryan W. Van Norden, *Taking Back Philosophy: A Multicultural Manifesto* (New York: Columbia University Press, 2017).

9. Linda Prieto and Sofia A. Villenas, "Pedagogies from *Nepantla: Testimonio*, Chicana/Latina Feminisms and Teacher Education Classrooms," *Equity & Excellence in Education* 45, no. 3 (2012): 411.

10. Dolores Delgado Bernal, "Using a Chicana Feminist Epistemology in Educational Research," *Harvard Educational Review* 68, no. 4 (Winter 1998): 556.

11. "Chicana Feminist Epistemology: Past, Present, and Future," *Harvard Educational Review* 82, no. 4 (Winter 2012): 511.

12. Guillermo Bonfil Batalla, *México Profundo: Reclaiming a Civilization*, trans. Philip A. Dennis (Austin: University of Texas Press, 1996), 17.

13. Andrés Reséndez, *Changing National Identities at the Frontier: Texas and New Mexico, 1800–1850* (Cambridge: Cambridge University Press, 2005), 1, 12.

14. Susy J. Zepeda, "Queer Xicana Indígena Cultural Production: Remembering

through Oral and Visual Storytelling," *Decolonization: Indigeneity, Education & Society* 3, no. 1 (2014): 123.

15.   James Diego Vigil, *From Indians to Chicanos: The Dynamics of Mexican-American Culture*, 3rd ed. (Long Grove, IL: Waveland Press, 2012), 324.

16.   Paul Spickard, *Almost All Aliens: Immigration, Race, and Colonialism in American History and Identity* (New York: Routledge, 2007), 463.

17.   Sanchez, "Why Student Group."

18.   Lourdes Diaz Soto et al., "The Xicana Sacred Space: A Communal Circle of Compromiso for Educational Researchers," *Harvard Educational Review* 79, no. 4 (Winter 2009): 755–56.

19.   Zepeda, "Queer Xicana," 121.

20.   Rebecca Romo, "'You're Not Black or Mexican Enough!': Policing Racial/Ethnic Authenticity among Blaxicans in the United States," in *Red and Yellow, Black and Brown: Decentering Whiteness in Mixed Race Studies*, ed. Joanne L. Rondilla, Rudy P. Guevarra Jr., and Paul Spickard (New Brunswick, NJ: Rutgers University Press, 2017), 129.

21.   Audre Lorde, "The Master's Tools Will Never Dismantle the Master's House," in *This Bridge Called My Back: Writings by Radical Women of Color*, ed. Cherríe Moraga and Gloria Anzaldúa (New York: Kitchen Table, Women of Color Press, 1983), 94–101.

22.   Juan González, *Harvest of Empire: A History of Latinos in America* (New York: Viking, 2000), 203.

CHAPTER FOUR

Women, Childbirth, and the Sticky Tamales

Nahua Rhetoric and Worldview in the Glyphic Codex Borgia

FELICIA RHAPSODY LOPEZ

PRIOR TO COLONIZATION, DIVERSE Indigenous populations across the area now known as Central Mexico had rigorous systems of glyphic and pictorial writing that they recorded in books now called codices (the plural of codex). According to Elizabeth Hill Boone, these texts "stand for an entire body of Indigenous knowledge, one that embraces both science and philosophy."[1] Of the multitude of precontact Indigenous books, only twelve codices from precontact Central Mexico remain. Using alphabetic texts in Nahuatl, the language of the Nahua people and the most widely spoken language in Central Mexico at the time of contact, I assess the glyphic and pictorial precontact texts as they relate to women's bodies and reproduction. In my examination of these diverse Central Mexican texts, or codices, most specifically the precontact glyphic Codex Borgia and the early colonial alphabetic Florentine Codex, I seek to further the decolonial project of recovering Indigenous rhetorical knowledge through methods that center Mesoamerican religious traditions, voices, documents, and language.

From the time of Spanish arrival, the legitimacy of Indigenous writing traditions has been questioned by non-Indigenous outsiders. The question of the value of Indigenous writing extended to other aspects of Indigenous life, from the perceived inferiority of native belief systems to the perceived inferiority of the Native populations themselves. As Boone states:

> There have always been those—historians and anthropologists alike— who deny historicity to pre-Columbian cultures, who have argued that the painted records are not history in the "proper" or "true" sense. As early as the sixteenth century, such arguments were surrounded by and inte- grated into the larger debates about the intelligence and humanity of the Mexicans and other American peoples—whether the Amerindians were rational and civilized. . . . Writing and history became conceptually braided together.[2]

While those debating the function and legitimacy of Nahuatl writing previously positioned themselves in direct opposition to each other, with one side dismissing the idea of any sort of precontact Nahuatl writing system, today most scholars agree that Nahuatl writing did exist.[3] With most now in agreement about the presence of Nahuatl and other Mexican writing systems such as those of the Mixtecs and Mayans at the time of contact, the academic debates have become more nuanced. Current issues of scholarly concern include questions about who among the Indigenous populations had access to and knowledge of these systems, and about the depth and prevalence of logographic and phonographic writing within these pictorial works.[4]

Like the debate over whether Nahua people had "true writing," contemporary scholars debate the rhetorical value of visual media like the perceived pictorial texts outside of written or glyphic language. Rhetoric scholar Maureen Day Goggin questions the line placed between the written word and other visual signs in her examination of embroidery:

> The continued bifurcation of visual and verbal aspects of rhetoric in subtle, and sometimes not so subtle, ways reified the *words*—written language— as a measure against, and somewhat above, all other potential resources for representation and communication. Thus, it tends to blind us to theoriz- ing and historicizing other kinds of semiotic resources and practices. As a result, the divide severely limits *what* counts as rhetorical practice and *who*

counts in its production, performance and circulation. (emphasis in original)[5]

This blinding to who and what counts as rhetoric, like the centuries-old arguments about the humanity of Indigenous people, continues to rob Indigenous people, especially those who did not use glyphic or other phonetic writing, of their full identities and knowledge. By privileging Euro-Western forms of rhetoric, specifically alphabetic texts, scholars fail to recognize the unique rhetorical strategies and theories of Indigenous people, such as those conveyed in glyphic, pictorial, sewn, gestural, and spoken forms of communication, some of which I will address here.

The use of rhetoric as persuasive speech among the Nahua people of Central Mexico constitutes one of the core subjects included in the Florentine Codex—a twelve-book, Nahua-authored alphabetic codex, written under the direction of Fray Bernardino de Sahagún in the early stages of Mexico's colonial period. The Florentine Codex, Book 6: Rhetoric and Moral Philosophy, focuses primarily on the speeches delivered to religious figures called *teteoh*; speeches given by the *tlatoani*, or rulers; and speeches made by parents and other various members of the community, women and men, during key moments in life, such as at the birth of a child.[6] Book 6: Rhetoric and Moral Philosophy ends with short collections of riddles, sayings, and metaphors.[7] However, the other volumes of the Florentine Codex contain a multitude of examples of what could be considered rhetoric despite the specific focus on rhetoric within this particular volume. Here I will focus on a short excerpt from Book 5: The Omens, which draws connections between a woman's body and a pot that cooks tamales.[8] Using parallels between this excerpt and the glyphic Codex Borgia, I will discuss what these texts reveal about the nature of Nahua rhetoric and their worldview. More directly, I will examine the use of what are commonly called metaphors within these Central Mexican texts and illustrate how they reveal literal connections between realms of existence and figures in the material world. Omens, framed as superstitions by the Spanish, represent an Indigenous form of knowledge, rooted in the interconnectedness of people with the world around them. This analysis furthers the ongoing movement toward anchoring glyphic decipherment of texts such as the Codex Borgia within a cultural and linguistic framework.

Background

Multiple scholars and texts have previously addressed the use of rhetorical strategies among diverse Mesoamerican people.[9] These works often address the use of specific language and word choice in creating rhetorical arguments or speeches.[10] Rhetoric among precontact Indigenous Mesoamerican groups, as well as encompassing spoken rhetoric, also included written forms of rhetoric that incorporated both visual imagery and logosyllabic writing. One of the most widely known books of Mesoamerican rhetoric is book 6 of the Florentine Codex, which contains speeches that Sahagún began collecting early in his proselytizing career alongside some visual texts drawn by Nahua scribes in forms more similar to those found in precontact texts. According to translators Arthur J. O. Anderson and Charles E. Dibble, book 6 of the Florentine Codex represents one of the more challenging texts to translate due to its "difficult, florid, formal language."[11] However, Nahua rhetorical speech, understood as the often flowery language used to convince or inspire a desired effect, can be found in degrees throughout the Florentine Codex. The twelve books of the Florentine Codex are believed to have been "molded after encyclopedic works known to the educated in Sahagún's time."[12] In other words, Sahagún's organization of the knowledge he collected from Nahua elders and scribes was modeled after previously published collections about other parts of the world. Sahagún specifically requested information that he recognized as rhetoric, a word that lacks a direct translation into Nahuatl— the word used in the Nahuatl text for "rhetoric" is the Spanish loanword *rethorica*. This has led some scholars to assert that the concept of rhetoric as a distinct form "would have been alien to a Nahua neophyte."[13] Others have stated, such as Sahagún's contemporary Fray Andrés de Olmos, that these types of rhetorical speeches are called by the Nahuatl term *huehuetlatolli*, or the words of the elders.[14]

However, persuasive and florid language among the Nahuas was not restricted to oral speeches, nor was it restricted to language labeled huehuetlatolli. Rather, any language that was meant to be persuasive shared elements in common with the huehuetlatolli. According to Louise Burkhart, persuasive modes of Nahuatl speech became important to friars as they sought out ways to convert more Nahua people to Christianity:

Nahuatl not only named but persuaded in a different way from Spanish or Latin. In order to use Nahuatl effectively, to persuade as well as to explain, the friars had to adopt the rhetorical forms of expression appropriate to Nahuatl. Christian precepts had to be expressed in a way that was not only grammatically correct but that would convince Nahua listeners to accept them. To this end, friars elicited and recorded native oratory, listed the figures of speech and adages contained therein, and strove to master the elegant speaking style of the native orators.[15]

While what Burkhart calls "figures of speech and adages" were initially adopted by the Spanish clergy in their attempts to more effectively convert Nahua and other Indigenous populations to Christianity, the use of such language in conversion was later abandoned. The problem, as the friars saw it, was that even though florid Nahuatl language was more convincing than literal Bible translations from Spanish or Latin, this more poetic form of Nahuatl also brought with it the embedded Nahua and other Indigenous beliefs. By the end of Sahagún's career, he and other friars "tended to avoid very elaborate figures of speech, which they could not fully understand and which might thus conceal unorthodox meanings."[16] Indigenous rhetoric and worldviews were so thoroughly embedded within Nahuatl words and expressions that the Spanish clergy who spoke Nahuatl grew to believe that the full conversion they sought would not be possible by continuing to speak in the ornate manner typical of Nahua rhetoric.

Similarly, Indigenous beliefs were inextricably tied to the preexisting written glyphic texts, and therefore their destruction was an integral part of the spiritual colonization process. While academics continue to debate the level to which the writing that appears in texts such as the Codex Borgia qualifies as a logosyllabic writing system, it is clear from early Spanish accounts that the Nahua people were able to read directly from these texts.[17] For example, regarding his questioning of Nahua people, Diego Durán stated, "The Indians find it difficult to give explanations unless they can consult the book of their village. So he went to his home and brought back a painted manuscript . . . [with this manuscript, the] native narrated the life of Topiltzin to me as I had known it but in a better manner than I had heard before."[18] While the Nahua people were practitioners of oral traditions, they also recorded and shared their diverse knowledge through books.

The accessibility of the knowledge contained within the Nahua codices varies along with the content of these texts. Precontact and early colonial maps and historical documents with their logosyllabic glyphs of people, places, names, and Spanish glosses have provided modern scholars with ways to begin to decipher these glyphic texts. However, texts such as those belonging to the Borgia group (a group of six codices that share iconographic style and content, and of which the Codex Borgia is the most elaborately illustrated) have yet to be thoroughly understood. Scholars such as Boone argue that these are examples of *nahuallatolli*, or Nahuatl sacred speech, in written form:

> The divinatory and religious codices, as in *nahuallatolli* and *iya* [Mixtec sacred speech], rarely state anything plainly. They are indirect, they obscure, they bring the past to bear by archaizing. The graphic images hold and release their meaning through euphemism, metonym, and metaphor; they show by analogy. Meanings themselves are layered.[19]

Scholar Katarzyna Mikulska Dąbrowska further emphasizes Boone's point, arguing that "in the Nahua culture oral expression of magical-religious type, termed *nahuallatolli*, has its parallel in the graphic form, *nahualicuilolli*."[20] Both Dąbrowska and Mercedes Montes de Oca Vega have written extensively on the glyphic representations of Nahuatl diphrasisms in Central Mexican texts.[21] The use of diphrasisms and similar rhetorical forms in precontact texts presents a challenge in decipherment. Rather than merely identifying what the imagery denotes, the intended meaning requires that contemporary audiences have an understanding of the diphrasisms, how they might be represented glyphically, and the meaning they hold for their intended audience in any given context. Currently, much of the decipherment of these religious *nahualicuilolli* offers a description of what has been presented rather than providing a layered cultural analysis, and therefore these analyses provide readings of glyphic texts that leave much of their meaning obscured.

Along with composing what could be called literal translations of both pictorial/glyphic Nahuatl codices and colonial alphabetic Nahuatl codices, scholars have explored the ways that Nahua and other Indigenous populations use what they label figures of speech, metaphors, and analogies.[22] Yet while these labels may work well in a Western context in differentiating between and categorizing statement types, these labels have the disadvantage of denying the veracity of these statements within an Indigenous framework. Anthropologist Joanna Overing, in discussing her fieldwork among Indigenous Piaroa people from Venezuela, has brought attention to the harm in the use of such terms, stating, "We often wiggle out of facing certain implications about the chaos in our data by resorting too quickly to such labels as 'metaphor', 'metonymy', and 'analogic' or 'figurative' thought: we say that our informants are rational, but because we do not truly understand their statements we construe their rationality as tropic creativity."[23] Similarly, Sally Rice, when discussing the use of what she labels metaphor and metonymy in Athapaskan, or Dené, languages, states that "it is neither paradoxical nor oxymoronic for speakers to insist that their very figurative languages are, in fact, very literal."[24] From Rice's use of the terms "figurative" and "literal," two terms that in the Western traditions are mutually exclusive categories, it is evident that these Western labels are problematic within an Indigenous context. Overing further explains:

> The Piaroa definition of metaphor, which for them depends upon the falsity of the statement, is identical to our normal judgment of whether or not a statement is figurative or literal. When a Piaroa assents to the truth of the statement that 'the tapir is their grandfather', a statement that to us sounds bizarre, we are nevertheless dealing with a literal statement about truths in the world as he knows them.[25]

Similar kinds of literal truths abound in Mesoamerican cultures, where corn is an ancestor to the people and, regionally, various other plants and animals are considered relatives to the people. This kind of interconnectedness with the natural world is fundamental to Indigenous worldviews in and beyond Mesoamerica, and as such it is integral to the function of Nahuatl rhetoric.

Rhetoric of Indigenous Realities

Central to Nahua rhetoric are appeals to the Nahua worldview, or *cosmovisión*. Appeals to the Nahua worldview draw on ancestral cultural knowledge about the lived world. The goals of these appeals often include showing respect to Indigenous teteoh, including ancestors, elders, and human and nonhuman relatives, and passing along this knowledge to others. When necessary, these appeals to the Nahua worldview can be used to re-create or reestablish the order mapped out in the Nahua worldview, either within a community or among community members. These appeals can also serve as warnings about proper behavior within the Nahua worldview. They can take a variety of forms and include rhetorical strategies such as repetition, parallelism, and diphrasisms, and these appeals could be delivered in the oral tradition or in the scribal tradition. In this way, the Nahua people access the sacred and ancient knowledge of the people and identify parallels, embodiments, and very real connections between seemingly, from an outsider perspective, disparate things or beings.

These Nahuatl expressions, although idiomatic and opaque to outsiders, are not disconnected to the material world. Rather, these expressions access connections found within the Nahua worldview, while also simultaneously accessing their spiritual beliefs since Indigenous Nahua beliefs are rooted in the material and natural world. The complex system of relationships and the resulting meaning behind phrases and expressions are what caused such difficulty for Spanish clergy engaged in attempts at spiritual conversion, as not only did the very language contain their ideologies, but also, as Burkhart points out, "Indigenous rhetoric emphasized interpersonal persuasion, with a tendency to relate the prescribed or proscribed behaviors to fundamental facts about reality."[26] Here it is important to recall that reality is not limited by what can be seen. Rather, Nahua reality was and is governed by understood relationships within the Nahua worldview, as passed down through the generations.

Book 5 of the Florentine Codex contains some of the *tetzaujtl*, or omens, of the Nahua people. Here I focus on how one omen about what happens to people when they eat tamales that stick to the side of the pot during cooking supports the Nahua religious belief concerning the interconnectedness of people and corn. Fray Bernardino de Sahagún, the commissioner of the Florentine Codex, recognized the strong link between these omens and the religious beliefs of the Nahua people, as book 5 ends with a short passage presented in Spanish, rather than the Nahuatl that comprises the vast majority of the text. Here he exhorts his fellow clergymen: "These superstitions harm the Faith, and therefore it is well to recognize them. Only these few have been recorded, though there are many more. But diligent preachers and confessors should seek them out, in order to understand them in confessions and to preach against them; for they are like a mange which sickeneth the Faith."[27] Documents recording precontact Nahua religious beliefs and practices are limited, and these recorded omens add to the body of religious knowledge available in contemporary recovery and revitalization efforts among Indigenous people today, as well as serving as an additional tool for glyphic decipherment. The following is an excerpt from book 5 of the Florentine Codex that discusses the dangers of eating tamales that stick to the side of the pot.[28] My translation follows.

The Cooking Pot and the Sticky Tamales (Nahuatl)

Injc chicuei capitulo, ytechpa tlatoa in jxqujuhquj tamalli.

In jtechpa in jxqujuhquj tamalli: oc no centlamantli inneztlacaviliz in njcan tlaca, qujlmach amo vel qujquazque, in oqujchtin, ioan cioa: qujlmach intla qujquazque toqujchti, amo axcan in qujçaz mjtl, injc qujmjnazque iauc: auh anoçe ic mjqujz, yoan aiaxcan tlacachioaz in jnamic.

Auh çan ie no yuhquj in jtechpa cioatl: intla qujquaz ixqujuhquj tamalli, amo vellacachioaz: çan itech ixqujviz ih jconeuh, ic mjqujz in ijti: ipampa cenca qujtecaoaltiaia in tenanoan, injc amo moquaz, in jxqujuhquj tamalli.

The Cooking Pot and the Sticky Tamales (Translated)

Chapter eight, which speaks about the tamales stuck [to the pot.]

About them, the tamales that were stuck [to the pot], still also there is another invention of the [Indigenous] people here. It is said that they, the men and the women, would not eat them. It is said that if they (we men) would eat them, then the arrows would not issue forth, so that they would not pierce one in battle, and with that he would die, and his spouse would have difficulty in childbirth.

And also, it is just so with the woman, if she would eat the stuck tamales, she would not be able to deliver. Her baby would only stick inside of her. Because of this, people's mothers used to greatly forbid them, so that the stuck tamales would not be eaten.

The Cooking Pot and the Sticky Tamales as Glyphic Representations

The connections made between the cooking pot and the bodies of the people (the woman in childbirth and the man in battle) are evident in this omen, as well as in the Nahuatl language and in glyphic texts such as the Codex Borgia. While the Nahuatl language provides many names for various body parts, Mesoamericanist Alfredo López Austin points out in his work on the human body and ideology among the Nahuas, the words *comitl* and *comic* ("the pot" and "in the pot," respectively) were used to refer to the abdominal cavity.[29] While the omen suggests that this association holds true for people of all genders, as does the use of the words comitl and comic, I will examine the use of the pot to signify the female abdominal cavity, specifically in its reproductive capacities as seen on the bottom half of page 20 in the Codex Borgia (CB20).[30]

The bottom half of CB20 (fig. 4.1) is the third of eight parts that begin on the bottom of page 18 moving left through the bottom half of page 19, 20, and 21, where the reader then moves up to the top half of page 21, traveling right until again reaching page 18. Given the accordion style of the Codex Borgia, pages 18 to 21 (CB18–CB21) comprise a set of pages that were likely viewed as a complete set, laid out for the reader to view simultaneously. Similarly, this set of pages has been examined by scholars as a whole.[31] According to art historian Boone, these pages present a "Tonalpohualli [260-day calendar count] organized as a compressed table. . . . Although there does not seem to be a single topical theme, the scenes on the top and bottom registers are iconographically related."[32] Similarly, Ferdinand Anders, Maarten Jansen, Luis Reyes García, and Eduard Seler see these pages as comprising a complete set, yet they examine each of the eight scenes separately. According to Anders, Jansen, and Reyes Garcia, these pages represent *los periodos aciagos*, or the ill-fated periods.[33] According to renowned scholar Seler, these pages present "los ochos dibujos, compuestos de figuras aisladas y grupos" (eight illustrations, comprised of isolated figures and groups), which are complexly divided to present six regions of the world.[34]

Karl Nowotny; Seler; and Anders, Jansen, and Reyes Garcia all provide details regarding the bottom half of CB20, with all three sources agreeing that the figure at the right of the cell is Chalchiuhtlicue, a *teotl* of water who is strongly associated with childbirth. Nowotny provides the least level of detail, commenting that the water vessel carried by Chalchiuhtlicue, the water goddess, "is broken in the customary manner, and the serpent appears through the break," and that the figures to her left illustrate "a nude woman and a cooking pot in which human flesh is cooked."[35] Anders, Jansen, and Reyes Garcia agree with Nowotny in the interpretation that the pot with a body inside in this scene represents the cooking of human flesh. According to Anders, Jansen, and Reyes Garcia (my translation):

Este tiempo es dominado por Chalchiuhtlicue, diosa de Ríos y Lagunas: malas consecuencias para la mujer que va por agua: se verá afectada en sus quehaceres diarios. La olla que carga se quiebra, porque tiene un coralillo dentro: está enviciada y no podrá contener el agua. En la jícara que lleva, un corazón sangra: muerte. Peligrosos coralillos, peligrosas rupturas, llamas destructivas amenazan en el camino, envician el pozo. El agua misma arde y humea: guerra, sequía, hambre y sed. Se cocina carne humana: la gente caerá en manos de sus enemigos. La olla sangra: pérdida y fracaso. La mujer liviana, desnuda y coronada de flores, se está lamentando. (This time is dominated by Chalchiuhtlicue, goddess of Rivers and Lakes: bad consequences for the woman who goes for water: she will be affected in her daily chores. The pot that she carries breaks, because it has a coral snake inside: it is corrupted and won't be able to hold water. In the cup she carries, a heart bleeds: death. Dangerous coral snakes, dangerous breaks, destructive flames threaten the road, poison the well. Water itself burns and smokes:

war, drought, hunger, and thirst. Human meat is cooked: people will fall into the hands of their enemies. The pot bleeds: loss and failure. The thin woman, naked and crowned with flowers, is lamenting.)[36]

Unlike Nowotny and Anders, Jansen, and Reyes Garcia, Seler provides an interpretation that draws upon intratextual analyses of the precise iconography, rather than merely seeing the image for what it appears to represent. Seler, rather than seeing an instance of cooking humans as meat, states that the figure within the pot in front of Chalchiuhtlicue is a glyphic representation of Nanahuatzin, as seen elsewhere in the Codex Borgia. Seler states (my translation):

> estoy seguro de que este símbolo o jeroglífico de Nanahuatzin figura aquí ... para simbolizar directamente a Nanahuatzin, el sifilítico, el numen excesivamente aficionado al placer sexual, cuyo castigo son las enferme- dades venéreas. Pues frente a la olla que contiene los miembros humanos vemos, igualmente sostenida por la línea de espuma del agua de la vasija, a su comparte femenina, Xochiquetzal, diosa del amor, representada como pecadora, como una mujer desnuda cuyo pelo, ceñido por una corona de flores blancas, forma por encima de ésta dos trenzas enhiestas parecidas a cuernos. (I am certain that this symbol or hieroglyph of Nanahuatzin ap- pears here ... to directly symbolize Nanahuatzin, the syphilitic, the numen excessively fond of sexual pleasure, whose punishments are venereal dis- eases. Then opposite the pot that contains the human body parts we see, equally supported by the line of foam on the water of the vessel, his female counterpart, Xochiquetzal, goddess of love, represented as a sinner, as a na- ked woman whose hair, fitted with a crown of white flowers, forms on top of these two erect braids, appearing like horns.)[37]

Seler supports his connection between the pot with a human figure and Nanahuatzin by pointing to page 10 of the Codex Borgia (CB10). Above a person he identifies as Nanahuatzin (here identified by the disfigurement of his limbs), a similar human figure is shown inside of a pot, this time with skulls presented at each side of the pot, with glyphic smoke elements rising from the skulls' mouths and from the top of the pot, and with a similar, though differently placed, bloody wound on the pot itself (fig. 4.2). While this iconography does share similar elements, I argue that both represent complications in utero, with the pot representing the woman's body. The association of this complex glyphic iconography with Nanahuatzin on CB10 and with Chalchiuhtlicue on CB20 need not mean that the two pages or the two teteoh presented upon them are directly related to one another, but rather both are related to the possible complications of childbirth, as Nanahuatzin is a teotl of deformities, and Chalchiuhtlicue is a teotl of the waters of childbirth.[38]

The interpretation of the pot as the woman's body is further supported by iconography presented within the bottom half of CB20, as well as in supporting iconography found throughout the Codex Borgia. The bottom half of CB20 contains diverse imagery related to a troubled birth. Across the bottom of this page are five Day Signs, which are read from right to left: Cuauhtli (Eagle), Mazatl (Deer), Quiahuitl (Rain), Ozomatli (Monkey), and Calli (House). The days 1 Eagle, 1 Deer, 1 Rain, 1 Monkey, and 1 House are elsewhere in the Codex Borgia associated with the Cihuateteoh, the spirits of the women who have died in childbirth.[39] Similarly, as already mentioned, Chalchiuhtlicue is prayed to during the mother's labor, and her waters washed the baby clean after the birth.[40] Additionally, as suggested by Thelma Sullivan, Chalchiuhtlicue was likely strongly associated with women's amniotic fluid, which like the rivers and lakes that she presides over, supports the life of the unborn child.[41] Chalchiuhtlicue herself, whose name means "her skirt is jade," is a teotl of water and often appears with water flowing from her skirt (as on Codex Borgia page 65) or beside a body of or container of water (as on Codex Borgia pages 14 and 20). The water within the container before her on CB20, atop which the woman and the person in a pot appear, is painted dark blue, with thick black lines alternating with thin wavy lines to form boxes and right angles. The top edge of the water and the lip of the container are lined with white waves of foam, as is seen atop containers of *pulque* (CB60), chocolate (CB58), and water (CB51). Below, to the right and to the left of this blue liquid, is a red layer, presumably the first layer of the container itself, followed by a thin white layer with very thin black lines throughout, then a thin yellow layer, and finally a thicker green outer layer. Spaced out through the green and yellow layers, a number of pot-shaped symbols appear in red, blue, and yellow. The design of this container is nearly identical to the fertile, corn-yielding land that Tlaloc, the teotl of rain, appears above on the upper left-hand corner of CB27. This similarity likely illustrates that the body of water on CB20, or the amniotic sac that it likely represents, is as fertile as the land that Tlaloc waters. However, on CB20, unlike in the representation of the fertile corn-producing land, foam tops the geometrically elaborate waters, and a dismembered snake winds through the waters. A dismembered snake likewise appears directly to the right of the vessel of water, and another fully formed snake appears emerging from the pot strapped to Chalchiuhtlicue's back at the far right of the page.

The combined representation of pots with snakes are not limited to this page of the Codex Borgia. Pages 58 to 60 of the Codex Borgia, or the "marriage prognostication" pages, contain a total of twenty-six scenes, which represent twenty-six possible unions based on birthday-based compatibility. According to Boone, these scenes contain iconography indicative of omens related to the unions, including "the birth of children."[42] These twenty-six possible unions show twenty-seven women (one man appears in the act of an affair, in between two women), and of these twenty-seven women, thirteen are shown with the same flowers in their hair as appear in the hair of the naked woman at the bottom of CB20. (That the flowers appear regularly upon the heads of these women likely signifies that it is not a distinguishing characteristic of the teotl Xochiquetzal, as Seler suggests above.) Within these twenty-six scenes, on four occasions the red snake and the curved pot appear to be iconographically joined. At the bottom right corner of CB58, a snake's head and tail can be seen within the break of the curved pot (fig. 4.3), the couple above them appear in the act of killing children. This representation of the snake and the pot together is most similar to that seen on CB20. Again on the right-hand side, at the middle of CB59 (fig. 4.4), a snake's body appears to move through the side walls of an unbroken pot, while the couple above them faces one another armed with weapons in their hands. On the left side of CB59 (fig. 4.5), opposite the last image, a snake's tail can be viewed above a man's head, and a broken pot above a woman's head, as the bodies of this couple face away from each other—between them lies a scorpion.[43] And at the bottom right of CB60 (fig. 4.6), an upside-down pot has a snake's tail visible at the opening of the unbroken pot. Here the woman appears with two children, and her male partner is Ehecatl, the teotl of wind. Interestingly, in a cognate text, the Codex

Vaticanus B, the woman appears alone with the two children, possibly suggesting that this union will leave her as a single mother.

The curved pot and the red snake appear individually (or seemingly unrelated to one another iconographically) alongside other couples on these pages as well, most notably in the scene where a man is caught engaging in an extramarital affair (fig. 4.7). In this particular scene, the snake takes the place of his loincloth and likely represents his phallus. The snake in the place of the loincloth or phallus thus stands as an indication of the man's sexual behaviors or proclivities. Among other couples, *cozcatl*, jewels or necklaces, are shown sticking out of unbroken pots on four separate occasions. This is significant, as newborn babies were called cozcatl as part of a diphrasism, *cozcatl quetzalli*, "the precious necklace/jewel [and] the precious quetzal feather/bird" forty times within the Nahuatl text of book 6 of the Florentine Codex.[44] Notably, CB65 (fig. 4.8) shows Chalchiuhtlicue's waters carrying a woman who holds a cozcatl below her in her right hand and *quetzalli* feathers above her in her left hand, likely signifying that the woman is with child. Given that these two items signify a newborn child, the presence of cozcatl, or jewels, within pots in various scenes on CB58–CB60 (fig. 4.9) likely represent favorable omens for pregnancy, while the presence of a snake within or emerging from a pot, likely suggests unfavorable omens of pregnancy.

Returning to the glyphic representations on CB20 (fig. 4.1), the imagery as presented within the page furthers the connection between the pot and the body of the expectant mother. The pot and the expectant mother's body have been painted in the same color, with the curve of the pot mimicking the curve of the expectant mother's waist and butt. The woman and her child (who emerges deceased, as illustrated by his closed eyes) face in the same direction, her upturned hands mirroring the hand and foot of her child. While she appears physically unharmed, the pot itself is bleeding. Whereas other representations of pots show a similar-shaped wound or gash at the very bottom of the pot (figs. 4.2, 4.3, and 4.5), the wound on the pot CB20 has been drawn on the right side, illustrating roughly where the blood would emerge given the posture of the mother as shown, just as the snake emerging from the pot on Chalchiuhtlicue's back issues from a wound on the pot's right side.

Flames and smoke, with the coloring and spots suggestive of a jaguar (who, according to creation narratives, was burnt by the sun), rise from a body of

Figure 4.1. Bottom half of Codex Borgia 20. Redrawn by Justin McIntosh.

Figure 4.2. Detail from Codex Borgia 10. Redrawn by Justin McIntosh.

Figure 4.3. Detail from Codex Borgia 58. Redrawn by Justin McIntosh.

Figure 4.4. Detail from
Codex Borgia 59. Redrawn
by Justin McIntosh.

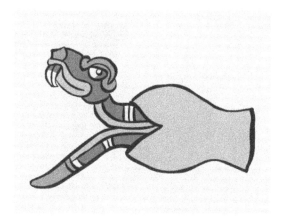

Figure 4.5. Detail from Codex Borgia 59. Redrawn by Justin McIntosh.

Figure 4.6. Detail from Codex Borgia 60.
Redrawn by Justin McIntosh.

Figure 4.7. Detail from Codex Borgia 59. Redrawn by Justin McIntosh.

Figure 4.8. Detail from Codex Borgia 65. Redrawn by Justin McIntosh.

Figure 4.9. Detail from Codex Borgia 59. Redrawn by Justin McIntosh.

water between the woman and her pot. This burning water is suggestive of the glyph for the diphrasism, *atl tlachinolli*, "water [and] burning," which signifies war. The connection between childbirth and battle has been widely addressed, and as scholars such as Elizabeth Brumfiel point out, "In many ways women who died in childbirth were the female counterparts of warriors who died in battle."[45] While this mother may appear alive on CB20, the death of a child in utero posed a great health risk to the mother. According to book 6 of the Florentine Codex, a child dies before birth when she or he *tlazaloa*, is stuck to something.[46] In this case, the physician uses an obsidian blade to remove the stillborn child in pieces in order to save the mother. This protective measure could account for the image of the person emerging from the broken pot as a head, foot, and hand.[47]

Pregnancies that potentially could result in death for both mother and child would actively be avoided if possible. As the Nahua people believed that the sticking of a child to the inside of the mother could be caused by eating a tamale that has stuck to the inside of the pot, the mothers actively warned against consuming them. It is unclear whether the knowledge related to the connection between the stuck tamale and the stuck child emerged from observational data or derived from the preexisting connection between humans and corn. Regardless of its origin, the Nahua people used their rhetorical strategies, in word, glyph, and imagery, to reinforce this connection, while also placing limits and providing guidance on human behaviors. As Burkhart points out, "To be effective, a rhetorical device must be 'felt' as well as 'thought.' That is, it must function cognitively in giving a name to a complex situation, classifying it in accordance with some ordering principle, but it must also evoke an emotional response."[48] To the ancient Nahua people, childbirth was a sacred act, and as women were the possessors of knowledge about both childbirth and food preparation, the knowledge of the women carried weight within their communities.

These texts, whether presented orally, in alphabetic texts, or in glyphic texts, employ the use of Indigenous rhetoric, which is deeply rooted in the Nahua worldview. As the excerpt from book 5 suggests, both men and women contribute to the success of a pregnancy, just as what either a mother or a father consumes can affect the health of a child. While this particular food (the stuck tamale) and its connection to a successful birth may seem irrational to outsiders, scholar Overing suggests that "we should view literal statements about the world as such, no matter how strange their content, rather than treat them as merely another example of the differentiating structure of the mind at work."[49] For the Nahua people, these narratives do not function as abstract metaphors, but rather function as yet another example of Nahua knowledge about how the ways we treat our food and the world around us have a dramatic impact on our health and the health of future generations.

Notes

1. Elizabeth Hill Boone, *Cycles of Time and Meaning in the Mexican Books of Fate* (Austin: University of Texas Press, 2007), 3.

2. Boone, *Cycles of Time*, 151–52.

3. Henry B. Nicholson, "Eduard Georg Seler, 1849–1922," in *Handbook of Middle American Indians*, ed. Robert Wauchope, vol. 13, *Guide to Ethnohistorical Sources: Part 2*, ed. Howard F. Cline and John B. Glass (Austin: University of Texas Press, 1973), 348–69; Elizabeth Hill Boone, *Stories in Red and Black: Pictorial Histories of the Aztecs and Mixtecs* (Austin: University of Texas Press, 2000); Alfonso Lacadena, "Regional Scribal Traditions: Methodological Implications for the Decipherment of Nahuatl Writing," *PARI Journal* 8, no. 4 (Spring 2008): 1–22; Marc Zender, "One Hundred and Fifty Years of Nahuatl Decipherment," *PARI Journal* 8, no. 4 (Spring 2008): 24–37.

4. Elizabeth Hill Boone, "In Tlamatinime: The Wise Men and Women of Aztec Mexico," in *Painted Books and Indigenous Knowledge in Mesoamerica: Manuscript Studies in Honor of Mary Elizabeth Smith*, ed. Elizabeth Hill Boone (New Orleans: Middle American Research Institute, 2005), 9–25.

5. Maureen Day Goggin, "From Visual Rhetoric in Pens of Steel and Inks of Silk: Challenging the Great Visual/Verbal Divide," in *Defining Visual Rhetorics*, ed. Charles A. Hill and Marguerite H. Helmers (Mahwah, NJ: Lawrence Erlbaum Associates, 2004), 88. Nahua scribes identified embroidery as a form of writing. See Felicia Rhapsody Lopez, "Mayahuel and Tlahuizcalpanteuctli in the Nahua Codices: Indigenous Readings of Nahuatl Pictorial and Alphabetic Texts" (PhD diss., University of California, Santa Barbara, 2016).

6. Teteoh, the plural form of teotl, is a complex religious term that may be applied to a being or force that is extraordinary. This term was applied to all ancestors and many plants, animals, and people, as well as figures who were widely revered throughout Mesoamerica, such as Quetzalcoatl and Tlaloc. For a more detailed explanation, see Felicia Rhapsody Lopez, "Case Study for the Development of a Visual Grammar: Mayahuel and Maguey as Teotl in the Directional Tree Pages of the Codex Borgia," *REvista: A Multi-Media, Multi-Genre e-Journal for Social Justice* 5, no. 2 (2017), https://escholarship.org/uc/item/4gm205sx.

7. As the Nahua people had no word for metaphor, the Nahua scribes use the

Spanish loanword, *metaphoras*, in this section of the text. The Nahuatl word given to describe these passages is *machiotlatolli*, which Alonso de Molina translates as *parabola*, or parable. Alonso de Molina, *Vocabulario de la lengua méxicana*, ed. Julius Platzmann, facsimile ed. (Leipzig, DE: B. G. Teubner, 1880), pt. 2, 50v.

8.   In diverse ancient and contemporary Nahua cultures, corn and foods made of corn hold associations with sexuality, fertility, and reproduction. For example, the Nahuatl words often have meanings relating sexuality to corn: *toca* can mean to plant corn seeds or to engage in sexual intercourse; *zonehua* can refer to the puffing action of a tortilla while it is cooking or to the enlarging of a woman's abdomen during pregnancy. In reference to the word for dragonfly, Jonathan Amith points out, "In Ameyaltepec, Guerrero, it is a:yoyontsi:n. This is derived from the root a:, water, and the verb yoma, which is the motion made by a woman as she is grinding nixtamal on a metate, sort of a concave swooping motion. The same motion is used to describe that of a man engaging in missionary position sex and is used in a riddle of doble sentido. [double meaning]." Jonathan Amith, "Dragonfly," NAHUAT-L electronic mailing list archives, June 2, 2014, http://listserv.linguistlist.org/pipermail/nahuat-l/2014-June/005699.html.

9.   Louise M. Burkhart, *The Slippery Earth: Nahua-Christian Moral Dialogue in Sixteenth-Century Mexico* (Tucson: University of Arizona Press, 1989); Thelma D. Sullivan, "The Rhetorical Orations, or Huehuetlatolli, Collected by Sahagún," in *Sixteenth-Century Mexico: The Work of Sahagún*, ed. Munro S. Edmonson (Albuquerque: University of New Mexico Press, 1974), 79–109; Don Paul Abbott, *Rhetoric in the New World: Rhetorical Theory and Practice in Colonial Spanish America* (Columbia: University of South Carolina Press, 1996); Davíd Carrasco, "Uttered from the Heart: Guilty Rhetoric among the Aztecs," *History of Religions* 39, no. 1 (August 1999): 1–31; Damián Baca and Victor Villanueva, eds., *Rhetorics of the Americas: 3114 BCE to 2012 CE* (New York: Palgrave Macmillan, 2010); Susan Romano, "Tlaltelolco: The Grammatical-Rhetorical Indios of Colonial Mexico," *College English* 66, no. 3 (2004): 257–77; Amara Solari, "The 'Contagious Stench' of Idolatry: The Rhetoric of Disease and Sacrilegious Acts in Colonial New Spain," *Hispanic American Historical Review* 96, no. 3 (August 2016): 481–515.

10.   Burkhart, *Slippery Earth*, 87–129; Sullivan, "Rhetorical Orations," 79–109; Carrasco, "Uttered from the Heart," 3–24; Gabriela Raquel Ríos, "In Ixtli In Yollotl/A (Wise) Face A (Wise) Heart: Reclaiming Embodied Rhetorical Traditions of Anahuac and Tawantinsuyu" (PhD diss., Texas A&M University, 2012), 24–26; Solari, "'Contagious Stench' of Idolatry," 502–3.

11.   Bernardino de Sahagún, *General History of the Things of New Spain: Florentine Codex*, trans. Arthur J. O. Anderson and Charles E. Dibble (Salt Lake City: University of Utah Press, 1950), 1:5.

12.   Sahagún, *General History*, 1:34.

13.   Cristián Roa de la Carrera, "Translating Nahua Rhetoric: Sahagún's Nahua Subjects in Colonial Mexico," in *Rhetorics of the Americas: 3114 BCE to 2012 CE*, ed. Damián Baca and Victor Villanueva (New York: Palgrave Macmillan, 2010), 73.

14.   Sullivan, "Rhetorical Orations," 79–109; Carrera, "Translating Nahua Rhetoric," 69–87.

15.   Burkhart, *Slippery Earth*, 12.

16.   Burkhart, *Slippery Earth*, 47.

17.   For more on this debate, see Lopez, "Case Study," 52–55.

18.   Diego Durán, *Book of the Gods and Rites and the Ancient Calendar*, ed. and trans. Fernando Horcasitas and Doris Heyden (Norman: University of Oklahoma Press, 1971), 65.

19.   Boone, *Cycles of Time*, 4.

20.   Katarzyna Mikulska Dąbrowska, "'Secret Language' in Oral and Graphic Form: Religious-Magic Discourse in Aztec Speeches and Manuscripts," *Oral Tradition* 25, no. 2 (October 2010): 355.

21.   Dąbrowska, "'Secret Language,'" 332–44; Mercedes Montes de Oca Vega, "Los Difrasismos En El Náhuatl Del Siglo XVI" (PhD diss., Universidad Nacional Autónoma de México, 2000). Diphrasisms, or *difrasismos* in Spanish, are a form of expression wherein the words for two different objects or ideas are used together to create new meaning. For example, in Nahuatl *in mitl in chimalli*, or "the shield [and] the arrow," combine to form an expression signifying war, and *in xochitl in cuicatl*, or "the flowers [and] the songs," refers to poetry. Diphrasisms are abundant in spoken, written alphabetic, and glyphic forms of Nahuatl.

22.   Burkhart, *Slippery Earth*, 12–14, 26–27, 44–45, 87–129; Sullivan, "Rhetorical Orations," 79–109; Abbott, *Rhetoric in the New World*, 32–40; Carrasco, "Uttered from the Heart," 3–24; Baca and Villanueva, *Rhetorics of the Americas*, 77, 158; and Solari, "'Contagious Stench' of Idolatry," 502–3.

23.   Joanna Overing, "Today I Shall Call Him 'Mummy': Multiple Worlds and Classificatory Confusion," in *Reason and Morality*, ed. Joanna Overing (London: Tavistock Publications, 1985), 150.

24.   Sally Rice, "Our Language Is Very Literal," in *Endangered Metaphors*, ed. Anna Idström, Elisabeth Piirainen, and Tiber Falzett (Amsterdam: John Benjamins Publishing, 2012), 23.

25.   Overing, "Today I Shall Call Him," 156.

26.   Burkhart, *Slippery Earth*, 191.

27.   Sahagún, *General History*, 6:195–96.

28.   Sahagún, *General History*, 6:185.

29.   Alfredo López Austin, *Cuerpo humano e ideología: las concepciones de los antiguos nahuas* (Mexico: Universidad Nacional Autónoma de México, Instituto de Investigaciones Antropológicas, 1980), 1:152, 2:148.

30.   Ferdinand Anders, Maarten Jansen, and Luis Reyes García, eds., *Los Templos del Cielo y de la Oscuridad: Oráculos y Liturgia Libro explicativo del llamado Códice Borgia* (Spain: Sociedad Estatal Quinto Centenario, 1993), 20. Page references to the Codex Borgia will refer to this work.

31.   Eduard Seler, *Comentarios al Códice Borgia*, trans. Mariana Frenk, 3 vols. (Mexico

City: Fondo de Cultura Económica, 1963); Boone, *Cycles of Time*; Anders, Jansen, and Reyes García, *Códice Borgia*; Karl Anton Nowotny, *Tlacuilolli: Style and Contents of the Mexican Pictorial Manuscripts with a Catalog of the Borgia Group*, ed. and trans. George A. Everett and Edward B. Sisson (Norman: University of Oklahoma Press, 2005).

32. Boone, *Cycles of Time*, 242.

33. Anders, Jansen and Reyes Garcia, *Códice Borgia*, 120.

34. Seler, *Comentarios al Códice Borgia*, 1:211.

35. Nowotny, *Tlacuilolli*, 23.

36. Anders, Jansen, and Reyes García, *Códice Borgia*, 128.

37. Seler, *Comentarios al Códice Borgia*, 213.

38. Congenital malformations such as the deformities that Nanahuatzin describe are strongly associated with and are currently the number one cause of death among infants in the United States, according to the Centers for Disease Control and Prevention. Sherry L. Murphy et al., *Deaths: Final Data for 2015*, National Vital Statistics Reports, vol. 66, no. 6 (Hyattsville, MD: National Center for Health Statistics, 2017), 1, 14. It is likely that deformities were a major contributor to infant death for ancient Nahua people as well.

39. Boone, *Cycles of Time*, 233.

40. Sahagún, *General History*, 5:175.

41. Thelma D. Sullivan, "Tlazolteotl-Ixcuina: The Great Spinner and Weaver," in *The Art and Iconography of Late Post-Classic Central Mexico*, ed. Elizabeth Hill Boone (Washington, DC: Dumbarton Oaks, 1982), 22.

42. Boone, *Cycles of Time*, 139.

43. The scorpion appears in the waters in the Codex Fejérváry-Mayer on page 27, the cognate of CB20. The glyph of the scorpion could be a representation meant to conjure the origin narrative of this animal. According to Nahuatl narratives as told to Hernando Ruiz de Alarcón, a man had taken a vow of sexual celibacy in preparation for turning into the scorpion. Yet the teteoh knew that his bite would prove fatal to people if they could not get him to break his vow. Xochiquetzal successfully ensured that the scorpion would not have a fatal sting by convincing him to break his vow. Hernando Ruiz de Alarcón, *Treatise on the Heathen Superstitions That Today Live among the Indians Native to This New Spain, 1629*, ed. and trans. J. Richard Andrews and Ross Hassig (Norman: University of Oklahoma Press, 1984), 204. Glyphic representations of the scorpion likely recalled to readers the nature of his origins, his broken sexual vows, and the remaining harm of his sting.

44. Sahagún, *General History*, 7:12, 44, 72, 80, 135, 137, 141, 146, 154, 176, 180–81, 185–87, 189–90, 192–95, 214.

45. Elizabeth Brumfiel, "Huitzilopochtli's Conquest: Aztec Ideology in the Archaeological Record," in *The Archaeology of Identities: A Reader*, ed. Timothy Insoll (London: Routledge, 2007), 275.

46. Sahagún, *General History*, 7:156.

47. Anderson and Dibble translate the word *ticitl* (*titicih*, plural) as "midwife" in this

section of the Florentine Codex to denote the type of medical work taking place and to correspond with the likely gender of these medical practitioners. See Sahagún, *General History*, 7:151–58 for examples of the use of the word ticitl in relation to childbirth. See Sahagún, *General History*, 11:29–30, 53 for general descriptions of male and female titicih, and where the term is translated by Anderson and Dibble as "physician."

48.   Burkhart, *Slippery Earth*, 13.
49.   Overing, "Today I Shall Call Him," 152.

CHAPTER FIVE

"O'odham, Too"

Or, How to Speak to Rattlesnakes

SETH SCHERMERHORN

Introduction

In the introduction to this book, Lawrence Gross discusses how most studies of Native American rhetoric have focused on how Native Americans have used rhetoric to resist colonization. "How Native Americans address one another," writes Gross, "is an area in need of further exploration." As such, most of this book is aimed at filling this gap within the academic literature. However, my goal in this chapter is to complicate what we might mean by "Native American rhetoric" spoken both by and for "Native American" audiences. My justification for this complication is linguistic, or more specifically, lexical. Some of the words that many Native American people use to refer to themselves within their own languages refer not only to humans but also to other entities. These may include various animals and plants, among other things, that A. Irving Hallowell called "other-than-human persons."[1] For example, among the Tohono O'odham, an indigenous people whose territory is now cut in half by the US–Mexico international border, a variety of plants and animals are regarded as "O'odham, too," including rattlesnakes. Rattlesnakes are potentially dangerous creatures, which human O'odham encounter with perhaps greater regularity than many O'odham, both human and rattlesnake, might prefer. Because rattlesnakes are "O'odham, too,"

103

human O'odham sometimes speak to rattlesnakes in order to persuade them. Sometimes this works. Sometimes it does not. If persuasion (rhetoric) does not achieve its intended goal, then it may become necessary to use coercion (force). If we understand speech intended to persuade as "rhetoric," then we must also understand such speech as Native American rhetoric.

O'odham, Too

When I began recording conversations with O'odham consultants in the course of conducting research for my doctoral dissertation on the now-transnational O'odham pilgrimages across the US–Mexico international border to Magdalena, Sonora, I had planned to study O'odham conceptions of personhood, which meant that I wanted to understand the semantic range of the word O'odham.[2] My earliest conversations were with Simon Lopez, an observant and knowledgeable cowboy and ritual curer in his seventies. After talking for several hours on July 2, 2011, I asked him specifically about the word O'odham and its various referents. He spoke for a few minutes about Tohono O'odham (Desert People), Akimel O'odham (River People), and O'odham in Mexico. He concluded, stating "and that's the only meanings of 'O'odham.'" I presumed that the semantic range was much wider, so I followed up with additional questions in the ensuing conversation, below:

> SS: Are there any other things that O'odham people would say are O'odham [people], like uh . . . maybe Ha:ṣañ [Saguaro], or Ba:n [Coyote], or other plants or animals, that in conversation, in O'odham, you would maybe say is O'odham?

> SL: Yeah, there's a lot, like I said, that you know. There is a lot of animals and things like that that are called O'odham. For instance that Ha:ṣañ, the Ko'oi, the Rattlesnake, the Woodpecker, and Ha:sañ, and other kinds of animal that they knew, that it's been here a long time ago. And those are the things that the O'odham, that they believe that they're O'odham. They're O'odham, too. . . . So there's all of those things that they believe that it's O'odham, too, in that area. Yeah.

SS: And, uh, all of those different O'odham that we're talking about, would they have *gewkdag* [roughly, "power"]? Do all of those different ones have something like that?

SL: [Nods his head] Yeah. Yeah, they do. They have all of these, that's concerned as O'odham. Like I said, you know, *during the Creation, there's only these kinds of animal people that were created, which is still here.* In *our* culture, we call them *Wi'ikam, Wi'ikam O'odham,* you know. And those are the people who survived the Creation, which we *respect.* For instance, like Rattlesnake, Woody Woodpecker, or, you know, some kind of things that were *O'odham* and that's what we *respect.* And a lot of times they'll say that they'll make you *sick.* If you treat them right. If you not treat them like you're supposed to, they'll make you *sick.*

A lot of times I heard, you know, they were telling me. Like right here, like right here at my house, I say, "You can't find any rattlesnakes." Or either the neighbors, you know, "You can't find any rattlesnakes." And my dad, he used to say, "When you go out at night, talk to them not to bother you, and they won't bother you. They'll be out there where they're supposed to be. Sometimes if you don't think different, yeah, they would strike you or something like *that.* Or if they come here, if you see them somewhere under that, where they'll come at night, or crawl at night. And then you'll find it, maybe you'll find it under that, or the wood, or somewhere around the house. If you see them, usually *just talk to them and tell them to go where they're at, where they belong,* instead of killing, killing it. And then [with raised voice] *they, they'll understand!* You show them out, and they'll go, they'll go where they're supposed to be out in the desert, not bothering people. *Unless* you tell them, "If you want the end of your day, you can do this, you know, and bother people." So, then you can kill it, kill it, *but* you have to talk to him to get a good reason *why* you're gonna.

Same way with what we call Horny Toad. Horny Toad. Those are really O'odham, too. And if you see them, you can't kill it. You can just take it and put it somewhere out in there where they can stay out there. And there's other things, like I said, that they're O'odham. *But* if you don't know and just kill 'em, just kill 'em away, in the long run or a short period of time, you'll find out. There's gonna be sickness in *you*. So, if you go see a medicine man, the medicine man will cure you. Mistreating a Rattlesnake, Horny Toad, or something like that. So, if you *cure* yourself of that, you'll be OK. *If you don't do that*, then in time you're gonna get it again. Sometimes, *it really will get you*, those kind of things, you know, like that. And that's what it's really important for the O'odham, O'odham like that, and most of them, they know, O'odham know that it's like that.[3]

To summarize, among various other entities, particularly those mentioned in O'odham origin stories, rattlesnakes are O'odham, too. If they are mistreated, they have "power" to make human O'odham sick, and therefore deserve respect. But Simon did not end there. Beyond discussing rattlesnakes as "O'odham, too," he went on to discuss the proper places for rattlesnakes. "Right here," he said, speaking to me under a *watto* (ramada) just outside of his bedroom door, "you can't find any rattlesnakes." Crucially, the spatial distance between human O'odham and rattlesnake O'odham is reinforced by talking to rattlesnakes. Voicing his father, Juan Baptisto Lopez, Simon said, "Talk to them not to bother you, and they won't bother you. They'll be out there where they're supposed to be." However, while rattlesnakes usually avoid O'odham, they may also "come here," even "around the house," where they may even strike human O'odham. However, Simon cautioned that in these close encounters, one should not rush to kill rattlesnakes, even when they clearly are not "where they belong." "*They'll understand!*" Simon exclaimed, "*just talk to them and tell them to go where they're at, where they belong.*" Even rattlesnakes out of place may be persuaded. "*Unless* you tell them," Simon's tone suddenly shifted, speaking now directly and more forcefully to a hypothetical rattlesnake, "If you want the end of your day, you can do this, you know, and bother people." Then, and perhaps only then, errant rattlesnakes who are not susceptible to persuasion may be killed. "*But*," Simon emphasized, "you have to talk to him to get [give] a good reason *why* you're gonna."

Killing a Rattlesnake

March 2014. Simon and I were talking and working together in his workshop behind the room where I often slept in the one-room house next to Simon's multiroom home. Suddenly, our conversations were interrupted by a scream. "*Snake!*" Simon's wife Florence shouted. Immediately, and without hesitation, Simon and I grabbed a few nearby shovels and rushed to the other side of the house. As we neared the spot, we slowed down, carefully looking for the snake. We found what looked like a baby Western Diamondback rattlesnake (*Crotalus atrox*), coiled up next to the house, not far from where women had been working and children playing. My conversation with Simon from nearly three years earlier about rattlesnakes was not foremost on my mind. So, I raised my shovel and prepared to chop the rattlesnake into pieces. Simon gestured that I should instead turn my shovel upside down, holding it by the blade, pinning the rattlesnake down with the end of the handle. I then asked if I should place the handle directly on his head, or at the base of his neck. He instructed me to crush the rattlesnake's head. Placing the handle at the base of his neck would simply make the rattlesnake's body thrash around in pain. He said that I could chop up other snakes into pieces, but that rattlesnakes should be killed by crushing their heads. Before I brought down the shovel onto the head of the rattlesnake, Simon spoke to the snake in O'odham. Then, I quickly and firmly crushed its head. I held the shovel down tightly for several moments. Again, Simon spoke in O'odham, explaining why we had to kill the rattlesnake. He also explained in English, briefly, that Rattlesnake is "mean" and knows that he should not be coming around the house. He then instructed me to carry the snake with the shovel away from the house, out to what looked like a mesquite tree, where he assured me that a bird or something else would eat it. I executed those directives and returned to the house, where Simon's grandchildren asked me what had happened.

Talking about Rattlesnakes and Killing Rattlesnakes

October 6, 2016. I had just finished my fifth year of walking to Magdalena during my sabbatical leave from Hamilton College, where I teach in the religious studies department. I finally had the opportunity to discuss rattlesnakes again with Simon Lopez, bringing together his previous discussions about rattlesnakes, my experience killing a rattlesnake under his tutelage, and any further explanation that he might offer. This follows my standard method, which I have previously outlined elsewhere, in which I begin with participation and observation, following up with informal conversations like the one below discussing previous events and culminating with video oral history interviews.[4]

> SS: Can you maybe explain that, you know, the right way to, to kill a rattlesnake, and to dispose of it?

> SL: Yeah. *Yeah* [louder], there's, I mean, uh, there's, it *is* [higher pitched] very, very, you know, *cultured* [louder] for *us* [louder]. We say that, that rattlesnake is, is O'odham, too. Rattlesnake is human. The same, same way with this other *birds* [louder] and things like that, that I told you, you know. How what I'itoi, cause it's I'itoi that made the rattlesnake.[5] Rattlesnake is the only one that, that was around. Like the rest, black whip, the other black, red racer, snakes, and other things like that, that we can see them. *Rattlesnakes* [louder] have been here before. Because that's how, that's how we understand. And that's why it'll make you sick. A lot of times when, when, uh, somebody kill the rattlesnake, and his wife's pregnant or something like that. And then *it'll* [taps on table] make the, when the child is born, or things like that, it'll make him sick because of what they did with the rattlesnake. *So* [louder] what we were told, and what they were, you know, that you have to *talk* [louder, higher pitch] to the snake. *Talk* [louder, higher pitch] to the rattlesnake first, before you kill it. And this way, he won't come, try to make, make anybody sick. *Or* [louder] if you know that your wife is pregnant or something like that, leave him alone. And tell somebody else to, to kill it or something like that. And there's different ways that, that they can be killed. Because like, like we say that the rattlesnakes are O'odham, too. They are living.

Without skipping a beat, Simon's preliminary explanation about how to kill a rattlesnake launched straight into an episode from O'odham oral history known as "Ho'ok A:gita."[6]

> SL: There's a story, story about the *Siwañ* ["chief"], the ruins, Casa Grande Ruins National Monument. That, that the people live over there, a lot, a

long ways this Hohokam, Hohokam in this that used to be there. And, uh, and there's, uh, there's this *guy* [louder] who's, they call it, Siwañ. *Siwañ Ma:kai.* And, he, he's some kind of, uh, my understanding is he's some kind of, uh, like, uh, like I would say, like, uh, a deer or something like that. That his name is Siwañ, and he lives there. There at that ruins which you can still see *now* [louder], the ruins that's there, that the *Siwañ Wa'aki:*, that means that's where that Siwañ live, lives there. And he's the one who takes care of *all* [louder] the people that's there. And uh, at the, Casa Grande ruins, uh, the monument. And, and he has, uh, he got, uh, uh, a rattlesnake, a rattlesnake, that, that lives with him. And he's *always* [louder] sittin', coiled up, right there on the, uh, on his, on his back, his front door, I guess. And the Ha:sañ [Ṣaguaro] stands on this other side. Cactus, saguaro cactus, stands there. And which he is O'odham, too. O'odham, too. The O'odham, you know, the, the saguaro cactus is O'odham, too. From our understanding, from our story, creation story, that's, the I'itoi make that. And the rattlesnake was like *that* [taps on table]. And he's always sittin' there at the corner. And so, when people comes visit him, he bothers that snake. He *plays* [louder] with him.[7] And he *hits* [louder] him with rocks and, and everything like that. And he'll try to do what he can, but he can't do anything, the rattlesnake.

So, he told the I'itoi. The I'itoi came over and took some of his mustache off, and put it on the, the snake, like his teeth, two of them. And he told that snake, "If he try to bother you, you bite him with that so they'll leave you alone." And so, they already did, somebody tried to come and hit, strike at him, and bother him, and, and then he got sick. And he, I think they said that he die, or, uh, he, they create him again, and, uh, so, cured him. And, and he was OK. And *that's* [louder] what he said, what to do with the snake, if he bothers you or other way around. And that means that you guys leave him alone. So, that's how rattlesnake got its poison and its teeth and things like that.

SS: Oh, OK, yeah.

SL: And so, a lot of times that's how they, they. That's why they say if you *kill* [higher pitch] the rattlesnake, you have to get him by the head, and really kill him. Not anywhere *else* [makes circular motion with hand], like chop, chopping in half. Or, *yeah* [higher pitch], you can chop in half, and you say, "OK, that's it. He's dead. He's dead." *Yeah* [higher pitch], he might be, but his head is still alive. And that'll get you in, in *ways* [louder], they say. That, that they'll get you in ways if that's still alive. So, what you have to *do* [taps on table repeatedly], is you have to kill him by the head. And make sure that *he* [knocks on table, louder] *is* [higher pitch] dead. And that's how they were, we were told.

And *also* [louder, higher pitch], like I said, you have to *talk* [knocks rapidly on table]. Talk to him [pause]. Like if you see him around the house, or anything like that, then you have *to* [knocks rapidly on table], if you *have* [higher pitch] to *kill* [higher pitch] him. *Or* [louder] if you can be able to just "ṢA:ʼ" him. Try and make him go where he belongs, out in the desert area, or things like that. But tell him, you know, "This is where you belong. And you stay here. Otherwise, *if* [louder, higher pitch] you go around somebody's *house* [knocks rapidly on table] and you know how, what you do, so you have to be *killed* [higher pitch]. You have to *die* [louder], if you go to some people's house. But if you just stay where you belong, that's OK, you can stay there forever." But if you have to kill him, you can't go. You have to talk to the rattlesnake and tell him why you *have* [higher pitch] to kill him. "Because you don't belong here." And he knows that he's no good. He knows that if somebody bothers him or something like that, he's gonna strike and make him sick, or even kill them with his poison. And that's no good. We don't want that, so you have to, you have to, have to kill him because, "You don't belong *here* [higher pitch], you belong in the desert area," and things like that. So [knocks rapidly on table], you have to kill him like *that* [louder, knocks on table]. And then take *him* [gestures away], take him, uh, you know, out in the desert and let him do what. And you know, the birds, and things like that. And that's how *we* [knocks rapidly on table], we deal with the rattlesnakes.

And a lot of times, they knew, the people knew. And if they're like that, their wives or, or their monthly periods or something like that, the ladies, they're not gonna bother him and, or the husband or somebody. They'll just tell somebody to, to go kill him or something like that. And, so, because they knew that they're told that you can't do that if you're like that, you know, and 'cause the snakes are . . . [trails off]

I have a lot of people that come here for me to do the, uh, the *wusot*, you know, the curing for the rattlesnakes or things like that. So, I have the, uh, rattler, or the image, image of a snake that, that I use, to, uh, to cure people that come here and ask me to do it for the rattlesnakes. Yeah.

[pause]

SS: So, yeah, you mentioned that you can, and you should, talk to the rattlesnake. And sometimes you can, uh, "S̩A:!" it away. Other times, if you need to kill it, then you explain to it why you're doing that. Um, and, just to be clear, what language do you talk to the rattlesnake in, when you're speaking to the rattlesnake? Do you talk in English, or in O'odham?

SL: *O'odham* [louder]. Yeah, O'odham. Like I *said* [gestures away], way back, the people don't understand English. And so that's how, but they understand. Just for instance, if you *go* [points out the window] to Children's Shrine. And those children that's there are from the Hohokam, way, way back. And they don't know, they don't see the *Milga:n* [white people] or whatever that's there. And so, they don't know English. They know O'odham. So, if you go down there and talk to them, talk to them in O'odham.

[pause]

But *there is some* [higher pitch] others that they say they just go *out* [makes gestures with both hands] and talk like English and talk to them. And I . . . maybe they understand. Or I don't know. But there's a lot of other things, like I said, way, way back, that these creations that the I'itoi made. And at that *time* [louder], there's no Milga:n or *S-cukcu* [black people] or something like that. They're all O'odham. And so, they don't know. Even the, uh, the *I'itoi* [louder]. He was O'odham. And that's why when he bring these people *alive* [louder] from, from the Eagle's, uh, killings, he tried to talk to them. And, and he answered them, *but* [gesture, like a shrug] won't understand what they're saying. So, that's why he sent them out somewhere [to Europe and Africa, presumably]. And I guess they're Milga:n. I don't know, but yeah. And there's others that, that said, you know, different things. But maybe that's what he *said* [louder, higher pitch]. And this, uh, this old man, he knows English, that was saying, saying when he said that he tried to get him. And he tried to talk to him. And he talked back. But he didn't know what. And this old man said, maybe he said, "*Goddamnit!*"[8] [laughs]

SS: [laughs]

SL: So, you know, so I'itoi don't even know that, you know, the Milga:n language.

Simon went on to talk about I'itoi (a powerful being sometimes also referred to as Elder Brother) and I'itoi Ki for a few minutes, until I brought him back to our discussion of rattlesnakes, and how to talk to them.

SS: Another thing that I was thinking about was that word. I don't really know if it is a word, but that, that sound, "ṢA:!" [louder]. I know that that's what you said to, uh, you know, dogs if they're causing problems and getting too close. Trying to eat your food or something.

SL: *Yeah* [quietly].

SS: And you were saying that that's what you say to, uh *rattlesnakes* [higher pitch] as well. So, can you tell me about that? Uh, you know, I don't, I don't know if that's a word. If it's something that would be in the dictionary. What, what does that, that mean, when you say that? Since I'm, I'm guessing it's O'odham?

SL: *Yeah* [louder], I really, I really can't, can't say. But *according* [louder, higher pitch] to, uh, Saxton, Dean, or is it his wife, Lucille, late Lucille, that

I *ask* [higher pitch] that cause I have his book. You know, that dictionary. And I look *and* [makes sweeping gestures with both hands] everything, you know. And that's what I was asking . . . And *that's* [louder, higher pitch] what I was asking all the time, *too* [louder]. You know, somebody, what about when we say "ṢA:!"? You know, to a dog, or something like that. That all you know is, is you say "ṢA:!" And just to, you know, get him away or something like that. I don't know what, how O'odham would say it. Or maybe, maybe in a way, like, they say "*HIJI!*" [louder]. You know. But that's, um, that's, uh, Milga:n way. You say, "Get away!" You know, "Get away!" You know, "*HIJI!*," "Get away!" But, like, "ṢA:!" or something like that, I won't know what, how to say it in, uh, in English. I mean, yeah.

SS: Yeah, I guess the point to me is that I've seen the dogs *listen* [higher pitch]. When, when *you* [louder, higher pitch] say that to dogs. And when other people say it to dogs, they *know* [higher pitch]. They know what that means. They listen. They go.

SL: *Yeah* [very quiet].

SS: And so, is it, in your experience, the same thing with, uh, rattlesnakes?

SL: Yeah, they did the same thing. That's why I, I say a lot of times. And, and, you know, this one time when I was working for the, uh, at Ki:ki Association [Tohono O'odham Ki:ki Association, formerly known as the Papago Housing Authority], in the old building at the Baboquivari District offices now, that they have. And we started. And we were parked. *He* [louder, higher pitch] was parked right there. And we were standing there. I came out. And we were standing there. And I was looking down this way. And I saw that rattlesnake came out under his truck, going down *that way* [points downward]. And I went like *this to Ed Kisto* [points downward multiple times, as if pointing to rattlesnake]. And I went, pointed at him, at the rattlesnake. And he went, "ṢA:!" [louder, drawn out]. He said that, you know, and went like *this* with his feet. And the rattlesnake kinda *coiled up* [forms circle with both hands] and went *back* [moves hands away] out that way. And then he just, uh, started talking to me. "Oh, he'll go away!" He said that. So I was, *I* [louder, higher pitch] was surprised. I mean, you know. It seems like he really heard or listened what he said 'cause he just kinda coiled up, and turned around, and went back under the truck. And, and he said, "Oh, go away!" And sure enough, I guess, after that I tried to look for it and he's gone. So that's surprising. I mean, you know, I got *surprised* [higher pitch, almost laughing]. *I was wondering, you know* [quieter], did he really listen? *"I heard what he said"* [higher pitch], or something like that? But he's the one who always says that those people can listen. You know, you tell them, "Stay away from us!" and, "Stay where you belong!" And, and they won't come around.[9]

Discussion

Missionary-linguists Dean Saxton, Lucille Saxton, and Susie Enos translate *ko'owi* or *ko'oi* as "rattlesnake."[10] According to ethnobiologist Amadeo Rea, *ko'i* or ko'oi may refer to any poisonous snake.[11] However, O'odham have different names for other snakes, both in O'odham and in English, so ko'oi generally refers specifically to rattlesnakes. Writing at the dawn of the twentieth century, anthropologist Frank Russell claimed that O'odham only related their origin stories in the winter, when rattlesnakes hibernate, fearing that rattlesnakes would bite them for telling these stories in the summer. "No information was obtainable that the Pimas believe that the snakes then carry venom, nor why the snakes should bite those who disregard the tabu. The Pimas do not hesitate to kill rattlesnakes except in certain cases."[12] So, O'odham are said, by Russell, to simultaneously avoid offending rattlesnakes, and to generally not hesitate to kill rattlesnakes, with only a few exceptions. Rattlesnake is sometimes credited with causing the first death, usually under I'itoi's directives, but Coyote is often ultimately credited with making "all web-footed animals, snakes, and birds."[13] Many O'odham oral traditions, some of which seem to draw upon the stories of their PeePosh, or Maricopa, neighbors, tell of Rattlesnake as a person who speaks to O'odham, usually in O'odham, and who is also to be spoken to in O'odham. Moreover, snakes are not always spoken to in calm voices and calm words. In particular, Simon Lopez's brother, David Lopez, told a story about speaking very harshly to a black whip snake who wanted to be his sister, Daisy Lopez's, husband. In that story, the possibility of persuading the snake to stay away from Daisy is long past. So, the snake is violently killed in a manner not altogether unlike the rattlesnake that I killed. However, when I killed a rattlesnake in March 2014, when baby rattlesnakes are prone to leave their mothers and consequently experience high mortality rates, I killed dispassionately, more as a matter of public safety. David Lopez's story, by contrast, tells of a deeply personal, even vengeful, killing of a snake who could not be reasoned with.

Conclusion

Because rattlesnakes are "O'odham, too," according to Simon Lopez, human O'odham sometimes speak to rattlesnakes in order to persuade them. Sometimes this works. Sometimes it does not. When persuasion (rhetoric) is insufficient, coercion (force) may become necessary. If we understand speech intended to persuade as "rhetoric," then we must also understand such speech, even cursing, swearing, threatening, as well as cajoling, as Native American rhetoric.

O'odham Rattlesnake Lore in Story and Song[14]

1. THIN LEATHER, 1901–1902

Frank Russell, *The Pima Indians* (Washington, DC: Government Printing Office, 1908), 215–216. In the public domain.

For a time after the creation of the four tribes of men and the animals they were confined in a great house together. Rattlesnake was there, and was known as Mâ'ik Sol'atc, Soft Child.[15] The people liked to hear him rattle, and little rest or peace could he obtain because of their continual prodding and scratching. Unable to endure it longer, he went at last to Elder Brother to ask help of him. Elder Brother took pity upon him and pulled a hair from his own lip to cut in short pieces to serve as teeth for Soft Child.

"Now," said he, "if anyone bothers you again, bite him." In the evening
Tâ'âpi,[16] Rabbit, came to Soft Child as he sat at the door and scratched him
as he had so often done before. Soft Child raised his head and bit his
tormentor as Elder Brother had instructed him to do. Feeling the bite,
Rabbit scratched Soft Child again, and again was bitten; then he ran about
telling that Soft Child was angry and had bitten him twice. Again he went
to him and again he was bitten twice. During the night his body swelled
and the fever came upon him. All through the dark hours he suffered and
throughout the next day; often he called to those around him to prepare a
place that might give him rest. No bed that they could make brought any
ease to his stricken frame. He asked for sea sand that he might lie upon it
and cool his fevered body. Coyote was sent to the sea to fetch the cooling
sand, but it gave no relief. Rabbit asked for a shade of bushes that the
cooling breeze might blow beneath them upon him, but this, too, failed to
help him. The traveling shade likewise brought no relief. His agony
increased until death came to give him peace.

For the first loss of life the people blamed Elder Brother, because he had
given Soft Child the teeth that made him a menace to all who approached
him.

2. WILLIAM BLACKWATER, 1927

*O'odham Creation & Related Events as Told to Ruth Benedict in 1927 in Prose,
Oratory, and Song* by Donald Bahr. ©2001 The Arizona Board of Regents.
Reprinted by permission of the University of Arizona Press. Pages 22–23.

The people lived at the navel of the earth and there was no death. Earth
Doctor returned to his people as a poor man, and no one knew that it was he.
He built a village council house and gathered the people together. He spoke
to them as a great orator, and people came from all directions to hear him. He
made a snake for his pet and the snake had rattles but no poison. The people
played with this snake. They would throw it into the air and listen to its rattle.
One day when they were alone, Earth Doctor said to his snake, "Does it hurt
you to have them throw you about?"

"Yes, but I do nothing about it."

"I will do something to help you." Before sunrise he went out and built a fire. When the sun came up he took one of his [the sun's] rays and made a fang. He took another and made another fang. And he put the heat of the sun in the teeth of his pet snake. He took more rays and decorated the snakes back, and he said to the snake, "When anyone troubles you, bite him. If you kill him you will also be the one to help him back to life again."

Next day the people came again to the council house and played with the snake. He bit at them and the people left him alone. Rabbit came, however, and he was not careful. The snake bit him. He lay without moving and the people said, "What is the matter?" Rabbit answered, "Snake bit me and the pain is growing worse." They took him to his house and at exactly the time of day when the snake had bitten him, he died. This was the first death.[17]

3. KUTOX, 1929–1932

Leslie Spier, *Yuman Tribes of the Gila River* (Chicago: University of Chicago Press, 1933), 348–49. In the public domain.

When everybody could speak, that is including rabbits and all other kinds of animals, he built a big house for them. This held all the beings he had created. When morning came they would all go out to play together; all the games of which they could think. Toward evening they would all go into the house. Then he also made a snake. It had no teeth. It was gentle. Its name was kinyama's kåsu$_R$, meaning fragile and limp. They would take the snake and hit each other with it. The rabbit always got the snake and played with it. He would bring it out, so that they could play, hitting each other with it until it was half dead. Then they would replace it.

They had no axe nor anything else with which to cut wood. The creator had power to reach out to the north and seize an axe. So they then had an axe to cut wood. As they had fire enough to keep them happy, they were well content in their home.

Early in the morning they all went out to play. The creator was lying right by the door. The snake crawled up to him. The creator asked him what he wanted. The snake said he only crawled up because of his poor condition; he was not being treated right. He had life just like the others: he did not see why he was roughly treated by everyone in that house. The creator told him to sit there and wait for the sun to rise. Then the creator took some coals and chewed them into tiny bits. They both sat there; the snake facing the east as the sun rose. Then the creator told him to open his mouth. This he did. Then the creator put the coal and sun rays together in it for teeth. The snake now had teeth, so he went back able to protect himself.

Toward evening when everybody returned to the house, they sent the rabbit again to get the snake. As she reached for the snake, she was bitten. She suffered with pain for just a short time and died at midnight.[18] (When a snake really means to bite, it kills at once. If you tread on him accidentally and he strikes, there is time to be cured. The reason he bit that rabbit first was that rabbits are his food.)

After the rabbit died they felt bad over their great loss. So instead of going out to play, they remained quiet mourning their sister. Then they began to wonder who had put teeth in the snake's mouth. They discovered who it was: their father, who had taken pity on the poor snake. Then they wondered why he did not feel sorry for the rabbit. Then they said they would kill their father, if only someone knew how. They thought he, too, ought to die.

4. UNNAMED COMPOSITE STORYTELLERS, 1900S

Dean Saxton and Lucille Saxton, *Legends and Lore of the Papago and Pima Indians* (Tucson: University of Arizona Press, 1973), 6–8. Used by permission.

Along came Black Beetle and said, "Soon the living things will multiply and crush me with their feet because I'm not a fast runner and have no possible way to save myself. I think that when someone has lived a long time he should die and go away and never come back here again. That way the earth will never get overpopulated and no one will crush me."

At that time Rattlesnake's bite was harmless. The children would play catch with him and take out his teeth. He could never sleep and always cried, so he went to First Born and said, "The children are making life miserable for me. You must make me different so I can live contentedly somewhere."

First Born changed many of the animals. When he finished them, he took Rattlesnake, pulled out his teeth and threw them far away. They landed and grew into what we now call "Rattlesnake's Teeth."

As the sun was about to rise, its rays beamed over the horizon. First Born got them and threw them in the water. Then he took them out and made teeth for the rattlesnake and said, "Now that I have done this for you, when anything comes near you, you must bite it and kill it. From now on the people will be afraid of you. You will not have a friend and will always crawl modestly along alone."

5. UNNAMED STORYTELLER, 1920S

Harold Bell Wright, ed., *Long Ago Told (Huh-Kew Ah-Kah) Legends of the Papago Indians* (London: D. Appleton & Company, 1929), 118. In the public domain.

[During preparations for the first *nawait i:'i*, or wine feast, in the Ha:ṣañ story.]

Oo-oo-flick ['u'uwĭ]—the birds—were the quickest to get ready for the feast. They came dressed in red and black and yellow. Some of the smaller ones were all in blue. Then Kaw-koy' [ko-owi]—the rattlesnake—came crawling in. And Kaw-koy' was all painted in very brilliant colors.

The birds did not like it because Rattlesnake was painted so bright. They gossiped and scolded and were jealous. Rattlesnake heard O-oo-flick [the birds] talking and rolled himself in some ashes. And that is why, even in these days, you will find the skin of Kaw-koy' marked with gray. The gray markings are where the ashes were caked onto his new paint.

6. ANNA MOORE SHAW (1930–1963)

"The Rattlesnake Receives His Fangs" from *Pima Indian Legends* by Anna Moore Shaw. ©1968 The Arizona Board of Regents. Reprinted by permission of the University of Arizona Press. Pages 17–19.

The Rattlesnake Receives His Fangs

Once the Rattlesnake was a gentle and timid little snake. His maker, the Sun God, had made him very beautiful. But he forget [*sic*] to give him a weapon with which to defend himself. Therefore he was the most abused and miserable little snake in the desert land of the red men.

In the evenings when the people's work was done, there would be merrymaking in the village ceremonial grounds. Sometimes there was singing, dancing, and playing of games. Other times Owl Ear, the storyteller, would recount legends of long ago.

Rattlesnake attended the gatherings because he liked to sing. But best of all he liked to hear the legends. Everything went very well with the little snake until one evening a prankster attended the merrymaking.

The prankster, whose name was Rabbit, wanted to have some fun, so he picked up the little snake and tied him in a knot as if he were a piece of rope. With much merriment, the young braves tossed the snake back and forth over the campfire like a ball. This rough treatment went on every evening, and the poor little Rattlesnake would crawl home in pain.

"I'll stay away from the meeting place," he would moan. But the whoops and the beating of the drums always upset his intentions, and the Rattlesnake would again crawl to the merrymaking.

This rough treatment from the men went on and on. Rattlesnake would cry, "My bones ache and I cannot sleep."

Early one morning, after a sleepless night, Rattlesnake asked the Sun God to help him. "Have pity on me and help me!"

The Sun God answered, "I will help you. You have been badly treated, and I must put a stop to it at once." Like a flash of lightning the Sun God appeared before the ailing little snake.

"Now open your mouth wide and I will place two of my powerful rays in your upper jaw. Hereafter you are going to be the most powerful of the desert snakes. But first you must give a warning with your rattle. When your warning is not heeded, then you may strike with your sun-ray fangs."

"I will do just as you've ordered," said Rattlesnake, feeling very important.

The next evening, Rattlesnake attended the meeting. "I wonder who will be my first victim?" he thought, coiling himself in a dark corner away from the crowd. But he didn't have to wait long, for at that moment naughty Rabbit saw him and came over to have some more fun with Rattlesnake. Rabbit kicked Rattlesnake and laughed when he heard the snake's rattle.

"Are you sounding off with your rattle like the medicine man?" asked Rabbit, and again he kicked Rattlesnake. Like a flash, Rattlesnake bit him.

"My foot! My foot!" cried Rabbit, limping to one corner of the grounds to nurse his wounds.

The astonished men rushed up to see what had happened.

Owl Ear, the storyteller, defended Rattlesnake. "Rattlesnake has always been a gentle little fellow. I have watched the ill treatment of our little friend, and I must say that Rabbit has received his punishment at last."

The news of Rattlesnake's sun-ray fangs went all over the land.

Thereafter the people were afraid of Rattlesnake, whose maker had given him such powerful fangs to use for his protection.

7. MANUEL HAVIER, 1976–1978

Donald M. Bahr, "Four Rattlesnake Songs," in *Speaking, Singing, and Teaching: A Multidisciplinary Approach to Language Variation: Proceedings of the Eighth Annual Southwest Areal Language and Linguistics Workshop*, ed. Florence Barkin and Elizabeth A. Brandt, Anthropological Research Papers, no. 20 (Tempe: Arizona State University, 1980), 118. Used by permission.

Song 1

Grey rattlesnake
Wash across zigzag goes.
Tree below rustles:
Sounds of crying.

Song 2

Green rattlesnake
Road across zigzag goes.
Green grass enters:
Sounds of crying.

Song 3

Little rattlesnake
Road in circularly sits:
Sounds of rattling.

Song 4

Straight going rattlesnake
Straight going rattlesnake
From the side across goes:
Sounds of rattling.

8. RAFAEL MENDEZ, 1920

Frances Densmore, *Papago Music*, Smithsonian Institution. Bureau of American Ethnology, Bulletin 90 (Washington, DC: US Government Printing Office, 1929), 97–98. In the public domain.

Song 1. "A Painted Snake Comes Out"

Here we begin to talk.
We call a name toward the east and a snake comes out, nicely painted.

Song 2. Song to a Little Yellow Wasp

Little yellow wasp, you throw dirt in my eyes.
I do not know what to do with you.
All I can do is to make a long-drawn breath, hoping you will die in four days.

9. MARIE DOMINGO, 1989

Jane H. Hill, "What Is Lost When Names are Forgotten," in *Nature Knowledge: Ethnoscience, Cognition, and Utility*, ed. Glauco Sanga and Gherardo Ortalli (New York: Berghahn Books, 2003), 176. Used by permission.
[In a study of dialect variation in Tohono O'odham conducted from 1986 to 1990 by Jane Hill and Ofelia Zepeda, with assistance from Mary Vernice Belin and Molly DuFort, O'odham words were elicited by showing speakers images of various plants, animals and cultural items. Marie Domingo offered the following narrative without solicitation, code-switching throughout, after she had been shown a picture of a western diamondback.]

"Yuucch![19] RATTLESNAKE![20] Yuucch! *Ko'oi! Ko'oi.* [When there are many?] *Ko:koi.* One almost bit me; these are real bad some of them. Here's right where it fell, right here (gesturing to her shin), and tore MY DRESS. It even got all the way to my SLIP. I thought perhaps, if my DRESS had been short, it would have fallen against my leg and bitten me, and yet I always wear a long dress; so it happened to fall right here. It didn't bite me. IT WAS A BIG RATTLESNAKE. It crawled back there, UNDER A BENCH IN THERE which is there in that little shed from where I was trying to take some PAINT . . . it almost bit me. I just took my DRESS straight off and threw it right away. I GUESS IT'S THE POISON, a sort of, a sort of GREENish-YELLOW,[21] just ran down there, where it presumably squirted out from where it fell and struck. Where it fell, presumably thinking that it fell against my leg, and squirted out all that poison. And when I had thrown it away, I said to MY AUNT, "Bring me something so I can put MY DRESS ON!"[22]

10. DAVID I. LOPEZ, 1992[23]

David Kozak and David Lopez, "Echoes of Mythical Creation: Snakes, Sex, Voice," *Wicazo Sa Review* 10, no. 1 (1994): 54–55. Published by the University of Minnesota Press. Copyright 1994 by the Association for American Indian Research. Used by permission.

[The punctuation reflects the original text.]

Snakes, rattlesnakes, I mean not really rattlesnakes, but like black whip, red racers, they're the <u>bad</u> ones. . . .

So, sure enough, one time we was sitting there—me and her—under the **watto** (ramada) and I guess at times, certain time like at noon, he (snake) comes out and she can feel it. Something like dizziness go like that—she can feel it that somebody's coming. And like I said, here's my bed and here's her bed, and she's just sitting there and just finally just laid down. I said, "you tired?" "No, I think something is coming to me, I feel dizzy." I said, "OH SHIT" I said. I'm just sitting there and just going like that and I thought "what am I going to do?" "Go get the medicine man (**ma:kai**) again and sure enough from here to that tire there (20 feet) I saw a black snake sticking out of a little hole. Went up high like that (imitating the snake's motions). O.K. I see you. I see you. YAHH! I went like that (shooing motion) and he went down there again. And I told Mom, I called Mom, "Mom, come here" I said. And she came and said "what happened?" and I said "she got sick again, but I think I find out who's doing that. Bring the waterhose over here, bring the hose and turn the water on" I said. Turn the water on, bring my rifle, bring the rifle, I think I saw that son of a bitch, that nasty old thing" I said. So, she did, brought my rifle and I loaded up, loaded and soaked that snake out, put water in there—it went in there and went in there and went in there. And I told Mom, "just sit over here and watch here, sit over her [*sic*], aim at the little hole, and nobody around. Just me and her and my late Mom. And others are not over here.

I said, "just watch over there but don't move, don't move, just watch over there." And I was just sitting there aiming, already aiming, and I guess the water got him finally, just stick his head like that and I aimed, BANG!, I got him good. Boy, he started jumping up and down, up and all around. I said, "I got you, you son of a bitch. How come you're bothering my sister? We don't want you nasty thing." And my late Mom was just cussing it and cussing, got a mop and just smashed its head. And I throw it away. Throw it away and say every time when you kill something like that, you talk to it. Say "I'm going to hang you over here and let the birds eat you for lunch." And I took it over there. That time it was just greasewood trees here. And I took it over there and just hang it on a tree and I said "I'm going to hang it on a tree and I said "I'm going to hang you over here you son of a bitch. Now the birds are going to eat you."

And that (black snake sickness) just went away. She was cured. "Boy, I don't have no dizziness anymore since when you killed that damn nasty old thing" she said. Then she sleeps pretty well after that. So that's how bad snakes are and all . . . them chuckwalla (lizard).

Notes

1. A. Irving Hallowell, "Ojibwa Ontology, Behavior, and World View," in *Culture in History: Essays in Honor of Paul Radin*, ed. Stanley Diamond (New York: Columbia University Press, 1960), 21.

2. Seth Schermerhorn, "Walking to Magdalena: Place and Person in Tohono O'odham Songs, Sticks, and Stories" (PhD diss., Arizona State University, 2013).

3. Simon Lopez, interview by author, July 2011, Santa Rosa, AZ.

4. Seth Schermerhorn and Lillia McEnaney, "Through Indigenous Eyes: A Comparison of Two Tohono O'odham Photographic Collections Documenting Pilgrimages to Magdalena," *Religious Studies and Theology* 36, no. 1 (2017): 23.

5. This assertion is disputed within O'odham oral traditions.

6. Simon Lopez, interview by author, March 2016, Santa Rosa, AZ.

7. "Playing" is a disrespectful offense that is usually paired with the consequence of "sickness." See Donald M. Bahr and Juan Gregorio, *Piman Shamanism and Staying Sickness (Ká:Cim Múmkidag)*, ed. Albert Alvarez, trans. David I. Lopez (1974; repr., Tucson: University of Arizona Press, 1981); Seth Schermerhorn, "Walkers and Their Staffs: O'odham Walking Sticks by Way of Calendar Sticks and Scraping Sticks," *Material Religion* 12, no. 4 (October 2016): 496; and Seth Schermerhorn, "Walkers and Their Staffs," chap. 3 in *Walking to Magdalena: Personhood and Place in Tohono O'odham Songs, Sticks, and Stories* (Lincoln: University of Nebraska Press, 2019), 94.

8. One interesting aspect of this story, found specifically in the punch line, is how Simon Lopez narrates the origin of the English language, blasphemy, and taking God's (or to be more accurate, I'itoi's) name in vain, as taking place in this single moment in O'odham oral tradition. One might also note here, as others have elsewhere, a pervasive language ideology among indigenous peoples that one cannot swear in indigenous languages whereas English, as a model of improper ways of speaking, is uniquely suited to this purpose. Anthony K. Webster, "'Everything Got Kinda Strange after a While': Some Reflections on Translating Navajo Poetry That Should Not Be Translated," *Anthropology and Humanism* 40, no. 1 (2015): 82–83.

9. Lopez, interview, 2016.

10. Dean Saxton, Lucille Saxton, and Susie Enos, *Dictionary: Tohono O'odham/Pima to English, English to Tohono O'odham/Pima*, ed. R. L. Cherry, 2nd ed., revised and expanded (Tucson: University of Arizona Press, 1998), 34.

11. Amadeo M. Rea, *At the Desert's Green Edge: An Ethnobotany of the Gila River Pima* (Tucson: University of Arizona Press, 1997), 112.

12. Frank Russell, *The Pima Indians*, Annual Report of the Bureau of American Ethnology to Secretary of the Smithsonian Institution 26 (Washington, DC: Government Printing Office, 1908), 206.

13. Russell, *Pima Indians*, 214.

14. Citations for the following works are in the *Chicago Manual of Style*, seventeenth edition, footnote style unless the holder of the copyright requested a specific format for the citation. In those cases, the format of the citation follows the respective requests of the copyright holders.

15. Moik Sulaj.

16. Tobĭ, or Toobĭ.

17. According to Bahr, this story and another are "practically the same as stories told by the Maricopas (Spier 1933: 347–52). . . . I think it likely that many Maricopas and Pimas would have criticized them for stealing, or, as an academic would say, 'plagiarizing,' this story from the Maricopas" (citation in original). Donald Bahr, ed., *O'odham Creation & Related Events as Told to Ruth Benedict in 1927 in Prose, Oratory, and Song [. . .]* (Tucson: University of Arizona Press, 2001), 22n. Therefore, the Maricopa story appears next. For the Spier citation, see Leslie Spier, *Yuman Tribes of the Gila River* (Chicago: University of Chicago Press, 1933), 347–52.

18.   Spier notes, "The tale was interrupted at this point." Spier, *Yuman Tribes*, 348n.

19.   Hill notes that "here, Marie Domingo begins with a unique case of the associa-tion of [ʔi::] 'Yuucch,' the Tohono O'odham sound for disgust about rattlesnakes, with the English name." Jane H. Hill, "What Is Lost When Names Are Forgotten," in *Nature Knowledge: Ethnoscience, Cognition, and Utility*, ed. Glauco Sanga and Gherardo Ortalli (New York: Berghahn Books, 2003), 176.

20.   Hill notes that "code switching into English is marked with SMALL CAPS." Hill, "What Is Lost," 179.

21.   Hill draws attention to Domingo's use of "'green-*ma* yellow, using English words with the Tohono O'odham derivational element –*ma* 'somewhat, resembling'" in order to provide "the gruesome detail of the exact color of the venom." Hill, "What Is Lost," 179, 176.

22.   Hill notes, "One of its rather interesting points is that the story is partly about Marie Domingo's appropriate O'odham female modesty; she always wears a long dress, and so is saved from being bitten, and even knowing that the snake is still nearby under a bench, her first thought is for a clean dress to cover herself." Hill, "What Is Lost," 176.

23.   Kozak and Lopez date this event to the early 1960s. David Kozak and David Lopez, "Echoes of Mythical Creation: Snakes, Sex, Voice," *Wicazo Sa Review* 10, no. 1 (1994): 55.

CHAPTER SIX

Sounding Navajo

Bookending in Navajo Public Speaking

MEREDITH MOSS

MUCH OF THE PUBLIC discourse promoting Navajo language revitalization and language programs takes place in English, both on and off the reservation, as in many other indigenous communities whose heritage languages are endangered. Although the Navajo language is commonly discussed as being central to the identity of a Navajo person, this claim may contradict other linguistic and social means Navajos use to construct Navajo identities, which exist within a wide spectrum of demographic categories as well as communities of practice relating to religion, occupation, and other activities.[1] The connection of language and identity is increasingly important as fewer and fewer children are learning Navajo as a first language. According to *The Ethnologue*, the Navajo language is spoken by 169,000 people, with 7,600 monolingual Navajo speakers.[2] However, the shift to English is proceeding rapidly. Therefore, the ways in which English usage and code-switching help to construct Navajo identity, particularly in public settings, are important to recognize and document.

In this chapter, I introduce the concept of "bookending" as it relates to the speech used in public performances by Navajos in front of other Navajos, in speech events largely composed of speech in the English language. By bookending the English speaking with Navajo language at the beginning and end, as well as routinely inserting recognizable Navajo phrases and pronunciations of English words, speakers create a Navajo performance from beginning to end that establishes both their authenticity as Navajos while also demonstrating capability with English and with speaking to a diverse audience of Navajos. The overall form of a bookended speech event is in effect its function as well: to be Navajo through and through, in a number of different and strategic ways.

Self-Introductions: Form as Function

Beginning with "Yá'át'ééh" ("Hello") or another greeting or opening, the first element of bookending is the tradition of self-introduction, which includes the listing the individual's clans, beginning with the mother's. As I first witnessed as a student of Navajo (Diné) language at Diné College, the tribal college on the Navajo Nation, and later in Arizona State University Navajo classes, the self-introduction is ubiquitous, if not mandatory, when making a public presentation or introducing oneself in a language class. Although sometimes employed in one-on-one conversations, the self-introduction is more often used in public contexts in which an individual speaks before a class or audience, due to its nature as a cohesive block of speech with a predictable pattern of clans and other information such as origin and profession.

The ubiquity of the self-introduction as a means of explaining some of the ways in which a person fits into Navajo society is often discussed as being necessary to find one's relatives in the audience, but more importantly to ensure that individuals avoid dating within the same clans. In fact, the ubiquity of the self-introduction in Navajo, taught in many Navajo Nation schools and serving as an obvious opener in much public speech, is problematic for those Navajo speakers who cannot produce the self-introduction because they struggle with either the language or the content, but yet they are aware it is appropriate and/or expected of them. In the first day of any level of Navajo language classes I have taken, for example, the ability of some students to rattle off a fluent-sounding self-introduction creates an awkward juxtaposition with the students who struggle or offer an embarrassed silence. The problem is not necessarily facility with the language. Instead, noting that one's mother, father, maternal grandmother, or paternal grandmother might share a clan is extremely uncomfortable to admit in public, although it is quite common and is the subject of many jokes about the Navajo Nation today. Besides, some individuals might not know all of these family members, much less their clan affiliations.

For outsiders like me, a white scholar trained in linguistics, the list of clans is easy to produce. I might list each clan as "Bilagáana" (white), having to say "Bilagáana" four times straight as more and more individuals smile or laugh with its repetition. According to some teachers, however, even Bilagáanas come from somewhere and so they should list their ancestors' countries of origin, some of which have Navajo names or Navajo borrowings for their names. At Arizona State University, the insistence on using European or other non-Bilagáana "clans" might have been a reflection of the demand for other options due to the mixed ancestry of numerous, so-called urban Navajo students.

A larger difficulty occurs when a non-Navajo's self-introduction yields uncomfortable comparisons between an outsider who can perform the self-introduction and any Navajos who cannot, sometimes resulting in a scolding or shaming of those perceived to be too lazy to learn their heritage language, as documented by Kimberly Marshall and Kristina Jacobsen.[3] By contrast, the late Martha Jackson, an instructor of Navajo language at Diné College, delighted in all of her students making the effort to practice and deliver the self-introduction. In fact, at least 25 percent of class time in the course I took with her in 2009 was devoted to instruction in the self-introduction. Certainly, seeing students acquire Navajo as a second language is a great comfort to those who have witnessed such rapid decrease in fluency rates as compared to earlier generations. Furthermore, the self-introduction claiming Navajo identity rooted in their Navajo genealogy provides some reassurance to older Navajo speakers that young people prize their heritage language as well as their ancestry and culture.

In addition to classroom performances, the symbolic importance of the self-introduction during public events for speakers and listeners cannot be overstated. In a changing linguistic landscape, beginning with the heritage language is a treasured practice that reminds the participants that the Navajo language is still alive. The primacy of its use indicates, however accurately or inaccurately, that the speaker's stance is oriented toward the use of Navajo and that the audience members may—or should—share that stance.[4]

Moreover, as a rhetorical device (a persuasive strategy), the self-introduction functions as a *persuasive entreaty to the audience for acceptance of one's identity as a Navajo* (or as a qualified outsider) in a distinctly Navajo context, as well as to establish some element of authority to speak on the subject due to that self-presentation of identity. In addition to other strategies, discussed later in this chapter, the self-introduction in Navajo showcases both cultural and linguistic authenticity—a clever solution to the difficulties of a society with many different cultural practices and linguistic proficiencies, all associated with Navajoness.

Due to its role in establishing authenticity and credibility as a speaker—at least some of which is predicated on being able to memorize and deliver a few structured sentences in the Navajo language—the self-introduction is notable in its consistent use of the Navajo language even when the subject matter of the rest of the presentation or conversation is exclusively conducted in English. The sudden switch to English can be abrupt, especially when a speaker is clearly not fluent in Navajo, and often the first words of English serve as an apology for needing to switch, or an explanation of one's plans to improve their fluency in Navajo because the self-introduction is the extent of their performative capabilities in Navajo. Establishing intent to learn the heritage language can be quite persuasive, as in the case of Chris Deschene, a candidate for Navajo Nation President in 2014, when the Nation still required candidates to speak Navajo. Deschene, a veteran and lawyer, promised to surround himself with fluent speakers and learn the language by the end of his first term, which endeared him to many monolingual English-speaking Navajos who could relate to his struggles to be taken as seriously as Navajo speakers. Debates about authenticity abounded as lawsuit after lawsuit was filed. Although Deschene was ultimately disqualified from the race, the language requirement was removed the next year in an election, showing the great divide between language hard-liners struggling to prove that Navajo language is essential to Navajo identity and those who, despite being affected by the same ideology, struggled for recognition with additional forms of Navajo authenticity.[5]

The political role of Navajo language ideologies in managing language shift certainly deserves more scholarly attention as Navajos recalibrate their definitions of Navajo identity. In the case of self-introductions, the disconnect between some fluent-sounding lines of Navajo and the fluency of one's English can be ignored when the assumed stance of the speaker and audience is that Navajo should be elevated above English for the common good of the Navajo people. When Navajo bookends English speech, as discussed above, a number of misunderstandings can arise, including assumptions that:

1. The speaker is, in fact, fluent in Navajo, and therefore
2. The ease with which a self-introduction is given should be a testament to the ease with which fluency in Navajo language might be attained, meaning that
3. Individuals (especially youth or middle-aged Navajo) who have not acquired Navajo proficiency should be ashamed of not working hard enough to learn their heritage language.

Furthermore, the widespread use of memorized self-introductions contributes to a sense of overall Navajo language speaking that may not accurately reflect the demographics of the Navajo Nation. As Deborah House has demonstrated, the widespread appearance of Navajoness, of which the genre of self-introduction is a part, allows for the dismissal of indications to the contrary; language loss is happening rapidly and language education is not in fact halting the shift to English.[6] Using Judith Irvine and Susan Gal's model of iconicization, fractal recursivity, and erasure, House explains that in the Navajo Nation's attempt to incorporate Navajo traditions and cultural concepts into everyday life, the myth of stable diglossia (equal bilingualism) is upheld and the recognition of the realities of language shift is erased.[7]

On the other hand, public speakers in Navajo contexts face numerous challenges, including managing audience expectations and language-speaking abilities as well as the need to establish their own identity and authority as speakers. A practiced public speaker can use both English and Navajo to manage the expectations of monolingual English speakers, the decreasing number of monolingual Navajo speakers, and the bilinguals in between. With this kind of mixed audience in a community that is shifting to English, the most important expectation is arguably that the speaker follows norms of politeness and respect for others' personal autonomy. As Ronald Scollon and Suzanne Scollon, Keith Basso, and many others have documented among speakers of other Athabaskan languages, Athabaskan communicative norms dictate respect for personal autonomy in conversational speech. In some cases, this approach results in holding back from forcing a view on another person.[8] Another manifestation of this phenomenon involves speaking indirectly so as to allow the listener to make individual sense of the utterance.[9] This routine allowance for personal autonomy in others means that a speaker should make maximal efforts to include the needs of all audience members, which often means choosing mostly English for the bulk of the speech and employing bookending and code-switching strategies. Furthermore, the ability to show politeness to the audience and allow for their language needs—especially when speaking as an authority figure to a younger audience—demonstrates the speaker cares for the audience and proves himself or herself to be a responsible contributor to society and to the gathering at hand. Strategies that show the speaker to be a thoughtful superordinate (as in a grandparent-grandchild relationship) may enhance the speaker's ethos (credibility) and may be particularly welcome in a society such as the Navajo Nation fraught with generational divisions relating to language, communication, and identity.

The "Rez Accent": Sounding Navajo in English

After beginning a speech with a self-introduction, an English translation of the self-introduction is often provided, which serves as a transition to the English portion of the speech. As discussed previously, bookending English with a Navajo beginning and ending indexes Navajoness using the heritage language, even for speakers and listeners with limited Navajo proficiency. Throughout the speaker's performance in English, the very sound of the English used, along with the structure of the talk, further index Navajo belonging and provide evidence for the speaker's Navajoness in a number of ways. Therefore, the speaker's individual idiolect of English becomes another index of Navajoness through the use of discourse markers and discourse particles typical in Navajo speech. Furthermore, Navajoness is indexed through the grammatical and phonological features that are "enregistered" (i.e., convey social meaning) as belonging to Navajo groups.[10]

The variety of English that is used is influenced by Navajo phonology as well as grammar, including the structure of sentences and the typical features of Navajo discourse that are indexical, or indicative, of Navajo identity. Navajo English can be considered globally as a variety of English affected by speakers' proximity to the Navajo language speakers, to bilingual speakers of both English and Navajo, and to other speakers of Navajo English. Navajo English is a rule-governed system spoken (albeit with variation) by wide and diverse populations of Navajo people. However, Navajo English is often stigmatized for various reasons, including anti-Navajo discrimination and stereotyping from non-Navajo as well as Navajo sources. In my own research, I have found that it is common even for successful Navajo professionals and academics to still decry their own speech as "bad" or "broken" English, and the language ideologies active both on- and off-reservation show conflicting beliefs about what "good" language might be.[11]

At the same time that usage of Navajo-influenced English is stigmatized in many contexts, the sounds and structures of Navajo English are quite recognizable to other Navajos, both above and below the level of consciousness. Some features that act as higher-order "indexicals" are consciously recognizable and so are employed for the distinct purpose of sounding like a Navajo; to be specific, this entails not "sounding white."[12] Particularly for the practiced public speakers in my research and experience, care is taken to pronounce certain words in a so-called "correct" way with extra attention to word-medial or word-final /t/ in a word such as "correct." Another salient feature of Navajo English that may be conscious or not, depending on the speaker, is on-glide deletion or initial /j/ cluster reduction, such as pronouncing the word "particularly" without the [ju] or "you" sound in the middle—a distinctly non-"white" pronunciation.[13] Other pronunciations are easy to recognize in Navajo English speech due to their frequent use on the Navajo Nation, such as the towns of Shiprock and Rough Rock pronounced with a glottal stop at the end rather than /k/.[14] Additionally, this word-final glottalization is seen in other words ending in the sound /k/ such as "barbaric." A list of common Navajo English features and their documentation in linguistic literature, if previously identified, can be found in my dissertation.[15]

Discourse Particles: Code-Switching for Structure and Stance

In addition to sounding Navajo, uses of specific words and phrases from both Navajo and English can index Navajoness in speech. In his analysis of Navajo and English poetry by Rex Lee Jim, Anthony Webster notes that the particle *jiní* ("they say" or "it is said") is used in Navajo stories as an indexical tool that links the narrative to a vast intertextual system of stories: "a shared stock of knowledge, a shared—or potentially shared—corpus of oral literature."[16] Furthermore, using jiní to structure a story allows the speaker to disavow direct knowledge of the events narrated, instead acting as a reporter providing information relevant to the situation at hand or the people present. I have heard many Navajos code-switch and use jiní when speaking English, particularly when telling a joke, as well as an English translation such as "they say." Hence, jiní can be defined as a discourse particle, a word that has "functions that are primarily interpersonal" and creates shared understanding or attitude between interlocutors.[17]

In providing commentary on a story related by Paul Ethelbah, M. Eleanor Nevins states that the Apache *ch'idii* ("it's said" or "they say") functions similarly as a discourse particle, noting:

> These frame the content of the utterance as something that is known to the speaker through the speech of others, not from personal experience. It is a very precise way of orienting to narratives about the distant past. Repeated use of these particles creates an orienting frame and can function as a narrative genre marker.[18]

Ethelbah, the Apache storyteller who performed a narrative in English for Nevins's benefit, used the English discourse particle *you know* in a similar way. Nevins argues:

> A discussion of these is worth the trouble if it reveals the presence of Apache poetic style in a largely English-language performance and if it draws attention to Paul Ethelbah's agency in bringing English into the service of his Apache storytelling.[19]

In public speech, much can be accomplished by bringing distinctly Navajo narrative traditions such as discourse particles into English; namely, the performance becomes a Navajo speech through its recognizably Navajo features as well as the interpersonal function of the phrases establishing shared stance. By using rhetorical devices such as bookending, code-switching (using both languages), Navajo English, and discourse particles, a speaker can make a clear argument for the social positioning of the speaker's identity and establish the speaker's ethos, or credibility, in speaking on the topic. As Ronald Scollon and Suzanne Scollon note, "discourse patterns are among the strongest expressions of personal and cultural identity."[20] In communities undergoing rapid language shift, where language ideologies affect personal relationships as well as politics, the strategic use of Navajo and English both reflects and builds the relationship the speaker has with the audience and is a vital part of strengthening ties between members of changing communities.

Finally, of course, a closing:

Axéhee'! Hágoónee'.

Notes

1.   Margaret C. Field, "Changing Navajo Language Ideologies and Changing Language Use," in *Native American Language Ideologies: Beliefs, Practices, and Struggles in Indian Country*, ed. Paul V. Kroskrity and Margaret C. Field (Tucson: University of Arizona Press, 2009), 31–47; Wendy Baker and David Bowie, "Religious Affiliation as a Correlate of Linguistic Behavior," *University of Pennsylvania Working Papers in Linguistics* 15, no. 2, Article 2 (2010), https://repository.upenn.edu/pwpl/vol15/iss2/2.

2.   "Navajo," *Ethnologue*, accessed August 25, 2019, https://www.ethnologue.com/language/nav.

3.   Kimberly Jenkins Marshall, *Upward, Not Sunwise: Resonant Rupture in Navajo Neo-Pentecostalism* (Lincoln: University of Nebraska Press, 2016), 85; Kristina M. Jacobsen, *The Sound of Navajo Country: Music, Language, and Diné Belonging* (Chapel Hill: University of North Carolina Press, 2017), 10.

4.   Alexandra M. Jaffe, "Stance in a Corsican School: Production of Bilingual Subjects," in *Stance: Sociolinguistic Perspectives*, ed. Alexandra M. Jaffe (Oxford: Oxford University Press, 2009), 119–45.

5.   Meredith Genevieve Moss, "English with a Navajo Accent: Language and Ideology in Heritage Language Advocacy" (PhD diss., Arizona State University, 2015), 63.

6. Deborah House, *Language Shift among the Navajos: Identity Politics and Cultural Continuity* (Tucson: University of Arizona Press, 2002), 85–103.

7. Judith T. Irvine and Susan Gal, "Language Ideology and Linguistic Differentiation," in *Regimes of Language: Ideologies, Polities, and Identities*, ed. Paul V. Kroskrity (Santa Fe, NM: School of American Research Press, 2000), 35–83.

8. Ronald Scollon and Suzanne B. K. Scollon, *Narrative, Literacy, and Face in Interethnic Communication* (Norwood, NJ: Ablex, 1981).

9. Keith H. Basso, "'To Give Up on Words': Silence in Western Apache Culture," *Southwestern Journal of Anthropology* 26, no. 3 (1970): 213–30.

10. Asif Agha, "The Social Life of Cultural Value," *Language & Communication* 23, no. 3 (2003): 231–73.

11. Moss, "English with a Navajo Accent," 126.

12. Michael Silverstein, "Indexical Order and the Dialectics of Sociolinguistic Life," *Language & Communication* 23, nos. 3–4 (July–October 2003): 193–229.

13. Guy Bailey and Erik Thomas, "Some Aspects of African-American Vernacular English Phonology," in *African-American English: Structure, History, and Use*, ed. Salikoko S. Mufwene et al. (London: Routledge, 1998), 85–109.

14. Charlotte C. Schaengold, "Bilingual Navajo: Mixed Codes, Bilingualism, and Language Maintenance" (PhD diss., Ohio State University, 2004), 43.

15. Moss, "English with a Navajo Accent," 92–112.

16. Anthony K. Webster, "Coyote Poems: Navajo Poetry, Intertextuality, and Language Choice," *American Indian Culture and Research Journal* 28, no. 4 (2004): 74.

17. Alexandra D'Arcy, "Canadian English as a Window to the Rise of *Like* in Discourse," in "Focus on Canadian English," ed. Matthia Meyer, special issue, *Anglistik* 19 (2008): 125–40.

18. Paul Ethelbah, Genevieve Ethelbah, and M. Eleanor Nevins, "'Ndah Ch'ii'n,'" in *Inside Dazzling Mountains: Southwest Native Verbal Arts*, ed. David L. Kozak (Lincoln: University of Nebraska Press, 2012), 203.

19. Ethelbah, Ethelbah, and Nevins, "'Ndah Ch'ii'n,'" 205.

20. Scollon and Scollon, *Narrative, Literacy, and Face*, 37.

CHAPTER SEVEN

Agency of the Ancestors

Apache Rhetoric

INÉS TALAMANTEZ

APACHE RHETORICAL THEORY, WHETHER or not we think of it as such, is demonstrably present in the use of what we consider sacred language, which is embedded in the Apache belief system. The importance of this linguistic protocol to practitioners of Apache religious traditions is that it compels us to learn how to listen carefully and effectively. This is critically important as we absorb the wisdom our elders reveal to us, the wisdom that we inherit from them. Ancient knowledge connects us to our cultural values, ceremonies, and philosophical traditions. This essay will examine Apache rhetoric and its importance for our survival. I am focusing on the idea that the sacred power, *diiyii*, in language, in nature, in the water, the plants, and the animal world is considered numinous by the Apache. Indeed, the diiyii in our language is a potent force that the people have utilized for contending with ongoing traumas, such as missionary fervor for our conversion, political subjugation, and environmental degradation.

The idea of thinking and speaking about nature and language as numinous comes to us from the blood memories of our thoughtful ancestors.[1] In the Apache language we have no word for religion, nor for rhetoric. Religion for us is how we live our lives. And similarly, we think of something like rhetoric as our way of speaking our language, which we inherit from our ancestors.[2] Human nature and our language teaches us that we are integrated with nature; we are not apart from it. We sense a dependence on the fact that nature is sacred and that everything we need in life comes from the sacred power of nature. Embedded in this way of careful thinking, we learn from most Native American communities that our languages emphasize respect, ethics, and protocol, while also providing the way we are to use concepts of cosmology and ontology for cultural continuity.

Apache theory, for example, holds that wisdom consists of acquiring a heightened mental capacity for prescient thinking that is produced by three conditions. A clear mind when creating rituals and ceremonies, chanting, singing, and telling sacred narratives, and through the movement of dance, is called *bini godlkooh*. The second is resilience of mind, *bini gontliz*; and the third is steadfastness of mind, *bini gonldzil*. Each must be cultivated in a conscientious manner by acquiring religious bodies of knowledge and applying them critically to one's mind. This is how one acquires wisdom. The following presents arguments for maintaining the integrity of Apache rhetoric. The goal is to organize ideas and theories that are Apache about the loss of land, languages, and theologies, for the purpose of defining the current order or spiritual relationships as symbolic forms of religious meaning that allow for the creation of sacred spaces. I propose a new interpretation of Native American religious history focused on an awareness of Indigenous rhetoric.

I agree with Thomas Berry's emphasis on these issues, on learning together by calling for a new vision of Christian traditions as well as a true understanding of Native American religious beliefs.[3] My work now offers a new perspective for validating and respecting the religious tradition and oral histories that Native American elders tell us, the process of talking with the people of knowledge about their memories as they recall their ethnohistories embedded in their oral traditions, sacred narratives, songs, chants, dance movements, dreams, and visions. Their memories I have learned are often about trauma, fear, poverty, sorrow, and anger. This research method represents forty years of fieldwork among the Mescalero Apache Sun Clan in New Mexico, primarily and also among the Navajo in the Four Corners area as well as work on Nahuatl, that is, Aztec, language and religious traditions. My task attempts to account for resurrecting Indigenous discourses within cultural, religious, and political contexts. Since my work is in a Western institution that they do not believe in, it took a long time to gain the trust of my consultants, who are the keepers of this knowledge. I had to prove I was trustworthy. I had to learn how to gain their trust, how knowledge is shared often in a sacred space, which requires seriously understanding protocol. Once I was seen as someone who should be taught, I discovered that these elders were willing to share with me their own theories for preserving the culture.

Our talk about the ecological crisis of the present is focused on our belief system and lived experiences. We often compare the sacred power of nature with the power of the church that, through missionization, continues to use its rhetoric to convert us to Christianity. The power of the church in religious conversion has created the genocide experienced by every Native nation from the Aztecs to the Zuni people. In this time of drastic climate changes, droughts, flooding, massive melting of glaciers, earthquakes, nuclear damage, and global warming, our societies must work together in our interconnectedness to nature and the land where we live. Scholars need to look at and integrate the ecological truths of the environment and global ecology in order to build on the fruitful movement of ecocentrism. For the Apache, nature is theology, and our way of speaking about it has always been associated with our sacred narratives. The ideas of belonging, healing, and the full value of life are encoded in our ceremonial system. As the late Yupiac scholar A. Oscar Kawagley reminded me in a personal communication, we follow the memories of our people, who raised us with stories of the respectful knowledge of the reciprocity of nature.

Kawagley told me that since the philosophy of religion as we know it has been primarily an enterprise that arose in Europe and is influenced by a text on Christianity as practiced in Europe, it is now time to begin a serious conversation as to why Native American religious traditions still remain underrepresented. Arvind Sharma asserted to me in personal communication that despite the absence of written texts, primal religions have an implicit philosophy. They can offer a fresh perspective on controversial philosophical issues. His work demonstrates ways in which various elements of primal religious experience can be incorporated into the categories of modern religious philosophy.

The Apache belief system furnishes a persuasive understanding of a particular way of thinking built upon a language that is, unfortunately, endangered. This conceptual set of beliefs aims to remain private for obvious reasons, given the political realities we face. Yet, at this point in history we are likely on our way to becoming more exposed to etic interpretation by religious philosophy scholars and others. John S. Mbiti reminds us that one of the difficulties of studying African religions and philosophy is that there are no sacred scriptures. Similarly, in the past, the dearth of written texts led religious scholars and anthropologists alike to form the mistaken impression that Native Americans did not have literacy, nor a body of oral narratives that conveyed a system of thought. Some earlier studies even concluded erroneously that we did not have languages at all, nor religious traditions. Today, of course, the assumptions have changed. Take the idea of sustainability, for example. Sustainability has become a major, multifaceted topic tied to the plant and animal world. So now it is critical for religious scholars to factor in the relationship of Native American belief systems to the natural world into their thinking.

It is not at all surprising to the Apache that gathering and hunting, which are still important to us today, are ceremonially overlaid with religious significance. This is for us the key difference between survival and death. The specific ways of thinking about and going about the task of procuring food in nature are vital to the people. It is their "ultimate concern," what the theologian Paul Tillich characterized as the tendency of religions to emphasize something as of the utmost importance.[4] Throughout history the successful hunt was definitely a matter of ultimate concern, not only in the pragmatic sense but the philosophic as well, underscoring the inseparability of the belief system from symbolic consciousness.

The Mescalero Apache origin story speaks to the unsafe and unhealthy conditions of our people. Taking control of these immediate concerns required consulting Ìsánáklésh, our Earth Mother and Land Giver. Ritual actions are used to overcome misfortunes and overcome and restore health. We know that the Apache ethos of our rituals and ceremonies renews our people's commitments to our way of life. The teaching of Apache ethics and values finds expression in the rhetorical practices considered sacred language. The fundamental importance of religious protocol and sacred rhetoric requires that we learn how to listen carefully, to absorb many layers of meaning embedded in the language, and to detect nuance in repetition. Our struggle continues to be to preserve our language, our culture, and our religion. Insider (emic) perspectives reveal indignation about ongoing religious conversion efforts, cultural assimilation, and genocide. Yet we have hope for the future, and count on the support of our allies dedicated to building sustainability and justice.

Long before European contact, Native Americans were already considering the powerful significance of the world of nature and were enriching their lives with substantive ecological knowledge. The Tewa projected their cultural, social, and religious beliefs "outward and upward to encompass the whole of their physical world as well by imbuing that world with a three-tiered spiritual meaning, one both reflecting and reinforcing their social order. The fit among their ideas of order in society, in the physical world, and in the spiritual realm is ingenious, for these three orders interlock and render order into everything within the Tewa world."[5] This understanding and respect for the natural world and its sanctity creates a feeling of kinship with environmentalists and the conservationists today.[6] Environmentalists express a remarkable sincerity in their research for the truth and their desires to work toward changes within American culture and the world. They also express an interest in understanding Native Americans as a diverse multifaceted population with different perceptions of American history, as people with whom they share this land and national identity. Berry, mentioned earlier, sees value in engaging in dialogue for understanding and respecting the religious traditions of other cultures. While environmentalists may not find it necessary to pray to the sun themselves, they can see the value in studying why solar power and energy are sacred to so many Native Americans. The late Ninian Smart once reminded me that what we need to do is to break down that simplified opposition between learning about religion and feeling the power of religion.

For traditional Native Americans, moral and ethical behavior is learned at a young age, using language and rhetoric as necessary means for survival, stressing individual responsibility, resourcefulness, and diligence. When I entered graduate school as a reentry Native American woman in 1971 at University of California, San Diego, it was a time when students and other members of the community were beginning to demand courses in Native American studies. This was a transformative time for me, as I became a student activist eager to enrich my life and learn more about Native American religious traditions. Fortunately, I had some excellent mentors, both in school and in life. Revelations of our Apache ancestors inform our concept of history and shape our understanding of religion. Western theoretical interpretations are open to debate yet continue to be applied to assess the validity of studying Native American religious traditions in universities. Learning about Native American topics, I discovered as a graduate student, involved mastering various non-Native theories used to challenge Indigenous ideas of nature, art, knowledge, and truth.

The forced relocations of Native Americans from their ecosystems have impacted other unknown ecosystems, and new revelations about nature are often devastating. The ancestors' wisdom about the spirit of the cosmos in songs, the spiritual dimension of prayer, the importance of the community working together for sustenance, and the significance of knowing the land reflect the nature of ritual and ceremony in knowing the ecosystem. A reinterpretation of how non-Native thinkers have used their own belief systems and observations as outsiders to define how Native Americans live their lives requires Indigenous responses. Westerners' theoretical interpretations are open to debate, yet their reflections continue to be applied to determine the validity of studying Native American religious traditions in universities. They are utilized to challenge Indigenous ideas of nature, truth, art, and knowledge. Earlier scholars used their work to fortify the missionaries' efforts in their quest to Christianize Native Americans. The work of divinity scholars often relies on American social science to define Native American belief systems. Divinity school students, upon completion of their studies, frequently become Christian missionaries. Like contemporary pious Muslim women who struggle to maintain religious and ethical traditions deemed unfashionable by Western standards, Native Americans continue to struggle with expressing their own religious identity. The Constitution grants all Americans freedom of religion, yet Native Americans are not free to practice their religious beliefs as related to hallucinogenic medicinal plants or confiscated sacred lands, to cite just two examples. Cultural subjugation fosters defiance in Native cultures surrounding issues of racial identity. It is time for us as scholars to determine why these biased assumptions have been allowed to remain pervasive. Today, a new direction is emerging in the academy, whereby "Indian White History" is challenged from a variety of perspectives and is called out for its misinterpretation of Native American worldviews.[7]

Smart noted, "The image of many academics of the study of religion is a pious dogmatism, girding its loins with the cloth of obscure scholarship."[8] This is certainly true for the study of Native American religious traditions. This is why it is essential, if one is to understand Indigenous cultures, to support Smart's ideas, as well as the work of a growing cadre of Indigenous scholars, by expanding the scholarship on tribal knowledge by using Indigenous research frameworks and epistemologies, decolonizing methodologies, qualitative fieldwork, and language study. Ethics and Native American rhetoric occupy a central role in placing Indigenous research within the academy, and we are always at risk when we do. However, the academy is facing an environment of emerging discourses of inclusiveness and theoretical perspectives. These perspectives are testing the Western philosophical system and its tradition of dominance.

Today, Native American belief systems are taken seriously after an era when they were treated with suspicion and even hostility. The time has come for Indigenous religions, which represent symbolic thinking and an appreciation for the rhetoric of sacred narratives as ways of thinking and being, to be justified based on the logic inherent in their traditions. The past and present ethnocentric bias to study and interpret other cultures using one's own cultural values as a central point of reference is a delusion. Still today, too many of the Judeo-Christian traditions deny the cosmological perspectives of Native American religious traditions still alive in many of our communities that revere the blood memories of our ancestors and their ancient histories. European Americans continue to impose the power of their reality within this nation, which in many ways reveals their inability to define themselves on this land. A good start would be to admit that there is a legitimate way to interpret American history, but first it must eliminate its historical colonialism. We must "dig deeply" to get at our ancestral memories, as Robert Perez of the University of California, Riverside, told me recently, to arrive at our truths about how our people lived here on this land for centuries. He also stated that these ancient histories reveal the importance of living in a sustainable, respectful manner in our ecosystems, an understanding that all of the natural world is sacred, and therefore our religious traditions developed within this understanding.

The history of distortion has impeded the formation of a well-rounded understanding of Native American theologies. When we examined the social, religious, and historical contexts within which Native American religions can best be understood, we learned we must preface our own work with the realization that the first obstacle is the persistence of miscomprehension between the majority of the American nation and Native American people. In spite of a vast literature that at varying times has encompassed myriad historical, "frontier," and "accommodationist" treaties, this land remains locked in political struggle.

While teaching Native American religious traditions at the University of California, Santa Barbara (UCSB), some of my dedicated students and I have attempted to create a place on campus that would allow us to get together socially to develop a new and more profound way for understanding each other. Finally, last year the American Indian and Indigenous Studies Group came to life. Combining the results of deep research and qualitative fieldwork experience, and working with Chumash communities and Native American elders, we developed a community whose flexibility allows for the diversity of our beliefs, practices, and cultures. Our work has been motivated by a concern for the need to construct a new basis for understanding these traditions from a Native American perspective, for all of the students at UCSB. A sense of the intrinsic importance of these cultures and practices, which are often thought of as historical rather than contemporary, is a significant motivator for implementing the university's curriculum in relation to these topics. I came to graduate school in the seventies with already formed ideas and perspectives on Native American worldviews and encountered a unique opportunity for me to engage in Native rhetorical practices and to pursue further research and study on Native people. Most students know very little about Native Americans, and when in seminars we attempted to open up the issues through an analysis of the metaphysical and epistemological questions, their sense of wonder, guilt, and frustration was overwhelming. Today in my classes my own teaching and field research reveals theories about Native Americans that often awaken in my students their own ideas and perceptions of the world, and the need to work to understand each other in the classroom.

An example from my own teaching experience will illustrate this awakening. During the academic year 1981–1982, I was an Andrew W. Mellon Faculty Fellow for the Committee on the Study of Religion at Harvard

University, invited by Professor Wilfred Cantwell Smith to teach a course entitled "Introduction to Native American Religious Traditions: Myths, Symbols, and Transitions." The course was the first of its kind at Harvard; it was designed as a multidisciplinary thematic exploration of the nature, structure, and the meaning of ritual and language in the religious life of Native American cultures of the Southwest. The class included religious studies majors, graduate students from the Harvard Divinity School, a variety of Native American students from other disciplines, and a Harvard faculty member, a Jesuit scholar of "American Indian religions" trained in Europe. There were about eighty people attending the class. Since this was the first time the course was being offered at Harvard, I decided to poll the students at the beginning of the semester to discover their reasons for taking a course of this nature, and to ask what they expected to gain from the experience. Their responses fell into three categories, each representative of broader cultural responses to Native Americans in America's life and history. (1) Most of the students expressed concern about the search for knowledge and truth about Native Americans; (2) their own interests in learning about spirituality as the key to personal life philosophies seemed to be an unresolved ongoing quest; and (3) they were concerned about the destruction of the natural world and its ecosystems.

It is not unusual for some students to search for meaning in their lives as they try to understand the lives of other students in their classes. What was apparent is that there seemed to be something missing in their lives. There seemed to be a desire for a more meaningful life experience. This is how it was expressed by one of the Harvard students:

> I want to know the truth about Native American cultures and peoples because I'm interested in comparative psychological healing systems and Native American religious art forms.

Another stated,

> My interests in studying Native American spirituality are concerned with how it might improve my ways of thinking, and how it may provide an opportunity for me to know more about myself. I also want to know more

about how other people express their religious beliefs in their day-to-day life and how this might help me on a personal level.

Yet another student wrote of her interest in gaining

An understanding of the value of mystical experiences and forms of meditation, as I feel there is a lack of ritual in my own life, and that there is not much that I respect in my own culture; this makes me feel alienation.

Another sought an opportunity to compare

Native American values, which are nature and community oriented, while European values are rooted in individualism, progress and Christianity, as a way to achieve a better understanding between us.

One undergraduate expressed a different interest, related more to concerns about the destruction and pollution of the natural world and its ecosystems:

Learning to interpret is the main reason I am here. I want to learn to live in harmony with people and nature. I am interested in learning more about the relationship between religion, nature, pilgrimage to sacred places and rites of passage. My love for the earth and my curiosity about the real Native American traditional ways of understanding the world brought me to this course.

Another wrote,

I am essentially ignorant of Indian culture both past and present. I don't know if the knowledge I already have is correct or not. For the most part I am taking this course to enhance my own knowledge and to clear up misconceptions. It strikes me as very odd that here in America we give so little attention to the religions of our country as well as to the struggles of Native Americans. We need to break the chain of arrogance in our culture and to stop the oppression of Native Americans.

What is apparent in interpreting these responses is that a primary concern of the students seemed to be understanding Native American ritual forms, which are usually expressed in a religious rhetoric that in English is elusive, complex, and not easily translated into ready-made responses to our technological society. In addition, these students were quite willing to admit that although they did not know much about Native American cultures, they were sympathetic toward the struggle of Native Americans. The students made clear their disdain for the violations by the federal government of land claims, treaties, and civil rights. They realized that survival for Native Americans relies on the conscience of the American people and the commitment to work together. These students also hoped to learn how dreams, visions, and ritual transformations could be tools for personal spiritual growth. They expressed interest in rites of passage as ritual frameworks for guiding young Native American men and women into adulthood. Unlike traditional young Native Americans, who are told what to expect at different periods of their lives in terms of daily duties to self, family, and community, the students in my Harvard class sought sources for personal growth and spirituality that did not seem to be available to them in American society.

During the course I offered a set of Indigenous concepts and methods as a particular approach to understanding Native American cultures. By focusing on rhetoric and ritual in a number of distinct societies, we examined various symbols, languages, and philosophies. Although this approach placed serious methodological requirements on both the students and the professor, there was a great payoff in terms of learning how people organize their world to live in balance. As in nature, where environmental conditions change over time and beget other changes in the ecosystem, so rituals for Native Americans contain teachings that pertain to trauma in society. Being displaced from traditional lands is one trauma; being forced into religious conversion is another; genocide is yet another, most egregious trauma. Rituals, drawn as they are from the words of our ancestors, and the power of all of nature, bring back harmony and balance to our lives. Ceremonies are concrete, directly applicable to everyday life; they require close contact with primary physical and spiritual realities. Many Native Americans still sing and dance for the Earth Mother and have reverence for all sources of life.

Although extended consideration of American history is beyond the scope of this essay, it is interesting to note that the Harvard students working on

American history had studied Native American cultures (as one of them said) "as a monolith of struggling conquered peoples." The fact that Native American cultures have a land-based cultural identity was not taught to these students. In textbooks on American history, the rich diversity of Native American cultures is often overshadowed by the fact that most of these cultures are being subjected to the idealized concept of assimilation. By the end of the course, many of the students expressed a keen interest in understanding Native Americans as a diverse, multifaceted population with different perceptions of American history, as peoples with whom they share this land and the identity of this country and with whom they coexist. Some of the graduate students have continued to be allies in this struggle and are now professors that I meet with at our annual meeting of the American Academy of Religion.

A guest lecturer, Cordelia B. Attack Him, a traditional healer and instructor at the Lakota Studies Department, Oglala Sioux Community College, talked about the preservation of Lakota culture and religion. It became apparent that traditional morality, ethics, and rhetoric is also learned as a necessity for survival in the Lakota world. She focused her talk on the responsibility of the individual to self as well as to community. She stressed the importance of knowing one's own language and culture as well as maintaining one's own spirituality through ritual and discipline. She spoke of the presence of Christian churches on the reservation and their influence on the Lakota people, and described how some Catholic priests on the reservation have used the Lakota sacred pipe at Catholic funeral rites and how these non-Lakota ideas and practices deeply affect the Lakota religious tradition. Jesuit priest Father Paul Steinmetz, a member of the class who had spent many years on the Lakota reservation, later spoke to the class about how he had been given the pipe and how he used it at Catholic funerals. This rare opportunity allowed the students to observe two different approaches by two people, one Lakota, the other non-Lakota, both responsible for specialized sacred knowledge and practices. When Mrs. Attack Him returned home, she wrote a long letter to my class that included statements from her Lakota students to my students.

Her students wrote about their own feelings and concerns. The Lakota students were concerned primarily with one overall plea for respect for the Lakota way of life. Their concerns were for respect for Lakota culture and religious traditions as well as for self-determination. Research and publications about Lakota culture were criticized for their inaccuracy, distortions, and derogatory tone. The students' desire for the return of the sacred Black Hills, taken by the federal government, was of central importance. One of the Lakota students put it this way:

> We have a deep respect for our religious traditions and for nature, yet you do not recognize that we are all the same and you fail to respect us as human beings. You must see us as a people and not as a minority group. Our values are as good as yours and so is our religion. We have a strong cultural heritage, language and religion. Our children have difficulty with English, yet they end up learning more than one language. If asked about water the Indian child thinks of lakes, ponds, rivers; the non-Indian thinks of the faucet. Our children are being taught the Lakota way, they have many teachers: grandparents, aunts, uncles, cousins, and parents. What we need from you is support in our fight to gain sovereignty as an Independent Lakota Nation. Support us in our fight for freedom from persecution and oppression by the Federal Government.

Another student felt this way about his people:

> We have always been a generous people; generosity is the most esteemed value in Lakota culture. Success in your world means accumulating wealth and possessions, now you want our water and mineral rights. By putting us on reservations you have made us dependent on you. I hope you (the majority culture) understand and realize your predicament.

There is an obvious need for a correct American history. How did all of this come to be now? It seems that both Indians and non-Indians have taken from nature what they needed and converted it with their creativity into cultural manifestations which fulfilled their needs.[9] Indian societies, before the discovery of America by Europeans, were in the process of significant development in the areas of religious practices, concern for living in balance with nature, as well as artistic and material accomplishments. Archaeological records and oral traditions alike attest to concerns for knowing their ecosystem. Ceremonial exchange such as burial practices, rites of passage, ritual transformations, concepts of healing, and diagnoses of illness were already a part of the life experiences of these societies. The order and structure of ecological relationships were already understood. All of the tribal belief systems knew both their geographic and spiritual or sacred boundaries. And most still have a strong sense of belonging to a specific land that was given to them by the Creator. On this land the sacred histories of their religious lives have taken place. The people are obligated to protect the ecological balances of the plant and animal life of these areas. Destroying these delicate balances means destroying what is held to be sacred.

On the other hand, the settlers who came to this land felt the need to claim the land and exploit it in the name of Western civilization. The settlers' views and attitudes were unlike the views of the diverse tribal societies that had already come into contact with each other. The sharp contrast in ideals and values affected the way the newcomers viewed the religious practices of Indian societies. The colonists feared the wilderness; they were after all from another land and from different ecosystems. Some argue that they were haunted by memories of former times and feared going back in time to the earlier, uncivilized states in Europe if they did not civilize this strange new land. Why they acted as they did toward the environment had to do with their ideals of individualism, independence, and the chance for a new beginning in the New World. In shaping their own adjustment to this new environment, they inherited much from the Indigenous societies they encountered, but they were more concerned with conquering than understanding. Their belief that God had given them this natural world to exploit allowed them to rationalize their behavior in the New World. Progress through exploitation and conversion was the formula for gain. Everywhere, in every direction, the souls and the raw materials of the earth that existed in profusion were ripe for exploitation.

What is clear from the students' comments and from the lessons of history is that the lack of understanding between the majority population and Native American societies is both political and religious. For the Lakota students and the Harvard students alike, the political and spiritual issues are significant; both groups seemed to realize that the only way we will survive is through spiritual awareness and respect of self, each other, community, and our environment. As I write these last few lines, the sky is at the time just before dawn when the silvery light spreads quickly across the landscape. I realize that we cannot expect or allow anyone to give shape to our thoughts or to find the path for us; to uncover the natural world for us or to give power to our words. However, the need to encourage students to ask the questions that open the dialogue that will lead to more intercultural understanding is one of my primary concerns. I ask myself: What have I learned from the way these students impacted my research and teaching? What have we gained by exploring this material? Is it possible for us to step out of the worldview we inherited to see some of our own strengths and deficiencies, and to truly understand the beliefs of others? What is needed is persuasive rhetoric which leads to understanding and provides us with a personal perspective that allows respect for each other.

The study of Native American religious traditions need not and must not entail a violation of that which is sacred to its practitioners. I am aware that the religious expression of the rhetoric of Native Americans is much more than what has been published to date. The future holds a more promising view, namely, to see Native American religious belief systems as distinct, each with its own religious characteristics emerging from and responding to their own individual historical experience and their specific social and cultural connection to nature, both with regard to the past as well as the present. In each case, of course, I am referring to a variety of traditions rather than a single one. Since the colonial historical experience for most Native Americans has been one of oppression, religious conversion, and assimilation, it is critical to recognize that what is happening to these religious traditions today is as important as what happened to them in the past. In other words, continuity and change should be seen as equally valid elements of preservation, adaptation, and renewal. To my knowledge no one has written a complete Native American religious history, although some have tried. The spiritual and aesthetic dimensions of these individual belief systems when taken together reveal the qualities of wholeness and interconnectedness of the social, cultural, and mythological categories of these traditions across time.

Although American Indian belief systems have been observed and studied since the seventeenth century, it is only with the most recent published works in this field that they have finally begun to come into their own and gain a long overdue and justly deserved recognition in the study of religion in America.[10] As early as 1884, Washington Matthews, a medical officer in the United States Army, published the first major work on a Navajo ceremony.[11] Yet Franc Newcomb and Gladys Reichard make clear almost sixty years later their surprise that Matthews's work did not spur on investigators to exert greater efforts in obtaining more complete information on Navajo ritual.[12] Reichard widens the horizon through her ethnography on Navajo religion complemented by her experiences living with the Navajo (Diné, as they call themselves), learning and speaking their language and by making the frame of meaning of Navajo religious traditions intelligible to non-Navajos.[13] More recently Gary Witherspoon has provided important linguistic analysis of the Navajo language and worldview.[14] But too many of the earlier introductions to Native American religious traditions provide only descriptive data, while the process of interpretation unfortunately is left to the reader. The exegesis when not provided by "the Native point of view" is left to the eyes and hands of future researchers. In view of such an impossibly diverse amount of material, one wonders where to start. What is the intellectual fabric that binds studies of American Indian belief systems together? The basic methodological and epistemological questions need to be asked and answered within an appropriate framework: What is a religious reality? What do we mean by religious behavior?

Although scholars of religion have attempted to answer these and other questions about religion in America, we have until now understood very little about Native American spirituality. The Protestant religion of the English colonists and the Roman Catholic belief of later European immigrants have been the most influential religious forces in most of America's communities. The many other diverse groups of peoples who settled in America also affirmed their religious independence. The peoples who are native to this land, the Native Americans, must also be recognized as having a diversity of religious traditions that have been the core and substance of their identity and survival. The collisions of cultures and the misunderstandings that resulted between different groups of immigrants and diverse Indigenous groups form a political-historical reality defined by Catherine Albanese as resting on the foundation of their understanding of religion.[15] She notes that Indians believed that every people had their sacred stories and rituals on which their world was based. Euro-American Christians believed in the primacy of their own religion—not just for themselves but for all peoples— as *the* universal truth. In theory, at least, Christianity transcended culture. In my research I have found that any study of this intricate relationship should seriously consider Roy Harvey Pearce, as his thesis initiates analysis of the dominant attitudes and ideas about American Indians from 1609 to 1851.[16] In his analysis of the immigrant American mind, Pearce presents the history of the concept of savagism alongside the idea of progress of civilization over savagism as an American belief. This belief came to life as the immigrants tried to figure out a way to contend with Native Americans and the wilderness. Convinced that their own destiny required civilizing "the Indian," the settlers' self-concept was shaped by the symbolic intertwining of the ideas "savage" and "civilized." Images and ideas about Indians formed by European philosophers, explorers, travelers, missionaries, and, later, Indian agents coalesced with everyday frontier experiences and created the historical complex of ideas that shaped the thinking and perceptions of nineteenth-century Euro-Americans in the New World. The concepts of savagism, civilization, Manifest Destiny, and Christianity—without any knowledge of Native languages—provided the basis for most people's notions about what they referred to as "the Indian." This period of tension produced the following racist suppositions: "the Indian" was idealized as a noble and virtuous hunter, a brave warrior, possessed of the freedom to roam unhindered, simple and childlike, the predecessor of civilized America. Yet, as savage and pagan, "the Indian" was to be feared for his cunning and cruelty, disdained for resisting civilization and Christianity, pitied for the inevitable loss of his land and culture and his probable extinction.[17] Robert Sayre described these attitudes toward "the Indian" thus: "He was, according to these stereotypes, solitary and ancient, simple and heroic, and doomed by a fate he could but rarely see."[18] This prophesied extinction went hand in hand with what was considered the Pilgrims' Progress, that is, the God-given idea of taming the land through conquest and saving souls through conversion. By reinterpreting American history and empire building as well as the metaphysics of Indian hating, Richard Drinnon makes it clear that in the twentieth century the presumption that one may expropriate land and natural resources was carried out even beyond the boundaries of this country.[19]

It is important to note that the Apache language, like most Athapaskan languages, resists borrowing from other languages as a way of enlarging the lexicon. This reveals how Apache experience mediates linguistic patterning.[20] Special attention is required in the linguistic organization of both daily and ceremonial life, kinship and its ideological aspects, politics and the encounters between Apache culture and American society. This requires a comprehensive understanding of Apache rhetoric, the ability to analyze and dissect speech in all of its artistic portrayals in the community. Understanding symbolic and cultural perspectives as well as kinship regarding the speaker allows for cross-cultural analysis and the possibility of looking at social change. My experience has involved all of the above in my ongoing research and study of the language, songs and chants, and dance of our girls' rite of passage, and especially in my efforts to understand the fascinating process of "trance" in the initiation dance in its social, psychological, and religious dimensions. This meditative, hypnotic trance when the initiate is carefully prepared brings on the ecstatic religious revelation, "possession" by the female deity, Ìsánáklésh. This rhythmic sensory stimulation combined with stress, exertion, and hyperventilation while dancing predominates this ceremony and is associated with trance behavior. The female initiation ceremony on the Apache reservation is the main surviving element of the Apache ceremonial system, which is centered on the visionary experience for acquiring diiyii, supernatural power; it is an intense religious experience that occurs during an altered state of consciousness. Initiation into this ceremony has become important in helping our young women achieve a positive Apache identity as exemplary women. A strict initiatory program of running, dancing, gathering traditional foods, ceremonial rocks, and minerals, as well as learning the Apache language and ceremonial rhetoric, is continued until the initiate, through the ceremonial singing, finds herself dancing in the ceremonial tipi, her feet softly touching the deerskin carefully placed at her favorite tipi pole. The late chanter Willeto Antonio told me during a ceremony in the summer of 2000 that the chanting holds the diiyii, the sacred power, of our language given to the initiate as she becomes the deity in the last day of her rite of passage.

The ceremony gives the initiates a process and new learning experience, which will allow her to reenter this altered state of consciousness without further preparation in order to reexperience her personal numinous power in future ceremonies focused on the meaning of Apache life. Possessors of diiyii learn to express religious thoughts that come from their imagination, and minute details provide insights into religious traditions and the shifting of human consciousness during ceremonies. This argument infers the rhetorical method used to explain or reach a conclusion or clarity. This shared consciousness connects us to our ancestors; their insight provides the Indigenous theory that informs our current-day observations. In my fieldwork and research on a non-written language, knowledge comes when my elders' Native theory interacts with my current data. Again, the study of language is important for all studies of Native American societies. Many of us are aware that our ancestors created sounds with meanings, and they managed to speak about the past and the future as well. They were skilled, and it is still obvious that they convey abstract ideas and speak intelligent sentences that had never been spoken before about the integration of religious beliefs and visions of the cosmos and life. As a Native scholar, I am interested in elucidating our oral narratives, especially our sacred narratives with other aspects of our culture. In my search for truth I have found that the metaphors in Apache have a heuristic function. However, they can also be used as rhetorical devices, especially when the speaker wants to protect information of a numinous nature or of a political stripe. In this case, my methodology provides different ways of looking at the culture and utilizing non-written rhetoric, especially since our language, belief system, and culture are still endangered. Calvin Martin's abstract of his journal article on Indian-White history reads,

> The writing of Indian-White history is impaired because Angloamerican historians in general have not familiarized themselves with the mythic world of North American Indians. In our historiography we tend either to project our thoughtworld onto the past or to accept and perpetuate that of contemporary White commentators and in doing so we seriously misrepresent what Indians themselves may have thought about the issue at hand. Increased attention and sensitivity to the Amerindian thoughtworld might result in our emphasizing different, generally ignored themes in the Indian-White dialogue, such as Power/Powerlessness, or revitalization/declension.[21]

He is referring to the ongoing "ethnocentric bias" utilized in interpreting other cultures using one's own culture as the point of reference. He insists that they should stop deluding themselves about the value of such history because it is essentially "White history": White reality, white "thoughtworld." As we seek to understand our own humanity to see the deeper meanings inherent in our sacred narratives and oral traditions, we see our belief system, deeply embedded in the world of nature and in our dreams and visions, as "power-full" symbolic wisdom. At that point, we enter responsibly into the lives of our familiar community and our ecosystem and come to understand our cosmological perspective. Deep study of our Indigenous history has taught us that the reality imposed on us by European-Americans is their perception of this land and its peoples. It is the opposite of our reality.

My study of religious expression and ritual rhetoric is designed to bring together ideas and methods from interdisciplinary fields to improve the understanding of the religious significance of Native American female rites of passage and their religious significance for my people. The initiate in her intense dance and rhythmic sensory stimulation brought about by the repetitive singing and chanting by the chanter Willeto Antonio and the singers of the ceremony creates a condition of emotional hyperarousal. The initiate is focused and alert, and clearly in an altered state of consciousness. I have also observed this condition in the Navajo girl's puberty ceremony and at the ceremony of the San Carlos Apache in Arizona. These sources of stimulation are also a feature of most rituals associated with trance behavior in other Native American cultures. An important work by Vivian Walter and W. Grey Walter included the comment that "rhythmic stimulation of the organ of hearing as a whole can be accomplished only by using a sound stimulus containing components of supra-liminal intensity over the whole gamut of audible frequencies—in effect, a steep fronted sound such as that produced by an untuned percussion instrument or explosion."[22] In the Apache case the instrument is an untuned deer-hoof rattle.

Silencing or ignoring our epistemologies has been devastating. Yet, in welcome contrast, there are some historians, like Robert Perez in his work on the Cuelgahen Nde, who excel at utilizing Native voices to cut through etic background noise. Cuelgahen Nde land is located on a vast area in Texas and Mexico. Perez clearly elucidates how the peoples' relationships to their land

and its sacred power, diiyii, comprise the underpinnings of a long-surviving culture. With respect for the people's metaphysics and what they say about themselves, his work becomes exemplary for today. Of course, the late Vine Deloria Jr.'s body of work honored in the book *Native Voices: American Indian Identity and Resistance* is of principal importance in all of its varied topics. My essay in that volume and all of the other contributions in the book were written by a cadre of scholars who are engaged in much needed intellectual insights and scholarship.[23] In her two books, *Gathering Moss: A Natural and Cultural History of Mosses* and *Braiding Sweetgrass: Indigenous Wisdom, Scientific Knowledge, and the Teachings of Plants*, Robin Wall Kimmerer, a scientist of Native American heritage, writes about the nature of mosses and sweetgrass from both a Native American and a scientific perspective, and she discusses exquisite metaphors for how to live close to nature.[24] I will always remember her work when I see moss or lichens on rocks, because my people consider them sacred healers. Finally, many Native American scholars and our allies are today sometimes pressured by academic disciplines to rely on trendy theories of the moment that are believed to accurately interpret Native American realities. As Bernard McGrane reminds us,

> Analytically, the desire of every "rational practice" is to cultivate and make reference to its reason for existence (Blum 1974). Hence, from this perspective, the decisive feature of anthropology is not the concrete state-of-affairs it speaks about, but rather the reason for its speech and the context, conditions and possibility of its speech. Its interest is itself, its being, and the maintenance of the conditions of its possibility (or, as Marx would say, the reproduction of the conditions of production). Its subject matter is concretely "primitive cultures"; analytically, itself. Anthropology as a contemporary discursive practice having a disciplinary identity has become institutionalized (Stocking 1987): as such it is an institution fundamentally involved in the reproduction of Western society. (citations in original)[25]

I would add that it has functioned primarily to misrepresent Indigenous peoples all over the world by calling them primitive. It is metaphorically time to go to Confession.

We are working to change this pressure in our academic endeavors. I have seen some new efforts and new approaches that are developing on the role of the ethnographer, as they enter a culture, in McGrane's book quoted above, *Beyond Anthropology*. How does one participate in qualitative field research without offending the people? How necessary is the language? Why is the belief system so important and what is its relationship to nature and the ecosystem? As my teacher Willeto Antonio once said to me in conversation, "You know what to do. You are doing it. You are on the pollen path." Richard Nelson, in his incisive work with the Koyukon people, tells us that the natural universe is nearly omnipotent, and it is only through acts of respect and propitiation that the well-being of humans is ensured.[26] Because spiritual power is everywhere in nature, gestures of reverence are nearly constant as people interact with their environment.

Another disruptive element for Native American cultures is the long convoluted geopolitical history of the Roman Catholic Church's rhetoric in our country up to the present. It is used to justify how the politically powerful have engaged Christianity to claim their divine right to control and govern the Native people of this land in order to exploit its rich resources. This Christian racist attitude persists to this day. Many people continue to think that there are no more Indians and that the land is here to be exploited. Today we can clearly see the devastation to the earth by this creed of exploitation. We live with the perils of climate change, rising seas, polluted air, fires, floods, and toxic food.

In discussing my study of religious expression and ritual rhetoric above and thinking about the challenges we have faced, I recollect with gratitude all of those who taught me and generously permitted a Native American woman academic to probe the nature of their scholarship and their private lives. My long-term relationships with them have considerably enriched my life. With respect I have followed their desire that I not use some of their names.

Apache oral traditions and philosophies at the most fundamental level are beliefs that nature and the supernatural world are interconnected. The rhetoric of origin stories defines proper human relationships and how nature functions. The origin stories explain why all of nature provides diiyii, sacred power. The Apache are in a constant search to recognize this power in the natural world because it is believed that if one uses the appropriate language, culture practices, ritual, and religious principles, one may acquire diiyii for a good, long life. The Apache worldview teaches that these the physical and spiritual worlds work together since nature has consciousness. The beginnings of our understanding of the origin and function of nature are revealed in our thoughtfully recorded sacred narratives and the extensive oral traditions that contain the rules for the proper use of language, religion, rhetoric, and behavior. These oral traditions reveal how the world came into being and how it and its natural entities transformed over time, which led the Apache to the idea that now we are related to all of nature and not better than nature. Animals and plants are to be treated with great respect because they have diiyii. The stories of our elders continue to reinforce these rules for appropriate speech and behavior.

This is what we have acquired and what we believe. The connection between the people and the cosmos is focused on everyday religious ritual and ceremony. When speaking to natural entities, religious rhetoric and careful thinking about whom one is addressing is necessary for a successful spiritual interchange. These traditions are still present-day beliefs and practices at Mescalero. Many Apache today are also Christians. Those that I have spoken with say that for them they are still also committed to Apache beliefs. What works for one person may not work for another, but they are all respected. While they express sentiments like this, many of my people are concerned with current-day American problems, especially those that concern the young people. Some of my Sun Clan relatives say to me that probably the young people are not following Apache belief system and are too focused on Western values. This is why it is imperative that we continue our rites of passage that teach them how to be good Apache by strengthening their Native identity in learning our language and history and following our lifeway. Watching the facial expressions of my granddaughter, Emily, when she sat in my class on religion and ecology during winter quarter of 2019, I realized that my work will continue, and for that I am forever grateful.

This wisdom provides the framework for our current studies of Native American culture, history, astronomy, and biology.[27] These efforts allow us to focus on Native American realities that our ancestors charged us with remembering. It is their blood memory that guides and shapes our scholarship. As students, we are trained to ask questions about nature with the tools of science. As Native Americans, we know that plants and animals are our oldest teachers. Why? Because we are taught to pay deep and careful attention to our ecosystems. Today we should work to bring these two views of knowledge together. What can we learn from the respectful environmentalist Christian monk, Thomas Berry?[28] We can learn that all people need the awakening of a wider ecological knowledge and consciousness. This requires the celebration of our reciprocal relationships with the rest of the living world so that we can attentively listen to the languages of other beings or to their silence. This is how we begin to be capable of understanding the generous beauty of the earth. This is how we begin to know how to give our gifts in return. This requires passion and takes us on a journey, both religious and scientific, as sacred as it is historical, as clever as it is wise. We can begin to understand that the factual objective approach of science can be learned and combined with the ancient knowledge of Indigenous peoples. Everyone who cares about the environment, everyone on earth, needs to understand reverence for the earth. It is what we need to survive. We must learn to be the keepers of the fire with allegiance to each other and gratitude for the gifts of creation. We must become Indigenous to our place.

Hold out your hands and let me lay upon them sacred cattail pollen— personally gathered. Breathe it in and remember things you did not know that you forgot, such as properly building a fire, caring for the land, and holding your grandmother in your arms and listening to her wisdom.

We have only to look at the struggle to maintain the land and religious beliefs of the Oglala Sioux of the Black Hills in South Dakota, the Chumash of Point Conception in California, and the Hopi of Black Mesa in Arizona, just to name a few of many religious sites that are threatened, to see the egregious effects of misunderstanding nature and Indigenous religious traditions. Institutional policies of both church and state continue to wreak cultural extinction upon Native Americans. As the book *Native Voices* mentioned above makes clear, Native American responses to these policies are evident today in the organized effort to stop the destruction and exploitation of the land and natural resources, and in the effort to correct insensitive and disrespectful attitudes toward Native American beliefs and their corresponding sacred lands.[29]

In many of these traditions, land acquisition by others is still seen as a violation of the sacred. Native Americans are often taught at a young age to be caretakers of this land and that wealth is measured by the way one's life has been lived, by one's generosity, by one's knowledge of the ecosystem, and by how one treats others, and not by how much land one owns. Wisdom and rhetoric are generally considered a form of power to persuade others with the goal of helping others to maintain the ecological balance of the natural world. Native American attempts at survival over the past two centuries have been, and continue to be, a struggle to preserve these sacred values. Our religious protocol teaches us how to live in balance. This is critically important since Apache is not a written language and we must attentively listen to our elders reveal the wisdom that we inherit from our oral traditions. This knowledge connects us to and is informed by our cultural values, rituals, ceremonies, and our philosophical traditions.

Notes

1.   N. Scott Momaday, *House Made of Dawn* (New York: Harper & Row, 1968), 140.

2.   Annette Angela Portillo, *Sovereign Stories and Blood Memories: Native American Women's Autobiography* (Albuquerque: University of New Mexico Press, 2017), 2–4.

3.   Simon Appolloni, "The Roman Catholic Tradition in Conversation with Thomas Berry's Fourfold Wisdom," *Religions* 6, no. 3 (2015): 794–818.

4.   Paul Tillich, *Dynamics of Faith* (New York: Harper, 1957), 4–5.

5.   Alfonzo Ortiz, "San Juan Pueblo," in *Handbook of North American Indians*, ed. William C. Sturtevant, vol. 9, *Southwest*, ed. Alfonzo Ortiz (Washington, DC: Smithsonian Institution, 1979), 283.

6.   Robert F. Heizer and Albert B. Elsasser, *The Natural World of the California Indians* (Berkeley: University of California Press, 1980), 220.

7.   Calvin Martin, "The Metaphysics of Writing Indian-White History," *Ethnohistory* 26, no. 2 (Spring 1979): 153–59.

8.   Ninian Smart, *The World's Religions*, North and South American ed. (Englewood Cliffs, NJ: Prentice Hall, 1989), 14.

9.   Calvin Martin, *Keepers of the Game: Indian-Animal Relationships and the Fur Trade* (Berkeley: University of California Press, 1978), 157–88.

10.   See Åke Hultkrantz, *The Religions of the American Indians* (Berkeley: University of California Press, 1979); Åke Hultkrantz, *The Study of American Indian Religions* (New York: Crossroad Publishing, 1983); Peggy V. Beck and Anna Lee Walters, *The Sacred: Ways of Knowledge, Sources of Life* (Tsaile, AZ: Navajo Community College, 1977); Black Elk, *The Sacred Pipe: Black Elk's Account of the Seven Rites of the Oglala Sioux*, ed. Joseph Epes Brown (Norman: University of Oklahoma Press, 1953); Vine Deloria Jr., *God Is Red* (New York: Grosset & Dunlap, 1973); Sam D. Gill, *Native American Traditions: Sources and Interpretations* (Belmont, CA: Wadsworth Publishing, 1983); Gary Witherspoon, *Language*

and Art in the Navajo Universe (Ann Arbor: University of Michigan Press, 1977); and Keith H. Basso, *Wisdom Sits in Places: Landscape and Language among the Western Apache* (Albuquerque: University of New Mexico Press, 1996).

11.   Washington Matthews, "The Mountain Chant: A Navajo Ceremony," *Annual Report of the Bureau of American Ethnology to the Secretary of the Smithsonian Institution* 5 (1883–1884): 385–467. The work was published as a stand-alone book in 1888. See Washington Matthews, *The Mountain Chant: A Navajo Ceremony* (Washington, DC: Government Printing Office, 1888).

12.   Franc J. Newcomb and Gladys A. Reichard, *Sandpaintings of the Navajo Shooting Chant* (New York: Dover Publications, 1975), 1. Newcomb and Gladys attribute the date for Matthews, "The Mountain Chant: A Navajo Ceremony," as 1887. But, as referenced in note 11, the standalone book was actually published in 1888.

13.   Gladys A. Reichard, *Navaho Religion: A Study of Symbolism* (New York: Pantheon Books, 1950).

14.   Witherspoon, *Language and Art*, 13–149.

15.   Catherine L. Albanese, *America, Religions and Religion* (Belmont, CA: Wadsworth Publishing, 1981), 19–38.

16.   Roy Harvey Pearce, *The Savages of America: A Study of the Indian and the Idea of Civilization* (Baltimore: Johns Hopkins Press, 1953), 3–49.

17.   Pearce, *Savages of America*, 3–49.

18.   Robert F. Sayre, *Thoreau and the American Indians* (Princeton, NJ: Princeton University Press, 1977), 6.

19.   Richard Drinnon, *Facing West: The Metaphysics of Indian-Hating and Empire-Building* (New York: New American Library, 1980), xvii–xviii.

20.   Sally Rice, "Our Language Is Very Literal," in *Endangered Metaphors*, ed. Anna Idström, Elisabeth Piirainen, and Tiber Falzett (Amsterdam: John Benjamins Publishing, 2012), 23–25.

21.   Martin, "Metaphysics of Writing," abstract, 153.

22.   Vivian J. Walter and W. Grey Walter, "The Central Effects of Rhythmic Sensory Stimulation," *Electroencephalography and Clinical Neurophysiology* 1, no. 1 (February 1949): 82. See also Wolfgang G. Jilek, "Altered States of Consciousness in North American Indian Ceremonials," *Ethos* 10, no. 4 (Winter 1982): 326–43.

23.   Richard A. Grounds, George E. Tinker, and David E. Wilkins, eds., *Native Voices: American Indian Identity and Resistance* (Lawrence: University Press of Kansas, 2003).

24.   Robin Wall Kimmerer, *Gathering Moss: A Natural and Cultural History of Mosses* (Corvallis: Oregon State University Press, 2003); Robin Wall Kimmerer, *Braiding Sweetgrass: Indigenous Wisdom, Scientific Knowledge, and the Teachings of Plants* (Minneapolis: Milkweed Editions, 2013).

25.   Bernard McGrane, *Beyond Anthropology: Society and the Other* (New York: Columbia University Press, 1989), 5.

26.   Richard K. Nelson, *Make Prayers to the Raven: A Koyukon View of the Northern Forest* (Chicago: University of Chicago Press, 1983).

27.   For two examples, see Kimmerer, *Gathering Moss*; and Kimmerer, *Braiding Sweet-grass*.

28.   See, for example, Thomas Berry, *The Dream of the Earth* (San Francisco: Sierra Club Books, 1988).

29.   Grounds, Tinker, and Wilkins, eds., *Native Voices*.

CHAPTER EIGHT

Why We Fish

Decolonizing Salmon Rhetorics and Governance

CUTCHA RISLING BALDY

Introduction

In 2002 I was standing just up the hill from the shores of the Trinity River looking out over the water with my grandfather, Milton Baldy. Our communities were still reeling from the recent fish kill, where thousands upon thousands of adult Chinook salmon had died along the shores of the Klamath River as they were returning home to spawn. The higher-than-normal water temperatures and low water flows had contributed to this man-made disaster that demonstrated how ongoing policies of water seizure were not only disastrous for our fish, but also were disastrous for our people.[1] My grandfather was a strong and stolid man. He was born and raised on the Hoopa Valley Indian Reservation. His strength and fortitude had come from years in the military as well as his well-known work ethic. He was also a fisherman and a hunter. His stories about the fish in our rivers were much like the other elders I have spoken to: the rivers used to run silver with salmon; you could walk along the backs of the fish; it was a sight to behold. But standing with him that day as we looked over the river, my grandfather's voice cracked. "What do you think this means for our world?" he asked me. "What does this mean for the next generations?"

There was a palpable mourning that happened in Native communities in

Northwest California because of the 2002 fish kill. This was yet another demonstration of the ongoing impacts of settler colonial government regulations and policies that threaten not only the environment, but also the health and well-being of our people and future generations. The seizure and diversion of water from our rivers has resulted in ongoing environmental impacts that clearly demonstrate how water diversion is detrimental and often goes against the tenets of sustainability and environmental justice that are supposed to be a part of California public policy.[2] We know that our rivers are suffering because of the continued seizure and diversion of water. We live with the impacts every day. There are many sociocultural and health impacts that result from water diversion policies that prioritize the economy rather than the protection of endangered species and environmental justice.[3] Our communities not only understand the sociocultural and health connections to our water and environment, but also we live them. We are people of place, and our connections have been forged for time immemorial. Our interconnection and interrelationship to our worlds is, as Mark Rifkin so deftly explains, "Beyond Settler Time."[4]

This chapter begins by highlighting a history of salmon governance in California that has ignored rhetorics of relationship for rhetorics of economy and science, which has in turn led to devastating consequences not only for the salmon but also for Native peoples. I then turn to exploring the role of rhetorical sovereignty in relation to protecting the salmon. As Scott Lyons so deftly explores in his work on rhetorical sovereignty, this chapter will now examine the history of rhetorical imperialism that attempts to dismantle the relationship between salmon and Indigenous peoples through violence and genocide while justifying these actions through legislative terminology and public discourse that devalues Indigenous epistemological relationships with more-than-human beings. However, I also investigate how salmon rhetorics are building and shaping rhetorical sovereignty among California Indian people who continuously "determine their own communicative needs and desires . . . to decide for themselves the goals, modes, styles and languages of public discourse."[5] My goal is to articulate how California Indian salmon rhetorics demonstrate rhetorical sovereignty and to emphasize "our full archive" to "recognize its possibilities."[6] Through my discussion of Northwest California salmon rhetorics, I aim to demonstrate how we are intervening on policy that would decenter our salmon rhetorics. We are utilizing the way we talk about salmon to build better salmon governance and policy. As Lyons so clearly argues, "he who sets the terms, sets the limits," and my hope is that validating California Indian salmon rhetorics in this chapter's analysis can help inspire reclamation of terms and discourse that frame rhetorical sovereignty through relationships to salmon and other more-than-human relatives. As Lisa King explains, "To claim rhetorical sovereignty is to claim the right to determine communicative need and the right to participate in the process of public image making and meaning making."[7] In California, our rhetorics of salmon relationship and ancestral connection can bring us toward environmental and social justice, and my hope is that this chapter can inspire and support ongoing efforts for California Indian peoples to build a decolonized salmon governance.

I would like to begin with an observation about our more-than-human relatives. The general convention is to refer to nonhuman relatives as "other-than-human" based on the work of A. Irving Hallowell.[8] However, in my estimation, that terminology has shortcomings. Instead, I draw here from and honor the work of Metis Indigenous feminist scholar Zoe Todd, who writes that through her work she has "finally come to understand that my Métis dad and non-Indigenous mom's work in teaching me about the lands, waters, fish, berries, invertebrates and other beings of where I grew up was an instructive form of philosophy and praxis which imbued within me a sense of my reciprocal responsibilities to place, more-than-human beings and time."[9] In our Hupa tradition, we recognize "more-than-human beings" as our relatives. But, on the other hand, we also recognize our dependence on them and so regard them in a way that understands this relationship as complex, dynamic, and informed by our practices of reciprocity and respect. The term "more-than-human" places the respect for these our relatives as not just in comparison to what it means to be "human" and does not place them into the realm of "other," but instead as relatives whose lived knowledges afford them great respect.

In Northwest California, Native peoples, much like Indigenous peoples around the world, see ourselves as interconnected with the environment, and we often speak of more-than-human beings (animals, flora, fauna, water, rocks, etc.) as relatives. The rivers that run through all lands connect us; they are the circulatory system of this world. We learn about our rivers as veins, or arteries, as necessary to the basic functioning of our world. "What happens," our elders will ask us, "when you dam up your artery? You can cause major damage to your entire body. Each and every part of this system works together to keep you healthy and functioning. It is the same with our rivers." It is also the same for the species that share our rivers. Coho salmon (*qehs* in the Hupa language) and Chinook salmon (*chwulo:q'e'*) are born in the Trinity River that runs through the center of the Hoopa Valley (*Na:tini-xw:*, where the trails lead back). They travel from the Trinity down to the Klamath River, and finally to the mouth of the Klamath, where they live until they return in the spring and fall to spawn. Our salmon, much as our people, return. Our trails (including the river) lead us back to Na:tini-xw:, where the trails return.

The Native peoples of Northwest California rely on salmon, and in Northwest California salmon are central to several ceremonies, cultural practices, creation stories, and even political and social movements. The Trinity River for the Hupa is a spiritual/cultural center of the valley. We perform many of our ceremonies along or with the river. Our world renewal ceremonies include the *ta:'ułtul* (the boat dance) that is performed in canoes on the river. Some of our ceremonies require that participants ceremonially bathe in the river. Many of our ceremonies also include the ritual praying for and eating of salmon. Salmon are not only a central species to our way of life, but they are also a keystone species for our waters. The ecosystem depends on them so much that if they go extinct there will be wide-ranging disastrous environmental impacts. According to the Wild Salmon Center, at least 137 different species depend on wild salmon. Salmon runs are also key to pushing vast amounts of marine nutrients from the ocean to the headwaters of "otherwise low productivity rivers."[10]

Indigenous peoples' understanding of the natural environment, ecosystems, botany, and animal species have been broadly encapsulated in the commonly used term "Traditional Ecological Knowledge" (TEK). In a TEK framework, "all things are connected" and "all things are related."[11] Our knowledge is based on thousands upon thousands of years of empirical evidence.[12] And as Western science continues to explore the interconnectedness of the environment, we can now see many connections between the field of ecology and TEK. While the concept of interconnected environmental systems is less than 150 years old in Western science, TEK is a "practical methodological tool for investigating the natural world and drawing conclusions about it that can serve as guides for understanding nature and living comfortably within it."[13] Several leading Indigenous scholars have explored the pitfalls and pratfalls of defining TEK. Kyle Powys Whyte notes, "There is a tendency to want to determine one definition for TEK that can satisfy every stakeholder in every situation. Yet a scan of environmental science and policy literatures reveals there to be differences in definitions that make it difficult to form a consensus."[14] Whyte's foundational work understands TEK as a "collaborative concept" that invites "diverse populations to continually learn from one another about how each approaches the very question of 'knowledge' in the first place, and how these different approaches can work together to better steward and manage the environment and natural resources."[15] Seafha Ramos notes that for the Yurok people in Northwest California TEK is considered a "way of life" and "a system where Yurok people and wildlife collaboratively strive to create and maintain balance of the Earth via physical and spiritual management in tandem."[16] Melissa K. Nelson reminds us that TEK is made up of "millennia-old" knowledge systems that are "tribally and geographically specific."[17] Nelson alternates between referring to TEK and "native science" throughout her work. Noted Indigenous activist and scholar Winona LaDuke adds that TEK is "culturally and spiritually" based and "is founded on spiritual-cultural instructions from 'time-immemorial' and on generations of careful observation within an ecosystem of continuous residence."[18] LaDuke pointedly argues that "this knowledge represents the clearest empirically based system for resource management and ecosystem protection in North America."[19] Much of the work in defining TEK done by Indigenous scholars has been to bridge rhetorics and methodologies of "traditional knowledge" and "scientific knowledge." Most Western scientific research still does not recognize or include TEK understandings, practices, or findings in their research methodologies, though TEK methodologies and findings are consistently proven to not only mirror Western scientific findings but also strengthen their outcomes and better inform their results and conclusions. Ramos provides an overview of studies in "forestry, fire ecology, and fisheries" as well as wildlife management and conservation that have applied TEK in their research.[20] Ramos concludes that "there is a need for natural resource managers and policymakers to gain a clearer understanding of the perspectives of Indigenous peoples in TEK and natural resources matters."[21] Ramos ties this to "using equitable terminology when referencing TEK in conjunction with Western Science."[22]

Ramos recognizes that terminologies or the rhetorics of "science," which is consistently separated from Traditional Ecological Knowledge, is problematic as it creates an idea that TEK is not science, or not equal to science. The rhetorics of science have been used to separate nature and humans and to dispossess Native people of relationships to the more-than-human world.[23] Relatives become "resources" under a Western scientific framework, and the separation between human and more-than-human beings is solidified through the language and rhetorics of science that dominate policies, laws, and governance. Currently, policies involving natural resource management solidify the rhetorics of Western science as critical to policy making and governance. As Native people, our interrelationship with a "natural resource" is often considered romantic or New Age, and our knowledges, our complex philosophies, theories, and methodologies of research are categorized as myths, legends, or "fables of a prehistoric Noble Savage."[24]

The rhetorics of Western science continue to influence salmon governance throughout the United States. Historically, the rhetorics of Western science have been deeply intertwined with rhetorics of colonization and capitalism that seek to both quantify and monetize relationships between more-than-human relatives and human beings. Contemporary issues of salmon governance have often focused on what can be "scientifically proven" or what kind of impacts can be quantified. Enshrined in the rhetorics of salmon governance in the State of California is not only a reliance on Western scientific conclusions, but also a classification of salmon as "economic resources" or "natural resources." Salmon are also constantly treated as impediments to economic development, and though they have recently been added to the endangered species list in several regions, this does not mean that government agencies make decisions that incorporate salmon protection. Native tribes who are constantly fighting as allies of the salmon are often treated as stakeholders rather than sovereign nations or as relatives of the salmon. Their deep interpersonal relationships with salmon are not acknowledged in salmon governance. Coleen Fox, Nick Reo, et al. argue that

Indigenous communities need to be present physically and intellectually in restoration and governance—not just as consultants—but present politically and spiritually.[25] Currently, in the state of California, the rhetorics that shape the interpretations, statutes, and policy decisions do not recognize tribal relationships with salmon but instead treat tribal involvement in salmon governance as "consultation" rather than as integral and ancestral.

Native peoples see salmon as relatives, or as kin. To acknowledge that interrelationship is paramount to living a healthy and balanced lifestyle. Todd refers to the many ways that fish are understood in Native epistemologies as "pluralities." Fish are kin, food, identity, health, family, teachers, and are key to spiritual practices, social health, and political sovereignty.[26] Fish and humans have a shared history, and throughout Northwest California, fish are important parts of gauging the health of the natural environment. Tribes throughout Northwest California developed complex systems of politics and governance that were informed by their ongoing relationship through fish. Tribes had to negotiate and manage spatial and temporal relationships through fish. Indigenous people also managed and monitored fish, much as scientists do today. Native people monitored numbers of fish, the impact of fishing practices on spawning and migration, and the impact of water quality during various fish seasons.

The relationships between human and salmon were generative and iterative. The iterative nature of salmon relationships is found in the complex understandings of salmon life cycles by Indigenous peoples from many different regions. Tribal people usually have multiple terms for salmon that can denote species classifications and also illustrate the relationship between people and salmon. In the Hupa language, terms for salmon were prolific and demarcate how Hupa people were documenting species classifications as well as species behavior. The generalized term for fish or salmon (*Oncorhynchus*) is *ło:q'*, while the more specialized term, *da:jahl*, is how the Hupa refer to the salmon that runs in the late fall, or the dog salmon, which is likely a reference to male chum salmon (*Oncorhynchus keta*). Additionally, *chwulo:q'e'* specifies the Chinook salmon (*Onchorhynchus tshawtscha*), and *xulo:q'e'* designates silverside salmon, or the first part of the spring run of king salmon. Finally, qehs refers to the hookbill salmon, likely referencing coho salmon. The Hupa were also adept in their understanding of the differing runs of salmon, with one in the fall and one in the spring. Aside from denoting xulo:q'e' as the "first part of the *spring run* of king salmon," their word for mockingbird or nightingale, *ło:q'-chwo*, is specifically tied to the story of "Salmon's Grandmother" and explains how this yellow-breasted bird comes up the river in May with the first spring run of king salmon, which also marks a difference between the spring and fall runs. It was just in 2017 that researchers from the University of California, Davis, led by Michael Miller published their findings of the genetic differences between spring run Chinook (king) salmon and fall Chinook. Miller found that "the difference between spring and fall run chinook is a small change in a single gene. This change occurred only once in Chinook's evolutionary history."[27] The classification of spring Chinook as a genetically separate species from the fall Chinook could be key to ongoing efforts for protecting the spring salmon, who often suffer from high temperatures in the water due to dams and the ongoing seizure of water from the rivers. In 2017 when these findings were released, Leaf Hillman, the Karuk natural resources director, was quoted in a Karuk Tribe press release as saying, "We have known all along that fall Chinook and spring Chinook, or ishyâat, are a distinct species. . . . It's about time Western science catches up to traditional wisdom since that's what is needed to make the policy changes necessary to save this part of our culture."[28]

Indigenous peoples have distinct, informed, ancient knowledges about the natural world as a result of their ongoing interconnection to land and more-than-human relatives. This includes a science that has matured over thousands of years, building empirical evidence and methodologies based on much longer relationships with our more-than-human relatives. I can recall speaking with my elders growing up about their ongoing work with Western scientists, ethnographers, and anthropologists. They would often refer to them as very "young," not only in terms of their age or maturity, but also in terms of their respective discipline's knowledge of the world. "Their science is young; their knowledge is young." They would remark how the 150 years of knowledge these Western scientists and scholars were building in their academic disciplines was still in the early phases of understanding the world. The more I thought about it, the more it made sense to me. Western disciplines were just beginning to build knowledge about this place and about the more-than-human beings that we share the world with, knowledge that we had developed over many thousands of years. This understanding of the Indigenous present as not necessarily existing in a common timeframe with a settler present is deftly explored by Rifkin in his book *Beyond Settler Time*. Rifkin also explores how the relationship between settler and land is new, so that Indigenous knowledge and Indigenous modernity is actually much different in its temporal existence than a settler modernity. He names this as "discrepant temporalities."[29] At one point, I was listening to my great-uncle explain about his experiences working with an anthropologist when he exclaimed, "It's like working with a toddler sometimes! They just think they know." The generosity and humor by which elders would work with academics and scientists still puts a smile on my face to this day.

As Western science continues to make "new discoveries" of knowledges that are already a part of an Indigenous ecological knowledge, Indigenous peoples are also utilizing these scientific findings to help protect our more-than-human relatives like the salmon. The Karuk Tribe has started the process to have the spring Chinook in the Klamath River added to the endangered species list.[30] In the past, federal agencies have declined to add the spring Chinook because they argued that the fall Chinook is the same species and could therefore develop the same behavior to maintain the spring run. With these scientific findings, it becomes easier for tribes to argue for continued protection of salmon. Once again, salmon governance seemingly hinges on Western science confirming traditional knowledge before that knowledge can be enveloped into policies, laws, and procedures for salmon conservation, protection, and management. This happens despite there being examples across tribes throughout Northwest California of specific and integral knowledges of salmon species.

In this chapter I am chiefly concerned with Indigenous salmon rhetorics, with a particular focus on Northwest California, in part because I am tied to three tribes (the Hupa, Yurok, and Karuk) that live along significant California rivers. I offer my words here not only as a researcher, but also as someone who grew up on the shores of the Trinity and Klamath Rivers, who fished these rivers with my father and grandfather, and who has seen the impact on our communities as we are faced with toxic water, the continuing threats of fish kills, and the ongoing efforts to prevent adequate water flows for our cultural and ceremonial practices.[31] The Hupa, Yurok, and Karuk, along with other tribes, have been central to work being done throughout Northwest California to protect salmon. We continue to honor our interrelationship with our salmon relatives, to testify at public hearings, to protest and plead with legislatures, and to fight for the rights of salmon. We also, importantly, are reinforcing our relationship to salmon, making this relationship central to our testimonies and our public activism. We have also begun work to envelop our salmon relationship into our own laws, policies, resolutions, and constitutions.

We must continue to take responsibility for our relationships with our more-than-human relatives by demonstrating and utilizing our salmon rhetorics to dismantle settler colonial rhetorical logics that value salmon only as a "resource." As Nelson writes, "Knowing, remembering, practicing, and implementing these place-based native sciences also comes with a great responsibility. Greg Cajete has called this a practice of sacred ecology or sacred sciences."[32] And Andrea Riley-Mukavetz and Malea Powell further explain: "This orientation to that set of relations, and the responsibilities that arise from maintaining 'right' relations, then forms the ambiguous boundaries of something we call *indigenous rhetorical practices.*"[33] I am interested in this chapter in exploring how analyzing our salmon rhetorics reveal the central role of our relationships with our salmon in our histories and our communities. Considering that much of our recent history has been dominated by attempts to shame, disrupt, and sever our salmon relationships, it is important to recognize how we continue to practice salmon rhetorics that utilize our ancient interconnections with salmon to solidify our current interrelationships with salmon.

This exploration and analysis of rhetorics that includes California Indian rhetorical strategies and community discourse is also important for the future development of policy, law, and political governance. Salmon rhetorics as political and legal frameworks has been previously explored by Todd, who acknowledges that "Indigenous relationships to 'other-than-human' [are] concrete sites of political and legal exchange that can inform a narrative that de-anthrpocentrizes current Indigenous-State discourse."[34] Todd explores these relationships with salmon as disrupting current policy frameworks that only see fish as a resource meant for extraction. She looks at fish as "active sites of negotiation" and as facilitating "discussions about history, governance, cosmologies, and legal orders that community members actively seek to address in a variety of ways. In this manner, fish and the act of fishing may initiate difficult conversations that may be avoided in other contexts."[35] Lori Biondini explains in her own exploration of salmon pluralities and the Hoopa Valley tribe that "people and fish are, again, agents in political landscapes and both equally affected by the processes of colonization and decolonization."[36] Leontina Hormel and Kari Norgaard echo this sentiment, explaining that "strong spiritual and emotional bonds to all life forms, and an instilled sense of responsibility to them, have served as counter-hegemonic tools."[37] Biondini concludes, "It follows that fish pluralities can be mobilized in ways that place social and cultural relationship [*sic*] on par with or above economies, to resist and provide alternatives to a capitalist structure."[38]

Salmon are at the forefront of some of the biggest environmental and economic development issues that continue to be hard fought in courts and have major impacts on water policy, land use, and development. Indigenous peoples throughout the United States face some of the harshest consequences of climate change, as they are also confronted with ongoing challenges to their sovereignty and self-determination and they must still attempt to navigate Western political frameworks that are based on Western worldviews. Glen Coulthard argues that the state uses discourses of "cultural rights," and then dictates the nature of those rights—often to the detriment of Indigenous peoples and the more-than-human beings who share this world with us.[39] Coulthard's rejection of state rhetorics and political governance systems reminds us that decolonization is not going to be built with Western frameworks. Instead, we need to stress our own knowledges and frameworks to build governance that values relationships and connectedness and cultural, social, spiritual practices. If we are to reclaim political spaces, we need to reclaim our political rhetorics, like our salmon rhetorics, to build salmon governance. It is fish that sustains us, it is fish that will sustain us as we move toward our decolonial futures.

From Gold Rush to Fish Kill[40]

Humboldt County, in far Northern California, is often touted for its pristine landscapes and world-renowned recreational activities. It is home to coastal redwood forests that are almost mythological in scope, with towering giants that have been written about by explorers, naturalists, and eco-adventurers. Ask about Humboldt County, and you are likely to hear about the "hippies" or the liberal activists. You may even learn about how the city of Arcata had, at one point, a majority Green Party city council. The Humboldt County mythology is centered around the protection of "nature," and we are often praised for how we prevent development of our beaches or our careful considerations of building big-box stores or allowing corporations into our small towns. Humboldt County's history is also steeped in romanticizing the California Gold Rush, which continues to be taught in our state school curriculum and often reenacted in theme parks or museums. California as a state exalts the Gold Rush as a time of great prosperity, a chance for settlers to fulfill their American Dream. Humboldt County was founded as part of the Gold Rush. Thousands of people flooded into the region once gold was discovered. The mentality of this massive influx was that of exploitation, a willingness to do whatever it took to extract as much gold and resources as they could from the region. This meant that California Indians were considered in the way, and the immediate response by this "marauding horde" of people rushing into California was an attempted extermination of California Indian people.[41] Brendan Lindsay describes early California settlers as having "a culture organized around the dispossession and murder of California Indians."[42] Sherburne Cook estimates that close to 90 percent of the California Indian population died during the years between 1770 and 1900, and Hupa scholar Stephanie Lumsden notes that "during California's transition into US statehood, a series of heinous laws were passed to protect settlers' land interests and desire for gold. These laws of the 1850s and 1860s legalized Indian slavery, directly funded genocide, allowed for blatant land theft, and facilitated the kidnapping of Indian children."[43] The efforts to eradicate California Indian people included passing laws that legalized volunteer militias that were paid for killing Native people and turning in their scalps and heads; laws that legalized the kidnapping, selling, and enslavement of California Indian people (which was primarily exercised against children and women); and laws that prevented Native people from leaving their reservation through threats of being "shot on sight."[44] Benjamin Madley notes that "California governors called out or authorized no fewer than 24 state militia expeditions between 1850 and 1861, which killed at least 1,340 California

Indians. State legislators also passed three bills in the 1850s that raised up to $1.51 million to fund these operations—a great deal of money at the time—for past and future anti-Indian militia operations."[45]

Humboldt County citizens participated in this legalized genocide as well. Jack Norton's seminal work, *Genocide in Northwest California: When Our Worlds Cried*, describes Humboldt County as a "deranged frontier." He notes, "These crimes were often directly incited by people who held political as well as economic power within the community. . . . In addition, the public was continually urged to commit genocide by the local newspaper."[46] Norton also highlights how the Gold Rush required the removal, enslavement, and indiscriminate killing of Native people in order to build the "prosperity" of the Humboldt County region. "Its goal," he writes, "was to appropriate the lands and resources of the original owners. It was assumed that if the native had no legal rights, and no guarantees of human dignity, then clearly he had no claim to hold the land."[47] The Gold Rush era not only included the outright killing and enslavement of Native peoples, but also it was extremely detrimental to the environment, effectively constituting an "ecocide," as discussed by Chisa Oros.[48] Oros explains:

> The treatment of Indigenous peoples in the region worked in tandem and as an echo of the violence against the natural world during this period. During the Gold Rush in northern California, it is estimated that gold miners dug up twelve-billion tons of earth. Some examples of destructive mining practices here in northern California include water cannon strip mining with massive and powerful cannons (sometimes called monitors), dredging, sluice mining, explosive mining of hillsides and canyons, unreinforced tunneling, river and stream damming, and the manual digging out [of] hillsides. In many of these situations, sediment gathered was treated with methylmercury, also called mercury or quicksilver, in order to gather the gold bits and separate the lucrative product from other minerals the miners did not have interest in. The mercury, a highly toxic metal, was washed away or discarded on the banks of rivers or outside the mines in large pits. I identify this type of destruction as being aligned with the concept of ecocide, and I find ecocide to best define the environmental destruction and exploitation committed by settlers in northern California during the Gold Rush.[49]

Along with the attempts to destroy the environment in the name of seizing as much gold as possible, miners also began clear-cutting the old-growth forests, which often resulted in soil collapse that led to disastrous results for the local ecosystem. Oros notes, "The bioaccumulation of mercury in fish and other water species in local rivers such as the Klamath, Trinity, Salmon, Mad, Eel, Van Duzen, Eel, Elk, Mattole, and Smith occurred in tandem with the massive impacts of debris and sediment, called slickens, run-off from mountain and hillside destruction and also the soil erosion from clear cuts."[50] These methods of destruction also led to habitat loss, contamination of waters, and contamination of fish and other wildlife. Settlers were not concerned with sustainable practices, often overfishing, overharvesting, and overhunting various regions. Fish canneries were established along some of the rivers, and there were instances where settlers took hundreds or thousands of fish from the river.[51]

Ultimately, gold would prove less profitable in the region than expected, and many of the Gold Rush migrants would instead turn to the seizing and claiming of Indigenous lands as private property. Lands that were the sites of immense violence and forced removal were claimed or sold. Rights to water, streams, and other natural resources were "claimed" to build private property ownership in the region. To this day, there are landowners who trace their rights to land and water back to deeds that were made at the end of the Gold Rush. The lasting effects of the "ecocide" of the Gold Rush are still wreaking havoc on the environment as well. High levels of mercury can still be detected in some lakes, streams, and fish.

The founding of California, and by extension Humboldt County, demonstrated how the settler colonial worldview included ongoing genocidal policies that not only attempted to kill California Indian peoples but also their more-than-human relatives. Diminishing the fish not only affected the food supply of Native peoples, but it also enacted a cultural genocide intended to separate humans from nature and build private property ownership. Continuing policies of the federal government, like allotment, were instituted to assimilate Native peoples and force them to adopt capitalistic views of the land, fish, and other "natural resources." These assimilative policies also included boarding schools, the establishment of military forts, and the outlawing of Native religious practices. "Rushing" also continued throughout the region: the timber rush and various mineral rushes continued the exploitation of both the land and resources. This mentality was also foundational to development projects that followed. The Bureau of Reclamation finished the Klamath Project in the 1960s, which built multiple irrigation and hydroelectric dam projects. Four large dams were installed on the Klamath River that resulted in lower water flows and worsening conditions for salmon. Farming and ranching practices continued to cause major problems with natural resource management in Northern California. Much of the water that is seized from the rivers in the Humboldt County region is used for supporting Central Valley farming. Throughout the history of California, agriculture has been privileged as foundational to ongoing economic development. Following the Gold Rush, farming became one of the fastest-growing industries in California. Settlers began to dam, dike, and drain watersheds for farming. Agriculture became a key way that settler colonial dominance could be demarcated, solidified, documented, and archived so that "rightful claims" to ownership were traced back to settlers and pioneers. Eve Tuck and K. Wayne Yang argue that settler colonialism remakes land into property and restricts human-land relationships to property and capital.[52] Further, Indigenous relationships to land are made primitive, abnormal, and abhorrent. This justifies the dispossession of land from Indigenous peoples by making it seem like they were not utilizing the land and also that their continuing interrelationship with land and more-than-human relatives is not legally sound or even "real," but instead is considered primitive and backward. The rhetoric of landownership, property rights, development, and natural resources became important to further degrade Native claims to the land. Our rhetorics of relationship and interrelationship were treated as less-than and primitive, replaced by rhetorics of terra nullius, wilderness, Manifest Destiny, and "discovery."

Settler colonial rhetorics like the above were not only enshrined in law and policy. They became part of an assimilative education system meant to, in the famous words of Richard Pratt, the architect of the Indian boarding school system, "kill the Indian, save the man."[53] Native children were forcibly removed from their families and taken to boarding schools that attempted to teach them Christianity and capitalistic values focused on training students to engage in domestic service (for girls) and manual labor (for boys). Dian

Million also notes how the boarding school system was designed to shame Native children about their cultural, spiritual, and storytelling traditions. Million argues that because of the violent treatment of Indigenous children in these schools, they began to "feel" bad about being Indian.[54] They were not only separated from their families and cultures, but also they were separated from their spiritualities and epistemological beliefs about the world. It became shameful to identify with Native epistemological frameworks about the world. Rhetorics of "relationship" to salmon and other more-than-human relatives were now associated with being primitive and backward.

According to Yurok scholar Kaitlin Reed's research on the Gold Rush and ongoing "Green Rush" of the cannabis industry in Humboldt County, as of 2008, there are 47,000 abandoned mining sites that date back to the Gold Rush. Close to 87 percent of these sites have safety hazards, and 11 percent are environmental hazards.[55] These potential hazards include contaminated runoff and pollutants like mercury, arsenic, lead, and other heavy metals.[56] This continues to affect how Native people in Northwest California are able to consume fish, like salmon. Dams also continue to threaten salmon. In 2002, salmon returning home to spawn on the Klamath and Trinity rivers were confronted with low water flows and higher-than-normal temperatures, resulting in a mass infection of a parasite called "Ich." Thousands upon thousands of salmon died. Estimates of the total number of salmon vary, but the Yurok Tribe estimates that over 34,000 salmon died.[57] The rhetoric surrounding the "Fish Kill," as it will be referred to here, focused on the divide between "farmers vs. fish." And much of the discussion was about how California "feeds the world" and how reliant the state is on the economic development brought about by the large farms in the Central Valley.[58] Tribes were rarely mentioned in the first press releases and reports about the Fish Kill, where the focus seemed to be mostly on the economic development consequences of providing water to support farming interests or to support the needs of the salmon fishing industry. There was little, if any, discussion about the impact on tribal peoples who live on the river, except for passing mention about the "cultural significance" of salmon.[59] Native peoples, however, were reeling from the impact of experiencing the Fish Kill on the ground and in real time. We were once again reminded of the ongoing apocalyptic consequences of capitalism. There was a palpable mourning in many of our communities that was also a reminder of how powerless we are often made to feel about determining and influencing policy, though we are the most likely communities to be adversely affected by these environmental disasters. We also had a renewed sense of urgency and commitment to our relationship to the salmon. Much as Native peoples in our region had done in the 1970s with the Fish Wars, Native people throughout the region began to organize responses, demand representation, and seize opportunities to speak on behalf of the salmon and to put front and center our interrelationships with salmon in our testimonies, research, and creative actions to protect the future of the salmon.[60]

Salmon Rhetorics for Salmon Futures

Born out of this contemporary massacre of fish is the enacting of rhetorical sovereignty as defined and explored by Scott Lyons. It became clear after the Fish Kill that we must once again utilize our salmon rhetorics to set the tone and (re)claim space in the discussion and policy about and the politics of salmon governance. Our stories, our knowledges, and our continued ceremonial connection to the salmon were a central part of our responses to the Fish Kill. We once again brought to the forefront our salmon rhetorics to build salmon governance. Million argues that Indigenous peoples must "recognize orally based communal knowledge as organized epistemic systems that *do exist* and whose influence is active even though they might not be legitimized by academia."[61] We began to use methodologies of storytelling and creative action in order to intervene in politics and governance. Our stories were centered on the salmon, emphasized our relationship to the salmon, and did so in a manner that validated our long history and knowledges. The texts, articles, films, and creative actions following the 2002 Fish Kill were based on Indigenous perspectives and localized knowledges about salmon. This was a resurgence of Indigenous salmon rhetorics, one that featured our stories and our histories. As Million points out, "Story has always been practical, strategic, and restorative. Story *is* Indigenous theory."[62]

In California, water use continued to be skewed toward protecting corporate agricultural farms that blanket the Central Valley. In 2014, tribal scientists and water monitors documented that the conditions of the rivers were once again mirroring the conditions that happened during the 2002 Fish Kill.[63] Conservation advocates, as well as tribes and tribal organizations, rallied to call attention to the potential catastrophe. The Bureau of Reclamation "announced that it would not release the preventative flows needed to avert a fish kill. Instead, they will wait until salmon show signs of disease and start dying, and would only release an "'emergency flow'" that would take at least four days to reach infected salmon in the Lower Klamath and up to a week if a die-off is discovered over a weekend."[64] Indigenous peoples throughout the region sprang into action, and they did this in part by exercising their rhetorical sovereignty, showing up to hearings and speaking in public spaces about the relationship between salmon and people. We even went to dance and sing on top of the Lewiston Dam, bringing in our own forms of direct action, which included prayers and songs for the fish and the water.[65]

Research and scholarship inspired by the activism and ongoing work to protect salmon in our region also began to feature our interrelationship with the salmon in order to provide a clear and effective foundation for our rhetorics in support of the salmon. LaDuke's work on the Klamath River included interviews with Native people. Leaf Hillman (Karuk) stated, "We have lived there since time began and so have the fish. Our dependence is reciprocal. The fish and the river have provided for us for all those years. Now it is our turn to pay them back."[66] Continuing scholarly research also makes clear Indigenous salmon rhetorics are key to understanding the interconnection of salmon to the health of the people, that is, the sociocultural impact of salmon governance. Several studies have been published that explore the connection between environmental decline and ongoing social issues like high rates of suicide, diabetes, and stress. A 2016 article written by Miranda Willette, Kari Norgaard, and Ron Reed (Karuk) argues that the decline of fish and fish habitats "appears to be associated with younger age of death, leading to further reductions in cultural reproduction within families."[67] This foundational research has also started to become part of the conversation in mainstream media about the importance of protecting salmon. An article in *The New York Times*, "Sick River: Can These California Tribes Beat Heroin and History" included interviews with several tribal people from the Humboldt County region to draw connections between the growing opioid and heroin epidemics in these communities with the ongoing environmental disaster facing the water and the salmon. The Yurok Tribal General Counsel Amy Cordalis is quoted as saying, "It's no coincidence to me that this opioid problem and the river crisis are happening at the same time; when that resource is gone, it leads to a sense of despair."[68] Yurok Chief Justice Abby Abinanti is quoted later in the article as he explains, "Our worldview is that we're here in partnership with these other beings, the river, and the fish. We have obligations to them."[69]

Aside from research and scholarly studies, many documentary films have also been made to tell the story of Indigenous peoples' connection to salmon. *River of Renewal* was coproduced by and features local filmmaker Jack Kohler.[70] It explores his lifelong involvement with the rivers and the salmon. *Dancing Salmon Home* is an important story of the Winnemem Wintu, who are contending with the extinction of salmon in the McCloud River.[71] In the film they travel to New Zealand to visit salmon relatives who are direct descendants of fishery specimens from the McCloud River that were sent around the world. The crux of the film is watching how the Winnemem Wintu reconnect to their salmon relatives who are now living and thriving in New Zealand and also how they attempt to negotiate with the US federal government to return these salmon home. They are unsuccessful in the film, as there are still a number of bureaucratic negotiations that must happen, although the Winnemem have noted that the Bureau of Reclamation has expressed great interest in this possible collaboration. This fight for the return of salmon to the McCloud River continues to this day.[72] *Upstream Battle* premiered in 2008 and received numerous international awards.[73] The film features several local Native people and tribal leaders who discussed their relationship to the salmon and followed them as they traveled to Warren Buffett's Berkshire Hathaway annual shareholder's meeting in Omaha, Nebraska, in the hopes of testifying on behalf of salmon interests regarding the decommissioning of the Klamath River dams. In addition, Hupa tribal member Brittani Orona put together a museum exhibit and documentary film about memory on the Klamath River basin that is available online.[74] *Stories of the River, Stories of the People* features tribal people reflecting on the impact of the 2002 Fish Kill and their interrelationship with the salmon. Yurok tribal youth worked with the Seventh Generation Fund to make a film about the Fish Kill during the 2014 threat to salmon. The short film interviewed tribal members about their reactions to the 2002 Fish Kill and their worries about the current status of the fish and the river. "We have a responsibility to this place," Oscar Gensaw states in the film. "We need to educate our people in this process, try to get our voices out there, and make it count."[75] In a 2016 documentary series called *Tending the Wild* made by KCET, the "Keeping the River" episode explored the connection between the Yurok people and the Klamath River.[76] A follow-up KCET series, *Tending Nature*, featured an episode that explored river restoration with the Yurok, Hupa, and Karuk. The episode includes interviews with several tribal peoples from the Northwest California region who speak about the river, the salmon, and the condor as "relatives." Charley Reed, Karuk/Yurok/Hupa Indigenous scholar and traditional dip-net fisherman, explains in the episode that "our people and fish have a symbiotic relationship, meaning that if they're unhealthy, we're unhealthy because we very much depend on each other to thrive. Now we're finally getting back to revitalizing who we are as people, our responsibilities, and I think that's where I see a lot of hope."[77]

Telling these stories of our interrelationship to salmon has become an important way for us to (re)claim our rhetorical sovereignty and to provide a basis for our understandings of salmon in salmon research and salmon discussions. We were once again telling our stories using our salmon rhetorics. As Leanne Simpson explains, "Storytelling is an important process for visioning, imagining, critiquing the social space around us, and ultimately challenging the colonial norms fraught in our daily lives."[78] Creative projects like the play *Salmon Is Everything* have continued this long tradition of storytelling to envision, imagine, and critique. This play was created in partnership with local tribes and community members and tells the story of the Fish Kill and the community response. In the introduction to the play, Suzanne Burcell, then director of the Indian Tribal Education Personnel Program at Humboldt State University, writes about working with the play's creator Theresa May to build the production.

> Toward the end of the second year, Theresa May asked me to read the near-final scripts. She said, "I think we've captured the perspectives of most of the stakeholders—tribal peoples, farmers, ranchers, environmentalists, government agencies, even the news media—can you think of anyone else?"

"What about the fish?" I asked.

"The fish?" Theresa's eyes widened.

"The fish," I said again. "It occurs to me that in all of this discussion about the fish kill, the perspective of the fish themselves is lost. I mean, the fish are living, breathing, and life giving—part of Creation and procreation. What if you were one of these beautiful salmon, just trying to swim upriver, to return to your birthplace and spawn? Isn't that what this whole drama is about—reverence for life?"[79]

Aside from creative interventions on salmon governance, there were also many instances of Indigenous peoples getting further involved in the politics and policy of salmon throughout the state. We were no longer going to apologize or silence our salmon rhetorics; instead, we were going to utilize our salmon rhetorics to build new policy and to take politics and policy into new directions. As Rifkin explains, "Native peoples remain oriented in relation to collective experiences of peoplehood, to particular territories (whether or not such places are legally recognized as reservations or given official trust status), to the ongoing histories of their inhabitance in those spaces, and to histories of displacement from them. Such orientations open up 'different worlds' than those at play in dominant settler orderings, articulations, and reckonings of time."[80] Biondini explores one poignant example in which Native people reclaiming salmon rhetorics also shaped the implementation of policy in the Hoopa Valley. Biondini's research focuses on the Hoopa Fish Commission in 2011. The commission was charged with "developing commercial fishing regulations with input from tribal membership." Biondini analyzes two public hearings where she examines how "the hearings show tribal members intervening and reframing the task of creating regulations away from a focus on resource management to acknowledging the complex relationship Hupa people have with salmon, and the dissonance between the expressed relationships and commercial fishing activities.[81]

With all of the work being done to (re)claim and (re)inscribe salmon rhetorics across law, policy, and governance, there was some potentially good news announced on November 17, 2020, when Berkshire Hathaway (owner of PacificCorp Power and the Klamath Dams) announced an agreement with the states of Oregon and California and the Klamath River Renewal Corporation that would move the process of Klamath Dam removal "one step closer."[82] While this was a moment of celebration for Native peoples in the region, it was also a reminder that there is still work to be done. Yurok Tribal Chair Joseph James commented during the press conference, "We are connected with our heart and prayers to these creeks, lands, animals, and our way of life will thrive with these dams being out. . . . It is our duty and our oath to bring balance to the river and this effort is fulfilling that duty." But he also reminded those watching: "It's been a long road. We still have a long road to go."[83] The next steps in salmon governance will hinge on how we communicate our vital relationships with salmon, our more-than-human relatives, and the natural world. These types of movements toward governance that understands interrelationships are happening all over the world. In New Zealand, the Whanganui River was declared as possessing "all the rights, powers, duties and liabilities" of a legal person. In Toledo, Ohio, citizens voted to grant legal rights for people to Lake Erie, "the first time a natural resource has been granted legal status in the United States."[84] In July 2019, Bangladesh became the first country to grant all rivers the same legal status as humans.[85] It is partially through the reclamation of our rhetorics, and our constant push to claim our rhetorical sovereignty over how we talk about the natural world and our interrelationship with more-than-human beings that we are now beginning to also (re)claim a legal system that speaks to the complexity of how these relationships can and should build governance structures.

Decolonizing Salmon Rhetorics and Governance

I began writing this chapter well after the due date requested by our esteemed editor for this collection. After an overbooked and sometimes turbulent summer, I finally sat down with my many scribbled notes, surrounded by books, articles, and a jar full of peanut M&M's, hoping that I could "bang out" the chapter in just a few nights. Each night someone would call and ask how I was doing, first my husband, then my friends, and finally my mother. "It's painful!" I told each and every one of them. "Writing this chapter is so painful."

I meant this to be flippant. Writing is hard. Writing sucks. Writing takes forever. Writing is never convenient. Most of the time when I would lament about the painfulness of spending hours into the night in my lonely office, people would laugh politely and say, "Well, you can do it!" I would sip some more caffeine and go back to work.

When my mother called and asked me how it was going, I went right into my jokey excuse for why I was watching a YouTube video about how to make a chocolate chip Bundt cake instead of writing. "It's painful!" I said, "Writing this chapter is painful."

She agreed. "Of course it's painful. It's hard to put out there these things that we know. We know them, but we don't know if we believe them anymore. And sometimes we believe them, but we don't know how to claim them, how to make them ours again. I always use the example, Indian people used to sing to their plants. We used to sing to our corn, to our acorns, to our trees. But people told us we were crazy. They said we were stupid for doing that. Some of us have adopted that belief, that maybe it makes us seem superstitious or woo-woo. And it doesn't seem real, so we feel awkward. I mean, you've watched people when they pray for the first time when they go gathering. They always get shy, and they go, 'But what do I do? How do I talk to a fern?' But scientists now, they suddenly say, 'Oh, did you know plants respond to your voice, or music, or singing? Did you know they talk to each other?' Yeah, we know. We have to implement these things that we already know and that's painful. Because there's an anger there because we gave it up in the first place, and maybe it wasn't a conscious decision, but we participated in that decision. And there's a sadness there, because it took so much violence and trauma to wrest that from us as a people. So, wanting to write that, to put that into words, to say, 'No, this is real. We know this'—that is painful. But it's important."

I typed it while she was talking. Not having thought about my own impetus for exploring salmon rhetorics, not having wanted to truly connect with why this chapter was about more than a line item for my curriculum vitae or an addition to my collection of articles on "Why We . . ."[86] In my mind, I had been composing an article that I thought was to clearly and concisely explore rhetoric through a California Indian lens because I wanted to make sure that a California Indian perspective was included in a discussion of Native American rhetoric. And I also thought this would simply be a straightforward and analytical exploration of salmon rhetorics.

"What are you trying to say?" my mother asked me.

"I'm trying to say that when we stop apologizing or decentering our relationship with salmon when it comes to governance and policy, that's when we are changing the world. And that our salmon rhetorics can be what builds our decolonized futures. 'Cause we are doing that, we've done that. The Fish Wars, the videos, the plays, the creative writing, our testimonies, our written comments. In my experience, I think we sometimes walk into situations like public hearings, and we don't think that they want to hear about our stories. You can tell, they think the science is the most important, the numbers. But I want us to remember that our science is relationships and that we solidified this in our languages, in our stories, in our theories and our practices and methodologies and in our rhetorics. So, we have to do that again. Our policies, our laws, our resolutions have to say that governance is about relationship and responsibility. Because decentering that didn't work and we lost so many salmon relatives and now our salmon relatives are endangered. So, let's talk about our relatives like they matter to us."

"Well then," she said, "say that."

Salmon navigate sometimes hundreds of miles to return home to spawn; they live by their relationship to their homelands. They know intrinsically and biologically where they come from and where they have been. Salmon cross borders fluidly; they build relationships across Indigenous cultures and also across nations, counties, and states. The Hupa people believe that it was the K'ixinay (First People) who taught humans how they were supposed to live so that the earth would remain balanced and good. The salmon became a part of that, and the Hupa were told that salmon "will be good wherever it grows."[87] The Hupa also say that when the K'ixinay left the world, they went into "everything," like the rocks, rivers, trees, plants, and salmon. Salmon are our First People; they are much older, much wiser, and here for us, embodying our spirituality and our culture. We pray for them to return when we do our ceremonies. We are grateful for what they give to us, and we build ceremony to remind ourselves not to take them for granted. "Let the salmon return" goes one of our prayers. We have always been told salmon must return so that we can live. And we live so that we can make sure they return. Hayah-no-nt'ik'.

Notes

1.   Michael Belchik, Dave Hillemeier, and Ronnie M. Pierce, *The Klamath River Fish Kill of 2002; Analysis of Contributing Factors* (Klamath, CA: Yurok Tribal Fisheries

Program, 2004), https://www.waterboards.ca.gov/waterrights/water_issues/programs/bay_delta/california_waterfix/exhibits/docs/PCFFA&IGFR/part2/pcffa_155.pdf.

2.   Will Houston, "Toxic Blue-Green Algae Detected in Trinity River," *Times-Standard*, August 20, 2014, https://www.times-standard.com/2014/08/20/toxic-blue-green-algae-detected-in-trinity-river/.

3.   Mirranda Willette, Kari Norgaard, and Ron Reed, "You Got to Have Fish: Families, Environmental Decline and Cultural Reproduction," *Families, Relationships and Societies* 5, no. 3 (2016): 375–92.

4.   Mark Rifkin, *Beyond Settler Time: Temporal Sovereignty and Indigenous Self-Determination* (Durham, NC: Duke University Press, 2017).

5.   Scott Richard Lyons, "Rhetorical Sovereignty: What Do American Indians Want from Writing?," *College Composition and Communication* 51, no. 3 (February 2000): 449.

6.   Chadwick Allen, *Trans-Indigenous: Methodologies for Global Native Literary Studies* (Minneapolis: University of Minnesota Press, 2012), xv.

7.   Lisa King, "Sovereignty, Rhetorical Sovereignty, and Representation: Keywords for Teaching Indigenous Texts," in *Survivance, Sovereignty, and Story: Teaching American Indian Rhetorics*, ed. Lisa King, Rose Gubele, and Joyce Rain Anderson (Logan: Utah State University Press, 2015), 26.

8.   A. Irving Hallowell, "Ojibwa Ontology, Behavior, and World View," in *Culture in History: Essays in Honor of Paul Radin*, ed. Stanley Diamond (New York: Columbia University Press, 1960), 21.

9.   Zoe Todd, "Fish, Kin and Hope: Tending to Water Violations in Amiskwaciwâskahikan and Treaty Six Territory," *Afterall: A Journal of Art, Context and Enquiry* 43, no. 1 (Spring/Summer 2017): 106, https://doi.org/10.1086/692559. The article may also be found at https://www.journals.uchicago.edu/doi/full/10.1086/692559. For Todd's original discussion of the term "more-than-human," see Zoe Todd, "An Indigenous Feminist's Take on the Ontological Turn: 'Ontology' Is Just Another Word for Colonialism," *Journal of Historical Sociology* 29, no. 1 (2016): 4–22.

10.   Guido Rahr, "Why Protect Salmon," Wild Salmon Center, accessed December 26, 2019, https://www.wildsalmoncenter.org/why-protect-salmon/.

11.   Raymond Pierotti and Daniel Wildcat, "Traditional Ecological Knowledge: The Third Alternative (Commentary)," *Ecological Applications* 10, no. 5 (2000): 1333, https://doi.org/10.1890/1051-0761(2000)010[1333:TEKTTA]2.0.CO;2.

12.   Pierotti and Wildcat, "Traditional Ecological Knowledge," 1336.

13.   Vine Deloria Jr., *Spirit & Reason: The Vine Deloria, Jr., Reader*, ed. Barbara Deloria, Kristen Foehner, and Samuel Scinta (Golden, CO: Fulcrum Publishing, 1999), 34.

14.   Kyle P. Whyte, "On the Role of Traditional Ecological Knowledge as a Collaborative Concept: A Philosophical Study," *Ecological Processes* 2, Article 7 (April 2013): 1, https://doi.org/10.1186/2192-1709-2-7.

15.   Whyte, "On the Role," 2.

16.   Seafha C. Ramos, "Considerations for Culturally Sensitive Traditional Ecological

Knowledge Research in Wildlife Conservation," *Wildlife Society Bulletin* 42, no. 2 (2018): 358, https://doi.org/10.1002/wsb.881.

17. Melissa K. Nelson, ed., *Original Instructions: Indigenous Teachings for a Sustainable Future* (Rochester, VT: Bear & Company, 2008), 12.

18. Winona LaDuke, "Traditional Ecological Knowledge and Environmental Futures," *Colorado Journal of International Environmental Law and Policy* 5, no. 1 (1994): 127.

19. LaDuke, "Environmental Futures," 127.

20. Ramos, "Considerations for Culturally Sensitive," 362.

21. Ramos, "Considerations for Culturally Sensitive," 362.

22. Ramos, "Considerations for Culturally Sensitive," 363.

23. Mark D. Spence, *Dispossessing the Wilderness: Indian Removal and the Making of the National Parks* (Oxford: Oxford University Press, 1999).

24. Dan Shilling, "Introduction: The Soul of Sustainability," in *Traditional Ecological Knowledge: Learning from Indigenous Practices for Environmental Sustainability*, ed. Melissa K. Nelson and Dan Shilling (Cambridge: Cambridge University Press, 2018), 12.

25. Coleen A. Fox et al., "'The River Is Us; the River Is in Our Veins': Re-Defining River Restoration in Three Indigenous Communities," *Sustainability Science* 12, no. 4 (July 2017): 521–33.

26. Zoe Todd, "Fish Pluralities: Human-Animal Relations and Sites of Engagement in Paulatuuq, Arctic Canada," *Études/Inuit/Studies* 38, nos. 1–2 (2014): 217–38, https://doi.org/10.7202/1028861ar.

27. Karuk Tribe, "Study Reveals New Salmon Species," August 17, 2017, https://yubanet.com/california/study-reveals-new-salmon-species/.

28. Karuk Tribe, "Study Reveals."

29. Rifkin, *Beyond Settler Time*, 3.

30. Rifkin, *Beyond Settler Time*, 3.

31. Matt Mais, Jan Hasselman, and Glen Spain, "Judge Rejects Agribusiness' Water-Grabbing Lawsuit over Trinity River Flows," Earthjustice, October 1, 2014, https://earthjustice.org/news/press/2014/judge-rejects-agribusiness-water-grabbing-lawsuit-over-trinity-river-flows.

32. Nelson, *Original Instructions*, 12.

33. Andrea Riley-Mukavetz and Malea D. Powell, "Making Native Space for Graduate Students: A Story of Indigenous Rhetorical Practice," in *Survivance, Sovereignty, and Story: Teaching American Indian Rhetorics*, ed. Lisa King, Rose Gubele, and Joyce Rain Anderson (Logan: Utah State University Press, 2015), 141.

34. Todd, "Fish Pluralities," 222.

35. Todd, "Fish Pluralities," 231.

36. Lori Biondini, "Salmon Pluralities: The Politics of Commercial Fishing on the Hoopa Valley Reservation" (master's thesis, Humbolt State University, 2017), 17, https://digitalcommons.humboldt.edu/cgi/viewcontent.cgi?article=1123&context=etd.

37. Leontina M. Hormel and Kari M. Norgaard, "Bring the Salmon Home! Karuk Challenges to Capitalist Incorporation," *Critical Sociology* 35, no. 3 (2009): 362, https://doi.org/10.1177/0896920508101502.

38.   Biondini, "Salmon Pluralities," 18.

39.   Glen Sean Coulthard, *Red Skin, White Masks: Rejecting the Colonial Politics of Recognition* (Minneapolis: University of Minnesota Press, 2014), 75.

40.   This section draws inspiration from Yurok scholar Kaitlin Reed's foundational work connecting the Gold Rush to the "Green Rush" of marijuana cultivation in Humboldt County. Her dissertation in progress at the time of this writing, "From Gold Rush to Green Rush: Marijuana Cultivation on Yurok Tribal Lands" at the University of California, Davis, will explicate how Humboldt County continues its "rush mentality" and how this continues to affect Native peoples throughout the region. A PowerPoint presentation of her work may be found at http://northamericancannabissummit.org/wp-content/uploads/2019/03/E1-68_REEDslides.pdf.

41.   Jack Norton, *Genocide in Northwestern California: When Our Worlds Cried* (San Francisco: Indian Historian Press, 1979), 115–31.

42.   Brendan C. Lindsay, *Murder State: California's Native American Genocide, 1846–1873* (Lincoln: University of Nebraska Press, 2012), 2.

43.   Sherburne Friend Cook, *The Population of the California Indians, 1769–1970* (Berkeley: University of California Press, 1976); Stephanie Lumsden, "Reproductive Justice, Sovereignty, and Incarceration: Prison Abolition Politics and California Indians," *American Indian Culture and Research Journal* 40, no. 1 (2016): 35.

44.   Kimberly Johnston-Dodds, *Early California Laws and Policies Related to California Indians* (Sacramento: California State Library, California Research Bureau, 2002), https://www.library.ca.gov/Content/pdf/crb/reports/02-014.pdf.

45.   Benjamin Madley, *An American Genocide: The United States and the California Indian Catastrophe, 1846–1873* (New Haven CT: Yale University Press, 2016), 354.

46.   Norton, *Genocide in Northwestern California*, 127–28.

47.   Norton, *Genocide in Northwestern California*, 127–28.

48.   Chisa Oros, "The Role of Fort Humboldt during the California Gold Rush: A Focus on Local Indigenous Women's Struggle, Resistance and Resilience" (master's thesis, Humboldt State University, 2016), http://humboldt-dspace.calstate.edu/bitstream/handle/10211.3/176139/oros_chisa_Sp2016.pdf?sequence=1.

49.   Oros, "Role of Fort Humboldt," 11.

50.   Oros, "Role of Fort Humboldt," 12. The repetition of the Eel River is in the original text and is not a typographical error here.

51.   Kari M. Norgaard, "The Effects of Altered Diet on the Health of the Karuk People: A Preliminary Report," The Karuk Tribe of California: Department of Natural Resources Water Quality Program, 2004.

52.   Eve Tuck and K. Wayne Yang, "Decolonization Is Not a Metaphor," *Decolonization: Indigeneity, Education & Society* 1, no. 1 (2012): 5.

53.   Richard Henry Pratt, *Battlefield and Classroom: Four Decades with the American Indian, 1867–1904*, ed. Robert M. Utley (1964; repr., Norman: University of Oklahoma Press, 2003), xi.

54.   Dian Million, *Therapeutic Nations: Healing in an Age of Indigenous Human Rights* (Tucson: University of Arizona Press, 2013).

55. Sierra Fund, "Mining's Toxic Legacy: An Initiative to Address Mining Toxins in the Sierra Nevada" (Nevada City, CA: The Sierra Fund, 2008), https://www.sierrafund.org/wp-content/uploads/MININGS_TOXIC_LEGACY_2010printing_4web.pdf.

56. Sierra Fund, "Mining's Toxic Legacy," 48.

57. Belchik, Hillemeier, and Pierce, *Klamath River Fish Kill of 2002*, 4.

58. Steve Hymon, "Salmon Die-Off Reignites Feud Over Klamath River Water," *Los Angeles Times*, September 25, 2002, https://www.latimes.com/archives/la-xpm-2002-sep-25-me-deadfish25-story.html.

59. Hymon, "Salmon Die-Off."

60. Andrew H. Fisher, "Defenders and Dissidents: Cooks Landing and the Fight to Define Tribal Sovereignty in the Red Power Era," *Comparative American Studies* 17, no. 2 (2020): 117–41, https://doi.org/10.1080/14775700.2020.1724017.

61. Dian Million, "There Is a River In Me: Theory from Life," in *Theorizing Native Studies*, ed. Audra Simpson and Andrea Smith (Durham, NC: Duke University Press, 2014), 35. Emphasis in original.

62. Million, *Therapeutic Nations*, 35. Emphasis in original.

63. Amber Shelton, "Klamath Basin Facing Catastrophic Fish Kill," *Times-Standard*, August 8, 2014, http://www.times-standard.com/general-news/20140808/klamath-basin-facing-catastrophic-fish-kill.

64. Shelton, "Klamath Basin."

65. Cutcha Risling Baldy, "Water Is Life: The Flower Dance Ceremony," *News from Native California*, Spring 2017, https://www.cutcharislingbaldy.com/uploads/2/8/7/3/2873888/water_is_life_the_flower_dance_ceremony.pdf.

66. LaDuke, "Environmental Futures," 63.

67. Willette, Norgaard, and Reed, "You Got to Have Fish," 375.

68. Jose A. Del Real, "Sick River: Can These California Tribes Beat Heroin and History?," *The New York Times*, September 4, 2018, New York edition, sec. U.S., https://www.nytimes.com/2018/09/04/us/klamath-river-california-tribes-heroin.html.

69. Real, "Sick River."

70. Carlos Bolado, *River of Renewal*, DVD (Pikiawish Partners and Specialty Studios, 2009).

71. *Dancing Salmon Home*, DVD (Eugene, OR: Moving Up Productions, 2013), https://dancingsalmonhome.wordpress.com/.

72. "Salmon Return: The Story of the New Zealand McCloud Salmon," Winnemcm Wintu, 2019, https://www.winnememwintu.us/mccloud-salmon-restoration/.

73. Ben Kempas, *Upstream Battle* (Preview Production GbR, 2008).

74. "Stories of the River, Stories of the People: Memory on the Klamath River Basin," The Native Women's Collective, accessed December 27, 2019, https://www.nativewomenscollective.org/storiesoftheriver.html.

75. SevenGenFund, "Fish Kill 2014? Yurok Youth Seek Answers," August 13, 2014, YouTube video, https://www.youtube.com/watch?v=CbHUb6aLizw&t=130s.

76. Christine Yuan, *Keeping the River*, Tending the Wild (KCETLink and the Autry

Museum of the American West, 2016), https://www.kcet.org/shows/tending-the-wild/episodes/keeping-the-river.

77.   Anna Rau and Corbett Jones, *Restoring the River with the Yurok, Hupa and Karuk*, Tending Nature (KCETink and The Range, 2019), 8:21–8:39.

78.   Leanne B. Simpson, *Dancing on Our Turtle's Back: Stories of Nishnaabeg Re-Creation, Resurgence and a New Emergence* (Winnipeg, MB: Arbeiter Ring Publishing, 2011), 34.

79.   Theresa J. May, *Salmon Is Everything: Community-Based Theatre in the Klamath Watershed* (Corvallis: Oregon State University Press, 2014), 20.

80.   Rifkin, *Beyond Settler Time*, 3.

81.   Biondini, "Salmon Pluralities," ii.

82.   Thadeus Greenson, "New Deal Brokered to Remove Klamath Dams," *Northcoast Journal*, November 17, 2020, https://www.northcoastjournal.com/NewsBlog/archives/2020/11/17/new-deal-brokered-to-remove-klamath-dams.

83.   Brian Gailey, "New MOA on Klamath Dams Results in Further Divided Views and Questions Authority," *Klamath Falls News*, November 17, 2020, https://www.klamathfallsnews.org/news/new-moa-on-klamath-dams-results-in-further-divided-views-and-questions-authority.

84.   Jason Daley, "Toledo, Ohio, Just Granted Lake Erie the Same Legal Rights as People," *Smithsonian Magazine*, March 1, 2019, https://www.smithsonianmag.com/smart-news/toledo-ohio-just-granted-lake-erie-same-legal-rights-people-180971603/.

85.   Ashley Westerman, "Should Rivers Have Same Legal Rights As Humans? A Growing Number of Voices Say Yes," *NPR*, August 3, 2019, https://www.npr.org/2019/08/03/740604142/should-rivers-have-same-legal-rights-as-humans-a-growing-number-of-voices-say-ye.

86.   Cutcha Risling Baldy, "Why We Gather: Traditional Gathering in Native Northwest California and the Future of Bio-Cultural Sovereignty," *Ecological Processes* 2, Article 17 (June 2013): 17, https://doi.org/10.1186/2192-1709-2-17.

87.   Pliny Earle Goddard, *Hupa Texts*, University of California Publications American Archaeology and Ethnology, vol. 1, no. 2 (Berkeley, CA: The University Press, 1904), 268, https://digitalassets.lib.berkeley.edu/anthpubs/ucb/text/ucp001-004.pdf.

CHAPTER NINE

"Hey, Cousin!"

Rhetorics of the Lower Coast Salish

DANICA STERUD MILLER

haʔɬ slax̌il
Danica Sterud Miller ti dsdaʔ spuyaləbš čəd.
syab Bill Sterud ti sdaʔ ʔə dbad spuyaləbš.
Carl William Sterud ʔə tudscapa hidastabš.
Marjorie Mathewson Sterud tsi sdaʔ ʔə tudkaya spuyaləbš.
ɬuɬaal ɬiɬ Young syayayə.

Hello.
I am Danica Sterud Miller, Puyallup.
My father is respected Puyallup Elder Bill Sterud.
My Puyallup grandmother is Marjorie Matheson Sterud.
My Hidatsa grandfather is Carl William Sterud.
I am of the Puyallup Young family.

As a child, I grew up introducing myself much more casually: "I'm Danica Sterud. I'm Puyallup. My dad is Bill." Now as an adult, I introduce myself formally, as per the epigraph above, but both introductions serve the same purpose, that is, among the Coast Salish, we introduce ourselves with our lineage to understand how we are related to each other. In Lushootseed, which is the name of our language, there is no word for a nuclear family. The

195

closest word, *syayayə*, broadly encompasses a familial feeling of love and respect. Despite settler colonialism, we continue to introduce ourselves according to one's parents and grandparents and further on. This is less a power posturing and more a meeting ground for establishing who a person is within the tangled web of Coast Salish relations. You don't have to go too far back before you realize that this new person you are introducing yourself to is, indeed, a cousin. As an American Indian studies professor at a university located on my Indigenous territory, I am both of my people and, as expected by my largely western colleagues and students, to be a representative of my people. This means I am expected to understand myself and my people outside of my Puyallup lens and to don a western one in its stead.[1] This type of doubling is well-known within marginalized communities, though in a different time and space, I would be very comfortable arguing that this doubling is especially fraught for American Indians. Due my position, then, I have been thinking more consciously about the Coast Salish as a people of clans. What does it mean to be of a clan, and how do we practice our clan epistemologies today?

Coast Salish peoples live and lived west of the Cascade Mountains between what is now central Oregon and the southern portion of what is now British Columbia, Canada. I myself am Puyallup, and I grew up on one of the last allotments on the Puyallup Reservation. What I know is Puyallup, but I am comfortable discussing the rhetoric of Lushootseed-speaking people, which ranges along the Salish Sea from Nisqually up to Skagit Territory.[2] My comfort in my ability to speak about, though certainly not for, Lushootseed-speaking peoples stems from the clan structure of Coast Salish people more generally. Coast Salish peoples understood themselves as clans of people related to other clans by ties of culture, language, and family. The clans themselves consisted of strong kinship-based people. Between the Coast Salish clans, there was no central authority or government, but the Elders and others with strong personal spirits were considered to be the just and generous guides for the clans.[3] Each clan had a series of landholdings upon which they had the exclusive rights to fish, hunt, gather. Equally important within Coast Salish epistemology, each clan also had rights to nonmaterial possessions, such as spirits, ceremonies, and songs. A quick look at the Medicine Creek Treaty, which involved the Puyallup, Nisqually, and Squaxin Island people, shows over a hundred Indigenous leaders signed the document. A single, centralized nation within a westernized framework we were not, and yet we understood the importance and value of shared kinship and clan interdependence.

Multiple clans lived together during the colder months in longhouses of cedar, some of which could hold up to a thousand people. We were small clans that could join together to form larger communities and live together harmoniously, not because we were of one mind and habit, but because we understood the value of respect, the interdependency of community, and the importance of our family relations. Our rhetoric of familial clan kinships continues this longhouse tradition of mutual understanding. Yet, in the warmer months, our clans removed themselves from the longhouses to travel. During the spring and summer, we left the villages and moved to temporary camps near the mountains, on the riverbanks, and along the Salish Sea to collect the winter supply of food. Lower Coast Salish are of the Salish Sea and of the rivers that stem from takobid.[4] Via and near these extensive waters, we traveled and we travel. Traditionally, the farther away a spouse originated, the more prestigious the clan member was. This is still the case today, and when introducing yourself within in your familial clan, you are likely to find a cousin not just over the mountain in Yakama, but perhaps down to the Laguna or over to the Ojibwe. We traveled and travel for visiting, for trading, and for hunting and gathering. From what my Elders tell me, however, and what I see around me, not to mention practice myself, I believe that trading and food gathering were convenient excuses to see distant syayayə, even syayayə unknown as of yet. Our seemingly complicated clan structures mean we can trust to be welcomed by our clan relations and be trusted to welcome them in return. The summers are spent traveling, which is a continuation of our clan interdependence. We understand each other within our kinship webs. The small clans traveled together, which was a both a nice respite from longhouse living and another way the Coast Salish were respectful of the local environs. The food that was gathered, hunted, fished, and prepared during the summer was brought back to the permanent winter village. We were multiple clans who lived together in longhouses, and also were people who understood the importance of spending time away to meet new people and renew old kinships.

In addition to the importance of clan kinship rhetoric, Coast Salish people also utilize a rhetoric of friendly, warm teasing. To be teased by an Elder is to be welcomed and loved. To be able to tease an Elder means your familiarity is deeply enmeshed and loving. A Coast Salish funeral, especially for an Elder, generally turns into a tearful, sidesplitting roast. The loving teasing of the Elder who has passed on speaks to why we will miss them and why we love them. Within this Coast Salish teasing between Elders, younger community members, and across generational lines there exists another dimension in regard to elder women. Elder women were recognized as possessing unique and powerful spirits, which only became more powerful as they grew older. As I mentioned earlier, the Medicine Creek Treaty had over one hundred Indigenous leaders sign it, but none of the signatories were women. I am constantly astounded by the limited patriarchal vision of the United States, yet I cannot help but laugh when I think of all the powerful female leaders who were undoubtedly in that treaty audience as well, and who were not asked or expected to sign by those shortsighted colonizers, who could not even conceive of the power in front of them. So, it is our elder women who are slower to tease and be teased. They are the acknowledged backbone and strength of our community, and that burden and that blessing often creates a more serious discourse with and between them.

Much like all Indigenous peoples, the Coast Salish have a strong rhetoric of respect for our Elders, which carries over into our community rhetoric. Elders are honored in specific, formal ways, and so that rhetoric contains a formal acknowledgment of their power and our debt to their wisdom and guidance. Less formally, though just as important, we show our respect to our Elders by not speaking. Our Elders speak to us and for us, and we listen. This rhetorical strategy does not only mean that we listen to our Elders, learn from our Elders, and obey our Elders, though that is the main goal. Listening to our Elders without speaking and without interrupting means that we gain their wisdom, and we also gain patience while listening, and patience if their wisdom and guidance does not agree with our own point of view. Thus, the rhetoric of our Elders speaking also becomes a rhetoric of clan listening. Clan members learn to integrate the wisdom of the Elders within their own desires and ambitions. The two do not necessarily have to agree, but they must, within clan rhetoric, eventually meld.

Historically, the Coast Salish prided themselves on their shrewd trading skills. Being a powerful trader was indicative that one had a powerful spirit. We could not have been less of a warlike people. The land was too generous for aggressive conflict over goods and land. Trade was mainly focused on decorative goods, region-specific foods, and marriage, although stories and songs were also traded. Today, we are much less of a trade-based people, although an informal economy still flourishes among us. To some extent, our trade discourse remains today in our generous gift-giving. Gift-giving was not exclusive to trade interactions, but it was certainly a part of them. More than gift-giving, however, trade rhetoric today is utilized by our leaders when they calmly, provocatively, and wisely work with the settler colonial government to continue, renew, and push for our ancestral sovereign and treaty rights. Much like trade began with gift giving, so do our negotiations with the settler colonial government. This signifies both that we continue our epistemologies of welcome and generosity, and it also acknowledges that we are welcoming these foreign leaders to what continues to be and will always be our land. Much like the trading days of the past, which would be led by a specifically gifted trader, the goods would be made and gathered through a clan-wide effort. Certainly, within our rhetoric today, our leaders depend, and vocally acknowledge, the work of all within our community as we support our leaders as they prepare for their meetings and negotiations. This might be a meeting between leaders, but it is also the work of the clan.

Initially, when conceiving of this chapter, I was uncomfortable with the term "rhetoric," as rhetoric is a field largely consisting of western academics who glorify a tradition of dominance through argumentative speech. Dominance, through speech or otherwise, is foreign to Coast Salish traditional beliefs. We were, and to a large extent, still are gently competitive, but this not about making another person lesser, which dominance implies. Instead, competition among the Coast Salish is more of an acknowledgment of a person's powerful spirit. Damián Baca explains that for non-western thinkers "every communicative act is tied to rhetorical production, and as such works to influence specific audiences to some action whether material or epistemological."[5] While I agree with this overall definition, even "influence" seems a bit of a harsh way to describe Coast Salish rhetoric. For the Coast Salish, rhetoric is used to convey meaning, which is akin to a discursive nudging. Perhaps then, when gently prodded by an auntie, or warmly teased by an Elder, that nudge does become a clan-wide nudge of influence.

Clan rhetoric is based on the relations we all share and shared. Everyone was related, which is so beautiful it almost hurts. I think about the expectations, the trust, and the safety that must have guided and led our people, and when I am with my cousins today, I am not only reminded of this loving warmth as a remnant of pre-settler colonialism, I am reminded of how we continue our clan epistemologies concurrent to, and sometimes indifferent to, the settler colonialism that surrounds us. By introducing ourselves by our Indigenous lineage to other Indigenous peoples, we are welcoming them, and inviting ourselves to be welcomed, into the clan communities. The Puyallup are known as the "Welcoming People," though all Coast Salish are well known for their generosity and hospitality. On paper, especially ones that deal with deeds and treaties, welcoming all to our land and our table seems not to have worked out that well for the Puyallup. And yet, continuing the clan rhetoric of who we are, who we were, and who you are, and how together we share a common ancestry is a rhetoric that defines and sustains us.

Notes

1. I am currently an associate professor at the University of Washington Tacoma.
2. The Salish Sea is also known as the Puget Sound.
3. Coast Salish peoples had three fairly permeable classes: nobles, commoners, and slaves. Rank was determined by kinship and, to a more complicated extent, through wealth (which was measured by a different materialism than contemporary capitalism).
4. Takobid is one of the indigenous names for Mount Rainier.
5. Damián Baca, "Te-Ixtli: The 'Other Face' of the Americas," in *Rhetorics of the Americas: 3114 BCE to 2012 CE*, ed. Damián Baca and Victor Villanueva (New York: Palgrave Macmillan, 2010), 4.

CHAPTER TEN

The Two-Spirit Tlingit Film Rhetoric of Aucoin's *My Own Private Lower Post*

GABRIEL S. ESTRADA

Introduction

For over a decade, Duane Gastant' Aucoin has been both the Yanyédi (Wolf) Clan representative on the Teslin Tlingit Executive Council and a media spokesperson for the two-spirit/queer Indigenous community. Preceding his 2009 International Two-Spirit Male Warrior award, Duane Gastant' Aucoin made rhetorical Teslin Tlingit inroads in his 2008 film *My Own Private Lower Post*.[1] This thirty-five-minute video exemplifies Indigenous film directing, acting, and production sovereignty. It also demonstrates how to heal historical trauma with a two-spirit rhetorical focus on Teslin Tlingit language, sobriety, and post-Indian residential school rematriation. Before delving into a visual rhetorical analysis of *My Own Private Lower Post*, this chapter first reviews how the explanation of "Anishinaabe rhetoric" by Lawrence Gross (White Earth Anishinaabe) theoretically informs a two-spirit Teslin Tlingit film rhetoric. The discussion then situates the title rhetoric of *My Own Private Lower Post* within Two-Spirit Media and New Queer Cinema history. The main two-spirit film analysis emphasizes Aucoin's rhetorical depictions of Teslin Tlingit healing, parenting, alcoholism, and a genderqueer Raven performance as a means to achieve post-Indian residential school healing interventions. I end the chapter with my own reflections on healing as a two-spirit person rhetorically impacted by the Northeast Two-Spirit Society's 2013 screening of Acoin's film in New York City.

Answering Gross's call for more scholarly work on Indigenous Nation–specific rhetoric and Angela Haas's advocacy for "digital and visual modes of rhetorical sovereignty," this introduction outlines the two-spirit Tlingit rhetorical sovereignty of the Indian residential school film *My Own Private Lower Post*.[2] In "Anishinaabe Rhetoric," chapter 8 of *Anishinaabe Ways of Knowing and Being*, Gross offers important insights into Anishinaabe rhetoric, particularly in terms of Anishinaabe rhetors speaking: 1) with the spirit, 2) from personal knowledge, 3) for a specific audience's larger needs, and 4) from the heart.[3] While Gross emphasizes specific examples of Anishinaabe language and culture for each of these four main rhetorical devices, he also recognizes that these four rhetorical interventions are generally applicable to broader "Native American rhetoric."[4] These four Native American rhetorics allow for a departure from Greek, Western, and US settler colonial applications of rhetoric that erase Indigenous ways, sovereignty, and culture. Within US Native American and Canadian Indigenous film analysis, however, the use of the term "rhetoric" has not been indigenized. In fact, notable scholars such as Michelle Raheja only mention settler colonial visual "rhetoric" in direct opposition to Indigenous "visual sovereignty," or media self-representation as envisioned by Indigenous directors and performed by Indigenous actors.[5] Following Gross, this article wrests the term "rhetoric" from purely Eurocentric film analysis by suggesting a visual rhetoric of Indigenous sovereignty.

Gross's Native American rhetoric helps explain how the "spiritual" Native American rhetoric of "speaking from the heart" and "personal experience" is central in Aucoin's healing film plot. Gross writes, "So the main concern in speaking from the heart is the question of how are we going to keep our relationships healthy and strong?"[6] Clearly, maintaining the health and strength of the Teslin Tlingit matrilineal Clan connection that Aucoin develops with his mother Vicky Bob is the central relationship of the film's plot. In *My Own Private Lower Post*, Aucoin and Bob visit the Lower Post Indian Residential School in British Columbia where Bob was interned as a child. Returning home to Teslin Tlingit Nation in the Yukon Territory, the two discuss the traumatic impact of those early residential school years upon their subsequent experiences of domestic violence, alcoholism, and struggles with parenting. Aucoin ends the first section of the film with forgiveness for his mother after Bob apologizes for her drunken years while raising him. In the film finale, Aucoin reenacts and narrates a completely Tlingit-language story of how Raven frees the stars, moon, and sun from three boxes to light the sky. This last linguistic and temporal shift is but another aspect of the Teslin Tlingit matrilineal spiritual force of creation that is needed to balance contemporary Teslin Tlingit relationships, in this case centering on Vicky Bob and her director son Duane Gastant' Aucoin. To keep "relationships healthy and strong" also includes the widening circles of Indigenous relationships so that all those Tlingit and non-Tlingit impacted by Indian residential schools can find digital models of Indigenous healing. This larger Indian residential school survivor audience is "who is going to profit most from a certain course of action," an important audience component of Native American rhetoric as Gross defines it.[7] In addition, as this chapter details, two-spirit people and their families are also impacted by Aucoin's strong presence as a two-spirit Teslin Tlingit filmmaker, politician, child, parent, partner, and singer.

Title Rhetoric and Two-Spirit Film History

A two-spirit identity shift occurs across the documentary works of Mona Smith (Sisseton-Wahpeton Dakota). Smith features gay- and lesbian-identified Ojibwe (Anishinaabe) speakers in the 1988 *Her Giveaway: A Spiritual Journey with AIDS*, but then switches to include two-spirit-identified interviewees in her 1990 *Honored by the Moon*.[8] The two-spirit term for Indigenous mixed-gender traditions was adopted at the 1990 International Gay/Lesbian Gathering in Winnipeg, Manitoba, an annual event that was thereafter called the International Two-Spirit Gathering. Two-spirit signaled a more gender-conscious reclamation of Indigenous spiritual traditions than had occurred with the mid- to late 1900s identifications of gay or lesbian sexualities and with the 1970s–2010s transgender gender identity. As an Ojibwe lesbian mother, Carole LaFavor spoke of her AIDS healing path through American Indian ceremonies in *Her Giveaway*. She went a step further in *Honored by the Moon* to state that two-spirit people were often seen as "spiritual leaders" and "doctors," more radically challenging the intensifying settler Christian cis-heteropatriarchal discrimination of the 1980s–1990s early AIDS pandemic.[9]

With a similar challenge, the two-spirit Sayisi Dene Zachery Longboy directed *Water into Fire* (1994), a film about queer Indigenous healing during the onslaught of deaths due to AIDS during the 1990s. Dancing to his own drumming and poetry, the openly HIV+ Longboy confronts the harshness of Western AIDS medicine and community deaths with a performance as a bird moving across a floor scattered with candles, Indigenous art, and smashed bottles of AZT HIV medication. Longboy draws upon Indigenous modes of healing with his drumming, poetry, and dancing to critique the Western AIDS medicine AZT that was often overdosed, ineffective, and deadly. Although AIDS was not a topic in *My Own Private Lower Post*, Aucoin demonstrates a related two-spirit film emphasis on traditional healing in his film that greatly distinguishes it from non-Indigenous queer film.[10] Building upon the 1990 Two-Spirit Media movement of openly depicting contemporary two-spirit people and AIDS healing, Aucoin reclaims Teslin Tlingit tradition, language and two-spirit healing roles.

Often, Indigenous healing and humor go together. Through the title *My Own Private Lower Post*, Aucoin makes a pun on the 1991 independent hit film title *My Own Private Idaho* by gay Euro-American director Gus Van Sant.[11] Aucoin's pun features the incongruity between the internationally famous title of a Van Sant's white queer Idaho movie and the relatively lesser-known film depictions of Lower Post (Daylu Dena) First Nation near the British Columbia and Yukon border. Given that Van Sant's film follows two male sex workers' searches for familial integration in a queer buddy road film across Oregon, a second aspect of the pun is that "My Own Private" queers "Lower Post," countering the cis-heteronormative image of First Nations.[12] The title *My Own Private Lower Post* reflects a two-spirit film history of Indigenous humorous critique. Aucoin's previous documentary on queer Indigenous British Columbia and Vancouver in his 2003 *Kichx Anagaat Yatx'i: Children of the Rainbow* uses such irreverent humor.[13] In one film scene, the locally famous duo Cashcreek Charlie (Duane Gaston' Aucoin) and Grandma Suzie (Sharon Shorty, Teslin Tlingit) are elders who do a nontraditional grouse dance in which Sharon plays the male grouse who catches Charlie. After visiting queer dance clubs and the very campy nightlife, Charlie also tries out dancing to Madonna's song with X-rated themes, "Express Yourself." This film title and content uses two-spirit humor and contemporary realities to affirm two-spirit identity in a way similar to Thirza Cuthand's (Little Pine Cree Nation) notable short films. While Cuthand's *Lessons in Baby Dyke Theory: The Diasporic Impact of Cross-Generational Barrers* (1995) introduces a desire to increase lesbian youth representation, her *Through the Looking Glass* (1999) humorously addresses the barriers in achieving a mixed-race Red/White identity in conjunction with queer identity.[14] These films utilize in-your-face Indigenous humor to approach serious Indigenous topics like identity alienation rooted in genocidal settler colonial policies.

Through Indigenous humor, Aucoin rhetorically codes both the Indigenous and queer historical traumas in his film title. Aucoin's 1998 two-spirit work follows Van Sant's 1991 depiction of queer desire that radically opposed the Classic Hollywood 1934–1968 censorship in which the majority of visibly LGBTQ characters either had to commit suicide or die a particularly violent death, a film history well documented in *The Celluloid Closet*.[15] For B. Ruby Rich, *My Own Private Idaho* was among a critical 1990s cohort of unapologetic "New Queer Media" that worked "as a response to the stigma and shame wrought by a culture that continued to pathologize gay men and blame them for the devastating HIV/AIDS epidemic."[16] Working off the queer B-52's 1980 song title and song chorus "Private Idaho" that represents a fearful state of mind, *My Own Private Idaho* makes public the private queer "hustling" lives of Mike Waters (Joaquin Phoenix) and Scott Favor (Keanu Reeves) in a time when male sex workers with male clientele faced high mortality rates from AIDS. Not only is Mike's profession of erotic love for Scott shameless and unrequited, but also the film makes public that Mike was born from the incestuous union of his older brother and his institutionalized mother without resounding judgments on the familial chaos that ensues. In turn, the "private" matter that Aucoin reveals in his film is the ongoing context of cultural genocide and domestic violence into which he was born as a two-spirit person. Aucoin's French-Arcadian Canadian father was part of the institution that normalized violence against Indigenous children in the traumatic Lower Post Indian Residential School where Aucoin's Tlingit mother was interned. This school violence became normalized as domestic violence once Aucoin's parents married and had mixed French-Tlingit children in an alcoholic environment. Like *My Own Private Idaho*, *My Own Private Lower Post* foregrounds themes of queer memory, neglect, and mental illness, along with revelations of profound familial and state abandonment.

Unlike Van Sant who made settler colonial depictions of the Chinook Portland and the Tenino/Warm Springs Deschutes River stops on his Oregon/Idaho buddy road film, Aucoin chose a rhetorical film title that exposes how settler colonial places are made through the genocidal State policies and programs aimed to assimilate and disappear Indigenous peoples. Unfortunately, white settler colonial conventions that ruled 1900s Hollywood films largely continued on in the 1990s New Queer Cinema and into postmillennial LGBTQ+ cinema, including *My Own Private Idaho*. When the young white male sex workers Mike and Scott first appear under the Elk iron sculpture of Chapman Park in Portland, they do so with the director's addition of a sculptured Native American man (a white actor in patina paint redface) in a loincloth riding the elk. This appropriation of the Native Americans as a symbol of wilderness and queer erotic freedom repeats as a non-diegetic Native American drumming and song intensifies the iconic campfire climactic scene in which Mike professes his desire to kiss Scott and explore homoerotic love with him. *My Own Private Idaho* displays New Queer Cinema's ongoing settler colonial fantasy that appropriating "Indian" freedom in nature equates to white queer sexual freedom. Substituting "Lower Post" for "Idaho" in the film title *My Own Private Lower Post*, Aucoin is rhetorically referencing the unapologetic queerness in Van Sant's 1991 film as well as indicting Canada's Indian residential schools traumatic assimilation programs. That Lower Post completes Aucoin's title is important as the title is the most public part of a film. Chief Robert Joseph of the Kwakwaka'wakw First Nations explained the need for public Indian residential school recognition that Aucoin and his mother demonstrated so that "there would be no one in Canada who didn't know the issue or who would say, 'I forget.'"[17] Through his title, Aucoin ensures that the public cannot forget the damaging legacy of the Lower Post Indian Residential School and its Christian settler cis-heteropatriarchy.

For Aucoin to seamlessly integrate his two-spirit presence throughout all levels of production in his own film speaks to a high level of sovereign Tlingit two-spirit visual rhetoric only sometimes seen in comparative two-spirit films of the 1990s and 2000s. Aucoin's central position in the film's healing scenes contrasts with decades of media in which two-spirit people are merely trying to gain access to ceremony in Indigenous communities where they are initially not wanted. For Aucoin to position himself as a two-spirit protagonist, narrator, and director is itself a strong rhetorical move that shows that two-spirit people have an established place in healing their Clans and Nations. In contrast, Shelly Niro (Mohawk) directed *Honey Moccasin* (1998) and featured a male-bodied two-spirit jingle dress dancer Zachery John (Billy Merasty, Cree) who actually dances in stolen women's regalia in a basement, which functions as the two-spirit–phobic "closet." While Niro's two-spirit representation is sympathetic, the fact remains that the two-spirit character is a thief and the antagonist of the film. Male-bodied jingle dress dancing is still an issue in Sharon Desjarlais's (Cree/Métis/Ojibwe) 2007 *Two-Spirited* short produced within the National Film Board of Canada's First Stories series.[18] *Two-Spirited* features a male-bodied Stoney Nakoda jingle dress dancer Rodney "Geeyo" Poucette who returns to the Kamloops Powwow arena to compete five years after being thrown out of the competition there for having danced and won in the women's jingle dance category. This rejection of two-spirit people from healing dances in *Honey Moccasin* and *Two-Spirited* is an unspoken result of the very Indian residential schools that forced Christian cis-heteropatriarchy onto Indigenous children and forbade two-spirit genders from being supported as the generations went forward.[19]

That the 2008 film director Duane Gastant' Aucoin is a two-spirit Yanyédi (Wolf Clan) representative of the Teslin Tlingit Council uniquely speaks to an important reclamation of two-spirit land, Nation, and healing within the genre of First Nations media. Filming on Teslin Tlingit Nation's land, Aucoin is able to make rare and critical two-spirit rhetorical interventions in the maintenance of two-spirit Teslin Tlingit language, kinship, healing, singing, and sovereign oral traditions. While it is important to have urban Indigenous media, Euro-American film scholar Lisa Tatonetti was correct in writing that film audiences should be not be "forced to choose" between seeing clearly queer but vaguely Indigenous characters and viewing clearly Indigenous protagonists who are only out as queer in off-reservation/reserve spaces. For example, she criticizes *Johnny Greyeyes* (2000) for only portraying First Nations lesbians in a Canadian prison while letting the reserve act as a sanctuary for non-queer families.[20] Longboy filmed *Water into Fire* in Vancouver, where he was adopted and raised by Euro-Canadians far from his parents' Sayisi Dene reserve, and so also does not address this split between the queer city versus the straight reserve. Longboy never converses directly with his Dene family as he sorts out the intense AIDS violence he is confronting as an urban two-spirit person. In contrast, Aucoin films oral traditions on his own reserve, with his own family, and in his own Indigenous language. He also went through an urban Indian experience outside of Teslin, but eventually moved back from Vancouver to help with the Teslin Tlingit Heritage Center. Aucoin's reserve setting helps to heal that urban/reserve split and show wholeness for two-spirit people living and working openly within their own First Nations.

Part of what is so powerful about *My Own Private Lower Post* is that it is one of the few two-spirit films to this day to depict intergenerational Indigenous alcoholism as stemming from the Christian heteropatriarchal Indian residential school programs of Canada. More often, contemporary "realistic" two-spirit films like those of Sherman Alexie's (Spokane/Coeur d'Alene) *The Business of Fancydancing* (2010) or Adam Garnet Jones's (Cree/Métis) *Fire Song* (2015) present widespread alcoholism on the reserve/reservation without grounded references to the historical causes of today's illnesses.[21] While two-spirit director Clint Alberta was brave to depict the identity disruption left in the wake of his absent alcoholic father in his queer anti-ethnographic *Deep Inside Clint Starr*, he also did not delve into the historical causes of his Dene Métis father's addictions and violence.[22] The immensely talented Alberta, who reports memories of child abuse in his film, committed suicide in 2002, an example of the high suicide and sexual abuse rates that remain as some of the many unresolved issues among two-spirit people and Indigenous communities. Documenting historical trauma, Karina Walters finds key correlations: where there is land separation and loss of culture, two-spirit people suffer more mental and physical health issues, often exacerbated by cycles of unemployment, poor housing, alcoholism, gendered/sexual violence, and drug use.[23] Aucoin's film makes plain intergenerational trauma, integrating an historical context rarely offered amid the dysfunctions commonly portrayed in two-spirit films.

My Own Private Lower Post Film Apologies and Rhetoric Analysis

Aucoin's foregrounding of the Tlingit language in the beginning and end of the film makes important rhetorical statements about linguistic sovereignty that counter the Indian residential school's attempt to eradicate Indigenous language and culture through Christian and English language assimilation projects. That Aucoin's film begins and ends with his own Tlingit language singing signals an arc of recovery of Tlingit rhetoric through the incorporation of Tlingit song and drumming that welcomes and bids farewell to the listener. While the first Tlingit song plays, black-and-white historical photos of Tlingit communities, celebrations, boating, and games flash in succession across the screen. Some of these images are reclaimed from settler archives, returning ownership of the images back to the Tlingit gaze.

When the richness of Aucoin's Tlingit singing stops, it marks the cultural interruption in Tlingit narrative and language use that occurred through the restriction of Tlingit language in residential schools. In this silence, black-and-white photographic images of Indigenous residential school children begin to fade in and out as Canadian prime minister Stephen Harper stridently states,

> Mr. Speaker, I stand before you today to offer an apology to former students of Indian residential schools. The treatment of children in Indian residential schools is a sad chapter in our history. We now recognize that, far too often, these institutions gave rise to abuse or neglect and were inadequately controlled, and we apologize for failing to protect you. Not only did you suffer these abuses as children, but as you became parents, you were powerless to protect your own children from suffering the same experience, and for this we are sorry.

This apology formally offered by Canadian prime minister Harper in 2008 was a cornerstone of the Settlement Agreement and the Indian Residential Schools Truth and Reconciliation Commission that attempted to address cultural genocide and Indigenous child abuse. This exact moment was a victory for many Indian residential school survivors such as Chief Robert Joseph, who explained that "when the apology came, I was so happy, so liberated. . . . I suddenly recognized that it wasn't our fault . . . these misconstrued policies that were intended to destroy our Indianness. When you discover that attempt, then you're not ashamed anymore."[24] This moment of apology is an Indigenous victory that Aucoin includes with emotional triumph.

And yet the State apology only begins a healing journey for survivors to tell their own story, and to maintain control over how the response to that historical trauma would be realized. Rather than letting the official Canadian apology become the central rhetorical moment in the film's narrative, Aucoin ultimately features his mother's apology to him for her years of alcoholic parenting. Aucoin does not free the government from its responsibility in formulating the destructive residential school policy from the late 1800s well into the 1900s, but he does emphasize what he can do within the teachings that his mother and mother's Yanyédi Clan instilled in him, even through her difficult years. His film really is about rematriation, reclaiming his matrilineal Wolf Clan place and power. While *My Own Private Lower Post* makes evident the scars of cultural genocide that the settler colonial Canadian government inflicted upon Aucoin's family, the film also centers the absolute need for Indigenous people to initiate their own family and Clan healing process in their own way. Aucoin focuses on Teslin Tlingit language, songs, medicine, narratives, and rhetoric rather than relying upon the State to step in with only Western modes of therapy, drugs, and jurisprudence.

Aucoin responds to Harper's apology by recounting the specific traumas within his Tlingit family, and especially that of his mother, Vicky Bob. By taking active steps to heal in the film, Aucoin minimizes the potential that Harper's settler rhetoric diminishes Indigenous peoples' sovereignty by continuing to situate the residential school survivors as passive victims of the State. Echoing Sarah Deer's analysis of violence against Indigenous women, Tanana Athabaskan scholar Dian Million notes how the settler colonial State rhetorically situates Indigenous people as officially recognized "victims" of a failed, past State policy in order to increase Indigenous dependency upon the settler State's anti-Indigenous therapeutic and policing programs as the mode of therapy.[25] As further proof of Harper's anti-sovereign intent, Million outlines how Harper's choice to battle the domestic violence that resulted from residential school trauma involved increasing State police and State social work centers while defunding Indigenous women's own programs to serve their own communities of abused women.[26] Million countered neoliberal Canadian rhetoric by advocating for local Indigenous movements to heal the scars of residential school internments and related domestic violence with the help of Indigenous sovereign legislation, policy, traditional medicine, language, feminism, and story.[27] Her anti-State and pro-Indigenous health sovereignty parallels much of the Tlingit rhetoric that Aucoin explores through his film.

Aucoin translates "Ha Kus Teyea" as "Our Way" in his film and in his "Truth and Reconciliation" essay.[28] Ha Kus Teyea is a key rhetorical signal of a Teslin Tlingit language and healing departure from the State's logics of patriarchal English-only Christian education and the Indian residential school system. In *My Own Private Lower Post*, Aucoin travels with his mother to the now-defunct Lower Post Indian Residential School to make peace with her culturally and physically abusive school and work experiences there. Once back home at Teslin, both smudge with protective sage and sing a prayer in Tlingit before discussing the difficult Catholic Lower Post memories. After Aucoin and his mother enter the mother's Teslin home similarly dressed in blue jeans, button-down shirt, and distinctive embroidered and shell-beaded vests with the highlighted Yanyédi (Wolf Clan) crest, Aucoin lights sage on an abalone shell and explains, "*Ha Kus Teyea*, Our Tlingit Way, has the medicines that will cleanse and protect us." As both begin to bless themselves with the smoke, he explains, "We smudge with sage to purify our spirits and to lift our spirits up to the spirit world. We sing our song so our voices will be heard in a good way. The truth needs a safe place to be heard." Aucoin sings, and both he and his mother face in one direction and then turn clockwise to the next direction as Aucoin continues the song and the scene fades to black. It is important to note that Aucoin does not portray the full ceremony and song. Rather, he intimates a longer ceremonial process that those within the culture may recognize. To follow Tlingit healing protocol before looking through the potentially triggering black-and-white family photographs of Lower Post is significant. It demonstrates how Ha Kus Teyea is at work decolonizing and healing Aucoin's family and community. Reencountering the historical trauma of domestic violence and alcoholism could re-traumatize Aucoin, his mother, and the audience who watches. For a Tlingit and Indigenous audience especially, this visual rhetoric of singing, smudging, and finding safe spaces in confronting residential school experiences is an important reminder of how to begin to safely heal from historical traumas. Here we are reminded again of Gross's Native American rhetoric, in which speakers draw upon the spirit before speaking.[29] Both Aucoin and Bob smudge and pray with the spirit to help with the speaking and healing of traumas.

Teslin Tlingit Parenting and Rhetorics of Healing Historical Trauma

In his "Truth and Reconciliation" essay, Aucoin explains how he was angry at his mother most of his life because he never understood how residential school history and policy shaped her hurtful behavior. He merely blamed her for what she did to him as a mother, an attitude he overcomes from the first moments of the film. With her son at her side, Vicky Bob narrates the patterns of physical abuse that the Lower Post Roman Catholic nuns established and were then carried on by her Catholic white husband, who helped run the Lower Post boy's school. She tearfully narrates her own subsequent alcoholism, her grief due to the death of a child who was injured during delivery, and her eventual sobriety. She apologizes to Aucoin for her behavior. Aucoin then cites his own drinking and lack of parenting skills as a direct result of the abuses that were normalized at Lower Post Indian Residential School, exemplifying how historical trauma travels across generations. He recounts in the film that his subsequent lack of parenting skills made his own two-spirit parenting with his male partner difficult. After a rebellious youth, he alternated between the harshly restrictive and negligently permissive ways of his father's and mother's respective modes of parenting. In the end, Aucoin forgives his father for the domestic abuse. He also thanks his now sober mother for trying as best she could to parent. Although Aucoin forgives his deceased white father, the film demonstrates that the matrilineal Tlingit cultural, linguistic, and spiritual sovereignty, or "Ha Kus Teyea" (Our Way), is the only lasting salve for those harrowing residential school experiences. In the final scene, both Aucoin and his mother are crying, but both are also embracing each other.

This film's parenting scene receives commentary in Aucoin's essay as well. Aucoin returns to the idea of facing the four directions to improve parenting. He writes, "Parents, the most important thing we can say to our kids is within four directions. 1) I did my best for you. 2) I made mistakes. 3) I'm sorry. 4) I love you."[30] The reason why these words are important is that they can lead to decreasing dysfunction when it comes to parenting. His essay traces a trajectory of hope for the Tlingit future. Aucoin shares that his parenting was less dysfunctional than that of his mother, and that his kids have even better parenting skills than he provided for them. Aucoin was born at Lower Post, but never knew how the abuse of that place impacted his life until after his kids were grown. He would have remained angry at his parents had he not known the history of residential school policy that forced his mother from her culture and home, a story that impacted decades of Indigenous children from the late 1800s up until the mid-1900s when Aucoin was born. In writing the essay and making the film, Aucoin not only heals his mother and himself, but also helps the next generations understand why Indigenous parenting is often so lacking due to the government's residential school policy.

Aucoin's personal statements rhetorically improve the ethos of his film. He can see the improvement in the parenting skills in his own family across three generations, and so the path of healing and hope is one that others will be more liable to follow given his personal narratives of success. Part of the effectiveness of Aucoin's visual film rhetoric is that the story is so very personal and protected at the same time. When Gross explains Native American rhetoric saying, "Knowledge that is personal is preferred," he qualifies in the next page, "while it is true that we can have shared experiences, the exact nature of the experience will depend on what the Creator put there for us to experience individually."[31] The rhetorical impact that personal experience allows is for the rhetor to be potentially more believable, for one's experiences, difficult or joyous, are ultimately facilitated by the Creator. In speaking from personal experience and from the heart, a political leader such as Aucoin is better able to meet the rhetorical criteria of his audiences to answer in the affirmative a central question that Gross says Indigenous people pose to their Native American rhetors: "Can I trust this person?"[32] If Aucoin as a leader was suggesting that we heal historical trauma without demonstrating that healing process himself, who would believe him? That Vicky Bob as his mother elder supports him also speaks to his credibility or ethos. She is ultimately allowing him to film her and thus demonstrate that the path they took to heal can be a good one for others who have experienced similar traumas.

Enter Teslin Tlingit Language and Yéil (Raven) Visual Rhetoric

To make the point clear about Tlingit health, visual, and linguistic sovereignty, the conclusion of the film is a transformative and genderqueer Raven story of creation that is performed in Tlingit with English subtitles. Gross would see this sudden shift from contemporary mother-son story to an ancient Raven narrative as a natural form of Indigenous rhetorical "digression" based upon "spiritual values" that creation stories relate.[33] As Indigenous rhetoric supports the philosophy that all things are connected across time and space, one could expect that creation narratives would appear alongside an Indian residential school narrative in an Indigenous film. This reliance on creation narratives is also part of what Gross calls speaking "with the spirit," which include the spirits of animals and creation narratives. He states that "the speaker tries to be guided by the spirits as much as possible and, if not the spirits directly, by spiritual values and ways of thinking."[34] For Aucoin to return to the creation of the sky luminaries realigns the healing narrative at hand back to Tlingit spiritual origins.

In the film's concluding Raven story, Aucoin plays the lead role Nashakaankowu as he retells the release of the sun, moon, and stars by Raven. Raven is played by the two-spirit ally and celebrated performer Sharon Shorty, who is herself of the Teslin Tlingit Kùkhhittàn (Raven Child) Clan, further establishing the importance of Clan-based knowledge. That the Tlingit woman Shorty plays the male Raven adds to the humor of the story as Raven tricks everyone by playing the role of a human crybaby. Just as Raven transforms into a human, the Raven Clan woman Shorty transforms into a male Raven for the sake of the story, showing how adaptation and transformation are alive and well within Tlingit culture as originally taught by Raven. In the two-spirit media context, Shorty is a key two-spirit ally as she embodies the often-humorous transformation from human to Raven and from feminine to masculine.

In the *My Own Private Lower Post* Raven story, the world begins in darkness and shadows, "as dark as the wings of the Raven himself," narrates Aucoin as he spreads his arms out like Raven wings in a shot above Teslin Lake. As he takes on the role of the Tlingit leader Nashakaankowu, he explains that Raven desires the sun, moon, and stars and that Nashakaankowu kept them in boxes as great treasures. In the story, Raven transforms into a spruce needle, is ingested by Nashakaankowu's daughter, and is born nine days later as a fast-growing human child. The Raven-grandchild receives the treasured three boxes only after crying for them incessantly. The following English subtitles accompany Aucoin's completely Teslin Tlingit–language narrative of what happens once Raven freed the stars, moon, and sun from their boxes into the sky:

> . . . Raven regained his true form and flew away happy.
> . . . Nashankaankowu was sad over what he lost.
> . . . But then a ray of light shown down on him.
> He felt its warmth and it felt good.
> And, he finally accepted and understood.

Aucoin concludes that just as Raven improved the world by releasing the luminaries that were once locked away in boxes, so must residential school survivors share their once-hidden stories to heal their respective Nations and Clans. He prefaces the story saying, "The legend of Raven stealing the sun teaches me something new every time. Like Raven, I was tired of the darkness. And like Nashakaankowu, I didn't want to share my light. But in the end, the box is now open and everything is made clear. My hope is that Raven's light will shine down upon you, too." Both Raven and residential school stories tell of recovery after incredible theft. Here Aucoin shows how the use of stories can shift in meaning depending upon one's perspective. In agreement, Gross shares that the Native American rhetoric of storytelling is not meant to have one moral, but many teachings as one evolves. He states, "Stories become like seeds planted in one's mind that can grow and then be revisited from time to time to harvest the new wisdom they present."[35] The Raven story that draws upon human parenting instincts told since time immemorial gains new rhetorical meaning for Aucoin in the context of healing Indian residential school trauma in his film.

Aucoin's mother returns in the final scene wearing a Yanyédi crest cape to hug her son at the shore of Teslin Lake, their aboriginal home from which she was once forcibly removed by the Canadian State. This image of both being on Teslin Lake and Tlingit land after forced removal is one of the more striking visual rhetorical devices that the film uses. Walters documents the centrality of land in healing historical trauma for Indigenous people, noting the ways in which "place and land are directly tied to indigenous identity and health."[36] Being on the homeland and water itself are healing, as the waterways recall the stories that can help resituate the present-day Tlingit with the help of Haa Kusteeyi.

While Vicky Bob's Teslin Tlingit land and culture had all the medicine needed to begin to heal those rifts of State-mandated familial, land, and cultural separation, it took time, experience, and Raven to access it. With a sharp beak and bright eyes, Raven gets into things like the chief's daughter's womb and the rich man's boxes of luminaries. Raven sets in motion the first changes in the cosmos that resonate with all the subsequent changes of learning and enlightenment. For Aucoin's people, half of the Clans are under the Raven moiety while the other half are under the Wolf/Eagle moiety. Traditionally, these Tlingit matrilineal moieties marry each other. For the Tlingit and many Indigenous peoples, there is no regeneration and continuity without Raven's strong imprint.

Personal Reflection on Raven Rhetorics

Having considered the Teslin Tlingit two-spirit visual rhetoric of the film in general, I will now share reflections on how the Indigenous rhetoric of Aucoin impacts my own healing journey as a two-spirit person. Gross's observation that Anishinaabe and Native American rhetors, especially elders, often speak to the "larger needs" of their audiences can apply to screening Indigenous films at two-spirit gatherings.[37] In other words, the two-spirit event coordinators can choose to screen particular films and schedule elders they feel will speak to the larger of needs of a two-spirit audience, even when the audience may not be able to voice those needs. I can make this rhetorical connection having first viewed Duane Gastant' Aucoin's *My Own Private Lower Post* while attending the 2013 Northeast Two-Spirit Society (NE2SS) "Two-Part Two-Spirit Training" in Manhattan. After NE2SS organizer Harlan Pruden (Saddle Lake Cree Nation) outlined the two-spirit identity as a reclamation of mixed-gender and queer Indigenous traditions, he screened the thirty-five-minute video. Pruden framed the screening within the larger goals of reinforcing two-spirit "traditional practices" as a way to begin healing the "historical trauma" that "led to the dissolution of the role and the displacement of Two-Spirit people from within their Nations and Native communities."[38] He initiated a personal discussion about the themes in the film of healing, sovereignty, historical trauma, Indian residential schools, rage, alcoholism, and dysfunctional parenting—and how these themes intersect with two-spirit healing. Some of those present related their own two-spirit experiences within their respective Nations to the themes of the film. Others connected the film's healing message to the real needs of two-spirit clients within their urban, community-based, behavioral health, mental health, and HIV/AIDS service provider organizations. Even after several years of reviewing two-spirit media and film history, I maintain my original impression that *My Own Private Lower Post* is an important two-spirit media to share. And here is where I digress into a family story I originally shared in the Denver 2018 American Academy of Religion paper I gave on this film. It was Native American audience members who responded to this story, which surprised me at that time. With their encouragement, I include it now and then expand on its context.

When I was in third grade, I moved in with my mom's parents on 67th Street in south Sacramento, on Nisenan lands. Even when my mom, sisters, and I relocated to the next neighborhood, I would find myself back there after grammar school while my mom worked. My grandparents Joe and Sarah Villalobos had a California black walnut tree by their front yard sidewalk, and I liked walnuts. But those nuts were especially tough, not like the dried treated ones in the store bins I could scoop out and break into easily. The street walnuts' outsides were fleshy green, and even after those parts rotted black and fell off, the tan walnuts inside were hard to crack. I remember trying to get at them one year during grammar school. I tried throwing them against the street asphalt with all my might, hitting them with rocks, and stomping on them with my tennis shoes, but those walnuts would just bounce and not break. Seeing no success, I gave up. My grandpa liked to sit in the garage with the door up and smoke his pipe, I guess watching me while I played in the front yard. One day he spoke to me in an encouraging voice that I now know he only used when I was a kid. Smiling and nodding and motioning with his pipe toward the walnut tree with some crows in it he said, "Watch those crows.

Watch them. They're smart." I knew those crows would peer at me from the walnut tree, but it hadn't occurred to me to return their gaze. So, I went out to watch them another day where they gathered in the walnut tree. There, I saw it. Carefully, one crow swooped down to the street and picked up a tough walnut already ripened and fallen. Quickly, ze returned to a perch on a walnut branch that hung over the street and waited. At just the right moment, ze dropped zir walnut in front of a car speeding down the road and under that walnut tree. I heard the smash and crack as the heavy car tires flattened out the nut. Once the car passed a safe distance, ze swooped back down and picked out the fleshy walnut parts scattered on the road. Amazed, I stood and watched the crows do this several times with success, more success than I'd had as they'd watched me.

Years later, I'd take my lunch breaks from my Hiram Johnson High School by walking down the street, past that walnut tree, and into my grandpa's open garage, never thinking too much about those crows or about Indigenous cultures. Local Nisenan and Miwok dances and Nations made a comeback during my youth, but Nisenan and Miwok weren't taught about in my urban schools except for a brief mention in Sutter's Fort Gold Rush history. I was just beginning to see the Harry Fonseca (Nisenan Maidu) Coyote series, but didn't know then that he and I were what would be called two-spirit people. I hadn't yet really thought about what protocols the local Valley Nisenan and Plains Miwok had for gathering, even after Gold Rush settlerism decimated their populations and only some regained federal recognition decades after the federal Rancheria Acts in 1959.[39]

An Indigenous namelessness extended into my own family. As my Grandpa Joe on my maternal side was a light-skinned Mexican-American World War II veteran born in Clifton, Arizona, it didn't occur to me that there was anything Zacateco about him or me, even though he admitted that he was part Indian from Zacatecas. In segregated California, my Grandpa Joe identified more with his Basque Mayagoitia patrilineage, although he took his mother's last name Villalobos. I was a contrast in that, like my father and paternal grandfather, I grew up racialized as "indio/Indian/dark-skinned," and not white-passing. However, while I was born after the 1964 Civil Rights Act during the Black, Chicana/o, American Indian Movement eras of Washington, Idaho, and California history, my parents and grandparents lived through the earlier US legal segregation eras built on localized Indigenous genocides. It wasn't until I went to my Grandpa Joe's mother's pueblo Jerez in Zacatecas years later that I was greeted with "Bienvenidos a tierra indígena" (Welcome to Indigenous land). When I asked my *tía* (aunt) in Jerez what our Indigenous lineage is, she said, "Chichimeca," what is also called more specifically Zacateco, a Nahuatl-speaking desert peoples who tend toward matrilineal descent. Four decades after watching those crows on the walnut tree, I lived to see my Grandpa Joe slowly decline and pass away in his nineties. At his grave in Orange, California, in the Tongva coastal region where I was born, I offered the Burley and Bright Half and Half pipe tobacco that my Grandpa Joe smoked in his garage so many years ago.

As I'd watched those crows crack walnuts, I wasn't aware that both my grandfathers also had roots from the Caxcan borderlands of Zacatecas and Jalisco in which Mother Crow is a central creatrix figure in ceremonies celebrating the summer monsoon rains.[40] In my paternal *abuelo* (grandfather) Santiago's Caxcan pueblo, Juchipila, Zacatecas, the Mother Crow's flower or *cacalotxuchil* (crow flower) is the main offering to give Xochipilli (Flower Child) thanks for the monsoon rains, for nature's regeneration, and for the ability to procreate and enjoy life.[41] My abuelo Santiago told stories of *La Aguila Blanca* (The White Eagle Woman) and *El Don Coyote* (Old Man Coyote/ Huehuecoyotzin), who were clever, strong, and transformational. There, in sight of the Caxcan Creation Mountain Tlachialoyantepec outlined by the Juchipila River, my pueblo elders affirmed, "¡Sí somos Caxcanes!" ("Yes, we are Caxcanes!") when I returned to Juchipila with my dad as a young adult. All I knew about crows while growing up in the Palouse lands of Pullman, Washington, and Idaho, is that my dad would "CAAA CAAA" at the crows, and they'd "CAAA CAAA" back. In fact, *cacalot* is the Caxcan Nahuatl variant word for crow/raven, and to me that word sounds like their raucous calls, something I've also only wondered about when I've heard or read the Navajo word for crow *gáagii*, the Lakota crow word *kȟaŋǧí*, and the Nisenan words for crow and raven, a·k and ka·k, respectively.[42] Mixing Edgar Allen Poe, my love of cornflakes and strawberries, and Indigenous crow stories, my dad once frightened me in Idaho with a story of a crow who plucked out a blind old man's eye and fed it to him in his cornflakes like a bloody strawberry. Although this story was different from the Caxcan eagle, rabbit, and coyote stories my dad's great-grandfathers passed across generations, it still reflected the larger sense that Raven and other transformers can both make us pay dearly for our lack of vision and give answers to problems that we sometimes did not know even existed.

Other memories are sometimes harder to recall. As a five-year-old child, I once woke up terrified and alone in the dark of my Dad's VW van outside a bar in the Idaho woods where he'd left me to get drunk. During his Chicano activism days, he would somehow survive a series of drunken car crashes, blackouts, and even waking up in a Folsom Prison holding cell. Yet, even when my dad drank daily, he dreamed and wrote of healing. I remember the Schitsu'umsh (Coeur d'Alene) and Nimiipuu (Nez Perce) college students acting in my dad's play in Moscow, Idaho. With arms outspread and draped in an Indian blanket, the Nimiipuu play protoganist cried, "I am the Human Spirit!" and it took everyone in the play to finally hold and heal the spirit who had been slowly dying. I also remember Don Gregorio, the Mexican Indigenous curandero (healer) and his bird-bright eyes as he'd watch me eat the blackened scrambled eggs he'd cooked for me while my dad worked as a college counselor in Moscow. The elderly Don Gregorio stayed with us as he helped to heal my dad from alcoholism, for a time filling the void left by my abuelo Santiago's passing and opening up a spiritual link to a larger world. When Don Gregorio once joked that he could fly to my dad, he was drawing upon an Indigenous knowledge that healing is mysterious, unbound by ordinary human consciousness and perceived physical limitations. When I was six, I saw crows silently gather on the wintering tree outside a hotel window on a trip with my dad back to California. It was the first year of what would become my dad's decades-long sobriety supported by 12-step programs.

Like my dad, both my grandfathers were alcoholics, and our families fractured in different ways because of that. My grandparents remained together, but my parents divorced when I was five years old. For my grandfathers, it wasn't Canadian Indian residential schools that prompted alcoholism; it was centuries of Mexican Indian colonial-induced epidemics, enslavements, wars, racialized mixing, and forced migrations. The widespread alcoholism and drug addictions we see in many of our Peoples today aren't indigenous to the Americas. Our seasonal Chichimeca/Caxcan medicines like tequila, sacred datura, tobacco, corn beer, and peyote were once respected only in ceremonies guided by strict protocols that ensured community health and well-being. As colonization progressed, Indigenous and Mestizo men in Mexico have been more apt to fall into alcoholism than women. The machismo of drinking is now something of a cult in many places in Mexico and the United States, but it has many roots. Chichimeca Wars, the Mexican Revolution, World War II, and the Vietnam War are the string of wars in which my father, grandfathers, and ancestors fought that impacted their drinking and mental health. What remains is a paradox. My dad and grandfathers were alcoholics and heavily impacted by colonialization, and yet they also taught me about crows, eagles, hawks, and other birds central to our Chichimeca belief systems of Zacatecas. While their drinking days made them erratic, they also cared for me when few others did. They cared enough to share their stories with me as their parents and grandparents had shared stories with them. Even after decades of effort, I am still in the process of understanding this wide sweep of changes.

Although Aucoin's matrilineal Raven story makes me think of my Grandpa Joe, crows, drinking, and walnuts, I acknowledge a different matrilineal balance in my family. While my mom was busy working, I spent a lot of time with her mother. Grandma Sarah Villalobos fed me in a different way than my Grandpa Joe could. As a two-spirit person, I found that she strengthened the feminine spirit within me. My Grandma Sarah also loved all birds. Her mindful care was the balance to my father's and grandfathers' drinking. Because she did not have addictions, it was easier to assimilate her teachings: to find beauty inside and around us, and to care for one another. It was my Grandma Sarah who watered and maintained the yard, medicine plants, and trees. She followed her mother Amada, who we called Grande and who raised corn, beans, and squash in Namiquipa, Chihuahua, on her own land that held an interrelated mix of Rarámuri and Apache matrilineal lines. Like my older sister and mother, I never became a drinker. But I lived in fear of becoming one, and I harbored resentments toward those who did in my family and communities. This was the feminine pattern in my family. I now see how my sobriety was still unbalanced because I hadn't forgiven, learned to move on, and focused instead on the underlying medicine within the Indigenous relationships that my dad and grandfathers were subtly teaching. With this realization comes a further decolonization of healing from the gendered and intergenerational effects of alcoholism.

What Aucoin showed and what I believe is that with effort, we as two-spirit people can retain our roles as mediators, teachers, and healers between different genders and generations. As two-spirit people, it is important for us to balance masculine and feminine, and to heal the harms in both that our histories present to us. Cis-heteropatriarchal colonization has made two-spirit familial balance tricky. The alcoholic legacies, Indigenous/settler–mixed families, and anti-Indigenous policies that Aucoin begins to uncover make this balancing act even more complicated. Yet Aucoin's film visualizes two-spirit Tlingit-specific modes of healing from alcoholism and residential school historical trauma. For two-spirit audiences, the film is inspirational as Aucoin seamlessly weaves himself as a two-spirit person throughout the central parenting and healing Haa Kusteeyi narrative in a manner that is rarely achieved in two-spirit film history.

While I don't have the skills to do the translation from Tlingit needed to really understand the Tlingit-language rhetoric, that wasn't the point of screening *My Own Private Lower Post* to an urban, non-Tlingit, and largely two-spirit audience. We were to make of it what we could from various perspectives that did not necessarily correspond to the sovereign understandings of the Teslin Tlingit reserve settings of the film. Gross notes that a common reaction to hearing stories is for Native people to associate them with other stories that are the same or related to the one told.[43] I think the Northeast Coast Two-Spirit Society organizers showed the film knowing that it would cause many of us to think about our families and the ways that colonialism created the conditions for alcoholism and domestic violence. Understanding the ways in which historical trauma can resurface across generations shifts the way that one can begin to heal. Returning to Gross's statement, "Stories become like seeds planted in one's mind that can grow and then be revisited from time to time to harvest the new wisdom they present,"[44] I can see that my grandfathers implanted walnut-seed memories that I would gather in a different way upon my seeing *My Own Private Lower Post*. But the cacalot/raven/crow are also sowers of memory and stories. Now, I think they were showing me how to crack through a tough walnut exterior of a Mexican/American/Indian alcoholic family to get to the Chichimeca and Caxcan medicine stories inside.

Up and down North America's Pacific coasts, from Mexico to California to the Pacific Northwest, the cacalot/raven/crow hold ancient keys to our ancestral ceremonies, healing, and regeneration of the world that we as two-spirit people continuously strive to balance. While I've written about the Tlingit and Caxcan Raven/Crow stories, many more persist. Above the Sacramento Valley where I grew up, the Sierra Miwok were created from Ravens; as one account goes, after a great flood, black-feathered crows turned into the dark-skinned Miwok.[45] Here in Los Angeles where I live in sight of Hollywood, the two-spirit Tongva activist L. Frank Manriquez shares how crows taught her a gender-neutral way and to connect to Tongva ancestors across time despite colonial erasures.[46] When I see crows and ravens in the coastal Tongva village sites, I'm aware that they will likely be here long after Los Angeles has disappeared as they were here long before it appeared. It wouldn't be the first time that the rhetor Raven gets the last laugh.

Conclusion

Two-spirit Tlingit rhetoric shapes *My Own Private Lower Post* from its title to its visual modes of healing and rematriation. Aucoin's Ha Kus Teyea–informed visual rhetoric responds to the alcoholism, domestic violence, and cultural loss that followed in the wake of the Indian residential school system in Canada. It also plots out a return to a Teslin Tlingit culture in which two-spirit people remain political leaders, Clan members, co-parents, storytellers, rhetors, and healers. Through subtly drawing upon two-spirit and queer references in the title and film content, Aucoin weaves himself into media history as a two-spirit protagonist facing the intergenerational consequences of residential school traumas in the most intimate family settings. The Northeast Two-Spirit Society shared Aucoin's film as a rhetorical move to activate our own two-spirit culture and healing. While I went to New York to find out how to organize a two-spirit society that the community had asked me to lead, I came back to Los Angeles with a latent two-spirit Tlingit Raven film rhetoric that had other impacts that would take a decade to unravel. With the aid of many two-spirit people, near and far, I did help establish the City of Angels Two-Spirit Society (CATSS) in 2014. But without the ability to hear the stories from Raven, my grandfathers, and other Indigenous rhetors, I wouldn't have had the heart to begin my two-spirit activism.

Notes

1.   Duane Gastant' Aucoin, *My Own Private Lower Post* (Teslin, YT: DGA Media and T'senaglobe Media Inc., 2008).

2.   Lawrence W. Gross, "Anishinaabe Rhetoric," chap. 8 in *Anishinaabe Ways of Knowing and Being* (Farnham Surrey, UK: Ashgate, 2014), 200–201; Angela Haas, "Toward a Decolonial Digital and Visual American Indian Rhetorics Pedagogy," in *Survivance, Sovereignty, and Story: Teaching American Indian Rhetorics*, ed. Lisa King, Rose Gubele, and Anderson Joyce Rain (Logan: Utah State University Press, 2015), 197.

3.   Gross, "Anishinaabe Rhetoric," 170.

4.   Gross, "Anishinaabe Rhetoric," 169.

5.   Michele Raheja, *Reservation Reelism: Redfacing, Visual Sovereignty, and Representations of Native Americans in Film* (Lincoln: University of Nebraska Press, 2010), 90.

6.   Gross, "Anishinaabe Rhetoric," 177–78.

7.   Gross, "Anishinaabe Rhetoric," 178.

8.   Mona Smith, *Her Giveaway: A Spiritual Journey with AIDS*, VHS (Minneapolis: Minnesota American Indian AIDS Task Force, 1988); Mona Smith, *Honored by the Moon*, VHS (Minneapolis: Minnesota American Indian AIDS Task Force, 1990). Both documentaries were funded by Native American AIDS education funds, one of the few US funding sources for two-spirit film in the 1990s. Gabriel S. Estrada, "Ojibwe Lesbian Visual AIDS: On the Red Road with Carole LaFavor, *Her Giveaway* (1988), and Native LGBTQ2 Film History," *Journal of Lesbian Studies* 20, nos. 3–4 (2016): 399–400.

9.   Estrada, "Ojibwe Lesbian Visual AIDS," 403.

10.   Estrada, "Two-Spirit Film Criticism: *Fancydancing* with Imitates Dog, Desjarlais and Alexie," *Post Script: Essays in Film and the Humanities* 24, no. 3 (Summer 2010): 107.

11.   Gus Van Sant, *My Own Private Idaho* (Los Angeles: Fine Line Features, 1991).

12.   While Waugh cites Annamarie Jagose in defining "queer" as "incoherences in the allegedly stable relations between chromosomal sex, gender, and desire," his queer Canadian film history mostly subsumes First Nations into broadly queer Canadian film. Thomas Waugh, *The Romance of Transgression in Canada: Queering Sexualities, Nations, Cinemas* (Montreal: McGill-Queen's University Press, 2006), 8, 13.

13.   Duane Gastant' Aucoin, *Kichx Anagaat Yatx'i: Children of the Rainbow* (Teslin, YT: DGA Media and T'senaglobe Media Inc., 2003).

14.   Lisa Tatonetti, "Affect, Female Masculinity, and the Embodied Space Between: Two-Spirit Traces in Thirza Cuthand's Experimental Film," in *Sexual Rhetorics: Methods, Identities, Publics*, ed. Jonathan Alexander and Jacqueline Rhodes (New York: Routledge, 2015), 122.

15.   Vito Russo, *The Celluloid Closet: Homosexuality in the Movies* (New York: Harper & Row, 1987), 261–64.

16.   Nathan Smith, "Representations of the Defiant," *Times Higher Education*, February 5, 2015.

17.   Chief Robert Joseph, quoted in Vivian Belik, "Putting the Legacy of Residential

Schools to Rest," *Yukon News*, November 2019, https://www.yukon-news.com/news/putting-the-legacy-of-residential-schools-to-rest/.

18.   Sharon Desjarlais, *Two-Spirited: First Stories Volume III* (Montreal: National Film Board of Canada, 2007).

19.   Estrada, "Ojibwe Lesbian Visual AIDS," 396.

20.   Lisa Tatonetti, "Forced to Choose: Queer Indigeneity in Film," chap. 4 in *The Queerness of Native American Literature* (Minneapolis: University of Minnesota Press, 2014), 123.

21.   Estrada, "Two-Spirit Film Criticism," 115; Gabriel S. Estrada, "Obscuring Two-Spirit Deaths in the Films *Conversion* and *Fire Song*," in *Religion and Sight*, ed. Louise Child and Aaron Rosen (Bristol, UK: Equinox Publishing, 2020), 59.

22.   Karina L. Walters et al., "Dis-Placement and Dis-Ease: Land, Place and Health among American Indians and Alaska Natives," in *Communities, Neighborhoods, and Health: Expanding the Boundaries of Place*, ed. Linda M. Burton et al. (New York: Springer, 2011), 166, 173.

23.   Walters et al., "Dis-Placement and Dis-Ease," 164, 189.

24.   Belik, "Putting the Legacy."

25.   Dian Million, *Therapeutic Nations: Healing in an Age of Indigenous Human Rights* (Tucson: University of Arizona Press, 2013), 38.

26.   Million, *Therapeutic Nations*, 186.

27.   Million, *Therapeutic Nations*, 184.

28.   Duane Gastant' Aucoin, "Truth and Reconciliation," in *International Queer Indigenous Voices*, ed. Ahimsa Timoteo Bodhrán, special issue, *Yellow Medicine Review: A Journal of Indigenous Literature, Art, and Thought* (Fall 2010): 35.

29.   Gross, "Anishinaabe Rhetoric," 175.

30.   Aucoin, "Truth and Reconciliation," 35.

31.   Gross, "Anishinaabe Rhetoric," 172–73.

32.   Gross, "Anishinaabe Rhetoric," 185.

33.   Gross, "Anishinaabe Rhetoric," 171.

34.   Gross, "Anishinaabe Rhetoric," 170.

35.   Gross, "Anishinaabe Rhetoric," 183.

36.   Walters et al., "Dis-Placement and Dis-Ease," 173.

37.   Gross, "Anishinaabe Rhetoric," 176.

38.   "Two-Part Two-Spirit Training," *The Audre Lorde Project*, March 16, 2013, https://alp.org/two-part-two-spirit-training.

39.   Jesus Tarango, "Now that Columbus' Statue is Gone, Let's Replace It with a Native American Monument," *Wilton Rancheria*, September 21, 2020, http://wiltonrancheria-nsn.gov/Home/News/TabId/562/ArtMID/2929/ArticleID/1174/Now-that-Columbus'-statue-is-gone-let's-replace-it-with-a-Native-American-monument.aspx.

40.   Daisy Ocampo, "Spiritual Geographies of Indigenous Sovereignty: Connections of Caxcan with Tlachialoyantepec and Chemehuevi with Mamapukaib" (PhD diss., University of California, Riverside, 2019), 83.

41. Ocampo, "Spiritual Geographies," 83.

42. "Tsídii—Translation—Navajo-English Dictionary," Glosbe, accessed December 10, 2020, https://glosbe.com/nv/en/tsídii; "Kȟaŋǧí in English—Lakota-English Dictionary," Glosbe, accessed December 10, 2020, https://glosbe.com/lkt/en/k%C8%9Fa%C5%8B%C7%A7%C3%AD; Alfred L. Kroeber, *The Valley Nisenan* (Berkeley: University of California Press, 1929), 284. The main example of (Yéil) Raven that Aucoin narrates from *My Own Private Lower Post* does not follow this pattern.

43. Gross, "Anishinaabe Rhetoric," 183.

44. Gross, "Anishinaabe Rhetoric," 183.

45. C. Hart Merriam, "How Kah'-kah-loo the Ravens became People," in *The Dawn of the World: Myths and Weird Tales Told by the Mewan Indians of California* (Cleveland: Arthur H. Clark Company, 1910), 101.

46. Paul Christiaan Klieger, *L. Frank Manriquez* (Sacramento: California Museum, 2011); Lydia Nibley, *Two Spirits* (Los Angeles: Say Yes Quickly Productions, 2010).

CHAPTER ELEVEN

Think Kodhamidh!

Cultural Continuity through Evaluative Thinking

PHYLLIS A. FAST

THIS ESSAY TACKLES CULTURAL continuity through the evaluative and rhetorical practices of the Koyukon Athabascans in Alaska. Previously, these practices centered around riddles, which have fallen out of use since the colonial period. I argue that parents who encourage their children to think beyond the immediate are able to promote the child's intelligence as well as maintain cultural continuity. My mother was one such person. She was sent to a boarding school near Salem, Oregon (Chemawah Indian School, 1920 to 1930). She and her siblings entered as Koyukon speakers and exited during the Great Depression speaking English. She had a Koyukon accent, so while the title of this essay contains a common three-word American English expletive, I have written the words to mirror the way it sounded. In Athabascan languages *g* sounds like *k*, and *t* sounds are like the soft *d* as in the word "this" rather than the harder sound of the word "talk," although both sounds are acceptable in Denaakk'e.[1]

Following Koyukon behavioral patterns, my mother did not raise her voice or appear angry, but rather sounded more like she was teasing me. She teased me and everyone she met. When I asked my brother if he remembered the phrase "Think Kodhamidh!," he said it seemed to him that she used it as my name, while he got the second part of the phrase as his middle name: Richard Dhamidh. We both chuckled. No matter what, her teasing style worked on me,

as it goaded me to the top of the educational ladder. Later, I learned that
Mom's style of teasing is what makes an Athabascan real to other Native
Americans. I suggest that those who know each other through jokes or teasing,
whether consciously nor not, replicate patterns of thought represented in the
old Athabascan riddles of a century ago. I further suggest that such patterns
of thinking are embedded in works like Keith Basso's *Portraits of the
Whiteman*, which is funny to most Native Americans, but sometimes beyond
the ken of others.[2] Because of my mother's constant demand that I try to guess
what she meant with each vague instruction, I contend that she was expecting
me to figure out what she meant—just as her own mother might have insisted
that she figure out the meaning of Koyukon riddles. In other words, "Think
Kodhamidh!" provided a vehicle to the evaluative thinking habits of
Athabascans, and became a rhetorical device that escaped the political
attention of outsiders. The second word is not in any language. My Koyukon
mother probably learned it on playgrounds in Oregon rather than in Rampart,
Alaska, where she was born and learned Denaakk'e. Her indigenous language
is now known by the colonial term, Koyukon. Twentieth-century English
speakers made up the term "Koyukon," which refers to the language spoken
around the confluence of the Koyukuk and Yukon Rivers. Along with that
new word came more forceful colonial events, including language change.
Why invent a word like Kodhamidh when Denaakk'e is no longer in common
usage? I suggest there is more to language than speech. Rather, it is part of an
evaluative method of being and thinking as an Athabascan.

Many Koyukon cultural practices and cultural logic have persisted after at
least four nation-states invaded Alaska over that past many centuries. The
three most recent colonial powers have been Russia, Spain, and the United
States. There is evidence showing that Asian populations have comingled
with North Americans for many centuries as well. What makes a Koyukon
Athabascan distinctively different from a mainstream American? I argue that
the Alaska Native Claims Settlement Act of 1971 (whose four original Alaska
Native architects included Koyukon Athabascan Emil Notti) is proof of the
power to maintain Native American difference successfully in politics and
business as well as in other social situations.

I have argued elsewhere that the Gwich'in Athabascans of northeast
Alaska use many rhetorical styles with precision, some to maintain internal

social control while other styles promote resistance to outside forces.[3] Most such teaching methodologies are intended to maintain quiet in a hunting world where edible species are very leery of human voices. The most common silencing lessons include teasing, social silence, shunning, and riddles. In this paper I talk about methods of teaching young people to think instead of talk by having them guess at the answers to riddles. Just like every other Native group on the North American continent, Koyukons have endured the tragic loss of the complexity of political conventions, indigenous education theories, and language. I argue that loss of language itself has not included losing the customs of thought and logic. Rather, silence has guided Koyukon people to a particularly insightful level of evaluative thinking. Riddling was a fun way to move between the small populations of Koyukons in northwestern Alaska as the year opened into spring. Sadly, the Koyukon people rarely practice riddling any more. There are opportunities to learn such subjects in schools, but it is hard to change intergenerational family dynamics in order to practice languages at home. It is not simple, as in the sense of substituting nouns or verbs as we do in the common world languages. Moreover, Koyukon verbs are complex, especially when certain cultural activities are no longer frequently practiced, such as snowshoeing. Verbs, for instance, require intricate conjugations that time and former customs made easy and enjoyable.

As many linguists have observed, the Koyukon language (hereafter used interchangeably with "Denaakk'e" with respect to the language, whereas I use "Koyukon" to refer to the people) tends to be very verb-oriented rather than object-oriented. A simple example is the idea of lifting something. In English, a single verb suffices. In Denaakk'e, the choice depends on what one chooses to lift, the person's intentions, the type of object, and even what it looks like. Such themes determine the verb to be used, and often reveals the function and nature of the object before a riddle-maker can finish a sentence. In contrast to such complicated grammar, verbs in English are limited by the type of action, while Koyukons select the verb depending on the type of object or objects in question, and conjugations vary significantly thereafter. Quoting Jules Jetté, James Kari described the Koyukon verb as follows: "Not only does it express the person and number of its subject, and the time and dependence of its action as our verb does, but it has also to denote the number and the gender of its object, as well as qualities inherent to it, such as its circular, spherical, or cylindrical shape, circumstances such as it being in a sack or a dish."[4] Jetté, who was a careful scholar, called my forebears Ten'a because the term "Koyukon" had not come into being when he served the Roman Catholic Church. At that time, many people knew Denaakk'e well. Sent to northern Alaska in 1898 by the Roman Catholic Jesuits, Father Jetté found his scholarly fascination with language to be richly rewarded until 1922, when he fell ill and left Alaska for a few years. Later, he spent time in southwestern Alaska to work among the Yupiat until his death in 1927.[5]

Later generations of Koyukon people are grateful to pour over the work of Jetté. As a Jesuit priest, Jetté's mission in Alaska was to convert indigenous people to Catholicism rather than to amass volumes of linguistic material. And, true to his profession, he devalued Koyukon religious traditions as superstitions, observing, "The beliefs of the Ten'a, as known to the writer, are few. They are centered on the existence and dispositions of spirits. The Ten'a do not conceive the spirits as really spiritual, or immaterial, substances. For them, the spirits have a sort of subtle body, a kind of aerial fluid, so to speak, capable of endless transformations."[6] Fortunately for later generations, there have been many people who have written or spoken otherwise about our culture. Newer investigators have examined Athabascan religious traditions either as scholars or as practitioners. However, the question persists, what did Koyukon Athabascans retain after European and American domination? For my own knowledge and comfort, I first sought answers in kinship studies, gender studies, and political activism. I regret that I did not pursue rhetorical work and action as Patrick Moore has done, given my own mother's industrious invention of names for her children. Moore's recent work on personal naming systems among the Tha and Kaska Dene in Canada reminds me of the many people who proudly told me their Gwich'in (upriver Alaskan Athabascans) or Koyukon (downriver Alaskan Athabascans) names.[7] At the time, I thought it was part of the revitalization efforts following the Alaska Native Claims Settlement Act of 1971 rather than long-standing efforts to maintain cultural continuity in the face of obstruction from outsiders. In this essay I suggest that some of that resistance occurred in the interethnic practices of riddling among Alaska's Athabascans.

Nineteenth-century Koyukon Athabascans of Alaska used riddles to entertain each other just as the snow-filled spring awakened the land. While more southerly places expect snow to melt away in spring, Athabascans along the Yukon River looked forward to Spring Carnivals with games like snowshoeing, sled-dog races, and other social events. The Koyukon welcomed the lengthening hours of daylight by saying *Tla-dzor-karas'ana,* or "Riddle me."[8] Few continue to riddle, partly because it called for expert knowledge of Denaakk'e.

Contemporary Koyukon people and scholars of varying backgrounds agree that the original Koyukon people probably moved frequently for multiple reasons, including seasonal hunting rounds, occasional environmental catastrophes, and political strife with other indigenous Alaskans and, later, with colonial forces. While populations may have been stronger prior to colonialism, in the twenty-first century there are only a few thousand Koyukon people in Alaska or elsewhere. It is my contention that for those who wish to do so, Koyukon culture perseveres even if the language does not. Nonetheless, speakers of the Koyukon language are few, but persistent. For example, Eliza Jones, who lives in Huslia, Alaska, is one of the few Koyukon people who has worked throughout her life on translations and training systems regarding the language of her birth. Jones has imparted to her family and others an equally strong passion for Koyukon. For instance, Jones has worked with her elder, Chief Henry, to scour the scholarly work by Father Jetté. Jones and Chief Henry found dozens of riddles from the more northerly part of the Koyukon world, a world that has a complex precolonial history that appears to involve intertribal warfare between the Inupiat of both the northwestern and the northern coastal areas. The results of their work reveal a distinctively different knowledge of the river environment. Future scholars may be able to unravel the linguistic and archaeological evidence that has amassed over the past century to expose earlier movements around the Kotzebue Sound area, which may have witnessed more ethnic activity than is known at this time. Archaeological findings reveal that Kotzebue's economy centered on trade with many neighboring peoples, both in northern Alaska as well with more distant neighbors from Asia.

Moving back to the environmental aspects of the Koyukon riddles, I draw upon the work of Athabascan scholar Tim Ingold, who encourages us to let go of the confines of Western categorization of plants and animals, and think of the riddles as "moments of activity" in which each being is an instantiation of a way of being alive.[9] Imagine, as he does, that the object of the riddle is caught in a network of other entities, not merely to be seen as a name in a list of fixed types confined to a fixed set of behaviors. An example of such a moment of activity is spotting a sudden shaft of sunlight glimmer through a raindrop on a bit of intricate spiderweb. Such beauty lasts an instant, and is one that cannot be replicated or confined by words. Moreover, it does not mean anything to say that it is part of a single environment or place unless one examines atmospheric conditions at a certain point of latitude and longitude with the sun hitting the viewer's eyes exactly so at that moment. In other words, such a moment of activity is a performance by several entities, including the sun, a precise place on the earth, rain, and a spider. By making the same point using an example in English, it should be obvious that this is not domination of thought through language. Following this, Koyukon people use riddles to force those so challenged to think beyond the moment. Hence, instead of thinking of Koyukon riddles as an environmental descriptor of an object, search the riddle for external features of the environment, including the season of year, all rendered in Denaakk'e.

Jetté was fascinated with riddling because of how the customs of riddling fit within the annual social cycle of the Koyukon. Midwinter, which is the coldest and darkest part of the year, was the time for sharing the traditional cycle of legends that were generally known to Athabascans in Alaska as well as Canada. It was also the time when the last of the stored food was consumed, possibly followed by starvation. Riddling season (corresponding to the time of increased sunlight, warmer weather, and some hunting) came next. Riddling involved unusually heavy use of a much older and intensely metaphorical language reserved for riddles. Jetté wrote, "One may be able to converse freely with the natives on current topics, and still find himself in the impossibility of grasping even the main idea of the riddle-questions."[10] Successful riddles thus became teaching tools for language, nature, and possibly for maintaining ethnic boundaries. Jetté found that while different villages spoke a common Koyukon language, they chose to tell riddles that were significantly different from each other in both topic and solvability. In other words, it was a way of maintaining village identity through riddles, suggesting that Koyukon people found riddling useful in maintaining social boundaries and as a way to maintain internal cultural continuity despite not knowing the neighbors as well as they should.

The following is an example transcribed and translated by Jetté in 1913. While seemingly simple, it provides a good example of the evaluative thought process in Athabascan culture.

Tłaatsaa ḵaraa'ana: Riddle me: my shovel in-the-trail I-am-dragging.

Answer: a beaver's tail.[11]

While the riddle seems to be straightforward, it demands that the people listening show their understanting of key subtleties of the Koyukon environment in riddling season. This example differs from a similar riddle in both the version of Denaakk'e and the environmental expertise expected of the audience. The riddle collected years later by Jones from along the Koyukuk River, many miles to the north of Kokrines, where Jetté first worked, reveals significant differences caused by the passing of time and being told in a different region. Jetté, who died a decade before Jones's birth, noted many such changes as he moved from village to village and consulted with people of different generations. In common with all Koyukon people, the riddle here as well as others are intented to stimulate thought about one's own knowledge of the evnironment. For instance, the ideas about the beaver-tail riddle that village-dwelling Kaska Dene would ask about concern the notion of a shovel. A village dweller would remember to think of a shovel as a tool to smooth snow or mud, and not as a digging device. A beaver's tail is flat, comparatively heavy, and not used as a tool for digging, but rather for smoothing mud on their partially aquatic lodges. Since the entryways are usually under water until spring, they are generally not seen until riddling season. Hence, seeing traces of beaver tails also speaks to the longer sunlight hours and warmer temperatures replacing the frigid weather of midwinter.

Here is Chief Henry's version as translated by Eliza Jones.[12] Those guessing the answer were expected to understand what the rivers in Alaska were like in other seasons, along with what seeing a cache of sticks might mean in terms of life on the rivers. Note that like their human companions on the Koyukuk River, the beaver spent the brief summer harvesting as much food as possible. In terms of colonization, the beavers of North America suffered even more than Native Americans simply because the wealthier Europeans sought beaver hide and sometimes beaver oil, but rarely the meat. That and money meant that few people understood that the loss of the beaver usually involved the loss of educational role models, invasion of alcohol-bearing strangers, and guns.

Riddle: Wait, I see something: at the headwaters it looks like a cache of sticks sticking in the water.

Answer: Beaver feed pile.

Not only is the riddle about another aspect of beaver life, but also the language Chief Henry used over fifty years after Jetté was on the Yukon River is so different as to be nearly incomprehensible to younger riddle answerers, just as Jetté would have expected the same to be true of people who live in different parts of the region. In both samples, the expectation is about knowing the environment the same way that the beavers knew it and respecting how to benefit from that knowledge. While both Jones and Jetté had intimate knowledge of the environment, it was knowledge that changed with the limited incursion of outsiders—mostly due to the freezing weather and exteme distances from other amenities. Changes between the two versions boil down to distrust of people in other locations as well as advances in travel technology, such as using motorized boats on open summer water rather than treking to snow-covered beaver dens in winter primarily by snowshoe or sled. Not stated in Jones's version is the subtle message inherent in the date of her work, 1976, five years after the Alaska Native Claims Settlement Act, an act which provided money to counter the rise in language loss; the rise in communicable diseases, such as tuberculosis; and, of course, the rise in alcoholism. Jones and Chief Henry worked hard to remind their friends and relatives to heed the value of older ways of living in Alaska. Note the difference in presentation, further denoting issues related to ethnic and temporaral boundaries.

An ever present fear in villages north of the Yukon River is heating homes and other places in the winter. Wood is usually the main source since oil has to be shipped in and there are no electrical grids connecting homes to the metropolitan world. Beavers are thus an important species because they cut down wood for their own needs, and leave chips and stumps that industrious humans find and salvage. In terms of ethnic issues, outsiders best beware when it comes to taking necessary resources away from impoverished people whose economy has a different kind of existence than those of mainstream Americans.

Koyukon riddles also gave elusive medicinal cures that have been rendered complex since the advent of modern chemically based medicines in the twenty-first century. Consider the following, brought to us from Jones of Huslia on the Koyukuk River:

They would say[,] "Wait, I see something! Because we don't want to choke on smoke we're hiding our faces." Who's going to figure this out? At least at that time it was their own frigid environment that they used as a basis for their riddles. They would name different things and try to figure them out. If they came close, the one who was riddling would say, Hakhu![13]

The riddle is about the tips of black spruce, which are common throughout northern Alaska. Spruce trees in general contain more vitamin C than other plants, and much of it is in the spruce tips, which point downward from the end of their generally short branches. I have found that simply chewing on a spruce tip will prevent a cough from getting worse or turning into a severe case of influenza. Additionally, spruce pitch, which seems to drain lethargically out of black spruce trunks, is good for healing small cuts, steeping as a tea, and as a temporary patch for leaks in plumbing. Any of those answers would seem correct to the riddle-maker. As Jones writes, the topic of the riddle is using spruce tips or pitch to heal a cough, and also a subtle reminder of the season in which to find and harvest such tips.

Hidden in this riddle is the question of where one goes to cure the common cold. The Alaska Native Medical Center (ANMC) in Anchorage, Alaska, or the Chief Andrew Isaac Health Center in Fairbanks have become meccas for more complicated health threats. It is easier and less stressful if the Koyukon individual can make use of nature to get over ordinary ailments, and they do if they know how. Going to ANMC or Chief Andrew Isaac is the simple, and often, free way to go, since those who have a Certificate of Indian Blood (CIB) showing they have more than one-quarter

Native American ancestry can get medical treatment for free. As always, anything "free" calls for great caution.

A final example demonstrates how riddling has been used to reveal ethnic identifiers through both arcane language and the intricacies of snowshoe netting, which includes understanding gender relations and related work relations. In the following extremely short riddle, one has to know the gender and tool issues related to the product, here the snowshoe. Men net coarse rawhide for the center part of the snowshoe where the foot rests. The women do the tedious work that requires a specialized shuttle. In other words, some of the work is to be done by the man who will use the snowshoe, and the bulk of the effort belongs to his wife. In the old days, wives came into the household as members of an opposite clan, usually from a distant village, thus creating within the home awareness that the married couple had to be cognizant of interethnic issues over the most important domestic work. With that specialized knowledge in mind, Jetté correctly observes the two possible answers are both incomprehensible and equally acceptable as an answer.[14]

> *Tla-dzor-karasána: ko kun, kokun.—a) Ketseneror-tsen; b) oix belil*
> Riddle me: here also, here also—Netting-the-snowshoes; or, snowshoe needle. [diacritical markers omitted][15]

Answer number one requires conveying the tediousness of the using the shuttle, or *oix belil*. Answer number two is to identify the shuttle, or *nesnor*. Besides knowing the tensions underlying the wife's compaints that her work is endless and tedious, it is also important to know that in a northern environment the best means of transportation was by snowshoe, even in the era of dogsledding. It was just much quicker than going by sled—which requires both hitching the dogs to the sled and knowing how to make the dogs go the way you want them to go. And, because both dogs and humans eat, it was much less expensive. It also requires knowing something about family dynamics as well as how to train youth for the complex tools needed to live in such a world.

Denaakk'e, or the Koyukon language itself, gives rise to complex thinking simply by its complicated verbs. Many people remark that few people take the trouble to learn it because of the verbs. The use of riddles makes it obvious that the language demands the participants know both a colloquial version of the language and an ancient form that has to be taught during the riddling season. Jetté noted that in older times the riddles were used as a tool to reinforce ethnic identity. I further suggest that they were also tools to show off one's skill at observation and thinking as riddles were once used as the second stage of education after traditional tales. Now that both language and education has been changed by colonial forces, I have asked if there is anything that helps individuals maintain their Koyukon identity. Many people live in the Koyukon region, but reportedly few speak the indigenous languages. It is my contention that it is the evaluative thinking required by riddling and which is continued by joking or teasing that happens constantly between friends and people who are tested through teasing to determine if they think like other Koyukons do.

Notes

1. For more on the Denaakk'e language, see Jules Jetté and Eliza Jones, *Koyukon Athabaskan Dictionary*, ed. James M. Kari (Fairbanks: Alaska Native Language Center, University of Alaska Fairbanks, 2000).

2. Keith H. Basso, *Portraits of "The Whiteman": Linguistic Play and Cultural Symbols among the Western Apache* (Cambridge: Cambridge University Press, 1979).

3. Phyllis Ann Fast, *Northern Athabascan Survival: Women, Community, and the Future* (Lincoln: University of Nebraska Press, 2002).

4. James Kari, "Appendix A: The Koyukon Verb: Jetté's Terminology and Contemporary Terminology," in *Koyukon Athabaskan Dictionary*, ed. James Kari (Fairbanks: Alaska Native Language Center, University of Alaska Fairbanks, 2000), 753–59.

5. Jetté and Jones, *Koyukon Athabaskan Dictionary*.

6. Julius Jetté, "On the Superstitions of the Ten'a Indians (Middle Part of the Yukon Valley, Alaska)," *Anthropos* 6, no. 1 (1911): 95. For a sample of the primary documents of Julius Jetté, see Jules Jette, S.J., Collection, Jesuit Oregon Province Archives Alaska Mission Microfilm Collection, microfilm AM roll 35, frames 357–87, Foley Library, Gonzaga University, Spokane, Washington.

7. Patrick Moore, "Negotiated Identities: The Evolution of Dene Tha and Kaska Personal Naming Systems," *Anthropological Linguistics* 49, no. 3/4 (Autumn–Winter 2007): 283–307.

8. Julius Jetté, "Riddles of the Ten'a Indians," *Anthropos* 8, no. 1 (January–February 1913): 181–201; Julius Jetté, "Riddles of the Ten'a Indians (Concluded)," *Anthropos* 8, no. 4/5 (July–October 1913): 630–51.

9.   Tim Ingold, *Being Alive: Essays on Movement, Knowledge and Description* (London: Routledge, 2011), 170.

10.   Jetté, "Riddles of the Ten'a Indians," 182.

11.   Jetté, "Riddles of the Ten'a Indians," 187.

12.   Chief Henry, *Koyukon riddles = K'ooltsaah ts' in'*, ed. Eliza Jones (Fairbanks: Alaska Native Language Center, University of Alaska, 1976), 60.

13.   Chief Henry, *Koyukon riddles*, 60.

14.   Jetté, "Riddles of the Ten'a Indians (Concluded)," 647.

15.   Jetté, "Riddles of the Ten'a Indians (Concluded)."

CHAPTER TWELVE

Coyotean Rhetoric

A Trans-Indigenous Reading of Peter Blue Cloud's
Elderberry Flute Song

INÉS HERNÁNDEZ-ÁVILA

In Honor of the Memory and Spirit of Peter Blue Cloud Aroniawenrate (Mohawk)

So, it wasn't me crying after all,
Creation thought.
Then it thought again,
but it is me because I dreamed it.
So, I have begun Creation with a cry.
When I begin to create the universe,
I must remember to give the cry
a very special place.
Perhaps
I'll call the cry
Coyote.

—Peter Blue Cloud, "The Cry"

FOR THIS ESSAY, I am reading the late Peter Blue Cloud Aroniawenrate's *Elderberry Flute Song: Contemporary Coyote Tales* from a trans-Indigenous Niimiipuuean perspective as a "daughter of Coyote."[1] *Elderberry Flute Song* is a collection that, to me, is indispensable in the field of Native American and Indigenous studies.[2] I want to pursue what I am calling a Coyotean scholarly/ creative tracking that maps the connections between N. Scott Momaday's idea of "the word"; a Coyote story told to me by my uncle, Frank Andrews; Chadwick Allen's idea of "trans-Indigenous"; and Blue Cloud's revelatory Coyotean tradition. Allen, in *Trans-Indigenous: Methodologies for Global Native Literary Studies*, asks: "What can we see or understand differently by juxtaposing distinct and diverse Indigenous texts, contexts, and traditions?"[3] He develops an interpretive methodology for trans-Indigenous literary studies that reads across and through different texts.[4] Following the lead of Maori scholar/activist/artist Ngahuia Te Awekotuku, who writes about *"innovation and improvisation"*[5] in Maori arts practice (emphasis in original), Allen also addresses the significance of Te Awekotuku's idea of a "critical, knowing audience" as central "to developing new modes of inquiry, appreciation, and interpretation for Indigenous arts in all media, including written literatures."[6] This "critical, knowing audience" is what I want to highlight to demonstrate my agreement with Cutcha Risling Baldy when she says that "Coyote First Person...embodies...[sovereignty] and futurity for Indigenous peoples."[7] For me, this message regarding Indigenous sovereignty and futurity is embedded in Blue Cloud's collection. Coyote is a central figure in the Niimiipuu/Nez Perce belief-system. This is one of the reasons I was first drawn to Blue Cloud's collection.[8]

Blue Cloud (1933–2011), from the Turtle Clan of the Mohawk, lived in California for a time, so he, too, does a trans-Indigenous interpretation of Coyote, since some of his pieces reference California Indian traditions. On the site, *Zócalo Poets: Nos Vemos en el Zócalo/Meet Us in the Square*, Blue Cloud is described thus:

> He participated in the craziness of Beat and Hippy cultures in the Cali-
> fornia of the early 1960s through the mid-'70s [*sic*]—learning from those
> amorphous "movements" yet distancing himself from their excessive
> self-absorption. Spending time with Maidu Elders in California, he was
> strengthened by their wisdom and their stories. In 1972 his history of
> the 1969 Native "Occupation" of the former Alcatraz Prison/Island—
> "Alcatraz is not an Island"—was published. In 1975–76—and again from

1983–85—he wrote for and edited *Akwesasne Notes*, a Native journal published out of Akwesasne, New York.[9]

I remember voraciously reading *Akwesasne Notes* in the 1970s when I was hungrily searching for anything written on or about Native peoples. Blue Cloud represents that fascinating combination that draws my attention: activist, poet, public intellectual, visual artist (painter, sculptor), carpenter, cultural worker, and Coyotean. On the Oyate (Native) website, *Elderberry Flute Song* is described as the following: "In these 56 poems and stories, Coyote is the comic, the amoral, and the obscene."[10] This statement is true, to a certain extent—there are stories of how Coyote lost his penis; how he takes it upon himself to teach Saucy Duckfeather to not be so smug and sure of her charms; how the old, legless woman frightens him, yet she still fixes his broken tail; how Gopher Woman tricks him into eating his own roasted penis to pay him back for eating several of her children; how he always seems to get his way with the women, even though often he must resort to trickery; how Coyote "gives birth" to Gopher (after Coyote, because he is hungry, swallows Gopher whole and Gopher decides to chew his way out); how Hawk has to put Coyote back together when all that is left of him is his anus, which is why, according to Hawk, Coyote is an asshole. Yes, there are these stories, but I spend more time here on some of Blue Cloud's writings that offer a much deeper and complex rendition of Coyote and his/her/their rhetorical strategies, which end up being Blue Cloud's Coyotean rhetoric. In particular, I want to point to the pieces where Coyote, through Blue Cloud, is articulating the themes that have to do with the "rhetorical problematic" as described by Richard Morris and Philip Wander: "Who am I? What am I? How did I come to be this way? Who are we? What do we do now?"[11]

Allen's concept of the "trans-Indigenous" is particularly useful to frame my essay for several reasons. As a Nez Perce woman, I grew up with Coyote stories, two of the most important of which are the story of Coyote defeating the Monster, slaying the Monster, and flinging the Monster's body parts far and wide to create the human peoples, including the Niimiipuu; and the story of Coyote causing the permanence of Death by disobeying the rules he was given to *not look back*.[12] In neither of these stories is Coyote amoral, comic, or obscene, nor is he/she the flat, one-dimensional, and very predictable entity that characterizes the stereotype of Coyote. He/she is a sacred being, an ancient being who is central to some traditions, such as the Niimiipuu (Nez Perce) belief-system. As Dan Flores points out in *Coyote America: A Natural and Supernatural History*, "as far south as the Aztecs, [they] knew him as Huehuecoyotl, Old Man Coyote, or Old Man America."[13] From the oral tradition of danza Conchera, I know that Huehuecoyotl is the one who gave us the first sound, the first dance.[14] All of my life I have been "trans-ing" between Coyote and Huehuecoyotl; s/he is the one who helps me make sense of myself. My closeness to Coyote draws me to the multiplicitous renditions of this sacred being, and I have known Blue Cloud's collection for some time; I use it often in various courses, including my courses on Indigenous poetry and Indigenous religious traditions. There is much to be said about how the often reiterated "trickster" energy (to use the problematic term in English) works from Indigenous perspectives in the Americas; this energy, the awareness of it, the naming of it, the integration of it within many Native belief-systems, is perhaps one of the grandest gestures of rhetorical strategy that gives (back) life, that renews, and reminds us who we are, and what we know from the beginning of time, as Indigenous peoples.[15]

It is precisely Blue Cloud's interpretation of Coyote that represents for me a Native American rhetoric, a Coyotean rhetoric that, to use Flores's words, "operates as shorthand for the greatest story ever told, the miracle of ongoing evolutionary adaptation to an endlessly changing world."[16] Flores writes what many Indigenous peoples know: "Coyotes have been in North America far longer than we, they are not going anywhere, and history demonstrates all too graphically that eradicating them is an impossibility. This is truly an instance in which any desire on our part to control nature is perfectly countered by a profound inability to do so."[17] Or, as Blue Cloud says, in the story of Jackrabbit's Daughters, where Coyote manages to avail himself of the largesse of the daughters (in every way), without having to make any commitment, "That's Coyote for you. Just when you think you got him in sight all that's really there is a sound going somewhere else" (65). There is also the Nez Perce understanding that Coyote can resuscitate from the throes of death if there is one hair, one bone, one even tiny piece of him left (Fox is often the one who brings him back to life).

I agree with much of what Damián Baca says when he critiques "Rhetoric and Composition's [quite shortsighted] macro-narrative [that] imagine[s] the origins of rational thought and communication in the minds of Western thinkers, [which is a] foundational myth [signifying] a colonial supremacy that is incompatible with the very possibility of achieving cultural pluralities."[18] However, I do take issue when he writes, "Moves toward decolonizing the field's horizons, toward moving beyond its cultural and epistemological flaws, require rhetorical mediations that operate out of Western reason, mediations that originate from te-ixtli, from the voices, testimonies, communicative strategies, and perspectives *of the colonized*" (emphasis mine).[19] The Coyotean rhetorical mediations I am presenting here, which do "operate out[side] of Western reason," do not emerge from the colonized. If anything, they represent what Laura Perez calls a "politics of memory"—or "more precisely, a politics of the will to remember: to maintain in one's consciousness, to recall, and to reintegrate a spiritual world-view about the interconnectedness of life, even if it is fragmented, circulating, as its pieces have, *through* colonial and neocolonial relations" (emphasis mine).[20] They are ancient strategies, eminently compatible over the centuries with the creative impulses of Native artists and Native peoples. The related question to remember: Who is the audience? The audience is a vital component of any rhetorical strategy(ies)—certainly the audience can be seen, considered, or rendered in ever-expanding ripples (what Lata Mani calls "multiple mediations").[21] The audience is not simply the receptor of the story (or his/her/ their story). The audience, depending upon their awareness, adds to, or limits, the nuance(s) of the story. Coyotean rhetoric assumes an intimately aware audience, again, the "critical, knowing audience" referenced above. Blue Cloud knew this, just as most Native writers do. They/we are talking to each other first, and then, to anyone and everyone else. Scott Lyons calls "rhetorical imperialism: the ability of dominant powers to assert control of others by setting the terms of debate."[22] Blue Cloud, like other Native writers, exercises rhetorical sovereignty to rigorously subvert rhetorical imperialism, and to remind us what we knew before institutionalized mindsets (from the state, the church, the schools) were imposed on us.

I call attention to N. Scott Momaday's elaboration of "the Word" in the sermon by his character, the Reverend John Big Bluff Tosamah, the Priest of the Sun, in *House Made of Dawn*.[23] Consider the intimately aware Native

American readership that delighted in this 1969 Pulitzer Prize–winning novel, published in 1968—a novel that many Native writers have said "saved their lives."[24] I myself remember reading the novel when it first came out, and in spite of the work centering on a male protagonist, my initial impression was literally to realize that I was/am possible as a human being, as an Indigenous human being. How did Momaday achieve this if not with his amazing and bold rhetorical strategy(ies)? How did he know to trust that there would be readers who would understand him? Perhaps the trust had much more to do with his trust in his own word, his own creation(s), which is, as we will see, a theme of Blue Cloud's. (They are of the same generation of heightened consciousness, and they were in tune with what was happening in Indian Country.) The scene with the Priest of the Sun takes place in a ramshackle building that houses the Los Angeles Holiness Pan-Indian Rescue Mission, where a Native American Church ceremony is taking place. Tosamah's sermon is a critique of the Gospel according to John:

> "In principio erat Verbum." . . . There was a single sound. Far away in the darkness there. . . . Nothing made it, but it was there; and there was no one to hear it, but it was there . . . it took hold of the darkness and there was light; it took hold of the stillness and there was motion forever; it took hold of the silence and there was sound. It was almost nothing in itself, a single sound, a word—a word broken off at the darkest center of the night and let go in the awful void, forever and forever. And it was almost nothing in itself. It scarcely was; but it *was*, and everything began. (emphasis in original)[25]

Tosamah calls attention to how John, "because he was a preacher," should have stopped after he acknowledged "the essential and eternal Truth, the bone and blood and music of the Truth," but he kept on talking instead.[26] He criticizes John for talking "through and around" the Word, saying, "He builds upon it with syllables, with prefixes and suffixes and hyphens and accents. He adds and divides and multiplies the Word. And in all of this he subtracts the Truth."[27] Tosamah contrasts this way with his grandmother's stories, and how she knew language. "She had learned that in words and in language, and there only, she could have whole and consummate being."[28]

This refrain regarding the significance of language, of the word, is familiar to those who know Momaday's work.[29] His rhetorical strategy is to (re)present his ancestral ways in contrast to what he observes in the world, in this way rendering the ancestral ways as viable and preferable alternatives, and a signal, if you will, to other Native peoples that the time has come for change. Given that this text was published more than fifty years ago, readers today can imagine what the impact of this novel must have been on Native readers back then. In a passage that tellingly, and chillingly, foresees our recent political situation in this country, Tosamah goes on to say, "[the white man] has diluted and multiplied the Word, and words have begun to close in upon him. He is sated and insensitive; his regard for language—for the Word itself—as an instrument of creation has diminished nearly to the point of no return. It may be that he will perish by the Word."[30] In contrast, for his grandmother, "words were medicine; they were magic and invisible. They came from nothing into sound and meaning. They were beyond price; they could neither be bought nor sold. And she never threw words away."[31] Storytellers (read broadly) in Indian Country, whether they are from the oral or written traditions, do their best, I believe, to not throw words away.

My late uncle Frank Andrews, Nez Perce elder from Nespelem, Washington, told me once, "In the longhouse there would be a lot of speakers, and much information, teaching. Much of the things [were] told in remembrance. Things to remember and not forget. To ... plant them within their hearts, within their mind[s]. That when it came their time to give a speech, or their time to tell a story, that there would be no faltering for words."[32] Uncle Frank was a pretty wonderful storyteller. He was always happy to share with me, and he would delight in the telling. A Pentecostal preacher, he said that once he told his congregation how much Coyote was like Jesus, which upset them very much; he chuckled when he told me. He told me a story about "Coyote and the Goose Brothers," which I remember in this way: Coyote was married to Goose Woman, and he loved the sumptuousness of his lot in life. He had a good woman who catered to him, tasty food, a comfortable home, and a full sexual life. Goose Woman treated him just right, but her sons were not so generous in their feelings toward him. They saw him as a leech, but they abided by their mother's choice of a mate, even though they would love to have sent Coyote packing.

One day the Goose brothers begin discussing an upcoming hunting trip, and their enthusiasm and planning intrigues Coyote, who has been overhearing from the other room. He immediately comes up to the brothers and asks to go with them. They groan and say no, many, many times, but in the end, their mom comes to them and asks them to take Coyote along, to do it for her. Only because she asks in this way do they reluctantly agree.

The next morning, Coyote jumps onto the back of the elder Goose brother and they all fly off to hunt elk. As they near the spot, though, they dump Coyote on the ground, in a clearing, and instruct him to wait for them; they tell him not to move. They fly higher up the mountain and stay for hours. Coyote, as to be expected, gets restless, and he is mad anyway for being left behind, so in short time, he starts moseying around. He comes upon some white-tailed deer and inspiration strikes him: "I know what I'll do, I'll kill these deer and have them ready when those guys come back, they'll see I was able to hunt without them! Hmmmppphh!"

He did just as he said, and then he found a comfortable rock to lean against and took a nap. After a little while, he wakes up to the sounds of the wings of the Goose brothers as they return from their successful hunt. At first, they are laughing and happy with accomplishment, when suddenly they are shocked speechless to see the piled-up carcasses of the deer. They turn as one on Coyote and yell at him, "What did you do, you idiot?!" He stands up, stretching and yawning, saying smugly, "*I* hunted as well, and as you can see, I was quite successful!" They look at him for a long, long moment, then they look at each other, and then back at Coyote, with fury in their eyes. "You *stupid!* You killed our *pets!*"

Exasperated and sad, they bury their little brothers and sisters, then they load the elk onto their backs, and Coyote jumped on as well, assuming his entitlement. As they fly home, the brothers seem to communicate with each other telepathically (or they reached an agreement before they began the journey back). As they fly over a valley on the way home, the Goose brother who is carrying Coyote abruptly shakes him off his back, causing him to fall perilously to the earth. Coyote hits ground with an enormous thud, which knocks him out for a while. When he wakes up, he shakes himself off, somewhat bewildered. Then, remembering what happened, he shrugs his shoulders and, as is his custom, he moseys along, away from his former home.

What is the Coyotean rhetoric in this story? Flores says, "Humans delight in Coyote's exploits because we recognize how they shine a light on motives we struggle with. Coyote has always showed us truth."[33] What is the truth in this story? There are many levels working within the narrative. The story reveals the well-known Coyote tendency to look for (often, not always) the easy route, or the easy out. He is happy with Goose Woman—all his needs are served—and yet he wants something else, some excitement, something to keep his instincts sharp. He knows the Goose brothers cannot stand him, but he also knows he has their mom on his side, so he is clear about his advantage. When he meets his comeuppance with the Goose brothers, he is okay. He is familiar with things not working out, so he goes on his way. The Coyotean rhetorical strategies embedded in this story? The Goose brothers showing respect for their mom, putting up with Coyote as much as they can, until he crosses the line; the brothers' (apparently) unspoken agreement about how to deal with Coyote, communicating as they did through body language, letting him fall to his own destiny, without resorting to undue violence; Coyote's own shrug of his shoulders (as opposed to him having a tantrum, or swearing revenge, or feeling defeated) when things fall apart; and perhaps, the two most important points, the way the story ultimately has to do with tenderness toward the deer in an unfolding drama of ecological sustainability, and the way that Coyote shows his nature to be one that gets up and keeps going, *no matter what*, especially in the face of failure (or his own atrocious foolishness). What is unsaid, of course, is as important as what is said, just as what is not done is as important as what is done. Implicit in Coyote stories is the need for listeners/readers to assume their own responsibility in filling in the blanks, and, as my grandpa Thomas Andrews Ukshanat used to say, "to stay with the beat" (i.e., to not *miss* a beat). The more aware a listener/reader is, the more s/he will be able to "stay with the beat."

Interestingly, in Flores's "Epilogue: Coyote Consciousness," he briefly mentions Blue Cloud and *Elderberry Flute Song*, but his assessment is that most of the stories "tend to head off into coyoteroticism."[34] Like the Oyate assessment of the collection being mostly about "the comic, the amoral, the obscene," Flores's reading is limited. Yes, there is coyoteroticism in the collection. How could there not be? He's Coyote! But there are stories like Coyote becoming enthralled with Spider Weaver's web (that Spider Weaver intentionally weaves to intrigue and overcome Coyote, who is wasting away from not eating, not caring one iota for himself), showing that Coyote, the great manipulator, can be manipulated quite easily, such that Grey Fox has to use all his wits to save his friend; frustrated that Coyote is not listening, Grey Fox finally decides to cut Coyote in two, to create his better half, Coyote Woman. In "The Drum," Coyote patiently exercises wisdom and consistently guides Badger's Son on the integrity of making a drum from his own vision, rather than relying on someone to tell him exactly how to do it, and without buttering anyone up (like Coyote Old Man) to get them to teach him how to do it. When Badger's Son is asked how he came by "such a fine drum," Badger's Son responds, "Oh, it was Coyote Old Man who refused to teach me how to make this fine drum!" (70). Both Oyate and Flores "miss the beat" in terms of many of the pieces in this collection. Indeed, there are stories that have to do with Coyote as creator or teacher, or even the one who sacrifices his life for others.

Baca writes, "Every communicative act is tied to a rhetorical production, and as such works to influence specific audiences to some action whether material or epistemological."[35] In Blue Cloud's story, "The Battle," Coyote sacrifices himself to attempt to teach a lesson about the rules of engagement, and the ethics of those rules, to the animal people who are at war with each other. (Little did I know when I first read this collection, many years ago, how much this piece would resonate with our recent political situation in this country.) Fox, Badger, Cougar, Jackrabbit, Mole, Mouse, Deer, and Bear all are in the midst of menacing each other, such that "the smell of hate and future bloodshed permeated the very air" (66), when Coyote arrives. He listens and then says, "in a very soft voice: 'No, I cannot allow this great fight to happen just yet. There has been no battle preparation dance. There has been no pipe of cleansing. No, the Creation does not wish this battle to take place just yet'" (66). The other animal people have no patience with him so one of them summarily slays Coyote, and the fighting resumes. Coyote appears again, this time with a club, and hitting his own slain body, he yells at the others, "Who killed this person? Who struck him down before I did? Was that person purified? Did he sweat himself and think of the children? Did he dance to ensure that the life cycle continue?" (66). Momentarily startled, the others pause, and then again strike Coyote dead. Again, he (re)appears, repeating the beating of his slain selves, and suddenly dancing a victory dance to claim the kills. His dancing again gives the others pause as they engage in questioning who can claim the kills. While they are so engaged, Coyote instructs the "women of these great warriors" to prepare a feast for everyone, "and soon, the recent anger was set aside for the more important battle of words leading to reason" (68). For Coyote's part, once the menacing battle has ended, he takes his selves to a sweat bath, where he sings a special song "known only to himself," and he and his selves are all revived. One of his selves comments, "Now, . . . that's what I'd call making your point the hard way" (68). Another self reminds them they have to take turns getting killed, because, as Coyote says, "Oh, it will happen again. . . . It always seems to happen again" (68). He merges into his selves and moseys away, "far away" (68).

In "The Battle," Coyote is not the instigator, but the peacemaker, even though it costs him two lives to "make his point." He is a listener, an observer, and a teacher. I am reminded of our late elder here in Native American studies at the University of California, Davis, David Risling Jr., and a story he used to tell about being sent by the elders to Alcatraz to tell the activists that they had to walk a spiritual path in order to know how to proceed with their activism. The Coyotean rhetorical strategy in this story is intended to remind Native peoples of (some of) the cultural practices they must keep uppermost in their hearts, minds, bodies, and spirits. Purification is a necessary first step (and last step, at least for Coyote) to any great undertaking—purification and ceremony, the battle preparation dance, the pipe of cleansing, the sweat ceremony (depending, of course, on the tradition). In any act, the children, the future generations must be remembered, and the life cycle must be protected. There is no room for egos, for base competitions, for pettiness. Coyote knows also to involve the women in creating a space where the dialogue can move toward a peaceful discourse. Once he accomplishes his goals, he leaves, unnoticed, to go about his own self-healing. This is not Coyote the fool, not Coyote the obscene or amoral. Yes, there is an element of the comic in this story, although it is one that can cause readers to laugh while wincing.

Lyons writes that "rhetorical sovereignty is the inherent right and ability of *peoples* to determine their own communicative needs and desires in this pursuit, to decide for themselves the goals, modes, styles, and languages of public discourse" (emphasis in original).[36] Blue Cloud was quite clear about this right, as he shows over and over in *Elderberry Flute Song*. Coyote is the one who counts coup, who sets the terms in these stories, although sometimes it is Coyote Woman who (sort of) bests him, as in "Why the Moon Dies," where Coyote Woman punishes Coyote by cutting herself where he likes it so much, in order to bring Moon, who is her sister, back from the death she is experiencing when Wolf (unwillingly) chases her, taking bites out of her as he cries all the while (Wolf is unhappy at his task, but he bows to Coyote's power and instructions). Coyote Woman only wins so much, though, because Coyote decides he likes the back-and-forth "dying and returning" of the Moon. His intentions at the start of the story are good; he wants some nights to be darker, in order to hunt, and to sleep, but he does not consider Moon's rights, so Coyote Woman intervenes for her sister to defend and protect her. Inadvertently, her cutting of herself creates the practice of women bleeding to bring back Moon, and of course, menstrual cycles. There is a tension here between Coyote and Coyote Woman, and yet the two are one, two aspects of the same self, and what they produce does serve the earth and their relations.

Baca tells us that "rhetorical traditions of the Americas and the Caribbean evidence a rich discourse of critique of Anglo- and Eurocentric ideologies. In a real sense, modernity begins with the encounter of the 'New World' and the creation of a new 'Other Within,' so that rhetorical practices of the Americas stand in a unique position vis-à-vis the development of that modernity—and its concomitants of colonialism, of racialized subjectivities, of the crisis of European reason, and of late global capitalism."[37] The "New World" and the "new 'Other Within'" are not "new," but rather have an ancient rootedness in this hemisphere, a rootedness that sustains the Indigenous rhetorical practices of the Americas. In *Elderberry Flute Song*, Blue Cloud takes on anthropologists and New Age aficionados in his critique of Anglo- and Eurocentric ideologies. While many of the pieces in the collection do not reveal or even feign an overt interest in "dominant" ideologies, in these pieces the rhetorical strategy is direct confrontation with the legacies of colonialism. In "Coyote's Anthro," Blue Cloud could have been anticipating Craig Womack's pronouncements about the way anthros invented the idea of "trickster," when he focuses on a newly minted anthro who penned "The Mythology of Coyote: Trickster, Thief, Fool, and World-Maker's Helper." The anthro is sitting at a campfire, preparing for fieldwork, when Coyote Old Man suddenly appears to him. The poor befuddled young anthro is beside himself as Coyote Old Man gets inside his head, reads his mind, taunts, tests, and confuses him. Coyote Old Man has little patience with the one who wants to know the stories, "the reasons behind the reasons . . . interrelationships, the problem of special paradox, sexual taboos, those kinds of things" (118–19). The anthro is not a keen observer. He is so intent on what he wants to see that he fails to see what Coyote shows him. In the ultimate test, Coyote Old Man demonstrates for him how to reach the moon, singing first to set things in motion, but when the anthro tries to follow suit, he fails, because, as the elder tells him, "You, my friend, forgot to sing" (120). Such is Coyote's summary dismissal of the anthro. It is clear in this story that Coyote's identity, his being, and, by extension, the identity and being of Indigenous peoples, do not depend on anthropologists; on the contrary, anthropologists are the bane of Native peoples (and Coyotes), enacting as they do dominant ideologies that oppress, distort, misrepresent, and presume. Blue Cloud reinforces the idea that Native peoples have the wit and power to meet any anthro face-to-face and more than hold their own.

In "Coyote's Discourse on Power, Medicine, and Would-Be Shamans," Blue Cloud is much more deliberate in his critique. He has Coyote giving an invited talk one evening, a talk that begins with casual chatting. Then, he continues by telling teaching stories. He has been asked to talk about "medicine and those some call shamans" (126), and he is doing the talk for pay. He continues by telling his audience about a young woman he met at some university campus, a self-styled "medicine woman," one named "Shamaness Fast Walker." Looking at Coyote through a crystal she invites him to meet her later, and because she is "good-looking" he agrees. After they finish up "the business of the two-backed dance and other forms of strenuous frivolity," she proceeds to "do" Coyote with her crystal. Coyote says, "I'd learned very young to counteract powers I had not requested. I stared back at her through the crystal. She began fading. I could see the moon thru her body. Her eyes dimmed and her mouth opened to plead with me. But it was too late. I couldn't stop myself. She faded completely away, not even leaving the trace of a shadow" (126). The Coyotean rhetorical strategy is clear: to let the audience know how dangerous it is to "play" and pretend power, and again, to remind Native people how to respond to presumptive arrogance however it manifests itself.

Coyote continues his storytelling by remembering another event he attended at the same campus, a poetry reading by a proclaimed "Shaman Poet." Intrigued, Coyote listened attentively: "Every other line spoke of his powers to understand all things within the Creation. His choruses called on his powers to hear him, to reaffirm these powers" (127). Coyote is impressed at first, but then he says, "I reached for him with my mind, to share some of that strength. I touched a shell and put my ear to it. I heard the echoes of his own words bouncing back and forth within a hollow shell. Then I probed his mind. I went inside of it to find a tight bundle of self, a bursting ball of energy looking out of eyes which were intent only on seducing his audience" (127). Filled with sadness at his discovery, Coyote withdraws and stops listening. The Coyotean rhetorical strategy revealed here shows us that Coyote listens with an open mind, he does a critical and deep listening as a co-participant in the reading, searching for the integrity of the poet's word(s), and the poet is found lacking. As co-participants ourselves, we are reminded to read/listen carefully. Coyote tells us also that "power and wisdom are universal," just as "phonies are universal, but then perhaps, like decay, the phonies are necessary compost to the growth of real power" (127), which is a very Coyotean thing to say!

As he continues with his discourse, Coyote contrasts two stories that actually are the lead-in to the finale of his talk. The first is about a young man who decides to "improve" the drum he will play, changing the designs on the drum, changing the songs themselves, doing "variations on the theme until the theme itself has been lost, swallowed up in his frenzy" (128). The young man only confuses himself and the people. In a way, his obsession with "newness" causes him to scatter himself asunder, disperse himself, much in the same way Momaday describes what has happened to the white man and his (mis)use of words. (This story, of course, also contrasts with the learning that Badger's Son receives in "The Drum.") In the second story, Coyote tells us about a little girl who walks into the forest alone, sad and worried about her father whose leg is swollen badly with pus. The "little people" of the woods decide to let her see them, because "they liked her very much and felt a deep respect for her sorrow" (128). They talk to her and listen to her tell them the source of her sorrow. They send her on her way with instructions to "pay close attention to everything she passed" (129). As she walks, she hears a plant calling to her and stops to listen. "The plant explained that the little people had asked it to help her. . . . It would teach the girl its powers if she would take the time to learn how to use it properly. . . . It included a cleansing, a chant, a song, a slow process of preparation, a further singing to be shared by the person being cured, and this was to be followed by a thank-you feast for the Creation" (128). The young girl accepts the teachings and is able to return home with the medicine that saves her father. As she grows up, she learns more and more, and becomes a "curing person," always following "the first instructions given by the plant, step by step slowly, so that she made no mistake" (129). Obviously, the young girl's experience is distinct from the impatient, frivolous young man. (Again, I am reminded of Momaday's description of the grandmother, above, who has a resemblance to this little girl-become-"curing person.")

Coyote's focus on the young girl becoming a medicine woman is the perfect lead-in to his main point about how real healers do not go around announcing themselves: "Even within a tribe or nation, the people know who to see for their particular needs, so why give them titles? / When porcupine goes night walking, he doesn't look behind himself and say, 'Ah, yes, I got my quills with me.' He knows what he's got" (130). Here is Coyote the teacher, ironically, some might say, because he can himself be the arch manipulator and deceiver, which is fascinating, because it means he can actually recognize (sometimes) what is true and what is not.

Flores describes "coyote power [as] surviving by one's intelligence and wits when others cannot: embracing existence in a mad, dancing, laughing, sympathetic expression of pure joy at evading the grimmest of fates; exulting in sheer aliveness; recognizing our shortcomings with rueful chagrin."[38] A careful consideration of this description reveals an individualistic approach to Coyote, surviving when others cannot, sheer joy at escaping "the grimmest of fates." Never mind anyone else, those others who cannot survive. Yes, Coyote exults in being alive, especially after narrowly managing to extract himself from danger. And yes, absolutely, he recognizes his own (and others') shortcomings. However, we need to return to the "rhetorical problematic" described by Morris and Wander in "Native American Rhetoric: Dancing in the Shadows of the Ghost Dance": "Who am I? What am I? How did I come to be this way? Who are we? What do we do now?" I want to suggest that these are the questions that Blue Cloud addresses in *Elderberry Flute Song*, particularly in certain pieces that do not fit Flores's description at all, but instead reveal a Coyotean consciousness (and, in a way, a mapping) of where Indigenous peoples began, what we have been through, where we are, and where we are going (or where we could go if we remember ourselves).

Going back to the poem that opened this essay, "The Cry," Blue Cloud very clearly situates "the cry" as a central motif, one that opens a space for us into understanding what I call a cosmic grief that gives resonance to who we are and how, over these last centuries, we have responded culturally and spiritually to historical experience. At the same time, this cosmic grief is generative of the activism that burst forth in the late sixties, early seventies (an activism that has always been palpable, sometimes just beneath the surface), a multifaceted activism nourished and sustained by spirit, distinct culture(s), and yes, laughter. Most importantly, "the cry" reminds us of our beginnings, of the knowledge and wisdom that we held before the devastation of colonialism. "The Cry" is immediately followed by the prose poem "I Cry Often and Long," in a persuasive move to have us associate the cry that is called Coyote with the "I" of the piece that follows. Blue Cloud opens this "I" piece with the following lines:

> There is a great aloneness in me, swirling like captured smoke within. I look around and look around again. It is an emptiness now, this land. It is an emptiness of the dead creatures and plants. It is a ghost land, a spirit land of keening winds. And the winds are the voices, *the whispering sorrow of creations gone before their time.* (emphasis mine) (10)

Coyote, the "I," is surveying the landscape, listening to the sorrow. After this opening stanza, each following one begins with "I cry often and long," until the last two stanzas. The "I" says that none of his relatives hear him. He is a "grey shadow" who reflects himself "on the underbelly of a cloud" (10). He is speaking to a "you": "I am what you think you saw behind a blackened stump, . . . I am the one who watches you from many eyes and directions" (10). As the piece progresses, it appears that he is talking to human people, human Indigenous people (and then, anyone else). He says, "I am you when you fear to gaze at your reflection"; "my cry is the echo of the anguished cry you hide in your own breast. I walk the many footpaths of your fears" (10). His voice is ultimately one of compassion as he says to the "you":

I cry often and long, because you were never a child. I mourn the fact of your empty seed. I am part of the mystery you refuse to recognize. I am waiting for you. I am waiting for you and have been waiting for you from the time of your great-great-grandfather's parched lips. I am waiting for the promise you once gave to a land and a people. I am waiting for the return feast I gave your unborn children. (10)

One reading of the above passage would suggest an allusion to those of our Indigenous peoples who are of the "stolen generations," as Aboriginal peoples in Australia would say, our peoples who were sent to boarding schools or residential schools. The reference to "your empty seed" could be a reference to the forced sterilization of Native women. The term "mystery" reminds me of how I have heard Native elders remind us that the Supreme Being at the very highest is a mystery, after which we give him/her names. Coyote tells this "you" that he is waiting, through the generations, for the promise to be fulfilled, for Native peoples to recover their wisdom traditions and their resilience. Blue Cloud's rhetorical strategy allows us to see this other facet of Coyote, a Coyote who is like those elders who understand the depths to which people can go because they themselves have been there. They have lived what they are observing, or something very similar, which is life experience that allows them to see more quickly, more precisely, both the depths and the heights. By the end of the poem, the "I" tells the "you": "This robe I spread before this campfire is for your warmth. Why do you stand way back there in the shadows and cold? / Come here: yes, that's it, slowly. Yes, now take my hand. Yes, now sit, stop trembling. Gently now, this robe I place about you, softly. There. / 'It is done, / now sleep, and do not fear your dreaming'" (11). This poem is the story of return, a difficult return, but a return that is sustained, that has been sustained, by this cry, this Coyote song, this sacred spirit being.

It is a matter of seeing Coyote in a different way. Blue Cloud's collection serves to help us train our eyes to see this difference, as the award-winning Mexican photographer Federico Gama would say.[39] While one of Coyote's less admirable but more notorious traits is to lead others astray, sometimes Coyote does the exact opposite, which is to be expected of him, after all. "Black Coyote" is a cautionary tale focusing on Snowfox and the transformation he is seeking. Snowfox has known from very young that he wants something other than what he is; as a baby, "he whimpered an unknown hunger his mother's milk could not quench" (85). When he is grown he becomes a skilled hunter and learns how to dream. Once he hears a song "brought to him on the wind of ice-breaking which gave him strange powers to see into the beyond," a song with instructions for him to sing four times, for he is to become "a shadow cast upon unknown stone" (85). He brings sorrow to his family and tribe because they are sure he is speaking about his own death. He leaves them and searches for Coyote Old Man, who has already foreseen what Snowfox's petition will be. When Snowfox arrives seeking Coyote Old Man's help, Coyote frowns "at what was to be / having seen the whole process / in his lately dreaming sleep" (86). Yet he reluctantly agrees to help him. As he prepares for the ceremony, Coyote takes his time and works patiently, all the while instructing Snowfox on how he is changing him into moon shadows, "part of but separate, merging / like day into night, season / into season, back and forth a running rhythm" (87). Coyote takes fresh charcoal and begins erasing Snowfox, taking away his voice, his body, making him a nameless shadow "moving slowly across the cool night sand" (87). In these lines there is a memory of "I Cry Often and Long," when Coyote makes reference to himself as a "grey shadow [moving] on the underbelly of a cloud." Coyote tells the nameless one, "Yes, you are a shadow now / yes as one with that which is me we run barking / look / now I will give you a dance, / a moon dance, take it, it / is yours, and / look / now I will give you a song: / take that too, and sing: / and watch me as you sing as I / tear you from me / see?" (88). At this point Coyote Old Man is laughing as he calls the nameless one his brother, "shadow of shadow / echo of further echo" (88). As he sends the nameless one into the world, Coyote gives him instructions: "you will turn the humans / sleeping with your voice, and / they will worry in their dreams / and wonder, and create a dance, / and form a Coyote Clan of / hunters and scouts, and all / because they heard your voice / and let it tell them what / they wished to think they heard" (89). Coyote tells the nameless one that his voice will be "more penetrating" than his own (88). He promises the nameless one that they will sing together even though "they never meet again"—they will sing "even until / the last human may perish / from having forgotten to dream / for the benefit of tomorrow" (89). At the end of this transformation ceremony, Coyote Old Man says, "and I name you Black Coyote, / dancer and singer of shadows,

/ disturber of human dreaming, / Go, the seasons await you!" (89). Blue Cloud's Coyotean rhetoric presents us with Snowfox, who has a vision of what he wants to become. The vision comes to him through a song, he seeks Coyote Old Man, and *because* the elder has tapped into the story and the vision, he acquiesces. We are shown an elder who is the one sought after for this change; he works carefully, and he instructs carefully. Black Coyote becomes a part of him, "part yet separate" but a helpmate to Coyote, who, like Coyote, will remind humans of the need to dream "for the benefit of tomorrow," who will create restlessness among humans when they forget to dream, and who, in the best of circumstances, will help them dream. Black Coyote is taught to echo Coyote's "inner thoughts;" to enter Coyote's dreaming, "become as one with [Coyote's] ears and nose," and he sees from Coyote's "eyes and think[s he] think[s] from Coyote's mind" (88). As the readers of this story, we are met with a Coyotean rhetoric that tasks us with remembering to dream, and remembering the fullness of the cry that is Coyote. This particular story is also a warning to be careful what you ask for; at the same time, we are presented with the very real, and sacred, direction that Snowfox, who becomes Black Coyote, receives through his dreams.

In "As I Sit Here Writing Down His Words," Blue Cloud presents us again with an "I" and a "he" who is referenced in the title—the "I" is writing down "his" words, which suggests that the "I" is either listening to the "he," or "his words" are coming to Blue Cloud, the poet, or to Coyote himself, to write. Or does the piece itself represent the words that are "his," that is, Coyote's? In some ways, the Coyotean rhetoric working here is revealed in the language that distinguishes the characters. The voice, the "I," makes reference to "a ragged human wearing an old army long coat," walking around, stumbling, in the rain—this seems like Coyote's voice, since a human writer might say "a ragged man" rather than "a ragged human" (90). Later in the piece, the voice references "the human" several times. On this dark, rainy night, "the blackest night," the "I" hears "coyotes . . . barking and keening very close," but also "a moaning like that of a wolf" (90). It is then that the "I" sees the ragged man; he says, "He is sobbing now as he realizes he may never find those he seeks. They should be camped right near here, but there are no signs of a fire. Wasn't it just yesterday that they . . . but no, it was much longer. He moans again from deep in his chest" (90). The old army long coat suggests that the human is a veteran, and definitely a longhair, which alerts us that the human is a Native man. He is searching for his people, but from a "much longer" time ago. As I read this piece, I am reminded of what I have heard from Native men when they explain what it means to be a warrior, particularly Galeson Eagle Star (Oglala Lakota) and Nando Slivers (Diné). It is much like what an American Indian Movement (AIM) member is quoted as saying in Morris and Wander: "Warrior society . . . means the men and women of the nation who have dedicated themselves to give everything that they have to the people."[40] To be a warrior is to protect the people, to defend them, care for them, give your life for them. But the longhair in this piece is struggling because he cannot find his people.

The "I" is observing this human and so are a bunch of coyotes, "watching and wondering and wanting in some way to help. The younger ones begin a yapping, hoping the others will join in" (90). The man sits on his haunches to rest. He is crying. "He stares at the ground before him as if emptied now of all emotion" (90), as if the young ones' yapping has helped him to know he is not alone. We are told then that "the oldest coyote studies the human for a while, then raises his head and begins a few deep, starting barks. He looks at the human and repeats the barks" (90–91). We can wonder if this "oldest coyote" is indeed the "I" who has been observing all of this all along. It is possible, after all, for Coyote to speak about himself in the third person. It would not be the first time. In the opening lines, we are told, "I put more wood on the fire and turn to see my eyes reflected on the window" (90). His "eyes" could be his "I's." We are told that the "human slowly raises his head to listen. Then he raises his head further back and from very deep within begins a low wolf moaning, and then the others join the song. The human's eyes are closed and head still back, and rain and tears stream down his face" (91). And so, we come back again to another story of return and renewal, signaled by the rain and the tears, and the Coyote songs of solidarity with the ragged human with the low wolf moaning. It is Coyote and the coyotes as a group who help the human, who acknowledge his existence, who are concerned for him, who accompany him, who stay with him, and, in the end, who sing with him. This is the story that Blue Cloud wants us to know.

In the conclusion to *Coyote America*, Flores registers hope for America regarding what he calls Coyote consciousness, although he also speaks about how Coyote has become a "Continental Everyman," "a social critic and a philosopher of human nature."[41] I contend that Indigenous peoples who know Coyote have always known this about him; he is an acutely keen observer. In celebrating Coyotean resiliency, Flores further notes, "They have . . . survived our own attempt to wipe them off the planet, and we were pretty damned dedicated to that. As our future unveils, I for one am going to be watching coyotes very, very closely to see just what they do."[42] He could be talking about Indigenous peoples, and of course, his "our" and "we" must be qualified. Indigenous peoples have not tried to wipe Coyote off the planet. For me, Coyote is an important link between Indigenous peoples in the United States and Mexico. We do not begin to know everything there is to know about him/her, but we Indigenous peoples do have stories—not the Hollywood or anthro versions, and not the stereotypical flat versions (no offense to Wile E.). Morris and Wander remind us that "the degree to which the dominant society has displaced tribal identities in favor of the 'Indian' has at times been so severe that Native Americans have become unrecognizable."[43] They point out that for the dominant society to see, or recognize Native Americans, they must fit the formula; they "must talk and act like 'real Indians.'"[44] By extension, Coyotes "must talk and act" like "real Coyotes," that is, fulfill the generic "Trickster" stereotype. Blue Cloud presents us with a Coyote who embodies the spirit of the sacred being as much more complex and multidimensional than any member of the dominant society can imagine. Two of the questions for which this volume on Native American rhetoric offers responses are: What does it mean for Native Americans to talk to each other? What do Native Americans sound like when they address their own people? *Elderberry Flute Song* offers us a lens by which to contemplate these questions. If we remember, in "The Battle" Coyote asks the ones who are doing the killing (of him), "Did he sweat himself and think of the children?"

In "Coyote's Song," Blue Cloud portrays Coyote at his most tender. In this piece, the children (little Coyotes) ask their Grandfather to sing them a song and tell them a story, also saying to him, "How was it when you was young like us, Grandfather?" Grandfather sits on the ground and picks beads of mud from his tail, flicking them behind himself so that they can "roll towards world's end," to entertain them for a moment, then he begins a story about sky-fish and "half-water-thing," who are curious and end up at a roundhouse looking for food, when they are caught by the old woman who is cooking inside. She throws sky-fish into the fire first, then half-water-thing, and bakes them for her son. The story is a teaching story to warn the young ones to take care when they are out and about, to not let their curiosity get the best of them, so they will not get baked, keeping in mind Coyote knows these lessons himself all too well. The children are not expecting such a story; they prefer the funny ones. Little Grandson breaks the uneasiness suddenly. "He tried to imitate Grandfather's deep voice and very solemnly said, 'Don't bake sky-fis, don't bake sky-fis!'" They all start laughing, Grandfather the hardest. He tells the little one, "Oh, yes, you are a coyote, no doubt." He then proceeds to sing them to sleep. As he begins playing his gourd rattle, he says, "Before there was a beginning there was another beginning to join the old one. Before the sky people there were the spirit people. The spirit people dreamed of night and sky, and the dream became real" (30). To the shushing sound of the rattle, Coyote sings a song four times, "each time a little softer," until the children sleep. He sings, "Our sleep is of dreaming, / we go back to the spirit, / and we sleep with the spirit, / we go back to the spirit, / and we sleep with the spirit" (31). He watches over them and keeps the rattle going, as he sits, "gazing into the fire" (31). In this piece, Blue Cloud presents us with Coyote the Grandfather, the elder, the gentle one who thinks of the children, teaches them, sings for them, protects them, watches over them.

Lyons notes the "key to . . . [the] rhetorics of sovereignty is an adamant refusal to disassociate culture, identity, and power from the *land*" (emphasis in original).[45] He says further that the "special relationship with the land . . . is made truly meaningful by a consistent cultural refusal [by Indigenous peoples] to interact with that land as private property or purely exploitable resource."[46] In Blue Cloud's "For Rattlesnake: A Dialogue of Creatures," we have a performance piece scripted for Snow Plant, Cedar, Woodpecker, Oak Tree, Flicker, Fox, Squirrel, Coyote, Blue Jay, Lizard, Rattlesnake, and Bear that affirms the relationship to the land, to the earth. The rhetorical strategy in this piece is to bear witness to the voices and presence of our more-than-human relations and to hear what they are living and suffering, and to remember they communicate with each other—they bear witness for each other. Snow Plant, "child of winter," begins by calling attention to the changing of the seasons, "the curving brownness emerging from snow / as earth her winter robe begins to fold" (92). Cedar tells us it is dawn. As they wait for the others to arrive, Woodpecker mentions "bear-who-used-to-be," and Oak Tree says, "yes, brothers and sisters, / bear, no more his soft and heavy walk / bear, no more / his strange and sacred manner" (92). Flicker interjects to ask, "Are we going to speak of THEM / again?"—and Fox continues, chanting: "I remember the last of bear's tribe / dragged / by fear-sweating horse / foaming from whip and smell / eyes rolling and bear / great clots of blood / and the human a most awful smell / of hate / and fear and lust / and the thought-pictures / of his mind / hurting all, / and we wondered at such cruelty / for his thought-pictures / were of himself / torn and devoured / by others of his likeness" (93). At this point in the narrative, it almost seems like we as readers are entering a funeral space. We are given the story of the extinction of Bear and his tribe, and the forced and violent enlistment of Horse in the atrocity. We are told of the smell of the human that is recognized by all the animals, a smell of hate, fear, lust, and the unfortunate horse. The human is disturbed by his own thought-pictures that reveal or betray a consciousness of his own acts, an immense fear that he could very likely suffer as he is causing others to suffer. The humans are the "THEM" that Flicker references.

Squirrel suddenly asks Coyote to explain what is happening, saying, "Wasn't this get together supposed to be for Rattlesnake?" (93). Coyote explains that Rattlesnake is on the way, but he also tells everyone, "Don't forget / it's said / that we are here to stay / as long as one of us remains" (93). Blue Jay responds, "Who said that?" to which Coyote responds, innocently, we are told, "I guess I just did" (94). Coyote, by the way, is described as a "man in old long coat, floppy hat, long tail he strokes" (93), making us as readers recall "As I Sit Here Writing Down His Words." The brief exchange is pretty much all of Coyote's intervention in this piece, other than to announce Rattlesnake when he finally arrives. But the intervention is an important one: "we are here to stay as long as one of us remains," which is the message of hope underlying the sadness and crisis of having to live on the same planet with the kind of humans they are describing. When Rattlesnake appears, he is carrying his head; he is "cut in half / and cut again headless / with strong heart beating a constant pulse . . . a nightmare of man's genius" (94). Acknowledging the seasons, he says, "I too am springtime / like my brother bear / for together we emerge / from sleep / to the dancers pounding feet / and the wormwood smell" (94). Rattlesnake tells of how he is a helpmate to humans, a fountain of wisdom and memory. "I teach them the necessary lesson / of alertness / of mind and body ever ready / for the tribal will," but the humans "have forgotten the allness / of the creation in their eager quest of vanity" (95). He says, "I lie headless and bloody at their feet / who am / their former brother" (95). He chants, "I dream bear / I vision bear / I call bear / we must all become bear," at which point Bear enters their space, dancing/shuffling, "four times in a circle, slowly, humming, as to himself" (95).

Bear testifies to what the humans have done to him, killing him, skinning him, then leaving his body "as in shame." He tells his relatives, "let us / then / begin again the praise / forgotten by man," as he asks Snow Plant to begin. Snow Plant returns to the praise prayer she offered at the beginning, describing the beauty in the changing of the seasons. Cedar continues, saying, "Yes my friend, / and dawn breeze lends me voice / and my branches whisper / a weeping as from an evil dream / of creatures born of hate / let us again / then / chant the evil back / into earth's womb / to be reborn / or not / as will be" (96). The rhetorical strategy in this piece turns our attention to the ability of the animal peoples, the sky peoples, to exercise their own agency to try to bring about transformation, the transformation of human people. At the same time, the piece ends with all of the voices joining in to offer the following prayer: "Man no more / look / he is fading, / man no more / see / he lies in dreaming, / man no more / forever / let us forget the pain, / man no more / forever / his bones of dust / the wind is taking / to scatter / to scatter / to scatter / to scatter" (96). We must recall that in "Coyote's Discourse on Power, Medicine, and Would-be Shamans" Coyote was able to easily "do" Shamaness Fast Walker, making her fade "completely away" (126). Here the animal and sky relations also know "how to counteract power" as Coyote does (126), making "Man" fade, and the dust of his bones scatter to the four winds. We are also shown a solidarity between the more-thanhuman peoples; they are clear about their own sacred natures, and they are clear about what each of their peoples brings to the whole "peopled universe," to use Lawrence Gross's term.[47] They are also clear about the impact "Man" has had on their lives and their worlds.

In *Elderberry Flute Song*, Peter Blue Cloud presents us with a Coyote realized by a writer who was likely a Coyote himself. Either that, or he was an immensely keen observer and philosopher of not only Coyotes, but also human Coyotes. I like to think he was/is the first. Morris and Wander state that they "seek to trace in Native American rhetoric significant efforts to revitalize tribal cultures by creating an 'ethos' [according to Clifford Geertz's definition] capable of transcending cultural difference among different tribal cultures and of forming coalitions sufficiently powerful to resist encroachments by the dominant society."[48] The figure and being of Coyote, as he/she is understood by Indigenous peoples, certainly can contribute to this ethos. We come back now to the beginning, to the cry, as the poet tells us, "It was all darkness and always had been / There was nothing there forever. / Creation was a tiny seed awaiting a dream. / The dream came to be / because of the cry. A howling cry which was / an echo in the emptiness of nothing. / The cry was very lonely and / caused the dream to / turn over in its sleep" (8). We are told that "Creation was the cry / seeking to begin something, / but it didn't know what, / and that is why it cried" (8). The cry, Coyote's cry, the cry who is Coyote, is the thread that keeps this collection together. Before the often foolish behavior of Coyote, before his risk-taking (also known as gambling), before his triumphs and failures as a lover, before everything, is the cry. This cry, represented in many of the pieces in this collection by Coyote the teacher, the healer, the elder, is what can help transcend cultural differences and build coalitions. The cry who is Coyote, Coyote's cry, is the secret to knowing Coyote, and the key to understanding Coyotean rhetoric. This is Blue Cloud's gift to us.

Notes

Note to Epigraph: Peter Blue Cloud, "The Cry," in *Elderberry Flute Songs: Contemporary Coyote Tales*, 4th ed. (Buffalo: NY: White Pine Press, 2002), 8–9.

1. For purposes of transparency, I did not grow up on the Colville Reservation, where I am enrolled. I grew up in Galveston, Texas, with a Nez Perce mother and a Tejano father. I have been taught about being Nez Perce throughout my life by members of my family, especially my mom, my uncle Frank, my auntie Tillie Red Elk, and other members of our community. I also want to acknowledge that in Niimiipuutímtki (the Nez Perce language), Coyote has several names, some for "common use" and some for "myth" (or sacred narratives, I would say). For coyote names in Niimiipuutímtki, see Haruo Aoki, *Nez Perce Grammar* (Berkeley: University of California Press, 1970), 7.

2. Peter Blue Cloud, *Elderberry Flute Song: Contemporary Coyote Tales*, 4th ed.

(1982; repr., Buffalo, NY: White Pine Press, 2002). In this essay, page numbers in parentheses will refer to this work.

3. Chadwick Allen, *Trans-Indigenous: Methodologies for Global Native Literary Studies* (Minneapolis: University of Minnesota Press, 2012), xix.

4. Gregory Younging, *Elements of Indigenous Style: A Guide for Writing by and about Indigenous Peoples* (Edmonton, AB: Brush Education, 2018), 64. I am following Younging in choosing to capitalize "Indigenous" as a matter of style.

5. Allen, *Trans-Indigenous*, 104.

6. Allen, *Trans-Indigenous*, 105.

7. Cutcha Risling Baldy, "Coyote Is Not a Metaphor: On Decolonizing, (Re) Claiming and (Re) Naming Coyote," *Decolonization: Indigeneity, Education & Society* 4, no. 1 (2015): 5. In her essay, Risling Baldy distinguishes between the indiscriminate (Western) use of the term "Coyote," and "Coyote First Person," who is the entity intimately related to Indigenous epistemologies (as with California Indian peoples). She also reminds us that "Coyote" has distinct names depending on the Indigenous culture that represents him/her. Risling Baldy, "Coyote Is Not," 2–3.

8. I am not writing in absolutes. I recognize that Coyote may not be central, nor indeed present, in all Indigenous traditions. But I, like Risling Baldy, align myself with the need to "complicate [trickster] discourse by demonstrating how Coyote First Person is not only a Trickster, but also a complex embodiment of Indigenous decolonizing epistemologies." Risling Baldy, "Coyote Is Not," 2.

9. "Peter Blue Cloud: Tales and Poems of Coyote," *Zócalo Poets* (blog), May 12, 2015, https://zocalopoets.com/2012/05/15/peter-blue-cloud-tales-and-poems-of-coyote/.

10. Oyate, "Elderberry Flute Song: Contemporary Coyote Tales," 2019, http://oyate.org/index.php/component/hikashop/product/282-elderberry-flute-song-contemporary-coyote-tales?Itemid=177.

11. Richard Morris and Philip Wander, "Native American Rhetoric: Dancing in the Shadows of the Ghost Dance," *Quarterly Journal of Speech* 76, no. 2 (May 1990): 184. Morris and Wander suggest that this "rhetorical problematic [is] faced by marginalized groups whose self-definition is inscribed by and communicated through an unaccommodating dominant society." Morris and Wander, "Native American Rhetoric," 184.

12. The following stories are particularly compelling: "Coyote and the Swallowing Monster," in *Coyote Was Going There: Indian Literature of the Oregon Country*, ed. Jarold Ramsey (Seattle: University of Washington Press, 1977), 9–12; and "Coyote and the Shadow People," *Coyote Was Going There*, 33–37. For an indispensable text on Niimiipuu language and storytelling traditions, including many on Coyote, see Haruo Aoki and Deward Walker Jr., *Nez Perce Oral Narratives* (Berkeley: University of California Press, 1989). These are stories that still live in the oral tradition.

13. Dan L. Flores, *Coyote America: A Natural and Supernatural History* (New York: Basic Books, 2016), 25. Huehuecoyotl means "Ancient Coyote," but Flores calls Coyote "Old Man America." However, the Aztecs, or ancient Nahuatl peoples, did not call Huehuecoyotl "Old Man America," because the name Huehuecoyotl predates what we know as "America."

14.   I have been involved with the Conchero dance tradition of central Mexico since the late 1970s, and I am acknowledged as a dance captain, a *capitana*, of this tradition, although since the death of my elder, the late María Teresa Osorio, a General, a *Generala* of La Mesa del Santo Niño de Atocha, I have participated less and less.

15.   I am aware of Craig Womack's critique of the term "trickster." Craig S. Womack, "A Single Decade: Book-Length Native Literary Criticism between 1986 and 1997," in *Reasoning Together: The Native Critics Collective*, ed. Janice Acoose et al. (Norman: University of Oklahoma Press, 2008), 19. My response is twofold: (1) the term is in the English language, but if we were to pursue the meaning of this entity in our original languages, the *idea* of this entity would have an enriched complexity, and (2) perhaps the anthropologists' invention of the term "trickster" is more the "indiscriminate" stereotype of what they think of as "trickster." Risling Baldy, "Coyote Is Not," 3n2.

16.   Flores, *Coyote America*, 229.

17.   Flores, *Coyote America*, 228. Flores's use of "our" and "we," I think, do not indicate an awareness of Native American readership who would not find themselves in the "our" or "we."

18.   Damián Baca, "Te-Ixtli: The 'Other Face' of the Americas," in *Rhetorics of the Americas: 3114 BCE to 2012 CE*, ed. Damián Baca and Victor Villanueva (New York: Palgrave Macmillan, 2010), 12.

19.   Baca, "Te-Ixtli," 12.

20.   Laura Perez, "Spirit Glyphs: Reimagining Art and Artist in the Work of Chicana Tlamatinime," in *Rhetorics of the Americas: 3114 BCE to 2012 CE*, ed. Damián Baca and Victor Villanueva (New York: Palgrave Macmillan, 2010), 203.

21.   Lata Mani, "Multiple Mediations: Feminist Scholarship in the Age of Multinational Reception," *Feminist Review* 35, no. 1 (July 1990): 24.

22.   Scott Richard Lyons, "Rhetorical Sovereignty: What Do American Indians Want from Writing?," *College Composition and Communication* 51, no. 3 (February 2000): 452.

23.   N. Scott Momaday, *House Made of Dawn* (1968; repr., New York: Harper Perennial Modern Classics, 2010), 79–87.

24.   Paula Gunn Allen is one of the writers who said this of N. Scott Momaday and this novel, *House Made of Dawn*. In a visit to my campus more than twenty years ago, in conversation with her audience, she said, "When I read *House Made of Dawn*, I realized, 'I'm not crazy. I'm Indian!'"

25.   Momaday, *House Made of Dawn*, 80–81.

26.   Momaday, *House Made of Dawn*, 82.

27.   Momaday, *House Made of Dawn*, 83. Scott Lyons begins his seminal article on rhetorical sovereignty with a version of the same passage. Lyons, "Rhetorical Sovereignty," 447.

28.   Momaday, *House Made of Dawn*, 83.

29.   The importance of the Word, and the sacredness of language, is a significant refrain in Indigenous literatures from early on. In reference to the "duplicitous interrelationships between writing, violence, and colonization developed during the nineteenth-century . . . [which] would set in motion a persistent distrust of the written word in

English," Lyons says, "If our respect for the Word remains resolute, our faith in the written word is compromised at best." Lyons, "Rhetorical Sovereignty," 449.

30.   Momaday, *House Made of Dawn*, 84–85.

31.   Momaday, *House Made of Dawn*, 85.

32.   Frank Andrews, in discussion with the author, Nespelem, Washington, on the Colville Reservation, late 1990s.

33.   Flores, *Coyote America*, 51.

34.   Flores, *Coyote America*, 243.

35.   Baca, "Te-Ixtli," 6.

36.   Lyons, "Rhetorical Sovereignty," 450.

37.   Baca, "Te-Ixtli," 2.

38.   Flores, *Coyote America*, 51.

39.   Diana Delgado Cabañez, "Federico Gama: Retratos de Identidades Indígenas en Tránsito por la CDMX," *Chilango* (blog), March 1, 2018, http://www.chilango.com/ciudad/federico-gama-fotos. In this article, the photographer Federico Gama is quoted as saying that the obligation of the photographer is to innovate, to ground concepts and to offer better alternatives; in summary, to train the eye to see differently.

40.   Morris and Wander, "Native American Rhetoric," 178.

41.   Flores, *Coyote America*, 246.

42.   Flores, *Coyote America*, 248.

43.   Morris and Wander, "Native American Rhetoric," 165.

44.   Morris and Wander, Native American Rhetoric," 165.

45.   Lyons, "Rhetorical Sovereignty," 457. Lyons makes the statement specifically in reference to the works of the scholars, in order, Vine Deloria Jr., Robert Warrior, and Elizabeth Cook-Lynn. The works cited by Lyons, again in order, are Vine Deloria Jr., *We Talk, You Listen: New Tribes, New Turf* (New York: Macmillan, 1970), 115; Robert Allen Warrior, *Tribal Secrets: Recovering American Indian Intellectual Traditions* (Minneapolis: University of Minnesota Press, 1995), 1–3, 91; and Elizabeth Cook-Lynn, *Why I Can't Read Wallace Stegner and Other Essays: A Tribal Voice* (Madison: University of Wisconsin Press, 1996), 90–91.

46.   Lyons, "Rhetorical Sovereignty," 458.

47.   Lawrence W. Gross, "Cultural Sovereignty and Native American Hermeneutics in the Interpretation of the Sacred Stories of the Anishinaabe," *Wicazo Sa Review* 18, no. 2 (2003): 132.

48.   Morris and Wander, "Native American Rhetoric," 166. Clifford Geertz defines ethos as "the tone, character, and quality of [a people's] life." Clifford Geertz, *The Interpretation of Cultures: Selected Essays* (New York: Basic Books, 1973), 127. This reference to Geertz also appears in Morris and Wander, "Native American Rhetoric," 188.

BIBLIOGRAPHY

Abbott, Don Paul. *Rhetoric in the New World: Rhetorical Theory and Practice in Colonial Spanish America.* Columbia: University of South Carolina Press, 1996.

Acoose, Janice, Craig S. Womack, Daniel Heath Justice, and Christopher B. Teuton, eds. *Reasoning Together: The Native Critics Collective.* Norman: University of Oklahoma Press, 2008.

Agha, Asif. "The Social Life of Cultural Value." *Language & Communication* 23, no. 3 (2003): 231–73.

Albanese, Catherine L. *America, Religions and Religion.* Belmont, CA: Wadsworth Publishing, 1981.

Alexander, Jonathan, and Jacqueline Rhodes, eds. *Sexual Rhetorics: Methods, Identities, Publics.* New York: Routledge, 2015.

Allen, Chadwick. *Trans-Indigenous: Methodologies for Global Native Literary Studies.* Minneapolis: University of Minnesota Press, 2012.

Anders, Ferdinand, Maarten Jansen, and Luis Reyes García, eds. *Los Templos del Cielo y de la Oscuridad: Oráculos y Liturgia Libro explicativo del llamado Códice Borgia.* Spain: Sociedad Estatal Quinto Centenario, 1993.

Anzaldúa, Gloria. *Borderlands/La Frontera: The New Mestiza.* 2nd ed. San Francisco: Aunt Lute Books, 1999.

Aoki, Haruo. *Nez Perce Grammar.* Berkeley: University of California Press, 1970.

Aoki, Haruo, and Deward E. Walker. *Nez Perce Oral Narratives.* Berkeley: University of California Press, 1989.

Appolloni, Simon. "The Roman Catholic Tradition in Conversation with Thomas Berry's Fourfold Wisdom." *Religions* 6, no. 3 (2015): 794–818.

Aucoin, Duane Gastant'. *Kichx Anagaat Yatx'i: Children of the Rainbow.* Teslin, YT: DGA Media and T'senaglobe Media Inc., 2003.

———. *My Own Private Lower Post.* Teslin, YT: DGA Media and T'senaglobe Media Inc., 2008.

———. "Truth and Reconciliation." "International Queer Indigenous Voices." Edited by Ahimsa Timoteo Bodhrán. Special issue, *Yellow Medicine Review: A Journal of Indigenous Literature, Art, and Thought* (Fall 2010): 34–35.

Baca, Damián. "Te-Ixtli: The 'Other Face' of the Americas." In *Rhetorics of the Americas: 3114 BCE to 2012 CE,* edited by Damián Baca and Victor Villanueva, 1–13. New York: Palgrave Macmillan, 2010.

Baca, Damián, and Victor Villanueva, eds. *Rhetorics of the Americas: 3114 BCE to 2012 CE.* New York: Palgrave Macmillan, 2010.

Bahr, Donald M. "Four Rattlesnake Songs." In *Speaking, Singing, and Teaching: A Multidisciplinary Approach to Language Variation: Proceedings of the Eighth Annual Southwest Areal Language and Linguistics Workshop,* edited by Florence Barkin and Elizabeth A. Brandt, 118–26. Anthropological Research Papers, no. 20. Tempe: Arizona State University, 1980.

——, ed. *O'odham Creation & Related Events as Told to Ruth Benedict in 1927 in Prose, Oratory, and Song [. . .].* Tucson: University of Arizona Press, 2001.

Bahr, Donald M., and Juan Gregorio. *Piman Shamanism and Staying Sickness (Ká:Cim Múmkidag).* Edited by Albert Alvarez. Translated by David I. Lopez. 1974. Reprint, Tucson: University of Arizona Press, 1981.

Bailey, Guy, and Erik Thomas. "Some Aspects of African-American Vernacular English Phonology." In *African-American English: Structure, History, and Use,* edited by Salikoko S. Mufwene, John R. Rickford, Guy Bailey, and John Baugh, 85–109. London: Routledge, 1998.

Baker, Wendy, and David Bowie. "Religious Affiliation as a Correlate of Linguistic Behavior." *University of Pennsylvania Working Papers in Linguistics* 15, no. 2, Article 2 (2010). https://repository.upenn.edu/pwpl/vol15/iss2/2.

Bolado, Carlos. *River of Renewal.* DVD. Pikiawish Partners and Specialty Studios, 2009.

Barkin, Florence, and Elizabeth A. Brandt, eds. *Speaking, Singing, and Teaching: A Multidisciplinary Approach to Language Variation: Proceedings of the Eighth Annual Southwest Areal Language and Linguistics Workshop,* Anthropological Research Papers, no. 20. Tempe: Arizona State University, 1980.

Basso, Keith H. *Portraits of "The Whiteman": Linguistic Play and Cultural Symbols among the Western Apache.* Cambridge: Cambridge University Press, 1979.

——. "'To Give Up on Words': Silence in Western Apache Culture." *Southwestern Journal of Anthropology* 26, no. 3 (1970): 213–30.

——. *Wisdom Sits in Places: Landscape and Language among the Western Apache.* Albuquerque: University of New Mexico Press, 1996.

Beck, Peggy V., and Anna Lee Walters. *The Sacred: Ways of Knowledge, Sources of Life.* Tsaile, AZ: Navajo Community College, 1977.

Belchik, Michael, Dave Hillemeier, and Ronnie M. Pierce. *The Klamath River Fish Kill of 2002; Analysis of Contributing Factors.* Klamath, CA: Yurok Tribal Fisheries Program, 2004. https://www.waterboards.ca.gov/waterrights/water_issues/programs/bay_delta/california_waterfix/exhibits/docs/PCFFA&IGFR/part2/pcffa_155.pdf.

Berry, Thomas. *The Dream of the Earth.* San Francisco: Sierra Club Books, 1988.

Biondini, Lori. "Salmon Pluralities: The Politics of Commercial Fishing on the Hoopa Valley Reservation." Master's thesis, Humboldt State University, 2017. https://digitalcommons.humboldt.edu/cgi/viewcontent.cgi?article=1123&context=etd.

Black Elk. *The Sacred Pipe: Black Elk's Account of the Seven Rites of the Oglala Sioux.* Edited by Joseph Epes Brown. Norman: University of Oklahoma Press, 1953.

Black, Jason E. "Native Resistive Rhetoric and the Decolonization of American Indian Removal Discourse," *Quarterly Journal of Speech* 95, no. 1 (2009): 66–88.

Blue Cloud, Peter. *Elderberry Flute Song: Contemporary Coyote Tales.* 4th ed. 1982. Reprint, Buffalo, NY: White Pine Press, 2002.

Bonfil Batalla, Guillermo. *México Profundo: Reclaiming a Civilization.* Translated by Philip A. Dennis. Austin: University of Texas Press, 1996.

Boone, Elizabeth Hill. *Cycles of Time and Meaning in the Mexican Books of Fate.* Austin: University of Texas Press, 2007.

———. "In Tlamatinime: The Wise Men and Women of Aztec Mexico." In *Painted Books and Indigenous Knowledge in Mesoamerica: Manuscript Studies in Honor of Mary Elizabeth Smith,* edited by Elizabeth Hill Boone, 9–25. New Orleans: Middle American Research Institute, 2005.

———, ed. *Painted Books and Indigenous Knowledge in Mesoamerica: Manuscript Studies in Honor of Mary Elizabeth Smith.* New Orleans: Middle American Research Institute, 2005.

———. *Stories in Red and Black: Pictorial Histories of the Aztecs and Mixtecs.* Austin: University of Texas Press, 2000.

———, ed. *The Art and Iconography of Late Post-Classic Central Mexico.* Washington, DC: Dumbarton Oaks, 1982.

Brumfiel, Elizabeth. "Huitzilopochtli's Conquest: Aztec Ideology in the Archaeological Record." In *The Archaeology of Identities: A Reader,* edited by Timothy Insoll, 265–80. London: Routledge, 2007.

Burkhart, Louise M. *The Slippery Earth: Nahua-Christian Moral Dialogue in Sixteenth-Century Mexico.* Tucson: University of Arizona Press, 1989.

Burton, Linda M., Susan P. Kemp, ManChui Leung, Stephen A. Matthews, and David T. Takeuchi. *Communities, Neighborhoods, and Health: Expanding the Boundaries of Place.* New York: Springer, 2011.

Carrasco, Davíd. "Uttered from the Heart: Guilty Rhetoric among the Aztecs." *History of Religions* 39, no. 1 (August 1999): 1–31.

Carrasco, David, and Scott Sessions. *Daily Life of the Aztecs.* 2nd ed. Santa Barbara, CA: Greenwood, 2011.

Carrera, Cristián Roa de la. "Translating Nahua Rhetoric: Sahagún's Nahua Subjects in Colonial Mexico." In *Rhetorics of the Americas: 3114 BCE to 2012 CE,* edited by Damián Baca and Victor Villanueva, 69–87. New York: Palgrave Macmillan, 2010.

"Chicana Feminist Epistemology: Past, Present, and Future." *Harvard Educational Review* 82, no. 4 (Winter 2012): 511–12.

Child, Louise, and Aaron Rosen, eds. *Religion and Sight.* Bristol, UK: Equinox Publishing, 2020.

Cook, Sherburne Friend. *The Population of the California Indians, 1769–1970.* Berkeley: University of California Press, 1976.

Cook-Lynn, Elizabeth. *Why I Can't Read Wallace Stegner and Other Essays: A Tribal Voice.* Madison: University of Wisconsin Press, 1996.

Coulthard, Glen Sean. *Red Skin, White Masks: Rejecting the Colonial Politics of Recognition*. Minneapolis: University of Minnesota Press, 2014.

Dąbrowska, Katarzyna Mikulska. "'Secret Language' in Oral and Graphic Form: Religious-Magic Discourse in Aztec Speeches and Manuscripts." *Oral Tradition* 25, no. 2 (October 2010): 325–63.

Dancing Salmon Home. DVD. Eugene, OR: Moving Up Productions, 2013. https://dancingsalmonhome.wordpress.com/.

D'Arcy, Alexandra. "Canadian English as a Window to the Rise of *Like* in Discourse." In "Focus on Canadian English." Edited by Matthia Meyer. Special issue, *Anglistik* 19 (2008): 125–40.

Debassige, Brent. "Re-Conceptualizing Anishinaabe Mino-Bimaadiziwin (the Good Life) as Research Methodology: A Spirit-Centered Way in Anishinaabe Research." *Canadian Journal of Native Education* 33, no. 1 (2010): 11–28.

Delgado Bernal, Dolores, Rebeca Burciaga, and Judith Flores Carmona. "Chicana/Latina Testimonios: Mapping the Methodological, Pedagogical, and Political." *Equity & Excellence in Education* 45, no. 3 (2012): 363–72.

Delgado Bernal, Dolores. "Using a Chicana Feminist Epistemology in Educational Research." *Harvard Educational Review* 68, no. 4 (Winter 1998): 555–83.

Deloria, Vine, Jr. *God Is Red*. New York: Grosset & Dunlap, 1973.

———. *Spirit & Reason: The Vine Deloria, Jr., Reader*. Edited by Barbara Deloria, Kristen Foehner, and Samuel Scinta. Golden, CO: Fulcrum Publishing, 1999.

———. *We Talk, You Listen: New Tribes, New Turf*. New York: Macmillan, 1970.

Densmore, Frances. *Papago Music*. Smithsonian Institution. Bureau of American Ethnology, Bulletin 90. Washington, DC: US Government Printing Office, 1929.

Desjarlais, Sharon. *Two-Spirited: First Stories Volume III*. Montreal: National Film Board of Canada, 2007.

Diamond, Stanley, ed. *Culture in History: Essays in Honor of Paul Radin*. New York: Columbia University Press, 1960.

Drinnon, Richard. *Facing West: The Metaphysics of Indian-Hating and Empire-Building*. New York: New American Library, 1980.

Durán, Diego. *Book of the Gods and Rites and the Ancient Calendar*. Edited and translated by Fernando Horcasitas and Doris Heyden. Norman: University of Oklahoma Press, 1971.

Estrada, Gabriel S. "Obscuring Two-Spirit Deaths in the Films *Conversion* and *Fire Song*." In *Religion and Sight*, edited by Louise Child and Aaron Rosen, 46–66. Bristol, UK: Equinox Publishing, 2020.

———. "Ojibwe Lesbian Visual AIDS: On the Red Road with Carole LaFavor, *Her Giveaway* (1988), and Native LGBTQ2 Film History." *Journal of Lesbian Studies* 20, nos. 3–4 (2016): 388–407.

———. "Two-Spirit Film Criticism: *Fancydancing* with Imitates Dog, Desjarlais and Alexie." *Post Script: Essays in Film and the Humanities* 29, no. 3 (Summer 2010): 106–18.

———. "Two Spirits, *Nádleeh,* and LGBTQ2 Navajo Gaze." *American Indian Culture and Research Journal* 35, no. 4 (2011): 167–90.

Ethelbah, Paul, Genevieve Ethelbah, and M. Eleanor Nevins. "'Ndah Ch'ii'n.'" In *Inside Dazzling Mountains: Southwest Native Verbal Arts,* edited by David L. Kozak, 197–239. Lincoln: University of Nebraska Press, 2012.

Fast, Phyllis Ann. *Northern Athabascan Survival: Women, Community, and the Future.* Lincoln: University of Nebraska Press, 2002.

Field, Margaret C. "Changing Navajo Language Ideologies and Changing Language Use." In *Native American Language Ideologies: Beliefs, Practices, and Struggles in Indian Country,* edited by Paul V. Kroskrity and Margaret C. Field, 31–47. Tucson: University of Arizona Press, 2009.

Fisher, Andrew H. "Defenders and Dissidents: Cooks Landing and the Fight to Define Tribal Sovereignty in the Red Power Era." *Comparative American Studies* 17, no. 2 (2020): 117–41. https://doi.org/10.1080/14775700.2020.1724017.

Flores, Dan L. *Coyote America: A Natural and Supernatural History.* New York: Basic Books, 2016.

Fox, Coleen A., Nicholas James Reo, Dale A. Turner, JoAnne Cook, Frank Dituri, Brett Fessell, James Jenkins, et al. "'The River Is Us; the River Is in Our Veins': Re-Defining River Restoration in Three Indigenous Communities." *Sustainability Science* 12, no. 4 (July 2017): 521–33.

Geertz, Clifford. *The Interpretation of Cultures: Selected Essays.* New York: Basic Books, 1973.

Gill, Sam D. *Native American Traditions: Sources and Interpretations.* Belmont, CA: Wadsworth Publishing, 1983.

Goddard, Pliny Earle. *Hupa Texts.* University of California Publications American Archaeology and Ethnology, vol. 1, no. 2. Berkeley, CA: The University Press, 1904. https://digitalassets.lib.berkeley.edu/anthpubs/ucb/text/ucp001-004.pdf.

Goggin, Maureen Day. "From Visual Rhetoric in Pens of Steel and Inks of Silk: Challenging the Great Visual/Verbal Divide." In *Defining Visual Rhetorics,* edited by Charles A. Hill and Marguerite H. Helmers, 87–110. Mahwah, NJ: Lawrence Erlbaum Associates, 2004.

González, Juan. *Harvest of Empire: A History of Latinos in America.* New York: Viking, 2000.

Gross, Lawrence W. "Anishinaabe Rhetoric." Chap. 8 in *Anishinaabe Ways of Knowing and Being.* Farnham Surrey, UK: Ashgate, 2014.

———. *Anishinaabe Ways of Knowing and Being.* Farnham Surrey, UK: Ashgate, 2014.

———. "Bimaadiziwin, or the Good Life of the Anishinaabeg." Chap. 9 in *Anishinaabe Ways of Knowing and Being.* Farnham Surrey, UK: Ashgate, 2014.

———. "Cultural Sovereignty and Native American Hermeneutics in the Interpretation of the Sacred Stories of the Anishinaabe." *Wicazo Sa Review* 18, no. 2 (2003): 127–34.

Grounds, Richard A., George E. Tinker, and David E. Wilkins, eds. *Native Voices: American Indian Identity and Resistance.* Lawrence: University Press of Kansas, 2003.

Haas, Angela. "Toward a Decolonial Digital and Visual American Indian Rhetorics Peda-
    gogy." In *Survivance, Sovereignty, and Story: Teaching American Indian Rhetorics,*
    edited by Lisa King, Rose Gubele, and Anderson Joyce Rain, 188–208. Logan: Utah
    State University Press, 2015.
Hallowell, A. Irving. "Ojibwa Ontology, Behavior, and World View." In *Culture in His-
    tory: Essays in Honor of Paul Radin,* edited by Stanley Diamond, 19–52. New York:
    Columbia University Press, 1960.
Heizer, Robert F., and Albert B. Elsasser. *The Natural World of the California Indians.*
    Berkeley: University of California Press, 1980.
Henry, Chief. *Koyukon riddles = K'ooltsaah ts' in'.* Edited by Eliza Jones. Fairbanks: Alaska
    Native Language Center, University of Alaska, 1976.
Hill, Charles A., and Marguerite H. Helmers, eds. *Defining Visual Rhetorics.* Mahwah, NJ:
    Lawrence Erlbaum Associates, 2004.
Hill, Jane H. "What Is Lost When Names Are Forgotten." In *Nature Knowledge: Ethnosci-
    ence, Cognition, and Utility,* edited by Glauco Sanga and Gherardo Ortalli, 161–84.
    New York: Berghahn Books, 2003.
Hormel, Leontina M., and Kari M. Norgaard. "Bring the Salmon Home! Karuk Challenges
    to Capitalist Incorporation." *Critical Sociology* 35, no. 3 (2009): 343–66. https://doi.
    org/10.1177/0896920508101502.
House, Deborah. *Language Shift among the Navajos: Identity Politics and Cultural Conti-
    nuity.* Tucson: University of Arizona Press, 2002.
Hultkrantz, Åke. *The Religions of the American Indians.* Berkeley: University of California
    Press, 1979.
———. *The Study of American Indian Religions.* New York: Crossroad Publishing, 1983.
Hund, Wulf D. "'It Must Come from Europe': The Racisms of Immanuel Kant." In *Racisms
    Made in Germany,* edited by Wulf D. Hund, Christian Koller, and Moshe Zimmer-
    mann, 69–98. Zurich: LIT-Verlag, 2011.
Hund, Wulf D., Christian Koller, and Moshe Zimmermann, eds. *Racisms Made in Ger-
    many.* Zurich: LIT-Verlag, 2011.
Idström, Anna, Elisabeth Piirainen, and Tiber Falzett, eds. *Endangered Metaphors.*
    Amsterdam: John Benjamins Publishing, 2012.
Ingold, Tim. *Being Alive: Essays on Movement, Knowledge and Description.* London: Rout-
    ledge, 2011.
Insoll, Timothy, ed. *The Archaeology of Identities: A Reader.* London: Routledge, 2007.
Irvine, Judith T., and Susan Gal. "Language Ideology and Linguistic Differentiation." In
    Regimes of Language: Ideologies, Polities, and Identities, edited by Paul V. Kroskrity,
    35–83. Santa Fe, NM: School of American Research Press, 2000.
Jacobsen, Kristina M. *The Sound of Navajo Country: Music, Language, and Diné Belong-
    ing.* Chapel Hill: University of North Carolina Press, 2017.
Jaffe, Alexandra M. "Stance in a Corsican School: Production of Bilingual Subjects." In
    Stance: Sociolinguistic Perspectives, edited by Alexandra M. Jaffe, 119–45. Oxford:
    Oxford University Press, 2009.

———, ed. *Stance: Sociolinguistic Perspectives*. Oxford: Oxford University Press, 2009.

Jetté, Jules, and Eliza Jones. *Koyukon Athabaskan Dictionary*. Edited by James M. Kari. Fairbanks: Alaska Native Language Center, University of Alaska Fairbanks, 2000.

Jetté, Julius. "On the Superstitions of the Ten'a Indians (Middle Part of the Yukon Valley, Alaska)." *Anthropos* 6, no. 1 (1911): 95–108; 6, no. 2 (1911): 241–59; 6, no. 3 (1911): 602–15; 6, no. 4 (1911): 699–723.

———. "Riddles of the Ten'a Indians." *Anthropos* 8, no. 1 (January–February 1913): 181–201; 8, no. 4/5 (July–October 1913): 630–51.

Jilek, Wolfgang G. "Altered States of Consciousness in North American Indian Ceremonials." *Ethos* 10, no. 4 (Winter 1982): 326–43.

Johnston-Dodds, Kimberly. *Early California Laws and Policies Related to California Indians*. Sacramento: California State Library, California Research Bureau, 2002. https://www.library.ca.gov/Content/pdf/crb/reports/02-014.pdf.

Kant, Immanuel. *Lectures on Anthropology*. Edited by Allen W. Wood and Robert B. Louden. Translated by Robert R. Clewis, Robert B. Louden, G. Felicitas Munzel, and Allen W. Wood. Cambridge: Cambridge University Press, 2012.

Kari, James. "Appendix A: The Koyukon Verb: Jetté's Terminology and Contemporary Terminology." In *Koyukon Athabaskan Dictionary*, edited by James Kari, 753–59. Fairbanks: Alaska Native Language Center, University of Alaska Fairbanks, 2000.

Kimmerer, Robin Wall. *Braiding Sweetgrass: Indigenous Wisdom, Scientific Knowledge, and the Teachings of Plants*. Minneapolis: Milkweed Editions, 2013.

———. *Gathering Moss: A Natural and Cultural History of Mosses*. Corvallis: Oregon State University Press, 2003.

King, Lisa. "Sovereignty, Rhetorical Sovereignty, and Representation: Keywords for Teaching Indigenous Texts." In *Survivance, Sovereignty, and Story: Teaching American Indian Rhetorics*, edited by Lisa King, Rose Gubele, and Joyce Rain Anderson, 17–34. Logan: Utah State University Press, 2015.

King, Lisa, Rose Gubele, and Joyce Rain Anderson, eds. *Survivance, Sovereignty, and Story: Teaching American Indian Rhetorics*. Logan: Utah State University Press, 2015.

Klieger, Paul Christiaan. *L. Frank Manriquez*. Sacramento: California Museum, 2011.

Kovach, Margaret. *Indigenous Methodologies: Characteristics, Conversations and Contexts*. Toronto: University of Toronto Press, 2009.

Kozak, David L., ed. *Inside Dazzling Mountains: Southwest Native Verbal Arts*. Lincoln: University of Nebraska Press, 2012.

Kozak, David, and David Lopez. "Echoes of Mythical Creation: Snakes, Sex, Voice." *Wicazo Sa Review* 10, no. 1 (1994): 52–58.

Kroeber, Alfred L. *The Valley Nisenan*. Berkeley: University of California Press, 1929.

Kroskrity, Paul V., ed. *Regimes of Language: Ideologies, Polities, and Identities*. Santa Fe, NM: School of American Research Press, 2000.

Kroskrity, Paul V., and Margaret C. Field, eds. *Native American Language Ideologies: Beliefs, Practices, and Struggles in Indian Country*. Tucson: University of Arizona Press, 2009.

Lacadena, Alfonso. "Regional Scribal Traditions: Methodological Implications for the Decipherment of Nahuatl Writing." *PARI Journal* 8, no. 4 (Spring 2008): 1–22.

LaDuke, Winona. "Traditional Ecological Knowledge and Environmental Futures." *Colorado Journal of International Environmental Law and Policy* 5, no. 1 (1994): 127–48.

Larrimore, Mark. "Sublime Waste: Kant on the Destiny of the 'Races.'" In *Civilization and Oppression,* edited by Catherine Wilson. Calgary, AB: University of Calgary Press. Supplement, *Canadian Journal of Philosophy* 25 (1999): 99–125.

Lindsay, Brendan C. *Murder State: California's Native American Genocide, 1846–1873.* Lincoln: University of Nebraska Press, 2012.

López Austin, Alfredo. *Cuerpo humano e ideología: las concepciones de los antiguos nahuas.* 2 vols. Mexico: Universidad Nacional Autónoma de México, Instituto de Investigaciones Antropológicas, 1980.

Lopez, Felicia Rhapsody. "Case Study for the Development of a Visual Grammar: Mayahuel and Maguey as Teotl in the Directional Tree Pages of the Codex Borgia." *REvista: A Multi-Media, Multi-Genre e-Journal for Social Justice* 5, no. 2 (2017). https://escholarship.org/uc/item/4gm205sx.

———. "Mayahuel and Tlahuizcalpanteuctli in the Nahua Codices: Indigenous Readings of Nahuatl Pictorial and Alphabetic Texts." PhD diss., University of California, Santa Barbara, 2016.

Lorde, Audre. "The Master's Tools Will Never Dismantle the Master's House." In *This Bridge Called My Back: Writings by Radical Women of Color,* edited by Cherríe Moraga and Gloria Anzaldúa, 94–101. New York: Kitchen Table, Women of Color Press, 1983.

Lumsden, Stephanie. "Reproductive Justice, Sovereignty, and Incarceration: Prison Abolition Politics and California Indians." *American Indian Culture and Research Journal* 40, no. 1 (2016): 33–46.

Lyons, Oren, ed. *Exiled in the Land of the Free: Democracy, Indian Nations, and the U.S. Constitution.* Santa Fe, NM: Clear Light Publishers, 1992.

Lyons, Scott Richard. "Rhetorical Sovereignty: What Do American Indians Want from Writing?" *College Composition and Communication* 51, no. 3 (February 2000): 447–68.

Madley, Benjamin. *An American Genocide: The United States and the California Indian Catastrophe, 1846–1873.* New Haven CT: Yale University Press, 2016.

Maggio, Jay. "'Can the Subaltern Be Heard?': Political Theory, Translation, Representation, and Gayatri Chakravorty Spivak." *Alternatives* 32, no. 4 (2007): 419–43.

Mani, Lata. "Multiple Mediations: Feminist Scholarship in the Age of Multinational Reception." *Feminist Review* 35, no. 1 (July 1990): 24–41.

Mann, Barbara A., and Jerry L. Fields. "A Sign in the Sky: Dating the League of the Haudenosaunee." *American Indian Culture and Research Journal* 21, no. 2 (January 1997): 105–63. https://doi.org/10.17953/aicr.21.2.k36m1485r3062510.

Marshall, Kimberly Jenkins. *Upward, Not Sunwise: Resonant Rupture in Navajo Neo-Pentecostalism.* Lincoln: University of Nebraska Press, 2016.

Martin, Calvin. *Keepers of the Game: Indian-Animal Relationships and the Fur Trade.* Berkeley: University of California Press, 1978.

———. "The Metaphysics of Writing Indian-White History." *Ethnohistory* 26, no. 2 (Spring 1979): 153–59.

Matthews, Washington. "The Mountain Chant: A Navajo Ceremony." *Annual Report of the Bureau of American Ethnology to the Secretary of the Smithsonian Institution* 5 (1883–1884): 385–467.

———. *The Mountain Chant: A Navajo Ceremony.* Washington, DC: Government Printing Office, 1888.

May, Theresa J. *Salmon Is Everything: Community-Based Theatre in the Klamath Watershed.* Corvallis: Oregon State University Press, 2014.

McGrane, Bernard. *Beyond Anthropology: Society and the Other.* New York: Columbia University Press, 1989.

McGregor, Deborah. "Coming Full Circle: Indigenous Knowledge, Environment, and Our Future." *American Indian Quarterly* 28, no. 3/4 (Summer–Autumn 2004): 385–410.

Merriam, C. Hart. *The Dawn of the World: Myths and Weird Tales Told by the Mewan Indians of California.* Cleveland: Arthur H. Clark Company, 1910.

Million, Dian. *Therapeutic Nations: Healing in an Age of Indigenous Human Rights.* Tucson: University of Arizona Press, 2013.

———. "There Is a River in Me: Theory from Life." In *Theorizing Native Studies,* edited by Audra Simpson and Andrea Smith, 31–42. Durham, NC: Duke University Press, 2014.

Mohawk, John. *Iroquois Creation Story: John Arthur Gibson and J. N. B. Hewitt's Myth of the Earth Grasper.* Buffalo, NY: Mohawk Publications, 2005.

Molina, Alonso de. *Vocabulario de la lengua méxicana.* Edited by Julius Platzmann. Facsimile ed. Leipzig, DE: B. G. Teubner, 1880.

Momaday, N. Scott. *House Made of Dawn.* New York: Harper & Row, 1968.

———. *House Made of Dawn.* 1968. Reprint. New York: Harper Perennial Modern Classics, 2010.

Montes de Oca Vega, Mercedes. "Los Difrasismos En El Náhuatl Del Siglo XVI." PhD diss., Universidad Nacional Autónoma de México, 2000.

Moore, Patrick. "Negotiated Identities: The Evolution of Dene Tha and Kaska Personal Naming Systems." *Anthropological Linguistics* 49, no. 3/4 (Autumn–Winter 2007): 283–307.

Moraga, Cherríe. "La Güera." In *This Bridge Called My Back: Writings by Radical Women of Color,* edited by Cherríe Moraga and Gloria Anzaldúa, 27–34. Watertown, MA: Persephone Press, 1981.

Moraga, Cherríe, and Gloria Anzaldúa, eds. *This Bridge Called My Back: Writings by Radical Women of Color.* Watertown, MA: Persephone Press, 1981.

Morris, Richard, and Philip Wander. "Native American Rhetoric: Dancing in the Shadows of the Ghost Dance." *Quarterly Journal of Speech* 76, no. 2 (May 1990): 164–91.

Moss, Meredith Genevieve. "English with a Navajo Accent: Language and Ideology in Heritage Language Advocacy." PhD diss., Arizona State University, 2015.

Mufwene, Salikoko S., John R. Rickford, Guy Bailey, and John Baugh, eds. *African-American English: Structure, History, and Use*. London: Routledge, 1998.

Murphy, Sherry L., Jiaquan Xu, Kenneth D. Kochanek, Sally C. Curtin, and Elizabeth Arias. *Deaths: Final Data for 2015*. National Vital Statistics Reports, vol. 66, no. 6. Hyattsville, MD: National Center for Health Statistics, 2017.

Nelson, Melissa K., ed. *Original Instructions: Indigenous Teachings for a Sustainable Future*. Rochester, VT: Bear & Company, 2008.

Nelson, Melissa K., and Dan Shilling, eds. *Traditional Ecological Knowledge: Learning from Indigenous Practices for Environmental Sustainability*. Cambridge: Cambridge University Press, 2018.

Nelson, Richard K. *Make Prayers to the Raven: A Koyukon View of the Northern Forest*. Chicago: University of Chicago Press, 1983.

Newcomb, Franc J., and Gladys A. Reichard. *Sandpaintings of the Navajo Shooting Chant*. New York: Dover Publications, 1975.

Nibley, Lydia. *Two Spirits*. Los Angeles: Say Yes Quickly Productions, 2010.

Nicholson, Henry B. "Eduard Georg Seler, 1849–1922." In *Handbook of Middle American Indians*, edited by Robert Wauchope, vol. 13, *Guide to Ethnohistorical Sources: Part 2*, edited by Howard F. Cline and John B. Glass, 348–69. Austin: University of Texas Press, 1973.

Norgaard, Kari M. "The Effects of Altered Diet on the Health of the Karuk People: A Preliminary Report." The Karuk Tribe of California: Department of Natural Resources Water Quality Program, 2004.

Norton, Jack. *Genocide in Northwestern California: When Our Worlds Cried*. San Francisco: Indian Historian Press, 1979.

Nowotny, Karl Anton. *Tlacuilolli: Style and Contents of the Mexican Pictorial Manuscripts with a Catalog of the Borgia Group*. Edited and translated by George A. Everett and Edward B. Sisson. Norman: University of Oklahoma Press, 2005.

Ocampo, Daisy. "Spiritual Geographies of Indigenous Sovereignty: Connections of Caxcan with Tlachialoyantepec and Chemehuevi with Mamapukaib." PhD diss., University of California, Riverside, 2019.

Oros, Chisa. "The Role of Fort Humboldt during the California Gold Rush: A Focus on Local Indigenous Women's Struggle, Resistance and Resilience." Master's thesis, Humboldt State University, 2016. http://humboldt-dspace.calstate.edu/bitstream/handle/10211.3/176139/oros_chisa_Sp2016.pdf?sequence=1.

Ortiz, Alfonzo. "San Juan Pueblo." In *Handbook of North American Indians*, edited by William C. Sturtevant, vol. 9, *Southwest*, edited by Alfonzo Ortiz, 278–95. Washington, DC: Smithsonian Institution, 1979.

Overing, Joanna, ed. *Reason and Morality*. London: Tavistock Publications, 1985.

———. "Today I Shall Call Him 'Mummy': Multiple Worlds and Classificatory Confusion." In *Reason and Morality*, edited by Joanna Overing, 150–78. London: Tavistock Publications, 1985.

Pearce, Roy Harvey. *The Savages of America: A Study of the Indian and the Idea of Civilization.* Baltimore: Johns Hopkins Press, 1953.

Pérez, Emma. *The Decolonial Imaginary: Writing Chicanas into History.* Bloomington: Indiana University Press, 1999.

Perez, Laura. "Spirit Glyphs: Reimagining Art and Artist in the Work of Chicana Tlamatinime." In *Rhetorics of the Americas: 3114 BCE to 2012 CE,* edited by Damián Baca and Victor Villanueva, 197–226. New York: Palgrave Macmillan, 2010.

Pesantubbee, Michelene E. "Religious Studies on the Margins: Decolonizing Our Minds." In *Native Voices: American Indian Identity and Resistance,* edited by Richard A. Grounds, George E. Tinker, and David E. Wilkins, 209–22. Lawrence: University Press of Kansas, 2003.

Pierotti, Raymond, and Daniel Wildcat. "Traditional Ecological Knowledge: The Third Alternative (Commentary)." *Ecological Applications* 10, no. 5 (2000): 1333–40. https://doi.org/10.1890/1051-0761(2000)010[1333:TEKTTA]2.0.CO;2.

Portillo, Annette Angela. *Sovereign Stories and Blood Memories: Native American Women's Autobiography.* Albuquerque: University of New Mexico Press, 2017.

Powell, Malea. "Rhetorics of Survivance: How American Indians Use Writing." *College Composition and Communication* 53, no. 3 (2002): 396–434. https://doi.org/10.2307/1512132.

Pratt, Richard Henry. *Battlefield and Classroom: Four Decades with the American Indian, 1867–1904.* Edited by Robert M. Utley. 1964. Reprint, Norman: University of Oklahoma Press, 2003.

Prieto, Linda, and Sofia A. Villenas. "Pedagogies from *Nepantla: Testimonio,* Chicana/Latina Feminisms and Teacher Education Classrooms." *Equity & Excellence in Education* 45, no. 3 (2012): 411–29.

Raheja, Michelle H. *Reservation Reelism: Redfacing, Visual Sovereignty, and Representations of Native Americans in Film.* Lincoln: University of Nebraska Press, 2010.

Ramos, Seafha C. "Considerations for Culturally Sensitive Traditional Ecological Knowledge Research in Wildlife Conservation." *Wildlife Society Bulletin* 42, no. 2 (2018): 358–65. https://doi.org/10.1002/wsb.881.

Ramsey, Jarold, ed. *Coyote Was Going There: Indian Literature of the Oregon Country.* Seattle: University of Washington Press, 1977.

Rau, Anna, and Corbett Jones. *Restoring the River with the Yurok, Hupa and Karuk.* Tending Nature. KCETink and The Range, 2019.

Rea, Amadeo M. *At the Desert's Green Edge: An Ethnobotany of the Gila River Pima.* Tucson: University of Arizona Press, 1997.

Reichard, Gladys A. *Navaho Religion: A Study of Symbolism.* New York: Pantheon Books, 1950.

Reséndez, Andrés. *Changing National Identities at the Frontier: Texas and New Mexico, 1800–1850.* Cambridge: Cambridge University Press, 2005.

Rice, Sally. "Our Language Is Very Literal." In *Endangered Metaphors,* edited by Anna Idström, Elisabeth Piirainen, and Tiber Falzett, 21–76. Amsterdam: John Benjamins Publishing, 2012.

Rifkin, Mark. *Beyond Settler Time: Temporal Sovereignty and Indigenous Self-Determination*. Durham, NC: Duke University Press, 2017.

Riley-Mukavetz, Andrea, and Malea D. Powell. "Making Native Space for Graduate Students: A Story of Indigenous Rhetorical Practice." In *Survivance, Sovereignty, and Story: Teaching American Indian Rhetorics*, edited by Lisa King, Rose Gubele, and Joyce Rain Anderson, 138–59. Logan: Utah State University Press, 2015.

Ríos, Gabriela Raquel. "In Ixtli In Yollotl/A (Wise) Face A (Wise) Heart: Reclaiming Embodied Rhetorical Traditions of Anahuac and Tawantinsuyu." PhD diss., Texas A&M University, 2012.

Risling Baldy, Cutcha. "Coyote Is Not a Metaphor: On Decolonizing, (Re) Claiming and (Re) Naming Coyote." *Decolonization: Indigeneity, Education & Society* 4, no. 1 (2015): 1–20.

———. "Why We Gather: Traditional Gathering in Native Northwest California and the Future of Bio-Cultural Sovereignty." *Ecological Processes* 2, Article 17 (June 2013): 17. https://doi.org/10.1186/2192-1709-2-17.

Romano, Susan. "Tlaltelolco: The Grammatical-Rhetorical Indios of Colonial Mexico." *College English* 66, no. 3 (2004): 257–77.

Romo, Rebecca. "'You're Not Black or Mexican Enough!': Policing Racial/Ethnic Authenticity among Blaxicans in the United States." In *Red and Yellow, Black and Brown: Decentering Whiteness in Mixed Race Studies*, edited by Joanne L. Rondilla, Rudy P. Guevarra Jr., and Paul Spickard, 127–43. New Brunswick, NJ: Rutgers University Press, 2017.

Rondilla, Joanne L., Rudy P. Guevarra Jr., and Paul Spickard, eds. *Red and Yellow, Black and Brown: Decentering Whiteness in Mixed Race Studies*. New Brunswick, NJ: Rutgers University Press, 2017.

Ross, Rupert. *Returning to the Teachings: Exploring Aboriginal Justice*. Toronto: Penguin Books, 1996.

Rossen, Jack, ed. *Corey Village and the Cayuga World: Implications from Archaeology and Beyond*. Syracuse, NY: Syracuse University Press, 2015.

———. "Epilogue: Challenging Dominant Archaeological Narratives of the Haudenosaunee." In *Corey Village and the Cayuga World: Implications from Archaeology and Beyond*, edited by Jack Rossen, 193–202. Syracuse, NY: Syracuse University Press, 2015.

Ruiz de Alarcón, Hernando. *Treatise on the Heathen Superstitions That Today Live among the Indians Native to This New Spain, 1629*. Edited and translated by J. Richard Andrews and Ross Hassig. Norman: University of Oklahoma Press, 1984.

Russell, Frank. *The Pima Indians*. Annual Report of the Bureau of American Ethnology to the Secretary of the Smithsonian Institution 26. Washington, DC: Government Printing Office, 1908.

———. *The Pima Indians*. 1908. Reprint, Tucson: University of Arizona Press, 1980.

Russo, Vito. *The Celluloid Closet: Homosexuality in the Movies*. New York: Harper & Row, 1987.

Sahagún, Bernardino de. *General History of the Things of New Spain: Florentine Codex.* Translated by Arthur J. O. Anderson and Charles E. Dibble. 12 vols. Salt Lake City: University of Utah Press, 1950–1982.

Sanga, Glauco, and Gherardo Ortalli, eds. *Nature Knowledge: Ethnoscience, Cognition, and Utility.* New York: Berghahn Books, 2003.

Saxton, Dean, and Lucille Saxton. *Legends and Lore of the Papago and Pima Indians.* Tucson: University of Arizona Press, 1973.

Saxton, Dean, Lucille Saxton, and Susie Enos. *Dictionary: Tohono O'odham/Pima to English, English to Tohono O'odham/Pima.* Edited by R. L. Cherry. 2nd ed., revised and expanded. Tucson: University of Arizona Press, 1998.

Sanchez, John, and Mary E. Stuckey. "The Rhetoric of American Indian Activism in the 1960s and 1970s." *Communication Quarterly* 48, no. 2 (2000): 120–36.

Sayre, Robert F. *Thoreau and the American Indians.* Princeton, NJ: Princeton University Press, 1977.

Schaengold, Charlotte C. "Bilingual Navajo: Mixed Codes, Bilingualism, and Language Maintenance." PhD diss., Ohio State University, 2004.

Schermerhorn, Seth. "Walkers and Their Staffs: O'odham Walking Sticks by Way of Calendar Sticks and Scraping Sticks." *Material Religion* 12, no. 4 (October 2016): 476–500.

———. "Walkers and Their Staffs." Chap. 3 in *Walking to Magdalena: Personhood and Place in Tohono O'odham Songs, Sticks, and Stories.* Lincoln: University of Nebraska Press, 2019.

———. "Walking to Magdalena: Place and Person in Tohono O'odham Songs, Sticks, and Stories." PhD diss., Arizona State University, 2013.

Schermerhorn, Seth, and Lillia McEnaney. "Through Indigenous Eyes: A Comparison of Two Tohono O'Odham Photographic Collections Documenting Pilgrimages to Magdalena." *Religious Studies and Theology* 36, no. 1 (2017): 21–53.

Schroeder, Susan, Stephanie Gail Wood, and Robert Stephen Haskett, eds. *Indian Women of Early Mexico.* Norman: University of Oklahoma Press, 1997.

Scollon, Ronald, and Suzanne B. K. Scollon. *Narrative, Literacy, and Face in Interethnic Communication.* Norwood, NJ: Ablex, 1981.

Seler, Eduard. *Comentarios al Códice Borgia.* Translated by Mariana Frenk. 3 vols. Mexico City: Fondo de Cultura Económica, 1963.

Shaw, Anna Moore. *Pima Indian Legends.* Tempe: Arizona State University, 1963.

Shilling, Dan. "Introduction: The Soul of Sustainability." In *Traditional Ecological Knowledge: Learning from Indigenous Practices for Environmental Sustainability,* edited by Melissa K. Nelson and Dan Shilling, 3–14. Cambridge: Cambridge University Press, 2018.

Sierra Fund. "Mining's Toxic Legacy: An Initiative to Address Mining Toxins in the Sierra Nevada." Nevada City, CA: The Sierra Fund, 2008. https://www.sierrafund.org/wp-content/uploads/MININGS_TOXIC_LEGACY_2010printing_4web.pdf.

Silverstein, Michael. "Indexical Order and the Dialectics of Sociolinguistic Life." *Language*

& *Communication* 23, nos. 3–4 (July–October 2003): 193–229.

Simpson, Audra, and Andrea Smith, eds. *Theorizing Native Studies*. Durham, NC: Duke University Press, 2014.

Simpson, Leanne B. *Dancing on Our Turtle's Back: Stories of Nishnaabeg Re-Creation, Resurgence and a New Emergence*. Winnipeg, MB: Arbeiter Ring Publishing, 2011.

Smart, Ninian. *The World's Religions*. North and South American ed. Englewood Cliffs, NJ: Prentice Hall, 1989.

Smith, Linda Tuhiwai. *Decolonizing Methodologies: Research and Indigenous Peoples*. 2nd ed. London: Zed Books, 2012.

Smith, Mona. *Her Giveaway: A Spiritual Journey with AIDS*. VHS. Minneapolis: Minnesota American Indian AIDS Task Force, 1988.

———. *Honored by the Moon*. VHS. Minneapolis: Minnesota American Indian AIDS Task Force, 1990.

Solari, Amara. "The 'Contagious Stench' of Idolatry: The Rhetoric of Disease and Sacrilegious Acts in Colonial New Spain." *Hispanic American Historical Review* 96, no. 3 (August 2016): 481–515.

Soto, Lourdes Diaz, Claudia G. Cervantes-Soon, Elizabeth Villarreal, and Emmet E. Campos. "The Xicana Sacred Space: A Communal Circle of Compromiso for Educational Researchers." *Harvard Educational Review* 79, no. 4 (Winter 2009): 755–76.

Spence, Mark D. *Dispossessing the Wilderness: Indian Removal and the Making of the National Parks*. Oxford: Oxford University Press, 1999.

Spickard, Paul. *Almost All Aliens: Immigration, Race, and Colonialism in American History and Identity*. New York: Routledge, 2007.

Spielmann, Roger. *"You're So Fat": Exploring Ojibwe Discourse*. Toronto: University of Toronto Press, 1998.

Spier, Leslie. *Yuman Tribes of the Gila River*. Chicago: University of Chicago Press, 1933.

Stokes, John, David Benedict, and Dan Thompson. *Thanksgiving Address: Greetings to the Natural World*. Corrales, NM: The Tracking Project; Onchiota, NY: Six Nations Indian Museum, 1993.

Struthers, Roxanne, Valerie S. Eschiti, and Beverly Patchell. "The Experience of Being an Anishinabe Man Healer: Ancient Healing in a Modern World." *Journal of Cultural Diversity* 15, no. 2 (Summer 2008): 70–75.

Struthers, Roxanne, and Cynthia Peden-McAlpine. "Phenomenological Research among Canadian and United States Indigenous Populations: Oral Tradition and Quintessence of Time." *Qualitative Health Research* 15, no. 9 (November 2005): 1264–76.

Sullivan, Thelma D. "The Rhetorical Orations, or Huehuetlatolli, Collected by Sahagún." In *Sixteenth-Century Mexico: The Work of Sahagún*, edited by Munro S. Edmonson, 79–109. Albuquerque: University of New Mexico Press, 1974.

———. "Tlazolteotl-Ixcuina: The Great Spinner and Weaver." In *The Art and Iconography of Late Post-Classic Central Mexico*, edited by Elizabeth Hill Boone, 7–35. Washington, DC: Dumbarton Oaks, 1982.

Tatonetti, Lisa. "Affect, Female Masculinity, and the Embodied Space Between: Two-Spirit

Traces in Thirza Cuthand's Experimental Film." In *Sexual Rhetorics: Methods, Identities, Publics,* edited by Jonathan Alexander and Jacqueline Rhodes, 121–33. New York: Routledge, 2015.

———. "Forced to Choose: Queer Indigeneity in Film." Chap. 4 in *The Queerness of Native American Literature.* Minneapolis: University of Minnesota Press, 2014.

———. *The Queerness of Native American Literature.* Minneapolis: University of Minnesota Press, 2014.

Tillich, Paul. *Dynamics of Faith.* New York: Harper, 1957.

Todd, Zoe. "Fish, Kin and Hope: Tending to Water Violations in Amiskwaciwâskahikan and Treaty Six Territory." *Afterall: A Journal of Art, Context and Enquiry* 43, no. 1 (Spring/Summer 2017): 102–7. https://doi.org/10.1086/692559. See also https://www.journals.uchicago.edu/doi/full/10.1086/692559.

———. "Fish Pluralities: Human-Animal Relations and Sites of Engagement in Paulatuuq, Arctic Canada." *Études/Inuit/Studies* 38, nos. 1–2 (2014): 217–38. https://doi.org/10.7202/1028861ar.

———. "An Indigenous Feminist's Take on the Ontological Turn: 'Ontology' Is Just Another Word for Colonialism." *Journal of Historical Sociology* 29, no. 1 (2016): 4–22.

Tuck, Eve, and K. Wayne Yang. "Decolonization Is Not a Metaphor." *Decolonization: Indigeneity, Education & Society* 1, no. 1 (2012): 1–40.

Van Norden, Bryan W. *Taking Back Philosophy: A Multicultural Manifesto.* New York: Columbia University Press, 2017.

Van Sant, Gus. *My Own Private Idaho.* Los Angeles: Fine Line Features, 1991.

Vigil, James Diego. *From Indians to Chicanos: The Dynamics of Mexican-American Culture.* 3rd ed. Long Grove, IL: Waveland Press, 2012.

Vizenor, Gerald. *Manifest Manners: Narratives on Postindian Survivance.* 1994. Reprint, Lincoln: University of Nebraska Press, 1999.

Walter, Vivian J., and W. Grey Walter. "The Central Effects of Rhythmic Sensory Stimulation." *Electroencephalography and Clinical Neurophysiology* 1, no. 1 (February 1949): 57–86.

Walters, Karina L., Ramona Beltran, David Huh, and Teresa Evans-Campbell. "Displacement and Dis-Ease: Land, Place and Health among American Indians and Alaska Natives." In *Communities, Neighborhoods, and Health: Expanding the Boundaries of Place,* edited by Linda M. Burton, Susan P. Kemp, ManChui Leung, Stephen A. Matthews, and David T. Takeuchi, 163–99. New York: Springer, 2011.

Warrior, Robert Allen. *Tribal Secrets: Recovering American Indian Intellectual Traditions.* Minneapolis: University of Minnesota Press, 1995.

Waugh, Thomas. *The Romance of Transgression in Canada: Queering Sexualities, Nations, Cinemas.* Montreal: McGill-Queen's University Press, 2006.

Webster, Anthony K. "Coyote Poems: Navajo Poetry, Intertextuality, and Language Choice." *American Indian Culture and Research Journal* 28, no. 4 (2004): 69–91.

———. "'Everything Got Kinda Strange after a While': Some Reflections on Translating Navajo Poetry That Should Not Be Translated." *Anthropology and Humanism* 40, no. 1 (2015): 72–93.

Whyte, Kyle P. "On the Role of Traditional Ecological Knowledge as a Collaborative Concept: A Philosophical Study." *Ecological Processes* 2, Article 7 (2013). https://doi.org/10.1186/2192-1709-2-7.

Willette, Mirranda, Kari Norgaard, and Ron Reed. "You Got to Have Fish: Families, Environmental Decline and Cultural Reproduction." *Families, Relationships and Societies* 5, no. 3 (2016): 375–92.

Wilson, Catherine, ed. *Civilization and Oppression.* Calgary, AB: University of Calgary Press. Supplement, *Canadian Journal of Philosophy* 25 (1999).

Witherspoon, Gary. *Language and Art in the Navajo Universe.* Ann Arbor: University of Michigan Press, 1977.

Womack, Craig S. "A Single Decade: Book-Length Native Literary Criticism between 1986 and 1997." In *Reasoning Together: The Native Critics Collective,* edited by Janice Acoose, Craig S. Womack, Daniel Heath Justice, and Christopher B. Teuton, 3–104. Norman: University of Oklahoma Press, 2008.

Womack, Craig S, Daniel Heath Justice, and Christopher B. Teuton, eds. *Reasoning Together: The Native Critics Collective.* Norman: University of Oklahoma Press, 2008.

Wright, Harold Bell, ed. *Long Ago Told (Huh-Kew Ah-Kah) Legends of the Papago Indians.* London: D. Appleton & Company, 1929.

Yuan, Christine. *Keeping the River.* Tending the Wild. KCETLink and the Autry Museum of the American West, 2016. https://www.kcet.org/shows/tending-the-wild/episodes/keeping-the-river.

Younging, Gregory. *Elements of Indigenous Style: A Guide for Writing by and about Indigenous Peoples.* Edmonton, AB: Brush Education, 2018.

Zender, Marc. "One Hundred and Fifty Years of Nahuatl Decipherment." *PARI Journal* 8, no. 4 (Spring 2008): 24–37.

Zepeda, Susy J. "Queer Xicana Indígena Cultural Production: Remembering through Oral and Visual Storytelling." *Decolonization: Indigeneity, Education & Society* 3, no. 1 (2014): 119–41.

CONTRIBUTORS

Philip P. Arnold is an associate professor and chair of the religion department and a core faculty member in Native American and Indigenous studies at Syracuse University. He is also the founding director of the Skä·noñh—Great Law of Peace Center. His books are *Eating Landscape: Aztec and European Occupation of Tlalocan* (1999); *The Gift of Sports: Indigenous Ceremonial Dimensions of the Games We Love* (2012); and *Urgency of Indigenous Values and the Future of Religion* (2020). He established the Doctrine of Discovery Study Group (www.doctrineofdiscovery.org) and Indigenous Values Initiative (www.indigenousvalues.org). He is coeditor of the Syracuse University Press series "Haudenosaunee and Indigenous Worlds" (https://press.syr.edu/haudenosaunee/).

Gabriel S. Estrada is a professor of religious studies at California State University, Long Beach, and cochair of the Indigenous Religious Traditions Unit of the American Academy of Religion. Author of "Obscuring Two-Spirit Death in the Films *Conversion* and *Fire Song*" in *Religion and Sight*, and "Ojibwe Lesbian Visual AIDS" in the *Journal of Lesbian Studies*, Dr. Estrada is currently writing the book manuscript *Two-Spirit Film: Restoring Trans* Indigenous Reelness*. Rarámuri and Chíhéne through zir Chicana mother and Chichimeca/Caxcan through zir Chicano father, ze is the City of Angels Two-Spirit Society (CATSS) cochair and Indigenous Pride LA secretary.

Phyllis A. Fast was a professor of anthropology and liberal studies at the University of Alaska Anchorage. She was Koyukon Athabascan and wrote extensively about her people. Her research interests included social anthropology, gender studies, and Alaska Native art. She was the author of *Northern Athabascan Survival: Women, Community and the Future* (2002). Dr. Fast was also an accomplished artist. Inspired by her Koyukon Athabascan heritage, her work has been featured in museums and other venues around the country.

Lawrence W. Gross (Anishinaabe) serves as the San Manuel Band of Mission Indians Endowed Chair of Native American Studies at the University of Redlands in Redlands, California. He is a member of the Minnesota Chippewa tribe, enrolled on the White Earth reservation. His research interest concerns Anishinaabe culture, and he has published extensively on the topic, including journal articles on silence, humor, and pedagogy. He is the author of *Anishinaabe Ways of Knowing and Being* (2014).

Inés Hernández-Ávila is Nimipu/Nez Perce, enrolled on the Colville Reservation, and Tejana. She is a professor of Native American studies at the University of California, Davis, and one of the six founders of the Native American and Indigenous Studies Association (NAISA). Dr. Hernández-Ávila is a scholar, poet, visual artist, and writer of creative nonfiction. Her research areas include contemporary Native American and Indigenous poetry of the US, Mexico, and Chile. She is a member of luk'upsíimey/North Star Collective, a Niimiipuu creative writers group, which was established in September 2020.

Felicia Rhapsody Lopez (Chicanx) is an assistant professor of literatures, languages, and cultures at the University of California, Merced. Her research focuses primarily on the written works of the Nahua of Central Mexico, specifically the development of productive and ethical models of decipherment and translation of glyphic and early alphabetic texts. As a scholar-artist-activist, her projects recover and advance Indigenous artistic and cultural traditions in order to make these rich Indigenous epistemologies accessible to diverse heritage populations today.

Danica Sterud Miller (Puyallup Tribe of Indians) is an associate professor of American Indian studies at the University of Washington Tacoma. She grew up on one of the last continuous allotments of Puyallup Territory in a family that was and still is very politically engaged, which is reflected in her research on constructions of Indigenous sovereignty and federal Indian law.

Delores (Lola) Mondragón (Chickasaw and Chicana) is a religious studies doctoral student at the University of California, Santa Barbara. She was raised, and learned to "straddle borders," in El Paso, Texas, and Ciudad Juarez, Chihuahua, Mexico. She is a daughter, mother, auntie, grandmother, community drum keeper, and song catcher invested in healing and recovery, from all forms of war, through rematriation, ceremony, and education. She cofounded the Veteran Women's Indigenous Healing Circle with the help of community Elders and sister veterans.

Meredith Moss is a lecturer in anthropology, linguistics, and religious studies at Hamilton College, which was founded on the ancestral territory of the Oneida Indian nation. Dr. Moss studies Indigenous language revitalization, language variation, and language ideologies. She has worked most extensively with off-reservation Navajo language advocates and Mohawk as well as other Haudenosaunee language advocates at the Kanatsiohareke Mohawk Community in the heart of the traditional Mohawk territory. Her research has been supported by the American Philosophical Society's Phillips Fund Grant for Native American Research and the Jacobs Research Funds at the Whatcom Museum, an affiliate of the Smithsonian Institution.

Cutcha Risling Baldy (Hupa, Yurok, Karuk) is an associate professor and department chair of Native American studies at Humboldt State University. Her research is focused on Indigenous feminisms, California Indians, and decolonization. She is the author of *We Are Dancing for You: Native Feminisms and the Revitalization of Women's Coming-of-Age Ceremonies* (2018). She cofounded the Native Women's Collective, a nonprofit organization that supports the continued revitalization of Native American arts and culture.

Seth Schermerhorn is an associate professor of religious studies and program director of American studies at Hamilton College, which sits on the traditional territory of the Oneida Indian nation. Schermerhorn specializes in the interdisciplinary study of Indigenous traditions, particularly in the Southwestern United States and northern Sonora. Although he has worked with several Indigenous nations, Schermerhorn works most extensively with the Tohono O'odham nation. His first book, *Walking to Magdalena: Personhood* *and Place in Tohono O'odham Songs, Sticks, and Stories*, was copublished by the University of Nebraska Press and the American Philosophical Society in 2019. He is cochair of the Indigenous Religious Traditions Unit of the American Academy of Religion.

Inés Talamantez was a professor in the department of religious studies at the University of California, Santa Barbara. She was responsible for their doctoral program in Native American religious studies. She trained over twenty-six PhD students in Native American religious studies and was influential in the careers on many other scholars in the field. She was a Centennial Scholar for the American Academy of Religion. Her primary area of research was the Apache girls coming-of-age ceremony. She worked on religion and ecology, Chicano and Chicana studies, women's studies, and dance. She coedited *Teaching Religion and Healing* (2006). Her book, *The Apache Pollen Path: Mescalero Female Initiation Ceremony*, is scheduled to be published posthumously by the University of New Mexico Press.

INDEX

Page numbers in italic text indicate illustrations.

Haas, Angela, 202
habitat decline, fish, 182
Hallowell, A. Irving, 52, 103, 167
Hanrahan, MB, 73
Harper, Stephen, 209, 210
Harvard University, 144–48, 150
Haudenosaunee Longhouse, 33, 34
Haudenosaunee (Iroquois) society, 3, 7–9;
    Confederacy, 32–34, 40, 45n7; Euro-
    pean contact and, 35–36, 41–43;
    Hiawatha Belt and, 32–34; Jesuit
    missionaries and, 35; pre-Colonial
    traditional clan systems retained
    by, 34; Skä·noñh—Great Law of
    Peace Center and, 34–44; terri-
    tory, 33. See also "Thanksgiving
    Address"
Havier, Manuel, 121–22
Hayenhwátha' (Hiawatha), 34, 36, 39–41,
    45n3
healers, 54–55, 57, 148, 157, 220, 222–23,
    253, 263
healing: of historical trauma, 202–3,
    212–13, 216–17; traditional, 204;
    two-spirit people and, 206–7
heart: heart-to-heart connections, 54;
    speaking from the, 48–49, 74, 202
Heidegger, Martin, 69, 75
Henderson, Battiste, 56
Henry (Koyukon Chief), 231, 233, 234
Her Giveaway (film), 203, 224n8
Hiawatha, 34, 36, 39–41, 45n3
"Hiawatha" (Longfellow), 45n3
Hiawatha Belt, 32–34
Hill, Jane H., 122–23, 126nn20–22
Hillman, Leaf, 172, 182
history, writing and, 80
HIV/AIDS, 203–4, 205, 208, 217
Hollywood, LGBTQ community, censor-
    ship and, 205
Honey Moccasin (film), 207
Honored by the Moon (film), 203–4, 224n8

"Ho'ok A:gita," O'odham oral history,
    108–9
Hoopa Fish Commission, 185
Hopkins, Sarah Winnemucca, 5
Hormel, Leontina, 175
Horny Toad, 105–6
House, Deborah, 131
House Made of Dawn (Momaday), 243–45,
    265n24
hoyane (male chiefs, good mind), 34, 39
Huehuecoyotl (Old Man Coyote, Old
    Man America), 242, 264n13
huehuetlatolli (words of the elders), 82
Huerta, Dolores, 66, 72
humans: animals with power to sicken,
    105–6, 108, 109, 110; fish and,
    171; flesh in pots in Codex Bogia,
    89–90; life cycle, 249; more-than-
    human beings, 166, 167, 170, 175,
    186. See also other-than-human
Humboldt County, CA: cannabis cultiva-
    tion in, 180, 191n40; genocide and,
    177; from Gold Rush to fish kill,
    175–81
humor, 173, 204–5, 214
hunting, gathering and, 140
Hupa Indians. See salmon rhetoric, Hupa
    Indians and
Hupa language, 171

I Am Joaquin (Gonzales, R.), 65, 66
Ich parasite, salmon and, 180
Idar, Jovita, 66
identity: Chicana/o/x rhetoric and, 65–72;
    doubling, 196; Navajo people and,
    12–13, 127, 130; rhetoric and, 5, 13;
    riddling and, 14, 232
Iethi'nisténha Ohóntsia, "Thanksgiving
    Address," 19
I'itoi (Creator), 108–9, 111–12, 114, 125n8
the ill-fated periods (los periodos aciagos),
    89

"Sick River," 182–83
silence, 3, 74, 128, 160, 185, 229, 244
Simpson, Leanne, 184
"A Single Decade" (Womack), 265n15
Six Nations, 32, 34, 45n4
Skä·noñh—Great Law of Peace Center:
    collaborative, 35; continuance and
    contribution, 43–44; Creation and,
    36, 37–38; European Contact and
    Genocide, 36, 41–43; Great Law
    of Peace, 36, 38–41; message of,
    36–44; Onondaga welcome greet-
    ing and, 35, 36; "Thanksgiving
    Address" and, 31–32, 36–37
Sky Woman, 37
slaves, 45n4, 176, 177
Slivers, Nando, 258
Smart, Ninian, 141, 143
Smith, Linda Tuhiwai, 65
Smith, Mona, 203
Smith, Wilfred Cantwell, 145
snakes, 92–93, 94–96, 114–15, 117–18. See
    also rattlesnakes
social change, 64, 69, 76, 154
social cohesion, 5, 7
social hegemony, colonization and, 5
social silence, 229
songs, 53, 66, 115–24, 125n17, 211
Soto, Lourdes Diaz, 72–73
sovereignty: production, 201; rhetorical,
    3–4, 166–67, 181–82, 184, 186, 249,
    260, 266n45; of Tlingit rhetoric,
    202
spaces: sacred, 70, 72–75; women and
    peaceful, 249
Spain, 42, 228
speakers, 3, 203; Anishinaabe, 2, 47–48,
    49, 58. See also public speaking,
    Navajo
Speaking, Singing, and Teaching (Barkin
    and Brandt), 121–22
speaking from the heart, 48–49, 74, 202

speech, 1, 3, 56–57, 84; talking to rattle-
    snakes, 105–6, 107, 108, 110–14, 124;
    Western rhetoric and dominance
    through, 199. *See also* public
    speaking, Navajo
Spielmann, Roger, 50, 51
Spier, Leslie, 117–18
spirits, religious practices and, 230
spirits of women who died in childbirth
    (Cihuateteoh), 91
spirituality, 152–53, 249; journeys, 53, 203,
    224n8; values, 2, 47, 48, 214
spiritualized, whole world as, 53
spruce trees, 215, 235
Squaxin Island people, 196
The Stars, "Thanksgiving Address," 27–28,
    37
State University of New York at Albany
    (SUNY Albany), 32
Steinmetz, Paul, 148
stereotypes, 133, 153, 170, 259
sterilizations, 75, 255
stillborn children, 97
stories, 54–55, 125n17, 134; "Ho'ok A:gita,"
    108–9; O'odham rattlesnake lore in
    song and, 115–24
Stories of the River, Stories of the People
    (film), 183
storytelling, 47, 48, 126n18, 181, 184
strategic positioning, 65, 66, 71
Stromberg, Ernest, 5–6
Struthers, Roxanne, 54–55, 57
Stuckey, Mary, 5
suicide, 182, 205, 208
Sullivan, Thelma, 91
The Sun, "Thanksgiving Address," 26, 37
SUNY Albany (State University of New
    York at Albany), 32
Supreme Court, US, 42–43
survivance, 3, 4, 5–6
swearing, 115, 125n8, 247
sweetgrass, 157

—— THE ——
TRIBE of
EPHRAIM

COVENANT
and
BLOODLINE

THE

TRIBE of

EPHRAIM

COVENANT
and
BLOODLINE

By
STEVEN D. GREEN

Horizon Publishers
Springville, Utah

ISBN 13: 978-0-88290-822-9

Published by Horizon Publishers, an imprint of Cedar Fort, Inc.
2373 W. 700 S., Springville, UT, 84663
Distributed by Cedar Fort, Inc., www.cedarfort.com

LIBRARY OF CONGRESS CATALOGING-IN-PUBLICATION DATA
Green, Steven D., 1944–
  The tribe of Ephraim : covenant and bloodline / Steven D. Green.
     p. cm.
  Includes bibliographical references.
  ISBN 978-0-88290-822-9
  1. Ephraim (Tribe of Israel) 2. Lost tribes of Israel. 3. Bible. O.T.—Criticism, interpretation, etc. 4. Church of Jesus Christ of Latter-day Saints—Doctrines. 5. Mormon Church—Doctrines. I. Title.
  BX8643.L66G74 2007
  230'.9332--dc22
                                    2007001131
Cover design by Nicole Williams
Cover design © 2007 by Lyle Mortimer
Edited and typeset by Annaliese B. Cox

Printed in the United States of America

10 9 8 7 6 5 4 3

Printed on acid-free paper

dedication

To the Blood of Ephraim
The Mystery
The Diversity
The Strength
The Persistence
Of the Birthright Tribe of Israel

table of contents

acknowledgments

This work has been on my mind for many years. I have felt for a long time that the complete story of the Tribe of Ephraim has never been fully told. I don't know if it ever will except in that day when all things will come to light. Why Ephraim, who had the birthright responsibility would just disappear from the annals of history with the scattering of Israel and not reappear until the Restoration, has bothered me for a long time. For some reason, I couldn't just let that thought go. Finally I decided that if I was ever going to be comfortable, I should take some time to really investigate and test whether Ephraim, after centuries of dormancy, just came to life again with the Prophet Joseph Smith or if the blood of Ephraim was involved in the preparation for the Restoration throughout the histories of the nations. The conclusion I came to was that yes, Ephraim was involved, and in fact was the driving force in the proceedings, movements, and many human contributions that led to the establishment of the environment for the Restoration. As we know, Ephraim then provided the leadership for the restoration and the gathering of Israel. The research and inspiration that led to my conclusion was both enlightening and somewhat astounding. There were many times when I was astonished at what I found in the research or the thoughts that would pop into my mind in the middle of the night sending me exploring down new roads. The search was a fascinating journey.

I am deeply indebted to my wife, Kathy, for her support and suggestions. My family was also a great help and encouragement. A special thanks goes to Shellie Harris, a neighbor and friend who volunteered to read the book and made many suggestions and corrected many errors. Monte Nyman also read the manuscript and offered much needed and valuable advice. Several other neighbors and friends read the manuscript and gave encouragement when it was needed.

I am grateful to Cedar Fort for consenting to publish the work and especially Annaliese Cox, who edited the work, making valuable suggestions and saving a first time author from many mistakes.

One who is in this role would be ungrateful if he did not recognize the efforts of so many who unknowingly contribute. I am grateful for the University of Utah Library, the Davis County Library, the LDS Church online library, and the many authors who I read and studied to accomplish this work.

The more one learns about Ephraim, the more one is fascinated and amazed. The journey writing this work was truly captivating. I can only hope the reader will find the same measure of anticipation, challenge, and delight in reading the book that I did researching and writing it.

introduction

Who is Israel?

What is the significance of the blood of Israel?

Israel was to be a chosen people for the Lord. Moses recorded: "For thou [Israel] art an holy people unto the Lord thy God: the Lord thy God hath chosen thee to be a special people unto himself, above all people that are upon the face of the earth" (Deuteronomy 7:6).

The Lord would watch over Israel as a shepherd would his flock. "He that scattered Israel will gather him, and keep him, as a shepherd doth his flock" (Jeremiah 31:10).

The Father, from the very beginning, had reserved special blessings for those of the house of Israel. "Come unto me, O ye house of Israel, and it shall be made manifest unto you how great things the Father hath laid up for you, from the foundation of the world" (Ether 4:14).

The Lord from ancient time made an exclusive covenant with Israel. He would recover them from a scattered state and facilitate their gathering to the lands promised to them from ancient times. "I have sent forth in these last days, the covenant which I have sent forth to recover my people, which are of the house of Israel" (D&C 39:11).

Israel had a special calling and work that the Lord was not going to trust to any other people. In the process of completing that work, Israel would themselves be saved. "For I have a great work laid up in store, for Israel shall be saved" (D&C 38:33).

So, who are these people that have been promised such abundance from the Lord? What is their original lineage?

In its simplest form, they are the descendants of Jacob, the son of Isaac and grandson of Abraham. The original House of Israel consisted of twelve tribes, who presently have millions of descendants scattered around the world. "The Lord hath chosen thee [Israel] to be a peculiar people unto himself, above all the nations that are upon the earth" (Deuteronomy 14:2).

What was Israel chosen to do?

Isaiah penned the answer: "Thou are my servant, O Israel, in whom I will be glorified. . . . Thou shouldest be my servant to raise up the tribes of Jacob, and to restore the preserved of Israel: I will also give thee for a light to the Gentiles, that thou mayest be my salvation unto the end of the earth" (Isaiah 49:3, 6). Israel was to assist the Lord in His "work and glory—to bring to pass the immortality and eternal life of man" (Moses 1:39).

The Bible first mentions Israel as a chosen and peculiar people shortly after they were freed from Egyptian bondage—but those destined to the lineage of Israel were chosen before their birth. They exhibited a spiritual characteristic in the premortal existence qualifying them to be born in the House of Israel. The Lord had a mission and expectation of those chosen. The spiritual qualities developed in the premortal existence would be renewed and put to use during their mortal probation on earth. They would be needed and expected to search for light and truth and perform many acts of diligence, discovery, courage, and sacrifice. Not everyone born through that lineage would live up to expectations, while others would willingly toil and sacrifice to motivate and move both individuals and civilizations along the path to furthering the Lord's work.

Those with the blood of Israel characteristically seek truth, knowledge, new discoveries, and freedom. The Holy Ghost has a unique effect on the blood of Israel, expanding those characteristics.

How could Israel, a group of interrelated tribes, slaves in Egypt for decades, few in number compared to other civilizations, affect the Lord's sons and daughters scattered on the continents of the world? "For it appears that the house of Israel, sooner of later, will be scattered upon all the face of the earth, and also among all nations" (1 Nephi 22:3). Israel would be scattered into every nation. That scattering would be a blessing to both the nations and families of the world (see Genesis 12:3 and 22:18).

What role does Ephraim play among the tribes of Israel?

Jacob designated Ephraim as the birthright tribe. Along with that designation came responsibilities and blessings. Ephraim would be accountable for leadership as Israel went about its mission. The Lord said of the posterity of Joseph, "For thou shalt be a light unto my people, to deliver them in the days of their captivity, from bondage; and to bring salvation unto them" (JST Genesis 48:11). Ephraim would play a critical leadership role in God's plan to offer immortality and eternal life to mankind.

Ephraim led the rebellion of the northern tribes when Israel split into two Kingdoms. The Northern Kingdom was known as Israel and the Southern Kingdom was Judah. After decades of grappling with sin and idol worship, the Northern Kingdom of Israel was conquered by Assyria and carried off to a land north of Nineveh, the Assyrian capital. After many years of captivity, Israel developed a new spirit and decided to depart the area of their conquerors and go where they could make a new start and get away from the idol worshippers all around them. Their only choice was north. We have no records of their journey to the north countries or locations where those tribes settled. The ten northern tribes just seemed to disappear from the annals of history—thus becoming the "lost ten tribes."

There are no records of activity from the tribe of Ephraim or any of the other lost tribes until the Prophet Joseph Smith began to discuss the role of Ephraim in the Restoration of Christ's Church. Ephraim's position as the birthright tribe suddenly became very apparent. Moses foretold: "For there shall be a day, that the watchmen upon the mount of Ephraim shall cry, Arise ye, and let us go up to Zion unto the Lord our God. For thus saith the Lord; Sing with gladness for Jacob, and shout among the chief of the nations; publish ye, praise ye, and say, O Lord save thy people, the remnant of Israel. . . . For I am a father to Israel, and Ephraim is my firstborn. Hear the word of the Lord, O ye nations, and declare it in the isles afar off, and say, He that scattered Israel will gather him, and keep him, as a shepherd doth his flock" (Jeremiah 31:6–7, 9–10).

Most members of the church have given little thought as to how Ephraim and Israel became positioned along the eastern coast of the United States and prepared to take on the challenges of restoring the gospel and organizing the Church of Jesus Christ in the latter days. The reader may wonder how, after two and a half millennia of dormancy, the blood of Ephraim suddenly sprang to life prepared to take on such a challenge.

It is my opinion that Ephraim was by no means dormant during those twenty-five hundred years. Dormancy goes against the grain of Israel's selection as a chosen people—a people carrying blood that is unwilling to accept the status quo.

When the Lord first designated Jacob's descendants as a chosen people, they had just been released from slavery to the Egyptians. They had had no experiences that developed their faith, nor had they experienced independence or governing themselves. When faced with a crisis, they complained to Moses that he should never have taken them out of Egypt. They cried to be taken back! Israel, God's chosen people, were unprepared for the tasks ahead of them. They had to wait forty years and have a whole generation familiar with life as a slave die off before the Lord would allow them to enter the promised land to establish Zion as the people of Enoch had done before them. Even then they were not equipped spiritually or physically to handle the task.

In the latter days when the Lord would gather Israel for the final time, failure would not be an option as it was with the children of Israel. The Lord would have a people and a land prepared for the task ahead of them. The preparation for Israel occurred during the three and a half millennia from the time Israel first entered the land of Canaan under Joshua to the Restoration in the latter days. It occurred among nations on the continents of the world and continues today.

What motivated Columbus to risk his life and that of his crews by sailing into the unchartered waters to discover America? What provoked the Greeks to experiment with democracy, or the Romans to form a republic, or Luther to protest excesses of the Catholic Church, or the Pilgrims to make a dangerous ocean crossing to seek political and religious freedom? Why did the early Christians face horrible deaths rather than renounce their belief in Christ, or men of the Renaissance, Reformation, or Enlightenment undertake the challenge of change when so many obstacles opposed them? Why were the founding fathers of the United States willing to take on the most powerful country in the world and seek independence? What moved a fourteen-year-old boy to go into a grove of trees and seek answers to his questions about religion? What motivated so many to seek the change that would help further the work of the Lord?

It is the author's opinion that the blood of Israel, particularly Ephraim, indirectly or directly influenced the people and events that prepared the world for the Restoration of The Church of Jesus Christ of Latter-day Saints and the gathering of all of Israel. The singular event necessary for all that to happen was the establishment of a country, free of monarchy, founded on the principle of a constitutional law which guaranteed a man the right to worship according to the dictates of his conscience. That was the land promised to Joseph and his descendants.

Does the land of Joseph belong solely to Lehi's lineage or do the descendants of Ephraim and Manasseh, who crossed the ocean during the colonial period of the United States, have an equal claim on the land?

What is the lineage of the Gentiles referred to on the title page of the Book of Mormon and throughout various verses in First, Second, Third and Fourth Nephi? Who are the Gentiles who were willing to go against mother country to provide a place for the Restoration and then brought the Bible and Book of Mormon to the descendants of Lehi living in America?

What did Nebuchadnezzar's dream, as interpreted by Daniel, tell us about Israel? Lehi and Nephi saw visions regarding the Gentiles' influence on the land on which they stood. Who were those Gentiles? If one reads carefully, he or she will discover many of those references to "Gentile" apply to the duties of the birthright tribe of Israel.

Are the modern-day descendants of Ephraim and Israel literal descendants, or are they adopted into the various tribes?

All these questions are explored within the chapters of this book. All with the thought in mind that descendants of Ephraim were preparing themselves, their descendants, their cities, their countries, and the promised land for the Restoration and Gathering of Israel. The preparation was both dramatic and simple. Some of the characters involved were recorded in the annals of history. For others, their contributions were known only to themselves.

Ephraim and Israel have a history rich in determination, courage, sacrifice, governing, exploring, experimenting, seeking liberty, and searching for truth. No matter what our lineage is, we have been both blessed and influenced by the those of Israel, particularly Ephraim, who have gone before us. As the current generation, we must stand amazed at all that the children of Israel has accomplished and reflect upon the eternal debt of gratitude we owe.

Part One

EPHRAIM:
ISRAEL'S BIRTHRIGHT TRIBE

chapter one

A PECULIAR TREASURE

Rise up, and get you forth from among my people, both ye and the children of Israel; and go, serve the Lord. . . . Also take your flocks and your herds" (Exodus 12:31–32). Those were the pressing words of a battered Pharaoh as he ordered Moses and the descendants of Jacob to leave Egypt before, as he lamented, the Egyptians all became "dead men." Rameses, the great Egyptian treasure city, was suddenly crowded with Jacob's descendants as they congregated in reply to Pharaoh's edict. Minds must have been racing with excitement, looking forward to enjoying liberty and new opportunities to worship the God of their choice. They gathered as families driving cattle, sheep, goats, and flocks of geese. They carried their own humble household goods augmented with rich spoils taken from Egypt. Six hundred thousand men plus women and children assembled among the great pyramids and buildings honoring the Egyptian ruling class. Some of those edifices had been built with captive Israel's own hands, coerced under the whips of the Egyptian taskmasters. For over two hundred years, they had made their homes in Egypt, first as welcomed guests and then as servants and slaves. Yesterday they were bondsmen and chattel; that day, Israel was a free people.

However, they were not left entirely to their own devices as they fled Egypt. "And the Lord went before them by day in a pillar of a cloud, to lead them the way; and by night in a pillar of fire, to give them light" (Exodus 13:21).

They were led through Succoth and Ethan, then down the western shore of the Red Sea, where they made camp. But they were not alone. Pharaoh sent spies to track them, searching for an opportunity to recapture his slaves. When he heard Israel was camped against the Red Sea with no safe route of escape, he launched his army. Pharaoh's army flew across the desert to overtake their former slaves.

Israel, unaware of Pharaoh's pursuit, was caught completely off guard when the army suddenly appeared in the desert behind them. They were terrified. Lashing out at Moses, they cried: "Because there were no graves in Egypt, hast thou taken us away to die in the wilderness? [W]herefore hast thou dealt thus with us, to carry us forth out of Egypt? Is not this the word that we did tell thee in Egypt, saying, Let us alone, that we may serve the Egyptians? For it had been better for us to serve the Egyptians, than that we should die in the wilderness" (Exodus 14:11–12).

Israel was learning the difficult lesson that freedom carries a burden of responsibility. They were suddenly faced with the prospect of defending themselves against their former masters, something they were both physically and mentally unprepared to do. At that moment, they would readily return to Egypt, give up their liberty, and accept bondage rather than face the prospect of defending themselves against the powerful Egyptian military.

Horrified that they might be massacred, the children of Israel awaited their fate. "And Moses said unto the people, Fear ye not, stand still, and see the salvation of the Lord, which he will show to you to day: for the Egyptians whom ye have seen to day, ye shall see them again no more for ever. The Lord shall fight for you, and ye shall hold your peace" (Exodus 14:13–14).

Moses ordered Israel forward toward the Red Sea. Their anxiety levels must have increased as they approached the shore. How would they be saved? The Lord instructed Moses to lift his staff and stretch it out over the sea. Unexpectedly, the sea parted, and Israel walked between the walls of water on dry ground. The Egyptians were held at bay by a cloud that prevented them from attacking. Once Israel was safely across, the cloud departed, and Pharaoh ordered his chariots and army into the sea in pursuit of Israel. Moses was then instructed by the Lord to stretch his hand over the sea, "that the waters may come again upon the Egyptians, upon their chariots, and upon their horsemen" (Exodus 14:26). The waters quickly engulfed Pharaoh's army and "the Lord saved Israel that day" and "the people feared the Lord, and believed the Lord, and his servant Moses" (Exodus 14:30–31).

The threat passed, and Israel moved on. It wasn't long before they ran out of the food and provisions they had carried out of Egypt. They again complained to Moses: "Would to God we had died by the hand of the Lord in the land of Egypt, when we sat by the flesh pots, and when we did eat bread to the full; for ye have brought us forth into this wilderness, to kill this whole assembly with hunger" (Exodus 16:3). Freedom lost its adventure and excitement when Israel faced the possibility of starvation in a lonely desert.

Again the Lord provided. As evening approached, the camp was inundated with quail providing meat for hungry souls. The next morning, the ground was covered with manna, which was gathered, baked, and eaten. The march continued only to encounter another crisis: the water supply was depleted. Once more, "the people murmured against Moses, and said, Wherefore is this that thou hast brought us up out of Egypt, to kill us and our children and our cattle with thirst" (Exodus 17:3). So violent were their cries that Moses feared for his life. He petitioned the Lord for help and was instructed to "smite the rock, and there shall come water out of it, that the people may drink" (Exodus 17:6). Another crisis was averted, but again, when faced with a challenge, Israel was more than willing to abandon their newly acquired freedom for the security Egypt offered, even if it meant returning to slavery.

Israel continued to the foothills of Mount Sinai where they made camp. Jacob's descendants were about to learn why the Lord was taking such interest in them. Moses went up into the mount, "and the Lord called unto him . . . saying, Thus shalt thou say to the house of Jacob, and tell the children of Israel; Ye have seen what I did unto the Egyptians, and how I bare you on eagles' wings, and brought you unto myself. Now therefore, if ye will obey my voice indeed, and keep my covenant, then ye shall be a *peculiar treasure* unto me above all people: for all the earth is mine: And ye shall be unto me a kingdom of priests, and an holy nation" (Exodus 19:3–6; italics added).

The Lord freed the children of Israel so that through their individual and community commitment and efforts they could become a "peculiar treasure" unto the Lord, "a kingdom of priests and a holy nation." The

Bible Dictionary defines peculiar as "one's very own, exclusive, or special; not used in the Bible as odd or eccentric."[1] Israel was being prepared to play a singular and distinctive role in the world. Abraham's, Isaac's, and Jacob's descendents would have the potential of impacting the families and nations of the world in a way no other people or nation ever would or ever could. Israel was on the verge of becoming a unique treasure and a holy nation if they were willing to serve and obey Him.

Moses anxiously hurried down the mountain to share with Israel the amazing news he had received from the Lord. Despite Israel's weaknesses, the Lord had great expectations for those he had chosen as his "peculiar treasure." "And the people answered together, and said, All that the Lord hath spoken we will do" (Exodus 19:8). Moses then returned to the mount to convey to the Lord Israel's commitment. For forty days on Mount Sinai, Moses was instructed about what would be required of Israel to reach the expectations of the Lord. Revelation after revelation poured down upon Moses, including the Ten Commandments, guidelines and regulations for governing, and specifications of the portable tabernacle that would serve as a sanctuary where the higher ordinances of the gospel could be administered. Moses learned how to organize Israel to develop a covenant people. Moses's training was suddenly interrupted when he learned from the Lord that the children of Israel had "corrupted themselves" (Exodus 32:7).

While Moses was on Mount Sinai receiving revelations, "the people gathered themselves together unto Aaron, and said unto him, Up, make us gods, which shall go before us; for as for this Moses, the man that brought us up out of the land of Egypt, we wot not what has become of him" (Exodus 32:1). In just forty days, Israel had abandoned the covenant they had made with the Lord and was ready to return to the gods of the Egyptians. Aaron complied and made a "molten calf," and Israel said: "These be thy gods, O Israel, which brought thee up out of the land of Egypt. . . . And they rose up early on the morrow, and offered burnt offerings, and brought peace offerings; and the people sat down to eat, and to drink, and rose up to play" (Exodus 32:4, 6).

Israel was struggling with faith and agency. When Moses was not personally present to lead them, they turned to what they had been accustomed to in Egypt—idol worship. They were more secure with the gods of Egypt, despite witnessing all the miracles God had performed to preserve them, and with the covenant they made just weeks earlier.

As Moses descended from Sinai, the people were reveling in the heathen fertility rites so often witnessed in Egypt. Moses was forced to destroy the golden calf. Those immediately involved in the fertility worship were slain and Israel was made ashamed of its behavior, but worse still, they lost and forfeited the prospect of immediately becoming the "peculiar treasure" the Lord had planned for them. Instead of the opportunity to live the higher law, Israel was relegated to the carnal commandments later revealed by the Lord to Moses.

Moses organized Israel into twelve tribes in preparation for the march to Canaan. When they were ready to travel, the Lord commanded Moses: "Behold, I have set the land before you: go in and possess the land which the Lord sware unto your fathers, Abraham, Isaac, and Jacob, to give unto them and their seed after them" (Deuteronomy 1:8). Israel left Sinai with hopes and aspirations of obtaining a land they could call their own and where they could raise their families in peace.

But it wasn't long before they were complaining again—the manna provided wasn't enough. "Who shall give us flesh to eat?" they cried. "We remember the fish, which we did eat in Egypt freely; the cucumbers, and the melons, and the leeks, and the onions, and the garlick: But now our soul is dried away: there is nothing at all, beside this manna, before our eyes" (Numbers 11:4–6). Even as slaves they had eaten vegetables and meats. Since leaving Egypt, all they had eaten was manna. Their newly acquired liberty didn't compensate for unsatisfied appetites.

The next semi-permanent encampment for Israel was at Kadesh-Barnea, which bordered Canaan. After setting up camp on the borders of the land promised to Abraham, Isaac, and Jacob, their confidence wavered. They said to Moses: "We will send men before us, and they shall search us out the land, and bring us word again by what way we must go up, and into what cities we shall come" (Deuteronomy 1:22; see also Numbers 13:1–16). Israel was not willing to expose themselves to the people of Canaan until they had a better idea of who and what they would be facing. The Lord commanded Moses to comply with their request and select twelve men, one from each of the tribes of Israel, to go and "spy out the land of Canaan." They were to check on the people to see if "they were strong or weak, few or many," and the land, "whether it be good or bad." They were to "bring of the fruit of the land" that the children of Israel could see for themselves what was in store for them (Numbers 13:17–20).

The spies traveled throughout the land for forty days. Upon their return they brought pomegranates, figs, a cluster of grapes so large it required two men to carry, and descriptions of a land flowing with milk and honey. But they also told of cities ringed by walls and strong people inhabiting them. The report caused a buzzing among the people. Caleb, of the tribe of Judah, quieted them, encouraging Israel to "go up at once, and possess it; for we are well able to overcome it" (Numbers 13:30). Joshua of the tribe of Ephraim concurred with Caleb's assessment. But the ten other spies were not so eager. They reported that the inhabitants of Canaan were stronger than Israel, the people of Anak, "which come of the giant" and how "we were in our own sight as grasshoppers" (Numbers 13:33).

Hearing of giants was just too much. "And all the children of Israel murmured against Moses and against Aaron: and the whole congregation said unto them, Would God that we had died in the land of Egypt! Or would God we had died in this wilderness. And wherefore that the Lord brought us unto the land, to fall by the sword, that our wives and our children should be a prey? were it not better to return into Egypt?" (Numbers 14:2–3).

Taking the land of Canaan was requiring too much of Israel. They were not prepared. Despite the efforts of Moses, Caleb, and Joshua to persuade them otherwise, Israel was not willing to risk all that would be required to obtain and occupy the land promised to their forefathers. Their hesitancy brought severe consequences. They were relegated to wander in the wilderness for thirty eight more years while the generation that hesitated, rebelled, and cried for Egypt all died off (Deuteronomy 2:14; see also Numbers 14:33–34).

The overnight freedom granted to Israel was a unique event in the history of the world. One day they were slaves toiling to make great edifices to honor their captors' dead, and the next day they were a free people. Israel did nothing to earn their own freedom. The Lord was responsible for their liberation. They were free physically but still captive to Egypt mentally and spiritually. Life as a slave was simple as long as they complied with their masters' wishes. Important decisions were made for them. They were fed, clothed, and sheltered. The work was difficult and taxing, but life was simple and secure.

Shortly after gaining freedom, Israel was faced with decisions with which they were unaccustomed. When Pharaoh's army appeared on the banks of the Red Sea, they complained that "it had been better for us to serve the Egyptians, than that we should die in the wilderness" (Exodus 14:12). The same story was repeated when they ran out of food, when water was scarce, when they wanted meat, and when they faced the challenge of conquering Canaan. Many readily forsook the covenant they had made with the Lord and willingly worshipped the golden calf while Moses was on Mount Sinai. One can only imagine how much different the history of the world would have been if the children of Israel had kept their covenant with the Lord. Living the higher law first given to Moses had the potential of producing a populace who could have reached great heights. A community living such a standard could have been an uplifting force for good to the people and nations of the world, with repercussions that would have been felt down to the present age. How different might the histories of nations have been written if Israel had only become what the Lord had intended for them. But that thought can only be left to speculation.

Israel was not prepared for the tough decisions and actions that freedom requires. They lacked faith in the Lord. Before the Lord could make them His "peculiar treasure," they would have to develop faith, patience, and trust in the Lord and learn how to deal with freedom—physically, mentally, and spiritually. The Lord would eventually accomplish His intended results, but instead of Israel becoming a "peculiar treasure" within generations; the passageway would take centuries and run through many divergent trails in scores of countries on the continents of the world. Today, Israel is still searching and forging down that path. Latter-day Israel can take many lessons from their ancient ancestors, the children of Israel, if they are truly to become the "peculiar treasure" the Lord has intended for them.

Notes

1   Bible Dictionary, "Peculiar," 748.

chapter two

AGENCY

Israel was not the first to grapple with freedom and agency. The issue began in the premortal existence. When the Lord presented the plan for organizing an earth to provide a place where the spirits could prove themselves and receive further glories, He asked, "Whom shall I send?" (Abraham 3:27). Two volunteers with very different versions of how to put the plan of salvation into effect put forth ideas. Satan offered, "Behold, here am I, send me, I will be thy son, and I will redeem all mankind, that one soul shall not be lost, and surely I will do it; wherefore give me thine honor" (Moses 4:1). Satan's plan was to guarantee that all would be saved. All would have to strictly follow his plan. Agency would be discarded and every decision would be made for those who chose to follow his plan; otherwise, Satan could not guarantee that every single spirit could be saved. A third part of the hosts of heaven agreed that Satan's proposal was the best arrangement for them to gain salvation. There would be no risk. Existence would be easier and risk free under that plan. Life's tough decisions would be made for them. Obviously agency and opportunities for personal growth were not important to them; their only care was that they would be saved, even if it meant selling their souls to Satan. They wanted an existence much like the children of Israel when they were slaves in Egypt.

The Lord rejected Satan's plan because he "sought to destroy the agency of man, which I, the Lord God, had given him" (Moses 4:3). So Satan became the "the devil, the father of all lies, to deceive and to blind men, and to lead them captive at his will" (Moses 4:4). Whenever and wherever Satan can reduce or eliminate agency and liberty, he has fertile ground to lead the children of God into captivity—a captivity that will not bring the blessings of salvation.

The Savior, offering the alternative to Satan's plan, simply said, "Father, thy will be done, and the glory be thine forever" (Moses 4:2). The Father's plan was: to "prove them herewith, to see if they will do all things whatsoever the Lord their God shall command them" (Abraham 3:25). The Father's will was to offer His spirit children agency during their mortal life. Mortality was to be a time of proving, testing, and decision making. To grow and develop in that mortal sphere, mankind had to have the ability to choose for himself.

Nephi, aware of the necessity of agency, wrote: "Because that they are redeemed from the fall they have become free . . . to act for themselves and *not to be acted upon*, save it be by the punishment of the law at the great and last day, according to the commandments which God hath given. Wherefore, men are free according to the flesh; and all things are given them which are expedient unto man. And they are free to choose liberty and eternal life, through the great Mediator of all men, or to choose captivity and death, according to the captivity and power of the devil" (2 Nephi 2:26–27; italics added).

President David O. McKay wrote a poignant reminder of the essential nature of agency:

> Think of it now—the value of freedom of choice! That was the great principle involved when war arose in Heaven when Lucifer would have deprived God's children of the right to choose. Lucifer said to the Lord: I'll go down and bring all your children back, but you give me the glory. Jesus however said: Send me and the glory be Thine. Satan's attempt to deprive the children of men of their free agency brought contention in Heaven—the only time about which we have any record that God would permit war in Heaven. And yet, the Lord would not deprive even the Adversary of the right to chose; and so Satan "turned away." But Christ came and died that you and I might have freedom of choice.[1]

Agency establishes an environment for the unfolding of each individual character. Agency involves opposition, testing, making choices, committing sin, repenting, overcoming trials, cultivating faith, spiritual awareness, and mental growth. Agency is absolutely necessary for spirits to move forward and reach their full potential. It is essential for the plan of salvation to work. People, nations, groups, families, and individuals lacking agency are denied the full possibilities for growth and development. The children of Israel were stymied as slaves in Egypt. Despite their pleas to return to Egypt whenever the going got a little rough, it was critical that they remain free if they were to ever become a "peculiar treasure" for the Lord.

Notes

1   David O. McKay, *Freedom of Choice*, 356. McKay's account of the war in heaven is a paraphrase of Moses 4:1–5 in the Pearl of Great Price as quoted from Gregory A. Prince and Wright W. Robert in *David O. McKay and the Rise of Modern Mormonism,* (Salt Lake City: The University of Utah Press, 2005), 41.

chapter three

A CHOSEN PEOPLE

The first mention of the word *Israel* in the Bible occurs in Genesis 32:28. Speaking to the prophet Jacob, the Lord said, "Thy name shall be called no more Jacob, but Israel." The Lord gave no indication why He changed Jacob's name to Israel, but He did pronounce a blessing upon Jacob: "A nation and a company of nations shall be of thee, and kings shall come out of thy loins; And the land which I gave Abraham and Isaac, to thee I will give it, and to thy seed after thee will I give the land" (Genesis 35:11–12). Jacob discovered that his lineage would produce a multitude of nations and kings to lead some of those nations. He and his posterity were to inherit the blessings and land promised his father Isaac and grandfather Abraham.

The Bible dictionary defines Israel as "One who prevails with God or Let God prevail. . . . The land of Canaan is also called Israel today. . . . The name Israel is therefore variously used to denote (1) the man Jacob, (2) the literal descendents of Jacob, and (3) the true believers in Christ, regardless of their lineage or geographical location."[1]

What did Jacob's blessing mean? What was significant about being a descendant of Abraham and Isaac? Why did the Lord tell Jacob that he would not only be "a nation" but a "company of nations?" (Genesis 35:11). To fully understand, we go back to the premortal existence. We know Satan influenced a third part of the host of heaven and caused them to be cast out, never obtaining the blessing of a mortal experience. But what about those who sided with the Savior? What motivated them to make that fateful decision? Did they make that choice with little knowledge or forethought? Or had experience in that existence taught them the absolute necessity of agency and the role a Savior who would atone for our sins as we slipped and faltered along the way?

Those spirits had experienced a long existence before they came to that defining moment. Elder Bruce R. McConkie described the circumstances of our premortal state: "From the time of their spirit birth, the Father's [premortal] offspring were endowed with agency and subjected to the provisions of the laws ordained for their government. The pre-existent life was thus a period—undoubtedly an infinitely long one—of probation, progression, and schooling."[2] Agency was an essential part of pre-earth life. Spirits had ample opportunities and time to make choices and prove themselves before ever having to make that consequential choice of whom to follow.

Even among the spirits choosing to follow the Lord's plan, some were more valiant than others. Certain spirits showed great capacity to follow the counsel given by the Father. Spiritual leaders matured and developed among those exhibiting such capacity. Abraham tells of a grand council held in the premortal existence in which all the spirits attended. In that council, the Lord selected some that He would make His rulers; Abraham was one of those rulers that was chosen before he was born. Of the spirits that the Lord would send to earth, there were "many noble and great ones" available to help bring about His "work and glory to bring to pass the immortality and eternal life of man" (Moses 1:39). Those spirits would be his "chosen people" on earth, and they would be born primarily through a singular lineage—the lineage of Israel. They would assist the Lord in bringing about His purposes among the inhabitants of this world.

> The greatest and most important talent or capacity that any of the Spirit children of the Father could gain is the talent of spirituality. Most of those who gained this talent were chosen, before they were born, to come to earth as members of the house of Israel. They were foreordained to receive the blessings that the Lord promised to Abraham and to his seed in all their generations.
>
> Israel is an eternal people. She came into being as a chosen and separate congregation before the foundations of the earth were laid;

she was a distinct and a peculiar people in preexistence, even as she is in this sphere.[3]

The Apostle Paul informed men gathered on Mars Hill in Athens that the Lord "hath made of one blood all nations of men for to dwell on all the face of the earth, and hath determined the times before appointed, and bounds of their habitation" (Acts 17:26). Based on this statement by Paul, all spirits awaiting the opportunity to come to earth would be appointed a specific time and place for their earthly sojourn. Moses further explains how the populations of the earth would be determined: "When the most High divided to the nations their inheritance, when he separated the sons of Adam, he set the bounds of the people according to the number of the children of Israel. For the Lord's portion is his people; Jacob is the lot of his inheritance" (Deuteronomy 32:8–9). Israel, God's chosen people both in the premortal and mortal existence, was a determining factor in how the world was populated. Those spirits meriting the blessing and opportunity to be of Israel would be sent to earth at strategic times and places to assist in bringing about the Lord's purposes.

He knew even these spirits would fail at times. Those failings would bring consequences as evidenced by the scattering of Israel (see chapter 7). But in most times and places, Israel would be a positive influence on people and events in this mortal life. During those times, Israel would assist the Lord in bringing about His purposes for His children.

Israel, God's chosen spirits, were woven into the tapestry of nations, peoples, and eras to help the Lord accomplish his purposes. The valiant servants were dispersed when the Lord needed them to accomplish a task. Some would spend a lifetime doing the Lord's errands; for others, their efforts would be brief. The Lord's work would be accomplished by individuals and nations, armies and kings, artisans and clergyman, tailors and merchants, slaves and explorers, and a fourteen-year-old boy seeking for the truth. Some would know their purpose in the plan; many would assist in ignorance of their role in the divine plan. There was simply a quality in their blood motivating them to push onward and forward. That determination and strength was and is inherent in the blood of Israel.

Notes

1   Bible Dictionary, "Israel," 708.
2   Bruce R. McConkie, *Mormon Doctrine*, 2nd ed. (Salt Lake City: Bookcraft, 1966), 590.
3   Bruce R. McConkie, *A New Witness for the Articles of Faith,* (Salt Lake City: Deseret Book, 1985), 510–12.

chapter four

COVENANTS

After Abraham learned of the premortal state of man and the opportunity to progress and become "noble and great" in that existence, the Lord Jehovah appeared to him and revealed promises and blessings concerning his mortal posterity.

He would be given a "strange land" for an "everlasting possession" if his seed would hearken to the Lord's voice (Canaan or modern-day Israel). The Lord would "make of thee a great nation," "bless thee above measure," and make Abraham's name "great among all nations." He would be "a blessing" to his own seed, his seed would "bear this ministry [preaching the gospel] and priesthood unto all nations," and "as many as received the gospel shall be called after thy name and shall be accounted thy seed." The Lord would "bless them that bless thee and curse them that curse thee." The right of the priesthood "shall continue in thee, and in thy seed after thee (that is to say, the literal seed, or seed of the body)." Through Abraham's seed "shall the families of the earth be blessed, even, with the blessings of the Gospel, which are the blessings of salvation, even of life eternal" (Abraham 2:6–12).

Abraham must have marveled at the breathtaking opportunities offered to his posterity. The promises included a distinctive land, the priesthood, temple blessings, eternal families, and an innumerable posterity. The promises must have been gratifying to the great prophet, but the responsibility of bearing the Priesthood and taking the gospel to "all the families of the earth" must have been staggering as he was shown the sacrifices and hard work that it would require. His posterity would ultimately be responsible for governing the Church on the earth. Among Abraham's seed would be Isaac, Jacob, Joseph, Ephraim, the Savior, the Apostles, Lehi, Nephi, Mormon, Moroni, Joseph Smith, and millions of others.

The covenant made with Abraham is often referred to as the Abrahamic covenant. That covenant passed to his son Isaac and his grandson Jacob and then to Jacob's twelve sons.

The Old Testament narrates how Jacob and his family moved from Canaan to Egypt to avoid starvation from a famine plaguing the area. An able administrator had spent seven years preparing Egypt for the famine by storing food and supplies. Unable to obtain local supplies, Jacob sent his sons to buy food from the Egyptians. They found that the administrator who had saved Egypt was none other than their brother Joseph, whom they sold into slavery years earlier. Joseph forgave his brothers and convinced them to bring Jacob and his entire family to Egypt where he could protect them during the famine (see Genesis 37–47).

Years later, as Jacob approached his final days, he desired to give Joseph's sons Manasseh and Ephraim a blessing. Though sick and aged, Jacob "strengthened himself" to give the blessing. He told his grandsons that the Lord had promised to "make a multitude of people" of his descendents. He then proceeded to adopt both Ephraim and Manasseh as his own children (Genesis 48:1–4). Addressing Joseph, he said, "And now of thy two sons, Ephraim and Manasseh, which were born unto thee in the land of Egypt, before I came unto thee into Egypt . . . behold, they are mine, and the God of my fathers shall bless them; even as Reuben and Simeon they shall be blessed, for they are mine; wherefore they shall be called after my name. . . . Therefore they were called the tribes of Manasseh and of Ephraim" (JST Genesis 48:5–6). Jacob then explained to Joseph what was destined for his posterity: "The fruit of thy loins . . . shall be blessed above thy brethren, and above thy fathers house . . . wherefore thy brethren shall bow down unto thee from generation to generation, unto the fruit of thy loins forever; For thou shalt be a light unto my people, to deliver them in the days of their captivity, from bondage; and to bring salvation unto them, when they are altogether bowed down under sin" (JST Genesis 48:9–11).

Jacob adopted Joseph's sons as his own and announced that one of Joseph's sons was to receive the birthright blessing in Israel. That blessing originally belonged to Reuben, Jacob's oldest son, but due to his indiscretion and adultery, he had forfeited the birthright. Instead, one of Joseph's sons would receive that blessing (see 1 Chronicles 5:1–2).

Jacob then offered to bless his newly adopted grandsons. Joseph took Manasseh, his eldest son, and set him at the right of Jacob. He then took Ephraim and set him at the left. Manasseh would then be in position to receive the birthright blessing. When Jacob stretched out his hands to give that blessing he crossed his arms, putting the right hand on Ephraim and the left on Manasseh (see Genesis 48:13–14). Joseph attempted to correct the placement, but Jacob refused and said, "I know it, my son, I know it." Then, referring to Manasseh, he said, "He also shall become a people, and he also shall be great: but truly his younger brother [referring to Ephraim] shall be greater than he, and his seed shall become a multitude of nations. And he blessed them that day, saying, In thee shall Israel bless, saying, God make thee as Ephraim and Manasseh: and he set Ephraim before Manasseh" (Genesis 48:19–20).

Later Jacob gave a blessing to each of his sons. He promised Judah that his descendants would maintain the political leadership role until Christ came: "The scepter shall not depart from Judah, nor a lawgiver from between his feet, until Shiloh come" (Genesis 49:10).

He prophesied that Joseph would be a "fruitful bough, even a fruitful bough by a well: whose branches run over the wall" (Genesis 49:22) and that God would "bless thee with the blessings of heaven above, blessings of the deep that lieth under, blessings of the breast, and of the womb: The blessings of thy father have prevailed above the blessings of my progenitors unto the utmost bound of the everlasting hills: they shall be on the head of Joseph and on the crown of the head of him that was separated from his brethren" (Genesis 49:25–26).

Ephraim's blessing told of how he was set before his older brother Manasseh, thus giving him the birthright. His seed would become a multitude of nations. His descendents would settle in a land adjacent to an ocean (this blessing also applied to Manasseh and was fulfilled in part when Lehi's and Ishmael's families crossed the ocean and settled in America). He would be a light unto the Lord's people, deliver them in the days of their captivity from bondage, bring salvation unto them when they were bowed down under sin, and have the blessing of heaven above (a reference to the blessing of the temple). His descendants would have blessings of the womb (referring to a great posterity), and he would be in a land with everlasting hills (the gathering of the Saints in the Rocky Mountains). Ephraim received the birthright—along with all the promises and obligations associated with the Abrahamic covenant.

From the time Jacob gave that final blessing to his sons and grandsons, the Bible is a narrative of Jacob's posterity, the House of Israel. It tells of Israel being captive in Egypt, gaining their freedom, being led by Moses to the promised land, and occupying the land. It mentions the ruling of Israel by judges and then kings and the division of Israel into the Northern Kingdom (ten tribes) and Southern Kingdom (Judah). And, especially, the Bible tells of prophets exhorting the people to repentance, warning of future calamities, and telling of the coming of Christ.

The Bible has served as the basis for Christian churches for centuries. But it only relates a portion of the story of Israel and its influence in the world. The Book of Mormon is the record of the branch of Joseph that settled in the Americas (see Jacob 2:35 and Alma 26:36). This record shows how many of the blessings given by Jacob were fulfilled.

chapter five

THE WATCHMEN

After wandering for forty years in the wilderness while the rebellious, adult generation of Israel all died off except for Moses, Joshua (from the tribe of Ephraim), and Caleb (from the tribe of Judah), Israel was finally preparing to enter the land of Canaan. The Lord offered again to make the new generation of Israel his "peculiar people": "The Lord hath avouched thee this day to be his *peculiar people*, as he hath promised thee . . . to make thee high above all nations which he hath made, in praise, and in name, and in honour" (Deuteronomy 26:18–19; italics added).

Previously the Lord, through Moses, told Israel that if they would not make or worship idols, would keep the Sabbath, reverence the sanctuary, walk in the Lord's statutes, and keep His commandments, then the Lord would bless them. He would give them "peace in the land" and "rain in due season, and the land shall yield her increase, and the trees of the field shall yield their fruit" (Leviticus 26:4, 6–7). He also assured them that when they chased their enemies, "they shall fall before you." In addition the Lord promised: "For I will have respect unto you, and make you fruitful, and multiply you, and establish my covenant with you. . . . And I will walk among you and will be your God, and ye shall be my people" (Leviticus 26:9, 12).

Israel's past was fresh in his mind as Moses exhorted the people to

23

strictly obey all of God's commandments. If they failed, they would be cursed in every imaginable way. They would be cursed in the city, the field, their posterity, and their resources. They would have children but "not enjoy them; for they shall go into captivity" (Deuteronomy 28:41). They would serve their enemies: "The Lord shall bring a nation against thee from far, from the end of the earth . . . whose tongue thou shall not understand. A nation of fierce countenance, which shall not regard the person of the old, nor shew favour to the young" (Deuteronomy 28:48–50).

One curse in particular should have been a motivator to always follow the Lord: "And thou shalt eat the fruit of thine own body, the flesh of thy sons and of thy daughters" (Deuteronomy 28:53). Israel would experience that very curse while under siege and surrounded by enemies as the verse foretold.

But that was not the end to the possible curses. They were warned that if they were not faithful, the Lord would scatter them among all nations. And in those nations, they would "find no ease, neither shall the sole of thy foot have rest: but the Lord shall give thee there a trembling heart, and failing eyes, and sorrow of mind: And thy life shall hang in doubt before thee; and thou shalt fear day and night" (Deuteronomy 28:65–66 see also Deuteronomy 4:25–28).

Unfortunately, the younger generation of Israel and their posterity often proved unfaithful and suffered the curses that Moses warned them about. They continued to struggle with their faith, their trust in the Lord, and the responsibilities that freedom demanded. During their wanderings in the wilderness, Moses had taken the place of their former Egyptian taskmasters by providing direction for Israel. Leadership among the ranks in general hadn't matured and was not on solid footing, leaving Israel vulnerable.

However, Moses did see a light at the end of the tunnel. He explained to the children of Israel that when these curses came upon them, they would recall both the curses and the blessings and "return unto the Lord [their] God" (Deuteronomy 30:2). They would once again obey Him, and He would "turn thy captivity, and have compassion upon thee, and will return and gather thee from all the nations, whither the Lord thy God hath scattered thee (Deuteronomy 30:3). The Lord promised that "he will not forsake thee, neither destroy thee, nor forget the covenant of thy fathers which he sware unto them" (Deuteronomy 4:31). Israel, despite their weaknesses, would not be left forsaken or forgotten.

Prior to his final departure from Israel, Moses pronounced a blessing on each of the twelve tribes. His blessing to Joseph gave Israel an idea of who would lead the tribes when the final gathering took place. At that future time, the seed of Ephraim would again be entitled to the full responsibilities of the birthright and to a land full of fruit, with ancient mountains and lasting hills (see Deuteronomy 33:13–17). Ephraim by the ten thousands and Manasseh by the thousands would stand at the head of Israel's gathering process and would "push the people together from the ends of the earth" (see D&C 58:45).

Centuries later, Jeremiah elaborated and confirmed Moses' prophecy, telling how "the watchmen upon the mount Ephraim shall cry, Arise ye, and let us go up to Zion unto the Lord our God. . . . and shout among the chief of the nations; publish ye, praise ye, and say, O Lord save thy people, the remnant of Israel" (Jeremiah 31:6–7).

The decendents of the tribe of Ephraim would be the "watchmen" when Israel was to be gathered a second time. Ephraim would lead the way for the scattered house of Israel.

chapter six

ISRAEL IS DIVIDED

Joshua marched ahead of the armies of Israel into the land of Canaan. It was a different army than the one that first viewed the land the Lord had promised them thirty-eight years earlier. This was a new generation, with new hopes and anticipations but not much stronger than their fathers in their dedication and faithfulness. They hadn't enjoyed freedom long enough to forge the hardened, steel-like character necessary to conquer and cleanse the land of Canaan as the Lord had directed. They were promised victory if they were faithful in keeping God's commandments and directions, but even that assurance was not enough. Israel gained a foothold and cleaned out pockets here and there, but that was as far as they were willing to go.

They didn't totally cleanse the land as directed by the Lord and instead settled among idol worshippers. Living among those who worshipped Baal soon had an effect on Israel: "And the children of Israel did evil in the sight of the Lord, and served Baalim: And they forsook the Lord God of their fathers, which brought them out of the land of Egypt, and followed other gods, of the gods of the people that were round about them, and bowed themselves unto them, and provoked the Lord to anger" (Judges 2:11–12).

When Israel entered Canaan, the Lord instructed Moses to select "wise men" that were "known among [their] tribes" to be leaders and help govern the people (Deuteronomy 1:13). They were to be the head of companies of tens, fifties, hundreds, and thousands. The Bible refers to the governmental structure as the judges. Israel operated under an organization of judges for four hundred years before they grew restless and desired change. They observed surrounding nations that were governed by kings and wanted to be like them. So the elders approached Samuel and pleaded, "Behold, thou art old, and thy sons walk not in thy ways: now make us a king to judge us like all the nations" (1 Samuel 8:4–5).

Samuel, aware of the consequences of their request, took the matter to the Lord. The Lord answered, "Hearken unto the voice of the people in all that they say unto thee: for they have not rejected thee, but they have rejected me, that I should not reign over them" (1 Samuel 8:7).

Israel, insecure as they measured themselves against the nations around them, wanted another security blanket—this time a king. Jacob's seed came to the conclusion that a monarchy would be good for them. They would be relieved of the burden of governing themselves, passing that responsibility to their king. They were comfortable with a monarchy because the king would be one of their own people. They assumed nothing could go wrong under such an arrangement. A king ruling Israel would give the appearance of strength and stability to the surrounding nations.

The Lord consented to their request—but not without a stinging warning about the consequences of having a king rule over them, "He will take your sons, and appoint them for himself, for his chariots, and to be his horsemen" (1 Samuel 8:11). A king would force the people to "ear his ground, and to reap his harvest, and to make his instruments of war, and instruments of his chariots" (1 Samuel 8:12). A king would also "take [their] daughters to be confectionaries, and to be cooks, and to be bakers" (1 Samuel 8:13). He would take their best fields and vineyards, and give them to his servants. He would tax them and give the proceeds to his government officials. He would take their servants, their "goodliest young men," and their animals and "put them to his work" (1 Samuel 8:16). The Lord's final warning was "Ye shall cry out in that day because of your king which ye shall have chosen you; and the Lord will not hear you in that day" (1 Samuel 8:18).

The people were more concerned about being like their neighboring nations than they were about giving up a portion of their liberty to a monarchy. Israel had its kings: first Saul, then David, followed by Solomon.

Israel reached its greatest heights under David. Solomon built the temple and made Israel known among the nations of the world. In the process of doing so, the king did exactly what the Lord had warned Israel about. Solomon devoted much of Israel's resources to building a lavish royal court including a number of heathen shrines. To take care of all the administrative duties required to maintain a royal lifestyle, the king formed a large bureaucracy. Young men and women were conscripted into the workforce and military. Heavy taxes were forced on the people to pay for all the luxury and opulence surrounding the royal court.

Upon Solomon's death, his son Rehoboam was to be crowned the new king of Israel. Law required that he obtain a vote of confidence from the people to legitimize his appointment. He was of the tribe of Judah in the southern area. Recognizing the need to win the approval of the northern tribes, he called for a conference and went to their headquarters. The spokesman for the northern tribes was Jeroboam of the tribe of Ephraim. Before Rehoboam arrived, the northern tribes held a counsel. The consensus of the counsel was that they were tired of the heavy tax burdens Solomon placed upon them to support his royal court. They were willing to accept Rehoboam as king but insisted that the taxes be reduced: "Thy father made our yoke grievous: now therefore make thou the grievous service of thy father, and his heavy yoke which he put upon us, lighter, and we will serve thee" (1 Kings 12:4).

Rehoboam appealed for time to think about their request while he counseled with his advisors. He first went to the older men to seek their advice. They counseled him to go along with their request and the people would "be [his] servants for ever" (1 Kings 12:7). Rehoboam wasn't satisfied with their advice and went to the younger members of his court. They advised him to increase the taxes, ensuring funds to maintain the royal lifestyle to which they had become accustomed. He agreed with the younger advisors.

When Rehoboam informed the northern tribes of his decision, they declined giving consent to his rule and returned to their tents in an act of defiance. Rehoboam, not realizing the extent of the northern tribes' discontent, sent his tax collector Adoram among Israel to collect the tribute. They replied by stoning Adoram to death. "So Israel rebelled against the house of David" (1 Kings 12:19) and formed the northern nation of Israel. Judah, with some of the tribe of Benjamin, became the southern nation. Israel was divided.

Jeraboam assumed the leadership of the ten northern tribes, eventually introducing heathen worship and fertility rites, leading Israel into apostasy and temporarily forfeiting Ephraim's right to exercise the birthright blessing of leading all the house of Israel. The tribe of Ephraim would not fully exercise that right until the latter days.

chapter seven

BRANCHES
OF THE OLIVE TREE

Israel is often compared to an olive tree "whose branches should be broken off and should be scattered upon all the face of the earth" (1 Nephi 10:12). The Book of Mormon prophet Lehi compared Israel to an olive tree whose branches were to be scattered throughout the Lord's vineyard (the world). Prophets from the Old Testament confirm the fate of Israel: "I will sift the house of Israel among all nations" and "I scattered them with a whirlwind among the nations whom they know not" (Amos 9:9; Zechariah 7:14).

George C. Reynolds, one of the early members of the Quorum of the Seventy, wrote a fascinating work entitled *Are We of Israel?* He describes the sifting of Israel throughout Europe and the rest of the world.

> The idea, though not until lately widely diffused, that many of the races inhabiting Europe are impregnated with the blood of Israel, is by no means a new one. Many writers, in their researches into the early history of that continent, have been forcibly struck with the similarity that existed between the laws, manners, customs, etc., of the ancient inhabitants of its northern and northwestern portions and those of ancient Israel. These writers have endeavored to account for this peculiarity in two ways. First by the supposition that Israelitish colonies for various causes, left the land of the inheritance and gradually worked themselves north and northwestward over Europe; and second,

by the argument that remnants of branches of the lost Ten Tribes had emigrated from Media into Europe, and through the ignorance of historians, disguised under other names, they had remained unknown until the present, their habits, customs, traditions, etc., having in the meanwhile become so greatly changed by time and circumstances, as to render them unrecognizable at this late day.[1]

In 2 Chronicles, Asa, while attempting to cleanse the Southern Kingdom of Judah of idol worship, related how many from the northern tribes of Ephraim, Manasseh, and Simeon had migrated to Judah to escape the idol worship in their own lands (see 2 Chronicles 15:8–9). That might explain why Lehi (from the tribe of Manasseh) and Ishmael (from the tribe of Ephraim) were living in Jerusalem around 600 BC.

Other members of the tribes of Israel left the land of Canaan voluntarily or involuntarily before Israel became a divided nation. Several of the tribes received an inheritance of land bordering the Mediterranean Sea. Commerce and trade would become natural aspects of their economy and livelihoods. Merchants and traders moved to surrounding countries, establishing temporary and permanent colonies. As they grew more efficient in shipbuilding and commerce expanded, the base of operations extended farther and farther from home.

> It must not be supposed that these maritime tribes were the only ones that would be found spreading abroad. The members of various tribes did not strictly confine themselves to the boundaries assigned their tribe by Joshua, but they intermingled for trade, etc., and many men of other tribes resided within the borders of Judah's inheritance and vice versa. We have a notable example of this (600 BC) in the case of Lehi and Laban, who were of the seed of Joseph, yet were residents of Jerusalem, and Nephi incidentally remarks that his father, Lehi, had dwelt in that city "all his days." The children of Ephraim, from their great enterprise and force of character, seem to have early spread, not only among other tribes, but also into foreign nations.[2]

Commerce was not the only phenomenon pulling Israel from Canaan. Many were carried from their homes and sold as slaves. Reynolds points out, "We are of the opinion that this wholesale slave trade of the Phoenicians is greatly underestimated as a factor in the diffusion of Israelitish blood throughout the world."[3] Other nations conquering across the Fertile Crescent would take Israelites from their homes and sell them as slaves, echoing the prophecy "Thou shalt beget sons and daughters, but thou shalt not enjoy them; for they shall go into captivity" and "the Lord shall bring thee into Egypt again with ships, by the way whereof I spake unto thee, Thou shalt see it no more again: and there ye shall be sold unto your enemies for bondmen and bondwomen, and no man shall buy you" (Deuteronomy 28:41, 68). Whether Israelites were seeking commercial opportunities or sold as slaves, they were spread into the countries surrounding the Mediterranean Sea, including present-day African nations, Greece, Italy, Spain, and France. Over time, they continued north into the German provinces and across the channel into England.

After first receiving their inheritance in Canaan, all the tribes passed through decades of apostasy, civil strife, and changes in government before Jacob's descendants divided into the Northern and Southern Kingdoms of Israel and Judah in 975 BC. Jeroboam (of the tribe of Ephraim) was appointed to be the first king of the Northern Kingdom. Concerned about establishing a unique character for the Northern Kingdom and differentiating it from Judah, he established a new capitol at Samaria and introduced idolatry among his people. So depraved did Israel become that they even offered human sacrifices to the heathen gods (see Psalm 106:34–38).

Over the next two centuries, prophet after prophet went among Israel calling the people to repentance and warning them of calamities to follow if they refused. Elijah, Elisha, Jonah, Amos, Micah, Joel, Hosea, and Isaiah all warned Israel. Occasionally, light came to darkened Israel, but only for brief periods. Civil war, royal assassinations, political upheaval, and foreign entanglements became the norm.

While Israel was embroiled in its own civil problems, a dark cloud formed to its east. Dormant for several decades, Assyria began to expand beyond its borders, incorporating whatever was in its path. Babylon, Chaldea, Syria, and a large portion of northern Israel would soon fall victim to conquering hordes. After a few years of consolidating their gains, Assyria was again hammering at the remaining portion of Israel, putting Samaria under siege. Three years into the siege Samaria fell and with it all of Israel was taken captive. Discovered centuries later, notes inscribed on a palace wall in Nineveh, Assyria's capital, describe King Sargon II breaking the siege and conquering Israel: "At the beginning of my rule, in the very first year I reigned . . . I set siege to and conquered Samaria . . . I carried away into captivity 27,290 persons who live there. I took fifty-five chariots for my royal equipment."[4] Thousands of Israelites were forced from their homes, carried off, and resettled in areas within the northern boundaries of Assyria. There they joined Israelites from previous deportations.

Assyria's policy, after conquering a nation, was to round up the leading citizens, governmental officials, upper class, and artisans and deport them to remote areas of the kingdom. Assyria would then import new people into the conquered area and place leaders of their own choosing over them. The imports mingled with the remnants of Israel left behind, eventually forming the people known as Samaritans in the New Testament (see 2 Kings 17:24).

In 721 BC, the Northern Kingdom of Israel came to an abrupt end. Israel was then scattered into two large groups located at Samaria and in captivity in Assyria and smaller groups throughout Africa, Asia, and Europe. With each passing decade, the blood of Israel was being sifted farther "among all nations."

Deported Israel spent several decades mourning their captivity. Disregarding their covenants with the Lord, idol worship, corruption in the government, pride, and a general indifference to the law of Moses stirred up the Lord's anger, and Israel was forced to pay as the Lord had forewarned them. Again they were held captive to a foreign power and regretted their negligence in keeping their covenant with the Lord. In captivity, Israel recognized the need for a new spirit; they needed to reject the heathen idol worship that plagued them for so long and turn to the Lord, the true God of their forefathers (see Hosea 10:1; Hosea 14:8–9; Hosea 10:6).

Jeremiah describes Israel's sentiments in Assyria: "Thou hast chastised me, and I was chastised, as a bullock unaccustomed to the yoke: turn thou me, and I shall be turned; for thou art the Lord my God. Surely, after that I was turned, I repented; and after that I was instructed" (Jeremiah 31:18–19).

Israel was ashamed of their past, but Jeremiah writes that the Lord would not forget Ephraim: "Is Ephraim my dear son? is he a pleasant child? for I spake against him, I do earnestly remember him still: therefore my bowels are troubled for him; I will surely have mercy upon him, saith the Lord" (Jeremiah 31:20).

In the Apocrypha, Esdras provides a more detailed account of captive Israel's decision to escape past mistakes and make a new start:

> And whereas thou sawest that He gathered another peaceable people unto Him. Those are the Ten Tribes which were carried away

34

captives out of their own land in the time of Oseas the king who Shalmaneser the king of the Assyrians took captive, and crossed them beyond the river; so were they brought into another land. But they took this counsel to themselves, that they would leave the multitude of the heathen, and go forth unto a further country where never man dwelt. That they might there keep their statutes, which they never kept in their own land. And they entered in at the narrow passages of the River Euphrates. For the Most High then showed them signs, and stayed the springs of the flood till they were passed over. For through the country there was great journey, even of a year and a half, and the same region is called Arsareth (or Ararath). Then dwelt they there until the latter time, and when they come forth again. The Most High shall hold still the springs of the river again that they may go through; therefore sawest thou the multitude peaceable.[5]

Reynolds explains why Israel decided to set its course north instead of attempting to return to the land of Canaan.

In their home of promise they had seldom kept the counsels and commandments of God and if they returned, it was probable they would not do any better, especially as the Assyrians had filled their land with heathen colonists whose influence would not assist them to carry out their new resolutions. Hency they determined to go to a country "where never men dwelt," that they might be free from all contaminating influences. That country could only be found in the north.[6]

Living in Egypt and the land of Canaan, Israel had proven that they were not strong when mixed with cultures indulging in idol worship. Twice in their past they had failed to keep a covenant with the Lord. This time, they chose to go into a land not previously inhabited by man to ensure that they would be away from evil influences. If alone, away from contaminating pressures, their chances of remaining faithful increased many fold. The only direction left to find that kind of peace was north. Once again, Israel left their captors with new anticipations.

Elder Bruce R McConkie depicts Israel as it marched into the unknown.

In their northward journeyings they were led by prophets and inspired leaders. They had their Moses and their Lehi, were guided by the spirit of revelation, kept the law of Moses, and carried with them the statutes and judgments which the Lord had given them in ages past. They were still a distinct people many hundreds of years later, for the resurrected Lord visited and ministered among them following his ministry on this continent among the Nephites.[7]

Reynolds explains how some left the main group during its northward journey and scattered throughout Europe.

> But we ask further, is it altogether improbable that in that long journey of one and a half years as Esdras states it, from Media, the land of their captivity to the frozen north, some of the back-sliding Israel rebelled, turned aside from the main body, forgot their God, by and by mingled with the Gentiles and became the leaven to leaven with the promised seed all the nations of the earth? And who so likely to rebel as stubborn, impetuous, proud and warlike Ephraim? Rebellion and backsliding have been so characteristically the story of Ephraim's career that we can scarcely conceive that it could be otherwise and yet preserve the unities of that people's history. Can it be any wonder then that so much of the blood of Ephraim has been found hidden and unknown in the midst of the nations of northern Europe and other parts until the spirit of prophecy revealed its existence?[8]

Reynolds attributes Ephraim's leaving the main body to rebellion and backsliding, but there is much more to the story. They were bearing course into a region of Europe that would play a crucial role in the future development of world events, the establishment of an independent country on the American continent and the Restoration of the gospel of Jesus Christ. They, however, were unaware that there was a great purpose for their wanderings. "For behold, the Lord God has led away from time to time from the house of Israel, according to his will and pleasure. And now behold, the Lord remembereth all them who have been broken off" (2 Nephi 10:22).

The Lord would remember Israel, particularly the birthright tribe of Ephraim, as they wandered into the European lands. He had a very important work for them to accomplish. The blood of Israel would exert great influence over the people and events that shaped Europe over the next two and a half millennia.

Notes

1   George C. Reynolds, *Are We of Israel?* (Independence, MO: Press of Zion's Printing and Publishing Company), 13–14.

2   Ibid., 15.

3   Ibid., 16.

4   Nelson Beecher Keyes, *Story of the Bible World,* (Independence, MO: Press of Zion's Printing and Publishing Company), 83.

5   *Apocrypha*, 2 Esdras 13:39–47.

6   Reynolds, *Are We of Israel?* 27.

7   McConkie, *Mormon Doctrine,* 457.

8   Reynolds, *Are We of Israel?* 10–11.

chapter eight

NATIONS AND FAMILIES
BLESSED

An anxious Israel fled the borders of Assyria north to find a country where no other inhabitants lived—one without the contaminating influences of idol worship. Repentant hearts were anticipating a new start, this time obeying the law of Moses. Along the journey, many of the tribe of Ephraim wandered away from the main body, fulfilling the prophecy that they would be scattered among the nations. Little has been said or written about Ephraim from that time long ago when they separated from the ten tribes as they journeyed north, until the nineteenth century and the Restoration of the Church of Jesus Christ in the latter days.

Those who carry Ephraim's blood might wonder what their ancestors were doing during the thirty-five centuries between the initial scattering of Israel after they first entered the land of Canaan and the Restoration of Christ's church in the latter days. Would those with Ephraim's blood hibernate and seclude themselves from the people of the world for three and a half millennia? If that were the case, why were they sifted and scattered among the nations so early in their history? Why were they dragged out of Canaan as captives and slaves to foreign nations? Would not their history have been better served if they remained in the land promised Abraham, Isaac, and Jacob for a thousand, or even two thousand years, and then dispersed in some grand manner for all the people of the world to witness?

Israelites themselves must have wondered why these things were

39

happening when there were so many promises and prophecies of their future role in the world. Why were they taken captive by the heathen Assyrians, and why did they have to flee to the north to feel secure in their attempts to worship the God of Abraham, Isaac, and Jacob? They, on many occasions, may have asked themselves what might have happened if they had remained faithful and not broken their covenant with the Lord. How different would Israel's history have been? How much different would the history of the world have been? They had been told that if they remained faithful, the Lord would "establish thee an holy people unto himself" (Deuteronomy 28:9). Israel had the potential to establish an Enoch-like city where the word of the Lord could have gone to the entire world. But that was not to be. Israel failed, and for that they were punished. Other routes would be established to fulfill the Lord's purposes. Those pathways would be long and difficult and would wind through many nations but over time would prepare Israel to do the Lord's bidding and bring salvation to mankind in the latter days.

Through Hosea, the Lord informed readers of the Old Testament that one of the reasons Ephraim was scattered was as punishment for failure to follow the Lord's counsel and for neglecting their covenants: "My god will cast them away, because they did not hearken unto him: and they shall be wanderers among the nations" (Hosea 9:17).

A second reason for Israel's scattering was, as Isaiah informed his readers, that Israel would change and be blessed because of the scattering: "And I will give them one heart, and I will put a new spirit within you; and I will take the stony heart out of their flesh, and will give them a heart of flesh" (Ezekiel 11:19). Israel would change over time in their new habitat. The ten tribes, after being captured by Assyria, fled to the northern countries to achieve that change and forget the indulgences of the past.

The Lord could have punished Israel where they were and brought about a change of heart without scattering them throughout the world. But that would not have accomplished the most important reason for sifting Israel among the nations.

As the reader further contemplates the scattering, he or she might ask what those nations would have been like without the influence of Israel, the Lord's chosen people. Blessings of the patriarch, Abraham, provide the answer to the Lord's rationale for allowing his chosen people to be removed from their promised land to wander around the world: "In thy seed shall all the nations of the earth be blessed" and "In thee and in thy seed shall all the families of the earth be blessed (Genesis 22:18; see Genesis 28:17).

Israel, particularly Ephraim, was scattered to bless the nations and families of the earth. Those blessings were not reserved just for the latter days. There were nations and people to prepare for those coming days.

Jacob's blessing to Joseph back in Egypt offers further enlightenment: "For thou shalt be a light unto my people, to deliver them in the days of their captivity, from bondage; and to bring salvation unto them, when they are altogether bowed down under sin" (JST Genesis 48:11). Joseph's posterity, the tribes of Ephraim and Manasseh, were to be a light during ages when darkness predominated. As sparks ignited and knowledge spread around the world, the other two promises could be accomplished—delivering the people from captivity and bringing salvation to those people. To accomplish that, Israel had to be among the families and nations of the earth.

Providing blessings to the nations didn't always require the presence of large numbers of Israel. Single individuals have often had astounding influence. One need look no further than the scriptures to find evidence of this.

Joseph, Jacob's son, was betrayed by his brothers, sold into slavery, and taken to Egypt. From a captive slave, he rose to a position second only to Pharaoh. His political administration prepared Egypt for seven years of terrible famine and, in the process, preserved his own father, Jacob, and his family. Joseph's very existence in the land of Egypt was expunged from the records by succeeding rulers, but his work brought blessings to millions.

Daniel was another who was taken captive as a young man to a strange land. From captivity in Babylon, he became a counselor to kings. His was the privilege of interpreting King Nebuchadnezzar's dream of the great figure representing important kingdoms and countries where Israel's presence would be manifested. Daniel foretold that those kingdoms would eventually fade from power, and then "shall the God of heaven set up a kingdom, which shall never be destroyed: and the kingdom shall not be left to other people, but it shall break in pieces and consume all these kingdoms, and it shall stand for ever. Forasmuch as thou sawest that the stone was cut out of the mountain without hands" (Daniel 2:44–45). Ephraim, the birthright tribe, would play the leadership role in Daniel's prophecy (see chapter 19).

Paul, the resourceful Apostle of the Lord, was the first to preach the gospel to the gentile nations. His missionary efforts blessed the lives of millions throughout the centuries. Alma, from the Book of Mormon, is another example. Fleeing for his life from King Noah's guard, he hid in the wilderness, drew men and women to him, preached the gospel, baptized followers, and organized the Church of Christ. He spent his life for the salvation of those seeking the gospel. These are just a few examples of the influence a single individual carrying the blood of Israel can exert. One can only imagine the influence of the children of Israel as they spread among the nations of the world.

The spirits that earned the privilege of being among chosen Israel probably pleaded for the opportunity to come to earth at favorable times, such as the latter days when Christ's church was fully functioning, so that they and their posterity could partake of all the blessings of the gospel. But that would not be possible for all the spirits who stood on the Lord's side in the War in Heaven. Some were called to bring light in times of darkness. They had proven their willingness to serve in the premortal life—now they were given the opportunity to assist in mortality.

Those spirits would need a special strength to live under the circumstances that existed between the time of Israel's scatterings and the Restoration of the gospel. This was an age of darkness and apostasy. Few were educated, access to information or scriptures was limited, living conditions were simple, and death and disease were prevalent. Yet Ephraim's calling to be a light unto the individuals, families, and nations staggering in darkness were sorely needed during the centuries before the gospel could be restored.

They were needed to forge new paths and prepare the way for those who would follow. What they accomplished must never be underestimated. Brigham Young describes Ephraim's unconquerable will:

> We are now gathering the children of Abraham who have come through the loins of Joseph and his sons, more especially through Ephraim, whose children are mixed among all the nations of the earth. The sons of Ephraim are wild and uncultivated, unruly, ungovernable. The spirit in them is turbulent and resolute . . . and they are upon the face of the whole earth, bearing the spirit of rule and dictation, to go forth from conquering to conquer. They search wide creation and scan every nook and corner of this earth to find out what is upon and within it. . . . No hardship will discourage these men; they will penetrate

the deepest wilds and overcome almost insurmountable difficulties to develop the treasurers of the earth, to further their indomitable spirit for adventure.[1]

The blood of Israel has a very distinctive quality, giving those who carry it an advantage during those darkened times. The Prophet Joseph Smith describes how that characteristic is influenced by the Holy Ghost.

> This first Comforter or Holy Ghost has no other effect than pure intelligence. It is more powerful in expanding the mind, enlightening the understanding, and storing the intellect with present knowledge of a man who is of the literal seed of Abraham, than one that is a Gentile, . . . for as the Holy Ghost falls upon of the literal seed of Abraham, it is calm and serene; and his whole soul and body are exercised by the pure spirit of intelligence.[2]

During those ages of darkness, Israel would be receptive to the influence of the Holy Ghost as minds were expanded and enlightened. Columbus testified to having been inspired by the Holy Ghost.

The words of Edmund Burke provide a premise for Ephraim during those ages: "The only thing necessary for the triumph of evil is for good men to do nothing."

The blood of Ephraim, scattered throughout the world, was unlikely to stand idle and do nothing when there was so much to accomplish before the light of the gospel could be fully extended to the people of the world. The record of how it was accomplished is full of intrigue, courage, persecution, diligence, industry, faith, and hope. It is a tale for which we of the modern era should become more knowledgeable and appreciative, both for what was accomplished by those who went before us, and also the difference it made in our own lives.

Notes

1   Brigham Young, *Journal of Discourses*, May 31, 1863, vol. 10 (London: Latter-day Saints' Book Depot, 1854–86), 188.
2   Joseph Fielding Smith and Richard D. Galbraith, *Scriptural Teachings of the Prophet Joseph Smith* (Salt Lake City: Deseret Book, 1993), 170–71.

Part Two

SCATTERED ISRAEL AND ITS EFFECTS

chapter nine

I WILL SAVE THE HOUSE OF JOSEPH

The lesson from Israel's first attempt to establish a Zion society in the land of Canaan was that neither the people (Israel) nor the land (Canaan) was prepared. After wandering thirty-eight years in the wilderness, and the older generation leaving this mortal existence, the children of Israel were still slaves to their past and lacked the strength, courage, faith, and dedication necessary to follow the Lord's instruction to the fullest. Tough choices had to be made. Leadership among the tribes hadn't matured.

The contaminating influences existing in the land presented difficult challenges. It was a land full of idol worshippers constantly offering enticements to return to old habits.

When the Lord would gather Israel for the second and final time, failure was not an option. The overnight freedom offered the children of Israel was a thing of the past. In the last days, freedom would be earned, so that those who enjoyed its benefits would appreciate the cost to acquire and sustain it.

The Lord set aside a special land for that people once they were prepared. They would have an opportunity to start anew, away from negative influences that might draw them in wrong directions. That exceptional venue would be a "land of promise . . . a land which is choice above all other lands" (1 Nephi 2:20). It would be "a land of liberty" so that "every man may enjoy his rights and privileges alike" (Mosiah 29:32).

A nation with a constitutional guarantee of religious freedom was the ultimate great hurdle in a long series of hurdles to prepare the world for the Restoration of Christ's church. It had to be a setting where a fourteen-year-old boy, claiming to have seen Heavenly Father and his Son Jesus Christ, in person, could survive without being beheaded or burned at the stake for blasphemy. In any other predominately Christian countries in the world, he would not have lasted long after making such a bold statement. Even in that promised land the path would not be painless for one making such a claim.

During the first 3,500–4,000 years of man's existence, the period of the Old Testament, the great advances in civilization came from Asia and the area known as the Middle East. From Egypt's Nile River in the West to the Tigris and Euphrates Rivers in modern-day Iraq, man made great strides. According to secular history, cities were born, animals were domesticated, the wheel was invented, writing was advanced, alphabets were introduced, and farming was improved. Trade, commerce, and travel by land and sea became more sophisticated. Nations and groups began to interact with each other for economic purposes. Great civilizations appeared, including Assyria, Babylon, and Persia. The first documented administrative laws were published in Babylon by Hammurabi. The secrets to making metals more useful were discovered. The first libraries were established. The continuing need for commercial interaction coupled with improved methods of travel fostered the spread of new ideas. Art, sculpture, and literature reached new heights. Many of those achievements filtered into Europe and around the world.

Around 500 BC, the spawning of new ideas and discoveries shifted from the original cradle of civilization to the continent of Europe—first to Greece and Rome and then into Western Europe. This shift occurred during the same time Israel, and particularly Ephraim, began migrating or were carried as slaves from Canaan to the European countries and were sifted among the nations. Those nations would be the birthplace to principles of democracy, coded law, representative government, and the emphasis on the importance of individual achievement. Dissemination of ideas and the spread of knowledge would occur at a rate never seen in the history of the world. The Christian religion would spread with its message of love, the concept of an afterlife and an emphasis on the individual member. Europe, for over two and half millennia, would be the initial proving ground for democratic thought and would prepare people to fulfill the Lord's purposes. The Lord said, "I will save the house of Joseph . . . and they shall be as though I had not cast them off. . . . And I will sow them among the people: and they shall remember me in the far countries; and they shall live with their children, and turn again (Zechariah 10:6–7, 9).

By 500 BC, the descendents of Joseph were scattered over a large area of Asia and Europe, even extending to other parts of the world. What we know of the scattering includes the following:

- After receiving their inheritance in the land of Canaan, the maritime tribes, including Ephraim and Manasseh, extended their commercial interests into the nations bordering the Mediterranean Sea, making new settlements. Others were taken as slaves by Phoenician traders. This scattering began around 1,000 BC and continued until Israel was taken captive by the Assyrians in 721 BC They migrated to the European countries of Greece and Italy and from there drifted north into Western Europe.
- In 721 BC, Assyria captured Israel and carried the ten northern tribes off to an area of northern Assyria. From there, many of them escaped and went north. Along the journey, members of the tribes, particularity Ephraim, broke away from the main camp and migrated into northern Europe.
- Not all the members of the ten northern tribes were carried into Assyria. Some were left in Israel where they mixed with other people imported by the Assyrians. They were known as the Samaritans in the New Testament times.
- Some members of the tribes taken captive by Assyria refused to take the journey to the north. They stayed behind forming colonies in northern Assyria. This group became a numerous force, eventually migrating into northern and central Europe and other parts of the world.

Lehi and Ishmael were of the tribes of Manasseh and Ephraim respectively, living in Jerusalem. Nephi informs us that his father Lehi had lived in Jerusalem "all his days," indicating that there were also members of the northern tribes living among the tribe of Judah in Jerusalem (1 Nephi 1:4). Around 600 BC, the Lord told Lehi to take his family and the family of Ishmael out of Jerusalem and to go to a land he would be shown. That land was the American continent. Lehi's sons, who were of Manasseh, married the daughters of Ishmael who were of the tribe of Ephraim. Those marriages meant that all descendents of Lehi living in America would carry the blood of Ephraim and Manasseh.

Concerning the tribes of Israel inhabiting early America, Apostle Erastus Snow commented:

> Whoever has read the Book of Mormon carefully will have learned that the remnants of the house of Joseph dwelt upon the American continent; and that Lehi learned by searching the records of his fathers that were written upon the plates of brass, that he was of the lineage of Manasseh. The Prophet Joseph informed us that the record of Lehi, was contained on the 116 pages that were first translated and subsequently stolen, and of which an abridgement is given us in the first Book of Nephi, which is the record of Nephi individually, he himself being of the lineage of Manasseh; but that Ishmael was of the lineage of Ephraim, and that his sons married into Lehi's family, and Lehi's sons married Ishmael's daughters, thus fulfilling the words of Jacob upon Ephraim and Manasseh in the 48th chapter of Genesis, which says: "And let my name be named on them, and the name of my fathers Abraham and Isaac; and let them grow into a multitude in the midst of the land," Thus these descendants of Manasseh and Ephraim grew together upon this American continent, with a sprinkling from the house of Judah, from Mulek descended, who left Jerusalem eleven years afterwards known as Zarahemla and found by Mosiah—thus making a combination, an intermixture of Ephraim and Manasseh with the remnants of Judah, and for aught we know, the remnants of some other tribes that might have accompanied Mulek.[1]

There were other scatterings to the Pacific Islands, Asia, Eastern Europe, Africa, and eventually to all nations of the world.

Brigham Young clarified the diffusion of the blood of Ephraim among the nations: "Israel is dispersed among all the nations of the earth; the blood of Ephraim is mixed with the blood of all the earth. Abraham's seed is mingled with the rebellious seed through the whole world of mankind."[2]

Israel, principally the tribe of Ephraim, was in Europe, where steps would be taken to develop a political thought eventually leading to the establishment of the Constitution of the United States. The path would begin in Greece and Rome before the birth of Christ. It would wind through Spain, where an explorer named Columbus would convince the monarchy to finance a project of sailing west. The path would go on to

Germany, where a monk would protest abuses in the church and post his objections for the world to see. Then it would go on to England, where preserving individual rights would be paramount in the foundation of its government. The path would then traverse the wide expanse of the Atlantic to a new land, "a promised land," set aside for the establishment of a "free people." A people free of the burdens of a monarchy, where guarantees for freedom of worship would be one of the final pieces of the puzzle to establish conditions for Ephraim to complete the calling described by the prophets of old preparing for the Restoration of the gospel of Jesus Christ.

James E. Talmage confirms the influence of Israel on the people and nations of the world:

> It has been said, that "if a complete history of the house of Israel were written, it would be the history of histories, the key of the world's history for the past twenty centuries" (*Principles of the Gospel, Based Largely Upon the Compendium,* The Church of Jesus Christ of Latter-day Saints, 1943; 1964 edition, p. 84). Justification for this sweeping statement is found in the fact that the Israelites have been so completely dispersed among nations as to give to this scattered people a place of importance as a factor in the rise and development of almost every large division of the human family. This work of dispersion was brought about by many stages, and extended through millenniums.[3]

The remaining portion of this narrative will trace events and people that contributed to the preparation. The pathway is filled with many notable contributions along with innumerable small offerings, each accumulating and building on the other.

Notes

1 Erastus Snow, *Journal of Discourses,* May 6, 1882, 23:184–85.
2 Brigham Young, *Journal of Discourses,* May 25, 1873, 16:75.
3 James E. Talmage, *Articles of Faith,* (Salt Lake City: The Church of Jesus Christ of Latter-day Saints, 1961), 316.

chapter ten

GREECE

—ooo-)⊗(-ooo—

"We alone regard a man who takes no interest in public affairs, not as a harmless, but as a useless character."

—Pericles, given at a funeral oration
for Athenians slain in battle

G*reece* was the third kingdom King Nebuchadnezzar saw in the dream that he related to Daniel. It was the first of the two European kingdoms in that dream. Greece was destined to play a noteworthy role in the latter-day gathering of Israel.

The era before 750 BC was known as Greece's Dark Ages. Little was accomplished or written during that period. What information passed down to later generations of those times came through two epic poems known as the *Iliad* and the *Odyssey*. The reportedly blind poet Homer is generally credited as the author of these epic tales, which have been read and studied from ancient times to the present. Around 700 BC, the Greeks adopted an alphabet from the Phoenicians (the first to use an alphabet system). The Greeks absorbed ideas from Egypt and Mesopotamia (Persia, the second kingdom in Nebuchadnezzar's dream), merged them with their own and forming a distinctive culture. From 500 BC forward, Greece experienced a period of exceptional political and cultural creativity. Its architecture, philosophy, science, arts, and literature influenced

Western Civilizations on a scale few understand or could imagine. Most important to their legacy was the unique political thought initiated by the Greeks.

Characteristic of the blood of Ephraim is to seek for avenues where agency can be practiced. From their first disagreement over taxes and their separation from the tribe of Judah after Solomon's death in Canaan, the tribe of Ephraim had searched for ways to allow men to exercise their agency. Ephraim's blood congregated in areas where experiments with liberty and democracy were conducted. Ephraim was duty bound to take a liberty loving people to a land where they could establish an atmosphere for the Restoration of the gospel. The long road to accomplish that assignment began in Greece.

From 750 to 550 BC, city states were established throughout Greece. Greece did not have a strong central government as did the preceding kingdom of Persia and succeeding kingdom of Rome. This lack of a strong central government, coupled with extraordinarily talented men, provided the catalyst for the exceptional cultural and political creativity that Greece fashioned over a period of four centuries.

The Greek city-states were free to experiment with various forms of government. Many of the city-states began as a monarchy then evolved into an oligarchy (rule by a few; i.e., nobles of the city states), and some even developed into a democracy. The various forms of government supplied firsthand experience and opportunities for Greek philosophers and historians to speak and write with an understanding of government that no other people of the world experienced.

During fifth and fourth centuries BC known as the the Classical Age, two city states stood out and dominated Grecian political history—Athens and Sparta.

Athens experimented with various forms of democracy while Sparta developed a unique way of life under totalitarianism. Athens democracy brought out the best and worst in those living within its environs. Citizens like Pericles, Socrates, Plato, Aristotle, and a host of other leaders, philosophers, scientists, and artisans generated new and unique ideas in the democratic atmosphere of Athens. Greek democracy was practiced differently than it is today, yet it offered the people of Athens more involvement in the decision making-process than any previous civilization.

Athens, Greece, and Europe were threatened by Persia's ambitious plans to expand its empire around 500 BC. The experiment in democracy may have come to an abrupt end had Darius, king of Persia, had his way. He captured the city states on the western coastline of Asia Minor across the Aegean Sea from Athens. Darius knew his newly acquired territory would not be secure with Athens thriving on the east coast of Greece. He decided to attack, capture Athens, and may have had aspirations to conquer Greece and the rest of Europe.

In 490 BC, a Persian army of twenty thousand sailed across the Aegean Sea to camp on the plain of Marathon just above Athens. Athens met the Persian threat with an army about half that size but came away with a stunning victory. The success of the Athenian army shattered the Persians' confidence that they were invincible and established a notion that free men could fight and win even against powerful monarchies. The Persian Wars continued for over a decade until a Grecian army defeated the Persians in 479 BC and sent the Persians scrambling back to Asia Minor. The effects of this defeat were enormous. This single war was "the most momentous conflict in European history, for it made Europe possible. It won for Western Civilization the opportunity to develop its own economic life—unburdened with alien tribute or taxation—and its own political institutions, free from the dictation of Oriental kings. It won for Greece a clear road for the first great experiment in liberty; it preserved the Greek mind for three centuries from the enervating mysticism of the East."[1]

Under the leadership of Pericles, Athens developed a direct democracy that offered large numbers of citizens the opportunity to participate in government. The guidelines required that at least six thousand people, chosen by lot, had to be present in the legislative body before they could conduct business. Pericles believed that male citizens of all social classes should participate in the governmental process, so he offered a stipend for their time spent in governmental service. Athenians also served on juries; often these juries were made up of hundreds and even thousands of jurors.

Though Athens was the birthplace of modern democracy, it was also home to thousands of slaves serving their Greek masters. It was the slave labor that gave Athenians leisure time to participate in the democratic process. The slaves did most of the work, freeing their masters' time to debate and discuss the political and philosophical issues of the day. Grecian slaves were afforded opportunities to be free. They could either purchase their freedom outright or earn it by serving their masters for a stipulated number of years. Once they gained their freedom, they were granted citizenship rights. Grecian policy toward its slaves may have allowed many, including those of the house of Israel, who were initially sold as slaves, the opportunity to gain freedom and become citizens of Greece.

Athenians loved beauty. They surrounded themselves with beautiful art and magnificent architecture. The buildings on the Acropolis, including the white marble temple known as the Parthenon, was built during the Golden Age of Greece. It was begun in 448 BC and completed in 432 BC. The majestic columns used by Greek architects in the Parthenon have been copied and adopted in architecture all over the world.

Greek philosophy began as an attempt to explain the universe in a way that man could understand. This philosophy was an attempt to help individuals appreciate who they were and stressed the need to discover order and meaning in life. The Greeks could be cruel, but at their best they were guided by high ideals. Socrates, Plato, and Aristotle were three great Grecian philosophers that raised questions about methods of governing, human nature, and society.

Socrates taught that evil could only result from man's ignorance and stressed the need for people to constantly question their suroundings. He was often critical of governmental officials and questioned democracy's ability to function. A student of Socrates, Plato, recorded many of Socrates's ideas and wrote the *Republic*, a work describing the ideal society based on an aristocracy (a government ruled by the upper class). Aristotle, another philosopher, was a collector of facts; he developed the initial process for scientific observation and experimentation. Aristotle was apprehensive about democracy and reasoned that in the wrong hands it could easily turn into a dictatorship.

The writings of these three Greek philosophers were translated and read throughout the Renaissance, Reformation, and Enlightenment periods of Europe and the Colonial and Revolutionary eras in America. The ideas of these philosophers deeply impacted and motivated all who read their works.

The Greeks also made important advances in medicine. Hippocrates, a pioneer in the medical field, is considered the founder of modern medicine. He taught that diseases came from natural causes rather than punishment from the Greek gods. Rest, fresh air, and proper diet were his recommendations for curing diseases. He emphasized the need to observe and interpret symptoms of diseases. Today, physicians take the Hippocratic Oath before they begin practicing medicine.

The achievements of the Classical Greeks can be attributed to several factors, including their geographic location, contributions from neighboring civilizations, the absence of an oppressive central government, the rise of the city state, an abundance of leisure time, and a relatively free environment to think critically.

The Mediterranean area provided many occasions for the exchange of ideas with neighboring civilizations due to its central location. Opportunities for trade and the accumulation of wealth grew on a grand scale. The climate allowed men to meet outdoors, mull over the latest philosophical idea, and communicate with each other with leisure.

The Greeks of the Classical era fashioned innovative ideas, political viewpoints, scientific observations, and mathematical equations not dreamed of in most of the world. "For if the collective, corporate city-state provided the framework and background for this lavish array of feats, they were actually undertaken and performed by a relatively few persons. Some forty or fifty of them created the classical Greek achievement. Without them, it would only have been a shadow."[2] The effect of a "relatively few persons" occured time and again as conditions were established for the Restoration of the gospel.

Phillip of Macedon gained the throne and set out to conquer the city-states of Greece. By 338 BC he had gained control of Greece and dreamed of controlling Persia. He was assassinated before his dream could ever be realized, but his son, Alexander, picked up where Phillip had left off. At the age of twenty, Alexander the Great set out to conquer Persia. Before he was finished, he controlled everything between Egypt and India. He died at the age of thirty-three in Babylon.

Although his empire soon crumbled, Alexander had initiated changes felt around the Mediterranean world for centuries to come. He spread the Greek culture throughout his holdings and absorbed ideas from other cultures. Great strides were made in medicine, mathematics, physics, astronomy, and geography during this time. Physicians at Alexandria dissected the bodies of executed criminals to learn how the human body works. They were able to perform delicate surgeries on patients. They used geometry to measure spheres, cones, and cylinders. Using mathematical theory, they discovered that the earth and other planets revolved around the sun, when the common belief at the time was that the sun and the other planets revolved around the earth. They calculated the circumference of the earth to within 1 percent of error. This combination of cultures made great strides in scientific discovery, reaching heights unmatched by any society until the modern era.

Two great unifying events of the modern world are the Olympic Games and the marathon. The Olympics began as athletic contests between Greek city-states, and marathon races began as the distance a messenger ran to spread the word of Greek victory at the Battle of Marathon.

Greek art, philosophy, architecture, and science set new standards that influenced Europe's development. The Greeks freed themselves from prior superstitions, experienced almost every kind of government, developed unique ideas about freedom, justice, governing, and citizen participation that influenced political thought all over the world. Their ideas spread throughout Europe and reached across the Atlantic Ocean to the founding fathers of an emerging nation in the New World two thousand years later. Their inspired influence is still notable in our lives today; in fact, "We ourselves, whether we like it or not, are the heirs of the Greeks and Romans. In a thousand different ways, they are permanently and indestructibly woven into the fabric of our own existences."[3]

These advancements had an especially profound effect on the Romans and Christians. "The Greeks were a highly educated race, and their civilization, culture, and philosophy were of great service to the Church. Every educated man in the Roman Empire spoke Greek, and it was in the Greek language that the gospel was preached as soon as it spread outside Palestine."[4]

Greece left a legacy impacting democracy that reached across oceans. The long, two-thousand-year journey from Greece to America would take many turns. The principles of democracy were distinguished for centuries only to be resurrected during Europe's Renaissance, Reformation, and Enlightenment. Under Ephraim's direction, Israel would be the driving force to see that the spirit of democracy would resurrect and continue to move forward until it reached the promised land and had the opportunity to blossom and bear the full fruits of the labors of the early Greeks.

Notes

1   Will Durant, *The Life of Greece* (New York: Simon and Schuster, 1966), 242.
2   Michael Grant, *The Founders of the Western World* (New York: Charles Scribner's Sons, 1991), 111.
3   Grant, *The Founders of the Western World*, 1.
4   Bible Dictionary, "Greece," 697.

chapter eleven

ROME

Paul, recounting the story of his conversion to a group of Jews, offended them when he told of seeing the resurrected Jesus. They demanded that he be punished. Jerusalem was under Roman rule, and Roman soldiers were responsible for maintaining law and order. The Jews "cried out" against Paul (Acts 22:23). Responding to the commotion, Roman soldiers took Paul with the intention of torturing him into explaining why the Jews were accusing him, but as they bound him, Paul boldly asked, "Is it lawful for you to scourge a man that is a Roman, and uncondemned?" There was obviously power in that question because,

> When the centurion heard that, he went and told the chief captain, saying, Take heed what thou doest: for this man is a Roman.
> Then the chief captain came, and said unto him, Tell me, art thou a Roman? He said, Yea.
> And the chief captain answered, With a great sum obtained I this freedom. And Paul said, But I was free born.
> Then straightway they departed from him which should have examined him: and the chief captain also was afraid, after he knew that he was a Roman, and because he had bound him. (Acts 22:25–29)

Why was a captain of the guard of the mighty Roman Empire so concerned about offending a Jewish rabble-rouser claiming Roman citizenship? Rome's commitment to law and order and rights of its citizens shielded Paul that day. Rome was an Empire so vast that it ruled a hundred million people on three different continents, yet it was concerned about protecting the rights of a single man—a Jew, not a Roman national—who claimed the rights of a Roman citizen. Rome's respect for law was the foundation of its greatness and proved an essential tool in bringing about the Lord's purposes.

Rome began as a small city-state in Italy and became the capital of a world-wide empire stretching from Britain in Europe to the Euphrates River in Asia Minor. In 509 BC, Rome drove out the Etruscan monarchy and set up an aristocratic republic. Rome was divided into two classes: the patrician upper class and the plebeians, or commoners (farmers, merchants, traders and artisans.) The three-hundred-man Senate was made up of patricians. They picked two men, called counsels, to run the government; one handled business affairs and the other led the army. The counsels served for a limited time and had to consult the Senate when making important decisions. In times of war, the Senate chose a dictator, giving him absolute control. However, they limited the dictator's service to six months or less to keep some control. Cincinnatus was the model dictator—he organized an army, led them to victory, and then returned to his farm shortly thereafter. Likewise, General Washington, commander of the Continental Army, made that same choice after the American Revolutionary War when pressure groups within the United States urged him to be king of the forming nation.

Over time the plebeians wanted more assurance from their government and demanded a written code of government. The Senate responded by issuing a written law on twelve bronze tablets known as the Twelve Tables. The Senate's need for commoners to serve in the army afforded the lower class some political power. When they began making further demands, the Senate had to meet their requests or watch their military ranks go unfilled. They gained the right to elect their own tribunes who could veto laws unfavorable to the plebeians. The upper class even opened the Senate to them. The plebeians steadily gained more power and more access to their government.

Important principles used and concessions gained by the common people of Rome were adopted by another group of commoners two thousand years later and an ocean apart. The framers of the U.S. Constitution wrote that document and included checks on each of the branches of government and veto power to the executive branch. Rome's influence was felt in many places long after the Empire disappeared.

The family was the basic unit in Roman society. The father was in control and strict discipline was the norm. Marriage was considered a lifelong union. The family included not only the currently living members but also ancestors and descendants. Loyalty to family spilled over into loyalty to Rome and respect for the law and authority. Self-control and courage were important to Roman citizens. Many, if not most, men served in the Roman Legions. The values learned at home made them solid, loyal soldiers as long as Rome remained true to its principles.

Around 390 BC, Rome was almost wiped out by the Gauls. After barely surviving this attack, Rome rebuilt their army and began fortifying the city. They then began a series of expansions and conquests of their own under the guise of self-defense. The Roman Legions were feared and respected wherever they marched. The soldiers were citizen soldiers, usually drafted, serving without pay and at times furnishing their own weapons. With loyalty, courage, respect for homeland, and authority as their core values, they weren't too much different than citizen soldiers fighting in the American Revolution.

But while Rome was ruthless in fighting, they were gracious in victory. They generally treated the conquered people with justice, allowing them to keep their customs, local governments, and money systems. For their generous terms, Rome required the defeated nations to acknowledge Rome as the ultimate authority and pay them taxes. Rome's lenient attitude toward conquered nations motivated the citizens of those nations to be loyal to Rome even in times of trouble. Latin and Greek were the principle languages of the Romans. Most of the conquered nations picked up and used the languages of Romans, most often Greek. As the Bible dictionary points out, Paul could use Greek in his missionary efforts in all except the Lycaonian mountain area.

To protect their holdings and handle any uprisings, Rome posted soldiers throughout its subjected holdings. The logistics of controlling and managing its vast empire required exceptional and efficient administrative skill. Engineers and administrators traveled with the armies to handle the requirements of governing far away nations from Rome. The sheer vastness of the empire required a new and extensive communication system. New paved roads, bridges, aquaducts, and public buildings were put in place. As an example of Rome's capabilities at the time, the city had fourteen aquaducts, spanning more than 225 miles.

Rome was not without its troubles. As Rome continued to grow, victorious leaders made slaves of some of the people they conquered; thus slave revolts were not uncommon. The most notable instance occurred when Spartacus led 70,000 slaves in a two-year revolt in southern Italy. Also, Roman legions fighting in remote places were no longer made up of draftees loyal to Rome but of volunteers from the conquered lands. A series of civil wars aided the decline of the Roman Republic.

Julius Caesar spearheaded one such war when he returned to Rome after a victory and forced the Senate to make him dictator. He initiated public work reforms and introduced the Julian calendar used in Western Europe for over sixteen hundred years. After his assasination, Octavian became dictator and the five-hundred-year-old Roman Republic came to an end. Octavian initiated new reforms in civil and postal services. He reorganized and established a government that operated very efficiently over the next two hundred years. Those years became known as the Pax Romana (Roman peace). Stability, peace, prosperity, unity, and order were established throughout the Roman Empire. That sheer strength of Rome allowed and induced people to move around freely within the empire spreading knowledge and new ideas to many people.

Although the Jews despised the Roman rule, they enjoyed the peace and prosperity it provided. During this period of peace and stability, the Son of God was born in a stable in Bethlehem. The peaceful conditions established an atmosphere where Jesus could grow to manhood and spend three glorious years teaching the gospel to the Jews. When the Jewish leaders felt threatened and plotted Jesus' death, law required Roman soldiers to make the arrest. When the Sanhedrin condemned Him to death, custom required Roman approval to execute the accused. The Sanhedrin was concerned that if Jesus was prosecuted according to Jewish law, which the Romans would have allowed, they might face a riot among the people. Instead of requesting that he be tried for the Jewish offense of blasphemy, they charged him with treason, an offense against Roman law, which would mean the Romans would have to execute the punishment. Even then, their plan almost failed. If the Roman procurator, Pilate, had had a stronger will, Jesus could have been released according to Roman law. He gave in to the Jewish leaders screaming for Jesus' death and ordered the crucifixion.

The Pax Romana also provided an environment for Christ's Apostles and disciples to spread Christianity throughout Judea and into the Gentile nations. The transportation system made travel assessable and convenient for early Christian missionaries. While Rome was responsible for the death of Jesus, Peter, and Paul, along with the crucifixion of thousands of Christians, it actually played an important role in the spread of Christianity. Three centuries later, Rome adopted Christianity as the state religion.

If the Jews had governed themselves, would their leaders have allowed the Savior to preach for three years, organize His church, and then sit by while the Apostles and disciples spread Christianity among the tribe of Judah? Unlikely! The new rabbi was a serious threat to their value and religious system and would have been stopped as soon as possible. Rome provided the peaceful environment for the Savior of the world to accomplish what He had been sent on earth to do, make atonement for the sins of mankind, establish His Church and send the disciples to preach the gospel to the nations.

Rome's contributions to the world are difficult to measure even today. The remains of the great Coliseum in Rome are a reminder of the Roman love for entertainment. Chariot races, gladiator fights, and sports events entertained tens of thousands, all a predecessor to our own sports stadiums. Roman literature influenced Medieval, Renaissance, and modern cultures. Cicero, Virgil, and Seneca were just a few of the Roman philosophers and writers whose works are studied today. Many of the founding fathers studied and incorporated these philosophers' ideas into the American governing system.

Roman law served as the basis for many other nations throughout Europe and the Americas. Today, twenty-three of the twenty-six letters of the English alphabet have Roman or Latin origins. Long after the Roman Empire ceased to exist, Latin was used all over Europe. Most universities taught in Latin. The Roman Catholic Church used Latin in its church services. About one half of English words have Latin origins.

Rome, though often cruel and ruthless, provided stability to a part of the world where important events were set to transpire, including the birth, death, and Atonement of Jesus the Christ. Modern governments, entertainment, education, culture, sports, architecture, and languages feel the influence of Rome. Israel, especially Ephraim, was sifted among the Romans to be a blessing and motivating force to provide a political heritage for later generations and a period of peace for the work of the Savior. Rome's contribution and influence are still being studied, put to use, and absorbed by individuals and nations around the world today.

chapter twelve

PREACH THE GOSPEL

$\mathcal{S}tudies$ of the early Christian church often focus on apostasy, corruption, the sale of indulgences, and power-hungry church leaders. But to the common man in early Europe, Christianity offered many of the principles that Christ had intended when He preached His gospel to the Jews. The Greek and Roman forms of worship were satisfying for the wealthy, but for the poor, they offered little. Those religious practices held no hope of rewards in an afterlife to strengthen the common man throughout the oppressive conditions of this life. There was comfort in the Savior's message of love, equality, human dignity, and a hope of eternal life. Christianity opened a whole new relationship between man and God, a personal relationship rather than a distant one with idols. All members, regardless of their station in life, were equal in the sight of God. Salvation was available to all who would accept the teachings of Christ and obey His commandments. Unlike other religious practices of the time, Christianity placed emphasis on the individual human being rather than some nebulous group. Each member realized that his growth and development were part of God's plan. This philosophy was important in the development of strong personal character needed to lead in future events and movements that would affect Europe, America, and the world.

As a religion, Christianity welcomed the oppressed and cared for those less fortunate. It offered a new optimism, if not in this life then in the next. Christianity among the rank and file was much different than Christianity among the leading hierarchy.

> It [Christianity] offered itself without restriction to all individuals, classes, and nations; it was not limited to one people, like Judaism, nor to the freemen of one state, like the official cults of Greece or Rome. By making all men heirs of Christ's victory over death, Christianity announced the basic equality of man. . . . To the miserable, maimed, bereaved, disheartened, and humiliated it brought the new virtue of compassion, and an ennobling dignity; it gave them the inspiring figure, story and ethic of Christ; it brightened their lives with hope of the coming Kingdom, and of endless happiness beyond the grave.[1]

Paul was the first great Christian missionary; he traveled throughout the Roman Empire, spreading the gospel of Jesus Christ. The Greek language was used extensively in the Mediterranean area, making it possible for Paul to communicate with many in Greek. In Romans 1:16 he said: "For I am not ashamed of the gospel of Christ: for it is the power of God unto salvation to everyone that believeth; to the Jew first, and also to the Greek." The early missionaries took the gospel first to the Jews and then to the Greek-speaking Gentiles.

At that time there were many Jews living outside of Judea in the area surrounding the Mediterranean Sea. Richard Lloyd Anderson wrote concerning Paul's preaching:

> What made this method strategically important was the wide dispersion of the Jews, for there is hardly a place in Paul's travels where there was not a synagogue, whether in Asia Minor, Greece, or Italy. In fact, the first public proclamation of the gospel after the resurrection was heard by pilgrims from nearly a dozen locations in the Roman provinces and some non-Roman areas. This highlights the tremendous leverage of the Jewish synagogues—places to meet Jews and many Gentile seekers that associated with such synagogues, places where converts could be made almost immediately, in each new city. This result was possible only after several centuries of political and commercial displacement of the Jewish people. In the first Christian century, the time was ripe.[2]

The Jews were not the only tribe of Israel scattered throughout the Mediterranean area. Ephraim and other members of the House of Israel were there when Paul and other missionaries preached the gospel. They had been scattered not only for political and commercial reasons, but also because it was the will of the Lord to mix the blood of Israel with the nations. Paul usually began his preaching at the local synagogue. From there he branched out to Gentiles, showing an interest. To a Jew like Paul, anyone not of the tribe of Judah (converted to Judaism or geographically from Judea) was considered a Gentile. Those of Ephraim and other members of the house of Israel would have been among the early converts referred to as Gentiles by Paul and others.

Rome originally tolerated Christianity because they considered the new religion a branch of Judaism. They allowed the Jews a degree of religious freedom not offered to any of their other conquests. Once it became evident that the Christians were different, Rome perceived them as a threat. Roman officials suspected Christians of disloyalty and treason because their belief in Christ did not allow them to make sacrifices to the Roman gods. Emperor Nero used Christians as scapegoats for the burning of Rome in AD 64 and began a series of persecutions against them lasting for over two centuries. During those persecutions, many people gave their lives rather than deny their testimony of Jesus Christ—Romans crucified Christians by the hundreds.

Foxe's Book of Martyrs describes very vividly the suffering of early Christians at the hand of the Romans. Persecutions began with the Apostles and continued periodically for three centuries. Several Apostles met violent deaths. Many had opportunity to deny their religion and avoid punishment but refused. Hundreds and thousands of individual acts of courage and heroism were displayed by early Christians as persecutors went about their evil work. Despite their best efforts, the Romans found they could not stop the spread of Christianity. Christians, willing to die for their beliefs, impressed many nonbelievers. Those nonbelievers were soon seeking answers about what made the Christian religion so different from the pagan worship of Rome and Greece.

Persecutions finally ended in AD 313 when the Emperor Constantine issued the Edict of Milan granting religious freedom to all of Rome's citizens. Constantine was converted, and within the next century, Emperor Theodosius made Christianity the official religion of the Roman Empire. In less than four hundred years, Christianity rose from avoiding persecutions by hiding in the underground passages outside Rome to the official religion of the great Roman Empire.

In New Testament times the rapid growth of the church created administrative problems. During the early decades, the leadership came from the ranks of the congregations. As the number of converts grew and spread over the Roman Empire, a more permanent type of church official evolved—one who could devote all his time to religious work. The first of these full-time officials were priests and bishops. The priest officiated over local congregations in a town or area and was responsible to a bishop, who administered an area called a diocese that included several congregations. An archbishop was over a province which was made up of several dioceses. The bishop at Rome gradually rose to a preeminent position in the church hierarchy and was given the title of pope.

With the recognition of a permanent and secular leadership, the simplicity of the church gradually disappeared. The early church was plain, with a lay leadership. Prayer, reading the scriptures, preaching from the lay leaders, and singing of hymns constituted worship services. Feeling pressure to justify and secure their positions, the church's hierarchy placed the church and priests as essential intermediaries between the members and God. Once that doctrine was fully established, the church leaders became more powerful in terms of governing, interpreting doctrine, and even influencing political decisions in the countries of Europe. As Roman structure and power declined, bishops and archbishops took the place of the Roman prefects and governors. Step by step the Catholic Church replaced the governing counsels of the Roman Empire. The church ruling class became a powerful force in many of the countries of Europe. Kings were often forced to bow to the will of the pope.

The church required funds to support the hierarchy, build cathedrals and monasteries, and to support the missionary effort. Practices used for raising funds encouraged corruption among church officials. The clergy became the interpreters of church doctrine further solidifying their position within the church. An example of this was the Council of Nicaea, which explained the nature of God the Father and His Son, Jesus Christ.

Despite problems created by growth and the institution of a secular clergy, many individual priests were attempting to do their best to keep the light burning for the countless individual acts performed by monks and lay members and helped take the message of Christ to those wallowing in darkness.

Some members in the church believed the best way to live a Christian life was to withdraw from the society around them, go into seclusion, and serve God through self denial, prayer, and fasting. They were known as monks and nuns. At first they lived a life of solitude, but over time they formed monasteries for the monks and convents for nuns. There was little organization in the monasteries until the early 500s when St. Benedict drew up a set of standards called the Benedict Rule, which regulated the daily life of those who had dedicated their lives to serving the church. Monasteries were established all over Europe over a two-hundred-year period.

Orders of monks practicing a lifestyle of poverty, chastity, and obedience had time and opportunity for personal study. Monks were often the most learned scholars of their time. The monasteries served as intellectual centers throughout Europe. The dedicated monks preserved the knowledge of Greece and Rome in the Latin language, including the works of Aristotle, Plato, and others. They spent many hours copying various valuable manuscripts to pass on to future generations.

The Franciscan and Dominican orders of friars were established based on a philosophy different than the Benedictine monasteries. Instead of living in isolated monasteries, these friars moved among the people, administering to their needs, teaching in the schools, and preaching church doctrine. St. Francis of Assisi (1182–1226) was the most recognized of these friars. Their example and message provided moral and intellectual leadership when it was needed.

Jerome (340–420), born in Dalmatia (Croatia), studied in Rome and then spent time living as a hermit in Syria, where he learned Hebrew from a Jewish rabbi and became fluent in Greek, Hebrew, and Arabic. Assigned the task of producing a Latin translation of the Bible, he finished this work around 404. He spent fifteen years just working on the Old Testament. It was an incredible achievement, opening the scriptures to Latin speaking people within the Roman Empire. Later, others would translate the Bible into many other languages, giving members an opportunity to experience the scriptures for themselves for the first time. At age thrity-two, St. Augustine found new implications for life in Christianity, something he had been seeking for many years. He taught that man, through searching and effort, could find meaning and importance in his own life.

Christian missionaries took the gospel to Ireland in the 400s. St. Patrick, the best known of the Irish missionaries, began his mission in 432. He traveled around Ireland when it was a wild and dangerous country, preaching and baptizing new converts. He worked to establish schools and monasteries throughout the country. Missionaries from these schools expanded the missionary effort.

In 597 Pope Gregory sent missionaries to England, led by a monk named Augustine, who converted the Anglo Saxon royalty. Many among the British were converted, and by 664 Christianity was accepted all over England. Augustine became the first archbishop, and Canterbury became the center of the Catholic Church in England.

Christian missionaries began reaching farther into Europe. Around 500, Clovis, the king of the Franks, was baptized. The northern portion of Italy became Christian about 653. In the 700s, Christianity stretched into the Germanic provinces and on into Scandinavia.

A Franciscan named Roger Bacon (1214–1292) introduced the notion of experimental science. He studied the works of Aristotle and Hippocrates, which had been preserved by diligent monks who spent many hours copying those records for future generations.

The Catholic Church promoted art and learning among its members. Orders of monks preserved knowledge of the Greek and Roman civilizations for future generations. Missionary efforts spread Christianity throughout the continent of Europe. Christian doctrine emphasizing the importance and dignity of the individual played an essential role in man's search for freedom and liberty. The Christian way of life was an essential quality in the men and women who, in the seventeenth and eighteenth centuries, left their homes in Europe and sailed for America and an opportunity for freedom and a new start in life. They were the beneficiaries of the myriad sacrifices and acts of labor of those who went before them, introducing and solidifying the Christian religion among their ancestors.

Members of Israel, and particularity the tribe of Ephraim, would have been among those early stalwarts spreading light to those who sat in darkness and captivity preparing for future events in the path to the Restoration. "And he said, It is a light thing that thou shouldest be my servant to raise up the tribes of Jacob, and to restore the preserved of Israel: I will also give thee for a light to the Gentiles" (Isaiah 49:6).

Notes

1   Will Durant, *Caesar and Christ A History of Roman Civilization and of Christianity from their beginnings to AD 325,* (New York: Simon and Schuster, 1944), 602.
2   Richard Lloyd Anderson, "The Church and the Roman Empire," *Ensign,* Sept. 1975.

chapter thirteen

THE JEWISH DIASPORA

Moses, prior to his final blessing of the tribes of Israel, had warned the people of the consequences that would befall the tribes if they were disobedient to the commandments they were given on Mt. Sinai: "The Lord shall cause thee to be smitten before thine enemies: thou shalt go out one way against them, and flee seven ways before them: and shalt be removed into all the kingdoms of the earth" (Deuteronomy 28:25).

All the tribes of Israel had failed in one way or another to keep those commandments and were thus scattered over the earth. Thirty-two hundred years later, when the Angel Moroni visited a young Joseph Smith, Moroni "quoted the eleventh chapter of Isaiah, saying that it was about to be fulfilled" (JS—H 1:40). Moroni explained to Joseph what was about to happen to scattered Israel: "And it shall come to pass in that day, that the Lord shall set his hand again the second time to recover the remnant of his people . . . and shall assemble the outcasts of Israel, and gather together the dispersed of Judah from the four corners of the earth" (Isaiah 11:11–12).

The two tribes mentioned in this scripture are Ephraim and Judah. The phrase "shall assemble the outcasts of Israel" refers to all the tribes of Israel. At the time of the separation of the Northern and Southern kingdoms, Judah held the leadership role of the Southern Kingdom and Ephraim in the Northern Kingdom. They were adversaries with hard feelings toward each other. Those feelings hadn't healed before the ten tribes were carried away by Assyria. Isaiah tells us that when the Lord "sets his hand again the second time to recover the remnant of his people" in the latter days, the enmity between Ephraim and Judah will be healed. Ephraim, as the birthright tribe, will lead the physical and spiritual gathering of Israel (the ten tribes) to the land of the Americas, and Judah will lead the physical gathering of Judah to the land of Israel.

Judah, like Ephraim, was dispersed among the nations. Concerning Judah, Isaiah wrote: "and gather together the dispersed of Judah from the four corners of the earth." This dispersion is often referred to as the Jewish Diaspora (scattering or dispersion). Judah's inheritance in Canaan bordered the Mediterranean Sea. For commercial and political reasons, members of the tribe of Judah went out as entrepreneurs and ambassadors to other countries bordering the Mediterranean and established communities. Many Jews migrated to Egypt during that period. This initial dispersion would have begun not long after Israel entered the land of Canaan, at about 1450 BC.

In 597 BC, Babylon attacked Judea and carried many of the leading Jews to Babylon. When Judea failed to pay tribute to Babylon, King Nebuchadnezzar struck again, putting Jerusalem under siege for a year and a half. A few Jews managed to escape during the siege and flee to other countries. The conquest of Judea was completed in 587 BC with the capture and destruction of Jerusalem. Those who survived the siege were taken captive into Babylon. Few, if any, Jews remained in Jerusalem, but several Jewish communities existed or were established outside the land of Canaan.

The Jews were allowed to return to Jerusalem when Persia defeated the Babylonians. Cyrus, king of Persia, permitted the Jews to return to Jerusalem in 538 BC, but many were comfortable with their lifestyle in Persia and decided to stay. Those who did return to Jerusalem rebuilt the city and temple.

The lure of the Greek culture attracted many Jews to areas outside Jerusalem. A colony in Alexandria translated the Old Testament, including the Apocrypha to the Greek version known as the Septuagint. It was accepted by many of the Jews of the Diaspora who spoke Greek. In AD 70 the Romans sacked Jerusalem, annexed Judea as a Roman province, again destroyed the city and the temple, and systematically forced the Jews to leave Palestine. The Jews were a minority in their own land. From that point, the history of the Jews was written from locations around the world where they were driven or migrated.

The tribe of Judah was different from that of the tribe of Ephraim. Judah was scattered—but not necessarily sifted among the nations. Whether they left through voluntarily migration or because they were driven out of Jerusalem, Jews tended to stick together in communities.

At first they married amongst themselves and had little interaction with their Gentile neighbors. The synagogue became the center of worship and community identity. This organization promoted good record keeping which was passed down from one generation to the next. Persecutions from Christians and Muslims only strengthened their unification. The Talmud was a major source of strength and identity.

Israel's blood ran through Jewish veins. It was a blood that loved liberty. They sought it wherever they were scattered and fought to maintain their right to be left alone and to worship as they pleased. "No other people in history fought so tenaciously for liberty as the Jews, nor any people against such odds. . . . the struggle of the Jews to regain their freedom has often decimated them, but has never broken their spirit or their hope."[1]

Their blinding hope was to someday return to their birthright country, Israel. "No other people has ever known so long an exile, or so hard a fate. Shut out from the Holy City, the Jews were compelled to surrender it first to paganism, then to Christianity. Scattered into every province and beyond, condemned to poverty and humiliation, unbefriended even by philosophers and saints, they retired from public affairs into private study and worship, passionately preserving the words of their scholars, and preparing to write them down at last in the Talmuds of Babylonia and Palestine."[2]

The Jewish system of record keeping has given the world a better knowledge of Judah's scattering than of any of the other tribes of Israel. Neither Ephraim nor the rest of scattered Israel had the unifying effects of the Talmud or local synagogues. Persecutions were not a motivating factor to unite or force them to stay among themselves as with the Jews. No known records were kept and passed from generation to generation.

The Jewish Diaspora illustrates that the Jews, even for a people who usually stayed to themselves, were scattered over many nations and continents. With that in mind, consider for a moment the effects of the scattering of the tribe of Ephraim and others of Israel who were sifted among the nations for over two millennia. The blood of Ephraim, over those many centuries, would have been flowing in the veins of hundreds of thousands, even millions of people throughout the world.

Notes

1 Durant, *Caesar and Christ,* 542.
2 Ibid., 549.

chapter fourteen

THE DARK AGES

For behold, the darkness shall cover the earth, and gross darkness the people" (Isaiah 60:2). As the Roman Empire declined, so did a civilized Europe. When the Roman Legions and the governing counsels vacated Western Europe, it left a large void. Local populations were not prepared to maintain the standards set by Rome. Lacking leadership, Western Europe took several steps backward. From the fifth to the eighth centuries, the period known as the Dark Ages, Europe was covered with a blanket of darkness. Stagnation, lack of centralized control, invasions from outside powers, war among tribes, and ignorance was the norm. Without the guidance of Apostles and prophets, the Christian church changed the doctrine and fell away from the original teachings and organization. Europe was isolated from the more advanced civilizations in the Middle East, China, and India. It was sparsely populated, generally undeveloped, and had no written law to govern. People lived in small communities with little or no contact with each other or the outside world. The roads built by the Romans were neglected, limiting travel to foot or horseback. Not many Europeans traveled more than a few miles from their homes in their entire lives.

But Europe was not destined to remain stagnant. The continent was designed to prepare the people who would establish a free country on a promised land an ocean away. Gradually, Europeans would pull themselves out of their vegetative state and set a slow but steady course toward progression.

Europeans were sitting on a continent, with an untapped potential. When the world was created, the Lord prepared Europe for His purposes. Forests, rich soils, mineral resources, and good harbors fed by wide rivers supported the expanding population and ever-changing culture.

Rome, before it fell, was pressured by Germanic tribes from the north and Muslims from the south. Roman legions retreated or were destroyed when the Germanic tribes attacked from the north. The mixing of the Germanic tribes and Greco-Roman people in the south produced a rather unique culture in Western Europe. The waves of migrating Germanic tribes sweeping across Europe further sifted Ephraim, along with other members of the tribes of Israel, among all European peoples.

What emerged from the vacuum left by Rome was a group of small unorganized kingdoms. The Franks surfaced as the strongest kingdom controlling the area that is now France and Germany. Clovis, the king, was converted to Christianity, making him the only Christian ruler among the Germanic tribes. He later had his whole army baptized. His conversion linked the Franks to the pope and Rome.

Charlemagne, who ruled the Franks from 768 to 814, expanded the empire and brought Christianity to the pagan people living in his kingdom. He spread Christianity into new areas of Europe while preventing invasions from foreign powers. His administration had a great effect on producing the unique European civilization.

The ninth and tenth centuries saw a new wave of invasions rock Europe, this time from the Scandinavian people in the north. The Vikings swept through parts of Europe, destroying much of what was in their path. Monasteries, abbeys, and small villages were often raided and burned to the ground. The Vikings eventually converted and played an important role in shaping the future of Europe. Viking invasions led to further fragmentation of the countries on the continent, while in England those invasions forced the people to unite if they were to have any chance of holding off these foreign invaders. The Viking migrations and invasions further mixed Israel among the European countries.

Fragmentation on the continent led to the breakup of the central government left from Charlemagne's rule, leaving the populace with little security or protection. The result was the formation of feudalism, a loosely organized system where the king and powerful Lord's divided up their land holdings to lesser lords. The grant of land ranged from a few acres to hundreds of square miles. Included with the grant would be the buildings, towns, and peasants working the land. The lesser lords promised to care for the land, give loyalty and service to the higher lord, and in return would receive protection from outside forces. The higher lords would form temporary armies from the serfs living on the sub-let land parcels and use the more permanent armies of knights to protect their holdings.

Large-land-holding nobles became very powerful, often rivaling the power of kings. While lords lived in castles, peasants lived in the villages and worked several days a week for the lord. With what remaining time they had, they would cultivate the small plot of land allotted to them. For the privilege of having a small plot, the peasants were committed to a lifetime of work and service. They were not slaves in the sense that they could be bought and sold, but they enjoyed little in the way of freedom or comfort. Life was hard, work hours were long, and famines, war, and disease were a constant threat.

People under this system lost much of their individual distinctiveness. They identified more with a collective group such as their village or church. Little emphasis was placed on personal growth. Too much individualism was a threat to both the village and church and was discouraged. It was a major reason for the stagnation plaguing Europe.

By about 800, Europe began an economic recovery. New inventions increased production and gave the peasant farmers and lesser lords a little extra money to spend. Trade began to revive throughout Europe. Centers for trade developed into cities. The cities were filthy, smelly, noisy, crowded places to live, with no sanitation and narrow streets, but they offered the peasants and traders an escape from the feudal system gripping Europe. They could get away from the manors and lords and enjoy more freedoms.

In 1050, while other civilizations around the world were thriving, Europe was just beginning to emerge from the Dark Ages and isolation. The Muslims to the south had dealt a devastating blow to European Christianity by capturing Palestine and had attacked Christian groups making pilgrimages to the Holy Land. The Crusades were organized to win back the Holy Land. Armies of knights marched south across Europe to fight the infidel that had taken Palestine. The First Crusade (1096–1099) almost achieved its goal. Several subsequent Crusades fell far short. Their marches promoted an exchange of culture among Europeans and brought new ideas from the Muslim-controlled areas in Asia Minor. Nobles and lords often volunteered their services to the Crusades and left Europe. Their departure left a power gap that was often filled by kings. Monarchies were reinvigorated and strengthened during this time.

As trade increased, so did manufacturing, banking, insurance, profits, and a market economy. More new towns sprang up all over Europe. More and more people gained new freedoms. Residents in the towns began to demand their own forms of government and won new rights—sometimes peacefully but often through violence. They broke ties with the feudal manors and enjoyed new freedoms both politically and economically.

The rise of the towns developed a new class of people—more self-assured, more independent, and more informed. They were a people hoping for stability in their lives and favored kings over the land-holding nobles. Kings were willing to consult with the common people in order to win their favor, giving them a new power.

With the decline of feudalism, national states began to form. Kings took opportunities to organize their holdings into nations, developing systems to tax the people, establish standing armies, and organize judicial systems and government bureaucracies. Most important, the kings won loyalty from their subjects, which instilled a feeling of patriotism never before felt in Europe. Gradually the nations of Europe emerged from the feudal system. England, France, Spain, the Netherlands, Portugal, Germany, and others formed the nucleus of Western Europe.

As nations developed, conflict between the pope and the monarchs of the various countries arose. The power to make appointments to both church and government positions caused constant conflicts between popes and kings. See-saw struggles raged all over Europe. Gradually, over the centuries, the impact of the pope declined as influence of national heads of state increased.

The revival of the economy brought other changes including new universities, monasteries, and abbeys. More books were available to enhance learning among those not attending universities. By the fourteenth and fifteenth centuries, the economy leveled off. Wars, famine, and disease took a constant and devastating toll. The Black Death struck Europe around 1350. It reoccurred over the next two centuries, wiping out one-third to one-half of the population. The towns and cities were usually hit the hardest. The plague showed no favor to the nobility, clergy, or middle class. Monasteries and universities felt the blow of the Black Death. There were fewer people to maintain and attend them. The manors had fewer laborers and tenants to manage the farms. The lords didn't have enough laborers to maintain their farms and eventually resorted to renting out their lands instead of holding them in a feudal state. The change negated the need for so many serfs and peasants. It was the beginning of the end of the feudal system. More and more people began to enjoy a small taste of freedom.

Emerging monarchies often faced a struggle for power with the nobility in their respective nations. While establishing a strong national monarchy, the English people also managed to secure curbs and controls on their kings and queens. In 1356, the German nobility won an important victory in controlling the power of the monarch. In Spain, when Ferdinand and Isabella came to power, just the opposite happened. They consolidated the power in the crown and believed the church should be subordinate to the royal government. To prove their point, they established a Court of Inquisition to intimidate their subjects, confiscated property belonging to Jews and Muslims, and cajoled Christians to accept the orthodox Christian philosophy. Jews fled the country by the tens of thousands. Spain became the strongest power in Europe in the sixteenth century, often using a heavy hand to control its colonies in America and around the world.

France and England were embroiled in a conflict lasting from 1337 to 1453 known as the Hundred Years' War. England won initial victories and captured some French territories. The war stirred a renewed nationalism among the French people. Patriotism was revived by a young peasant girl—Joan of Arc. She persuaded the king to let her lead the army to relieve the besieged city of Orleans. She inspired the French soldiers to a stunning victory over the English and rescued Orleans. She was allowed to continue the fight and was captured by the British. They accused her of witchcraft and had her burned at the stake. Her martyrdom proved a turning point in the war. France went on to win back most of the territories it had lost to England. It was important for future developments that France remained a strong, independent nation. The French would play an important role in the American Revolution.

Many nations were founded during this period as citizens began to show preference for country over prior feudal loyalties. The crack in the feudal system became larger as the decades passed. Most important, freedom and liberty were taking small steps forward for the people of Europe.

The spirit of Ephraim was working among the nations of Europe.

All that occured during this period fulfilled Nebuchadnezzar's dream—the crumbling of the image with legs of iron that represented the Roman Empire. The pieces from the fragmentation were the emerging nations of Europe. The disintegration of Rome and emergence of the nations were the most important part of Nebuchadnezzar's dream (see Daniel chapter 2). The complete crumbling of the statue was the initiation of the forces and actions that would prepare the people of Europe for the discovery and colonization of America. Important forces were about to be unleashed that would change the course of history.

The scripture quoted at the beginning of this chapter was from Isaiah: "For behold, the darkness shall cover the earth, and gross darkness the people." Isaiah then goes on to say: "But the Lord shall arise upon thee, and his glory shall be seen upon thee. And the Gentiles shall come to thy light, and kings to the brightness of thy rising" (Isaiah 60:2–3). The Gentiles and kings of Europe were coming to the light in preparation for the latter days. Change would occur slowly among monarchies. It was a light and understanding that evolved over many decades preparing minds for much greater events and changes to follow. And as Jacob informed Joseph, the "fruit of [his] loins" would "be a light unto my people, to deliver them in the days of their captivity" (JST Genesis 48:9, 11). Though not understanding the purpose at the time, Ephraim was among the people of Europe assisting in their efforts to pursue knowledge, strive for freedom, seek change, promote progress, and constantly follow the trail that would bring about the Lord's purposes and fulfill their calling as the birthright tribe of Israel.

chapter fifteen

THE RENAISSANCE

Europeans began focusing on the future instead of wallowing in the past. There were still many mountains to climb, obstacles to overcome, discoveries to be made, and minds to prepare before the calling they received from Moses could be accomplished. Europe was entering a critical period in the preparation of the world for the events the Lord had planned. The Renaissance (1300–1600) was a major leap in grooming the people of Europe. It was a revival in learning, artistic expression, creative literature, scientific discovery, and human development. The Renaissance transformed Europe from a medieval society to the modern world.

Renaissance means rebirth—and it was indeed a cultural and intellectual rebirth that revived the classical works of the Greeks and Romans. Those works were debated, studied, and copied over and over to acquaint Europeans with the celebrated philosophers of the past. The rebirth influenced painting, sculpture, architecture, ideals, intellectual thought, and how man viewed himself in the world in which he lived. It started in Florence, Italy, and was probably instigated by the interplay of the Crusades and a revival in ancient Greco-Roman culture. Florence was full of energy, abounding with gifted artists, scholars, architects, and scientists.

Similar appearances of talented men occurred in Athens as Greece entered its Golden Age and on the east coast of the United States at the beginning of the American Revolution—many of which were descendants of Ephraim. It is likely that descendents of Ephraim represented at the two other major jump starts in Western Civilization. Athens was the launching site for the great Greco-Roman civilizations, and Florence initiated the Renaissance. Both were important predecessors to the American Revolution. Both laid founding ideologies for government and the worth of individual achievement so essential to the American cause. All three of these gatherings of talented men were major steps in the progress of mankind and preparation for the Restoration of the gospel.

The Renaissance stressed the importance of man's life on earth. Previously, people focused on life after death and heavenly rewards. Renaissance thinkers and scholars were known as humanists. They expressed a confidence and belief in the worth of the individual and his ability to think and act for himself. Church and medieval customs were constantly scrutinized and questioned. Humanists were the forefathers of the Reformation and our modern world. It worked to free men from the superstitions and controls of the past, which for so long had held them back. The Renaissance spawned a whole new sense of artistic freedom. Artists, writers, and philosophers pioneered new paths, slowly moving through the unknown.

> The same century that saw the discovery of America saw the rediscovery of Greece and Rome; and the literary and philosophical transformation had far profounder results for the human spirit than the circumnavigation and exploration of the globe. For it was the humanists, not the navigators, who liberated man from dogma, taught him to love life rather than brood about death, and made the European mind free.[1]

The Italian Renaissance produced some writers of superb talent and ingenuity. Niccolo Machiavelli wrote his well-known work *The Prince*, which describes how to be a ruler. He promoted the doctrine that a ruler, in order to be successful, could and should use whatever means necessary to achieve his objectives. He wrote: "From this arises the following question: whether it is better to be loved than feared, or the reverse. The answer is that one would like to be both the one and the other; but because it is difficult to combine them, it is far better to be feared than loved if you cannot be both."[2] Many a monarch in Europe applied Machiavelli's doctrine to rule their nations.

Renaissance art took a decided shift to a more realistic representation of humans and landscapes. The artists used perspective and shading to add dimension and studied human anatomy in detail to be able to portray correct proportions. Florence produced three master artists whose genius is admired all over the world—Leonardo da Vinci, Michelangelo, and Raphael.

Leonardo da Vinci, born in 1452, was a genesis of modern thinking; most famous for his art, his work also extended to music, architecture, engineering, botany, and optics. His papers contained sketches of flying machines and submarines centuries before any were put to use.

Michelangelo was another multi-talented artist. He was a sculptor, architect, engineer, and poet. As an architect, he designed the dome for St. Peter's Cathedral in Rome. The dome was used as model for many other buildings including the United States Capitol in Washington DC.

Raphael arrived in Florence when Leonardo da Vinci and Michelangelo were in their prime. He learned from both masters. While in Florence, he executed a series of Madonnas distinguishing his own artistic creativity. Raphael spent his last twelve years in Rome where his works can be found in the Sistine Chapel even today.

From Italy, the Renaissance spread to northern Europe. The northern humanists were different from their Italian neighbors. The Italians wrote and spoke primarily to the upper class. Northern humanists addressed a much broader range of people and issues. They were critical of existing religious, social, political, and economic situations and constantly strived to reform social problems. They were especially critical of the church and of the loss of the simplicity of early Christianity. The church was a favorite target for reform issues.

Dutch humanist Erasmus was the most influential of the northern humanists. He wrote *The Price of Folly,* a critique of the evils existing in society. He took a keen interest in the scriptures, which led him to produce a new and more accurate edition of the Bible. His Greek edition of the New Testament was widely read and used by Martin Luther. Thomas More, an English humanist, wrote *Utopia*, the first book since Plato's *Republic* that made an attempt to describe the ideal society. He was critical of English capitalism, espousing a socialistic society where all things were held in common. King Henry VIII had him executed for treason.

In Spain, Miguel de Cervantes (1547–1616) wrote a satire entitled *Don Quixote de la Mancha* about a medieval knight who sets out on an adventure to right the evil he sees around him. Knights were a thing of the past by the time Cervantes wrote his satire, but it brought back some of the ideals Europe found in the mysticism of the knights. Don Quixote, the "knight of the woeful countenance," and his sidekick, Sancho, set about the countryside of Spain fighting windmills, mistaking inns for castles, and defending a lady's honor. The satire exposed the outdated medieval society but also expressed ideals that revitalized the idealist.

The apex of the northern Renaissance was reached in England by the playwright William Shakespeare (1564–1616). He was supreme among Renaissance writers and completed thirty-seven plays that are still studied in schools and performed thousands of times each year. History, comedy, tragedy, and romance were depicted in rich, flowing, poetic style. He created remarkable characters, intriguing stories, and wonderful lines that have influenced generation after generation.

John Adams reportedly carried *Don Quixote* in his saddlebags as he traveled the circuit as a new lawyer in Massachusetts. Adams, Jefferson, and many other founding fathers enjoyed reading Cervantes and Shakespeare. It was often a retreat for them when the business of winning independence and establishing a government weighed heavily upon their shoulders.

In 1454, Johann Gutenberg printed the first edition of the Bible using movable type. Development of movable type made the production of books faster, easier, and less costly. Thousands of books were printed and made available to a population who had been without for centuries. Prior to that time, books had to be copied by hand. Design work and illustrations were also done by hand, making books expensive and time-consuming to produce. Only the elite had access to explore the treasures contained in books. Once movable type was developed, a whole new world of reading was opened to Europeans. The Bible and religious materials composed much of the new printed materials, which gave people a personal access to the word of God. Previously, it was only obtainable through priests. There was an immediate demand for a broader base of reading, including travel books, almanacs, poetry, romances, medicine, science, and a variety of other topics. Europeans were exposed to new, innovative ideas. More of the population became literate. The better-educated populace began questioning the world around them, particularity the religious practices of the day.

The Renaissance was a rebirth for Europe, lifting it out of the Dark Ages. It generated new attitudes about learning and culture. With the new attitudes came an attention to individual learning and achievement and a renewed spirit of adventure, resulting in new developments in every subject. The Renaissance forced man to focus more on worldly things, but it also helped him understand his individual worth and potential. The individual was a free agent who could think, act, and reason for himself. Men became skeptical about religion and dissatisfied with the corruption in the church.

The Renaissance forged great advancements in culture and science. It was also a very important preparation period for the people of Europe. They gained a new sense of self-worth and were exposed to the scriptures and reading. The Renaissance paved the way for the next great movement that would continue to prepare Europeans for the destiny that lay before them.

Notes

1   Will Durant, *The Renaissance,* (New York: Simon and Schuster, 1953), 86.
2   Niccolo Machiavelli, *The Prince*, translated by George Bull, (Baltimore: Penguin Books, 1961), 96.

chapter sixteen

THE REFORMATION

Martin Luther's posting of the 95 Theses on the door of the Castle Church in Wittenberg, Germany, is usually considered the beginning of the Reformation. However, the practices of the Roman Catholic Church were being questioned for over a century before Luther challenged the church. Northern humanists had commented on how far the church had strayed from the teachings and mission of Jesus. They claimed the church leaders lacked moral leadership and seemed to be more concerned about making money for the church than the spiritual welfare of the members. Many priests were engaging in questionable practices. The clergy actually discouraged reading of the scriptures by members because it threatened their position in the church.

The concerns of those humanists were much like the reformers who followed a century later. Their desires were to return to the simple, early Christian church. They championed personal faith and spirituality.

As early as the 1300s, theologians in England and Bohemia were advocating many of the same principles set forth by Luther in 1517. John Wycliffe (1320–1384), a professor and theologian at Oxford University, believed that the Bible should have importance in the lives of the church members and that they should have personal access to God without the use of a priest acting as intermediary. He challenged the pope's right to rule and punish those who questioned papal authority. He even went so far as to dispute the validity of the sacrament in the church.

John Huss (1370–1415) agreed with many of Wycliffe's opinions. He believed that the scriptures should be the authority on church matters rather than decrees from the clergy, that reforms were needed to correct the corruption existing in the clergy, that the communion of bread and water was not the actual flesh and blood of Christ, and that Christians should have the Bible in their own language. The increased attention that the protesters were receiving was a threat to the Catholic clergy. Huss eventually became a martyr, but his doctrine continued to spread throughout Bohemia and Moravia.

Jerome (1370–1416) and others throughout England, Scotland, and the European continent received similar treatment for expressing convictions that differed from the Roman Catholic doctrine. Many were imprisoned prior to sentencing and were tortured for weeks or even months before receiving a final sentence. All were devoted to the cause of reforming existing conditions in a church which they determined was not in line with the scriptures or the original church established by Christ.

The scriptures were jealously guarded by the clergy. Latin was the language of the Bible used in Catholic Church worship services. To protect their standing as priests, the church decreed that they alone would be interpreters of the scared word. Only the learned could read and understand Latin, which meant that even many priests that lacked training could not read the vulgate version of the Bible.

One objective of the Reformation was to make the scriptures available to the lay members. To accomplish that, four things had to happen: (1) the scriptures had to translated from Latin to the native tongues, (2) translations had to be in a readable language for the common people, (3) translations had to be printed, and (4) translations had to be sold and distributed to the lay members. The Catholic hierarchy fought the distribution of the scriptures at all four levels.

William Tyndale (1494–1536) dedicated his life to translating the Bible into English and making it available for the people of England to read. His understanding of Latin, Greek, and Hebrew were crucial in translating existing scriptures into English. The clergy in England instigated laws forbidding anyone to translate scriptures into English without approval of a bishop's council. Throughout Europe, the New Testament was being translated into several different languages. But in England, Luther's works were burned in public demonstrations. Once he completed translating the New Testament, Tyndale attempted to get it published. Opposition was so great that he had to leave England and go underground in Germany, where the reforming spirit was alive and strong.

He went to Wittenberg, a Protestant stronghold in Germany, to continue his work. Leaving England didn't ensure his safety. Cardinal Wolsey sent agents from England to search him out, forcing Tyndale to keep a constant watch. In 1526, he published his first version of the New Testament. Copies had to be smuggled into England. Many of the smuggled books were confiscated and burned. Both sides used spies, bribes, and treachery to accomplish their ends. Englishmen caught smuggling or selling the translated New Testament were arrested, imprisoned, and, in some cases, burned at the stake. Tyndale worked to translate the Old Testament but was eventually discovered, arrested, and executed. Several of his associates met similar fates.

Tyndale's voice was silenced, but his translations lived on. The New Testament and what he finished of the Old Testament were made available to the English people and used during the translation of the King James Version of the Bible.

In 1517, Martin Luther (1483–1546) wrote his 95 Theses and requested the opportunity to debate certain issues within the Catholic Church. Luther's protests were primarily motivated by the church's policy to raise money for the construction of St. Peter's Cathedral in Rome. A monk named John Tetzel had been commissioned by the pope to sell indulgences in Europe as a money-raising project. He was in Germany at the time, offering indulgences and promoting the pope. Indulgences sanctioned the pope's authority to forgive sins while excusing people from the obligation of being good. Those with money could supposedly buy their way to salvation. Many took exception to his methods, among them was Martin Luther. His response was the 95 Theses, which questioned the practice of indulgences.

Luther's theses were translated from Latin to German and published throughout Germany. He wrote and preached about reforming the church. As with most of the reformers, he initially had no intention of rebelling against the church. His goal was to reform the church from within. Time and circumstances would prove that option unworkable—thus the Protestant Reformation had its beginning.

Luther's message appealed to those who wanted to return to the simpler and original Christian Church. Luther later translated the New Testament into German. As his ideas spread, the Catholic clergy became alarmed and levied charges of heresy against Luther. He was excommunicated by the pope, and King Charles declared him an outlaw, making it a crime for anyone to give him shelter or aid. Luther continued his work and teaching. He argued that the Bible should be the source of religious truth rather than the clergy, that salvation came through faith alone not good deeds, that the pope had no authority, the priests and pope had no special powers and all Christians had an equal access to God. He later organized the Lutheran church, breaking away from the church in Rome.

Luther's ideas found fertile ground in Germany and Scandinavia. Two other reformers, Ulrich Zwingli and John Calvin, challenged the authority of the Catholic Church. They stressed the importance of the Bible but rejected the ritualism of Catholicism. Calvin believed that salvation was gained through faith and the Bible was the true source of religious truth. He added the concept of predestination, the philosophy that God had already determined who would receive salvation before they were born. He stressed discipline, hard work, morality, and honesty. Calvin's ideas soon spread throughout Germany, France, the Netherlands, England, and Scotland, setting off new waves of protest across Europe. The Calvinist doctrine provided the basis for other Protestant churches, including Presbyterianism, Puritanism, and Congregationalism. In Scotland, John Knox, a Calvinist follower, led a religious revolt, overthrowing the Catholic queen and establishing the Scottish Presbyterian Church.

Kings, in the continental countries of Europe, generally supported the Catholic Church. In England, the king led the revolt against the church. The work of Wycliffe and others laid the foundation, but the actual act of revolt was the result of King Henry VIII's desire to divorce his wife and marry another who could give him a male heir to the throne. When the pope refused his request for divorce, Henry was furious. He appointed his own archbishop over England who in turn granted the king his desire for a divorce. He confiscated Catholic Church properties and organized the Anglican Church, patterned much like the Catholic Church but free of papal authority. The Church of England maintained much of the Catholic ceremony and ritual but placed the English monarch as the head of the Anglican Church. The church did incorporate some Protestant doctrine and made English the language used in church sermons and rituals rather than Latin.

Other reformers sprung up in various parts of Europe. One group, called the Anabaptists, rejected the practice of infant baptism and baptized adults by immersion after they had demonstrated that they had converted and exhibited the necessary faith.

In England, George Fox founded a unique religion known as the Religious Society of Friends, or the Quakers. Their lifestyle was based on simplicity, their clergy were not professional, and they believed in spiritual revelation. They opposed war, the taking of oaths, and titles of nobility.

Another reformer, who appeared in a later period, was John Wesley (1703–91), the Anglican clergyman who founded Methodism. He was trained at Oxford, where he began his methodical approach to religion. He studied the scriptures and lived a life of devotion to God. Excluded from preaching in the chapels of the Church of England, Wesley soon discovered that he didn't need a building but could preach in the open air. He rode throughout Britain on horseback, preaching tens of thousands of sermons and organizing Methodist Societies. He believed personal salvation came by faith in God. Lacking a trained ministry, Wesley inaugurated a lay ministry to administer to the societies spread throughout England. He later visited America and ordained Dr. Thomas Coke to be a superintendent in the New World.

As the Protestant Reformation swept across Europe, the Catholic Church was feeling pressure to make changes and win back the trust of its members. The Council of Trent was called in 1545 and continued to occasionally meet for almost twenty years. The council enacted programs to end corruption and abuses among the clergy and officers of the church. It established schools to better educate the clergy, especially to deal with the challenges of Protestantism. Pope Paul used the Inquisition to stem and root out heresy among the clergy. Spying, torture, and execution were often used to eliminate heretics and bring the clergy back into line. New religious orders like the Jesuits were used to combat the onslaught of Protestantism. The reform did much to eliminate corruption. The clergy that followed were better prepared and much more charitable toward their members. The Catholic Church made many positive strides within the church.

The Reformation wouldn't have been possible without sacrifice. Many suffered persecutions and gave their lives for the cause. Those advocating reform were often persecuted and executed. As John Foxe points out in *Foxe's Book of Martyrs*, many converts to Protestantism were harassed, tortured, murdered, and slaughtered in mass killings. The numbers were in the hundreds, thousands, and even hundreds of thousands, depending on the location in Europe. Many reformers paid the ultimate price for their religious convictions. Slowly Europeans developed a degree of religious toleration. That change of attitude didn't come overnight. In some countries, it took decades to allow even a semblance of tolerance.

The Reformation played a monumental role in the colonization of the United States and the American Revolution. Most of the American colonists were Protestant and had acquired different attitudes than their ancestors. The people moving to the American colonies had more tolerance and acceptance of people with differing political and religious views. They could work beside them, meet with them in public meetings, accept their differences, and get along socially. The tolerance was not perfect by any means; but it existed in a greater degree than in any other part of the world. Americans learned that to associate with one another—they would have to agree to disagree about some things. It was an attitude that was generations ahead of its time for most of the world.

The division between Protestants and Catholics in Europe was often a major motivator for different groups to immigrate to America. Protestants fled from Catholics in some areas, and Catholics fled from Protestants in others. Those fleeing for religious purposes made a major contribution to the population growth of the colonies. In America, they found space to practice their religion in peace.

The Reformation was principally a northern European movement, while southern Europe remained Catholic. The vast majority of the immigrants to America were from northern Europe and were Protestant; both were important factors in the development of the colonies. The sheer diversity of Protestant churches added a dimension to America not found elsewhere. No one church dominated the religious or political life. There was no monolithic head of church controlling minds and politics. If the British colonies had been dominated by the Catholic Church, as was South and Central America, the prospects of establishing a government free of outside influences from European church leaders would have been very difficult, if not impossible. The Reformation made substantial gains in preparing a people to fulfill the purposes of the Lord.

Zechariah describes how Judah and Joseph (Ephraim and Manasseh) would be sown among the people in far countries. The countries of Europe were among those far countries. He then prophesied: "And they of Ephraim shall be like a mighty man. . . . And I will sow them among the people: and they shall remember me in far countries; and they shall live with their children, and turn again" (Zechariah 10:7–9).

Ephraim was like a "mighty man" among the reforming elements in Europe. The blood of Israel continued to lead events and people step by step, generation by generation, to fulfill the calling given by the ancient prophets.

THE ENLIGHTENMENT

Preparation of the people of Europe was aided by an intellectual movement known as the Enlightenment, beginning around 1700. It was in part a result of the Scientific Revolution, emphasizing human reasoning as the method to solve the long-standing problems of ignorance, intolerance, tyranny, and superstition. Enlightenment thinkers questioned traditional beliefs. Their targets were religion, monarchs who believed they had a divine right to rule the people, and the aristocracy who dominated European society. The Enlightenment promoted the rise of natural religion or belief that God is known only through natural or scientific observation. They believed that God exists and that He created the world, but that the world is then governed by natural laws that God cannot break. They thought that men should attempt to be upright, decent, and good to others. Many rejected the divinity of Christ, the Atonement, and the Resurrection.

As the Enlightenment poured across Europe, traditional customs and beliefs were scrutinized. Enlightened thinkers found flaws in Christian theology, a monarch's claim of a divine right to rule, and the existing class systems and stratification of society. They couldn't justify through reason or the scientific method why any of these things existed. Tolerance and freedom were at the core of the Enlightenment. The attacks against religion were to weaken the psychological hold it had over so many people.

The Enlightenment thinkers would have been more direct in their attacks against monarchies, but it would have meant their demise.

Enlightenment emphasis on tolerance, freedom, and the individual accomplishment were important to the preparation of the people of Europe and America. Their claim that the individual had the right and ability to make a difference in the world was a carryover from the Renaissance and Reformation. The Enlightenment placed much greater emphasis on individual achievement, an idea that carried through to modern times.

Enlightenment thinkers employed science and reason to better understand society and suggest improvements. John Locke, Thomas Hobbes, Montesquieu, Voltaire, Rousseau, and Adam Smith promoted new ideas about how to govern, man's natural rights, the meaning of liberty, and how the economy should function. Individually they produced ideas that would affect European society and spark revolutionary flames in America. In the wake of the English Civil War, two English thinkers proposed two vastly different set of ideas that would become key to the Enlightenment.

Thomas Hobbes (1588–1679), England

Hobbes developed a political philosophy based on the view that the people first lived individually and were naturally selfish, greedy, and cruel and that to escape anarchy and a brutal life in such a situation they entered a "social contract" in which they agreed to give up their state of nature for an organized society. To maintain any kind of order in such a situation, a strong government was needed. His idea of strong government was an absolute monarchy with power to keep order and force compliance.

John Locke (1632–1704), England

Like Hobbes, Locke believed that people first lived individually and then entered a social contract. He differed from Hobbes in that he believed people were basically good, moral, and reasonable. They had certain "natural rights" that belonged to them at birth. These inherit rights were the right to live, to enjoy liberty, and own property. Those who ruled had an obligation to protect and preserve those rights. The best kind of government was one that was limited in its powers and acceptable to the people it governed.

A government that violated any of those natural rights broke the unwritten social contract, giving the people the right to overthrow the government and replace it with one which would preserve their natural rights.

Less than a century later, Locke's political philosophy was read and quoted up and down the east coast of the British North America as the colonists struggled with the decision to revolt against a government they felt was violating their natural rights.

Montesquieu (1689–1755), France

In 1748 Montesquieu published *The Spirit of the Laws,* which examined governments throughout history. He advanced the idea of separation of powers among the three branches of government, each being able to check the other two as a way to ensure liberty in a nation. His work had a great influence on later political thought and laid the foundation for modern democracies.

Voltaire (1694–1778), France

Voltaire was a writer, historian, and philosopher. He was a man of wit and used it to expose abuses and corruption among governmental officials. He was the most powerful propagandist of the eighteenth century. He advocated freedom of thought, speech, and conscience; equality in society; and the dignity of man. He was quick to criticize the slave trade, religious prejudice, the French government, and the Catholic Church. For his efforts, he was imprisoned and exiled.

Rousseau (1712–78), France

Rousseau, a controversial and difficult man, rebelled against many of the dominate values of the time. He believed that man in his natural state was basically good but was corrupted by the evil in society, particularly the unequal distribution of the world's goods. He favored feelings and emotion rather than reason and proposed a method of education where the pupil would be helped to grow and develop freely according to his own nature. In 1762 he published his philosophy about government and society in *The Social Contract.* It was a theory of government based on a contract where free individuals of their own accord entrusted a part of their freedom to the government. He believed that society placed too many controls on the individual. Controls were necessary but should be kept to a minimum. Controls that were necessary could only be established by governments that had been freely elected. His ideas played an important role in the development of democracy.

Adam Smith (1723–90), England

Smith championed free trade and a laissez-faire philosophy as the most efficient way to promote economic growth and produce wealth. He wrote the *Wealth of Nations,* arguing that the free market should regulate business activity. When demands for market goods were created, the market would meet those demands without the aid or interference of government. Government's sole purpose was to protect society, see that justice was administered, and provide the public services society required. His ideas spread across Europe as the Industrial Revolution took hold and would be adopted by other societies around the world as the most efficient way to stabilize and operate an economy.

The political ideas proposed by Locke, Montesquieu, Voltaire, and Rousseau occurred during an eighty-year period just prior to the American Revolution. Many of their ideas were incorporated into the American political thought and dynamics. Locke influenced some of the key founding fathers, including Benjamin Franklin, Thomas Jefferson, and John Adams. All three men were on the committee assigned by the Second Continental Congress to write the Declaration of Independence.

Was all this just coincidental? Or was it part of the overall design? The ideological reasoning for the colonies separating from Great Britain was formulated by a British Enlightenment thinker several decades before the actual event. Old World philosophers shared ideas and experiences with New World enlightened men of ideas. The blood of Ephraim flowed in the veins of men and women of ideas on both sides of the Atlantic Ocean, bringing the world a step closer to the time when the American Revolution and the Restoration could be accomplished.

chapter eighteen

BRITISH RIGHTS

England chose a different avenue for governing than the continental European countries. Feudalism developed in England, but monarchs managed to keep the country somewhat united under the feudal system. The Viking invasion tended to unite England while dividing the continental countries. Competition with feudal lords strengthened the monarch in England whereas it had the opposite effect on the continent. William the Conqueror had a complete census taken in 1086, the first in Europe. From it, he developed an efficient system for collecting taxes, strengthening the position of the monarch in England, and giving England an advantage over other European countries.

In 1154, under the leadership of an educated King Henry II, the justice system in England initiated a process of law that would affect legal systems all around the world. He expanded existing traditions and founded the English common law, a legal system based on existing customs and court rulings. It was a practice that proved adaptable to all of England. The English tailored a workable jury system, offering a measure of justice for the accused. Both practices became the basis for the legal systems in England and the United States.

As a result of oppressive tax measures, severe administrations of justice, and excessive requests to fulfill military service, the barons and bishops united and laid out demands for a better government. It was the first time in English history that any group had been bold enough to take such a stand against a monarch. At first King John refused, but more and more people began to side with the barons, leaving the king with few supporters. On June 15, 1215 he met with the council and under pressure granted a list of demands drawn up by the barons, bishops, and townspeople. The demands became known as the Magna Carta. The importance of this document was not just in what it contained—just as important was how it was obtained. The people of England let it be known that if the monarch refused to rule according to the will of the people, they could force his compliance. It was a monumental development in the arduous process leading to democratic forms of government.

Incorporated in the Magna Carta were clauses reminding the king that he had an obligation under prior feudal agreements that he had no right to break them and if he ever chose to break them, the tenants-in-chief could call him to account. It also reminded the tenants-in-chief that they had obligations to tenants under them. The benefits of the reminders had a positive effect throughout England.

The charter also laid down some protections for all Englishmen with the clause: "No free man shall be seized or imprisoned or dispossessed or outlawed or banished or in any way injured, nor will we attack him nor send against him, except by legal judgment of his peers or by the law of the land." This had a far-reaching effect. It formed the basis for what we now call "due process of law." The process became an integral part of English rights and the basis for an amendment to the Constitution of the United States.

The king was forced to agree not to raise new taxes without the consent of the Grand Council made up of lords and bishops from around England. No other monarch or country in Europe would have allowed those controls. England was far ahead of the European countries in offering a measure of protection to its citizens.

The decision forcing the crown to get Council approval for raising taxes later haunted England when it attempted to initiate new taxes on the citizens of the thirteen colonies in America. They cried, "No taxation without representation"—a reference to the fact that they had no representation in the English Parliament, and therefore new taxes imposed on their colonies were illegal according to British law.

Subsequent monarchs called the Grand Council more frequently as they needed advice or new taxes. The Council evolved into Parliament, who at times refused to grant the tax requests and even complained about the monarch's policies, the beginnings of fierce conflict and competition between crown and Parliament.

With the passage of time, representation in the Parliament broadened to include commoners. The commoners consisted of representatives of shires and towns and were usually knights. England's legislature developed into a two-house body: the House of Lords, composed of the nobles and bishops, and the House of Commons, composed of the knights and middle-class citizens. Parliament became a model and forerunner for the legislative branch formulated in the United States Constitution.

For centuries after the Magna Carta, England experienced a struggle for power between monarch and Parliament. Kings constantly argued that they had a "divine right to rule" which gave them absolute power. Parliament was always quick to remind the kings of the agreements made in the Magna Carta. It was one of the great documents of the world in forging liberty.

The power struggle came to a head in 1640. King Charles lashed out at Parliament, leading troops into the House of Commons and arresting radicals who opposed him. Those not arrested had to escape out the back door. They soon raised an army against the king, and the English Civil War followed. Oliver Cromwell led the forces siding with Parliament and defeated the king's forces. King Charles was beheaded in 1649. It was a first for a European nation. A king had been tried for improper conduct and executed by his own people. Parliament let the world know that even a king was not above the law in England. While other European monarchs were solidifying their right to absolute rule, England was limiting the power of the monarchs. England's civil war occurred 150 years before the French Revolution. The early start allowed time for England's government to stabilize before the colonization of America.

For a period after the civil war, Parliament abolished the office of king, and England became a republic with Cromwell, a military leader as its head. The English people soon tired of military rule, and Parliament in 1660 installed a new monarchy. Concerns about the Catholic leanings of the new monarchs brought about a bloodless revolution in 1688. The crowned king was forced to flee England, and his Protestant daughter, Mary, and her husband, William, were installed as monarchs. The queen and king were placed on the throne at the will of Parliament.

From that point on, the monarch in England could not act independently from Parliament. This was the Glorious Revolution for the English and settled the question of whether the crown was subject to the will of the people through their representatives in the Parliament. Parliament was composed of the upper-class citizens of England. The revolution did little to extend the base of representation, but England was ahead of the rest of Europe in protecting its people from despotic kings.

Before William and Mary were crowned, they were required to accept several acts of Parliament that became known as the Bill of Rights. Those acts upheld Parliament's power in relation to the crown and reinstated the traditional rights of Englishmen. Cruel and unusual punishment, excessive fines, excessive bail, keeping of standing armies without the consent of Parliament were abolished. The Bill of Rights confirmed the principle of habeas corpus (no person could be held in a prison without first being charged of a crime). Many of the principles stated in England's Bill of Rights found their way into the Bill of Rights in the United States Constitution.

Following the Glorious Revolution, two political parties emerged in England, each with different political opinions and each representing different classes. A cabinet to advise the king and the position of Prime Minister were added. Again, England's system served as a model for other governments.

The protected rights of Englishmen played a crucial role in the attitudes of Colonial America. Those rights traversed an ocean with the people migrating to the New World. When England began to violate those rights, the colonials turned to Locke's theory that if a government is oppressive, the people have a right to revolt and change that government. The philosophical reasoning for the American Revolution was developed in Europe, but the only place it could be explored and implemented was in the British North American colonies.

The British Isles, separated by the English Channel and North Sea, provided the English opportunities independent from the continental European countries. England was protected somewhat from interference, invasions, and the constant haggling that constantly occurred on the continent. The English unified earlier, developed different attitudes about how they should be governed, fought their civil war earlier, and developed ideas about the rights of their people that were vastly different from the continental nations. England developed a unique system of government and an attitude about protecting citizens. That attitude was carried across the Atlantic Ocean by immigrants seeking new freedoms and opportunities in the New World.

The British Isles were full of people with the blood of Ephraim. Joseph's descendents would lead the charge for a political arrangement where the crown and government were obligated to the will of the people and protecting the rights of Englishmen. From Old Testament times, Ephraim guarded its freedom and proved rebellious when that freedom was threatened. It is little wonder that the British early on set about making a nation different from their neighbors on the continent. Great Britain was destined to colonize the land that the Lord had told Lehi was "a promised land . . . a land which I have prepared for you . . . a land which is choice above all other lands" (1 Nephi 2:20).

chapter nineteen

EUROPE FULFILLS ITS DESTINY

Around 600 BC, Nebuchadnezzar, king of Babylon, was suddenly awakened from his sleep by a very troubling dream. He was perplexed that he couldn't remember it and called together his wise men to see if they could tell him what he had dreamed. To his disappointment, none could give him a satisfactory answer, so he condemned them to death. When the king's captain came to seize Daniel to be executed, he asked for some extra time so that he might give the king the answer to his troubling question. That night Daniel received a vision revealing Nebuchadnezzar's nocturnal dreams.

Daniel went before Nebuchadnezzar, proclaiming that although his astrologers, magicians, and soothsayers were unable to reveal the dream, "there is a God in heaven that revealeth secrets and maketh known to the king Nebuchadnezzar what *shall be in the latter days*. Thy dream, and the visions of thy head upon thy bed, are these" (Daniel 2:28; italics added).

Daniel then proceeded to describe the king's dream:

> Thou, O king, sawest, and behold a great image. This great image, whose brightness was excellent, stood before thee; and the form thereof was terrible.
>
> This image's head was of fine gold, his breast and his arms of silver, his belly and his thighs of brass,
>
> His legs of iron, his feet part of iron and part of clay.

Thou sawest till that a stone was cut out without hands, which smote the image upon his feet that were of iron and clay, and brake them to pieces.

Then was the iron, the clay, the brass, the silver, and the gold, broken to pieces together, and became like the chaff of the summer threshingfloors; and the wind carried them away, that no place was found for them: and the stone that smote the image became a great mountain and filled the whole earth. (Daniel 2:31–35)

Daniel then offered the interpretation: "Thou art this head of gold. And after thee shall arise another kingdom inferior to thee, and another third kingdom of brass which shall bear rule over the earth. And the fourth kingdom shall be strong as iron: forasmuch as iron breaketh in pieces and subdueth all things: and as iron breaketh all these, shall it break in pieces and bruise" (Daniel 2:38–40). The different parts of the image King Nebuchadnezzar saw represented different kingdoms that would follow each other in succession as major powers in Asia Minor and Europe.

The head of gold represented Nebuchadnezzar's Babylon. Earlier, Babylon had crushed Assyria, the kingdom that had taken the ten northern tribes of Israel captive, and then the Egyptians and Syrians, ending any hopes that either nation had of gaining dominance in the area. Those victories were important to maintaining the integrity of the area. He then continued on and captured Jerusalem in 587 BC, destroyed the temple, and took thousands of Jews captive into Babylon. Nebuchadnezzar rebuilt the city of Babylon, including a surrounding wall large enough at the top to contain two rows of small structures and a road. The city was famous for its hanging gardens, which the Greeks designated one of the Seven Wonders of the World. Despite outward appearances, the administration never won over the Chaldean priests of Babylon, who constantly worked to undermine the government. They entered into an agreement with Persia to open the city gates and let the Persian army in to sack the city. Once accomplished, Babylon, with all its glory, was destroyed.

Persia was the second kingdom in Nebuchadnezzar's dream: it was "the breast of silver," led initially by King Cyrus. Cyrus proved an able administrator, exhibiting an element of humanity not exhibited under previous ruling kingdoms in the region. Persia was the first conquering power to offer differing racial and national groups some form of equal rights. So long as taxes were paid and peace maintained, Cyrus and his successors did not interfere with local customs or religion. Cyrus allowed the Jews captured by Nebuchadnezzar to return to Jerusalem, rebuild the temple, and establish a homeland for the tribe of Judah. They would remain there until the Romans sacked Jerusalem in AD 70 when the temple was once again destroyed and Judah was scattered throughout the world not to return until the latter days (see chapter 13).

Assyria was the first kingdom to unite the Near East under one government. Babylon extended the Assyrian kingdom and unification of the area. Persia, its successor, extended its influence further, reducing ruthlessness and adding a state of humanness not seen in the area. The accomplishments of these early kingdoms were passed on to the Greeks and Romans who inherited the developments of the previous super powers.

Greece was the third kingdom in Nebuchadnezzar's dream, represented by the belly and thighs of brass. King Phillip began expansion, and his son Alexander continued extending Greek control to a wide area of Europe and Asia Minor. Greek culture flourished, producing great philosophers such as Socrates, Aristotle, and Plato. The basic principles of democracy and government advocated by those philosophers provided new insights for future nations (see chapter 10).

Greece was followed by the Roman Empire (legs of iron) extending both its domain and administration further than the previous kingdoms, covering Asia Minor and much of Europe. The Romans established peace to an area where wars had been fought for centuries. It opened communication links, built roads, and made ease of travel something never thought possible in previous empires. Rome created stability and peace when the Savior came into the world and established His Church. Initially, the Apostles were able to travel freely and preach the gospel throughout the Roman Empire, initiating the spread of Christianity. Despite the positive accomplishments of Rome, the empire was also responsible for misery and slavery for millions, persecutions of Christians, and the apostasy of Christ's Church (see chapters 11 and 12).

The Roman Empire represented by iron would "break in pieces." There would never be another kingdom in Europe like Rome. Instead, smaller nations would emerge from what was once the impressive Roman Empire. If liberty and diversity of religion were to have opportunities to sprout in Europe, the large monolithic empire of Rome had to dissolve. In Rome's place, a multitude of nations would emerge; some strong and some weak. The strong nations, namely Great Britain, France, Spain, Italy, Greece, and the Netherlands, played strategic roles in the progress of the thirteen colonies in America. Democracy could not have developed if Europe had remained under the control of Rome and the Roman Catholic Church. Different nations and religions allowed for diversity and eliminated dominance by any one single country or church. The competition between England and the countries on the continent of Europe diverted English attention away from America at critical times and was a major reason that thirteen upstart colonies managed to hold out against Mother England until independence could be won and a government established.

Once Rome fell, the Dark Ages engulfed Europe until the Renaissance dispelled the gloom. In Spain, Columbus convinced a king and queen to support an exploration to find a new route to the Orient. Instead, he discovered America, the "land of promise." John Locke, in England, proposed the notion that if and when a government violated man's natural rights of life, liberty, and property, the people have a right to overthrow that government and replace it with one that would preserve those rights. Locke's concept was the basic premise of the American Revolution. In Great Britain, a political system evolved limiting the power of the monarch and protecting basic rights of citizens. A quasi representative parliament was given powers to represent and protect the people. The parliament eventually became a two-house legislative body, and political parties emerged, representing differing opinions and keeping the other party in check. Many of the practices in Great Britain were embraced by the founders of the American political system.

The advent of many nations offered a climate and some protection to advocates of change, but it did not come easily. Advocates were harassed, persecuted, and often martyred by both national governments and church officials. Emergence of the nations in Nebuchadnezzar's dream stimulated the Renaissance, Reformation, and Enlightenment. A sense of nationalism and patriotism developed among the nations of Europe, all necessary for the physical preparation of Europe and America.

An emphasis concerning individual worth and achievement were essential to the preparation of the people of Europe to tackle the tasks ahead of them. They began looking to the future instead of being held back by the traditions and myths of the past. The existence of differing religious beliefs initiated by the Reformation fostered a more tolerant attitude. Traditional beliefs and prejudices, especially concerning religion, were carefully scrutinized. Men and women were more educated than previous generations and had access to more printed material including the Bible. Some experienced a taste of freedom. Though limited, it was enough to wet appetites even if it meant homes and security were sacrificed.

The enlightened Europeans were similar to the children of Israel in their desire for freedom, but they differed in their grounding. Generations of preparation were behind them. Many times during that grounding they took two steps forward and one backward and even at times took two steps forward and three steps backward, but slowly and surely the Lord was preparing a people to accomplish His purposes.

The preparation made those Europeans different than the children of Israel in what they were willing to endure to make the promised land a home for their families and their descendents. When faced with threats and challenges, they didn't immediately cry to be taken back to Europe like Israel did for Egypt. They tolerated death, starvation, diseases, freezing winters, threats from Native Americans, a three thousand mile ocean journey, and attacks by wild animals. They immigrated to a land dense with forests that had to be cleared, swamps drained, homes built, towns organized, and hundreds of other challenges. They were willing to face those challenges for the opportunity to improve their lives and the lives of generations to follow.

On the Western Hemisphere around 550 BC, Nephi's brother, Jacob, had a vision in which he was told the land he occupied was "a land of liberty" and the Lord would "fortify this land against all other nations" (2 Nephi 10:11–12). Then Jacob was reminded of how his own family had gotten there: "We have been led to a better land, for the Lord has made the sea our path, and we are upon an isle of the sea" (2 Nephi 10:20).

He acknowledged that his people were on "an isle of the sea," referring to the continents of America. Then he learned something of those back in the Old World. "Wherefore as it says isles, there must needs be more than this, and they are inhabited also by our brethren" (2 Nephi 10:21). The "isles of the sea" refer, among others, to the continents of Europe and Asia Minor. Those continents were "inhabited also by our brethren." Who were Jacob's brethren? They were descendants of the House of Israel, particularly the House of Joseph. The Lord made Jacob aware that he had brothers in the House of Joseph on other "isles of the sea." Then the Lord gave him some insights concerning those brothers: "For behold, the Lord God has led away from time to time from the House of Israel, according to his will and pleasure. And now behold, the Lord remembereth all them who have been broken off, wherefore he remembereth us also" (2 Nephi 10:22).

The Lord had not forgotten His people scattered throughout the world. Jacob was made aware of their existence. What he may or may not have understood is the role his brothers and sisters in Israel were about to play in the preparation of the people of Europe to fulfill promises given to Lehi, Nephi, and Jacob that their own posterity would be remembered when they fell into apostasy. It would be men and women with the blood of Ephraim who migrated from Europe who would be the Lord's tools in extending those blessings to Lehi's seed. There was much work to achieve before that could be accomplished. His brothers in the house of Joseph would be a driving force in Europe to accomplish the Lord's purposes.

Jacob recognized two of the branches of Israel that the Lord had led away. Both had important but different roles in accomplishing the Lord's ultimate purpose. Nephite prophets were informed that they were to keep a record (Book of Mormon) that would be of great worth to their seed and to the world. The record would be hidden for centuries before it came to the knowledge of the world. When that record did come to light, it would be their brethren from Europe who would immigrate to America; establish families; set up a government; and then translate, print, and offer that record to Lehi's posterity. While Ephraim and Manesseh were writing the record in America, and while it was preserved and hidden in the earth, descendants of Ephraim and Manasseh in Europe and others of the house of Israel were preparing themselves, their posterity, and the nations they inhabited to take the steps necessary to establish a free people on the promised land. Then, the European branch would be prepared to offer Lehi's posterity the restored gospel. Descendants of Ephraim in Europe and descendants of Israel would be the first to carry the Book of Mormon to descendants of Lehi and to the world.

The blood of Ephraim was a driving force constantly preparing the people of Europe to fulfill the Lord's purposes. Preparation was not accomplished without sacrifice. Sacrifices were made by countless individuals over thousands of years. Progress required change, and change did not come easily to established ruling circles, whether church or state. Men and women sacrificed time, talents, associations with families and friends, tortured bodies, and their very lives to further the work along. Each individual sacrifice was important in the overall plan. Few records were kept, so we know little of what they endured and accomplished. Someday current generations may gain a better understanding of their ancestor's role in pushing the work forward. Until then, we can only be grateful for their achievements and do all we can to ensure they have access to the blessings of the gospel that we, who live in the restored period, enjoy.

King Nebuchadnezzar's dream foretold events that had to occur before the stone could be cut out of the mountain: "And in the days of these kings shall the God of heaven set up a kingdom, which shall never be destroyed: and the kingdom shall not be left to other people, but it shall break in pieces and consume all these kingdoms, and it shall stand for ever" (Daniel 2:44). The time was fast approaching for the establishment of the kingdom Nebuchadnezzar saw is his dream. This kingdom would not be left to "other people." Israel, God's chosen, led by Ephraim, the birthright tribe, would be responsible for establishing that kingdom, under the Lord's direction. As the time approached for Nebuchadnezzar's dream to be fulfilled, the role and responsibilities of Ephraim, the House of Israel, and the Gentiles spoken of in the Book of Mormon intensified. The preparation period in Europe was basically complete by 1600. The remaining work would move to the New World in preparation for a new covenant the Lord had promised Israel.

> Behold the days come, saith the Lord, that I will make a new covenant with the house of Israel, and with the house of Judah:
>
> Not according to the covenant that I made with their fathers in the day that I took them by the hand to bring them out of the land of Egypt; which my covenant they brake, although I was an husband unto them, saith the Lord:
>
> But this shall be the covenant that I will make with the house of Israel; After those days, saith the Lord, I will put my law in the inward parts, and write it in their hearts; and will be their God, and they shall be my people.
>
> And they shall teach no more every man his neighbor, and every man his brother, saying, Know the Lord: for they shall all know me, from the least of them unto the greatest of them, saith the Lord: for I will forgive their iniquity, and I will remember their sin no more. (Jeremiah 31:31–34)

Part Three

Ephraim's Role in the Promised Land

chapter twenty

THE DISCOVERY OF AMERICA

—◦○◦ ⟨⟨◉⟩⟩ ◦○◦—

Nephi, in 1 Nephi 13, recounts a vision related to the discovery and colonization of America. His begins where Nebuchadnezzar's dream finished—the establishment of the nations of Europe: "And I looked and beheld many nations and kingdoms. And the angel said unto me: What beholdest thou? And I said: I behold nations and kingdoms. And he said unto me: These are the nations and kingdoms of the Gentiles" (1 Nephi 13:1–3).

Nephi saw the nations of Europe which were represented by the feet and toes of the image in Nebuchadnezzar's dream. He refers to them as "nations and kingdoms of the Gentiles." Nephi is considered a cultural Jew, though not of the tribe of Judah (see 2 Nephi 33:8). We know Nephi was of the tribe of Manasseh. In his eyes, the people living in the European nations were considered Gentiles, even though some were carrying the blood of Israel.

The nations Nephi observed in vision were about to play a vital role in the recorded and known discovery and colonization of America. Nephi was shown the struggles Christ's Church would experience after His death:

> And it came to pass that I saw among the nations of the Gentiles the formation of a great church.
>
> And the angel said unto me: Behold the formation of a church which is most abominable above all other churches, which slayeth

the saints of God, yea, and tortureth them and bindeth them down, and yoketh them with a yoke of iron and bringeth them down into captivity.

And it came to pass that I beheld this great and abominable church; and I saw the devil that he was the founder of it. (1 Nephi 13:4–6)

The early church experienced apostasy while the Apostles were still on the earth. Much of the New Testament is devoted to correcting errors and bringing members and groups back into the fold. Changes in doctrine, persecutions, and martyrdoms of church members continued for centuries thereafter. Nations, religious organizations, and misguided individuals were responsible for the apostasy that crept into the church.

Next, Nephi was shown the Atlantic Ocean, which separated him from the people he saw in his vision: "I looked and beheld many waters; and they divided the Gentiles from the seed of my brethren" (1 Nephi 13:10). The Atlantic Ocean played an important role in future events. The ocean offered pilgrims and colonists relatively easy and affordable journeys to America and would make possible the development of the economy and culture of what would become the United States. If those pilgrims and colonists would have had to travel by land, far fewer would have ever made the journey to America.

Nephi saw Christopher Columbus among the Gentile nations across the Atlantic Ocean. "And I looked and beheld a man among the Gentiles, who was separated from the seed of my brethren by the many waters" (1 Nephi 13:12). Here was a Gentile influenced by the blood of Israel. What set him apart from millions of other Gentiles was a burning feeling that God had chosen him to open a new path to the Indies (Asia and India). In a manuscript written by Columbus after his voyage, the *Book of Prophecies,* he addressed a letter to the king and queen of Spain:

> With a hand that could be felt, the Lord opened my mind to the fact that it would be possible to sail from here to the Indies, and he opened my will to desire to accomplish the project. This was the fire that burned within me when I came to visit Your Highnesses. All who found out about my project denounced it with laughter and ridiculed me. And the sciences . . . were of no use to me. Quotations of learned [men] were no help. Only Your Majesties had faith and perseverance. Who can doubt this fire was not merely mine, but also of the Holy Spirit who encouraged me with radiance of marvelous illumination from his sacred Holy Scriptures, by a most clear and powerful testimony from

the forty-four books of the Old Testament, from the four Gospels, from the twenty-three Epistles of the blessed Apostles—urging me to press forward? Continually, without a moment's hesitation, The Scriptures urge me to press forward with great haste.[1]

Columbus, Don Quixote of the Seas, quotes Columbus describing his inspiration and preparation years before the event: "Our Lord unlocked my mind, sent me upon the sea, and gave me fire for the deed. Those who heard of my enterprise called it foolish, mocked me, and laughed. But who can doubt but that the Holy Ghost inspired me?" Columbus tells that he prepared from his youth for what he felt was his calling:

> From my first youth onward, I was a seaman and have so continued until this day. . . . Wherever on the earth a ship has been, I have been. I have spoken and treated with learned men, priests, and laymen, Latins and Greeks, Jews and Moors, and with many men of other faiths. The Lord was well disposed to my desire, and He bestowed upon me courage and understanding; knowledge of seafaring. He gave me in abundance, of astrology as much as was needed, and of geometry and astronomy likewise. Further, He gave me joy and cunning in drawing maps and thereon cities, mountains, rivers, islands, and harbours, each one in its place. I have seen and truly I have studied all books—cosmographies, histories, chronicles, and philosophies, and other arts.[2]

The Lord prepared a man with knowledge, courage, and desire to set sail in uncharted waters. He could not have succeeded on courage and desire alone. The Renaissance created the spirit of adventure that motivated Columbus and other explorers to seek new waters, new lands, and new people. Prior to the 1400s, Europeans had little desire or ability to explore. Following the Crusades, Europeans were introduced to Asia and its spices, silks, jewels, and gold. To obtain the coveted items, traders had to make long and often dangerous journeys over land. To provide the cherished items in any kind of quantity and at affordable prices, a sea route had to be explored. New technology, changing political views, and demand from society made voyages by sea possible, practicable, and profitable. Obstacles were overcome with new and more accurate maps, improved navigational instruments, and faster ships.

The spirit of the Renaissance forced improvements in mapmaking. Informed Europeans knew the earth was not flat. European maps at the time included what they knew of the continents of Asia, Africa, and Europe. Europeans knew nothing about North and South America.

Columbus came to the conclusion that by sailing west he would eventually reach Asia. He had confidence that he could sail out into uncharted waters and return, debunking many superstitions of his time that somewhere out in the vast unknown a ship would fall off the earth.

By 1300, the compass had come into use. Later, the astrolabe was invented, allowing sailors to determine the ship's latitude. Both were necessary tools for keeping ships on course. By the 1400s, designers in Portugal and Spain began improving ship design, making them smaller with different shaped sails and having the rudder in the rear instead of at the side. These improvements made the ships faster, more maneuverable, and—most important—allowed them to sail against the wind.

Rivalries among the "many nations and kingdoms" that Nephi observed motivated governments in Europe to advocate exploration and colonization. Those governments wanted the prestige of new discoveries and the riches those discoveries would add to their treasuries.

Nephi learned in his vision that after the "Spirit of God . . . wrought on the man [Columbus] . . . he went forth upon the many waters, even to the seed of [his] brethren, who were in the promised land" (1 Nephi 13:12). As with many on the Lord's errands, Columbus found the journey full of challenges. In 1484, after years of preparation, he proposed his route to the Indies to King John II of Portugal and was turned down.

Despite his preparation and study, Columbus had two false concepts of the earth. He believed the world was smaller and the land portions of the earth much larger than reality. "Thus, he calculated the distance from the Canaries to Japan at about 2,400 miles. He was wrong, of course; the actual airline distance is 10,600 miles. But remarkably, what did lie about 2,400 miles west of the Canaries was an entirely new continent, unknown to anyone in Europe or Asia."[3]

If Columbus had known the truth about the distance to the Orient, over four times farther than he calculated, he may not have been as anxious to start his journey. Not knowing what lies ahead often has tremendous advantages. Columbus, like many other explorers, had no idea of what would be required to fulfill his dream; thus he was not afraid to begin the voyage.

The Portuguese had turned Columbus down because their experience had told them that the earth was larger than Columbus claimed. They figured his chances of success were slim if not impossible.

In 1485, Columbus left Portugal for Spain to lobby the Spanish monarchs, Fernando and Isabel, to support his endeavor. It took another seven years before he gained their confidence and financial support. The agreement negotiated with the Spanish monarchy provided Columbus with two small ships, the *Pinta* and the *Niña*. He managed to lease a third and larger ship, the *Santa Maria*. His next challenge was to find sailors willing to sail out into the Atlantic, where no man had sailed, and return to tell about it. Few were willing to take on such an adventure, but with the aid of another veteran sea captain, Martin Alonso Pinz'on, who agreed to go along, he managed to scrape up enough sailors to man the three ships. On August 3, 1492, the three vessels set out to fulfill Nephi's vision of the gentile discovery of America.

Carried by winds, the three vessels sailed west into uncharted waters. After thirty-two days, the sailors became restless and fearful, urging Columbus to turn around before the voyage ended in disaster. He persuaded the men to go on, but he did commit to turn around if land wasn't sighted soon. He was encouraged by the sightings of land birds and floating plants and sticks—signs that land couldn't be far off. Two days later, a lookout on the *Pinta* sighted land. Columbus and his crews were soon looking at a tiny island in the Bahamas that Columbus later named San Salvador. His twenty years of preparation and faith had finally paid off. He had no idea the effect his discovery would have on the world. During his lifetime, he was always under the impression that he had discovered a new route to the Indies. Little did he know that he played an integral role in preparing for the time when the stone could be cut out of the mountain and cover the whole earth. The plan of the Lord for the Restoration of the gospel was moving steadily forward.

Notes

1   Christopher Columbus, *Book of Prophecies,* translated by Delno C. West, and August Kling (Gainsville, FL: 1991).

2   Jacob Wassermann, *Columbus, Don Quixote of the Seas,* translated by Eric Sutton, (Boston: Little, Brown, and Co., 1930), 19.

3   De Lamar Jensen, "Columbus and the Hand of God," *Ensign,* October 1992, 6–13.

chapter twenty-one

A CHOSEN LAND

The prophet Ether wrote a brief record of a people who were led by the Lord from the Tower of Babel when the languages were confounded to a land of promise. That record was translated centuries later by the Nephite prophet Moroni, whose ancestors were also led to that land by the Lord. Ether described what he learned from the Lord about the land his people occupied: "After the waters had receded from off the face of this land it became a choice land above all other lands, a chosen land of the Lord; wherefore the Lord would have that all men should serve him who dwell upon the face thereof" (Ether 13:2).

Centuries after Ether, Nephi learned that the Lord was about to lead his father's family to a land of promise: "And inasmuch as ye shall keep my commandments, ye shall prosper; and shall be led to a land of promise; yea, even a land which I have prepared for you; yea, a land which is choice above all other lands" (1 Nephi 2:20).

After arriving in the New World with his family, Nephi's father, Lehi, stated: "We have obtained a land of promise, a land which is choice above all other lands. . . . And behold, it is wisdom that this land should be kept as yet from the knowledge of other nations; for behold many nations would overrun the land, that there would be no place for an inheritance" (2 Nephi 1:5, 8).

The Lord let it be known through different prophets: "After the waters had receded from off the land it became a choice land above all other lands, a chosen land of the Lord" (Ether 13:2); "The Lord poured out His blessings upon the land" (Ether 9:20); "It was a land of promise" (2 Nephi 1:5); "The existence of the land would be kept from the knowledge of other nations" (2 Nephi 1:8); and "A land prepared for those who would be led there" (1 Nephi 2:20).

The soil on which Lehi, Nephi, and Ether stood was truly "choice above all other lands." Their small colonies developed into great civilizations, and not until the people became wicked did those civilizations decline. The land supported the people while they were righteous. They were aware the land had a destiny far beyond their own people. Full realization of that destiny would be played out in the last days, after the discovery of America by Columbus and the colonization by European powers.

Monarchies ruled the countries of Western Europe for many centuries. Europe abounded in poverty, disease, crime, and despair. The elite aristocracy controlled most of the land and wealth, while those without were searching for a way to escape the stagnant conditions surrounding them. A constantly increasing population made for crowded surroundings. Few opportunities for change or release from the stagnant environment were available to the vast majority of Europeans.

Many had a hope that somewhere—out in the waters of the Atlantic—was a place where they would have opportunities to start over, make dreams come true, and change lifestyles. Little did they know that such a place existed, but its existence had been deliberately kept from them by the Lord for many centuries. It was a whole continent, where no monarch ruled, untouched by outside forces and inhabited by relatively few people. The land mass was blessed with an abundance of natural resources, fertile soil, blue skies, and space to roam. Forests were plentiful with game and rivers with fish. Literally hundreds of thousands of square miles of ground lay unclaimed, unspoiled, and available to support a people willing to work and sacrifice to bring it under cultivation. There was no other place like it in the world and yet no nation had claimed or settled the richest area of North America. As Nephi learned, the Lord truly had preserved and set aside a place on earth for a particular purpose.

The land would be a major contributor to the development of the people willing to colonize it. Opportunities for individual and group achievement were beyond comprehension to so many who had known only anonymity and poverty. The land helped mold a people more democratic in thought, more individualistic in action, more independent and more willing to sacrifice for liberty.

Three thousand miles of ocean separating the promised land from the Old World proved to be a great protective barrier. Until European sailors conquered their fear of the unknown and sailed west beyond chartered waters, the promised land was sheltered from foreign invaders except those the Lord led there. Travel distance between the Old and New Worlds served as a shield even after colonization. The distance disallowed strict control by the ruling Mother Country in Europe. Left to their own devices, the colonists of British North America developed strong habits of self government. Speed of travel by water while migrating to the New World prevented hindrance from many outside forces that could have occurred if travel had been by land. The escape of the children of Israel from Egypt had proven the dangers of such land journeys. The early immigrants to America had opportunities to transplant across the wide Atlantic, the seeds to a very unique political philosophy relatively free of corrupting influences.

North America was a land of abundance to support an ever expanding population. Fish and game were readily available, and copious forests supplied wood for homes, businesses, and shipping. The adjacent ocean provided a living for many. The coastline along the Atlantic was dotted with natural inlets and harbors not available along most seaboards. Settlements naturally grew along these inlets. Wide, slow moving, navigable rivers flowed into many of the harbors allowing shipping to traverse inland. Settlements sprang up all along many of those rivers.

The abundance of natural resources compared to the population was far different than the European countries. An area with a 3,000 mile coastline and millions of square miles of open space had as few as 300,000 native inhabitants, spread thinly over the continent. The early pilgrims and colonists did not face the contaminating influences plaguing the children of Israel as they entered the land of Canaan. The openness and sparseness of people was totally new to the immigrants. They had opportunities for a new life. The lack of inhabitants, potential converts for the countries of Spain and Portugal, made North America less desirable to them. Those predominately Catholic nations chose the southern continent where populations were denser and potential converts more abundant.

The land was an essential factor in the development of freedom of thought and action. It provided the means for political and economic independence. Land in Europe was owned by a few, leaving the poor and middle classes little or no opportunities for ownership. America, it seemed, had a never-ending supply at reasonable prices. The franchise (right to vote in political elections) was normally granted only to those with a certain amount of land.

More people owned land at this time than in any previous time. The land provided economic independence to more people than was available anywhere else in the world. It was incomprehensible to most Europeans that they could own and work their own land and take the profits from it. These opportunities for self-reliance were unavailable in Europe.

To make the ground profitable, early colonials had to clear trees and drain swamps, which required all their time and energy. The first years on farms were hard work. It was not for the weak or lazy, but it offered opportunities for families to work and live together, not always the case in Europe. The work was tough, not only for the head of the house but for all family members. The work made people strong in body and spirit. The soil provided food for families and often a little surplus to improve lifestyles. The land established an environment for strong family ties, independent thinking, and dignity that had not always been available in Europe.

The population grew at an astounding rate. From 1650 to 1770, it was estimated that the inhabitants of America doubled from one million to two million. An expanding population brought more and more land under cultivation. The ever-spreading populace made it difficult for the Mother Country to control and gave increasing economic power to the colonies.

The land played a vital role in creating the cadre of talented, educated, and principled men who formulated the political thought behind the American Revolution and devised a workable Constitution for the people. The wealth the land created brought opportunities for education and political expression on a scale never before thought possible.

The New World tolerated religious diversity. Isolation from church headquarters in Europe allowed more independent thinking. People were free, for the most part, to worship however they wanted. The abundance of sects made religious tolerance more necessary and important. That tolerance spilled over into politics and everyday life.

The Appalachian Mountains that ran the length of the eastern seaboard played a pivotal role. The mountain range served as a barrier to western movement, preventing populations from spreading too fast and allowing time for cities to grow and populations to increase. The time proved vital in stabilizing and maturing the American society. Local governments and a workable economy had time to develop. When expansion began, there was a stable foothold along the Atlantic seacoast. Explorers had models and established ideals to carry with them as they crossed the Appalachians.

The land played an important role in motivating the citizen soldiers of America fighting in the Revolutionary War to continue when their government was unable pay their due wages. The soldiers were offered inducements of land for service in the military. When the war was over, those who served could return to a farm or shop and continue making a living. Many similar revolutionary movements in other countries left the standing armies idle once the war was over. With nothing to do and nowhere to go, soldiers and officers often turned against the very governments they had fought to support. In America, the land provided an important outlet for retiring soldiers.

The land played a vital role in America winning the Revolution against Mother England. The British didn't have the resources or manpower to control all the land or seacoast of what became the United States. Often, when the American army was beaten and worn out, its leaders still found avenues of escape from the British juggernaut. The sheer vastness of America made for difficult planning and execution of British war plans and control of the population almost impossible. European powers had to fight a totally new kind of war than what they were accustomed. Great Britain simply did not have enough resources to bring the colonies back into the fold. The Americans used the land to their advantage—and what an advantage it gave them!

The land of promise continued to support an ever-expanding population for two centuries. It was raw, undeveloped, and required hard work to bring it under cultivation, creating strong individuals and families. The people developed an economy like no other. It served the American people well during those two centuries.

The land was an important factor in the Restoration of the gospel. As with the American Revolution, the land offered protection and opportunities to early Church members fleeing from persecutions. Those in flight could find new places to set down roots and continue the work of the Restoration and building up of the Church while leaving persecutors behind. When avenues within the territory of the United States were exhausted, the Saints traveled to the midst of the Rocky Mountains to build a temple and establish Zion. The land provided space and distance for the struggling church to consolidate, strengthen their members, and provide a place for the gathering of Israel. The path was not without challenges and difficulties, but there was no other location on earth where the Restoration could have been accomplished.

The land provided the atmosphere to build a strong nation, a beacon of liberty. Twice in the last century the nations of Europe called on the inhabitants of America to help preserved their own freedom during world wars.

When the Lord told Nephi the land had been prepared, He meant just that. Isolation, geography, mountain chains, natural resources, fertile soils, natural harbors, rivers, and what seemed to be a never-ending supply of land all played a role in the development of the people who were led to the land. The rugged untamed country produced a citizenry different than any on the earth. Opportunities for education and participation in the political process were on a scale never before seen. The colonists were able to apply what proved effective from their European past while they innovated and experimented with their own ideas and solutions. There was no king, dictator, or established bureaucracies to inhibit progress. Americans had new opportunities for lateral and forward movement. The chosen land produced a unique people out of transplanted Europeans.

The early American colonists in the promised land raised a posterity capable of dealing with the important responsibilities of winning independence for a new country, establishing a Constitution and the Restoration of the gospel of Jesus Christ. Each of these steps would require spirits the Lord had withheld and reserved for those specific purposes. The blood of Ephraim was on the threshold of taking on full responsibility as the birthright tribe of Israel.

chapter twenty-two

A PROMISED PEOPLE

Over five thousand years of traditions and history had been recorded before the Old World learned of the existence of the Americas: "And behold it is wisdom that this land should be kept from the knowledge of other nations; for behold many nations would overrun the land, that there would be no place for an inheritance" (2 Nephi 1:8). The Lord preserved America, the promised land, for those who had been promised an inheritance.

Unbeknown to the Old World, three groups of people had been led by the Lord to the promised land prior to Columbus—the Jaredities, the Nephities, and the Mulekites. The Lord informed Nephi: "There shall be none come into this land save they shall be brought by the hand of the Lord" (2 Nephi 1:6). The three migrations crossed the oceans long before Old World ships were ready for such an undertaking. From the Book of Mormon we learn the hand of the Lord was evident in bringing the groups safely across thousands of miles of ocean. Those crossings produced great civilizations, but each failed to stay true and "serve the God of the land who is Jesus Christ" (Ether 2:12) and all three fell; one to total destruction. Those civilizations never communicated with the lands from which they migrated so the Old World had no knowledge of their existence.

Columbus was not the first European explorer to set foot on the New World. Five hundred years prior to Columbus's voyage, Scandinavian explorers landed on American shores. They made settlements, explored, and made notes of the coastline but soon pulled up stakes, returned to their homes, and kept the existence of America to themselves. The Norsemen, Portuguese, Danish, French, Irish, and others visited America before 1492, but none made permanent settlements or bothered to publicize their findings. When the time was right, Europe would learn of the secret that lay out in the unexplored waters. That time was 1492.

Columbus made his voyage as the Renaissance mushroomed across Europe. The ideology of the Renaissance motivated men to glance into the future rather than cling to traditions of the past. The Reformation was about to break across Europe. Twenty-five years after Columbus set sail, Martin Luther posted his 95 Theses. The Enlightenment would follow, broadening the horizons of many Europeans.

Columbus's discovery was a spark that ignited an explosion of European exploration and discovery. Spain and Portugal were the first to send out explorers. The Spanish conquistadors brought a new culture to the seed of Lehi living in South America and carried gold and treasures back to Europe. The robbing of America's treasures had a rather unique effect in Europe. The new money the gold created in the European countries undermined the stifling effects of the feudal system that touched off a flurry of capitalist activity. The change had a dramatic effect on breaking down established systems and patterns, setting in motion new political and economic forces that would be in place to support the colonization of America.

The French explored North America in 1524. French ships skirted along the east coast but decided not to settle and continued north to what is now Canada. The French government was too preoccupied with internal problems and wars with other European countries to concentrate on discoveries an ocean away. Not until the early seventeenth century did they initiate colonization in Canada, and it was centered on the fur trade rather than permanent settlements.

Spain and Portugal dominated settlement of the New World for the first hundred years after Columbus. Spain controlled most of South and Central America and slowly worked north until they reached what is now southern Florida. About that time, Spain became embroiled in difficulties externally with England and internally attempting to stamp out the Protestant movement in their country. The monarchy made the decision to invade England and take control of the seas. A fleet of 124 vessels,

1,100 guns, and 27,000 men assembled in what became known as the Spanish Armada. The British defense consisted of 197 ships, 2,000 guns, and 16,000 men.

The Spanish ships were large and slow, while British vessels were smaller, faster, and more maneuverable. The British could fire their guns at greater distances, enabling them to keep their ships out of the range of the Spanish guns. England fired at the Spanish until they ran out of ammunition after firing an amazing 100,000 rounds. Shortly thereafter, strong winds came up and blew the Spanish Armada, first northward around Scotland and then southward toward Ireland. Many of the ships were wrecked, and parts washed ashore in both Scotland and Ireland. Only half of the Armada returned to Spain. The defeat had a devastating ting effect on Spain and forced the government to consolidate and reel in the colonization effort. Spain maintained its holdings in America but had little resources to extend into new areas; thus they went no farther than the southern areas of North America.

The French showed little interest in extending colonies south of the St. Lawrence River, and after the defeat of the Spanish Armada, Spain didn't have the resources to extend farther into North America. Both countries were ruled by absolute monarchies, and both were strong Catholic countries. Neither would have any part in the colonization of the richest part of North America. It would be up to England to colonize the land sandwiched between areas controlled by France and Spain.

Why England? (1) England was predominantly Protestant, (2) England had established a government that was hundreds of years ahead of the rest of Europe in its democratic form and protection of individual rights, and (3) England was full of people with the blood of Ephraim.

England finally awoke to the political and economic value of colonization and was soon active around the world. The English established America's first colony in Jamestown in 1607. For the next century and a half, England transported more people to the New World than either the French or Spanish. Both France and Spain adopted the policy that only Catholics in good standing could immigrate to their colonies, which strictly limited the number of immigrants. England, the strongest Protestant power in Europe, was willing to let anyone—regardless of their religious conviction—migrate to America. The English were happy to be rid of them. Many went to the colonies seeking opportunities to practice their religion without interference. More people went as families to the

English colonies, making the situation more stable and permanent. The mixture of the Protestant religions fashioned an atmosphere of acceptance for new immigrants. The diversity, attitude of tolerance, and concern for protecting the rights of Englishmen were essential in the development of independent political thought in America.

Colonization of America happened at the opportune time. England was racked with unrest and turbulence. For decades, the monarchy and Parliament had been hammering away at each other in a power struggle for supremacy. The British Civil War broke out in 1644, resulting in the overthrow of the government and execution of the king. Added to the internal turmoil, England was caught up in a series of wars with one or more of the countries of Europe. From 1689 to 1763, England fought as many as six wars. The first five wars settled nothing, making it necessary to fight another. Both the Crown and Parliament had little time to be bothered about what was going on in America. Through all that turmoil, England was racked by a series of weak governments.

For 150 years, the colonists were isolated from the power structures in England. Throughout that time institutions of self-government were established. Representative town and colonial assemblies were formed, often patterned after England's Parliament. The practice of self-government was without parallel anywhere in the world. More people were afforded opportunities to participate in the governmental process than anywhere in Europe. Americans came to cherish those established patterns of self-rule. Population increased rapidly. The economy quickly grew. America was indeed turning out to be a promised land.

European powers were constantly at war with each other. These wars often spilled over into America. Such was the case with the Seven Years' War, or the French and Indian War as it was called in America. England defeated the French in 1763 and brought an end to European engagements in North America. England acquired Canada and parts of Florida. The French pulled entirely out of North America, eliminating any threat of invasion or influence on the colonies by the French. With the French gone, the need for British protection greatly diminished. The colonies became much bolder and aggressive after the French evacuated Canada.

Great Britain accumulated an enormous debt in fighting the French and Indian War. The Ministry in London was compelled to hold the colonies responsible for part of the expenses of the war and proposed new and, for the first time, direct taxes on the colonists. The projected tax touched a nerve among the Americans. They were not about to submit to demands for taxation from a Parliament in which they had no representation and that was located three thousand miles away. The cry of "taxation without representation" was heard up and down the colonies. It became the rallying cry for defying Parliament's taxation proposals. Similar objections were expressed by the ten tribes of Israel led by Ephraim when they separated from Judah after King Solomon's death in the land of Canaan. Protecting liberty was always a characteristic of the blood of Ephraim.

After the war, Parliament was determined to maintain an army in America to protect England's interests and the colonies from outside threats or aggressors. For such protection, Parliament resolved that the Americans should be taxed. Friction between occupying British soldiers and American citizens soon developed. London's decision to keep a standing army in America was a serious point of contention between Mother England and her colonies.

Prior to the French and Indian War, England was the world's most formidable naval power. Its ships roamed the world. Countries respected and feared the power of the Royal Navy. With victory, the British government neglected its navy, decreased the number of ships, and let many slip into disrepair. Short on cash, the War Ministry decided it was safe to let the navy slide since no other European power was capable of challenging them.

The French, reeling from the horrific defeat, resolved to strengthen its navy, hoping for an opportunity to seek revenge against the British. The French navy was superior to Great Britain's only once during that period, and that was during the American Revolutionary War. The timing was opportune for America. The contribution of the French navy supplying America during the war proved indispensable and was the deciding factor in the American victory at Yorktown, the last significant battle of the war. The victory eventually forced England to negotiate peace and accept America's independence.

Nephi learned in vision that "the Lord hath covenanted this land unto me, and to my children forever, and also all those who should be led out of other countries by the hand of the Lord" (2 Nephi 1: 5). Timing in both world and local events was a major factor in protecting the land for those the Lord chose to lead there. The Lord was preparing both the Old World and New World for His purposes.

Nephi's seed was not alone among the tribes of Israel who would inherit the promised land. The Lord, when he visited America, said: "Ye are my disciples; and ye are a light unto this people, who are a remnant of the house of Joseph. And behold, this is the land of your inheritance; and the Father hath given it unto you" (3 Nephi 15:12–13). The Americas would be the land for Joseph's descendants to inherit. Members of the European house of Joseph were about to make their mark on America.

chapter twenty-three
THE GENTILES
SHALL BE BLESSED

The term *Gentile* appears in the Book of Mormon at least forty-four times. Those references to Gentile do not always have the same meaning. To a Jew the word *Gentile* has one meaning; to a Mormon, another. Nephi, who once lived in Jerusalem, may have used the term differently than Mormon, who lived a thousand years later and never knew the land of Jerusalem.

Gentile can be defined in many ways: (1) a non-Jewish person, (2) a Christian, as distinguished from a person who is Jewish, (3) a non-Mormon person, and (4) a heathen.

The Bible Dictionary adds further meaning to the definition of a Gentile: "The word *Gentiles* means the nations, and eventually came to be used to mean all those not of the house of Israel. It is first used in Genesis with reference to the descendents of Japheth (see Genesis 10:2–5). As used throughout the scriptures it has a dual meaning, sometimes to designate peoples of non-Israelite lineage, and other times to designate nations that are without the gospel, even though there may be some Israelite blood therein. This latter usage is especially characteristic of the work as used in the Book of Mormon."[1]

To summarize, a Gentile could be any one of the following: a person who is not Jewish, a Christian, a person who is not Mormon, a heathen, the nations of the world, people not of the house of Israel, those nations of the world without the gospel, and people in the nations of the world carrying both Gentile blood and the blood of Israel.

The last definition applies to how Gentile is often used in the Book of Mormon and would fit most of those who are members of The Church of Jesus Christ of Latter-day Saints today.

Elder Mark E. Peterson, an Apostle of the Lord, further explains the term Gentile:

> And who are these modern Gentiles? We are.
>
> We are they to whom the gospel was restored, and we have the keys of the gathering as brought back by Moses and committed to the Prophet Joseph Smith to be used for this very purpose (see D&C 110). And we are they who have been commanded to preach the gospel to the entire world (see D&C 68:8; 112:28; 133:37).
>
> We are also of Israel, however—mostly of Ephraim—but we are Gentiles too, inasmuch as Ephraim was widely scattered among the Gentiles in ancient times and intermarried with them.
>
> Ephraim now is the first of the scattered tribes to be gathered, since Ephraim holds the birthright in Israel.
>
> We are referred to in this prophecy as Gentiles, but we are the "believing Gentiles" because we have the "believing blood" of Ephraim in our veins as well as the blood of the Gentiles. Our pedigrees show that we come from many nationalities. In the revealed dedicatory prayer for the Kirkland temple, the Prophet used this expression: "concerning the revelations and commandments which thou hast given unto us who are *identified with the Gentiles*" (D&C 109:60; italics added).
>
> It is inspiring indeed to realize that we are the very ones to whom Nephi and the Christ referred some two thousand years ago. We have lived that prophecy.[2]

Based on Elder Peterson's statement, we could add one more important designation to the term *Gentile*—believing Gentiles who are gathered and carry the believing blood of Ephraim and Israel.

Ephraim was given the birthright by Jacob thousands of years ago. Connected with that birthright is the opportunity and privilege to be gathered first, and the awesome responsibility to prepare for the gathering of the remainder of the house of Israel. That preparation has been in progress for over three millennia and will continue until it is completed. It has occurred all over the world, an essential thread running through Canaan and Asia Minor, the nations of Europe, across the Atlantic Ocean, finally resting in the promised land of America. Leading the way through those nations and peoples were those with Ephraim's blood flowing through their veins, preparing both a land and a people. What a journey it has been, and it is by no means finished. The best is yet to come.

The Book of Mormon refers to that journey and to the role Ephraim, other members of the house of Israel, and the Gentiles would play in accomplishing the Lord's purposes: "Then shall the fulness of the gospel of the Messiah come unto the Gentiles and from the Gentiles unto the remnant of our seed—And at that day shall the remnant of our seed know that they are of the house of Israel and that they are the covenant people of the Lord; and then shall they know and come to the knowledge of their forefathers, and also to the knowledge of their Redeemer" (1 Nephi 15:13–14).

The Gentiles in these scriptures are predominately of Ephraim, as evidenced by the lineage of most of the early church members, including the Prophet Joseph Smith. They were the Gentiles that Nephi refers to in this scripture. The seed of Nephi also carried that believing blood of Ephraim and Israel. The Book of Mormon tells us Lehi's ancestors were from Manasseh (see Alma 10:3). The Prophet Joseph Smith said Ishmael was from the tribe of Ephraim.[3] Once Lehi's sons married Ishmael's daughters, all their posterity would carry the blood of both Ephraim and Manasseh.

The Mulekites, who came to America eleven years after Lehi, were mainly of the tribe of Judah, with perhaps a scattering of the other tribes mixed among them. The Native Americans inhabiting North America at the time the colonists settled the promised land carried the blood of Israel predominately Ephraim and Manasseh. They had custody of the promised land for centuries prior to the arrival of the early colonists. At first they shared with the new inhabitants the knowledge necessary for survival in the new land, including how to hunt, grow corn, methods of travel, how to build shelter to survive cold winters, and methods of fighting adaptable to America and not used in Europe. As more and more colonists arrived and took away the lands from the Native Americans, the relationship change and fighting broke out between the two groups. The colonists may not have survived those early years without the assistance of the Native Americans. The Book of Mormon describes how the Gentiles would someday return the favor by introducing the gospel of Jesus Christ and delivering a record of their ancestors to American branches of the house of Joseph.

Before the gospel could be introduced, the Gentiles would scatter the seed of Nephi.

> And it meaneth that the time cometh that after all the house of Israel have been scattered and confounded, that the Lord God will raise up a mighty nation among the Gentiles, yea, even upon the face of this land; and by them shall our seed be scattered.
>
> And after our seed is scattered the Lord God will proceed to do a marvelous work among the Gentiles, which shall be of great worth unto our seed; wherefore, it is likened unto their being nourished by the Gentiles and being carried in their arms and upon their shoulders.
>
> And it shall also be of worth unto the Gentiles; and not only unto the Gentiles but unto all the house of Israel, unto the making known of the covenants of the Father of heaven unto Abraham saying: In thy seed shall all the kindreds of the earth be blessed. (1 Nephi 22:7–9)

Nephi saw a group of Ephraim's posterity bringing the blessing of the gospel to his seed in America. This was a continuing fulfillment of the prophecy told to Abraham: "In thy seed all the kindreds of the earth be blessed."

The Savior, when he visited the American continent, made reference to Ephraim's role referring to them as Gentiles. "And blessed are the Gentiles because of their belief in me, in and of the Holy Ghost, which witnesses unto them of me and of the Father. Behold, because of their belief in me, saith the Father, and because of the unbelief of you, O house of Israel, in the latter day shall the truth come unto the Gentiles, that the fulness of these things shall be made known unto them" (3 Nephi 16:6–7).

In these verses, the Savior adds one more definition to the term *Gentile*: those in the gentile nations who were converted by the power of the Holy Ghost and believe in the Father and His Son Jesus Christ and have the fulness of the gospel. This then is the converted, gathered Gentiles, carrying the blood of Israel, as opposed to those Gentiles with the blood of Israel merely scattered in the Gentile nations.

The "house of Israel" referred to in 3 Nephi 16:6–7 is the seed of Nephi who gathered to hear the Savior. Their seed would fall into unbelief. It would be the Gentiles (Ephraim) who would bring them back to the true gospel.

Mormon adds his testimony: "And now behold this I speak unto their seed [descendants of Lehi], and also to the Gentiles who have care for the house of Israel [gathered Ephraim and Israel in the latter days], that realize and know from whence their blessings come" (Mormon 5:10).

He affirms: "Therefore repent [descendants of Lehi], and be baptized in the name of Jesus, and lay hold upon the gospel of Christ, which shall be set before you, not only in this record but also in the record which shall come unto the Gentiles from the Jews, which record shall come from the Gentiles [gathered Ephraim in the latter days] unto you" (Mormon 7:8).

The Gentiles who "care for the house of Israel" would be the birth-right tribe, Ephraim. They, assisted by other members of the house of Israel with that believing blood, would take the record of the Jews (the Bible) to the seed of the Lamanites.

Many sacrifices were made by Gentiles throughout the centuries to bring the word of God to the seed of Lehi. William Tyndall and others labored tirelessly to translate and make the Bible available in English. He was just one among many contributing to the cause. It would make sense that they too carried the "believing blood" of Ephraim and Israel in their veins and were answering that believing spirit when they made the efforts and sacrifices to give the record of the Jews to the English people who in turn would carry it to the seed of Joseph in America.

Notes

1   Bible Dictionary, "Gentile," 679.
2   Mark E. Peterson, *The Great Prologue*, (Salt Lake City: Deseret Book, 1975), 5–6.
3   Brigham Young, *Journal of Discourses*, 23:184.

Quote of Joseph Smith saying Ishmael was of the tribe of Ephraim.

chapter twenty-four

A FREE PEOPLE

In vision, Nephi described the coming of the Gentiles to the land of America: "And it came to pass that I beheld the Spirit of God, that it wrought upon other Gentiles; and they went forth out of captivity, upon the many waters. And it came to pass that I beheld many multitudes of Gentiles upon the land of promise" (1 Nephi 13:13).

Nephi noted that the Spirit wrought upon the Gentiles. Those Gentiles were receptive to the Spirit and were willing to "go forth out of captivity." Nephi explained that these Gentiles "were like unto my people before they were slain" (1 Nephi 13:15). The likeness referred to by Nephi may be attributed to the blood of Ephraim and Israel running through their veins.

The Spirit touched receptive spirits among those Europeans. The Old World had made many strides forward, but persecutions and lack of opportunity still prevailed over the entire continent. For many Europeans, the only hope for release from the darkness and stagnation was to brave crossing the Atlantic Ocean to put down stakes in the New World. Persecuted religious sects made decisions to move whole congregations. Families, individuals, speculators, indentured servants, criminals and a host of others left to get away from the past and venture into new beginnings. The largest percentage was English, but French, German, Dutch, and Scandinavian immigrants also poured in.

Many found what they were looking for—if they were willing to pay the price. For 150 years, the Gentiles developed and practiced institutions of government and free enterprise. Not until England attempted to exercise its powers and collect direct taxes from the colonies did the Gentiles become dissatisfied. England's Sugar Act of 1764, the Stamp Act of 1765, followed by the Townshed Acts, soon had the colonists protesting. Boston led the protest, which culminated in the Boston Tea Party. The citizens of Boston were not willing to let established privileges and rights slip from their grasp. Not even Mother England would be allowed to trample on these rights. For many, proud of their English ancestry, it was not an easy decision.

In the Virginia Assembly, an outspoken Virginia lawyer taunted fellow Virginians to take action against the affronts of the British.

> They tell us, sir, that we are weak—unable to cope with so formidable an adversary. But when shall we be stronger? Will it be next week or the next year? Will it be when we are totally disarmed and when a British guard shall be stationed in every house? Shall we gather strength by irresolution and inaction?
>
> Sir, we are not weak, if we make a proper use of those means which the God of nature hath placed in our power. *Three millions of people armed with the holy cause of liberty, and in such a country as that which we possess, are invincible to any force which our enemy can send against us.* Besides, sir we shall not fight our battles alone. There is a just God who presides over the destinies of nations; and who will raise up friends to fight our battles for us. The battle, sir, is not to the strong alone; it is to the vigilant, the active, the brave. The war is inevitable. And let it come! I repeat it, sir, let it come!
>
> Gentlemen may cry, "Peace! peace!"—but there is no peace. The war is actually begun. Our brethren are already in the fields. Why should we idle here? What is it that gentlemen wish? What would they have? Is life so dear, or peace so sweet, as to be purchased at the price of chains and slavery? Forbid it, Almighty God! I know not what course others may take; but as for me, give me liberty or give me death.[1]

Patrick Henry was wise enough to acknowledge the components necessary to risk war and make a run for independence. He exaggerated the situation with his remarks that peace with England could only "be purchased at the price of chains and slavery."[2] The colonists were neither in chains nor slaves. The simple fact was that the people living in America at that time enjoyed more freedom and liberty than any other people in the world, including their cousins in England. The American Revolution was fought in a different mind-set than any other movement of its kind. It occurred in a land prepared by the Lord and was led by men with very high ideals and intentions, men influenced by the blood of Israel. The goal for most American revolutionaries was to protect a people and nation of outside or foreign interference and hold on to established liberties.

The Lord had another purpose for the American Revolution: to establish a place where religious freedom would become a constitutional guarantee so that His Church could be restored and weather the storms that would oppose it. There was no other spot on the earth where the Restoration could have succeeded. Lehi prophesied: "Wherefore, this land is consecrated unto him whom he shall bring. And if it so be that they shall serve him according to the commandments which he hath given, it shall be a land of liberty unto them" (2 Nephi 1:7).

On several occasions George Washington acknowledged the hand of the Lord in preserving Americans and the cause for which they were fighting. In a letter to Benjamin Harrison on December 18, 1778, Washington wrote: "Providence has heretofore taken us up when all other means and hope seemed to be departing from us, in this I will confide."

In his first Inaugural Address on April 30, 1789, he acknowledged: "No People can be bound to acknowledge and adore the invisible hand, which conducts the Affairs of men more than the People of the United States. Every step, by which they have advanced to the character of an independent nation, seems to have been distinguished by some token of providential agency."

Washington also said to Reverend William Gordon on March 9, 1781: "We have . . . abundant reason to thank providence for its many favorable interpositions in our behalf. It has, at times been my only dependence for all other resources seemed to have fail'd us."

"For it is wisdom in the Father that they should be established in this land and set up as a free people by the power of the Father" (3 Nephi 21:4). But gaining that freedom would come at a very high cost.

Notes

1   William Writ, *Sketches of the Life and Character of Patrick Henry,* (Philadelphia: Clayton 1818), 120–23. Italics added.

2   Ibid.

chapter twenty-five

THE REVOLUTIONARY WAR

Thomas Paine, in his pamphlet *American Crisis*, written during one of the darkest hours of the American Revolution, penned the following:

> If there be trouble let it be in my day, that my child may have peace and this single reflection, well applied is sufficient to awake every man to duty.
>
> These are the times that try men's souls. The summer soldier and sunshine patriot will, in this crisis, shrink from the service of their country, but he that stands it now deserves the love and thanks of man and woman. Tyranny, like hell, is not easily conquered; yet we have this consolation with us that, the harder the conflict, the more glorious the triumph. What we obtain too cheap, we esteem too lightly; it is dearness only that gives every thing its value. Heaven knows how to put a proper price upon its goods, and it would be strange indeed if so celestial an article as freedom should not be highly rated.

Thomas Paine, an Englishman turned American patriot, captured the spirit of the American Revolution. His *American Crisis* became a powerful propaganda tool and motivating force in dark days when many questioned whether the revolt against England had any probability of success.

The Lord told Nephi that this would be "a land of liberty unto the Gentiles" (2 Nephi 10:11). If the Book of Mormon had been available in 1776, anyone reading those words would wonder how it would be possible.

The American colonies had existed for only a short 150 years, compared to Europe, which had been in existence for thousands of years. Great Britain was the most powerful country in the world both militarily and economically. England's military might was staggering compared to its colonies, having experienced officers, soldiers, and sailors. Its navy roamed the world. The American corps of officers had little or no experience. Some fought with England in the French and Indian War but were always under the supervision of the British. Americans had no united government. There was no treasury to fund a war, pay soldiers, or purchase supplies. The Continental Congress met for the first time in 1775, but it was nothing more than a confederation of states. It had no power to tax, raise funds to support the war, or pay soldiers. The American economy didn't have the maturity or strength to support a war. Military stores, if there were any, were inadequate. America had no way of manufacturing gun powder. Most of the gunpowder, ammunition, and cannons had to be imported. Colonial manufacturing produced few if any of those items. The colonies had no navy or standing army. A few militias were organized throughout the colonies but lacked any central coordination or control. No significant supply system existed to furnish an army with food, clothing, or provisions. During the revolution, many of those items were supplied by the individual soldiers out of their own funds. Most colonial families owned a musket, but there was no standardization. Often soldiers had to make their own ammunition to fit their unique muskets.

So how did a group of upstart colonists manage to wear down the mighty and mobile British Empire and win independence? "I beheld that their mother Gentiles were gathered together upon the waters and upon the land also, to battle against them. And I beheld the power of God was with them, and also that the wrath of God was upon all those that were gathered together against them to battle" (1 Nephi 13:17–18).

The power of God was with them. Many afflictions tried men's souls before independence was won. Success required sacrifice, deprivation, and some of the best blood the world had seen. Men and women would suffer from cold, heat, hunger and thirst, imprisonment, loss of property, lack of pay, terrible wounds, and too often death.

Those who offered themselves to the cause were a remarkable group. Only once has the world seen such a collection of dedicated, talented, selfless men and women appear in the same place at the same time. The assemblage included men like George Washington, Benjamin Franklin, John

Adams, Thomas Jefferson, Samuel Adams, Joseph Warren, Nathanael Green, and many more for whom we have names, but even more for whom we don't. They understood the words of Thomas Paine when he said: "What we obtain too cheap, we esteem too lightly; it is dearness only that gives every thing its value." In the truest sense, if freedom and liberty is to be understood and appreciated, it must be earned and achieved. The children of Israel were handed freedom and it didn't work for them. Americans inherited the basic values of individual rights and liberty from their ancestors, and then they went out and used those values in their own situations. There were no handouts for them.

A few examples will perhaps give the reader an idea of what they experienced and accomplished in winning independence.

When the call went out through Paul Revere and other messengers on that morning, April 19, 1775, the areas around Lexington and Concord, Massachusetts, responded. For what the British thought would be a relatively easy mission turned into a nightmare and was the spark igniting the Revolutionary War. Men left plows, farms, and shops to answer a call that the British were threatening to destroy or capture the military supplies at Concord. They gathered muskets, gunpowder, lead balls, and provisions; they left their families, joined local militias, and marched toward Lexington and Concord.

Isaac Davis, a farmer and captain of the minutemen in his town of Acton, was typical of those who left families that night. He and his wife, Hannah, were concerned as they put their children to bed earlier that evening. All were ill; two had symptoms of canker rash, a fatal childhood disease. The family was awakened by a warning gunshot. Hannah tried to calm the children as minutemen from the surrounding area gathered in her kitchen. For Isaac, it was not an easy decision to leave that night, but there was no hesitation to do his duty. As he was leaving the house, he turned to Hannah and said, "Take good care of the children." He then left to march at the head of his company. Hannah Davis had a premonition that she would never see her Isaac again. He was one of the first to fall when the British fired on the militia at the North Bridge in Concord.

Those defenders were not much different than a group of Nephite defenders answering the same sort of call issued by General Moroni as he marched to the aid of Pahoran and the government: "And he did raise the standard of liberty in whatsoever place he did enter, and gained whatsoever force he could in all his march towards the land of Gideon. And it came to pass that thousands did flock unto his standard, and did take up their swords in the defence of their freedom, that they might not come into bondage" (Alma 62:4–5).

The blood of Ephraim and Massasseh was answering the call to defend liberty in both instances. Americans, much like Moroni's defenders, flocked to the standard of liberty forcing the British back into Boston. Within a few days an army of twenty thousand men surrounded the Boston area, hemming British troops inside the city.

The great statesman Ben Franklin wrote: "It is common observation here that our cause is the cause of all mankind, and that we are fighting for their liberty in defending our own." Franklin was only moderately aware of the truth and significance of that statement.

Courage, cowardice, great battles, and heroic acts fill the pages of history books, but usually little is said of the wives and children left behind. Though not life threatening, their struggles while husbands and fathers are away were very important to the cause. They were often the motivation and reason for men to volunteer. They stayed at home caring for farms and shops, waiting for their men to return. Some women followed the army wherever it went and endured the same hardships, doing the cleaning, ironing, and various chores for the men. A few served as soldiers and spies, taking heavy personal risks. For all, the wait was long and trying. Many great and noble spirits served the cause in different ways. A wife and mother of the Revolution described her situation:

> And besides to tell the truth, I had no leisure for murmuring. I rose with the sun and all through the long day I had no time for aught but my work. So much did it press upon me that I could scarcely divert my thoughts from its demands, even during the family prayers, which thing both amazed and displeased me, for during that hour, at least, I should have been sending all my thoughts to heaven for the safety of my beloved husband and the salvation of our hapless country. Instead of which I was often wondering whether Polly had remembered to set the sponge for the bread, or to put water on the leach tub, or to turn the cloth in the dying vat, or whether wool had been carded for Betsey to start her spinning wheel in the morning, or Billy had chopped light wood enough for the kindling, or dry hard wood enough to heat the big stove or whether some other thing had not been forgotten of the thousand that must be done without fail, or else there would be a disagreeable hitch in the housekeeping.[1]

The plight of the common soldier during the Revolutionary War is seldom told from their own perspective. Generals and officers usually get the majority of attention. Those leaders marched at the head of armies made up of volunteer soldiers. Often, those soldiers served without pay, proper clothing, or enough ammunition, food, supplies, or—most hurtful—without the full support of the American population. Many brought to the service their own muskets, clothing, blankets, and supplies or they went without.

Joseph Plumb Martin, one of those citizen soldiers, wrote an insightful book about the time he served in the Revolutionary War. He entitled it, *Private Yankee Doodle Being a Narrative of Some of the Adventures, Dangers and Sufferings of a Revolutionary Soldier*. His descriptions of everyday life of the soldiers are eye opening.

> How often have I had to lie whole stormy, cold nights in a wood, on a field, or a bleak hill, with such blankets and other clothing like them, with nothing but the canopy of the heavens to cover me. All this too in the heart of winter, when a New England farmer, if his cattle had been in my situation, would not have slept a wink from sheer anxiety for them. And if I stepped into a house to warm me, when passing, wet to the skin and almost dead with cold, hunger, and fatigue, what scornful looks and hard words have I experienced.
>
> Almost everyone had heard of the soldiers of the Revolution being tracked by the blood of their feet on the frozen ground. This is literally true, and the thousandth part of their suffering has not, nor ever will be told.[2]

Washington's soldiers more often than not fought under trying conditions. They were usually outgunned, out-trained, and outsmarted. The cause for the misfortune was lack of training, weapons, and equipment. Too many times the Americans turned and ran when the British moved into formation like clockwork, fired a volley, and charged. It was a frightening experience for untrained troops. Fortunately, there were also times when the Americans displayed remarkable courage and fortitude.

Bunker Hill and Harlem Heights in New York were two battles where the Americans proved they could stand against a British charge. Colonel Thomas Knowlton and his Connecticut regiment were an integral part of the American operations at both engagements. At Bunker Hill his regiment was assigned to defend the American left side to prevent the British from making a flanking movement to get behind the defenders on

Bunker Hill. The first British attacks that day were against his position and all were repulsed. As the British brought more and more troops into the battle and the situation deteriorated for the Americans, Knowlton's troops covered the retreat, saving many lives.

After Boston, the fighting moved to New York. The British sailed an armada of ships and thirty thousand men to take the city and hopefully bring an end to the war. Washington had a third that many to defend the New York area. British General Howe first invaded Long Island, forcing the Americans to make a rushed retreat to Manhattan Island. Only the resourcefulness of Washington and his men made the retreat possible. The British pressed the Americans on Manhattan, forcing further retreats. As the Americans were pulling back from the British onslaught, Washington ordered Thomas Knowlton with 150 men to scout out the enemy lines. They inadvertently ran into two battalions of British and a fierce firefight commenced. Washington, hearing the gunfire, sent reinforcements to aid Knowlton. The fighting was furious as Americans forced the British to turn and run. It was the first time in such a confrontation that Americans saw the backs of the Redcoats rather than their bayonets charging at them. Thirteen hundred of Washington's men forced five thousand British soldiers to retreat from the battlefield. It was a minor victory, but one that proved a great morale booster. Thomas Knowlton gave his life that day. He was not only a good soldier and leader but a member of a family that has a great posterity of which some are part of the church today. Ephraim's blood flows in the veins of Thomas Knowlton's posterity, as with many others participating in the Revolutionary War.

Bloody tracks were often left where Washington's troops marched. The winter of 1776 was no exception. Reeling from the loss of New York, Washington led a ragged army across New Jersey, trying to stay ahead of Lord Cornwallis and the British army and hoping to catch and destroy him. Fortunately the Americans reached Trenton at the Delaware River and crossed to safety just as the British approached. Washington was soon planning a surprise attack against the British and Hessians (hired soldiers) left to guard Trenton. These were desperate times for the Revolution. Washington was hoping a successful assault would revitalize the army and the Revolution.

The plan required another crossing of the Delaware and a surprise attack against the Hessians guarding Trenton. As soldiers marched to load the boats for the river crossing that Christmas day in 1776, they looked like anything but a professional army. Most of their uniforms and clothing were in rags. Many were without shoes. Substituting were rags wrapped around cracked and cold feet. Some were even barefoot. Major James Wilkinson noted he could see on the path the men had trod "tinges here and there with blood from the feet of men who had broken shoes." It was cold; snow began to blow in the soldier's faces. These men had spent many a cold night just weeks before fleeing from the British in their rags, and yet that night they willingly followed their Commander in Chief in a bold and dangerous plan to strike back at the British.

In spite of the inclement elements, Washington led his ill-clad men to surprise the camp at Trenton and win a much needed and deserved victory. His men were too tired and worn to do anything but take their prisoners and booty back across the Delaware to a safe position and get some much needed rest.

On December 29, 1776, Washington again ferried his army to the New Jersey side of the Delaware. Only 1,500 soldiers had strength to go with their Commander. Washington soon learned that Lord Cornwallis and 5,500 troops were headed his way with revenge on their minds. He was concerned that his army was in danger of being trapped against the river by a far superior British force. What made matters more critical was the enlistments of the New England troops, which was the majority of his army, ran out on December 31, just two days away. His army would then dissolve and the men would exit to find their way home. He felt he could not take his armed forces back across the river for fear a retreat would have devastating repercussions on the morale of the army and country. He was about to lose much of his fighting force just as Lord Cornwallis and his British army approached. The men so wanted to return to families needing them.

Washington had little choice but to make an appeal for the men to stay. He knew better than anyone the hardships they had suffered. Desperate times called for desperate measures. He asked one of the New England regiments to form up. They stood in lines that cold December day waiting while Washington made an appeal for the men to stay one more month. A sergeant recorded the events:

> He alluded to our recent victory at Trenton; told us that our services were greatly needed and that we could now do more for our country than we ever could at any future period; and in the most affectionate manner entreated us to stay. The drums beat for volunteers, but nor a

man turned out. The soldiers, worn down with fatigue and privations, had their hearts fixed on home and the comforts of the domestic circle, and it was hard to forgo the anticipated pleasures of the society of our dearest friends.

The General wheeled his horse about, rode in front of the regiment and addressing us again said, "My brave fellows, you have done all I asked you to do, and more than could be reasonably expected; but your country is at stake, your wives, your houses and all that you hold dear. You have worn yourselves out with fatigues and hardships, but we know not how to spare you. If you will consent to stay one month longer, you will render that service to the cause of liberty and to your country which you probably never can do under any other circumstances.

A few stepped forth and their example was immediately followed by nearly all who were fit for duty in the regiment, amounting to about two hundred volunteers. An officer enquired of the General if these men should be enrolled. He replied: "No! men who will volunteer in such a case as this need no enrolment to keep them to their duty."[3]

At other camps officers made similar appeals with success. Militia from the surrounding area also joined the camp. Washington soon had five thousand troops to resist Lord Cornwallis's charging army.

Colonel Edward Hand of Pennsylvania delayed Cornwallis from reaching Washington's camp until nightfall. Greatly outnumbered, his men used whatever natural cover they could find and fired their long rifles at the oncoming enemy, forcing them to deploy and bring up the cannons. As soon as the British accomplished that, Hand and his men withdrew to a new position, each time successfully delaying Cornwallis's march toward Washington. The temperatures were above freezing, making the roads the British traveled a muddy quagmire slowing their advance. British cannons stuck in the mud and had to be pulled out, wasting both time and energy. Darkness arrived before Cornwallis reached Washington's camp. After convening a council of war among his officers, Cornwallis decided his own troops were too tired to risk an assault on a dug-in enemy at night. He was certain Washington was trapped and morning light would give the British a decided advantage.

Washington also held a council of war with his officers to determine a course of action. Their position was tentative at best. Someone suggested a plan to march the army silently around the left flank of the British camp, down a relative unknown path, and attack British troops stationed at Princeton, twelve miles to the north. The plan was adopted since there were no other promising alternatives.

The weather made an accommodating change for the Americans. A cold wind came up and temperatures dropped below freezing. The ground soon froze hard. Only a few hours earlier the muddy roads, which slowed the British, were now solid, enabling the Americans to move the cannon more easily and rapidly. The wheels were wrapped in rags to avoid noise which might alert the British lookouts.

Washington assigned four hundred men to keep the campfires burning brightly and to continue the appearance of digging in preparation for the British attack. The British were deceived while Washington made his escape. Again, bloody streaks in the snow and mud were left behind by the American army lacking shoes as it marched north. The blood of Ephraim was in the mix of red streaks left in the snow and mud that cold January night in New Jersey.

The attack on the British at Princeton began as the Americans approached the town. At one point, the British gained the advantage, forcing the Americans to retreat. Washington rode in, mounted on his white horse, rallied the troops, and with the aid of other officers got them to re-form and move against the British. He personally led the attack. When the two sides got within thirty yards of each other, they halted and fired a volley. One of Washington's staff officers saw the General disappear in a cloud of smoke and feared the worst. When the smoke cleared, Washington was still astride his horse, waving his soldiers forward. They went on to claim another victory, energizing the army and country. The victories at Trenton and Princeton were fitting tributes to the quality of men and officers of the Revolution.

The next winter brought similar circumstances to the American army. Earlier in the fall the British won two major battles against Washington's troops, took control of the capital, forced Congress to flee to York, and broke the American blockade of the Delaware River, giving them access to Philadelphia by the sea. Washington decided to spend winter camp in a place called Valley Forge. Dr. Albigence Waldo, a surgeon at Valley Forge, described conditions in the camp:

> I am sick—discontented—and out of humour. Poor food—hard lodging—cold weather—fatigue—nasty cloathes—nasty cookery— vomit half my time—smoaked out of my senses—the Devils in't—I can't endure it—Why are we sent here to starve and freeze?—What sweet felicities have I left at home: A charming wife—pretty children—good

beds—good food—good cookery—all agreeable—all harmonious! Here all confusion—smoke and cold—hunger and filthyness—a pox on my bad luck! There comes a bowl of beef soup, full of burnt leaves and dirt, sickish enough to make a Hector spue—away with it boys!

There comes a soldier; his bare feed are seen thro' his worn out shoes, his legs nearly naked from the tattered remains of an only pair of stockings, his breeches not sufficient to cover his nakedness, his shirt in strings, his hair disheveled, his face meager; his whole appearance pictures a person forsaken and discouraged.[4]

The winter at Valley Forge was mild compared to two years later when Washington's army camped at Morristown. The soldiers suffered the same privations, this time in six-foot snow drifts and temperatures constantly below freezing.

What motivated these soldiers and statesmen to sacrifice so much to win independence? They could have surrendered to the British, been forgiven of their treason, returned home, and lived relatively independent lives under British rule. Thomas Paine and John Adams indicated the primary motivation of those men was to pass on to their children the rights of independent free men. They had become accustomed to liberty and were not about to give it up without fully exhausting their strength, nerve, and will. They fully believed in the cause even when the odds seemed to be so heavily stacked against them. Many carried that believing blood of Ephraim, cherishing liberty above safety and freedom above the comforts of home. There are no words to fully describe who they were and what they accomplished.

Nephi wrote: "The Gentiles that had gone out of captivity were delivered by the power of God" (1 Nephi 13:19). Many forefathers prayed for the strength to survive the trials of winning freedom and recognized the power of God was with them in their struggle for independence.

Notes

1   Helen Evertson Smith, *Colonial Days and Ways, As Gathered from Family Papers*, originally published in 1900, (New York: Frederick Ungar, 1966), 226–7; this quotation is printed in *The American Revolutionaries: A History in Their Own Words 1750–1800*, edited by Milton Meltzer (New York:

Thomas Y. Crowell, 1987), 70.

2   Joseph Plumb Martin, *Private Yankee Doodle*, edited by George E. Scheer, (New York: Eastern Acorn Press, 1962), 284.

3   "Account of Princeton," *Pennsylvania Magazine of History and Biography*, 515–519, as quoted in the *The Spirit of Seventy-Six,* 519–20.

4   Albigence Waldo, "Valley Forge, 1777–1778, Diary of Surgeon Albigence Waldo, of the Connecticut Line." *Pennsylvania Magazine of History and Biography*, 1897, 305–310, as quoted in the *Spirit of Seventy-Six*, 639–642.

chapter twenty-six

FOR THIS PURPOSE

$\mathcal{D}uring$ Nephi's remarkable vision regarding the future state of America, he "beheld . . . that the wrath of God was upon all those that were gathered against them to battle" (1 Nephi 13:18). This scripture refers to the Gentiles who came to America and the Mother Gentiles who sent troops to keep them within the British Empire. The wrath referred to in this scripture was shown in unique, natural ways. There were a few instances when the Americans were aided by the weather such as happened as the Americans broke camp to attack the British at Princeton but the major reasons for lack of success on the part of the British came from poor internal decisions, futile policies, failed strategies and dissension within the army and country.

King George III, shortly after deciding to go to war, hired seventeen thousand Hessian mercenaries to augment his own Redcoats to squash the rebellion in America. That single act turned many of the loyalists and fence sitters in America to the patriot side. They asked themselves how they could remain loyal to a king willing to hire foreign mercenaries to fight against British citizens. The actions of British and Hessian soldiers—looting, burning homes, committing atrocities against citizens, and their own arrogance—turned many Americans away from the crown. The British often were their own worst enemies.

British commanders lacked aggression. Often after major victories, they neglected to follow up when they could have struck a death blow to the American cause. General Howe had two opportunities at New York to trap a sizable portion of the American army but refused to take advantage. Several times the British had opportunities to inflict catastrophic blows and failed to do so. British commanders allowed Washington and his army to survive when they could have ended the war. Their indecision, dissension among higher ranking officers, and lack of aggression was a major reason Washington managed to maintain an army under such trying circumstances.

Most British governmental officials and military officers thought the war would be over in a matter of months. One British General made the statement in Parliament that with five thousand men he could march from one end of the American continent to the other. At that time there were few who would have argued with him. Looking at the two sides on paper, no assessment would have given the Americans much of a chance to win independence. But the British didn't count on the war lasting for eight long years or the Americans putting up any real resistance. They were mistaken on both counts. British pride, ignorance, and arrogance among governmental officials and military officers led them to underestimate the staying power of their American cousins. The British were fighting a war at the end of a three-thousand-mile supply chain. Most supplies for their military came from England, an ocean away. It was time consuming and costly. The cost and the length of the war put a terrible strain on the British economy.

European nations formed alliances with the Americans, distracting the British from the war in America. France became an ally, furnishing badly needed money, military supplies, and men. The battle at Yorktown was as much a French victory as it was Washington's. Spain and the Netherlands provided money and aid to the colonies. All three countries made their contributions primarily to get revenge and weaken the British or to win back lost holdings the British had taken in previous wars. France and Spain entered treaties with America, causing stress in the British home front and disrupting British plans for executing the war in America. Britain was forced to keep part of its army in Europe to counteract threats from their long time enemies. Those resources could have been used against Americans making the odds much tougher for Washington. Support among the British citizens was hot and cold. Many factors, both internal and external, proved a detriment to the British cause. There were no great miracles performed against the British, as was done for the children of Israel, just the workings of the Lord through existing nations, animosities, geographical features and human nature to accomplish His purposes.

General Washington was forced to use the tactics of Roman statesman and general Fabius Maximus Verrucosus in the second Punic War with the Carthaginians (218–201 BC). Those tactics were to harass the enemy at every opportune moment but to avoid pitched battles where the winner could take all. Washington really didn't have a choice. He knew that as long as the army existed, the British could not claim victory. The British seemed oblivious to the strategy. Their strategy was to capture the large cities in America, as was usually done in the European wars, forcing the enemy to capitulate. They gained little except a place to house armies. A winter camp in Philadelphia actually weakened the British army. Washington's "Fabian tactics" eventually wore down the British both in America and London. Only once did he really abandon the tactic, and that was at Yorktown, where with the aid of French naval and ground forces, he had a decided advantage and made the most of it. The loss persuaded the British government to finally sue for peace and grant independence.

God informed Jacob in 2 Nephi that "there shall be no kings upon the land who shall raise up unto the Gentiles" (2 Nephi 10:11). There was only one person with the clout and respect of the people to either make himself king or have the people proclaim him king—George Washington. On at least two different occasions the Continental Congress gave him emergency dictatorial powers to execute the war. The wrong man may have been very tempted to establish a military dictatorship. Fortunately, Washington had no such desires. He always considered himself Commander of the army but subject to civil authorities. He was often very frustrated with Congress, but never to the point that he thought the military should take the reigns of government.

A movement among army officers in 1782 to establish a monarchy with Washington as the king was quickly squashed by the Commander. In a letter of reply to the leader of the movement, Washington wrote:

> With a mixture of great surprise and astonishment I have read with attention the Sentiments you have submitted to my perusal. Be assured Sir, no occurrence in the course of the War, has given me more painful sensations than your information of there being such ideas existing in the Army. . . .

I am much at a loss to conceive what part of my conduct could have given encouragement to an address, which to me seems big with the greatest mischiefs that can befall my Country. If I am not deceived in the knowledge of myself, you could not have found a person to whom your schemes are more disagreeable. . . . Let me conjure you, then, if you have any regard for your Country, concern for your self or posterity, or respect for me, to banish these thoughts from your Mind and never communicate, as from yourself or any one else, a sentiment of the like Nature.[1]

With such strong resolve, Washington quenched one dangerous attempt to establish a monarchy in America. Toward the close of the war, growing discontent arose among the officer corps for a perceived indifference toward pay and pensions of those who served during the Revolution. They threatened to either resign at the end of the war or disband if a peace agreement were signed, leaving the country without military leadership. Their actions were designed for a military takeover of the government. Washington was the only man in the country commanding the respect to ward off the threatened coup. He called for a meeting of the officers.

He personally prepared a speech, hoping to change the minds of the officers he had served with for many years. His arguments were eloquent and emotional. When finished, he felt like he had done little to change their minds. He paused for a moment and reached into his pocket to obtain a letter from a congressman. He stumbled as he began to read the letter. Slowly he reached into his pocket, found a pair of glasses, and put them on. He begged their indulgence for wearing the glasses: "Gentlemen, you must pardon me. I have grown grey in your service and find myself growing blind." Tears filled the eyes of many officers. Attitudes quickly changed. Washington finished the letter and immediately left the room. He again defused a threat that could have changed the course of history. Washington was committed to an America as a republic, not a nation ruled by a monarch. Times and events have often borne witness of the wisdom and greatness of the man who led the troops during those crucial times.

Brigham Young paid tribute to those men who laid it all on the line to ensure an independent America capable of creating a republic on the promised land.

We believe that the Lord had been preparing that when he should bring forth his work that, when the set time should fully come, there might be a place upon his footstool where sufficient liberty of conscience should exist, that his Saints might dwell in peace under the broad panoply of constitutional law and equal rights. In this view we consider the men of the Revolution were inspired by the Almighty, to throw off the shackles of the mother government with her established religion. For this cause were Adams, Jefferson, Franklin, Washington and a host of others inspired to deeds of resistance to the acts of the King of Great Britain, who might also have been led to those aggressive acts, for aught we know, to bring to pass the purposes of God, in thus establishing a new government upon a principle of greater freedom, a basis of self-government allowing the free exercise of religious worship.

It was the voice of the Lord inspiring all those worthy men who bore influence in those trying times, not only to go forth in battle but to exercise wisdom in council, fortitude, courage and endurance in the tented field, as well as subsequently for themselves and succeeding generations, the blessings of a free and independent government.[2]

Another prophet of the Lord, Wilford Woodruff, penned words giving tribute to "those worthy men who bore influence in those trying times": "I am going to bear my testimony to this assembly, if I never do it again in my life, that those men who laid the foundation of this American government, and signed the Declaration of Independence were the best spirits the God of heaven could find on the face of the earth. They were choice spirits, not wicked men. General Washington and the men that labored for the purpose were inspired of the Lord."[3]

It wasn't only the Lord who served as inspiration to our founding fathers. The efforts and sacrifices of thousands who had gone before them, laying the foundation for the forefathers, funneled down over the ages to those men who changed the course of history. The dedication and labor of literally hundreds of thousands who had gone before them were coming to fruition in that spot on earth that Brigham Young described as "a place upon his footstool where sufficient liberty of conscience should exist." Washington, Franklin, Adams, Jefferson, and a host of others felt not only the guiding hand of the Lord but the guiding inspirations from many who made contributions, both large and small, to further the Lord's purposes.

Thomas Jefferson was assigned the task of writing the document declaring independence. John Adams took on the task of pushing it through the Congress. The work of both men was brilliant and taxing. The words of the Declaration of Independence speak of their dedication:

We hold these truths to be self-evident, that all men are created equal, that they are endowed by their Creator with certain unalienable rights, that among these are life, liberty and the pursuit of happiness.

That to secure these rights, governments are instituted among men, deriving their just powers from the consent of the governed,

That whenever any form of government becomes destructive to these ends, it is the right of the people to alter or abolish it, and to institute new government. . . .

And for the support of this declaration, with a firm reliance on the protection of Divine Providence, we mutually pledge to each other our lives, our fortunes and our sacred honor.

Below that final paragraph, fifty-six men affixed their signature. They were "the best spirits the God of heaven could find on the face of the earth." Many of them proved their dedication during the course of the war, sacrificing homes, fortunes, farms and lives. Thomas Paine said: "Those who expect to reap the blessings of freedom must, like men undergo the fatigues of supporting it." John Adams knew the Declaration of Independence would not come without price. "I am well aware of the toil and blood and treasure that it will cost us to maintain this declaration and support and defend these States. I can see that the end is more than worth all the means and that posterity will triumph in that day's transactions." Benjamin Franklin may have made the most poignant of statements when debate raged about the Declaration of Independence. He was reported to have said: "We must all hang together or assuredly we shall all hang separately."

Washington was not present in 1776 when the Declaration of Independence was voted upon and signed. He was leading the troops and preparing for an attack by the British against New York. Despite all the odds, his troops outlasted the British, forcing England to acknowledge independence for its American colonies—but the great work was not finished. There was no law to define what that independence meant or to guarantee rights of the citizens. Washington put an end to the danger of monarchy, but the threat of the promised land becoming thirteen different states was looming over the country. The government under the existing Articles of Confederation had neither the unity nor strength to ward off external threats from other countries or internal threats from citizen groups. A central government, limited in power, protecting individual rights but strong enough to hold the nation together, was needed.

"Therefore, it is not right that any man should be in bondage to another. And for this purpose have I established the Constitution of this land, by the hands of wise men whom I raised up unto this very purpose and redeemed the land by the shedding of blood" (D&C 101:79–80). Who were these wise men the Lord raised up for the purpose of establishing the Constitution? Many had been involved in winning independence. The two most prominent were George Washington and Benjamin Franklin. John Adams and Thomas Jefferson were in Europe serving as ambassadors to Great Britain and France.

Washington was the one essential character to the Constitutional Convention. He served as president, seldom participating in deliberations and debate but adding a presence to validate the convention and win public support. Ben Franklin, usually not a man of many words in conventions, played the role of compromiser among the delegates. Both were essential roles to the success of the convention.

The men meeting at the Constitutional Convention were also inspired by the philosophical works of the Greeks and respect for law advocated by the Romans. Many had studied the Enlightenment thinkers: John Locke's advocacy of natural rights; Montesquieu's separation of powers among the three branches of government; Voltaire's freedom of thought, speech, conscience, and the dignity of man; Rousseau's limitation on governmental control; and Adam Smith's argument that laissez-faire philosophy as the most reasonable method of promoting strong and independent economic growth. Magna Carta, the English Bill of Rights, and England's bicameral system of governments were on their minds.

> The framers of the Constitution were mostly young men, aggressive and energetic. Their average age was forty-four. That included Benjamin Franklin who was eighty-one years old and at least fifteen years senior to everyone else. Five of the delegates were in their twenties. Many others, including James Madison and Alexander Hamilton, were in their thirties. James Wilson, Luther Martin, and Oliver Ellsworth were between forty-one and forty-five. George Washington and a few others were fifty-five. Only four were sixty or older.
>
> Most of the Constitutional delegates were lawyers; eight were judges. All were accustomed to making decisions that affected the courses of other men's lives. Each played important and complex roles in society.
>
> Half of the delegates to the Constitutional Convention had been members of the Continental Congress. Nearly half had been officers in

the army during the Revolutionary War. Six had signed the Declaration of Independence. Two had signed the Articles of Confederation. Sixteen had been or were later state governors. More than half would be elected to the United States Congress. Two were to become president and one would be vice-president. Two were to be chief justices of the Supreme Court. As the natural leaders of their society, they found themselves in a remarkably strong position to undertake the task before them.[4]

These men, carrying the blood and spirit of generations who went before them, absorbing the experiences and sacrifices of their ancestors, put on the earth at the right place and at the appropriate time, established a Constitution for a prepared and promised land. Their experience is one that no other people will ever live. Their accomplishments fulfilled many prophecies. They completed the last great act necessary for the Lord's gospel to once again come to earth. As great as their accomplishment was, it was only a preparation for a greater work to come. But, that work would never have been possible if they had not stayed the course and completed the task of making the promised land truly "a land of freedom." We must never forget who they were and what they accomplished. They truly have made a lasting contribution to who we are.

Notes

1 George Washington to Lewis Nicola, May 22, 1782, *Writings of George Washington*, John C. Fitzpatrick, vol. 24 (Washington, DC: 1931–39), 272.

2 Brigham Young, *Journal of Discourses*, 2:170, Feb. 18, 1855.

3 Wilford Woodruff, in Conference Report, 89–90, April 10, 1898.

4 Frank W. Fox and LeGrand L. Baker, "Wise Men Raised Up" *Ensign*, June 1976.

chapter twenty-seven

WHAT WE CAN DO FOR THEM

- There shall none come into this land save they shall be brought by the hand of the Lord. (2 Nephi 1:6)
- Gentiles who had gone forth out of captivity did humble themselves before the Lord and the Lord was with them. (1 Nephi 13:16)
- The Gentiles shall be blessed upon the land. (2 Nephi 10:10)
- The Spirit of the Lord, that it was upon the Gentiles and they did prosper and obtain the land for their inheritance. (1 Nephi 13:15)
- The power of God was with them. (1 Nephi 13:18)
- The Gentiles . . . were delivered by the power of God out of the hands of other nations. (1 Nephi 13:19)
- This land shall be a land of liberty unto the Gentiles. (2 Nephi 10:11)
- There shall be no kings upon the land. (2 Nephi 10:11)
- And I will fortify the land against all other nations. (2 Nephi 10:12)
- The Lord God will raise a mighty nation among the Gentiles, yea even upon the face of this land. (1 Nephi 22:7)
- Whatsoever nation shall possess it shall be free from bondage, and from captivity, and from all other nations under heaven. (Ether 2:12)

Fulfillment of the above scriptures was brought about by the Lord through the men and women who served Him. A group of men, representative of all those contributors through all the ages, called upon an Apostle of the Lord in the St. George Temple, demanding that he do something for them that they could get in no other place but a House of the Lord. They recognized the need for the ordinances of the temple. Wilford Woodruff in General Conference, April 10, 1898 reported:

> Another thing I am going to say here, because I have a right to say it. Every one of those men that signed the Declaration of Independence with General Washington called upon me, as an Apostle of the Lord, Jesus Christ, in the temple at St. George two consecutive nights and demanded at my hands that I should go forth and attend to the ordinances of the house of God for them. Men are here, I believe, that know of this—Brothers J. D. T. McAllister, David H. Cannon and James C. Bleak. Brother McAllister baptized me for all these men, and I then told these brethren that it was their duty to go into the temple and labor until they got endowments for all of them. They did it. Would those spirits have called upon me, as an Elder in Israel, to perform that work if they had not been noble spirits before God? They would not.
>
> I bear this testimony because it is true. The spirit of God bore record to myself and the brethren while we were laboring in that way.

The fifty-six signers of the Declaration of Independence plus George Washington were a diverse group. They were a representation of the Gentiles Nephi refers to in 1 Nephi 13 (see above noted scriptures). Those fifty-six signers and Washington were not just acting on behalf of themselves as they demanded the temple ordinances; they represented all those who participated with them and those who had gone before them. The influence of the blood of Ephraim and the promises made to him and his descendants were truly coming to fruition.

In his journal Wilford Woodruff wrote concerning the days the temple work was completed for those signers and several others who contributed.

> Aug 21, 1877 I Wilford Woodruff went to the Temple of the Lord this morning and was Baptized for 100 persons who were dead including the signers of the Declaration of Independence. . . .
>
> It was a vary interesting day. I felt thankful that we had the privilege and the power to administer for the worthy dead especially for the signers of the declaration of Independence, that inasmuch as they had laid the foundation of our Government that we could do as much for them as they had done for us.

In addition, temple ordinances were completed for Martin Luther and Abraham Lincoln.

The words of Wilford Woodruff, after completing the temple ordinances for the forefathers, summarizes our obligation to them, "We could do as much for them as they had done for us." There are many more whose contributions haven't received the public attention of those signers of the Declaration of Independence but who deserve the blessings of the temple. Efforts to complete the work for all those who have gone before would be an invaluable way of showing our gratitude for their individual contributions to so many blessings enjoyed today. Most notable among those blessings is the gift of liberty conveyed from generations past to our generation.

Part Four

Who Is Ephraim?

chapter twenty-eight

THE RESTORATION

September 17, 1787, the Constitutional Convention in Philadelphia surrendered to divine and human forces that had been in play for hundreds of years and approved the Constitution for the United States of America. By June of 1788, the necessary two-thirds of the states voted to accept the national Constitution. In 1791 a Bill of Rights was added to the Constitution. At long last, a setting existed on the earth where the Restoration of the gospel of Jesus Christ could transpire. The day was near that so many of the spirits of the dead had anticipated. The time had come for the "stone which is cut out of the mountain without hands shall roll forth, until it has filled the whole earth" (D&C 65:2). Joseph Smith Jr. was born just fourteen years after the Bill of Rights was adopted.

The Lord informed Joseph of Egypt that there would be one who would be responsible for the Restoration in the latter days: "And there shall rise up one mighty among them, who shall do much good, both in word and in deed, being an instrument in the hands of God, with exceeding faith, to work mighty wonders, and do that which is great in the sight of God, unto the bringing to pass much Restoration unto the house of Israel" (2 Nephi 3:24). The mighty one referred to would be a descendant of Joseph who was sold into Egypt and Joseph's son Ephraim.

Wherefore, Joseph truly saw our day. And he obtained a promise of the Lord, that out of the fruit of his loins the Lord God would raise up a righteous branch unto the house of Israel; not the Messiah, but a branch which was to be broken off, nevertheless, to be remembered in the covenants of the Lord that the Messiah should be made manifest unto them in the latter days, in the spirit of power, unto the bringing of them out of darkness and out of captivity unto freedom.

For Joseph truly testified, saying: A seer shall the Lord my God raise up, who shall be a choice seer unto the fruit of my loins.

Yea, Joseph truly said: Thus saith the Lord unto me: A choice seer will I raise up out of the fruit of thy loins; and he shall be esteemed highly among the fruit of thy loins. And unto him will I give a commandment that he shall do a work for the fruit of thy loins, his brethren, which shall be of great worth unto them, even to the bringing of them to the knowledge of the covenants which I have made with thy fathers. . . .

And he shall be great like unto Moses . . . to deliver my people O house of Israel. . . .

And out of weakness he shall be made strong, in that day when my work shall commence among all my people, unto the restoring thee, O house of Israel, saith the Lord. . . .

And his name shall be called after me; and it shall be after the name of his father. And he shall be like unto me; for the thing, which the Lord shall bring forth by his hand, by the power of the Lord shall bring my people unto salvation. (2 Nephi 3:5–7, 9, 13, 15)

Joseph of Egypt was told that his descendant would be a "choice seer," a messenger to prepare the way. Out of his weaknesses, he would be made strong. Many of the seer's greatest lessons came from mistakes he made. He would, by the power of the Lord, bring salvation to the people of the world. The latter-day seer would be named Joseph, after Joseph of Egypt and his father. The Restoration of the Lord's Church would lie on the shoulders of Joseph Smith.

Elder Bruce R. McConkie gave a unique insight into Joseph Smith's preparation:

Here is a man who was chosen before he was born, who was numbered with the noble and great in the councils of eternity before the foundations of this world were laid.

Along with Adam and Enoch and Noah and Abraham, he sat in council with the gods when the plans were made to create an earth whereon the hosts of our Father's children might dwell.

Under the direction of the Holy One and of Michael, who became the first man, he participated in the creative enterprises of the Father.

In his premortal state he grew in light and knowledge and intelligence attained a spiritual stature which few could equal, and was then foreordained to preside over the greatest of all gospel dispensations.

Here is a man who was called of God as were the prophets of old.

Born among mortals with the talents and spiritual capacity earned in preexistence, he is ready at the appointed time to perform the work to which he had been foreordained.[1]

In that premortal existence, Joseph was well aware of the earthly preparation necessary to get to the appropriate time and location where he could implement the mission to which he had been ordained. He would be sensitive to the fact that progress during those centuries required many individual sacrifices. Many before him had made individual contributions that made his mission possible. He was probably acquainted with many of those spirits in the premortal existence. He would have been buoyed, motivated, and felt a deep sense of responsibility to bring about conditions for their salvation in the postmortal world as well as those who were then on the earth and those spirits who were yet to come to earth. They would rejoice in every step he made as the Restoration was accomplished. Many of those spirits were his brothers and sisters in Israel.

Discussing his predecessor, Brigham Young said:

It was decreed in the counsels of eternity, long before the foundations of the earth were laid, that he, Joseph Smith, should be the man, in the last dispensation of the world, to bring forth the word of God to the people, and receive the fulness of the keys and power of the Priesthood of the Son of God. The Lord had his eye upon him, and upon his father, and upon his father's father, and upon their progenitors clear back to Abraham and from Abraham to the flood, from the flood to Enoch, and from Enoch to Adam. He has watched that family and that blood as it has circulated from its fountain to the birth of that man. He was foreordained in eternity to preside over this last dispensation.[2]

Brigham Young refers to the Lord having his eye on Joseph's father and father's father. Joseph's immediate progenitors possessed traits that were immersed in his own life, such as hard work, independent thought, service to others, and an intense love of liberty. Joseph recalled that the "love of liberty was diffused into my soul by my grandfathers while they dandled me on their knees." His father's side came from England and his mother's from Scotland. Joseph's father and mother were a constant support to their son, often suffering great tribulations while their son was involved in the work of the Restoration.

Joseph's great-grandfather, Samuel Smith II, was active in local politics in Concord, Massachusetts, and was a member of the provincial council and the Tea Committee. He was known as Captain Samuel Smith. He may well have been involved in events in Massachusetts that led to the war and the fighting around Lexington and Concord, the battles that started the Revolution. Smith was active throughout the war and gave much of himself to win independence. The Prophet's grandfather also served in the Revolution and was a man of strong religious conviction. He made a prediction that "God was going to raise up some branch of his family to be a great benefit to mankind." Smith lived to 1830 and witnessed the beginning of his prediction.

On his mother's side, Joseph's grandfather, Solomon Mack, was apprenticed to another family because of difficult times for his own family. He stayed as an indentured servant until the age of twenty-one, when he was set free. He fought in the French and Indian war and enlisted in the American Army when the Revolutionary War began. He served in the army and as a privateer with two of his sons.

In 1820, the shroud of darkness that had covered the earth for centuries was lifting. Young Joseph Smith responded to a scripture he read in the New Testament: "If any of you lack wisdom, let him ask of God, that giveth to all men liberally, and upbraideth not; and it shall be given him" (James 1:5). Seeking answers to questions, he retired to a grove near his house and prayed. There, in his own words, he "saw a pillar of light exactly over my head, above the brightness of the sun, which descended gradually until it fell upon me. When the light rested upon me I saw two Personages, whose brightness and glory defy all description, standing above me in the air" (JS–H 1:16–17). With that visit, the young Prophet learned that the existing ideas of the nature of God and his Son, Jesus Christ, were flawed. He realized that God, contrary to Enlightenment philosophy, was concerned about His children in their mortal state and would be involved in man's mortal existence by bringing about salvation for mankind. Joseph learned that he would be an instrument in restoring God's church to the earth and that he had been prepared in the eternities for his calling.

Joseph was now about to enter his mortal preparation. His training would come from heavenly messengers who had been patiently waiting to share their knowledge, keys, and experience with the Prophet of the last dispensation. Joseph Smith would be blessed with knowledge and powers like no other mortal.

The Prophet's instruction from those heavenly messengers began when he was seventeen. The Angel Moroni appeared to him four times during the night and day of September 21–22, 1823, telling him of a book written on gold plates deposited in the earth. The book contained "an account of the former inhabitants of this continent, and the source from whence they sprang" and "the fulness of the everlasting Gospel . . . as delivered by the Savior to the ancient inhabitants" (JS–H 1:34). Moroni then quoted several Old Testament scriptures to help the young Joseph understand the importance of the journey on which he was about to embark:

> Behold, I will send my messenger, and he shall prepare the way before me. (Malachi 3:1)

> Behold, I will reveal unto you the priesthood, by the hand of Elijah the prophet, before the coming of the great and dreadful day of the Lord. And he shall plant in the hearts of the children the promises made to their fathers, and the hearts of the children shall turn to their fathers. If it were not so, the whole earth would be utterly wasted at this coming. (JS–H 1:38–39)

> And it shall come to pass afterward, that I will pour out my spirit upon all flesh; and your sons and your daughters shall prophesy, your old men shall dream dreams, and your young men shall see visions. (Joel 2:28)

Moroni also quoted from Isaiah chapter eleven: "And in that day there shall be a root of Jesse, which shall stand for an ensign of the people; to it shall the Gentiles seek: and his rest shall be glorious. And it shall come to pass that the Lord shall set his hand again the second time to recover the remnant of his people. . . . And he shall set up an ensign for the nations, and shall assemble the outcasts of Israel and. . . . Ephraim shall not envy Judah, and Judah shall not vex Ephraim" (Isaiah 11:10–13). Moroni told Joseph that "the fulness of the Gentiles was soon to come in" (JS–H 1:41).

One can only imagine what was racing through the mind of a young seventeen-year-old Joseph Smith as he was visited by an angel. The angel informed him that he would be that messenger to prepare the way for the Savior's Second Coming. In the first visit he learned the role Ephraim would play in the Restoration, that there would be a turning of hearts to the fathers and from the fathers to the children, the time for the gathering of Israel would soon occur, and dreams and visions would be a part of the restoration process. References to the Gentiles in the above quoted scriptures would be those in whose veins the believing blood of Israel flowed. Ephraim and Judah would play significant roles in the gathering of Israel.

Joseph received directions to go to the place where the gold plates were buried. He wasn't allowed to take them at that time but was instructed that he should return each year to the spot. For four years he made the annual visit and received "instruction and intelligence" from Moroni "respecting what the Lord was going to do, and how and in what manner his kingdom was to be conducted in the last days" (JS–H 1:54). On September 22, 1827, Joseph obtained the gold plates from Moroni at the Hill Cumorah and soon began the process of translating the Book of Mormon. The learning process the young Prophet experienced as he translated the Book of Mormon can only be imagined. Only one who has read, studied, and pondered this book would understand the depth of learning available among its pages.

On May 15, 1829, John the Baptist conferred the Aaronic Priesthood on Joseph Smith and Oliver Cowdery, and later that month those same two received the Melchizedek Priesthood at the hands of the Apostles Peter, James, and John. By March of 1830, the first copies of the Book of Mormon were available. Then on April 6, 1830, The Church of Jesus Christ of Latter-day Saints was organized in Fayette, New York. Joseph received many revelations applicable to the Restoration and organization of the Church. Those revelations were later organized into the Doctrine and Covenants. The crowning revelation came on April 3, 1836, recorded in section 110. This revelation came to the Prophet and Oliver Cowdery in the Kirtland Temple:

> The veil was taken from our minds, and the eyes of our understanding were opened.
>
> We saw the Lord standing upon the breastwork of the pulpit, before us; and under his feet was a paved work of pure gold, in color like amber.
>
> His eyes were as a flame of fire; the hair of his head was white like the pure snow; his countenance shone above the brightness of the sun; and his voice was as the sound of the rushing of great waters, even the voice of Jehovah saying:

I am the first and the last; I am he who liveth, I am he who was slain; I am your advocate with the Father. Behold, your sins are forgiven you; you are clean before me; therefore lift up your heads and rejoice. (D&C 110:1–5)

Joseph and Oliver had three other visions that day in the Kirtland Temple; all were essential to the calling of the Prophet and the tribe of Ephraim fulfilling its responsibility as the birthright tribe. "After this vision closed, the heavens were again opened unto us; and Moses appeared before us, and committed unto us the keys of the gathering of Israel from the four parts of the earth, and the leading of the ten tribes from the land of the north" (D&C 110:11).

Moses, as he passed the keys on to Joseph, knew the gathering would not fail this time. He had watched from the yonder heavens as the Lord prepared the earth and Israel for the gathering in the last dispensation and the Second Coming of the Lord Jesus Christ. It must have been a special moment for Moses as he conferred those keys on the Prophet.

> And after this, Elias appeared, and committed the dispensation of the gospel of Abraham, saying that in us and our seed all generations after us should be blessed.
>
> After this vision had closed, another great and glorious vision burst upon us; for Elijah the prophet, who was taken to heaven without tasting death, stood before us, and said:
>
> Behold, the time has fully come, which was spoken of by the mouth of Malachi—testifying that he [Elijah] should be sent, before the great and dreadful day of the Lord come—
>
> To turn the hearts of the fathers to the children, and the children to the fathers, lest the whole earth be smitten with a curse—
>
> Therefore, the keys of this dispensation are committed unto your hands; and by this ye may know that the great and dreadful day of the Lord is near, even at the doors. (D&C 110:12–16)

Receiving those keys would be essential for Ephraim to accomplish its calling as the birthright tribe. It would be Ephraim, aided by other members of the house of Israel, particularly Manasseh, who would be the driving force in the gathering of Israel and leading the ten tribes from the north, blessing all the earth with the gospel and doing the essential work of turning hearts of the children to the fathers and the fathers to the children. Ephraim would also soon begin to gain an understanding of what their ancestors had accomplished over the past centuries to bring about the Restoration.

Brigham Young said: "The Book of Mormon came to Ephraim, for Joseph Smith was a pure Ephraimite, and the Book of Mormon was revealed to him."[3] Joseph was an Ephraimite, but he also carried Gentile blood. The introduction to the Book of Mormon states it was "sealed by the hand of Moroni, and hid up unto the Lord, to come forth in due time by way of the Gentile." Joseph Smith was chief among the Gentiles to bring the Book of Mormon to light. His ancestors came from a Gentile nation, a nation that long ago was sifted with the blood of Ephraim.

The prophet of the Lord was given the keys by three heavenly messengers to (1) send out missionaries to preach the gospel and offer the blessings of the covenant of Abraham (Elias), (2) gather Israel both spiritually and physically (Moses), and (3) weld the generations together to receive all the blessing the Lord has to offer (Elijah). The prophet would confer those keys on all the Twelve Apostles who in turn would pass those keys on to leaders who would follow. The President of The Church of Jesus Christ of Latter-day Saints holds those keys today.

Joseph Smith was a remarkable prophet called to open the work in the last dispensation. He gave his life in testament to his dedication. The following verses from the Doctrine and Covenants pay tribute to the life and work of the Prophet of the last dispensation.

> Wherefore, I the Lord, knowing the calamity which should come upon the inhabitants of the earth, called upon my servant Joseph Smith, Jun., and spake unto him from heaven, and gave him commandments. (D&C 1:17)

> The ends of the earth shall inquire after thy name, and fools shall have thee in derision, and hell shall rage against thee;
> While the pure in heart, and the wise, and the noble, and the virtuous, shall seek counsel, and authority, and blessings constantly from under thy hand. (D&C 122:1–2)

> Joseph Smith, the Prophet and Seer of the Lord, has done more save Jesus only, for the salvation of men in this world, than any other man that ever lived in it. He lived great, and died great in the eyes of God and his people; and like most of the Lord's anointed in ancient times, has sealed his mission and his works with his own blood. (D&C 135:3)

It is the blood of Ephraim and Israel testifying to the world that Jesus Christ's Church has been restored in these latter days.

Praise to the Man
Praise to the man who communed with Jehovah!
Jesus anointed that Prophet and Seer.
Blessed to open the last dispensation,
Kings shall extol him, and nations revere.

Praise to his memory he died as a martyr;
Honored and blest be his ever great name!
Long shall his blood which was shed by assassins,
Plead unto heaven while the earth lauds his fame.

Great is his glory and endless his priesthood.
Ever and ever the keys he will hold.
Faithful and true, he will enter his kingdom,
Crowned in the midst of the prophets of old.

Sacrifice brings forth the blessings of heaven;
Earth must atone for the blood of that man.
Wake up the world for the conflict of justice
Millions shall know brother Joseph again.

Hail to the Prophet, ascended to heaven
Traitors and tyrants now fight him in vain.
Mingling with Gods, he can plan for his brethren
Death cannot conquer the hero again.[4]

Notes

1   Bruce R. McConkie, "The Mighty Prophet of the Restoration," *Ensign*, May 1976.
2   Brigham Young, *Journal of Discourses, 7*:289.
3   Ibid., 2:268.
4   William W. Phelps, "Praise to the Man," *Hymns of The Church of Jesus Christ of Latter-day Saints*, (Salt Lake City: The Church of Jesus Christ of Latter-day Saints, 1985), 27.

chapter twenty-nine

THE GATHERING

With the preparation completed, the time had come for the Lord to once again gather His chosen people. The promised land was set to receive Israel. Hearts of those with Israel's blood were softened and receptive to the word of the Lord. Israel of the latter days was prepared and willing to overcome obstacles, face dangers, and make sacrifices for what they believed. A prophet of the Lord was called, tutored, and given "the keys of the gathering of Israel from the four parts of the earth."

Moses, Isaiah, Jeremiah, Ezekiel, Elias, Elijah, John the Baptist, Peter, James, John, Lehi, Nephi, Jacob, Ether, Moroni, the participants in the American Revolution, and many from the nations of Europe must have watched from the eternities with great anticipation. Prophecies of Israel's gathering were finally coming to fruition. What a time it must have been for so many as they observed from yonder heavens the Lord's workings among the house of Israel and nations of the world.

> For can a woman forget her sucking child, that she should not have compassion on the son of her womb? Yea, they may forget, yet will I not forget thee, O house of Israel.
>
> Behold, I have graven thee upon the palms of my hands; thy walls are continually before me. . . .
>
> Thus saith the Lord God: Behold, I will lift up mine hand to the Gentiles, and set up my standard to the people; and they shall bring

thy sons in their arms, and thy daughters shall be carried upon their shoulders.

And kings shall be thy nursing fathers, and their queens thy nursing mothers . . . and thou shalt know that I am the Lord; for they shall not be ashamed that wait for me. (1 Nephi 21:15–16, 22–23; Nephi is quoting Isaiah, compare to Isaiah 49)

The Lord truly had not forgotten His chosen Israel. Preparations for Israel's gathering had been in progress for centuries. "That thou mayest say to the prisoners: Go forth; to them that sit in darkness" (1 Nephi 21:9). The veil of darkness plaguing Israel since they departed from the ways of the Lord in Canaan was about to be lifted. "Neither will the Lord God suffer that the Gentiles shall forever remain in that awful state of blindness, which thou beholdest they are in" (1 Nephi 13:32). The Gentiles were about to see the light of the gospel, something missing in their lives for centuries. (The term *Gentile* as used in these scriptures refers to Gentiles whose blood is mixed with the house of Israel).

And it shall also be of worth unto the Gentiles; and not only unto the Gentiles but unto all the house of Israel, unto the making known of the covenants of the Father of heaven unto Abraham, saying: In thy seed shall all the kindreds of the earth be blessed.

And I would my brethren, that ye should know that all the kindreds of the earth cannot be blessed unless he shall make bare his arm in the eyes of the nations.

Wherefore, the Lord God will proceed to make bare his arm in the eyes of all nations, in bringing about his covenants and his gospel unto those who are of the house of Israel.

Wherefore, he will bring them again out of captivity, and they shall be gathered together to the lands of their inheritance; and they shall be brought out of obscurity and out of darkness; and they shall know that the Lord is their Savior and their Redeemer, the Mighty One of Israel. (1 Nephi 22:9–12)

The scattering of Israel was broad. Nephi tells us that Israel would be "scattered upon all the face of the earth and also among all nations" (1 Nephi 22:3). The sifting of Israel throughout Europe discussed in part one of this book is just a fraction of the total dispersion. Centuries were involved in Israel's diffusion. It continues today as the blood of Israel spreads further and further into the nations of the world. The scattering was a result of Israel's disobedience, but it was also part of the Lord's plan to leaven all the nations of the world with the blood of Israel.

> Speaking of the day of gathering and of the people who should bring it to pass, Moses said: "Joseph . . . shall push the people together to the ends of the earth." The tribe of Joseph shall do it! And who is Joseph? Moses continues: "And they are the ten thousands of Ephraim, and they are the thousands of Manasseh."

> Thus, if Israel is to be scattered in all nations upon all the face of the earth; if she is to be gathered by the tribe of Joseph; if Ephraim has the birthright and is the presiding tribe; if the other tribes are to receive their blessings from Ephraim—then Ephraim must also be in all nations upon the face of the earth, and Ephraim must be the first tribe to gather in the last days. And so it is.[1]

Jeremiah prophesied of Israel's gathering: "For there shall be a day, that the watchmen upon the mount of Ephraim shall cry, Arise ye, and let us go up to Zion unto the Lord our God" (Jeremiah 31:6). Ephraim the birthright tribe would be Israel's watchmen. They were an integral part of the preparation for the day of gathering and by right and obligation were the first to respond, first to gain testimonies and willingly share their testimonies with their brothers and sisters of Israel and with the Gentiles seeking the light of the gospel.

Jeremiah was aware that the gathering would require toil and sacrifice and a change of heart on Israel's part: "Behold I will gather them out of all countries. . . . And they shall be my people, And I will be their God: And I will give them one heart and one way, that they may fear me for ever, for the good of them, and of their children after them: And I will make an everlasting covenant with them, that I will not turn away from them" (Jeremiah 32:37–40). The Lord would be a sanctuary to those who would gather. When hearts changed Israel gained a desire to listen to missionaries, accept the gospel and feel the need to gather to the Church. It is a process that continues today. Due to conditions in some areas of the world, change occurs more slowly but is surely moving forward.

The great instruments which would change hearts are the Book of Mormon and the Bible. Ezekiel was made aware the effect the word of the Lord would have on gathering Israel.

> Moreover, thou son of man, take the one stick, and write upon it, For Judah, and for the children of Israel his companions: then take another stick and write upon it, For Joseph, the stick of Ephraim and for all the house of Israel and his companions.

And join them one to another into one stick; and they shall become one in thine hand. . . .

Thus saith the Lord God; Behold I will take the stick of Joseph, which is in the hand of Ephraim, and the tribes of Israel his fellows, and will put them with him, even the stick of Judah, and make them one stick, and they shall be one in mine hand.

And the sticks whereon thou writest shall be in thine hand before their eyes.

And say unto them, Thus saith the Lord God; Behold, I will take the children of Israel from among the heathen, whither they be gone, and will gather them on every side, and bring them into their own land. (Ezekiel 37: 16–17, 19–21)

Note Ezekiel's reference to the "stick of Ephraim." Ephraim, aided by others of Israel, would be responsible to carry the Book of Mormon to "all the house of Israel and his companions." The stick "which is in the hand of Ephraim" would go forth to "the convincing of Jew and Gentile that Jesus is the Christ, the Eternal God, manifesting himself unto all nations."[2]

Nephite prophets also foretold the scattering and gathering of Israel: "After all the house of Israel have been scattered and confounded, that the Lord God will raise up a mighty nation among the Gentiles, yea even upon the face of this land" (1 Nephi 22:7). The United States was established as the place for Israel's initial gathering. Even within the promised land the Church, to avoid persecution and seek security, would flee and gather in the untamed Salt Lake Valley to establish Zion and build her stakes. Isaiah described the gathering to the mountains of Utah:

And it shall come to pass in the last days, when the mountain of the Lord's house shall be established in the top of the mountains, and shall be exalted above the hills, and all nations shall flow unto it.

And many people shall go and say, Come ye, and let us go up to the mountain of the Lord, to the house of the God of Jacob; and he will teach us of his ways, and we will walk in his paths; for out of Zion shall go forth the law. (2 Nephi 12:2–3; also Isaiah 2:2–3)

Elder Bruce R. McConkie described three phases to the gathering of Israel.

Phase I—From the First Vision, the setting up of the kingdom on April 6, 1830, and the coming of Moses on April 3, 1836 to the secure establishment of the Church in the United States and Canada, a period of about 125 years.

Phase II—From the creation of stakes of Zion in overseas areas, beginning in the 1950s to the Second Coming of the Son of Man, a period of unknown duration.

Phase III—From our Lord's Second Coming until the kingdom is perfected and the knowledge of God covers the earth as the waters cover the sea, and from then until the end of the Millennium, a period of 1,000 years.

This gathering of Israel and this building up of Zion in the last days occurs in stages. The early part of the work, which involved gathering to the United States and building stakes of Zion in North America, has already been accomplished. We are now engaged in gathering Israel within the various nations of the earth in establishing stakes of Zion at the ends of the earth. This is the work that is now going forward in all of the nations.[3]

Isaiah informed his readers that when the Lord "set his hand again the second time to recover the remnants of his people . . . he shall set up an ensign for the nations, and shall assemble the outcasts of Israel, and gather together the dispersed of Judah from the four corners of the earth" (Isaiah 11:11–12). When Moroni first visited Joseph Smith, he told the young Prophet this scripture was about to be fulfilled (see JS–H 1:40).

According to Isaiah, two gatherings would occur in the latter days. Israel would gather to the land of Joseph or America. Ephraim and Manasseh would be the leading tribes in that gathering. The other gathering would be that of the tribe of Judah to the land of its inheritance, modern-day Israel.

Interestingly, both gatherings would proceed through a two-phase process. The first phase would be a necessary physical gathering preceding the more important spiritual gathering. The spiritual gathering could not occur without the physical gathering.

The physical phase of gathering began in the land of Joseph when the first pilgrim carrying the blood of Israel set foot in what would become British North America. He was followed by many other Gentiles with Israel's blood gathering to America. That gathering continued for decades. A nation had to be established, a government formed with a Constitution protecting individual and religious freedom, an economy and culture established before the Lord would initiate the spiritual gathering of Israel. That gathering needed committed Saints to manage and care for Israel gathering from around the world.

Judah is in the physical gathering stage of its tribe to the land of Israel, preparing for the time when the spiritual gathering will commence. That spiritual gathering will come under the direction of he who holds the keys of gathering as handed down by Moses.

The preparation phases or physical gatherings in both countries have required sacrifice, dedication, and hard work. Those who have participated in the physical gatherings make it possible for the spiritual gatherings to occur. Their labors should never be forgotten.

The work of gathering Israel has only begun. Ephraim, aided by other members of the house of Israel, has laid the foundation. There are still millions to gather to the stakes of Zion scattered throughout the world. Today, the blood of Israel can gather with the Saints in their own nations, growing in the gospel and strengthening the church. Modern-day Israel can rejoice within the wall of Zion around the world. The Church is making available the blessings of the temple to more and more Saints as new temples are constructed in many nations. One can only imagine what the blessing of the temple mean to those who have had to do without for so many years.

The words Moroni penned while translating the record of the Jaredites indicates the Lord's blessings for Israel as it gathers to Zion around the world: "Come unto me, O ye Gentiles, and I will show unto you the greater things, the knowledge which is hid up because of unbelief. Come unto me, O ye house of Israel, and it shall be made manifest unto you how great things the Father hath laid up for you, from the foundation of the world" (Ether 4:13–14).

Israel, Israel, God Is Calling
Israel, Israel, God is calling,
Calling thee from lands of woe.
Babylon the great is falling;
God shall all her towers o'er-throw.

Israel, Israel, God is speaking.
Hear your great Deliverer's voice!
Now a glorious morn is breaking
For the people of his choice.

Israel, angels are descending
From celestial worlds on high,

And to man their power extending,
That the Saints may home-ward fly.

Israel! Israel! canst thou linger
Still in error's gloomy ways?
Mark how judgments pointing finger
Justifies no vain delays.

Come to Zion, come to Zion!
Zion's walls shall ring with praise.
Come to Zion, come to Zion!
Zion's walls shall ring with praise.[4]

Notes

1   Bruce R. McConkie, *The Millennial Messiah* (Salt Lake City: Deseret Book, 1982), 191.
2   Introduction to the Book of Mormon.
3   Bruce R. McConkie, "Let Israel Build Zion," *Ensign,* May 1977.
4   Richard Smyth, "Israel, Israel, God Is Calling," *Hymns,* 7.

chapter thirty

A NEW SPIRIT

Soon after the Church was organized, missionaries were called to leave families and go out into the world to share the gospel. The first missionaries were sent to the United States and Canada, but by 1837 missionaries of the Church were sailing across the Atlantic to the British Isles. In 1840, members of the Quorum of the Twelve Apostles were called to expand the effort in Great Britain.

The British Isles were ripe for the coming of the members of the Twelve as missionaries. Most British subjects shared language, culture, and heritage with the missionaries from America. Freedom of religion was a strong tradition in Britain. There was not the strong reliance upon clergy typical on the European continent. The people loved to read the Bible, taking pride in the King James translation that the Apostles used in their preaching. England had a strong central government that ensured uniform application of the laws respecting the practice of religion. This meant that the missionaries were legally equal with other ministers wherever they went in the country. Moreover, the industrial revolution had shattered the social standing of the lower classes and left them feeling they had been abandoned by their ministers. Many were seeking spiritual and temporal satisfaction and support in their lives.

This was the preparation the Lord provided to take the gospel to Great Britain.[1]

Missionaries were sent to other areas of the world including nations on the continent of Europe and in the South Pacific. Orson Hyde was sent to Jerusalem in 1841 to dedicate the Holy Land for the return of the Jews.

The blood of Israel, particularly Ephraim, was awakening to the spirit many prophets had prophesied they would. It was a spirit felt by both missionary and convert. The believing blood scattered among the nations, centuries earlier, was at last being introduced to the restored gospel of Jesus Christ and accepting the restored truths. All the preparation in America and Europe over the centuries was finally coming to fruition. Many an ancestor must have looked from the heavens with hope as their posterity was introduced to a faith that promised eternal lives and eternal families. "And it shall come to pass that the righteous shall be gathered out from among all nations, and shall come to Zion, singing with songs of everlasting joy" (D&C 45:71).

> As the Church spread through Europe, tens of thousands of new converts immigrated to America, leaving everything behind them for their faith and desire to be with fellow members. Of the 60,000 to 70,000 who emigrated to the Salt Lake Valley in the late 1800s, more than 98 percent of the survivors were from Europe, and 75 percent were from Britain. The British converts began to emigrate with the arrival of Brigham Young to Britain in 1840. As American members faced persecutions, new European members brought strength and refreshment.[2]

One member in England described her feelings about the call to go to Zion:

> I believe in the principle of the gathering and felt it my duty to go although it was a severe trial to me in my feelings to leave my native land and the pleasing associations that I had formed there, but my heart was fixed. I knew in whom I had trusted and with the fire of Israel's God burning in my bosom, I forsook home.[3]

Brigham Young wrote a letter to his brother Joseph illustrating the spirit of gathering exhibited by the converts in Great Britain. "They have so much of the spirit of gathering that they would go if they knew they would die as soon as they got there or if they knew that the mob would be upon them and drive them as soon as they got there."[4]

By 1840, thousands had joined the Church and desired to gather to

Zion. They sacrificed all they had to book passage to America. The converts poured into Nauvoo, expanding the population, making it a vibrant, beautiful place to live. But peace and enjoyment were not to be the lot of the early Latter–day Saints. The Prophet Joseph Smith and his brother Hyrum were shot while imprisoned in Carthage Jail. Persecutions soon followed. The Church had been driven from New York, Ohio, Missouri and were now facing the prospect of leaving their beloved city of Nauvoo. On a bitter cold February 4, 1846, the Saints were forced to leave the city and escape west into Iowa. On barges and ferries they fled across the Mississippi River into Iowa, most unprepared for the cold winter conditions, trying the strength and courage of those stalwart Israelites. Mud, sleet, flooded tents, hunger, lack of shelter, sickness, disease, and fatigue were unwelcome companions. Thousands of Saints were scattered along a three hundred mile trail leading west across the state of Iowa.

They were a special people. The blood of Ephraim and Israel flowing in their veins had been tried many times in previous generations. It was a blood capable of meeting the challenges facing the Saints as they journeyed into the west.

> The glory of God is portrayed in the lives of the Latter-day Saint pioneer men, women, and children who placed all they had on the altar. They were prepared to give everything, including their lives. These pioneers forged lives that were fired white hot in the crucible of some of the most difficult suffering and tests. This was a magnificent generation of common, ordinary souls who were brought together through their faith in God and who moved forward to meet danger and trials. They were given a monumental work to do, and they did it.[5]

President Gordon B. Hinckley describes the faith of those pioneers as they were forced from their homes in Nauvoo:

> In the bone-chilling cold of that bitter winter, the exodus began. Many of the Saints gathered their belongings and closed the doors of their dwellings for the last time as they turned to what lay across the river—and west.
>
> How the Saints must have felt, leaving so much behind—the fields they had cultivated, the trees they had planted, the temple they had built. The men, women, and children walked out of their beautiful homes, climbed aboard their wagons, drove down to the river, there to cross and move slowly over the soil of Iowa, looking back now and again at what they were leaving and would never see again.

Leaving Nauvoo was a remarkable act of faith. There was much of hardship ahead for these pioneers, but they had faith in their leaders and faith in the Lord and His goodness—faith that He would once again lead His people to the promised land, faith that they would not falter or fall. So they walked out into the wilderness, their journey marked by faith in every footstep.[6]

Leaving Nauvoo in such haste left the Saints ill-prepared for the journey west. Lack of adequate food and supplies, disorganization in the camps, and an unusual wet spring constantly slowed forward progress. Illness, drenched clothes and bedding, flooded tents, cold temperatures, and deaths hampered movement. The call from the United States Government for volunteers to form the Mormon Battalion in June of 1846 took six hundred men from the ranks of the leading companies to go on a march to California. With the loss of so many men and the slowness of progress, the Saints had little choice but to delay the trek west until the following year. In the interval, they would prepare for the journey and for the gathering of Israel as other members would follow their trail across Iowa to Florence (Council Bluffs). Throughout the next two decades, tens of thousands of Mormons traversed the area in route to Salt Lake City.

The following year the first company of wagons, with Brigham Young at the head, crossed the plains into the Rocky Mountains and begin colonization in the Great Basin. It was the beginning of the fulfillment of the prophecy from Isaiah: "And it shall come to pass in the last days, that the mountain of the Lord's house shall be established in the top of the mountains, and shall be exalted above the hills; and all nations shall flow unto it. And many people shall go and say, Come ye, and let us go up to the mountain of the Lord, to the house of the God of Jacob; and he will teach us of his ways" (Isaiah 2:2–3).

While Saints were establishing a location "in the top of the mountains" for the gathering of Israel, the missionary work in Europe continued. The birthright tribe was fulfilling its responsibility on many different fronts on two continents to gather Israel both physically and spiritually.

The Saints in Utah began the process of transforming the desert to a home for gathering Israel. Irrigation ditches were dug to feed dry parched ground, crops were planted, and a city was laid out with a spot for a House of the Lord. It soon became evident to Church leaders that more members would be needed to build Zion and the Lord's temple. A call went out in 1847 from the First Presidency in an epistle to the Saints in Europe to immigrate to Salt Lake City. They were told to bring their strength and supplies to help build the communities of Zion. At last the Mormons had found a location where they could be at peace and offer a home for Israel's gathering.

In a second call to the members in Europe in an epistle dated October 12, 1849, Church leaders pleaded: "We want men; brethren, come from the States, from the nations, come! and help us build and grow, until we can say enough, the valleys of Ephraim are full."[7]

Brigham Young soon realized that many members in America and Europe wanted to follow the counsel to gather to Zion but lacked the means to make such a journey. With insight and foresight he established the Perpetual Emigration Fund to assist members financially. Over several decades the fund served as an aid for tens of thousands gathering to Zion.

During the years 1847 to 1856, most of the pioneers walked across the plains and through the Rocky Mountains beside covered wagons. The journey across the heartland of America held many challenges for those first groups of pioneers. Tired bodies, sore and swelling feet, sunburn, illness, disease, and death were always a threat, but the wagon companies worked their way to the Salt Lake Valley in relative safety. Communities began to grow and spread.

By 1856 a large number of convert emigrants with little means to contribute to their passage put a strain on the Perpetual Emigration Fund, forcing church leaders to economize. The European emigrants' passage involved travel by ship across the Atlantic then rail or boat to Iowa City. By the time they got to Iowa, neither the fund nor the immigrants could afford wagons, so they resorted to handcarts, a less expensive method of travel.

From 1856 to 1860 ten different handcart companies made the journey to the Salt Lake Valley, including 2,962 men, women, and children pulling a total of 653 handcarts. Each adult in the company was allowed seventeen pounds of clothing and bedding; the children were allowed ten pounds, which were loaded in the handcarts. The handcarts were then packed with food and provisions. A cart fully loaded weighed about five hundred pounds. Throughout the long and tiresome journey, bodies wore out, forcing the pioneers to discard the personal items to lighten the load. Several wagons loaded with tents, food, and supplies, pulled by oxen, accompanied each company. Tents accommodating twenty people were set up each night for sleeping, taken down the next morning, and loaded in the wagons.

The total number of estimated deaths from the ten handcart companies was 250, a much higher rate than among the wagon companies. The death toll for eight of those companies was not severe, but the cost of human suffering was extreme for the Willie and Martin companies.

The crossing and rescue of the Willie and Martin Handcart Companies were some of Ephraim's finest hours. Words are not available to totally describe the strength of spirit, the suffering, and sacrifice of the members of those companies and their rescuers. It is a testament to the conviction, fortitude, and power of the blood of Ephraim and Israel. Their story is one that deserves recognition equal to many other sacrifices that are written in the history books of this country and the nations of the world.

As handcart companies were organized, normal procedure was to select a missionary returning from Europe to serve as captain. One can only imagine what would have gone through the minds of those selected to lead, thinking their missions were completed and then to find they had the responsibility of getting a handcart company through to the Salt Lake Valley. James G. Willie, age forty-one, and Edward Martin, age thirty-seven, were selected to lead the fourth and fifth companies. For various reasons the companies were late leaving England and delayed in getting to Iowa City. Handcarts were not ready for them when they arrived, causing delays. A crash effort to build the handcarts made for shoddy workmanship, causing the need for constant repair along the trail and bringing further delays. The results proved tragic for the two companies.

The Willie Company pulled out of Iowa City July 15, with five hundred members in good spirits but short of oxen to pull the wagons. The shortage of animals made it necessary for the handcarts to carry an extra weight, wearing out both the carts and those who pulled them. As the Willie Company camped on the Wood River in Nebraska, their cattle stampeded when spooked by a herd of buffalo. By the time the men rounded up the animals, thirty were missing, creating even further problems. To compensate, each handcart was loaded with an extra sack of flour, adding a hundred pounds to an already heavy load. When they reached Fort Laramie, Wyoming, about the first of September, most of their supplies were depleted, and to their surprise there were no provisions for them to purchase. At the rate they were consuming food, they would run out about three hundred and fifty miles from Salt Lake City. Rations were cut and the Saints resolved to hurry the pace. That became more and more difficult as the men and women grew weaker due to the lack of nourishment and difficulty of the trail. Many a father and husband gave some of his share of food to his wife and family. Pulling the carts became more and more difficult.

John Chislett, a sub-captain in the Willie Company, recorded in his diary the sufferings of the members as food was running low and the weather was getting colder. The Martin Handcart Company, two weeks behind the Willie Company, was in a desperate condition. They had still to travel in the snowy cold winter conditions that hit the Rockies that winter of 1856.

October 4, 1856, Willard Richards rolled into Salt Lake with word that two handcart companies were still out wending their way to Zion. Brigham Young was surprised to learn that the two companies had left Iowa City so late in the year. Fortunately the word came just before the October semi-annual conference of the Church. President Young and other authorities admonished the members in Salt Lake to open their hearts and send aid to their brothers and sisters of the Willie and Martin companies who were still as many as seven hundred miles from Salt Lake. They asked for ox teams, wagons, horses, mules, flour, and food supplies. The women were asked to furnish blankets, stockings, shoes, and clothing.

The response was marvelous. Sixteen wagon loads were ready by October 7. The first of the rescue parties, consisting of twenty-seven young men, was on the way east to find the Willie and Martin companies. Others were soon to follow.

The rescuers moved east across the continental divide when they were hit by a severe snow storm that lasted three days. At the Sweetwater River they halted, hoping for better weather when Captain Willie and Joseph Elder rode into camp and urged them to push on with all possible speed to give aid to his struggling handcart company who didn't have the strength to go any further. The next day, October 21, the first rescue party reached the Willie Company and found members with frozen fingers, toes, feet, and ears, most too weak to continue. Aid was administered, food given to hungry souls, and all the members of the Willie Company loaded in the wagons for the remainder of the journey to Salt Lake. Of the five hundred men, women, and children who started the journey, sixty-seven died along the trail.

While some of the rescue party helped the Willie Company, others pushed east to find the Martin Company. For five days they traveled a hundred miles through snow and freezing temperatures. At Devil's Gate, they camped and sent three scouts ahead to search for the lost company. They rode another twenty miles before finally discovering the Martin Company. Over fifty of the company had died already. Many more were on the verge. With the knowledge that there was help ahead, the company pushed on to the base camp at Devil's Gate where the rescuers were preparing for them.

The ordeal was not over for members of the company or their rescuers. They had a limited supply of food and soon found themselves in a blizzard and sub-zero temperatures. The handcart company decided to move to a ravine, later named Martin's Cove, where they would be somewhat sheltered from the storm and could find wood for fires. It was a two and a half mile trip from Devil's Gate and required the crossing of the Sweetwater River. Fording one more river was just too difficult for many who had suffered so much to that point. Their strength gone and will broken, some wept at the thought of having to wade through the ice cold water.

Realizing the desperate situation, three eighteen-year-old members of the rescue party came to the aid of the handcart members. The three young men waded through the stream and one by one carried women, children, and men across the ice cold water. Most of the day, they waded back and forth across the Sweetwater River. One can only imagine the stress the ordeal must have put on their bodies both at the time and later in their lives. "When President Brigham Young heard of this heroic act, he wept like a child, and declared that this act alone would immortalize them."[8]

After crossing the river, the Martin Company rested in the cove for five days while temperatures dipped to eleven degrees below zero. There was little to eat for so many suffering from cold and hunger. When the temperatures warmed, the handcart got moving again. Many of the handcart members were in such a weakened condition that a decision was made to empty most of the wagons and load them with the weakest and sick members from the company. Those with sufficient strength would continue to walk, but they would no longer have to pull the handcarts. The company moved out on November 9.

The Martin Company was still not out of the woods. So many had to be put in the wagons; little room was left for food. There were still over three hundred miles of rugged mountainous territory to cover before they reached Salt Lake. The freezing temperatures continued to test the strength of those pioneers. Frozen fingers and toes, hunger, and death plagued the march. Food rations were again running out.

West of them, more rescue parties were struggling through the rough snow-covered trail to reach them. Heavy snow stopped their progress at the South Pass. Some of the rescuers turned back, thinking the Martin Company must have made winter quarters somewhere along the trail. Others stayed, faithfully waiting for their brothers and sisters to appear ahead of them.

A messenger was sent to the rescue party camped at the South Pass. Wagons filled with flour were soon headed to the company. A few days later, other wagons from Salt Lake greeted the company, carrying clothes and provisions. On November 30, the Martin Company reached the Salt Lake Valley. The number of those who died along the trail was between 135 and 150. Many from both the Willie and Martin Handcart Companies gave their last breath in their quest to gather to Zion. It is a testament to their strength and spirit.

George E. Grant described conditions in the Martin Company in a dispatch to Brigham Young in October of 1856:

> It is not much use for me to attempt to give a description of the situation of these people, for this you will learn from your son Joseph A and br. Garr, who are the bearers of this express; but you can imagine between five and six hundred men, women and children, worn down by drawing handcarts through snow and mud; fainting by the wayside; falling, chilled by the cold; children crying, their limbs stiffened by cold, and their feet bleeding and some of them bare to snow and frost. The sight is almost too much for the stoutest of us; but we go on doing all we can, not doubting or despairing.[9]

The members of the handcart companies were not the first to leave streaks of blood in the snow along a path they trod. Revolutionary soldiers were noted to have left the same kind of streaks from bare, cracked feet as they marched to the battles at Trenton and Princeton and into winter quarters at Valley Forge. Both the pioneers and soldiers of the Revolution carried the precious believing blood of Ephraim. That blood had been shed many times in many places over the centuries to prepare for the gathering of the House of Israel. This time those streaks in the snow were from Saints who were gathering to Zion. Ephraim finally had an inheritance in the land of Joseph where they could assemble and be at peace.

In an address given November 16, 1856, after the arrival of the Willie Handcart Company in Salt Lake City, Brigham Young said:

> My faith is, when we have done all we can then the Lord is under obligation and will not disappoint the faithful; he will perform the rest. If no other assistance could have been had by the companies this season, I think they would have had hundreds and hundreds of fat buffaloes crowding around their camp, so that they could not help but kill them. But, under the circumstances, it was our duty to assist them, and we were not too early in the operation.[10]

The participants in the latter-day journey across the plains of America were a different people from the children of Israel who followed Moses as they escaped from their Egyptian taskmasters. When they panicked at the sight of the Egyptian army at the Red Sea, or when their food supply ran out or when there was no water in the camp, they complained to Moses that they would be better off if they were back serving the Egyptians. They were not left to their own devices to solve the problems. They may have gone a little hungry or thirsty but never faced starvation. The Lord came to their rescue each time and satisfied their complaints. They were not prepared to face trials encountered along the way.

As President Young pointed out, the Lord could have done the same for the Mormon Pioneers if it had been necessary. But it was not. The blood of Ephraim had been tested and prepared for many centuries for trials encountered as they gathered to Zion. There were no cries to be taken back to Winter Quarters or Europe. Instead they constantly pressed forward, facing hardships, freezing temperatures, lack of food, tired bodies and spirits, and even death. The Lord knew there were Saints in Salt Lake willing to go to the aid of their brothers and sisters in Israel who were still out on the trail. They would do for the handcart Saints what the Lord did for the children of Israel. Ephraim and Israel had matured over the centuries. They were prepared to do what was necessary to bring the handcart companies to Zion. Brigham Young stated, "It was our duty to assist them," and that is exactly what they did.

The Mormon pioneers left a great legacy. That legacy has had an effect on the members of the Church to the present day. Their faith and actions had much to do with determining who Latter-day Saints are today. It is a humbling thought to think we are of the same blood of Israel as those pioneers and many others who went before them. A celebration of their lives should include words that describe the character traits they exhibited:

faithful, independent, hard working, obedient, courageous, willing to sacrifice, resourceful, devoted, grateful, hopeful, willing to serve, loving, unselfish, tough, charitable.

The Saints truly exemplify that who we are is who we were:

They, the Builders of the Nation

They, the builders of the nations, Blazing trails along the way;
Stepping stones for generation, Were their deeds of every day.
Building new and firm foundations, Pushing on the wild frontier,
Forging onward, ever onward, Blessed, honored Pioneer!

Service ever was their watch-cry; Love became their guiding star;
Courage their unfailing beacon, Radiating near and far.
Every day some burden lifted, Every day some heart to cheer
Every day some hope the brighter, Blessed, honored Pioneer!

As an ensign to the nation, They unfurled the flag of truth
Pillar, guide, and inspiration To the hosts of waiting youth;
Honor, praise, and veneration To the founders we revere!
List our song of Adoration, Blessed, honored Pioneer![11]

Notes

1   *Church History in the Fulness of Times*, prepared by the Church Education System, (Salt lake City: The Church of Jesus Christ of Latter-day Saints, 1989), 229.

2   The Pioneer Story, www.lds.org.

3   Jane Charters Robinson Hindly, "Jane C. Robinson Hindly Reminiscences and Diary," Family and Church History Department Archives (The Church of Jesus Christ of Latter-day Saints).

4   Brigham Young, quoted in Leonard J. Arrington, *American Moses*, (1985), 94.

5   Vaughn J. Featherstone, "Following in Their Footsteps," *Ensign*, July 1997, 8.

6   Gordon B. Hinckley, "Faith in Every Footstep: The Epic Pioneer Journey," *Ensign*, May 1997, 62.

7   "Second General Epistle," Oct. 12, 1849, in J. A. Little, *From Kirtland to Salt Lake City*, (Salt Lake City: 1890), 207–8.

8 Solomon F. Kimball, "Our Pioneer Boys," *Improvement Era*, July 1908, 679.

9 George E. Grant, as quoted in LeRoy and Ann Hafen, *Handcarts to Zion: the story of a Unique Western Migration 1856–1860,* (Spokane, WA: The Arthur H Clark Company, 1960), 116–17.

10 Printed in the Deseret News of Nov. 26, 1856, as quoted in Hafen, *Handcarts to Zion*, 250.

11 Ida R. Alldredge, "They, the Builders of the Nation," *Hymns*, 36.

chapter thirty-one

LATTER-DAY EPHRAIM

For I am the Lord thy God; I dwell in heaven; the earth is my footstool. . . .

My name is Jehovah; and I know the end from the beginning; therefore my hand is over thee.

And I will make of thee a great nation, and I will bless thee above measure, and make thy name great among all nations, and thou shalt be a blessing unto thy seed after thee, that in their hands they shall bear the ministry and Priesthood unto all nations. . . .

For I give unto thee a promise that this right shall continue in thee, and in thy seed after thee *(that is to say, the literal seed, or the seed of the body) shall all the families of the earth be blessed, even with the blessings of the Gospel*, which are the blessings of salvation, even of life eternal. (Abraham 2:7–9, 11; italics added)

Abraham learned from the Lord Jehovah that through the literal seed of his body, that is to say his descendants, all the families of the earth would be blessed with the gospel, salvation, and eternal life. That blessing and responsibility passed from Abraham to Isaac, Jacob, Joseph, and Ephraim. Ephraim was given both the blessing and responsibilities of the birthright among the twelve tribes of Israel. Those responsibilities included preparation for and winning independence for the promised land, custody and care of the Book of Mormon, raising a prophet for the latter days, accepting the priesthood keys, preaching the gospel of Jesus Christ to the world,

199

gathering Israel from the nations where it has been scattered, establishing the ordinances of salvation for the dead, building Zion and her stakes, overseeing the building of the New Jerusalem, welcoming the ten lost tribes when they return, and preparing for the Lord's Second Coming.

In a discourse to the members in 1855, Brigham Young spoke of the blood of Israel going out to the nations of the world:

> Recollect that we are now calling upon the Elders to go and gather up Israel; this is the mission given to us. It is the first mission given to the Elders in the days of Joseph. The set time is come for God to gather Israel, and for His work to commence upon the face of the whole earth, and the Elders who have arisen in this Church and Kingdom are actually of Israel. Take the Elders who are now in this house, and you can scarcely find one out of a hundred but what is of the house of Israel.
>
> Will we go to the Gentile nations to preach the Gospel? Yes, and gather out the Israelites, wherever they are mixed among the nations of the earth. Ephraim has become mixed with all the nations of the earth, and it is Ephraim that is gathering together.
>
> It is Ephraim that I have been searching for all the days of my preaching, and that is the blood which ran in my veins when I embraced the Gospel. [1]

Many members of the Church may not be aware that the preponderance of Latter-day Saints are the literal seed of Abraham and Ephraim. Joseph Fielding Smith wrote: "The great majority of those who become members of the Church are literal descendants of Abraham through Ephraim, son of Joseph."[2]

> Nearly all of the Latter-day Saints are of Gentile ancestry as well as being of the house of Israel. In this Dispensation of the Fullness of Times, the gospel came first to the Gentiles and then is to go to the Jews. However, the Gentiles who receive the gospel are in the greater part, Gentiles who have the blood of Israel in their veins.[3]
>
> Therefore, through the scattering of Israel among the nations, the blood of Israel was mixed with the Gentile nations, fulfilling the promise made to Abraham. Most of the members, although they are designated as descendants of Abraham, through Israel also have in their veins Gentile blood. Moreover we have learned that the Lord said that he would scatter Israel among the Gentile nations, and by doing so would bless the Gentile nations with the blood of Abraham. Today we are preaching the gospel in the world and we are gathering

out, according to the revelations given to Isaiah, Jeremiah, and other prophets, the scattered sheep of the house of Israel. These scattered sheep are coming forth mixed with Gentile blood from their Gentile forefathers. Under all the circumstances it is very possible that the majority, almost without exception, of those who come into the Church in this dispensation have the blood of two or more of the tribes of Israel as well as the blood of the Gentiles.[4]

Throughout Israel's history, members of different tribes mixed and married with each other, making it possible for families and individuals to carry the blood of more than one tribe of Israel. Israel was to bless the nations and families of the world with its blood and all the implications that would come with it. That was accomplished through the scattering of Israel as it mixed with the nations of the world. Many, if not most, of the members of the Church carry blood from more than one tribe along with Gentile blood. Those who are pure Gentile will be adopted into the House of Israel and receive all the blessings promised to Abraham and his posterity. Those carrying out the responsibilities of Ephraim in the latter days are then, for the most part, Abraham's literal descendants. They are fulfilling the promises made by the Lord to that great Patriarch, to the House of Israel and to the inhabitants of the world.

Ancient prophets were aware that effort, power, energy, strength and sacrifice would be required of Ephraim to affect the covenant given to Abraham.

> But, the Lord liveth, that brought up the children of Israel from the land of the north, and from all the lands whither he had driven them; and I will bring them again into their own land that I gave unto their fathers.
>
> Behold, I will send for many fishers, saith the Lord and they shall fish them; and after will I send for many hunters, and they shall hunt them from every mountain, and from every hill, and out of the holes of the rocks. (Jeremiah 16:15–16)

> Turn, O backsliding children saith the Lord; for I am married unto you: and I will take you one of a city, and two of a family, and I will bring you to Zion. And I will give you pastors according to mine heart, which shall feed you with knowledge and understanding. (Jeremiah 3:14–15)

> And ye shall be gathered one by one, O ye children of Israel. (Isaiah 27:12)

Gathering Israel would require many hunters to "hunt them out from every mountain and hill and even from the holes in the rocks." Israel will be found "one of a city and two of a family." No one knows better that the words of Jeremiah and Isaiah are true than our present-day missionaries. They are searching for Israel one by one throughout the world to bring them the blessings of Abraham and strengthen the stakes of Zion. They rely on the Spirit of the Lord to guide them in their efforts.

Wilford Woodruff, in a talk to the Saints, explained responsibility of those born in these latter days.

> We occupy a different position from any other generation; there has never been a generation since God made the world that has been called upon to perform the work the Latter-day Saints have.
>
> It is our lot to live in the great and last dispensation that God has given unto man, the dispensation in which a people is to be prepared to build up the kingdom of God on the earth, which is to thrown down or overcome no more forever.
>
> We are called of God. We have been gathered from the distant nations. . . . The Lord has been watching over us from the hour of our birth. We are of the seed of Ephraim and of Abraham, and of Joseph who was sold into Egypt, and these are the instruments that God has kept in the spirit world to come forth in these latter days to take hold of this kingdom and build it up. These are my sentiments with regard to the Latter-day Saints. I will repeat what I have often said—there is no power beneath the heavens that can remove Zion out of her place, or destroy this Church and kingdom as long as the people do the will of God, for he will sustain them and overrule the acts of their enemies for their good and for the final triumph of his truth in the earth. Then what manner of men and women ought we to be, who are called to take part in the great latter-day work? We should be men and women of faith, valiant for the truth as it has been revealed and committed into our hand. We should be men and women of integrity to God, and to his holy Priesthood, true to him and true to one another. Our aim is high, our destiny is high, and we should never disappoint our Father, nor the heavenly hosts who are watching over us. We should not disappoint the millions in the spirit world, who too are watching over us with an interest and anxiety that have hardly entered into our hearts to conceive of. These are great and mighty things which God requires of us. We would not be worthy of salvation, we would not be worthy of eternal lives in the kingdom of our God, if anything could turn us away for the truth or from the love of it.[5]

Isaiah foretold of the labor to strengthen the stakes of Zion.

> Enlarge the place of thy tent, and let them stretch forth the curtain of thy habitations; *spare not, lengthen thy cords and strengthen thy stakes*;
> For thou shalt break forth on the right hand and on the left, and thy seed shall inherit the Gentiles and make the desolate cities to be inhabited. . . .
> With everlasting kindness will I have mercy on thee, saith the Lord thy Redeemer. . . .
> For the mountains shall depart and the hills be removed, but my kindness shall not depart from thee, neither shall the covenant of my peace be removed, saith the Lord that have mercy on thee. (Isaiah 54:2–3, 8, 10; italics added)

The Lord instructed Joseph Smith in this dispensation concerning the need to search out Israel and strengthen the stakes of Zion.

> Send forth the elders of my church unto the nations which are afar off; unto the islands of the sea; send forth unto foreign lands; call upon all nations, first upon the Gentiles and then upon the Jews.
> And behold, and lo, this shall be their cry, and the voice of the Lord unto all people: Go ye forth unto the land of Zion, that the borders of my people may be enlarged, and that her stakes may be strengthened, and that Zion may go forth unto the regions round about. (D&C 133:8–9)

Among Ephraim's important assignments, in what Elder Bruce R. McConkie termed Phase II of the gathering, will be establishing atmospheres where the tent can be broadened to countries without the gospel. It is a work requiring much patience, love, duty, and a desire to offer all people of the earth the opportunity to partake of the blessings of Abraham's covenant. "The Spirit of the Lord God is upon me; because the Lord hath anointed me to preach good tidings unto the meek: He hath sent me to bind up the brokenhearted, to proclaim liberty to the captives, and the opening of the prison to them that are bound; . . . to comfort all that mourn; . . . to give unto them beauty for ashes . . . that they might be called trees of righteousness, the planting of the Lord, that he might be glorified" (Isaiah 61:1–3). It is one of the challenges for Ephraim in the latter days. Its accomplishment will be one of the great records told as the Millennium approaches.

Preaching the gospel, gathering Israel, and strengthening the stakes of Zion are just the beginning of Ephraim's responsibilities in the latter days. President Joseph F. Smith had the great vision of the spirits of the dead, their spiritual state and the preaching of the gospel to those who didn't have a chance to hear it during their sojourn on earth. He said he saw:

> The hosts of the dead, both small and great. I beheld that they were filled with joy and gladness, and were rejoicing together because the day of their deliverance was at hand. They were assembled awaiting the advent of the Son of God into the spirit world to declare their redemption from the bands of death. While this vast multitude waited and conversed, rejoicing in the hour of their deliverance from the chains of death, the Son of God appeared, declaring liberty to the captives who had been faithful; And there he preached to them the everlasting gospel, the doctrine of the resurrection and the redemption of mankind from the fall, and from individual sins on conditions of repentance. But behold from among the righteous, he organized his forces and appointed messengers, clothed with power and authority, and commissioned them to go forth and carry the light of the gospel to them that were in darkness, even to all the spirits of men; and thus was the gospel preached to the dead. The dead who repent will be redeemed, through obedience to the ordinances of the house of God. And after they have paid the penalty for their transgressions, and are washed clean, shall receive a reward according to their works, for they are heirs of salvation. (D&C 138)

Those dead described by President Joseph F. Smith must wait for ordinances of salvation that can only be accomplished here on earth. The ordinances of baptism, endowment, and sealing must be completed in the temples of the Lord by members of the Church before the resurrected beings in the spirit world can receive their eternal rewards. It is a daunting task but so necessary.

The signers of the Declaration of Independence appearing to Wilford Woodruff in the St. George temple were only a sampling of those hoping to have the ordinance and sealing work completed for them so they too can enjoy all the blessings promised to Abraham. Elijah, when restoring the keys for this work, warned latter-day Israel that the hearts of the fathers are turned to the children; now it is time that the children turn their hearts to the fathers (see D&C 110:14–16). They are waiting for a work that only the living members can do for them.

We have a great work before us in the redemption of our dead. The course that we are pursuing is being watched with interest by all heaven. There are fifty thousand millions of people in the spirit world who are being preached to by Joseph Smith, and the Apostles and Elders, his associates, who have passed away. Those persons may receive their testimony, but they cannot be baptized in the spirit world, for somebody on the earth must perform this ordinance for them in the flesh before they can receive part in the first resurrection, and be worthy of eternal life. *It takes as much to save a dead man as a living one.* The eyes of these millions of people are watching over these Latter-day Saints. Have we any time to spend in trying to get rich and in neglecting our dead? I tell you no.[6]

Ephraim must also prepare for the return of the lost ten tribes of Israel.

> And they who are in the north countries shall come in remembrance before the Lord . . . and shall no longer stay themselves. . . .
> And they shall bring forth their rich treasures unto the children of Ephraim, my servants.
> And the boundaries of the everlasting hills shall tremble at their presence.
> And there shall they fall down and be crowned with glory, even in Zion, by the hands of the servants of the Lord, even the children of Ephraim.
> And they shall be filled with songs of everlasting joy.
> Behold, this is the blessing of the everlasting God upon the tribes of Israel, and the richer blessing upon the head of Ephraim and his fellows. (D&C 133:26, 30–34)

Many questions and theories arise concerning the location of the lost ten tribes of Israel. There are not immediate answers to those questions. What matters is that Ephraim is prepared when they come. They will come seeking the blessings of the gospel and ordinances of the temples. They will bring their records to share, and Ephraim will have his to share with them. Ephraim will be their host, offering the blessings they have enjoyed since the Restoration with those of Israel who have been lost for almost 2500 years. What a meeting it will be. What a time it will be for Ephraim and his fellows.

President Joseph Fielding Smith accounted for Ephraim's great calling.

> It is Ephraim, today, who holds the priesthood. It is with Ephraim

that the Lord has made covenant and has revealed the fulness of the everlasting gospel. It is Ephraim who is building temples and performing the ordinances in them for both the living and the dead. When the "lost tribes' come—and it will be a most wonderful sight and a marvelous thing when they do come to Zion—in fulfillment of the promises made through Isaiah and Jeremiah, they will have to receive the crowning blessings from their brother Ephraim, the "firstborn" in Israel.[7]

The final great responsibility for Ephraim will be to prepare for the Second Coming of the Lord Jesus Christ.

> Wherefore, go forth, crying with a loud voice saying: The kingdom of heaven is at hand; crying Hosanna! Blessed be the name of the Most High God.
>
> Go forth baptizing with water, preparing the way before my face for the time of my coming.
>
> For the time is at hand; the day or the hour no man knoweth; but it surely shall come. (D&C 39:19–21)
>
> And for this purpose I have commanded you to organize yourselves. . . .
>
> For the purpose of building up my church and kingdom on the earth, and to prepare my people for the time when I shall dwell with them, which is nigh at hand. (D&C 104:58–59)

The return of the ten tribes, the building of the city of Zion and the Second Coming of Lord Jesus Christ lies in the future. Again it is an awesome and fearful responsibility but the Lord has told us "if ye are prepared ye shall not fear" (D&C 38:30).

Joseph Smith foretold of the great work going forth among the children of men.

> No unhallowed hand can stop the work from progressing; persecutions may rage, mobs may combine, armies may assemble, calumny may defame, but the truth of God will go forth boldly, nobly, and independent, till it has penetrated every continent, visited every clime, swept every country, and sounded in every ear, till the purposes of God shall be accomplished, and the Great Jehovah shall say the work is done. [8]

And the Lord told Nephi in vision: "And blessed are they who shall seek to bring forth my Zion at that day, for they shall have the gift and the power of the Holy Ghost; and if they endure unto the end they shall be lifted up at the last day, and shall be saved in the everlasting kingdom of the Lamb; and whoso shall publish peace, yea, tidings of great joy, how beautiful upon the mountains shall they be" (1 Nephi 13:37).

Now Let Us Rejoice

Now let us rejoice in the day of salvation.
No longer as strangers on earth need we roam.
Good tidings are sounding to us and each nation,
And shortly the hour of redemption will come,
When all that was promised,
The Saints will be given,
And none will molest them from morn until ev'n,
And earth will appear as the garden of Eden,
And Jesus will say to all Israel, "Come Home."[9]

Notes

1   Brigham Young, *Journal of Discourses*, 2:268.

2   Joseph Fielding Smith, *Doctrines of Salvation,* vol. 3, (Salt Lake City: Bookcraft, 1956), 246.

3   *Answers to Gospel Questions,* vol. 4, (Salt Lake City: Deseret Book, 1963), 38–39.

4   *Answers to Gospel Questions,* 3:62–63.

5   Wilford Woodruff, *Journal of Discourses*, 22:232–33, June 26, 1881.

6   Ibid., 234; italics added.

7   Smith, *Doctrines of Salvation,* 3:252–53.

8   Joseph Smith, *History of the Church*, 4:540.

9   William W. Phelps, "Now Let Us Rejoice," *Hymns*, 3.

chapter thirty-two

LEADERS OF THE RESTORATION

We began the study of Ephraim in the Old Testament as the children of Israel were about to escape Egyptian bondage. They were emancipated slaves searching for a place to live and enjoy the freedom won for them by the Lord. The final chapters have covered Ephraim's critical role in the scenes of the final dispensation. The tribe of Ephraim through the centuries has completed a transformation from slaves to prophets, leaders and teachers of the Restoration, preparing for the Second Coming of the Lord Jesus Christ.

This book has only traced the scattering and gathering of Ephraim through Western Europe and America. It is an essential trail to follow because it led to the land the Lord had prepared for the Restoration of the Church of Jesus Christ and the initial gathering of Israel. That promised land was the only site on the earth, at that time, where that Restoration could have succeeded, Zion established, and missionaries sent to preach the gospel to scattered Israel around the world.

The Lord told Zechariah that He would scatter Ephraim among all people and nations. "And I will sow them among the people: and they shall remember me in far countries; and they shall live with their children, and turn again" (Zechariah 10:9). Ephraim was scattered among the nations as a punishment for rejecting the Lord and failing to keep His commandments, to be a blessing that in time they would "turn again" and return to the Lord, and to bless the nations and families of the world with the blood of Ephraim the birthright tribe of Israel.

The Lord had a definite purpose in scattering Israel at such an early time. For two and a half millennia, Ephraim has been working around the world, fulfilling his responsibility as the birthright tribe to bring conditions for the gospel to be preached in all the nations. When all the records are finally brought to light, many more accounts will be told in various nations of dedication, sacrifice, and heroic acts of men and women who carry the blood of Israel and have spent lives struggling to bring the light to people grappling in darkness. Many acts have and will continue to open new channels for the preaching of the gospel, gathering of Israel, and building up of Zion. Records are still being written as men and women search for the truth. There is still a good deal to learn of Ephraim's work around the world.

Ephraim's early scattering was to bless the nations and families with the blood of Israel. It is a blood that cherishes and loves freedom, constantly searching for truth. In each nation and time period its effect was distinctive and irreplaceable. Progress was accomplished through a myriad of individuals in whose veins that unique, priceless blood flows. It is a blood that:

- Seeks change, advancement, and progress.
- Loves liberty and is willing to sacrifice for freedom.
- Has been shed around the world to encourage liberty.
- Looks to the good and strives to make the world a better place.
- Works to bring light and knowledge to people who sit in darkness.
- Cares for the individual souls of men and women.
- Preserves the good of the past.
- Looks forward to what must be completed to insure the future.
- Cares what it will pass on to its posterity.

For thou art a holy people unto the Lord thy God: the Lord hath chosen thee to be a special people unto himself, above all people that are upon the face of the earth. (Deuteronomy 7:6)

For the Lord hath chosen . . . Israel for his peculiar treasure. (Psalm 135:4)

Ephraim was sifted among the nations to be a driving force in the search for the principles and ideology to establish democracy, institute laws, foster learning, preserve knowledge of the past, and yet always looking forward for opportunities to improve life for his posterity. Ephraim:

- Influenced the great philosophers of Greece—Socrates, Plato, and Aristotle—as they espoused principles of democracy
- Met in the Senate in Rome as a written code of law was developed protecting Roman citizens
- Impressed Roman philosophers and writers—Cicero, Virgil, and Seneca—to write about the good and evil experienced by Rome
- Marched with Roman Legions as they brought peace and order to a barbarian world
- Was among the first to accept the gospel taught by the Apostles as they went forth to teach the Gentiles. "And they that escape of you shall remember me among the nations whither they shall be carried." (Ezekiel 6:9)
- Went forth as missionaries to spread Christianity to men and women throughout Europe. The spirit of Ephraim was felt by St. Francisis of Assisi, Jerome, Augustine, St. Patrick, and others who shared Christianity with their fellow beings
- Was shed as martyrs, accepting death rather than renouncing a testimony of the Savior
- Loved learning, despised ignorance, and did all in his power to preserve all the knowledge of the past to pass on to future generations

But thou Israel, art my servant. . . . I have chosen thee. . . . Fear thou not; be not dismayed; for I am thy God: I will strengthen thee; yea, I will help thee; yea, I will uphold thee with the right hand of my righteousness. (Isaiah 41:8–10)

And my people who are a remnant of Jacob shall be among the Gentiles, yea, in the midst of them as a lion among the beast of the forest. (3 Nephi 21:12)

The house of Joseph would suffer through the stagnation of the Dark Ages but would be leading elements to bring people and nations back to light and progress including:

- A concern that humankind develops a sense of self-worth to motivate them to rise above conditions, constantly attempting to drag them down or conform to outdated and corrupt ideologies.

- Joining armies of nations to protect against invaders who would destroy freedom, cultures, and nations.
- Wearing crowns of monarchs, sitting in cabinets, and leading armies throughout Europe protecting national identities and assisting the spread and stabilization of Christianity, including Clovis, Constantine, Charlemagne and King Henry VIII.

For have I not the fowls of heaven, and also the fish of the sea, and the beasts of the mountains? Have I not made the earth? Do I not hold the destinies of all the armies of the nations of the earth? (D&C 117:6)

The blood of Ephraim was mixed in the talented men initiating the Renaissance of Europe and the Reformation or reform of Christianity. Progress takes many forms, including art, writing, teaching, discovery, and even protest. Joseph's posterity would:

- Inspire artists, architects, philosophers, teachers, men, and women of ideas including Castiglione, Machiavelli, Leonardo da Vinci, Michelangelo, Erasmus, Cervantes, and Shakespeare.
- Be among the great scientists and discoverers—including Bacon and Newton—advancing knowledge.
- Develop printing and distribution of books to enlighten man, making the Bible his favorite choice of reading. Johann Gutenberg's development of movable type made great strides toward conquering ignorance.
- Have a desire to share the word of God with others, often at great risk to himself.
- Travel with the great discovery voyages of the world, the most important of which was Columbus's discovery of the promised land.
- Long to return to the simplicity of Christ's original church as evidenced by Wycliff, Huss, Jerome, and Tyndale.
- Walk in the footprints of the reformers. Rebellion and change were characteristics running in his veins as shown by the actions of Luther, Calvin, Zwingli, and Wesley.
- Accept persecutions, punishments, and even death to search for the truth and advance knowledge.

- Understand that change does not come without consequences and sacrifice.

Ephraim shall say, What have I to do any more with idols? I have heard him, and observed him: I am like a green fir tree. From me is thy fruit found. (Hosea 14:8)

Before Ephraim and Benjamin and Manasseh stir up thy strength, and come and save us. (Psalm 80:2)

The house of Joseph would be among the Enlightenment thinkers, often questioning the past and espousing democratic ideology on how society should be best governed. John Locke, Montesquieu, Voltaire, Rousseau, and Adam Smith set down principles in the era immediately preceding the American Revolution. Ephraim's blood:

- Would run in the veins of England's royalty, lords, and members of Parliament.
- Was present when the Magna Carta was approved.
- Constantly fought for the rights of Englishmen.
- Would always be willing to participate when questions of individual rights and liberty were involved.

And the Gentiles shall come to thy light, and kings to the brightness of thy rising. (Isaiah 60:3)

Israel's birthright tribe was drawn to a land of promise:

- Despite the fearful crossing of a three thousand mile ocean as evidenced by the pilgrims and colonists of America.
- Looking for space to start anew.
- To worship as they pleased.
- To offer their families and posterity opportunities never dreamed possible in the Old World.
- To experience a degree of democracy and quick to participate in local governmental councils in the New World.
- To accept hard work and sacrifice as a necessity to succeed as immigrants in a new land.
- To benefit from the fruits of his labors and gain a status as citizens.
- To enjoy the privilege of owning land or shop to provide for family.

And it came to pass that I beheld the Spirit of God, that it wrought upon other Gentiles; and they went forth out of captivity, upon many waters. And I beheld the spirit of the Lord, that it was upon the Gentiles, and they did prosper and obtain the land for their inheritance. (1 Nephi 13:13, 15)

Unlike the children of Israel after being freed from Egyptian task-masters, Ephraim's blood was willing to take on the dangers, risks, and hardships required to tame the new and unfamiliar, win independence, and institute laws concerning freedom of religion. Ephraim would be among the first to answer the call:

- At Lexington and Concord in 1775 to oppose the British march to capture supplies and weapons stored by local committees.
- At Philadelphia in the hot summer of 1776 to hammer out a Declaration of Independence informing the world and Mother England that American intentions were to be an independent nation. Men like John Adams, Thomas Jefferson, and Benjamin Franklin are just a few of the many who come to mind.
- At Trenton following the commander-in-chief on a stormy, cold night to make a surprise attack against the enemy during one of the darkest hours of the Revolution.
- At Trenton, Princeton, and Valley Forge, where he left behind bloody tracks in the snow where shoeless men trod, thinking of a cause more important than the comforts of a warm fireside with family.
- At many battlefields where his blood was shed and bodies buried in defense of a cause and country.

And I Nephi, beheld that the Gentiles that had gone out of captivity were delivered by the power of God out of the hands of all other nations. (1 Nephi 13:19)

Descendants of Ephraim sat in the great councils, forging a new country:

- In Europe, working out treaties and agreements to end the war and recognize the independence of the United States of America.
- In Philadelphia, at the Constitutional Convention, arguing for compromise and conciliation.
- In state conventions, winning approval of the constitution and

supporting the amendments which were to become the Bill of Rights.

> And for this purpose have I established the Constitution of this land, by the hands of wise men whom I raised up unto this very purpose, and redeemed the land by the shedding of blood. (D&C 101:80)

A descendant of Joseph and Ephraim entered a grove of trees on a beautiful spring day, seeking answers to questions. He received the most remarkable vision ever conceived in the mind of man and found answers to questions concerning the nature of God the Father and His Son Jesus Christ. The tribe of Ephraim:

- Went on to establish the Lord's Church in the latter days.
- Accepted the priesthood keys to administer and carry on the Lord's work on earth.
- Gave their blood for what they believed.
- Followed prophets from one settlement to another, searching for a place to worship in peace, without persecution.
- Left homes in Europe at great sacrifice when a call came from a Prophet to gather to Zion.
- Crossed the plains, leaving many unmarked graves, to aid in the establishment of Zion in the tops of the mountains in the west.
- Sent fathers out on missions at great sacrifice to various parts of the world to share the gospel of Jesus Christ, seeking out their brothers and sisters of the House of Israel and gather them to Zion.

> Wherefore, Joseph truly saw our day. And he obtained a promise of the Lord, that out of the fruit of his loins the Lord God would raise up a righteous branch unto the house of Israel; not the Messiah, but a branch which was to be broken off, nevertheless to be remembered in the covenants of the Lord that the Messiah should be made manifest unto them in the latter days, in the spirit of power, unto the bringing of them out of darkness and out of captivity unto freedom. (2 Nephi 3:5)

Modern-day Ephraim, assisted by other members of the House of Israel, are:

- Strengthening the stakes of Zion.

- Teaching the restored gospel to Sunday Schools, Primaries, Youth groups, Relief Societies, and Priesthood groups.
- Willingly giving of their time to do the work so essential for those who have gone before them.
- Sending sons and daughters to all quarters of the earth to share the gospel.
- Preparing for the coming of the Lord, Jesus Christ.

Ye shall be a blessing: fear not, but let your hands be strong. (Zechariah 8:13)

Thus saith the Lord; Refrain thy voice from weeping, and thine eyes from tears: for thy work shall be rewarded, saith the Lord. (Jeremiah 31:16)

Present-day Ephraim has a responsibility to those in the past, present, and future and can look to the past with great satisfaction as to what their brothers and sisters in Israel have accomplished. They have been builders of nations, churches, great philosophers, soldiers, and statesmen and are deserving of our dedication and respect. Despite past accomplishments, Ephraim's greatest role lies in the present and future. His past is recorded in the histories of the world; his future work will be recorded in the eternities. His past initiated progress and forged nations; his future will create eternal families and kingdoms.

Some spirit children had qualified for greater responsibilities here on earth by their diligence in the pre-earth life. Those noble spirit children foreordained to play a leading role during the last dispensation were formulated into the tribe of Ephraim even in the pre-earth life. Their assignment was to prepare the world for the Second Coming of Christ. They had the task of spreading the gospel to the rest of Father's children. They were given the responsibility in these last days to gather in the scattered remnants of The House of Israel. They had the responsibility of providing an opportunity for both the living and those who died without knowledge of the saving ordinances of the gospel. They were indeed chosen. Chosen to wear out their lives offering salvation to the rest of the children of Israel. Their promised rewards were both temporal and spiritual. They were to receive assistance from heavenly beings enabling them to accomplish their super-human task.[1]

And thy seed shall be as the dust of the earth, and thou shalt spread abroad to the west, and to the east, and to the north, and to the south: and in thee and in thy seed shall all the families of the earth be blessed. (Genesis 28:14)

Our past has influenced our present. Ephraim has a past like no other. Our current records contain only bits and pieces of a few of the branches of Ephraim. We still have much more to learn. The challenge lies in completing all the Lord requires of the scattered posterity of the birthright tribe to take the gospel to all nations and at the same time perfect the Saints and save our dead. Those of Israel have a unique quality earned in premortal life. That quality, if exercised and applied, has proven to accomplish unbelievable things. As Brigham Young reminds us:

The sons of Ephraim are wild and uncultivated, unruly, ungovernable. The spirit in them is turbulent and resolute . . . and they are upon the face of the whole earth, bearing the spirit of rule and dictation, to go forth from conquering to conquer. They search wide creation and scan every nook and corner of this earth to find out what is upon and within it. No hardship will discourage these men; they will penetrate the deepest wilds and overcome almost insurmountable difficulties to develop the treasures of the earth, to further their indomitable spirit for adventure.[2]

May Ephraim never lose that spirit and quality. There are many mountains to climb, rivers to ford, souls to save, and temples to build before we of Israel can accept the accolade, "Well done thou good and faithful servant." One thing very evident relative to those carrying the precious, believing blood of Ephraim and Israel is:

- Who we were is who we are!
- Who we are is who we will become!
- The eternities await Ephraim's diligence.

The words penned by William W. Phelps portray latter-day Ephraim:

The Spirit of God
The Spirit of God like a fire is burning!
The latter-day glory begins to come forth;
The visions and blessings of old are returning,
And angels are coming to visit the earth.

The Lord is extending the Saints understanding,
Restoring their judges and all as at first.
The knowledge and power of God are expanding;
The veil o'er the earth is beginning to burst.

We'll call in our solemn assemblies in spirit,
To spread forth the kingdom of heaven abroad,
That we through our faith may begin to inherit
The visions and blessings and glories of God.

How blessed the day when the lamb and the lion
Shall lie down together without any ire,
And Ephraim be crowned with his blessing in Zion,
As Jesus descends with his chariot of fire!

We'll sing and we'll shout with the armies of heaven,
Hosanna, hosanna to God and the Lamb!
Let glory to them in the highest be given,
Hence-forth and forever,
Amen and amen!

Notes

1 R. Wayne Shute, Monte S, Nyman, and Randy L. Bott, *Ephraim, Chosen of the Lord*, (Riverton, UT: Mellennial Press, Inc., 1999), 15.
2 Brigham Young, *Journal of Discourses*, 10:188, May 31, 1863.
3 William W. Phelps, "The Spirit of God," *Hymns, 2.*

A PECULIAR TREASURE, A CHOSEN PEOPLE

Premortal life

Now the Lord had shown unto me, Abraham, the intelligences that were organized before the world was; and among all these there were many of the noble and great ones; And God saw these souls that they were good, and he stood in the midst of them, and he said: These I will make my rulers; for he stood among those that were spirits, and he saw that they were good; and he said unto me: Abraham, thou art one of them; thou wast chosen before thou wast born.

Abraham 3:22–23

When the most High divided to the nations their inheritance, when he separated the sons of Adam, he set the bounds of the people according to the number of the children of Israel. For the Lord's portion is his people; Jacob is the lot of his inheritance.

Deuteronomy 32:8–9

And hath made of one blood all nations of men for to dwell on all the face of the earth, and hath determined the times before appointed, and the bounds of their habitation

Acts 17:26

And we know that all things work together for good to them that love God, to them who are the called according to his purpose. For whom he did foreknow, he also did predestinate to be conformed to the image of his Son, that he might be the firstborn among many brethren. Moreover whom he did predestinate, them he also called: and whom he called, them he also justified: and whom he justified, them he also glorified.

Romans 8:28–30

Blessed be the God and Father of our Lord Jesus Christ, who hath blessed us with all spiritual blessings in heavenly places in Christ. According as he hath chosen us in him before the foundation of the world, that we should be holy and without blame before him in love: Having predestinated us unto the adoption of children by Jesus Christ to himself, according to the good pleasure of his will, In whom also we have obtained an inheritance, being predestinated according to the purpose of him who worketh all things after the counsel of his own will.

Ephesians 1:3–5, 11

Abraham and a covenant with the Lord

And I will make thee exceedingly fruitful, and I will make nations of thee, and kings shall come out of thee, And I will establish my covenant between me and thee and thy seed after thee in their generations for an everlasting covenant, to be a God unto thee, and to thy seed after thee.

Genesis 17:6–7

And I will make of thee a great nation, and I will bless thee above measure, and make thy name great among all nations, and thou shalt be a blessing unto thy seed after thee, that in their hands they shall bear this ministry and Priesthood unto all nations; And I will bless them through thy name; for as many as receive this Gospel shall be called after thy name, and shall be accounted thy seed, and shall rise up and bless thee, as their father; And I will bless them that bless thee, and curse them that curse thee; and in thee (that is, in thy Priesthood), for I give unto thee a promise that this right shall continue in thee, and in thy seed after thee (that is to say, the literal seed, or the seed of the body) shall all the families of the earth be blessed, even with the blessings of the Gospel, which are the blessings of salvation, even of life eternal.

Abraham 2:9–11

And I will bless them that bless thee, and curse him that curseth thee: and in thee shall all families of the earth be blessed.

Genesis 12:3

And in thy seed shall all the nations of the earth be blessed.

Genesis 22:18

Jacob becomes Israel

And he said, Thy name shall be called no more Jacob, but Israel: for as a prince hast thou power with God and with men, and hast prevailed.

Genesis 32:28

But thou, Israel, art my servant, Jacob whom I have chosen, the seed of Abraham my friend.

Isaiah 41:8

And God said unto him, I am God Almighty: be fruitful and multiply; a nation and a company of nations shall be of thee, and kings shall come out of thy loins;

Genesis 35:11

And thy seed shall be as the dust of the earth, and thou shalt spread abroad to the west, and to the east, and to the north, and to the south: and in thee and in thy seed shall all the families of the earth be blessed.

Genesis 28:14

Israel, a chosen people of the Lord

For thou art an holy people unto the Lord thy God: the Lord thy God hath chosen thee to be a special people unto himself, above all people that are upon the face of the earth. The Lord did not set his love upon you, nor choose you, because ye were more in number than any other people; for ye were fewest of all people: But because the Lord loved you, and because he would keep the oath which he had sworn unto your fathers.

Deuteronomy 7:6–8

And I will take you to me for a people, and I will be to you a God: and ye shall know that I am the Lord your God.

Exodus 6:7

Now therefore, if ye will obey my voice indeed, and keep my covenant, then ye shall be a peculiar treasure unto me above all people: for all the earth is mine: And ye shall be unto me a kingdom of priests, and an holy nation.

Exodus 19:5–6

And I will walk among you, and will be your God, and ye shall be my people.

Leviticus 26:12

Only the Lord had a delight in thy fathers to love them, and he chose their seed after them, even you above all people.

Deuteronomy 10:15

For thou art a holy people unto the Lord thy God, and the Lord hath chosen thee to be a peculiar people unto himself, above all the nations that are upon the earth.

Deuteronomy 14:2

For the Lord hath chosen Jacob unto himself, and Israel for his peculiar treasure.

Psalm 135:4

But ye are a chosen generation, a royal priesthood, an holy nation, a peculiar people; that ye should shew forth the praises of him who hath called you out of darkness into his marvelous light.

1 Peter 2:9

And it shall come to pass, if thou shalt hearken diligently unto the voice of the Lord thy God, to observe and to do all his commandments which I command thee this day, that the Lord thy God will set thee on high above all nations of the earth. And all these blessings shall come on thee, and overtake thee, if thou shalt hearken unto the voice of the Lord thy God.

Deuteronomy 28:1–2

The Lord shall establish thee an holy people unto himself, as he hath sworn unto thee, if thou shalt keep the commandments of the Lord thy God, and walk in his ways.

Deuteronomy 28:9

For the mountains shall depart and the hills be removed, but my kindness shall not depart from thee, neither shall the covenant of my peace be removed, saith the Lord that hath mercy on thee.

3 Nephi 22:10

For as the new heavens and the new earth which I will make, shall remain before me, saith the Lord, so shall your seed and your name remain.

Isaiah 66:22

Israel's calling and mission to God's children upon the earth
In thee shall all families of the earth be blessed. [The Lord speaking to Abraham.]

Genesis 12:3

And in thy seed shall all the nations of the earth be blessed. [The Lord speaking to Abraham.]

Genesis 22:18

Thou art my servant, O Israel, in whom I will be glorified. It is a light thing that thou shouldest be my servant to raise up the tribes of Jacob, and to restore the preserved of Israel: I will also give thee for a light to the Gentiles, that thou mayest be my salvation unto the end of the earth.

Isaiah 49:3, 6

That thou mayest say to the prisoners, Go forth; to them that are in darkness, Shew yourselves. They shall feed in the ways and their pastures shall be in all high places.

Isaiah 49:9

And the Gentiles shall come to thy light, and kings to the brightness of thy rising.

Isaiah 60:3

And I will set a sign among them, and I will send those that escape of them unto the nations. . .to the isles afar off, that have not heard my fame, neither have seen my glory; and they shall declare my glory among the Gentiles.

Isaiah 66:19

Go ye therefore, and teach all nations, baptizing them in the name of the Father, and of the Son, and of the Holy Ghost: Teaching them

223

to observe all things whatsoever I have commanded you: and lo, I am with you alway, even unto the end of the world.

Matt 28:19–20

Go ye into all the world, and preach the gospel to every creature.

Mark 16:15

Wherefore, the Lord God will proceed to make bare his arm in the eyes of all the nations, in bringing about his covenants and his gospel unto those who are of the house of Israel.

1 Nephi 22:11

Israel failed to keep their covenant with the Lord because they were not willing to obey His commandments. For their transgressions they were driven from the promised land and scattered throughout the world:

1. As a punishment
2. To receive blessings because of the scattering
3. To bless the nations where they were scattered

Israel's scattering

And I will sift the house of Israel among all nations, like as corn is sifted in a sieve.

Amos 9:9

Even all nations shall say, Wherefore hath the Lord done thus unto this land? What meaneth the heat of this great anger? Then men shall say, Because they have forsaken the covenant of the Lord God of their fathers, which he made with them when he brought them forth out of the land of Egypt: For they went and served other gods, and worshipped them, gods whom they know not, and whom he had not given unto them. And the anger of the Lord was kindled against this land, to bring upon it all the curses that are written in this book: And the Lord rooted them out of their land in anger, and in wrath, and in great indignation, and cast them into another land, as it is this day.

Deuteronomy 29:24–28

I lifted up my hand unto them also in the wilderness, that I would scatter them among the heathen, and disperse them through the countries.

Ezekiel 20:23

And the remnant of Jacob shall be in the midst of many people as a dew from the Lord, as the showers upon the grass.

Micah 5:7

Concerning the house of Israel, that they should be compared like unto an olive-tree, whose branches should be broken off and should be scattered upon all the face of the earth.

1 Nephi 10:12

For it appears that the house of Israel, sooner or later, will be scattered upon all the face of the earth, and also among all nations.

1 Nephi 22:3

Israel's punishment

And the Lord shall scatter you among the nations, and ye shall be left few in number among the heathen, whither the Lord shall lead you.

Deuteronomy 4:27

And he said, I will hide my face from them, I will see what their end shall be: for they are a very forward generation, children in whom is no faith. I will heap mischiefs upon them; I will spend my arrows upon them. They shall be burnt with hunger, and devoured with burning heat, and with bitter destruction: I will also send the teeth of beasts upon them, with the poison of serpents of the dust. The sword without, and terror within, shall destroy both the young man and the virgin, the suckling also with the man of grey hairs. I said I would scatter them into corners, I would make the remembrance of them to cease from among men. For they are a nation void of counsel, neither is there any understanding in them.

Deuteronomy 32:20, 23–26, 28

And the Lord shall scatter thee among all people from the one end of the earth even unto the other; and there thou shalt serve other gods, which neither thou nor thy fathers have known, even wood and stone. And among these nations shalt thou find no ease, neither shall the sole of thy foot shall have rest: but the Lord shall give thee a trembling heart, and failing of eyes, and sorrow of mind.

Deuteronomy 28:64–65

So shall ye serve strangers in a land that is not yours. (The tribe of Judah)

Jeremiah 5:19

I will cause thee to serve thine enemies in the land which thou knowest not. (The tribe of Judah)

Jeremiah 17:4

My god will cast them away, because they did not hearken unto him: and they shall be wanderers among the nations. (Speaking of the tribe of Ephraim)

Hosea 9:17

For a small moment have I forsaken thee.

Isaiah 54:7

Israel's blessing resulting from their scattering

For behold, the Lord God has led away from time to time from the house of Israel, according to his will and pleasure. And now behold the Lord remembereth all them who have been broken off.

2 Nephi 10:22

That the house of Israel may go no more astray from me, neither be polluted any more with all their transgressions; but that they may be my people, and I may be their God.

Ezekiel 14:11

I will sow them among the people: and they shall remember me in the far countries; and they shall live with their children, and turn again.

Zechariah 10:9

Yet will I leave a remnant, that ye may have some that shall escape the sword among the nations, when ye shall be scattered through the countries. And they that escape of you shall remember me among the nations whither they shall be carried captives, because I am broken with their whorish heart, which hath departed from me, and with their eyes, which go a whoring after their idols: and they shall lothe themselves for the evils which they have committed in all the abominations. And they shall know that I am the Lord, and that I have not said in vain that I would do this evil unto them.

Ezekiel 6:8–10

And I will give them one heart, and I will put a new spirit within you; and I will take the stony heart out of their flesh, and will give them a heart of flesh.

Ezekiel 11:19

For thou shalt forget the shame of thy youth, and shalt not remember the reproach of the widowhood any more.

Isaiah 54:4

Therefore say, thus saith the Lord God; Although I have cast them far off among the heathen, and although I have scattered them among the countries, yet will I be to them as a little sanctuary in the countries where they shall come.

Ezekiel 11:16

Israel will prove a blessing to the nations where they were scattered

Remember these, O Jacob and Israel; for thou art my servant; I have formed thee; thou are my servant; O Israel, thou shalt not be forgotten of me.

Isaiah 44:21

And thy seed shall be as the dust of the earth, and thou shalt spread abroad to the west, and to the east, and to the north and to the south: and in thy seed shall all the families of the earth be blessed.

Genesis 28:14

And in thy seed shall all the nations of the earth be blessed.

Genesis 22:18

And it shall come to pass, that as ye were a curse among the heathen, O house of Judah, and house of Israel; so will I save you and ye shall be a blessing: fear not, but let your hands be strong.

Zechariah 8:13

For thou shalt be a light unto my people, to deliver them in the days of their captivity, from bondage; and to bring salvation unto them, when they are altogether bowed down under sin.

JST Genesis 48:11

Gathering of Israel

Behold I will gather them out of all countries, whither I have driven them in mine anger, and in my fury, and in great wrath; and I will bring them again unto this place, and I will cause them to dwell safely. And they shall be my people and I will be their God.

Jeremiah 32:37–38

Hear the word of the Lord, O ye nations, and declare it in the isles afar off, and say, He that scattered Israel will gather him and keep him, as a shepherd does his flock. For the Lord hath redeemed Jacob, and ransomed him for the hand of him that was stronger than he.

Jeremiah 31:10–11

For thus saith the Lord God; Behold, I, even I, will both search my sheep, and seek them out. As a shepherd seeketh out his flock in the day that he is among his sheep that are scattered; so will I seek out my sheep, and will deliver them out of all places there they have been scattered in the cloudy and dark day. And I will bring them out from the people, and gather then from the countries, and will bring them to their own land and feed them upon the mountains of Israel by the rivers, and in all the inhabited places.

Ezekiel 34:11–13

Therefore say, thus saith the Lord God, I will even gather you from the people, and assemble you out of the countries where ye have been scattered.

Ezekiel 11:17

For a small moment have I forsaken thee; but with great mercies will I gather thee.

Isaiah 54:7

And ye shall be gathered one by one, O ye children of Israel.

Isaiah 27:12

That then the Lord thy God will turn thy captivity, and have compassion upon thee, and will return and gather thee from all the nations; whither the Lord thy God hath scattered thee.

Deuteronomy 30:3

And he will lift up an ensign to the nations from far, and will hiss unto them from the end of the earth: and, behold, they shall come with speed swiftly.

Isaiah 5:26

And the Lord will set his hand again the second time to restore his people from their lost and fallen state. Wherefore, he will proceed to do a marvelous work and wonder among the children of men.

2 Nephi 25:17

And then will I gather them in from the four quarters of the earth; and then will I fulfill the covenant which the Father made unto all the people of the house of Israel.

3 Nephi 16:5

Come unto me, O ye Gentiles, and I will show unto you the greater things, the knowledge which is hid up because of unbelief. Come unto me, O ye house of Israel, and it shall be made manifest unto you how great things the Father hath laid up for you, from the foundation of the world; and it hath not come unto you, because of unbelief.

Ether 4:13–14

Wherefore, the Lord God will proceed to make bare his arm in the eyes of all the nations, in bringing about his covenants and his gospel unto those who are of the house of Israel. Wherefore, he will bring them again out of captivity, and they shall be gathered together to the lands of their inheritance; and they shall be brought out of obscurity and out of darkness; and they shall know that the Lord is their Savior and their Redeemer, the Mighty One of Israel.

1 Nephi 22:11–12

THE BIRTHRIGHT TRIBE

All the covenants and blessings and responsibilities given to Abraham, Isaac and Jacob, and God's chosen people Israel apply to Joseph and his sons Ephraim and Manasseh.

Joseph

Joseph is a fruitful bough, even a fruitful bough by a well; whose branches run over the wall.

Genesis 49:22

And the Almighty, who shall bless thee with blessings of heaven above, blessings of the deep that lieth under, blessings of the breasts, and of the womb. The blessings of thy father have prevailed above the blessings of my progenitors unto the utmost bounds of the everlasting hills: they shall be on the head of Joseph, and on the crown of the head of him that was separated from his brethren.

Genesis 49:25–26

Ephraim, Joseph's second son, received the Birthright Blessing of Israel from Jacob

And when Joseph saw that this father laid his right hand upon the head of Ephraim, it displeased him and he held his father's hand to remove it from Ephraim's head. And Joseph said unto his father, Not so, my father: for this is the firstborn; put thy right hand upon his head.

Genesis 48:17–18

And his father refused, and said, I know it, my son, I know it: he also shall become a people, and he also shall be great; but truly his younger brother shall be greater than he, and his seed shall become a multitude of nations. And he blessed them that day, saying, In thee shall Israel bless, saying, God make thee as Ephraim and as Manasseh: and he set Ephraim before Manasseh.

Genesis 48:19–20

Behold this is the blessing of the everlasting God upon the tribes of Israel, and the richer blessings upon the head of Ephraim and his fellows.

D&C 133:34

The Tribe of Ephraim rejects Gods commandments

Ephraim is joined to idols: let him alone. Their drink is sour: they have committed whoredom continually. . . .and they shall be ashamed because of their sacrifices.

Hosea 4:17–19

I know Ephraim, and Israel is not hid from me: for now, O Ephraim, thou committest whoredom and Israel is defiled. They will not frame their doings to turn unto their God: for the spirit of whoredoms is in the midst of them, and they have not known the Lord. They shall go with their flocks and with their herds to seek the Lord; but they shall not find him; he hath withdrawn himself from them. They have dealt treacherously against the Lord.

Hosea 5:3–7

Because Ephraim hath made many altars to sin, altars shall be unto him to sin. I have written to him the great things of my law, but they were counted as a strange thing.

Hosea 8:11–12

My people are destroyed for lack of knowledge: because thou hast rejected knowledge, I will also reject thee, that thou shalt be no priest to me: seeing thou hast forgotten the law of thy God, I will also forget thy children. As they were increased, so they sinned against me: therefore I will also forget thy children.

Hosea 4:6–7

Ephraim is smitten, their root is dried up, they shall bear no fruit.

Hosea 9:16

And I will cast you out of my sight, as I have cast out all your brethren, even the whole seed of Ephraim.

Jeremiah 7:15

Scattering of the tribe of Ephraim

My God will cast them away, because they did not hearken unto him: an they shall be wanderers among the nations.

Hosea 9:17

Therefore I will cast you out of this land into a land that ye know not, neither ye nor your fathers; and there shall ye serve other gods day and night where I will not shew you favor.

Jeremiah 16:13

For they have sown the wind, and they shall reap the whirlwind.

Hosea 8:7

Ephraim, he hath mixed himself among the people; Ephraim is a cake not turned.

Hosea 7:8

The tribe of Ephraim in its scattered state again turns to the Lord

Ephraim shall say, What have I to do any more with idols? I have heard him, and observed him: I am like a green fir tree. From me is thy fruit found. Who is wise, and he shall understand these things? prudent, and he shall know them? for the ways of the Lord are right, and the just shall walk in them.

Hosea 14:8–9

I have surely heard Ephraim bemoaning himself thus; Thou hast chastised me, and I was chastised, as a bullock unaccustomed to the yoke: turn thou me, and I shall be turned; for thou art the Lord my God. Surely after that I was turned, I repented; and after I was instructed, I smote upon my thigh: I was ashamed, yea, even confounded, because I did bear the reproach of my youth. Is Ephraim my dear son? is he a pleasant child? for since I spake against him, I do earnestly remember him still: therefore my bowels are troubled for him; I will surely have mercy upon him, saith the Lord.

Jeremiah 31:18–20

Therefore I will look unto the Lord; I will wait for the God of my salvation: my God will hear me. Rejoice not against me, O mine enemy: when I fall, I shall arise; when I sit in darkness, the Lord shall be a light unto me. I will bear the indignation of the Lord, because I have sinned against him, until he plead my cause, and execute judgment for me: he will bring me forth to the light, and I shall behold his righteous.

Micah 7:7–9

And I will strengthen the house of Judah, and I will save the house of Joseph, and I will bring them again to place them; for I have mercy upon them: and they shall be as though I had not cast them off: for I am the Lord their God, and will hear them. And they of Ephraim shall be like a mighty man, and their heart shall rejoice as through wine: yea, their children shall see it, and be glad; their heart shall rejoice in the Lord. I will hiss for them, and gather them; for I have redeemed them: and they shall increase as they have increased. And I will sow them among the people and they shall remember me in far countries; and they shall live with their children, and turn again.

Zechariah 10:6–9

Gathering of the tribe of Ephraim

And it shall come to pass in that day, that the Lord shall set his hand again the second time to recover the remnant of his people, which shall be left. . . . And he shall set up an ensign for the nations, and shall assemble the outcasts of Israel, and gather together the dispersed of Judah from the four corners of the earth. The envy of Ephraim shall depart, and the adversaries of Judah shall be cut off: Ephraim shall not envy Judah, and Judah shall not vex Ephraim.

Isaiah 11:11–13

For there shall be a day, that the watchmen upon the mount of Ephraim shall cry, Arise ye, and let us go up to Zion unto the Lord our God. For thus saith the Lord; Sing with gladness for Jacob, and shout among the chief of the nations: publish ye, praise ye, and say, O Lord save thy people, the remnant of Israel. . . . for I am a father to Israel, and Ephraim is my firstborn. Hear the word of the Lord, O ye nations, and declare it in the isles afar off, and say, He that scattered Israel will gather him, and keep him, as a shepherd doth his flock.

Jeremiah 31:6–7, 9–10

American continent given to house of Joseph for an inheritance

Ye are my disciples; and ye are a light unto this people, who are a remnant of the house of Joseph. And behold, this is the land of your inheritance; and the Father hath given it unto you.

3 Nephi 15:12–13

The tribe of Ephraim in the latter days

But, The Lord liveth, that brought up the children of Israel from all the lands of the north, and from all the lands wither he had driven them: and I will bring them again into their land that I gave unto their fathers. Behold, I will send for many fishers, saith the Lord, and they shall fish them: and after will send for many hunters, and they shall hunt them from every mountain, and from every hill, and out of the holes of the rocks.

Jeremiah 16:15–16

And it shall come to pass in that day . . . ye shall be gathered one by one, O ye children of Israel.

Isaiah 27:12

Turn, O backsliding children, saith the Lord; for I am married unto you: and I will take you one of a city, and two of a family, and I will bring you to Zion: And I will give you pastors according to mine heart, which shall feed you with knowledge and understanding.

Jeremiah 3:14–15

The Spirit of the Lord God is upon me; because the Lord hath anointed me to preach good tidings unto the meek: he hath sent me to bind up the brokenhearted, to proclaim liberty to the captives, and the opening of the prison to them that are bound. To proclaim the acceptable year of the Lord, and the day of vengeance to our God; to comfort all that mourn; To appoint unto them that mourn in Zion, to give unto them beauty for ashes, the oil of joy for mourning, the garment of praise for the spirit of heaviness; that they might be called trees of righteousness, the planting of the Lord, that he might be glorified. And they shall build old wastes, they shall raise up the former desolations, and they shall repair the waste cities, the desolations of many generations.

Isaiah 61:1–4

Wherefore the Gentiles shall be blessed and numbered among the house of Israel.

2 Nephi 10:18

And it meaneth that the time cometh that after all the house of Israel have been scattered and confounded, that the Lord God will raise up a mighty nation among the Gentiles, yea, even upon the face of this land; and by them shall our seed be scattered. And after our seed is scattered the Lord God will proceed to do a marvelous work among the Gentiles, which shall be of great worth unto our seed; wherefore, it is likened unto their being nourished by the Gentiles and being carried in their arms and upon their shoulders. And it shall also be of worth unto the Gentiles; and not only unto the Gentiles but unto all the house of Israel, unto the making known of the covenants of the Father of heaven unto Abraham, saying: In thy seed shall all the kindreds of the earth be blessed. And I would, my brethren, that ye should know that all the kindreds of the earth cannot be blessed unless he shall make bare his arm in the eyes of the nations. Wherefore, the Lord God will proceed to make bare his arm in the eyes of all the nations, in bringing about his covenants and his gospel unto those who are of the house of Israel. Wherefore, he will bring them again out of captivity, and they shall be gathered together to the lands of their inheritance; and they shall be brought out of obscurity and out of darkness; and they shall know that the Lord is their Savior and their Redeemer, the Mighty One of Israel.

1 Nephi 22:7–12

Wherefore Joseph truly saw our day. And he obtained a promise of the Lord, that out of the fruit of his loins the Lord God would raise up a righteous branch unto the house of Israel; not the Messiah, but a branch which was to be broken off, nevertheless, to be remembered in the covenants of the Lord that the Messiah should be manifest unto thee in the latter days, in the spirit of power, unto the bringing of them out of darkness unto light—yea, out of hidden darkness and out of captivity unto freedom. For Joseph truly testified, saying: A seer shall the Lord my God raise up, who shall be a choice seer unto the fruit of my loins. Yea Joseph truly said: Thus saith the Lord unto me: A choice seer will I raise up out of the fruit of thy loins; and he shall be esteemed highly among the fruit of thy loins. And unto him will I give commandment that he shall do a work for the fruit of thy loins, his brethren, which shall be of great worth unto them, even to the bringing of them to the knowledge of the covenants which I have made with thy fathers. But a seer will I raise up out of the fruit of thy loins; and unto him will I give power to bring forth my work unto the seed of thy loins—and not to the bringing forth my word only, saith the Lord, but to the convincing them of my word, which shall have already gone forth among them.

2 Nephi 3:5–7, 11

For it is wisdom in the Father that they should be established in this land, and be set up as a free people by the power of the Father, that these things might come forth from them unto a remnant of your seed, that the covenant of the Father may be fulfilled which he hath covenanted with his people, O house of Israel. Therefore when these works and the works which shall be wrought among you hereafter shall come forth from the Gentiles unto your seed which shall dwindle in unbelief because of iniquity; For thus it behooveth the Father that it should come forth from the Gentiles, that he may show forth his power unto the Gentiles for this cause that the Gentiles, if they will not harden their hearts, that they may repent and come unto me and be baptized in my name and know of the true points of my doctrine, that they may be numbered among my people, O house of Israel; And when these things come to pass that thy seed shall begin to know these things—it shall be a sign unto them, that they may know that the work of the Father hath already commenced unto the fulfilling of the covenant which he hath made unto the people who are the house of Israel.

3 Nephi 21:4–7

For behold, I say unto you that as many of the Gentiles as will repent are the covenant people of the Lord.

2 Nephi 30:2

Send the elders of my church unto the nations which are afar off; unto the islands of the sea; send forth unto foreign lands; call upon all nations, first upon the Gentiles, and the upon the Jews. And behold, and lo, this shall be their cry, and the voice of the Lord unto all people: Go ye forth unto the land of Zion, that the borders of my people may be enlarged, and their stakes may be strengthened, and that Zion may go forth unto the regions round about.

D&C 133:8–9

And it shall come to pass in the last days, when the mountain of the Lord's house shall be established in the top of the mountains, and shall be exalted above the hills, and all nations shall flow unto it.

And many people shall go and say, Come ye, and let us go up to the mountain of the Lord, to the house of the God of Jacob; and he will teach us of his ways, and we will walk in his paths; for out of Zion shall go forth the law, and the word of the Lord from Jerusalem. And he shall judge among the nations, an shall rebuke many people: and they shall beat their swords into plow-shares, and their spears into pruning-hooks—nation shall not lift up sword against nation, neither shall they learn war any more. O house of Jacob, come ye and let us walk in the light of the Lord; yea, come, for ye have all gone astray, every one to his wicked ways.

2 Nephi 12:2–5 (Isaiah 2)

But if they will repent and hearken unto my words, and harden not their hearts, I will establish my church among them, and they shall come in unto the covenant and be numbered among this the remnant of Jacob, unto whom, I have given this land for their inheritance. And they shall assist my people, the remnant of Jacob, and also as many of the house of Israel as shall come, that they may build a city, which shall be called the New Jerusalem.

3 Nephi 21:22–23

And blessed are they who shall seek to bring forth my Zion at that day, for they shall have the gift and the power of the Holy Ghost; and if they endure unto the end they shall be lifted up at the last day, and shall be saved in the everlasting kingdom of the Lamb; and whoso shall publish peace, yea, tidings of great joy, how beautiful upon the mountains shall they be.

1 Nephi 13:37

LITERAL SEED

Abrahamic covenant

And I will bless them that bless thee, and curse them that curse thee; and in thee (that is, in thy Priesthood) and in thy seed (that is, thy Priesthood), for I give unto thee a promise that this right shall continue in thee, and in *thy seed after thee (that is to say, the literal seed, or the seed of the body) shall all the families of the earth be blessed, even with the blessings of the Gospel, which are the blessings of salvation, even life eternal.*

Abraham 2:11

After this, *Elias appeared and committed the dispensation of the gospel of Abraham, saying that in us and our seed all generations after us should be blessed.*

D&C 110:12

And *as I said unto Abraham concerning the kindreds of the earth, even so I say unto my servant Joseph: In thee and in thy seed shall the kindred of the earth be blessed.*

D&C 124:58

Therefore, thus saith the Lord unto you, with whom the priesthood hath continued through the lineage of your fathers—*For ye are lawful heirs, according to the flesh, and have been hid from the world with Christ in God*—Therefore your life and the priesthood have remained, and must needs remain through you and your lineage until the restoration of all things spoken by the mouth of all the holy prophets since the world began. Therefore, blessed are ye if ye continue in my goodness, a light unto the Gentiles, and through this priesthood, a savior unto my people Israel.

D&C 86:8–11

The Lord speaking of John Johnson

For he is a descendant of Joseph and a partaker of the blessings of the promise made unto his fathers.

D&C 96:7

The Lord speaking about members of the Church in Jackson County

For ye are the children of Israel, and of the seed of Abraham, and ye must needs be led out of bondage by power, and with a stretched-out arm.

D&C 103:17

The Lord speaking to Joseph Smith

Abraham received promises concerning his seed, and of the fruit of his loins—from whose loins ye are, namely my servant Joseph—which were to continue so long as they were in the world; and as touching Abraham and his seed, out of the world they should continue; both in the world and out of the world should they continue as innumerable as the stars; or, if ye were to count the sand upon the seashore ye could not number them. *This promise is yours also, because ye are of Abraham*, and the promise was made unto Abraham; and by this law in the continuation of the works of my Father, wherein he glorifieth himself. Go ye, therefore, and do the works of Abraham; enter ye into my law and ye shall be saved.

D&C 132:30–32

And they shall bring forth their rich treasures *unto the children of Ephraim, my servants*. And there shall they fall down and be crowned with glory, even in Zion, *by the hands of the servants of the Lord, even the children of Ephraim*.

D&C 133:30, 32

The Lord speaking to Joseph Smith in revelation

And also with Joseph and Jacob, and Isaac, and Abraham, your fathers, by whom the promises remain.

D&C 27:10

What is the rod spoken of in the first verse of the eleventh chapter of Isaiah, that should come of the Stem of Jesse? Behold, thus saith the Lord: *It is a servant in the hands of Christ, who is partly a descendant of Jesse as well; as of Ephraim, or of the house of Joseph,* on whom there is laid much power. What is the root of Jesse spoken of in the tenth verse of the eleventh chapter. Behold, thus saith the Lord, *it is a descendant of Jesse, as well as of Joseph unto whom rightly belongs the priesthood, and the keys of the kingdom, for an ensign, and for the gathering of my people in the last days.*

D&C 113:3–6

What is meant by the command in Isaiah 52nd chapter, 1st verse, which saith: Put on thy strength, O Zion—and what people had Isaiah reference to? He had reference to those whom God should call in the last days, who should hold the power of priesthood to bring again Zion, and the redemption of Israel; and to put on her strength is to put on the authority of the priesthood, which she, *Zion, has a right by lineage*; also to return to that power which she had lost.

D&C 113:8

Wherefore, the Lord God will proceed to *make bare his arm in the eyes of all the nations, in bringing about his covenants and his gospel unto those who are of the house of Israel.* Wherefore, he will bring them again out of captivity, and they shall be gathered together to the lands of their inheritance; and they shall be brought out of obscurity and out of darkness; and they shall know that the Lord is their Savior and their Redeemer, the Mighty One of Israel.

1 Nephi 22:11–12

Wilford Woodruff

We are of the seed of Ephraim, and of Abraham, and of Joseph, who was sold into Egypt, and these are the instruments that God has kept in the spirit world to come forth in these latter days to take hold of this kingdom and build it up.

Journal of Discourses, 22:233, June 26, 1881

Wilford Woodruff

But the Lord has said that in restoring these blessings to the children of Abraham, that he would be inquired of by the house of Israel, to do it for them. But from what branch or part of the house of Israel will the Lord look for his petition or request to issue if not from the Latter-day Saints? For we are out of the tribe of Joseph through the loins of Ephraim, who has been as a mixed cake among the Gentiles, and are the first fruits of the kingdom, and the Lord has given unto us the kingdom and priesthood and keys thereof. Hence, the Lord will require us to ask for those blessings which are promised unto Israel, and to labor for their salvation.

Journal of Discourses, 4:232–33, February 22, 1857

Bruce R. McConkie

The Almighty Elohim is the father of billions of spirit children, all of whom lived for millions (perhaps billions) of years in his eternal presence. He ordained and established the plan and system whereby they might advance and progress and become like him. That plan is the gospel of God, known to us as the gospel of Jesus Christ because he is the chosen to put all of its terms and conditions into operation.

Our Eternal Father knows all of his spirit children, and in his infinite wisdom, he chooses the very time that each comes to earth to gain a mortal body and undergo a probationary experience. Everything the Lord does is for the benefit and blessing of his children. And each of those children is subjected to the very trials and experiences that Omniscient Wisdom knows he should have. Those who were entitled to an inheritance in Enoch's Zion came to earth in that day. Those whose spiritual stature qualified them for life among the Nephites during that nation's golden era found their inheritance with that people in ancient America. Apostles and prophets are sent to earth to do the work of Apostles and prophets at the time and season when their particular talents are needed. All of the elders of Israel were foreordained and sent to earth in the house of Jacob to minister to their kinsmen and to the Gentiles. Indeed, spiritually endowed souls, in large measure, have been born in the house of Israel ever since the day of Father Jacob. We are here now in latter-day Israel, scattered in all the nations of the earth, because that is where the Lord wants us to be, and that is where we need to be for our own development, advancement, and salvation.

The Mellennial Messiah, (Salt Lake City: Deseret Book, 1982) 660–61.

Era	CHAPTER	INFLUENTIAL EVENTS	YEAR	INFLUENTIAL PEOPLE
Democracy	10	Beginning of Greek classical philosophy	600 B.C.	
Democracy		Establishment of Democracy	505 B.C.	Socrates Plato Aristotle Phillip of Macedon Alexander the Great
Christianity		Establishment of the Roman Republic	509	
Christianity	11	Rome emerges as the most powerful state in Italy	264	Cicero Virgil
Christianity	12	Pax Romana (Roman Peace) Christianity spreads Persecutions of Christians	27 B.C.– A.D. 180	
Christianity		Edict of Milan grants religious freedom to all Roman citizens	313	Constantine
Christianity	12	Council of Nicea	325	
Dark Ages	11	Fall of Rome	476	
Dark Ages		Period known as the Dark Ages	500–800	Clovis
Dark Ages	14	Feudalism develops Emergence of nations Viking Invasions Europe's economy begins to recover		Charlemagne
Dark Ages	18	England initiates justice system	1154	
Dark Ages		First Crusade	1096	
Dark Ages	18	Magna Carta in England	1215	
Dark Ages	14	Nations emerge throughout Europe	1300–1400	
Dark Ages		Black Death	1350	
Dark Ages		Hundred Years War	1337–1453	Joan of Arc
Renaissance	15	Renaissance—a cultural and intellectual movement reviving Europe	1300–1600	
Renaissance		Movable type used in printing Age of Discovery	1454	Gutenberg
Renaissance	20	Discovery of America by Columbus	1492	Columbus
Renaissance	15	Humanism		Castiglione Machiavelli Leonardo da Vinci

CHAPTER	INFLUENTIAL EVENTS	YEAR	INFLUENTIAL PEOPLE
			Michelangelo
			Raphael
			Erasmus
			Cervantes
			Shakespeare
22	Defeat of the Spanish Armada	1588	
16	Preparation for the Reformation	1300–1536	John Wycliffe
			John Huss
			Jerome
			William Tyndale
	Reformation	1517	Martin Luther
			Ulrich Zwingle
			John Calvin
			John Knox
			John Wesley
17	Enlightenment		
18	Glorious Revolution in England	1688	
17	Scientific Revolution Promotion of new ideas		Thomas Hobbs
			John Locke
			Montesquieu
			Voltaire
			Rousseau
			Adam Smith
22	Establishment of the first English colony in America at Jamestown, Virginia	1607	
	Puritans settle near Boston	1629	
	French and Indian War		
	Parliament passes the Sugar, Stamp, and Currency Acts	1764–65	
24	American Revolution begins	1775	George Washington
			John Adams
25	Declaration of Independence	1776	Thomas Jefferson
	England Grants Independence	1783	Ben Franklin
	Constitution approved	1787	James Madison
	Bill of Rights approved	1791	A. Hamilton
28	Joseph Smith born	1805	
	The Church of Jesus Christ of Latter-day Saints organized	1830	Joseph Smith
30	Church moves to the Great Basin to facilitate the gathering of Israel	1847	Brigham Young

Reformation

Enlightenment (Europe)

Enlightenment (America)

OLD TESTAMENT TIME CHART
INCLUDING THE
SCATTERING OF ISRAEL

Year (B.C.)	Event	Prophets/ Leaders	Scattering of Israel
4000	The Fall of Adam		
2400	The Flood	Noah	
2200	Tower of Babel		
1996	Birth of Abraham		
1896	Birth of Isaac		
1836	Birth of Jacob		
1745	Birth of Joseph		
	Birth of Ephraim		
		Israel in Egypt	
1491	The Exodus from Egypt	Moses	
1451	Israel enters the promised land		
1429	Period of judges	Rule of judges	The initial scattering of Israel begins as members leave Cannan for commerical or political reasons or are taken captive as slaves to nations surrounding the Mediterranean Sea and into Southern Europe.
1095	Saul anointed king	Israel's first king	
1055	David anointed king		
1015	Solomon anointed king	Israel's last king	
975	Death of Solomon		
975	The ten northern tribes under Jerobooam revolt from Rehoboam and form the Northern Kingdom of Israel.		Two kingdoms separate.
873		Elijah	
851		Elisha	Israel continues to be sifted among the nations.
837		Joel	
792		Amos	
790		Hosea	

Year (B.C.)	Event	Prophets/ Leaders	Scattering of Israel
758		Isaiah	
721			Northern Kingdom of Israel taken captive by Assyria.
628		Jeremiah	Many escape captivity from Assyria and flee south. Some escape from the main body and scatter into Northern Europe
609		Daniel	
606			Fall of Assyria
598		Ezekiel	
587		King Nebuch- adnezzar	Jews taken captive into Babylon. Babylon captures the Southern Kingdom of Judah.
555	Fall of Babylon		Persia rules Africa and the Pacific Islands.
537			Cyrus allows Jews to return to Jerusalem. The blood of Israel continues to scatter throughout Europe and Asia.
510			Romans establish a republic.
505			Establishment of democracy in Athens.
490–479	Greek and Persian Wars		
470–399		Socrates	
428–348		Plato	
384–322		Aristotle	
330		Alexander the Great	Rome rules the area
101–144		Julius Caesar	
AD 1	Birth of Christ		

about the author

$\mathcal{S}teven$ D. Green is a native of Utah. He received a BA and MEd from Utah State University, where he served as student body president. After serving a brief tour in the United States Army, he taught in the public school system for two years before entering a career in real estate development. A student of history, he has served in many church callings; but the one he loves the most is that of teacher. He and his wife are the parents of five children and reside in Bountiful, Utah.